WHAT IS A WOMAN?

What is a Woman?
And Other Essays

TORIL MOI

OXFORD
UNIVERSITY PRESS

OXFORD
UNIVERSITY PRESS

Great Clarendon Street, Oxford OX2 6DP

Oxford University Press is a department of the University of Oxford.
It furthers the University's objective of excellence in research, scholarship,
and education by publishing worldwide in

Oxford New York

Athens Auckland Bangkok Bogotá Buenos Aires
Cape Town Chennai Dar es Salaam Delhi Florence Hong Kong Istanbul
Karachi Kolkata Kuala Lumpur Madrid Melbourne Mexico City Mumbai
Nairobi Paris São Paulo Shanghai Singapore Taipei Tokyo Toronto Warsaw

with associated companies in Berlin Ibadan

Oxford is a registered trade mark of Oxford University Press
in the UK and in certain other countries

Published in the United States
by Oxford University Press Inc., New York

British Library Cataloguing in Publication Data

Data available

Library of Congress Cataloging in Publication Data
Moi, Toril.
What is a woman?: and other essays/Toril Moi.
Includes bibliographical references and index.
1. Feminist theory. 2. Feminism and literature. 3. Women and
literature. I. Title.
HQ1190 .M64 1999 305.42'01—dc21 99–16111
ISBN 0–19–812242–X (hbk)
ISBN 0–19–818675–4 (pbk)

1 3 5 7 9 10 8 6 4 2

Typeset in Baskerville by
Cambrian Typesetters, Frimley, Surrey

Printed in Great Britain
on acid-free paper by
Bookcraft Ltd, Midsomer Norton, Somerset

For

DAVID

Preface

By a happy coincidence this book will be published in 1999, in time to mark the 50th anniversary of *The Second Sex*. *The Second Sex* is both a major philosophical text and the deepest and most original work of feminist thought to have been produced in this century. In Part I I set out to show that feminist thought can benefit immensely from serious reconsideration of *The Second Sex*, not as a historical document illustrating a long past moment in feminist thought, but as a source of new philosophical insights.

Although it would be wrong to say that it has been forgotten, *The Second Sex* has yet to be properly inherited by contemporary feminist theorists. By this I mean that it is still not generally drawn upon in contemporary theoretical discussions; that teachers of feminist theory and women's studies often tell me that they haven't read it since they were 18, or that they never finished it; that it is not usually taken seriously in seminars on feminist theory; that it tends to be either quickly dismissed or rapidly genuflected to in prefaces and introductions; and that when it is engaged with, the text is usually read from a stance of critical impatience and superiority. Where theorists turning to, say, Luce Irigaray assume as a matter of course that they have to be patient and attentive in their reading, and that the difficulties they encounter arise because of the challenging complexity of Irigaray's thought, critics of Beauvoir far too often demonstrate that they don't believe that *The Second Sex* deserves careful attention. Far from eliciting patience and thought, difficulties in the text are instantly assumed to be evidence of some particularly shallow and uninteresting contradiction of Beauvoir's. (I want to say here that I know of no critic or philosopher who has done a better job of showing what it means to approach Beauvoir attentively, patiently, and without self-defensiveness than Nancy Bauer, whose forthcoming book will be published by Columbia University Press.) Boundless intellectual possibilities open when I think of all the brilliant women who do feminist theory today, the depths of philosophical and theoretical experience they could bring to a reconsideration of Beauvoir, and the creative uses they could put her to, if only they were willing to approach the text with the care and patience it deserves. It has to be said, though, that the task of English-language critics is not helped by the philosophically deplorable English translation.[1] The best way to celebrate the fiftieth anniversary of *The Second Sex* would be to set up a well-funded project for a full-scale scholarly edition and retranslation of the text.

Making up roughly half of this volume, Part I is a book in its own right. It consists of two new essays, both concerned, in one way or another, with the way Simone de Beauvoir's thought illuminates contemporary theoretical problems. I have called this part 'A Feminism of Freedom' because I want to stress that freedom—not identity, difference, or equality—is the fundamental concept in Beauvoir's feminism. Contemporary feminist theory has yet to attempt the radical task of rethinking feminism from a vantage point outside the exhausted categories of identity and difference.[2] In these new essays I begin this task. It is a beginning that, at least to me, has made theory feel like fun again.

The new essays (Chapters 1–2 and Chapter 8) in this book are a continuation of my two previous books: *Sexual/Textual Politics: Feminist Literary Theory* (1985) and *Simone de Beauvoir: The Making of an Intellectual Woman* (1993). In *Simone de Beauvoir* I set out to produce a historically and socially grounded understanding of the factors that contributed to making Beauvoir the intellectual woman she became, and of the works she then wrote. I understood the book above all as a study of subjectivity, considered as a concrete, social and psychological phenomenon. Any theory of

---

[1] See Simons, 'Silencing' for a pioneering (1983) account of the problems with the Parshley translation. In this book I have provided an ample amount of footnotes showing exactly why the published English translation is a philosophical disgrace.

[2] Equality, on the other hand, is by no means an exhausted concept. It tends to be far too quickly dismissed, as if we all knew what it means to claim that women should be men's social equals. In another new essay included in this volume, 'Is Anatomy Destiny?: Freud and Biological Determinism' (Chapter 8), I try to show that the distinction between a feminism of equality and a feminism of difference is positively unhelpful to an understanding of Beauvoir.

subjectivity that fails when confronted with a concrete case is not going to be able to tell us much about what it means to be a man or a woman today. In my new essays I spend much time thinking about why concrete cases matter so much to theory. (I also write about that in Chapter 4.) In the book on Beauvoir I read some of her most important texts (including *The Second Sex*) both as representations of the factors that shaped her subjectivity, and as examples of her creative responses to those factors. In that book, then, my project was to understand the conditions that made Beauvoir and what she made of them. I also included a study of what her critics made of her: the reception of the work of one of the greatest intellectual women in this century is a chronicle of sexism, careless reading, and a desperate failure to take her philosophically seriously. The Simone de Beauvoir we know today was shaped by that reception, one that I do not wish upon any intellectual woman today. I hope that these essays, alongside the other new books on Beauvoir's philosophy which are now appearing, will help to change this situation.

In the two first essays I stage an encounter between a problem in recent theory and *The Second Sex*. Here, my purpose is not to produce a critique of Beauvoir, but to show how useful her work can be for feminist theory today. In different ways, I show that Beauvoir's answers to the questions I ask about the body, the personal and the impersonal, and about the political uses of theory, are based on a fundamental commitment to women's freedom. The title of the first essay echoes the question that launches *The Second Sex*. By calling the essay and the book *What Is a Woman?* I also mean to issue a small challenge to those who think that the answer to that question *must* be metaphysical, essentialist, or a case of biological determinism. Chapter 1 is, one might say, an attempt to liberate the word 'woman' from the binary straitjacket that contemporary sex and gender theory imprisons it in.

Taking my inspiration from Beauvoir on the one hand and from Wittgenstein on the other, in Chapter 1 I also try to show that Beauvoir's understanding of the body as a situation provides an alternative to sex and gender thinking, an alternative that while rejecting biological determinism, provides us with a strong historically and socially situated understanding of the concrete, material, living and dying body. At the same time I try to show that there is no reason at all to lay down theoretical requirements for what the word woman *must* mean. In short, I think that it is perfectly possible for contemporary anti-essentialist feminists to use the word woman without having to blush and instantly mumble something about 'strategic essentialism'. To be able to reach the conclusion that we actually do not have to assume that there is anything intrinsically wrong with the word 'woman', was immensely liberating to me. I hope it will be to others too.

In Chapter 2, ' "I Am a Woman": The Personal and the Philosophical'—the longest essay in the book—I present, among other things, an extremely careful reading of the first three paragraphs of *The Second Sex*. The point of this exercise is to show, in depth, just how much Beauvoir has to tell us about what it means to write philosophy (or theory) as a woman in a sexist society. In the process of doing this, I also show that the contemporary debates about the personal and the impersonal, about subjectivity and objectivity, about the terror of speaking *for* others and the belief that the only alternative is to self-consciously speak *as* instead (as a woman, as a white woman, as a white working-class woman, as a white, lesbian, working-class woman), are conceptually impoverished and rather unenlightening compared to the immense insights of *The Second Sex*. In this chapter I also set up an encounter between Beauvoir's way of thinking and the way of thinking I find in ordinary language philosophy such as this is understood by Cavell, Austin, and Wittgenstein. This encounter has given me a whole new understanding of what kind of enterprise theoretical and philosophical writing can be. No other writing I have done has taught me more.

After working on 'I Am a Woman', I am left with the question of exactly what it will take for a woman in a sexist society to be able to speak—or to remain silent—in a genuinely non-defiant way. Non-defiance is important because defiance is still a reactive stance, induced by sexist aggression. Although there is every reason for women to be defiant in response to sexist onslaught, the problem with the stance—particularly for women who want to write philosophy—is that it may block us from finding our own voice. As Beauvoir shows, the encounter with sexist aggression obliges the woman to reply *either* in ways that imprison her in her sexed subjectivity, *or* in ways that makes her eliminate that sexed subjectivity altogether. For Beauvoir both alternatives are deplorable. Sexism consists in giving a woman the 'choice' between having to believe that she is a woman through and through at all times and in all circumstances, and having to deny that she is one ('I am a writer, not a woman writer'). As I show in Chapter 2, Beauvoir's understanding of this dilemma and its implications is unparalleled. Contemporary feminist theory has never formulated this problem as well as Beauvoir did, and so tends to reproduce this sexist dilemma, for example by remaining fixated on the question of identity and its deconstruction, or by labelling some women 'woman-identified' and others 'male-identified'.

I said that my new work is the continuation of my two other books. Given that *Sexual/Textual Politics* has been quite a bestseller, many readers of this preface will probably have read it. Such readers might want to know what the connections between my new essays and my first book might be. The short answer to that is obvious: the texts themselves will tell. Here I shall only make a few observations. Rereading *Sexual/Textual Politics* for the purpose of writing this preface was an interesting experience. I sound younger, and more inexperienced, theoretically and humanly. But I am glad to report that I recognize the voice. Although it is a voice that fails me from time to time, there is a freshness to it, a willingness to say exactly what I think, which carries a feeling of freedom.

The failure of voice is noticeable in a sentence such as this one, about the problems with the idea of the 'humanist self' (much quoted, I am afraid): 'As Luce Irigaray or Hélène Cixous would argue, this integrated self is in fact a phallic self, constructed on the model of the self-contained powerful phallus' (8). I don't think I can have believed this when I wrote it. I don't understand why every integral whole must be phallic, which is what I am saying here. It doesn't help that I say I have it from Irigaray and Cixous. This in fact makes it worse, since my subsequent chapters on them show that I am by no means pleased by their understanding of what a woman is. Beauvoir would call such failures of voice moments of inauthenticity. Today I would say I fail to stake myself in such claims, which is to say that I fail to take my own writing seriously enough.

In the same way, the very last paragraph of the book, the final reference to Derrida's utopian vision in 'Choreographies', is a reasonably good example of theoretical alienation. I remember very well putting the paragraph there as an afterthought. What I wanted to do, was to give a man the last word of my book, in order to unsettle the 'woman-centred' feminists who thought that feminist theory would have to dismiss 'male theory' entirely. I certainly succeeded in annoying those who believe that there is such a thing as 'male theory'. But in order to score an easy rhetorical point, I unfortunately forgot that I actually did not think of myself as a deconstructionist at all, so that the choice of *that* man was not exactly very thoughtful. I have to take responsibility for the resulting misunderstandings.

But *Sexual/Textual Politics* is also full of sentences that I *did* believe in, and still do. In the chapter on Irigaray, I write that we should 'aim for a society in which we have ceased to categorize logic, conceptualization and rationality as "masculine", not for one from which these virtues have been expelled altogether as "unfeminine" ' (160). A very Beauvoirean point. I see that I— rightly or wrongly—attribute the equally Beauvoirean thought that femininity is a patriarchal construct to Kristeva (see 166), and give this as my reason for liking her work better than that of Irigaray and Cixous. Today, I think I have developed these ideas in deeper and more thoughtful ways, but they are still fundamental to my way of being a feminist. I also like my tendency to argue through concrete examples, as for instance in the discussion of under what circumstances Irigaray's 'mimicry' might be a useful, neutral, or reactionary strategy for feminists (see 141–3).

The crucial difference, however, concerns poststructuralism. *Sexual/Textual Politics* is marked by poststructuralism. My new work is an attempt to work my way out from under poststructuralism (particularly in Chapter 1), and to see what happens when one goes elsewhere (particularly in Chapter 2). Anyone interested in the question of how my thought on questions such as essentialism, femininity, subjectivity, and so on has developed since the early 1980s, can probably easily work it out for herself. My sense is that my views on these matters, which owe a lot to various forms of post-structuralism, have developed and deepened, but not undergone any radical change. In Chapter 4 in this volume (another very recent essay) I give a brief overview of the motivations for my continuous interest in the subject as a subject of praxis—as the subject of acts, including speech acts. This interest is what constantly sends me back to thinkers such as Freud, Lacan, Kristeva, Bourdieu, Sartre, and Beauvoir, and from there to Wittgenstein, Austin, and Cavell. From this list it appears that my most genuine investment in poststructuralist thought always came through psychoanalysis, and only rarely through Derrida or Foucault. Subjectivity (and agency) has always been at the heart of my interests. This contrasts with my attitude to the concept of identity. As far as I can see, everything I have written is marked by a radical disinterest in the concept of identity. I neither posit nor deconstruct it, I simply do not use the term. Only now do I fully realize that this fundamental fact is the most Beauvoirean aspect of my thought.

Finally, however, there is the question of what I now think of as the metaphysical presuppositions of poststructuralism. Rereading it, I was astonished to see to what extent I avoid engaging with such metaphysics in *Sexual/Textual Politics*. On the whole, the book turns poststructuralist thought into a workable set of tools for feminist critique, no more and no less. The major reason for this is, of course, the fact that it was written by a socialist feminist who was already thinking a lot about Simone de Beauvoir. These fundamental commitments made me read French theory quite differently from feminists (not least in the US) who did not share these political and theoretical commitments. The fact that the whole book is structured as a series of readings of different theoretical texts, from Kate Millett and Mary Ellmann to Hélène Cixous and Julia Kristeva, also saves me from metaphysical mischief. When I make points that still hold up in my eyes, it is usually because they are presented as concrete analyses of a given text, and not at all as general metaphysical commitments.

My lack of interest in the foundational claims of deconstruction is surely the reason why most deconstructionists, particularly in the United States, thought the book banal and quite insufficiently Derridean. As late as in 1995 one deconstructive critic found it worth her while to point out that I grossly misunderstand Cixous because I persist in thinking of women as 'social beings' (Kamuf 75), and also, apparently, believe that 'theory's political responsibility begins and ends in a present "reality" ' (Kamuf 74). Peggy Kamuf's thoughtful essay on Cixous, from which these quotes are taken, in fact raises all sorts of important issues—about what reading and writing as a feminist might mean, what we take words such as 'woman', 'style', 'reality', and 'social beings' to mean, and so on—issues that I would wish to engage with in a more serious fashion.[3] But sure: I do think it makes sense to say that women are social beings. And I certainly think that our political responsibility is to reality, which I take to mean the ordinary world we all inhabit. What I do not think, however, is that there is any need to speak of 'reality'.

My new essays are deeply concerned with the ordinary and the everyday. I now see poststructuralism as a form of thought that is too eager to lose itself in metaphysics (see Chapters 1 and 2 for this kind of claim). In short, the two new essays collected in Part I show why I would now challenge the mindset that produces the need to place scare quotes around words such 'reality' or 'social beings'. They also show how hard the task of justifying this feeling intellectually actually is. As Wittgenstein teaches us, the task of freeing ourselves from the intellectual pictures that hold us captive is not only immensely hard, it is never done, for we are always going to find ourselves held by new metaphysical mirages, fall for new temptations to forsake the ordinary.

In *Sexual/Textual Politics* I find many traces of the metaphysics I now want to escape. I appear to believe that there is something intrinsically wrong with being part of a binary opposition (on what evidence? I ask myself today), I am quite insufficiently nuanced about when essentialism is a bad thing and when it doesn't matter, and I spend too much time using words like 'signifier'

---

[3] In Chapter 2 I do discuss style, and Chapter 1 is full of considerations of what the word 'woman' might mean. But 'reality' will have to be left for another day.

when 'word' would have been quite adequate. I also fail to explain properly why it is so terrible to see the subject as a non-contradictory master of its own world. Clearly, there are many situations in which it doesn't matter in the least what one thinks a self or a subject is. This didn't occur to me in 1984. In short, I sometimes write as if it is self-evident that some theoretical idea or other is intrinsically bad for feminist politics. Today I would call that theoreticism.

Looking back on *Sexual/Textual Politics* I nevertheless think of it fondly. It is, mostly, a courageous and free book. It is as if I am arrogating voice to myself without thinking about it, without the slightest worry about what that act means (see Chapter 2 for extensive discussion of what it means for a woman to 'arrogate voice' to herself). I am sure that the fact that I was in England, freshly arrived from the Norwegian fjords and unemployed, helped to give me the insouciance required to write it. I am still astonished at my capacity to just sit down and write that book in two overworked and badly underpaid years. Now, as middle age is bearing down on me, I have become more self-reflexive. Writing takes much longer. I get paid leaves. I have read a lot more and lived a fair bit more too. *Sexual/Textual Politics* is a book of a particular moment in my history, and in the history of feminist theory. I do not feel a need to return to it in order to correct what I now see as various errors of judgement and momentary failures of voice. I am content to leave it in peace. The fact is that I like the young, slightly thoughtless, but passionate and strong woman's voice I hear in the book. I still agree with most of it. In short, I am glad I wrote it.

The next two parts of this collection contain essays written between 1980 and 1998. (Each previously published essay in Parts II and III has a date under the title. That date is the date of writing, not of publication.) Since each part has its own introduction, I shall not dwell on these essays here. In the essays from the 1980s I find, at times, some of the same uneasiness of voice as in *Sexual/Textual Politics*, but the essays I have collected here still appear to me to be valid and useful engagements with questions of abiding interest to me: the question of how to understand what a woman is (my interest in Bourdieu and in Freud, in particular, has a lot to do with this) and to understand how desire and knowledge are interwoven with each other (this is true for all the essays in Part III, but it is also a crucial concern in many of the essays on Freud—see Chapters 5, 6, and 7, in particular).

Over the years I have worked hard to develop clarity of thought and style. (I discuss the meaning of clarity and the question of style in Chapter 2.) All the essays in this collection are written in an effort to communicate with anyone who cares about the subject matters I write about. As Sartre puts it, by choosing one's subject matter one also chooses one's audience. Every act of writing entails a host of choices. There are so many things in the world one *could* write about: why *these* questions and not some quite different ones? Some questions can only be answered by retelling a whole life. In the end, all I can do—all anyone can do—is to take responsibility for the choices I actually have made, and hope that they will make sense to others as well.

All of the essays in this collection, from the earliest to the most recent, that is to say from the analyses of Freud and Girard in Chapters 5 and 6 to the commentary on *The Second Sex* in Chapter 2, have in common a constant preoccupation with the task of reading. To me it makes no difference whether the text I read is categorized as 'literature' or 'theory' or 'philosophy'. To find a way to listen to texts of whatever kind without traducing or belittling their concerns, but also without losing my own subjectivity in the encounter, is a far more difficult task than I once thought. This collection as a whole, then, is a record of almost twenty years of work on the question of how to read as a feminist.

Acknowledgements

In 1994–5 I was the fortunate recipient of a Rockefeller Fellowship at the National Humanities Center (NHC) here in North Carolina, and of a Senior Fellowship from the American Council of Learned Societies (ACLS). Duke University granted me sabbatical leave for the same year. The philosophical groundwork for my new essays—the intense study of Wittgenstein, Austin, and Cavell on the one hand, and the rereading of Beauvoir and Sartre on the other—was done at the National Humanities Center. At the NHC I profited immensely from ongoing conversations with my philosophical colleagues Richard Moran and George Wilson, and with my literary colleagues Sarah Beckwith and Jonathan Freedman. Above all, however, I owe great thanks to Martin Stone who first showed me what I could learn from reading Wittgenstein, Austin, and Cavell. I have learned a lot from his example. In the autumn of 1998 Duke University granted me another semester's leave, without which I could not have finished writing these essays. Further acknowledgements will be found in the notes to each essay, where I thank the friends and colleagues who were kind enough to provide comments on my innumerable drafts.

Over the past two decades a great number of audiences in various parts of the world have been exposed to lectures based on material included in this book. Although it is impossible to list them here, I do want to say how much I have learned and continue to learn from being allowed to present my thought to an audience and from the discussions that invariably follow. I also want to thank the students—graduate and undergraduate—in my various classes in Literature and French at Duke University over the past four years for participating so actively in my investigations of sex and gender, the personal and the philosophical, and the work of Stanley Cavell and Simone de Beauvoir. My research assistants Norbert Schürer, Alanna Thain, Christian Thorne, and Virginia Tuma all provided invaluable help in locating material, preparing the old essays for publication and, not least, endlessly going to the library for me. I have been particularly lucky in having such well-organized, energetic, and creative RAs. I also, finally, want to thank my publisher, Oxford University Press, in the persons of Kim Scott Walwyn, the Editorial Director for the Humanities, who waited for ten years for this book, and my new editor Sophie Goldsworthy who has been as responsive and helpful as any editor could be. Matthew Hollis and Rowena Anketell shepherded the manuscript through production in the most helpful and efficient way.

T.M.

Durham, NC
January 1999

Permissions and Bibliographical Information

The cartoon by Tom Cheney in Chapter 2 appears by permission from:

© *The New Yorker Collection* 1996 Tom Cheney from cartoonbank.com. All Rights Reserved.

Permission to reprint the following essays is gratefully acknowledged:

Chapter 3: 'Appropriating Bourdieu: Feminist Theory and Pierre Bourdieu's Sociology of Culture', *New Literary History* 22/4 (1991), 1017–1049. © 1991 Johns Hopkins University Press.

Chapter 4: 'The Challenge of the Particular Case: Bourdieu's Sociology of Culture and Literary Criticism', *Modern Language Quarterly* 58/4 (Dec. 1997), 497–508. © 1997 The University of Washington.

Chapter 5: 'The Missing Mother: René Girard's Oedipal Rivalries', *Diacritics* 12/2 (1983), 21–31. © 1993 Johns Hopkins University Press.

Chapter 10: ' "She Died Because She Came Too Late . . .": Knowledge, Doubles and Death in Thomas's Tristan', *Exemplaria* 4/1 (1992), 103–31. © 1992 The Center for Medieval and Early Renaissance Studies at the State University of New York at Binghamton.

The remaining essays were first published as follows:

Chapter 6: 'Representation of Patriarchy: Sexuality and Epistemology in Freud's *Dora*', *Feminist Review* 9 (1981), 60–74.

Chapter 7: 'Patriarchal Thought and the Drive for Knowledge', in Teresa Brennan (ed.), *Between Feminism and Psychoanalysis* (London: Routledge, 1989), 189–205.

Chapter 9: 'Desire in Language: Andreas Capellanus and the Controversy of Courtly Love', in David Aers (ed.), *Medieval*

Literature: Criticism, Ideology & History (Brighton: Harvester, 1986), 11–33.

Chapter 11: 'Intentions and Effects: Rhetoric and Identification in Simone de Beauvoir's "The Woman Destroyed" ', in *Feminist Theory and Simone de Beauvoir* (Oxford: Blackwell, 1990), 61–93.

Chapters 1, 2, and 8, and all prefatory and introductory material appear for the first time in this collection. © Toril Moi

Contents

A Note on the Text

Many of these essays were written at a time when there were no available translations of the French texts I work with. For example, since I published my first essay on Bourdieu in 1991, a great number of Bourdieu's books and essays have been translated into English. Throughout this volume, I have made every effort to update my references. Wherever possible I have substituted the new published English text for my own previous translations. I have also streamlined all references to Freud, so that they now all refer to *The Standard Edition*. Very occasionally I have added a footnote containing a clarification or a reference to more recent publications. Except for some very minor stylistic and editorial changes, I have not otherwise rewritten previously published essays.

I use the MLA reference system, as outlined in the *MLA Style Manual*. As far as possible references are given in the text. Cumbersome and very long references are nevertheless exiled to footnotes. The context is supposed to make it clear what author and what work is being cited. Full references can be located by consulting the list of Works Cited at the end of the book. Multiple entries under one author's name (Beauvoir, Bourdieu, Freud, Sartre) are organized alphabetically. I list quoted translations under their English title, but add the original reference whenever I feel it should be there.

Throughout this book the abbreviation 'TA' indicates that the published translation has been amended by me. This happens particularly often when I am quoting *The Second Sex*. In this volume I always refer both to the English translation and the French original of *The Second Sex*. Page references to some frequently used texts are preceded by the following abbreviations. The editions used are those listed in the 'Works Cited' section at the end of the book.

By Simone de Beauvoir:

ASD	*All Said and Done*
DSa	*Le deuxième sexe*, vol. i
DSb	*Le deuxième sexe*, vol. ii
FA	*La force de l'âge*
FC	*Force of Circumstance*
FCa	*La force des choses*, vol. i
FCb	*La force des choses*, vol. ii

FR	*La femme rompue*
MDD	*Memoirs of a Dutiful Daughter*
MJF	*Mémoires d'une jeune fille rangée*
PC	*Pyrrhus et Cinéas*
PL	*The Prime of Life*
TCF	*Tout compte fait*
WD	*The Woman Destroyed*

By Freud:

| SE | *Standard Edition* |

By Wittgenstein:

| PI | *Philosophical Investigations* |

More occasional abbreviations are signalled in footnotes to each essay.

The free woman is just being born.

> Simone de Beauvoir

In truth there is no divorce between philosophy and life.

> Simone de Beauvoir

PART I

A FEMINISM OF FREEDOM:
SIMONE DE BEAUVOIR

What Is a Woman? Sex, Gender, and the Body in Feminist Theory

INTRODUCTION

Since the 1960s English-speaking feminists have routinely distinguished between *sex* as a biological and *gender* as a social or cultural category. The sex/gender distinction provides the basic framework for a great deal of feminist theory, and it has become widely accepted in society at large.[1] Over the past ten years or so, the distinction has nevertheless become highly contentious among feminist theorists. Feminists inspired by psychoanalysis, French feminist theory, and queer theory have questioned its value.[2] Poststructuralist theorists of sex and gender such as Donna Haraway and Judith Butler have subjected it to merciless critique.[3]

I want to thank Kate Bartlett, Sarah Beckwith, Sara Danius, Terry Eagleton, Maria Farland, Sibylle Fischer, Sally Haslanger, Julia Hell, Alice Kaplan, Eva Lundgren-Gothlin, Diana Knight, Walter Benn Michaels, Mats Rosengren, Vigdis Songe-Møller, Martin Stone, Lisa Van Alstyne, and Jennifer Wicke for much needed critical feedback on earlier versions of this essay. The fabulous participants in my seminar on 'Sex, Gender and the Body' at the School of Criticism and Theory at Cornell University in the summer of 1997 helped me to put the finishing touches to this paper.

[1] Handbooks in non-sexist usage routinely recommend that we use 'sex to mean the biological categories of male and female and gender to designate the cultural and other kinds of identities and attributions associated with each sex' (Frank and Treichler 14).

[2] Moira Gatens's eloquent 1983 defence of the concept of sexuality is the best and earliest example of a psychoanalytic critique of the sex/gender distinction. Eve Sedgwick's discussion of the distinction in *Epistemology of the Closet* exemplifies the queer critique. Tina Chanter argues that the sex/gender distinction makes it impossible to understand French psychoanalytically inspired feminism, and particularly the work of Luce Irigaray.

[3] Here and throughout this essay, I use the term 'poststructuralist' to indicate English-language critics working on the sex/gender distinction from a poststructuralist perspective. (For obvious reasons, theorists who do not write in

For them, the original 1960s understanding of the concepts has the merit of stressing that gender is a social construction and the demerit of turning sex into an essence. Considered as an essence, sex becomes immobile, stable, coherent, fixed, prediscursive, natural, and ahistorical: the mere surface on which the script of gender is written. Poststructuralist theorists of sex and gender reject this picture of sex. Their aim is to understand 'sex or the body' as a concrete, historical and social phenomenon, not as an essence.[4] Although they want radically to change our understanding of sex and gender, they retain these concepts as starting points for their theories of subjectivity, identity, and bodily sexual difference. With respect to sex and gender poststructuralists are reformist rather than revolutionary.[5]

In this paper I too am trying to work out a theory of the sexually different body. Unlike the poststructuralist theorists of sex and gender, however, I have come to the conclusion that no amount of rethinking of the concepts of sex and gender will produce a good theory of the body or subjectivity. The distinction between sex and gender is simply irrelevant to the task of producing a concrete, historical understanding of what it means to be a woman (or a

---

English usually do not discuss this particular distinction. Foucault, for example, uses the word *sexe* in much the same way as Beauvoir.) I take the most influential of these theorists to be Judith Butler and Donna Haraway. Their analyses of sex and gender have been accepted by a great number of contemporary feminist critics and theorists. I also draw on Elizabeth Grosz's work on the body, since it provides a particularly clear example of the way Butler and Haraway's critiques of the sex/gender distinction have been taken up by other theorists.

4 The formulation 'sex or the body' is widely used in poststructuralist theory. It is theoretically confusing in that it makes us believe that it makes sense to ask questions such as 'Is sex the same thing as the body?', 'Will a theory of "sex" be the same thing as a theory of the "body"'? As this paper will show, such questions are based on a confused picture of sex, gender, and the body, and can have no clear answer.

5 Donna Haraway dreams of a deconstructed and reconfigured understanding of sex and gender (see 148). Judith Butler's two books *Gender Trouble* and *Bodies That Matter* come across as massive attempts to hammer the sex/gender distinction into poststructuralist shape. After showing that *gender* is performative, Butler aims to prove that *sex* is as constructed as gender. In her pursuit of a historical and political understanding of the body, Butler never asks whether the sex/gender distinction actually is the best framework for her own project.

man) in a given society. No feminist has produced a better theory of the embodied, sexually different human being than Simone de Beauvoir in *The Second Sex*. Because contemporary English-language critics have read Beauvoir's 1949 essay through the lens of the 1960s sex/gender distinction, they have failed to see that her essay provides exactly the kind of non-essentialist, concrete, historical and social understanding of the body that so many contemporary feminists are looking for. In short, Beauvoir's claim that 'one is not born, but rather becomes a woman' has been sorely misunderstood by contemporary feminists.[6] Lacan returned to Freud; it is time for feminist theorists to return to Beauvoir.

I do not mean to say that the distinction between sex and gender does no useful work at all. That we sometimes need to distinguish between natural and cultural sex differences is obvious. The feminists who first appropriated the sex/gender distinction for their own political purposes were looking for a strong defence against biological determinism, and in many cases the sex/gender distinction delivered precisely that. I agree that feminists have to reject the claims of biological determinism in order to produce a forceful defence of women's freedom. But feminists managed to make a convincing case against biological determinism long before they had two different words for sex to choose from. Even in a language without the sex/gender distinction it is not difficult to convey one's opposition to the idea that people in possession of ovaries are naturally unsuited to sports, intellectual work, or public careers. From the fact that Norwegian or French have only one word for sex (*kjønn*, *sexe*), it hardly follows that Norwegian or French feminists are unable to distinguish between sex and gender.[7] Working in German, another language with only

---

[6] Sara Heinämaa is an exception to this rule. See her excellent critique of the tendency to project the sex/gender distinction on to Beauvoir, particularly in 'What Is a Woman?'.

[7] In much feminist work in Norway expressions such as 'social sex' and 'biological sex' have been used. Swedish feminist theorists on the other hand introduced a distinction between *kön* and *genus* modelled on the English distinction in the 1980s. For a Swedish discussion of sex and gender, see Danius. In French neither Simone de Beauvoir nor Monique Wittig have had any trouble criticizing the belief that sex alone can explain social behaviour. Recently, however, Christine Delphy and other feminists have been struggling to introduce

one word for sex, in 1920 Freud had already developed a theory of subjectivity that explicitly distinguished between 'physical sexual characters', 'mental sexual characters', and 'kind of [sexual] object choice' ('The Psychogenesis of a Case of Homosexuality in a Woman', *SE* 18: 170).

I do not claim, then, that a distinction between sex and gender is irrelevant to every feminist project. Rather I start my investigation of sex and gender in feminist theory by asking: In what circumstances do we need to draw on distinctions of this kind? In this essay, my main project is to show that there is at least one case in which the distinction does no useful work at all, and that is when it comes to producing a good theory of subjectivity. In other contexts the sex/gender distinction nevertheless remains of crucial importance to feminism. In the first part of this essay I discuss biological determinism such as it emerged towards the end of the nineteenth century. At this time biological determinism is characterized by two features: (1) a sexual ideology which I shall label the 'pervasive picture of sex'; and (2) the belief that science in general and biology in particular both could and should settle questions about women's role in society. In my view, the combination of these two features created a historical and conceptual situation which made it necessary and urgent to respond by distinguishing between nature and social norms. I return to some significant texts from the late nineteenth century because Simone de Beauvoir still finds it necessary to argue against them, and because I think that the sex/gender distinction in contemporary feminist theory is designed to counter this kind of biological determinism. It follows that the distinction may not work as well for other purposes as it does for this one.

My account of biological determinism is followed by a discussion of the 1960s and 1970s formulation of the sex/gender distinction, particularly in the influential work of Gayle Rubin. In Section III the poststructuralist attempt to revise the 1960s formulation

---

the word *genre* as an equivalent to the English gender (see Delphy, 'Rapports'). Whatever one thinks of this as a feminist strategy, the attempt shows that in the 1990s the sex/gender distinction is still not operative in ordinary French language.

becomes the subject of critical analysis. In Section IV I show that Simone de Beauvoir's understanding of the body as a situation offers a powerful alternative to sex/gender theories, and in Section V I bring the Beauvoirean approach to bear on some legal cases. The point of this section is to show through concrete examples that Simone de Beauvoir's understanding of what a woman is makes a political and practical difference in the conflicts of everyday life. In contemporary feminist theory so much energy is spent keeping the spectre of biologically based essentialism at bay that it is easy to forget that generalizations about gender may be just as oppressive as generalizations about sex. In many situations today biological determinism is not the most pressing obstacle to an emancipatory understanding of what a woman is. *The Second Sex* shows that every general theory of gender or 'femininity' will produce a reified and clichéd view of women. The final afterword is subtitled 'The Point of Theory'. Here I summarize some of my findings, and ask what concrete investigations the theoretical work in this essay might lead to. I end by asking what kind of work feminist theory might usefully carry out, and what we need it for.

Finally, I want to say a few words about the wider feminist and theoretical issues I seek to engage with. Taking Wittgenstein's deceptively simple phrase 'the meaning of a word is its use in the language' (*PI* §43) as my source of inspiration,[8] I have tried to show that what Susan Gubar has wittily labelled feminist theory's 'bad case of critical anorexia', namely the tendency to make the word woman slim down to nothing (901), is a problem of our own (I mean 'us feminist theorists' own') making. Through a careful investigation of the concepts of sex and gender, this essay tries to show (rather than just claim) that the belief that any use of the word 'woman' (and any answer to the question 'What is a woman?') must entail a philosophical commitment to metaphysics and essentialism, is mistaken. It follows that efforts to rescue the word 'woman' from its so-called inherent essentialism, for instance

---

[8] To be exact, what Wittgenstein actually writes is this: 'For a *large* class of cases—though not for all—in which we employ the word "meaning" it can be defined thus: the meaning of a word is its use in the language.' In my view, all the cases in which feminists discuss the meaning of the words *woman*, *sex*, and *gender* belong to the '*large* class of cases' Wittgenstein has in mind.

by claiming that one only uses it 'strategically', or that one really thinks of it as an 'umbrella term', or that one really ought only to speak of various *kinds* of women, or that one always mentally must add quotation marks to the word in order to place it under deconstructive erasure, are misguided because they are unnecessary.

Whether it is to reaffirm or to deconstruct the concept, most feminist theories today rely on a universalized and reified concept of 'femininity'. In this essay I first show that a feminist theory that starts from an ordinary understanding of what a woman is, namely a person with a female body, will not necessarily be either metaphysical or essentialist. I also show that such a theory does not have to be committed to the belief that sex and/or gender differences always manifest themselves in all cultural and personal activities, or that whenever they do, then they are always the most important features of a person or a practice. Women's bodies are human as well as female.[9] Women have interests, capacities, and ambitions that reach far beyond the realm of sexual differences, however one defines these. Investigations of the meaning of femininity in specific historical and theoretical contexts are indispensable to the feminist project of understanding and transforming sexist cultural practices and traditions. Yet any given woman will transcend the category of femininity, however it is defined. A feminism that reduces women to their sexual difference can only ever be the negative mirror image of sexism. It is because Simone de Beauvoir never forgot that one of the many possible answers to the question 'What is a woman?' is 'a human being', that I have been able to make such extensive use of *The Second Sex* in this essay. Yet it is as oppressive and theoretically unsatisfactory to reduce women to their 'general humanity' as it is to reduce them to their femininity. Beauvoir herself writes: 'Surely woman is, like man, a human being, but such a declaration is abstract. The fact is that every concrete human being is always in a specific situation' (*SS* xx; *DSa* 13; TA).[10]

---

[9] None of this is meant to block serious inquiry into the question of sexually ambiguous or intersexed bodies. For a beginning of such discussions, see the analysis of various questions raised by the existence of transsexuals in this essay.

[10] In French: 'le fait est que tout être humain concret est toujours *singulièrement situé* (my emphasis). Parshley translates this as 'The fact is that every concrete human being is always a singular, separate individual'.

As Beauvoir shows, the question of what a woman is instantly raises the question of the relationship between the particular and the general.[11]

The answer to the question of what a woman is, is not one. To say this, moreover, is specifically to deny that the answer is that woman is not one.[12] It may be that, in some situations, it makes sense to understand a given woman or a given group of women as, say, plural and decentred. Yet to generalize this or any other view is to fabricate yet another reified concept of femininity. Too many forms of contemporary feminism appear unable to understand women who do not conform to their own more or less narrow vision of what a woman is or ought to be. The predictable result is the proliferation of accusations of 'exclusionism' against this or that theory. What we need today more than ever is a feminism committed to seeking justice and equality for women, in the most ordinary sense of the word. Only such a feminism will be able adequately to grasp the complexity of women's concrete, everyday concerns. That feminism, I am happy to say, exists. Moreover, usually even the most anti-metaphysical feminist theorists support it in practice. No feminist I know is incapable of understanding what it means to say that the Taliban are depriving Afghan women of their most elementary human rights just because they are women. The problem is not the meaning of these words, but the fact that too many academic feminists, whether students or professors, fear that if they were to use such sentences in their intellectual work, they would sound dreadfully naive and unsophisticated. Such fear, incidentally, is not only grounded on a certain theoretical confusion about sex and gender, but also on the idea that academic writing and ordinary language and experiences are somehow opposed to each other. (In a somewhat oblique way, Chapter 2 in this book is an attempt to undo the second belief; this essay is trying to deal with the first.)

This essay, academic and theoretical as it is, won't tell anyone

[11] I discuss this question at some length in Ch. 2, below.
[12] *Ce sexe qui n'en est pas un* (*This Sex Which Is Not One*) is the title of one of Luce Irigaray's most influential books.

what to do about the Taliban. It does show, however, that we do not have to believe that the word 'woman' always carries heavy metaphysical baggage. If I am right about this, then it follows that an anti-essentialist feminist may very well claim that the point of feminism is to make the world a better place for women without being caught in the slightest theoretical contradiction. For me, at least, this is an immensely liberating conclusion. My aim in this essay, then, is to show that the question of what a woman is, is crucial to feminist theory, and that anyone who is willing to think it through once more from the beginning stands to gain a real sense of intellectual freedom.

I. BIOLOGY AND SOCIAL NORMS

What was decided among the prehistoric Protozoa cannot be annulled by Act of Parliament.

Geddes and Thomson, 1889

Pervasive Sex

'Sometime in the eighteenth century, sex as we know it was invented', Thomas Laqueur writes in his illuminating study *Making Sex* (149). At this time Western culture was moving from what Laqueur calls a 'one-sex model' to a 'two-sex model' of sexual difference. From Antiquity to the Middle Ages women's anatomy was not seen as inherently different from men's, only as a different arrangement of the same parts: 'all parts that are in men are present in woman', wrote the sixteenth-century doctor Fallopius (Laqueur 97). The vagina was considered an inverted penis, the womb an interior scrotum. Since male and female reproductive organs were not taken to be fundamentally differ-ent, anatomical differences were pictured as hierarchical as opposed to complementary. Man was on top and woman at the bottom of the same scale of values. In this picture, biology or anatomy did not ground the social and cultural differences between the sexes. If the social order was a manifestation of God's plan for mankind, there was no need to appeal to biology to explain why women could not preach or inherit property. As

Laqueur puts it, in this situation gender precedes sex.[13] Although Lacqueur does not say so, the implication is that sexist ideologies based on appeals to what feminists today call gender are no less oppressive than those based on appeals to biological, anatomical, or genetic sex differences.

Under the 'one-sex model' anatomy and biology were ideologically insignificant compared to, say, theology. This changed dramatically with the shift to the 'two-sex model'. In 1913 a British doctor named Walter Heape produced a particularly representative expression of the 'two-sex' view of sexual difference:

> the reproductive system is not only structurally but functionally fundamentally different in the Male and the Female; and since all other organs and systems of organs are affected by this system, it is certain that the Male and Female are essentially different throughout. . . . [They are] complementary, in no sense the same, in no sense equal to one another; the accurate adjustment of society depends on proper observation of this fact (quoted in Laqueur 220).

Science has taken the place of theology or natural philosophy, and biology, as the science of the body, has been drafted into ideological service. Scientific truth, not divine revelation, is supposed to keep women in their place.

I am not turning to Laqueur because I am certain that he is right in his analysis of the history of sex. For all I know, the whole idea of a shift from a 'one-sex' to a 'two-sex model' is wrong. What interests me in Laqueur's fascinating book, however, is the way the 'two-sex model' produces accounts which over and over again picture biological sex as something that seeps out from the ovaries and the testicles and into every cell in the body until it has saturated the whole person. What this shows, to my mind, is that in the nineteenth century, biological sex is pictured as *pervasive*.[14] My

---

[13] '[I]n these pre-enlightenment texts, and even some later ones, *sex*, or the body, must be understood as the epiphenomenon, while *gender*, what we would take to be a cultural category, was primary or "real" ' (8). The formulation is helpful for contemporary readers, but should not be taken to mean that people actually thought in terms of a distinction between sex and gender in pre-modern times.

[14] Laqueur does not use the expression 'pervasive sex': I take responsibility for this interpretation.

claim is not that this was never the case before (I am not a historian and have not done the research to be able to say whether it was or not). My claim, rather, is that precisely at the time that modern feminism is born (in the period stretching from Mary Wollstonecraft through John Stuart Mill to Henrik Ibsen and the first women's movement) it does seem to be the case that sex is pictured as pervasive. Every feminist from Wollstonecraft onwards finds it necessary to oppose this idea. It is in the encounter with the pervasive picture of sex that the need for something like the sex/gender distinction is born.[15]

In the pervasive picture of sex, then, a woman becomes a woman to her fingertips: this is biological determinism with a vengeance. Because sexual desire is considered to trickle out from the reproductive glands, heterosexuality is taken for granted. Pervasive sex saturates not only the person, but everything the person touches. If housework, childcare, and selfless devotion are female, heroic exploits are male, and so are science and philosophy. Whole classes of activities are now endowed with a sex. The modern world is a world steeped in sex: every habit, gesture, and activity is sexualized and categorized as male or female, masculine or feminine. In the transition to the 'two-sex model', man and woman emerge as two different species.

Strindberg's 1887 play *The Father* provides a vivid example of this way of thinking about sexual difference. An avid reader of contemporary science, Strindberg was particularly well informed about contemporary debates concerning the nature of women and men.[16] In *The Father* man and woman, husband and wife, are two different species, the sexual relationship does not exist, and the truth of sexual difference is a struggle until death, where the most powerful wins:

---

[15] I am grateful to Chris Vanden Bossche at the University of Notre Dame for helping me to clarify what I want and do not want to use Laqueur for, and to Vigdis Songe-Møller for sharing with me her doubts about Laqueur's validity for Ancient Greek society.

[16] It is no coincidence that the Captain in the play is a scientist, whose work his wife Laura is not only incapable of understanding, but considers as a sign of his madness.

THE CAPTAIN. One last word about reality. Do you hate me?
LAURA. Yes, sometimes! When you are a man.[17]
THE CAPTAIN. This is like race hatred. If it is true that we're descended from apes, then it must have been from two different species. We're simply not like each other, are we?
LAURA. What is all this supposed to mean?
THE CAPTAIN. I realize that in this struggle one of us must go under.
LAURA. Which one?
THE CAPTAIN. The weaker, naturally!
LAURA. And the stronger is right?
THE CAPTAIN. He's always right, since he has the power!
LAURA. Then I'm right![18]

If sexual difference produces two different species, then only power—sexual warfare—will resolve the resulting impasse, Strindberg concludes. Either radical patriarchy or—as Strindberg feared—radical matriarchy would do the trick. The two-sex model, Strindberg realized, cannot produce a relationship between the sexes, at least not if the word 'relationship' implies mutual trust and understanding.

In the picture of sex resulting from the 'two-sex model' any transgression against sexual norms seems 'unnatural'. Since an 'unnatural' man or a woman is no longer a 'real' man or a woman, moreover, different concepts have to be forged to cover the proliferation of new sexual species: Krafft-Ebing's fabulous catalogues of sexual perversions come to mind. Foucault illustrates this logic in his stunning account of the invention of the modern homosexual:

> The nineteenth-century homosexual became a personage, a past, a case history, and a childhood, in addition to being a type of life, a life form, and a morphology, with an indiscreet anatomy and possibly a mysterious physiology. Nothing that went into his total composition was unaffected by his sexuality. It was everywhere present in him: at the root of all his actions because it was their insidious and indefinitely active principle; written immodestly on

---

[17] The play shows that in his relations to his wife, the Captain oscillates between behaving as a phallic, sexual male and regressing to a baby-like state. Laura's 'when you are a man' alludes to her impression that when he isn't a man, he is a baby.

[18] My translation from Strindberg, *Fadren* 72. A somewhat different translation may be consulted in *Strindberg: Five Plays* 35.

> his face and body because it was a secret that always gave itself away. It was consubstantial with him, less as a habitual sin than as a singular nature. . . . The sodomite had been a temporary aberration; the homosexual was now a species (43).

The pervasive picture of sex gives rise to essentialism, biologism, accusations of degeneration and 'unnatural' behaviour. It can certainly only consider two sexes. It sexualizes not only the whole person, whether this person is a woman, a man, or a so-called 'pervert', but the whole world of human activities. *This* is the picture of sex that the great majority of contemporary feminists, gays, and lesbians rightly oppose.

When one pictures sex as pervasive, there can be no difference between male and masculine, female and feminine, sex and gender. This would also, incidentally, be true for a pervasive picture of *gender*. As Laqueur's research shows, modern feminist theory was born at a time when sexist ideology often grounded its claims about the subordination of women on appeals to the sciences of the body, particularly biology. This explains why the question of the relationship between nature and social norms has become so important in modern feminist theory. But feminists have no reason to feel more sanguine about ideologies that ground their claims about sexual difference on gender, such as appeals to God's plan for women, or the belief that 'femininity' (whatever this is taken to mean) is eternally subversive because it is eternally 'outside discourse'. Whether it is gender or sex that is pictured as pervasive, the result is an unwarranted sexualization (or 'genderization') of women, and occasionally also of men.[19]

The encounter between the pervasive picture of sex and modern feminism produced the sex/gender distinction and its equivalents. (Here it does not matter what words one uses to express the distinction between these two ways of understanding sexual difference.) Trusting in the authority of science, however, many nineteenth-century biological determinists hoped that the question of women's rights, capacities, and duties could be settled

---

[19] See Sect. V, below, for a more extensive discussion of generalizations about gender.

once and for all. But the more science they read, the less obvious the meaning of the body became. For scientists disagreed about the scientific interpretation of the body, and even more about the correct *social* interpretation of the biological facts established by science (see Laqueur 193): 'The body could mean almost anything and hence almost nothing at all', Laqueur writes (217). Once the body was taken to be meaningful, it became possible for feminists, gays, and others to fight over its interpretation, to dispute just how much or how little meaning the body has in human society. Historically, then, *gender* emerged as an attempt to give to biology what belongs to biology, no more and no less. Gender may be pictured as a barricade thrown up against the insidious pervasiveness of sex.

Biological Determinism

Late nineteenth-century biological determinists drew on the pervasive picture of sex. A quick look at the claims such scientists routinely made about women and men will make it resplendently clear why feminists needed to introduce a distinction between biology and social norms. In 1883 W. K. Brooks, Professor of Biology at Johns Hopkins University, published a book entitled *The Law of Heredity*. The chapter discussing the intellectual differences between men and women was first published in the anti-feminist *Popular Science Monthly* in 1879.[20] Much quoted and much debated, Brooks's views were at the forefront of discussions of biology and women's rights in the last two decades of the nineteenth century.[21] His starting point was the observation that 'among the higher animals . . . the males are more variable than the females' (326). According to Brooks, this 'law is so pronounced and conspicuous that its existence has long been

---

[20] According to Cynthia Eagle Russett, the editor of the *Popular Science Monthly* scolded people promoting women's rights for their refusal to be guided by science: 'And yet the fundamental questions of this important movement belong solely to scientific investigators' (quoted in Russett 13).

[21] Russett discusses Brooks's influence on G. Stanley Hall, Havelock Ellis, and others (see Russett 92–6).

recognized by all naturalists' (323).[22] This 'fact' can best be explained, he writes, by assuming that the ovum transmits hereditary characteristics and sperm cells transmit acquired characteristics:[23]

> According to this view, the male element is the originating and the female is the perpetuating factor; the ovum is conservative, the male cell progressive. Heredity or adherence to type is brought about by the ovum; variation and adaptation through the male element; and the ovum is the essential, the male cell the secondary factor in heredity. . . . Like Aristotle and the ancients, we must believe that the two reproductive elements play widely different parts. Like Bonnet and Haller, we see that the structure of the adult is latent in the egg (84–5).

For Brooks it is obvious that social differences between the sexes are caused by their physiological differences: 'If there is fundamental difference in the sociological influence of the sexes, its origin must be sought in the physiological differences between them' (243).[24] Moving on to the intellectual differences between men and women, he claims that men's brains enable them to grasp the unknown: discoveries, science, the highest artistic and philosophical insights are reserved for them. Women's brains can deal with the known, the ordinary, and the everyday, keep track of traditions and social customs; in short, take care of everything

---

[22] The variability hypothesis, as it was called, was in fact widely accepted at the time. In *The Descent of Man* (1871) Darwin wrote that 'Numerous measurements were carefully made of the stature, the circumference of the neck and chest, the length of the back-bone and of the arms, in various races; and nearly all these measurements show that the males differ much more from one another than do the females. This fact indicates that, as far as these characters are concerned, it is the male which has been chiefly modified, since the several races diverged from their common stock' (638). Numerous commentators concluded that males were simply 'higher' on the evolutionary ladder than females.

[23] As Brooks himself points out, this theory, which sounds so bizarre to modern ears, positions him 'midway between Darwin's theory of natural selection and Lamarckianism' (80).

[24] He also writes that 'Our examination of the origin and significance of the physiological differences between the sexes, and of the parts which they have taken in the progress of the past, would therefore lead us to expect certain profound and fundamental psychological differences, having the same importance' (257).

that requires 'rational action without reflection' (258). Women preserve the old, men discover the new; 'the ovum is conservative, the male cell progressive'.

Science, Brooks continues, ought to determine social policy concerning women: 'If there is . . . a fundamental and constantly increasing difference between the sexes . . . the clear recognition of this difference must form both the foundation and super-structure of all plans for the improvement of women' (242–3). If his scientific conclusions give comfort to adherents of the status quo, this cannot be helped:

> It is hardly necessary to call attention to the obvious fact that our conclusions have a strong leaning to the conservative or old-fashioned view of the subject,—to what many will call the 'male' view of women. The positions which women already occupy in society and the duties which they perform are, in the main, what they should be if our view is correct; and any attempt to improve the condition of women by ignoring or obliterating the intellectual differences between them and men must result in disaster to the race (263).

Although it is tempting to continue by quoting Brooks's account of women's intellectual inferiority, his gloating over the fact that there has been no female Shakespeare, Raphael, or Handel, or his insistence that women cannot manage intellectual 'reflection', I shall restrain myself, since these themes do not add anything new to his general thesis of male variability and female stability.

Another influential text from the same period is *The Evolution of Sex* by the Scottish researchers Patrick Geddes and J. Arthur Thomson, first published in Britain in 1889. Geddes and Thomson's central claim is that males and females exhibit different 'metabolisms'. Females are 'anabolic', males 'katabolic'; males tend to expend, and females to conserve, energy. Males 'live at a loss', Geddes and Thomson write, 'females . . . live at a profit' (26); or in even more colourful language, males exhibit 'a preponderance of waste over repair' (50). Discussing Brooks's views, they stress that their own thesis is entirely compatible with his: 'The greater variability of the males is indeed natural, if they be the more katabolic sex' (29).

Working their way from a consideration of the adult organism down through the sexual organs and tissues, Geddes and Thomson finally arrive at the sex-cells themselves, or rather at the protoplasm 'that makes them what they are' (81). This induces them to launch into a lengthy discussion of protozoa (unicellular organisms): 'It is among the Protozoa that we must presently look, if we hope to understand the origin and import either of "male and female" or of fertilization' (89). If the protozoa contain the secret of sexual difference, it is because Geddes and Thomson believe that the ovum and the sperm cell *are* protozoa, the only cells in the body that date back to the earliest evolutionary stages. This is how they picture the reproductive cells:

> Just as the ovum, large, well nourished, and passive, is a cellular expression of female characteristics, so the smaller size, less nutritive habit, and predominant activities of the male are summed up in the sperm. As the ovum is usually one of the largest, the sperm is one of the smallest of cells (109).

Geddes and Thomson then drive the point home: 'If the anabolic and katabolic contrast, so plainly seen in the sex-elements, be the fundamental one, we must expect to find it saturating through the entire organism' (130). This is true for all higher animals as well as for humans. The conclusion is inevitable: 'It is generally true that the males are more active, energetic, eager, passionate, and variable; the females more passive, conservative, sluggish, and stable' (270). In other words: the world is full of hungry, lean males in energetic pursuit of large, sluggish females (who, by the sound of it, must be sorely tempted to gobble the little man up for breakfast: there is more than a little fear of the female in this picture).

Geddes and Thomson do not doubt that their theory has clear social and political consequences:

> We have seen that a deep difference in constitution expresses itself in the distinction between male and female, whether these be physical or mental. The differences may be exaggerated or lessened, but to obliterate them it would be necessary to have all the evolution over again on a new basis. What was decided among the prehistoric Protozoa cannot be annulled by Act of Parliament (267).

They deplore the fact that so many contemporary writers completely neglect 'the biological considerations underlying the relations of the sexes' (267). Politics and economics cannot solve the question of the 'subjection of women':

> The reader need not be reminded of . . . the attitude of the ordinary politician, who supposes that the matter is one essentially to be settled by the giving or withholding of the franchise. The exclusively political view of the problem has in turn been to a large extent subordinated to that of economic *laissez-faire,* from which of course it consistently appeared that all things would be settled as soon as women were sufficiently plunged into the competitive industrial struggle for their own daily bread. While, as the complexly ruinous results of this inter-sexual competition for subsistence upon both sexes and upon family life have begun to become manifest, the more recent economic panacea of redistribution of wealth has naturally been invoked, and we have merely somehow to raise women's wages (268).

Giving women the vote, or—even more thoughtlessly—paying them decent wages, are misguided attempts to impose a social order without foundation in nature. Just as Brooks predicts the end of the 'race' if women's position were to change, Geddes and Thomson believe that the 'species' will come to a ruinous end unless women are kept out of economic competition with men.[25]

Although Brooks and Geddes and Thomson harp on different leitmotifs (male variability versus anabolic and catabolic protozoa), the structure of their arguments is remarkably similar:

(1)   the characteristics of the reproductive cells saturate the adult human organism (this is the pervasive—and obviously heterosexist—picture of sex)

AND

(2*a*) biological facts justify social norms;[26]
or

---

[25]   Russett discusses Geddes and Thomson at length (see esp. 89–92), as does Sayers (see 38–50).

[26]   By 'social norms' here and in the following I mean 'social norms concerning sex roles and the relationship between the sexes'. I supply six different variations of the three authors' view of the relationship between biological facts and social norms since they seem to wander between all of them without much consistency, often producing circular arguments (first existing social norms are taken to be the aim of evolution, then evolution is used to prove that existing social norms are indeed the result of evolution).

(2*b*) science both can and should tell us what our social norms
should be;
or

(2*c*) social norms are expressions of biological facts;
or

(2*d*) social norms have their cause and origin in nature;
or

(2*e*) attempts to change the existing social norms will have disastrous consequences for humanity, since they are against the
natural law (the biological facts);
or

(2*f*) unless social norms are brought back into harmony with the
natural law (the biological facts), there will be disastrous
consequences for humanity.

The claims listed from 2*b* to 2*f* are really just variations on 2*a*, the
idea that *biological facts justify social norms.* In Brooks's and Geddes
and Thomson's texts, this belief draws massive support from the
pervasive picture of sex (claim 1). This picture of sex enables
them to overlook the difference between Plato and the protozoa,
between Raphael and the rhizopods, barnacles, beetles, and
butterflies that provide the evidence for their theses about
human sexual difference. For these writers, a man is essentially an
enormous sperm cell, a woman a giant ovum.

   Biological determinism presupposes a pervasive picture of sex
and considers that biology grounds and justifies social norms:

Biology

Social Norms

There is no distinction between male (sex) and masculine
(gender) or between female and feminine. Whatever a woman
does is, as it were, an expression of the ovum in her. This view,
clearly, is essentialist and heterosexist, and I take as given that all
feminists will want to oppose it.[27] I shall now examine three

---

[27] I am aware of the fact that some late 19th-cent. women tried to ground their
feminism on biological determinism. There are also feminists today who remain
biological determinists. Such feminists usually believe that women's biology make

different ways of responding to the biological determinists' pervasive picture of sex.

II. SEX AND GENDER IN THE 1960S AND 1970S

[I dream of] an androgynous and genderless (though not sexless) society, in which one's sexual anatomy is irrelevant to who one is, what one does, and with whom one makes love.

Gayle Rubin, 1975

Stoller and Rubin

The English-language distinction between the words sex and gender was first developed in the 1950s and 1960s by psychiatrists and other medical personnel working with intersexed and transsexual patients. The transsexuals' dilemma has been summed up as a sense of being 'trapped in the wrong body'. Transsexuals feel that the sex of their body does not correspond to the sex of their mind. Psychiatrists were intrigued by the question of how transsexuals came to develop their sense of belonging to the 'wrong sex'. Once the terms sex and gender had been introduced, doctors could claim that transsexuals suffered from a 'mismatch' between their sex and their gender. This had the advantage of making it look as if the solution to the problem was straightforward. All that needed to be done to cure transsexuals was to bring their sex and their gender into harmonious correspondence with each other by changing the body through surgery and hormone treatment. Why most doctors and all transsexuals consider that the obvious way to achieve this is to change the body and not the mind, is a question I shall not go into here.[28]

Thus, the distinction between sex and gender emerged from a

---

them superior to men, or if not superior, then fundamentally different from men spiritually, mentally, and ethically. They usually wish to inhabit a more 'natural' social order. I do not intend to discuss biological determinist forms of feminism any further in this essay.

[28] I doubt that the distinction between sex and gender actually explains very much about transsexuality, but that is another matter. For a good account of the medicalization of transsexual identity, see Hausman.

concern with individual identity. At its inception, the distinction medicalizes 'sex' and turns 'gender' into a purely psychological category. In 1963 the American psychoanalyst Robert Stoller first formulated a concept of *gender identity* in a paper presented at the 23rd International Psycho-Analytical Congress in Stockholm: 'Gender identity is the sense of knowing to which sex one belongs, that is, the awareness "I am a male" or "I am a female". . . . The advantage of the phrase "gender identity" lies in the fact that it clearly refers to one's self-image as belonging to a specific sex' ('A Contribution' 220).[29] But 'gender identity' is a term concerned only with a person's psychological experience of belonging to one sex or another. By 1968 Stoller had expanded his insights and developed four different concepts:

> I prefer to restrict the term *sex* to a biological connotation. Thus, with few exceptions, there are two sexes, male and female. . . . *Gender* is a term that has psychological or cultural rather than biological connotations. If the proper terms for sex are 'male' and 'female', the corresponding terms for gender are 'masculine' and 'feminine'; these latter may be quite independent of (biological) sex. . . . *Gender identity* starts with the knowledge and awareness, whether conscious or unconscious, that one belongs to one sex and not to the other, though as one develops, gender identity becomes much more complicated, so that, for example, one may sense himself as not only a male but a masculine man or an effeminate man or even a man who fantasies being a woman. *Gender role* is the overt behavior one displays in society, the role which he plays, especially with other people, to establish his position with them insofar as his and their evaluation of his gender is concerned (*Sex and Gender* 9–10).

Although the term 'gender role' soon faded from view in feminist theory, Stoller's other three concepts were quickly appropriated

---

[29] Although John Money and his colleagues coined the phrase 'gender role' as early as 1955 (see Money, Hampson, and Hampson 302), it was Stoller's explicit contrast between sex and gender that fired feminists' imagination. In fact, in 1985, Money polemicized against Stoller's definitions of sex and gender on the grounds that it destroyed his own original concept of 'gender role': 'Its outcome was to restore the metaphysical partitioning of body and mind. Sex was ceded to biology. Gender was ceded to psychology and social science. The ancient regime was restored!' (282).

by feminists. Crucial to Stoller's distinction between sex and gender is the idea that sex belongs to the realm of science, to biology and medicine. Sex is a category that requires scientific description. All the 1960s and 1970s feminist elaborations of the distinction between sex and gender, including that of Gayle Rubin, incorporate this understanding of sex.[30] The 1960s view of sex, then, is clearly at odds with the traditional or pre-feminist meaning of the word in English, where a reference to someone's sex is simply a reference to their being a man or a woman.[31]

When Gayle Rubin, in her path-breaking 1975 essay 'The Traffic in Women', appropriated Stoller's categories for her own feminist purposes, her aim was to develop conceptual tools that would combat sexism by explaining why and how women's oppression was maintained in widely different cultures:

> [Feminists need to] build descriptions of the part of social life which is the locus of the oppression of women, of sexual minorities, and of certain aspects of human personality within individuals. I call that part of social life the 'sex/gender system', for lack of a more elegant term. As a preliminary definition, a 'sex/gender system' is the set of arrangements by which a society transforms biological sexuality into products of human activity, and in which these transformed sexual needs are satisfied (159).

Rejecting the term 'patriarchy' on the grounds that not all sexist systems are ruled by fathers, Rubin nevertheless considers that 'sex/gender system' designates a system that oppresses women. For Rubin, bodily sexual differences and the sex drive are 'biological', the 'raw material' for the production of gender:

> Hunger is hunger, but what counts as food is culturally determined and obtained. Every society has some form of organized economic activity. Sex is sex, but what counts as sex is equally culturally determined and obtained. Every society also has a sex/gender system— a set of arrangements by which the biological raw material of human sex and procreation is shaped by human, social intervention and satisfied in a conventional manner, no matter how bizarre some of the conventions may be (165).

[30] Heinämaa ('Woman—Nature, Product, Style'), Chanter, and Gatens all discuss Stoller's sex/gender distinction.

[31] This, moreover, is also the meaning of *sexe* in French, as Beauvoir's title *Le deuxième sexe* makes clear.

What interests Rubin is not sex, but gender. For her, the fundamental meaning of gender is oppressive social norms: gender is the oppressive result of a *social* production process.[32] On the structural level, Rubin takes sex to mean biological sexual differences and gender to mean the oppressive social norms brought to bear on these differences. This is a classic example of a feminist rejection of biological determinism. It is important to stress that on Rubin's definition, gender is always oppressive, that in human society there can be no such thing as non-oppressive gender differences.

This assumption has been exceptionally influential in US feminism. Ideologically, it has been used to justify the idea that women are above all victims of male power. Perhaps the clearest intellectual elaboration of Rubin's view can be found in Catherine MacKinnon's understanding of what a woman is, namely the effect of the 'organized expropriation of the sexuality of some for the use of others'.[33] When Judith Butler

[32] Rubin's essay triggered much debate among Marxist and socialist feminists in the 1970s and 1980s. The question was whether her understanding of how the sex/gender system works was compatible with a Marxist analysis of production, economic relationships, and so on. As recently as 1996, Teresa Ebert claimed that Rubin's understanding of sex and gender allowed feminists to '[suppress] any knowledge of the economic relations of production in their theories of gender and sexuality' (47). It is certainly true that much recent US feminist work in the humanities has been spectacularly unconcerned by questions of class, economic production, conditions of labour, and so on. Whether this is a necessary consequence of Rubin's way of thinking about sex and gender, is a question I shall not venture into here.

[33] MacKinnon writes: 'the organized expropriation of the sexuality of some for the use of others defines the sex, woman' ('Feminism, Marxism' 2). I am not implying that Gayle Rubin would necessarily have to agree with such a radicalization of her own views. The problem with MacKinnon's definition of woman is that she tries to define woman in a structural way, to make the concept correspond to the Marxist concept of class. For Marx classes are fully defined by their antagonism to each other: the working class is per definition the class that is structurally bound to struggle against the bourgeoisie. Without the concept of class struggle, there is no proletariat. It hardly seems satisfactory, however, to define men and women simply in terms of their structural antagonism to each other. Such a definition makes any hope of non-patriarchy or reconciliation between the sexes meaningless. Or rather, a more complex understanding of how the power relations between the sexes

considers sex to be an effect of power, she too becomes one of Rubin's inheritors.[34] While such structural theories of what a woman is enable feminists to produce quite remarkable critiques of sexist ideology and misogynist abuse of power, they have notorious difficulties in explaining what the sexually different body has to do with being a woman, or with women's oppression, and in providing a sufficiently nuanced account of individual subjectivity. Nor are they well placed to provide analyses of power relations more complex than that of domination and subordination.

Although Rubin emphasizes structural social and cultural formations, she also includes personal identity within the sex/gender system. While immensely influential, it would seem that Rubin's attempt to theorize individual subjectivity introduces a number of unacknowledged ambiguities in her understanding of sex and gender. This is how Rubin's argument about individuals goes. All societies turn biological sex into gender in one way or another, she writes: 'Human sexual life will always be subject to convention and human intervention. It will never be completely "natural", if only because our species is social, cultural, and articulate. The wild profusion of infantile sexuality will always be tamed' (199). The individual men and women we meet in everyday life are products of the sex/gender system; no human being exemplifies 'raw' or 'natural' sex.

The problem with this observation is that it makes it all too easy to think of sex as a Kantian *Ding an sich* beyond the reach of

---

actually work, will not be able to use such a definition of gender. In *The Second Sex* Beauvoir compares the oppression of women to that of Jews, Blacks in America, and the proletariat. Unlike MacKinnon she concludes that while the oppression of women shares some features with all of these forms of oppression, it is nevertheless not theorizable in exactly the same terms: 'The proletariat can propose to massacre the ruling class . . . but woman cannot even dream of exterminating the males. The bond that unites [woman] to her oppressors is not comparable to any other. The division of the sexes is a biological fact, not an event in human history. Their conflict has emerged from within a primordial *Mitsein*, and woman has not broken it' (*SS* xxv; *DSa* 19; TA).

34 See Sect. III, below for an extensive discussion of Butler's work.

ordinary human experience.[35] To say that sex means chromosomal, hormonal, and anatomical sexual differences is perfectly
meaningful. But chromosomes are hardly the *Ding an sich*. Yet, in
poststructuralist sex and gender theory, such statements have
frequently given rise to the idea that there is an alarming conceptual gap between sex (chromosomes, hormones, etc.) and the
body (the concrete, historically and geographically situated
entity) that feminist theory now must bridge. Labouring under
this picture of sex, some feminists seem to believe that as soon as
the body acts, walks, and talks it becomes gender, that is to say an
entity *not* produced by chromosomes, hormones, and so on.
Interpreted in this way, sex becomes a uselessly abstract category,
whereas gender slides towards the traditional prefeminist sense of
sex, and so towards a usage in which the sex/gender distinction is
not operative. Recent poststructuralist theorists relentlessly criticize this understanding of the sex/gender distinction. Yet they
also promote it.[36] Spellbound by this understanding of sex and
gender, they labour to make its abstract and scientistic understanding of sex yield a good theory of the concrete body. As I shall
go on to show, this is a hopeless task.[37]

'Gender is between the ears, sex is between the legs', is a slogan
much used by contemporary transsexuals. In this slogan another
common feminist interpretation of the 1960s sex/gender distinction is at work: sex is the body, gender is the mind.[38] The philosophical and political drawbacks of this reintroduction of the

---

[35] Rubin herself never explicitly says that sex is 'outside language' or 'outside
history'. Such phrases are nevertheless common—and it has to be said, well-
founded—interpretations of her views. In her pioneering 1984 essay 'Thinking
Sex', Rubin herself criticizes 'The Traffic in Women' for not drawing a distinction between gender and sexual desire (what some would call sexual orientation). On my reading, Rubin is a little too hard on her earlier essay here.

[36] Eve Sedgwick generally refers to 'sex' in its 1960s sense as 'chromosomal
sex' (*Epistemology* 27). She also writes: ' "M. saw that the person who approached
was of the opposite sex." Genders . . . may be said to be opposite; but in what
sense is XX the opposite of XY?' (*Epistemology* 28).

[37] I discuss poststructuralist accounts of sex and gender in Sect. III, below.

[38] Here and in the rest of this essay I will refer to the '1960s distinction' for
short. I really mean to indicate the theories of sex and gender developed on the
basis of Stoller and Rubin's theories, which in fact date back to the 1950s and
find their fullest feminist expression in the 1970s and early 1980s.

body/mind distinction are only too apparent. Entirely divorced from the mind, the body is perceived as a mere object, subject to the mind's decisions, a blank slate on which gender writes its script. In this idealist view, the body (nature) is entirely subordinated to the mind. No contemporary feminist theorists favour this interpretation of the sex/gender distinction, and I will not discuss it further here.[39]

Rubin's pioneering work is more convincing as an analysis of social norms and practices than as a theory of individual subjectivity. In particular, Rubin's understanding of what would count as social liberation for women is suggestive. Armed with much anthropological data, Rubin denies that *any* social configuration of sex is based on or caused by biological facts. Whatever social norms rule the expressions we give to our sex and our sexuality, they are completely arbitrary and usually oppressive to women. Thorough understanding of the social relations of sex and gender will contribute to the feminist task of 'eliminating the social system which creates sexism and gender' (204). But this is not enough:

> I personally feel that the feminist movement must dream of even more than the elimination of the oppression of women. It must dream of the elimination of obligatory sexualities and sex roles. The dream I find most compelling is one of an androgynous and genderless (though not sexless) society, in which one's sexual anatomy is irrelevant to who one is, what one does, and with whom one makes love (204).

In Rubin's utopia gender would disappear. There would be *no* social norms for correct sexual and sexed behaviour. Moving beyond the question of the oppression of women towards a vision of a society where all sexualities may be freely expressed, she embraces a utopia that inspired many 1960s and 1970s critiques of stereotyped images of women.[40] To expect someone to be masculine (which here means 'to conform to socially normative notions of what a man should be like'), just because he is male, or to deny

---

[39] Moira Gatens 1983 essay on sex and gender contains an excellent critique of the body/mind reading of sex and gender.

[40] Mary Ellmann's *Thinking About Women* remains the best and most entertaining example of this trend.

someone the right to behave in 'masculine' ways just because she is female, is to reinforce the sex/gender system. Such stereotyping is oppressive to women, and also, albeit to a lesser degree, to men.[41]

Winning the right to mix and match stereotypes (so that a woman may choose between traditional femininity and traditional masculinity) does not liberate us from gender. When Rubin wishes to 'get rid of gender', she wishes for a society without *any* sexual stereotypes. Gender in her view is a negative term referring to arbitrary and oppressive social norms imposed upon sex and sexuality. While sex and sexuality will always be socialized in some way or other, there is no reason to pretend that the biological differences between men and women furnish the 'natural' organizing principles for that socialization. In so far as the word 'gender' refers to the systematic social organization of sexual difference—the imposition of only two general categories of being as normative for all people—in a non-sexist society gender will simply have to go. In Rubin's utopian world, instead of describing a specific behaviour as masculine or feminine, we would have to come up with more precise descriptions, to consider whether we think of the behaviour as wise, kind, selfish, expressive, or destructive *without* thinking of any of these terms as sex-specific.

In her essay 'Interpreting Gender' Linda Nicholson claims that Gayle Rubin is a 'biological foundationalist' (as opposed to a biological determinist). According to Nicholson, 'biological foundationalism' includes some measure of 'social constructionism', yet it still claims that there are 'real biological phenomena differentiating women and men that are used *in all societies in similar ways* to generate a male/female distinction' (80; my emphasis). Given that Rubin never claims that some aspects of gender are

---

[41] Perhaps one still needs to explain this point: feminists have usually not denied that men too may suffer from a sex/gender system that oppresses women. The point is that since the system fundamentally favours males, for instance by assuring them a better material situation, better working conditions, greater sexual freedom, and so on, it is not necessarily in most men's *interest* to oppose a system that in other ways may weigh heavily on them, for instance because it requires that men live up to stereotypical standards of masculinity.

absolutely invariable in all cultures, this is an unfair description of 'The Traffic in Women'. In fact, Rubin and Nicholson would seem to have a very similar understanding of the role of biological sexual differences. '[T]he position I would like feminists to endorse [is] that biology cannot be used to ground claims about "women" or "men" transculturally', Nicholson writes (89). The only difference between this formulation and Rubin's denial that biology grounds social norms is the word 'transculturally', which is superfluous in this context. To deny that biology grounds social norms *is* to deny that our sexed bodies produce *any* gender norms in whatever context.[42]

Politically, Rubin inherits Simone de Beauvoir's hope for a society where women will no longer be cast as Other. Like Beauvoir's critique of patriarchal femininity, Rubin's critique of gender bears a strong family resemblance to Marxist and socialist critiques of ideology. Gender is ideological in the precise sense that it tries to pass social arrangements off as natural.[43] Common to Rubin and Beauvoir's idea of what a non-oppressive society would look like is the thought that whatever biological differences exist between the sexes, they cannot ground any particular social norms or structures. Any attempt to invoke sex (biological or anatomical sex differences) as a pretext for imposing any specific social arrangement (gender) is ideological and ultimately oppressive. In this theory, a firm line is drawn between biology and social norms:

$$\frac{\text{Biology}}{\text{Social Norms}} \; \rightarrow \; \frac{\text{Sex}}{\text{Gender}}$$

---

[42] Nicholson is right to say that some so-called 'social constructionist' theories produce deeply oppressive generalizations about female or feminine difference (see 97). But such oppressive effects will be generated by any theory that reifies femininity or masculinity, regardless of its ideas about the role of biological, anatomical, or genetic sexual differences. If I believe that biological sex differences are an effect of 'regulatory discourses' *and* picture such discourses as all-encompassing, I am going to have just as oppressive a theory of femininity as if I were a biological determinist. I discuss the problems arising from generalizations about femininity in Sect. V below.

[43] I discuss Beauvoir's critique of 'patriarchal femininity' in Ch. 7 of my *Simone de Beauvoir*. Roland Barthes's critique of bourgeois ideology in *Mythologies* is written in the same spirit as Beauvoir's anti-naturalizing critique of sexism.

This figure works well on the general social level. Here 'sex' means something like men and women, or male and female bodies, and 'gender' means general social norms. Yet, as I have shown, Rubin does not fully acknowledge that she also uses sex and gender in a different, and far more problematic, sense. Applied to individual human beings gender appears to mean both individual gender identity and social gender norms, and the meaning of sex emigrates to the far reaches of hormones and chromosomes. Soon theorists following in Rubin's footsteps will think of sex as an ungraspable entity outside history and culture, and of gender as the only relevant term for sexual difference. This appears to leave a gap where the historical and socialized body should be, a gap taken to call out for theorization. But this is a theoretical problem that only arises if one assumes that the sex/gender distinction *must* be the axiomatic starting point for any theory of embodied and sexually differentiated subjectivity. It is this spurious gap that the powerful poststructuralist revision of the sex/gender paradigm steps in to fill.

III. THE POSTSTRUCTURALIST PICTURE OF SEX AND GENDER

> If the immutable character of sex is contested, perhaps this construct called sex is as culturally constructed as gender; indeed, perhaps it was always already gender, with the consequence that the distinction between sex and gender turns out to be no distinction at all.
>
> Judith Butler, 1990

Sex, Gender, and Sexual Difference

Poststructuralist theorists of sex and gender are unhappy with the way the 1960s understanding of sex and gender accounts for personal identity and the body. They consider, much as I do, that the 1960s understanding of sex easily turns sex into an ahistorical and curiously disembodied entity divorced from concrete historical and social meanings. Their critique of the sex/gender distinction has two major objectives: (1) to avoid biological determinism;

and (2) to develop a fully historical and non-essentialist understanding of sex or the body. These are aims shared by the great majority of contemporary feminists. The problem with the poststructuralist critique of sex and gender is not its ultimate goal. Rather, my argument is that the goal is not achieved, for two reasons: because the starting point for the poststructuralists' analysis is singularly unpromising; and because the theoretical machinery they bring to bear on the question of sex and gender generates a panoply of new theoretical problems that poststructuralists feel compelled to resolve, but which no longer have any connection with bodies, sex, or gender. The result is work that reaches fantastic levels of abstraction without delivering the concrete, situated, and materialist understanding of the body it leads us to expect.

Before showing how I reach these conclusions, I should stress that my subject in this section is the way the distinction between sex and gender works in poststructuralist feminist theory. I do not pretend to comment on all poststructuralist theory or on all poststructuralist feminist theory. In particular I am not going to analyse the many different ways in which poststructuralists have used the word 'gender'. The most common poststructuralist way of using the word is exemplified in Joan Scott's epochal essay 'Gender: A Useful Category of Historical Analysis'. 'The word [gender] denoted a rejection of the biological determinism implicit in the use of such terms as "sex" and "sexual difference"', she writes (29). Scott's concern is to analyse the historical and social effects of sexual difference. When she calls this subject matter 'gender', she is not necessarily opposing it to 'sex'. In her usage, the word 'gender' does the same work as the French *sexe* and the Norwegian *kjønn*, or the English *sex* in its traditional, pre-1960s meaning. Where Scott writes 'gender', Virginia Woolf would no doubt have written 'sex', and in all probability they would have meant pretty much the same thing.[44] In contemporary American academic language, Scott's usage has long since become normative, and I see no reason to deplore this.

The grounds on which Scott chooses 'gender' over 'sex' or

---

[44] '[I]t is fatal for anyone who writes to think of their sex', Virginia Woolf writes in *A Room of One's Own* (99).

'sexual difference' are nevertheless dubious. It appears that, for her, the word 'gender' in itself signals rejection of biological determinism, whereas the words 'sex' and 'sexual difference' in and by themselves signal acceptance of it.[45] In my view, no one word can serve as talismanic protection against ideological danger. The proof of resistance to biological determinism has to be established in the text as a whole. (Scott herself does so with elegance and verve.) And as soon as opposition to biological determinism has been established, it really does not matter whether one writes 'sex', 'gender', or 'sexual difference'. *The Second Sex* proves that one can be radically opposed to biological determinism without using the word 'gender' once. Conversely, it is obviously easy to say 'gender' and still be a biological determinist. Recent work in sociobiology tends to do precisely this.

In psychoanalytic theory, as opposed to poststructuralist theory, the most widely used concept is sexual difference, not sex or gender. As Moira Gatens has pointed out, the sex/gender distinction is incompatible with the psychoanalytic understanding—be it poststructuralist or not—of sexual difference. The psychoanalytic understanding of the sexually different body offers a challenging alternative to sex and gender thinking. When I started working on this essay, my intention was to include a long section on psychoanalysis. What interests me is the question of what 'femininity' means to different psychoanalytic theorists, and how different psychoanalytic views relate to Beauvoir's understanding of the body as a situation. Unfortunately, I soon realized that these are exceptionally difficult questions, and that I most certainly could not do them justice within the framework of this essay. I will return to them in another context.[46]

So far, I have shown that in Gayle Rubin's work the sex/gender distinction operates on two different levels: on a general social level, where gender becomes synonymous with

---

[45] I am not denying that words such as 'sex' or 'sexual difference' often are steeped in biological determinism, but the same is actually true for gender these days, particularly in everyday American usage. My point is that these words need not have such connotations, and that in some situations they do not have them.

[46] See Ch. 8, below, for a modest first step towards such a project.

social norms or ideology and sex means concrete human bodies; and on an individual level, where gender gets interpreted as personal identity or subjectivity, and sex is imagined to be an elusive entity inside or beyond the actual body. Although it is difficult to imagine a more unpromising point of departure, Butler and Haraway insist on taking the second, highly problematic understanding of sex and gender as the starting point for their attempts to escape identity politics, undo naive conceptions of subjectivity, and develop a concrete, materialist understanding of the body. As I will show, the theoretical difficulties produced by this choice are overwhelming. It is particularly surprising to note that poststructuralists entirely overlook Simone de Beauvoir's originality. They do not discover the enormous differences between *The Second Sex* and the 1960s understanding of sex and gender, and thus fail to appreciate that Beauvoir's understanding of subjectivity and the body offers exactly what they are looking for (see Section IV, below).

Here is a checklist of terms that regularly recur in Judith Butler, Donna Haraway, and Elizabeth Grosz's discussions of sex and gender:

SEX	**GENDER**
biological	political
natural	cultural
essence	construction
essentialist	constructionist
body	mind
passive	active
base	superstructure
being	doing
substance	performance
fixed	[mobile; variable]
stable	unstable
coherent	non-coherent
prediscursive	discursive
prelinguistic	linguistic
presocial	social
ahistorical	historical

The first thing to be stressed is that poststructuralists are *unhappy* with these dichotomies.[47] They take this binary structure to be inherent in the 1960s understanding of sex and gender, and see their own project as an immense effort to get out of this straitjacket. Judith Butler's project is to make us realize that sex is 'as culturally constructed as gender' (*Gender Trouble* 7). In terms of the checklist above, this means that we should realize that sex is as cultural, performative, unstable, discursive (and so on) as gender. In much the same way, Donna Haraway wants to 'historicize and relativize sex' (136), and also frequently refers to the need to deconstruct various binary oppositions relating to sex, gender, and the body:

> In all their versions, feminist gender theories attempt to articulate the specificity of the oppressions of women in the context of cultures which make a distinction between sex and gender salient. That salience depends on a related system of meanings clustered around a family of binary pairs: nature/culture, nature/history, natural/human, resource/product (130).

While this is an accurate account of Gayle Rubin's sex/gender system, Haraway's formulation leaves it unclear whether the terms sex and gender are themselves part of the objectionable 'family of binary pairs'. Poststructuralists certainly often interpret the pair as a variation on clear-cut binary oppositions, such as nature/culture, coherent/non-coherent, stable/unstable, and so on. Yet Gayle Rubin neither thinks of gender as the *opposite* of sex, nor does she define it as the *absence* of sex. The distinction between sex and gender cannot easily be assimilated to the kind of binary opposition that deconstructionists need to work on.

Here one might object that the distinction between writing and speech, which Derrida so memorably deconstructs, is not a binary opposition either. Yet whatever we make of Derrida's analysis of writing and speech, we may agree that these words *are* the key

---

[47] The words listed above are taken from Judith Butler, *Gender Trouble* (6–7, 24–5); Donna Haraway (134–5, 147); and Elizabeth Grosz, *Volatile Bodies* (17–18). I have suggested 'mobile' or 'variable' as the positive opposites of 'fixed'. Both terms are regularly used by poststructuralist theorists of subjectivity, but unlike 'unstable' and 'non-coherent' they do not occur on the pages I consulted.

terms in the field he is dealing with. This is not the case for sex and gender. Many non-English-speaking feminists manage very well without these particular terms, without becoming biological determinists for all that. If we find these words to be particularly troublesome for feminist theory, as many poststructuralist feminists do, the obvious strategy is to look around for a better set of concepts before investing an enormous amount of time and energy deconstructing the bad existing concepts.

The concepts sex and gender represent two different ways of thinking about sexual difference. They do not pretend to explain class, race, or nationality, or anything else. When it comes to thinking about what a woman is, therefore, the sex/gender distinction is woefully inadequate. Many critics appear to believe that a sexed human being is made up of the sum of sex plus gender. From such a perspective it does look as if everything in a woman or man that is not sex must be gender, and vice versa. Suddenly sex and gender start to look like a deconstructable 'pair'. But this analysis forgets that a sexed human being (man or woman) is more than sex and gender, and that race, age, class, sexual orientation, nationality, and idiosyncratic personal experience are other categories that always shape the experience of being of one sex or another.[48]

Whether I consider a woman to be the sum of sex plus gender, to be nothing but sex, or nothing but gender, I reduce her to her sexual difference. Such reductionism is the antithesis of everything feminism ought to stand for. In this context it makes no difference at all whether the woman's difference is taken to be natural or cultural, essential or constructed. All forms of sexual reductionism implicitly deny that a woman is a concrete, embodied human being (of a certain age, nationality, race, class, and with a wholly unique store of experiences) and not just a human

---

[48] No wonder that Haraway criticizes feminists who think in terms of sex and gender for being unable to include race in the category of gender. We shall only succeed in historicizing 'the categories of sex, flesh, body, biology, race, and nature', Haraway writes, if we ensure that 'the binary, universalizing opposition that spawned the concept of the sex/gender system ... implodes into articulated, differentiated, accountable, located, and consequential theories of embodiment, where nature is no longer imagined and enacted as resource to culture and sex to gender' (148).

being sexed in a particular way. The narrow parameters of sex and gender will never adequately explain the experience and meaning of sexual difference in human beings. This shortcoming is not repaired by adding on new factors. To think of a woman as sex plus gender plus race and so on is to miss the fact that the experience of being white or black is not detachable from the experience of being male or female.[49]

A major source of confusion in poststructuralist writings on sex and gender is the fact that many critics appear to think of the terms on each side of the checklist (see above) as interchangeable, or rather as one tightly packed bundle of concepts which can never be unpacked. All the terms on the left side of the checklist are projected on to anyone who uses the word sex, all the terms on the right side to anyone who uses the word gender. Particularly widespread is the assumption that anyone who says sex *must* be thinking of it as an essence or a substance, as ahistorical and prediscursive, and so on. There is often the implication that anyone who thinks of biology (or other sciences of the body) as producing valuable and reliable insights must be an essentialist too. In further elaborations, it usually appears that such poststructuralists think of anything natural as stable, fixed, and unchanging, and since sex in their scheme of things is natural, they assume that it follows that sex, unlike gender, is outside history, discourse, and politics. The next step, of course, is to propose various solutions to this 'problem'. The most common suggestion is that 'sex' itself must be considered to be as variable and historical as gender. My point is not that this is false, but that it is a solution to a problem produced by the poststructuralist reading of the sex/gender distinction in the first place.

The idea that sex *must* be ahistorical and outside discourse, for example, is not grounded in an analysis of the concept of sex itself. There is no good reason to assume that someone who thinks that it makes sense to speak of sex as natural must therefore be an essentialist in the bad, metaphysical, and political sense that poststructuralist feminists give the term. The kind of essentialism that

---

[49] Linda Nicholson also discusses the shortcomings of what she calls the 'additive' view of race and gender (see 83).

feminists usually worry about is the kind that claims that women's bodies inevitably give rise to and justify specific cultural and psychological norms. Poststructuralists are right to object to this view, but this is biological determinism, and although Simone de Beauvoir does believe that a woman can be defined by reference to the usual primary and secondary sexual characteristics, it is ludicrous to characterize her (or Gayle Rubin for that matter) as an 'essentialist' in this sense. For Beauvoir, the possession of the usual biological and anatomical sexual characteristics is what makes a woman a woman.[50] But given that she firmly demonstrates that this has no *necessary* social and political consequences, this is a kind of essentialism that has no negative consequences whatsoever for feminist politics. The only kind of essentialism that feminists need to reject is biological determinism.[51]

The fact that the usual understanding of sex often treats the concept as an ahistorical entity is no reason to think that it therefore must be 'outside discourse', or that it must operate as a Kantian *Ding an sich*. If we look at the way feminists use the terms feminine (gender) and female (sex), it is clear that they usually function as two different criteria of selection. Feminists assume that the word 'female' picks out a certain group of people, and that the word 'feminine' will not pick out exactly the same group

[50] It doesn't follow that there will be no ambiguous or difficult cases (see Sect. V, below, for some further discussion of transsexuality).

[51] Gayatri Spivak's famous injunctions to 'take the risk of essence', or to consider the 'strategic use of essentialism' ('In a Word', *Outside* 3–4) may be read in the light of this sentence. Perhaps Spivak may be taken to mean that not all essentialisms are *politically* equally harmful. I think that is right. But if that is so, it follows that there may be cases and situations where essence is no risk at all. Spivak's work on essentialism, particularly in the interview with Ellen Rooney entitled 'In a Word' exemplifies the tension between her allegiance to Derridean deconstruction on the one hand and her admirable grasp of concrete political situations on the other. Spivak's work is a remarkable attempt to hold these two ways of thinking about the world together without falling into theoreticism. The difficulty of the project—the tension between deconstruction and concrete political analysis—surfaces when she asks: 'Is essentialism a code word for a feeling for the empirical, sometimes?' (*Outside* 6), or when she writes: 'if one doesn't . . . consolidate ways of gathering the empirical, antiessentialism versus essentialism can prove a red herring' (*Outside* 7). Spivak's understanding of the relationship between theory and politics in general would be well worth further study.

of people. Why many poststructuralists believe that feminists who use the words in this way secretly consider 'female' the ground and essence of 'feminine' remains a mystery to me.[52]

In such claims there is a pronounced tendency to believe that if we accept that there are biological facts, then they somehow will become the ground of social norms. Consider the common post-structuralist argument that the belief that there are only two sexes, men and women, *must* be heterosexist.[53] This would be true if the speaker making the claim were a biological determinist. Given Rubin's or Beauvoir's—or indeed most feminists'—under-standing of the relationship between biology and social norms, however, this critique makes no sense at all. To deny that biology grounds social norms is to deny that the existence of two biologi-cal sexes justifies any specific socio-sexual arrangements, be they heterosexist or not.[54]

In fact, the idea that there must be something heterosexist about the belief that there are only two sexes presupposes that biology somehow gives rise to social norms. The same is true for the belief that if we can just turn sex into a more 'multiple' or 'diverse' cate-gory than it has been so far, then social norms will be relaxed. This is nothing but biological determinism with a liberal face. Even if we all agreed to have five sexes—Anne Fausto-Sterling has proposed adding 'herms', 'ferms', and 'merms' to the usual two—nothing guarantees that we would get more than two genders, or that we wouldn't be stuck with five sets of oppressive gender norms instead of two.[55] And what are the grounds for believing that a system of three, five, or ten genders (regardless of the number of sexes we decide there are) will be more liberating than two?

Sometimes the argument for a mulitiplicity of sexes is based on the idea that we have to challenge the oppressive binary opposition

[52] I don't mean to say that this usage is unproblematic, just that the problem with it has nothing to do with grounds and essences (see my discussion of femi-nist treatment of words such as 'femininity' and 'masculinity' in Sect. V, below).

[53] See Sedgwick, *Epistemology* 31; Sedgwick, 'Gender Criticism' 276 (essentially a reprint of the same passage); Butler, *Gender Trouble* 22, 33 (*et passim*).

[54] Joan Copjec has given a thoughtful critique of Butler's claims about heterosexism from a Lacanian perspective (see esp. 201–11).

[55] Fausto-Sterling proposes these terms as a way of acknowledging the main forms of intersexuality that naturally occur in human beings (see 21).

man/woman. The assumption is that if we can only show that there are third terms, categories that fall outside the two master terms, then the very meaning of man and woman, male and female will be shaken to the core. One example of this widespread belief may be found in Marjorie Garber's *Vested Interests*, where she claims that transvestism is a sign of a 'category crisis', that is to say that it represents

> a failure of definitional distinction, a borderline that becomes permeable, that permits border crossings from one (apparently distinct) category to another. . . . The binarism male/female . . . is itself put under erasure in transvestism, and a transvestite figure, or a transvestite mode, will always function as a sign of overdetermination—a mechanism of displacement from one blurred boundary to another (16).

Yet a concept ('man', 'woman') that is blurred at the edges is neither meaningless nor useless. Wittgenstein writes:

> One might say that the concept 'game' is a concept with blurred edges.—'But is a blurred concept a concept at all?'—Is an indistinct photograph a picture of a person at all? Is it even always an advantage to replace an indistinct picture by a sharp one? Isn't the indistinct one often exactly what we need?
>   Frege compares a concept to an area and says that an area with vague boundaries cannot be called an area at all. This presumably means that we cannot do anything with it.—But is it senseless to say 'Stand roughly there'? (*PI* §71).

Hermaphroditism, transvestism, transsexuality, and so on show up the fuzziness at the edges of sexual difference, but the concepts 'man' and 'woman' or the opposition between them are not thereby threatened by disintegration. Nor have all the usual ways of using the words suddenly become impossible: from the fact that the word 'game' doesn't have a clear and essential definition outside every language game, it does not follow that it does not have one within specific language games, nor does it follow that the absence of a clear definition makes the word 'game' more difficult to use, more ambiguous, more unstable, or more transgressive than other words. The existence of hermaphrodites and transsexuals proves that not all human beings can be easily categorized as either male or female, that there will always be ambiguous, unclear, or borderline cases, but I have not noticed that this has made our everyday handling of the terms 'man' and 'woman' more difficult, or the meaning of those words more inherently unstable or obscure. The fact that there are difficult cases doesn't prove that there are no easy ones. If gays, lesbians, transvestites, transsexuals, and intersexed people suffer discrimination in contemporary society, this is the fault of our social norms and ideologies concerning human sex and sexuality, not of the assumption that biologically speaking, there are only two sexes.[56]

If we are serious about denying that biology can justify social norms, it follows that the question of how many sexes there are or ought to be has *no necessary* ideological or political consequences whatsoever. It does not follow, however, that the material structure of our bodies has no impact on our way of being in the world. There is every reason to believe that the world would be vastly different if human beings had three arms and an extra pair of eyes in the back of the head. But bodily structures have no absolute meaning. For Simone de Beauvoir our bodies are an outline or sketch of the kind of projects it is possible for us to have, but it doesn't follow from this that individual choices or social and ethical norms can be deduced from the structure of the human body (see Section IV, below).

In a 1993 interview with Peter Osborne and Lynne Segal, Judith Butler demonstrates just how close the poststructuralist critique of the idea that there are only two sexes comes to biological determinism. Wondering whether Butler doesn't fail to register the 'constraints coming from the body itself', Osborne and Segal ask: 'Why is it that male bodies don't get produced as child-bearing?' (Osborne 112). In her reply Butler speaks of the social ideology that makes women feel they are failures if they do not have children:

> Why shouldn't it be that a woman who wants to have some part in child-rearing, but doesn't want to have a part in child-bearing, or who wants to have nothing to do with either, can inhabit her gender without an implicit sense of failure or inadequacy? When

---

[56] Suzanne Kessler has written a strong indictment of the thoughtless and ideologically suspect ways in which contemporary medicine treats intersexed infants.

people ask the question 'Aren't *these* biological differences?', they're not really asking a question about the materiality of the body. They're actually asking whether or not the social institution of reproduction is the most salient one for thinking about gender. In that sense, there is a discursive enforcement of a norm (Osborne 113).

Butler is perfectly right to stress that motherhood is a socially constructed institution regularly used to legitimize women's oppression. But her answer says more than this. It makes a second claim, one that I, unlike Butler, think is not necessary to secure the first. For Butler also insists that to define biological sex by reference to testicles and ovaries *is* to enforce the norm that only mothers are 'real women'. The question of biological sex differences is taken to be exactly the same as the question of social ideology ('discursive norms'). But this is precisely the assumption Geddes and Thomson make when they claim that the social roles of the sexes can be read off from the structure of the ovum and the sperm cell. Butler seems to believe that if one takes sexual difference to be determined by reference to the potential reproductive function of the body, then one simply *must* be caught up in repressive sexist ideology. Yet the whole of *The Second Sex* is evidence to the contrary. As a result, Butler ends up implying that most past and contemporary feminists (including Simone de Beauvoir) and just about all medical researchers and biologists are sexist oppressors, just because they accept that there are biological bases for the categorization of human beings into two sexes. Although Butler struggles against the social norm whereas Geddes and Thomson joyfully embrace it, the fundamental logic of their arguments appear to be perilously similar.

I am of course not claiming that poststructuralists working on sex and gender are biological determinists. The widespread tendency to criticize anyone who thinks that biological facts exist for their 'essentialism' or 'biologism' is best understood as a *recoil* from the thought that biological facts can ground social values.[57]

---

[57] In a seminar at UNC-Chapel Hill in Sept. 1996, Anne Balsamo told the audience that after a lecture where she had shown slides of bodies in the process of undergoing various technological interventions, someone came up to her and said: 'But you know, the body is only a *hypothesis.*'

Instead of denying that biological facts ground any such thing, as Beauvoir and Rubin do, poststructuralists prefer to deny that there *are* biological facts independent of our social and political norms.[58] To put this more clearly: I get the impression that post-structuralists believe that if there *were* biological facts, then they would indeed give rise to social norms. In this way, they paradox-ically share the fundamental belief of biological determinists (Figure A1). In their flight from such unpalatable company they go to the other extreme, placing biological facts under a kind of mental erasure (Figure A2):

(A1) Since:

Biological facts
↓
Social Norms

(A2) Therefore:

~~Biological facts~~
↓
Social Norms

Caught in the fantasy of a nightmarish, immobile, and timeless monster called sex, poststructuralists roll out the heavy theoreti-cal artillery for an all-out counterattack. Against what they take to be the bad 1960s picture of sex, they mobilize their own good 1990s picture of gender. No wonder that so many poststructural-ists express their misgivings about the very act of distinguishing between sex and gender. Thus Elizabeth Grosz rightly wants to escape the distinction by turning to theories of the 'lived body' or the 'social body', yet she does so seemingly without any awareness

---

[58] In the Osborne/Segal interview, Butler gives a fuzzy reply to the question of whether there are biological sex differences or not. On the one hand she '[does] not deny certain kinds of biological differences', on the other she claims that she is 'not sure that [the problematic of reproduction] is, or ought to be, what is absolutely salient or primary in the sexing of the body'. What is remark-able here is that it remains entirely unclear *what* 'kinds of biological differences' Butler accepts, or what *other* criteria for biological sexual differences she might want to propose. In the next sentence, she returns to the idea that reproductive differences are always the effect of social norms. If reproduction is central to the 'sexing of the body', she adds, 'I think it's the imposition of a norm, not a neutral description of biological constraints' (Osborne 113).

that Simone de Beauvoir's concept of the body as a situation provides exactly what she is looking for.[59] Others seek a more radical solution and claim that sex is constructed by gender, or by the same regulatory discourses that produce gender, so that, ultimately, there is no difference between sex and gender; sex turns out to have been gender all along:

(B)

Biological facts ⇔ Social Norms
Sex ⇔ Gender

Because they think that to speak about biological facts is the same as to speak about essences or metaphysical grounds, many poststructuralists believe that in order to avoid biological determinism one has to be a philosophical nominalist of some kind. In their texts, philosophical realism becomes a *politically* negative term. This is obviously absurd. To avoid biological determinism all we need to do is to deny that biological facts justify social values, and even the most recalcitrant realist can do that. In a parallel move, poststructuralists often conflate a nominalist position concerning the *general* relationship between our categories and the world with a *specific political* interpretation of the world. The assumption is always that if only we would become aware of exceptions and hard cases, then we would necessarily be led to question the very meaning of our concepts, politically as well as theoretically. Or to put it the other way round: the assumption is that *political* exclusion is coded into the very concepts we use to make sense of the world. It is this idea that makes some poststructuralists assume that the word 'woman' can never be used in non-ideological ways, that 'woman' *must* mean 'heterosexual, feminine and female'.[60] In this view, all concepts become bundle concepts: mention one word and hosts of others are taken to be implied.

But if political oppression is taken to follow from the fact that every concept draws a boundary, and thus necessarily excludes

---

[59] See Grosz, *Volatile* 18; on Beauvoir see esp. 15–16.

[60] Carrie L. Hull gives a clear, critical account of why Judith Butler thinks that every positive statement will be performative of a political exclusion (see esp. 29–30).

something—i.e. from the very fact that words have a meaning, and that meaning is normative—then it becomes difficult to see what political alternative poststructuralists intend to propose. The incessant poststructuralist invocations of the slippage, instability, and non-fixity of meaning are clearly intended as a way to soften the exclusionary blow of concepts, but unfortunately even concepts such as 'slippage' and 'instability' have fairly stable meanings in most contexts. It follows from the poststructuralists' own logic that if we were all mired in exclusionary politics just by having concepts, we would not be able to perceive the world in terms other than the ones laid out by our contaminated concepts.[61] If oppressive social norms are embedded in our concepts, just because they are concepts, we would all be striving to preserve existing social norms. As a result poststructuralists have difficulty explaining how it can be that a fair number of people *fail* to become 'suddenly and significantly upset' when they encounter phenomena that deviate from conservative (normative) expectations about gender.[62]

Of course language in general and concepts in particular often carry ideological implications. But as Wittgenstein puts it, in most cases the meaning of a word is its use.[63] Used in different situations by different speakers, the word 'woman' takes on very different implications. If we want to combat sexism and heterosexism, we should examine what work words are made to do in different speech acts, not leap to the conclusion that the same word must mean the same oppressive thing every time it occurs, or that

[61] Diana Fuss exemplifies the belief that there is something *politically* wrong with the very word woman, whether it occurs in the singular or the plural: 'hasty attempts to pluralize do not operate as sufficient defenses or safeguards against essentialism. The plural category "women", for instance, though conceptually signaling heterogeneity nonetheless semantically marks a collectivity; constructed or not, "women" still occupies the space of a linguistic unity' (4). Fuss believes that the very existence of a concept 'woman' or 'women' must be essentializing, exclusionary, and therefore politically oppressive simply by virtue of being a word ('a linguistic unity'). No wonder she argues that we can't ever fully escape essentialism.

[62] The quotation is from Butler, *Gender Trouble* 110.

[63] 'For a *large* class of cases—though not for all—in which we employ the word "meaning" it can be defined thus: the meaning of a word is its use in the language' (*PI* §43).

words oppress us simply by having determinate meanings, regardless of what those meanings are.[64]

Perhaps Sex Was Always Already Gender?

The subheading is taken from Judith Butler's *Gender Trouble*, and this section will focus on her attempt to show that sex is a cultural construct, the effect of regulatory discourses. Judith Butler has produced by far the most important work on sex and gender in the 1990s. Precisely because her work is such a principled development of poststructuralist thought, it enables me to show why I think alternatives are needed. My analysis of Butler's understanding of sex and gender does not entail a critique of her politics. Butler's important work has given an intellectual voice to gay and lesbian critics. Her critique of heterosexism and homophobia has inspired thousands, and for good reason. Writing as I am in a country where gays and lesbians are shot, tortured, and beaten to death by rabidly homophobic terrorists, I fully realize the importance of Butler's political task. What concerns me in this essay, however, is not Butler's powerful account of heterosexism, homophobia, and of various forms of homosexual and lesbian sexuality, but the question of how she understands sex, gender, and the body. In my view, but possibly not in Butler's, her understanding of the sex/gender distinction and the body does not, or not to any significant extent, ground either her account of sexuality or her politics. In my view, then, Butler's political aims are not

---

[64] As I will show below, for the purposes of understanding how and when the body is political and historical it is not necessary to enter into protracted arguments about the nature of meaning and reference. If I reject the poststructuralist insistence on entering into this problematics when they discuss sex, gender, and the body, it is because I think that certain readings of Wittgenstein propose convincing philosophical alternatives to their post-Saussurean view of language. In a forthcoming book, tentatively entitled *Wittgenstein and Deconstruction*, Martin Stone shows what the differences between Derrida's and Wittgenstein's understanding of language, meaning, and interpretation actually are. I should add that Martin Stone's graduate seminar on Wittgenstein at Duke in the spring of 1997, as well as my many conversations with him about Wittgenstein have been immensely helpful to my work. Over the past few years my understanding of Wittgenstein has also been deepened through discussions with Richard Moran and David Finkelstein.

threatened by my project, which is to show that one may arrive at a highly historicized and concrete understanding of bodies and subjectivity without relying on the sex/gender distinction that Butler takes as axiomatic, and particularly without entering into the obscure and theoreticist debates about materiality and meaning that her understanding of sex and gender compels her to engage with.

In my view, poststructuralist theorists of sex and gender are held prisoners by theoretical mirages of their own making. This becomes starkly evident in Butler's attempt to show that 'sex' or 'nature' or 'biology' or 'the body' is as constructed as gender:

> If the immutable character of sex is contested, perhaps this construct called sex is as culturally constructed as gender; indeed, perhaps it was always already gender, with the consequence that the distinction between sex and gender turns out to be no distinction at all. . . . The production of sex *as* the prediscursive ought to be understood as the effect of the apparatus of cultural construction designated by *gender* (*Gender Trouble* 7).

When sex is seen as a cultural construct, Butler argues, the traditional sex/gender distinction has been undone. Both are now the product of the same discursive norms; sex is not the ground of gender, but the effect of it. This analysis presupposes the 'bad' picture of sex and the 'good' picture of gender discussed above. Anyone who doubts that sex and gender *have* to be described in this way, or anyone who thinks that sex and gender are useless starting points for a theory of the body and subjectivity will find Butler's theoretical exercise empty.

If we enter into the poststructuralist perspective outlined by Butler, it now looks as if we have to solve a new problem. For if sex is as 'discursive' as gender, it becomes difficult to see how this fits in with the widespread belief that sex or the body is concrete and material, whereas social gender norms (discourses) are abstract and immaterial. This is the starting point for Butler's extraordinary attempt, in *Bodies That Matter*, to show by theoretical argument that the body is material and yet constructed. Her major claims concerning the body may be summarized as follows: (1) Essentialists claim that sex determines gender. Butler opposes them by claiming that 'regulatory discourses' determine biological facts: sex is the performative effect of gender. (2) In order to explain how this can be, she concludes that a general theory of 'materiality' is required. (3) Butler then provides one by claiming that matter is an effect of power. (4) This proves that the body is material and constructed, and that it is therefore inside culture, history, and society as well. According to Butler, the body has now been shown to be at once an effect of regulatory norms, concretely material, and fully historical.

I shall take a closer look at some of these arguments. Butler believes that unless she can show that matter (the matter the body is made of) doesn't exist in the form of brute given facts, she will be stuck with an essentialist picture of sex or the body. In her recoil from positivism and biological determinism, she insists that matter cannot possibly be natural or given:

> What I would propose . . . is a return to the notion of matter, not as site or surface, but as *a process of materialization that stabilizes over time to produce the effect of boundary, fixity, and surface we call matter.* That matter is always materialized has, I think, to be thought in relation to the productive and, indeed materializing effects of regulatory power in the Foucaultian sense (*Bodies* 9–10).[65]

By proposing that power produces matter, Butler makes 'power' sound a little like the *élan vital,* or God, for that matter; power becomes a principle that works in mysterious ways behind the veil of appearances.[66] Whether power is of God or man, it does sound as if it ought to be capable of producing any number of differently sexed bodies, and not only two. The question of why we stubbornly think there are only two sexes is not answered by appeals

[65] John McDowell's analysis of the consequences of either denying or accepting the 'myth of the given' might apply to Butler's understanding of the relationship between concepts and world (see John McDowell, esp. chs. 1–2).

[66] I would like to acknowledge here my debt to Sara Danius's instructive essay on the sex/gender distinction in poststructuralist theory. In her essay 'Själen är kroppens fängelse' ('The soul is the prison of the body') Danius discusses Foucault, Laqueur, Butler, and queer theory, and although she is more optimistic about the philosophical value of Butler's arguments than I am, Danius too questions the political value of Butler's understanding of 'materialization' precisely because she can't quite see how the theoretical understanding of matter solves the difficulties that Butler thinks that the distinction between sex and gender produces (see esp. 162–3).

to 'power'. (It remains unclear to me whether Butler thinks that our discursive concepts—'regulatory power'—produce the material world, or whether they just organize it.[67])

A far better starting point would be to ask *when* (under what circumstances) the problem of the 'materiality of the body' might arise. Imagine an inebriated reveller desperately trying to figure out whether those pink elephants really are material. Or a computer specialist who on finding herself face to face with a space invader, starts to wonder whether she really turned off the virtual reality equipment she was testing. The inebriated reveller will perhaps find that the problematic elephants go away when she sobers up, whereas a good night's sleep and a strong cup of coffee will do nothing to solve the other woman's problem. As Stanley Cavell puts it: 'how I make sure is dictated by what I want to know, which in turn is dictated by what special reason there is for raising the question' (*Claim of Reason* 59). Different reasons for raising a question require different kinds of answers.

Butler's reason for asking about the materiality of the body is that her own theoretical description of sex and gender has made this look like a compelling necessity. In the preface to *Bodies That Matter*, Butler writes: 'This text is offered, then, in part as a rethinking of some parts of *Gender Trouble* that have caused confusion' (xii). In *Gender Trouble* Butler claimed that sex was as constructed as gender. In the preface to *Bodies That Matter*, Butler writes that readers of her previous book constantly asked: 'What about the materiality of the body?' (ix). She continues: 'if I persisted in this notion that bodies were in some way constructed, perhaps I really thought that words alone had the power to craft bodies from their own linguistic substance?' (x). *Bodies That Matter* comes across as the author's attempt to deny that she ever denied that the body was material.[68]

Although there clearly are situations in which we need to

[67] Sally Haslanger discusses the obscurity of Butler's view at length in her paper 'Natural Kinds'.

[68] In *The Claim of Reason* Stanley Cavell writes: 'And it is startling to remember how many modern philosophers have seemed to be denying the obvious, and then denied they were denying it. Nothing is more characteristic of the skeptic's position' (103).

establish whether a body is material, it is significant that Butler does not mention any. On the contrary, to her, the 'materiality of the body' is a problem situated outside any conceivable situation, an assumption that makes her treat the body as an abstract epistemological object, that is to say that she treats it just like traditional epistemologists treat their 'material objects' (a table, a tomato, a bit of wax, and so on). What she is interested in is 'materiality' in its purest and most general form, not anything specific about any particular body. Stanley Cavell suggests that such an approach turns objects into 'generic objects': 'What is at stake . . . in the object is materiality as such, externality altogether' (*Claim of Reason* 53). The 'materiality of the body' is a problem produced by the poststructuralist picture of sex and gender, not by any concrete question feminists have asked about sex or the body. Ultimately, Butler loses sight of the body that her work tries to account for: the concrete, historical body that loves, suffers, and dies.

One of Butler's attempts to explain the 'materiality' of the body nevertheless deserves some attention, since it relies on one of the most widespread—and most mistaken—poststructuralist arguments around: I am referring to the old cliché about the 'materiality of the signifier'. At one point in *Bodies That Matter*, Butler tries to show that there is no reason to worry that 'linguistic constructivism' turns the body into nothing but a linguistic effect. Because the language in which we speak of the body is material, her argument goes, there can be no opposition between the body and language:

> the materiality of the signifier . . . implies that there can be no reference to a pure materiality except via materiality. Hence, it is not that one cannot get outside of language in order to grasp materiality in and of itself; rather, every effort to refer to materiality takes place through a signifying process which, in its phenomenality, is always already material. In this sense, then, language and materiality are not opposed, for language both is and refers to that which is material, and what is material never fully escapes from the process by which it is signified (*Bodies* 68).

But this is implausible, to say the least. Butler would seem to have been led astray by the assumption that the word 'materiality' means the same thing in relation to language as in relation to the body or other material phenomena. Clearly, signifiers consist of acoustic waves or black marks on a page, and, clearly, nobody would deny that such traces or patterns are material. But Saussure never thought that language was a matter of signifiers alone. Merleau-Ponty tells a good story about this:

> Language takes on a meaning for the child when it *establishes a situation* for him. A story is told in a children's book of the disappointment of a small boy who put on his grand-mother's spectacles and took up her book in the expectation of being able himself to find in it the stories which she used to tell him. The tale ends with these words: 'Well, what a fraud! Where's the story? I can see nothing but black and white!' (*Phenomenology* 401).

In themselves, the black and white patterns on the page signify nothing. It is only by leaving out that which gives our sounds and signs meaning—that is to say, that which makes them *language*—that Butler can persuade herself that she has proved her point. If one really wants to know what makes the body similar to language, or what makes language similar to the body, the answer that both are material is not going to give much satisfaction.

The belief that since language or discourse are material, then any discourse-based theory must be materialist has a long tradition in feminist theory by now. One example that comes to my mind is Elizabeth Grosz's claim that Luce Irigaray's discursive strategies amount to 'a strikingly materialist position, at least insofar as language is regarded as material' (*Sexual Subversions* 241). This is taken to be a conclusive counterargument to my own observation that 'the material conditions of women's oppression are spectacularly absent from [Irigaray's] work' (*Sexual/Textual Politics* 147). The point I was making was that Irigaray spends no time at all discussing the specific ways in which patriarchy oppresses women. To her, both patriarchy and the feminine work in much the same ways in Freud's Vienna as in Plato's Athens. In Grosz's response, clearly, the argument about the materiality of the signifier is at work. But even if language and discourse were material in the sense Butler and Grosz suggest, they surely would not be material in quite the same way as educational institutions, women's wages, women's legal and political status, or women's access to contraception and abortion.[69] The belief that the words 'material' or 'materialist' alone, without further specification, can secure any political claims is destructive to serious discussion of feminist politics.

Butler's intense labours to show that sex is as discursively constructed as gender are symptomatic of the common post-structuralist belief that if something is not discursively constructed, then it must be natural. In keeping with the check-list of terms listed under 'sex' above, nature is taken to be immutable, unchanging, fixed, stable, and somehow 'essential-ist'.[70] It is also assumed that everything cultural is linguistic, discursive, constructed, and so on. When sex is claimed to be 'as constructed as gender', this is an attempt to help nature escape from the tyranny of fixed identities and stable essences. This is also taken to be a radical political claim. The hypothesis is that if something is constructed, then it will be cultural as opposed to natural, and therefore easy to change by political action. But this is a rash conclusion, since it seems far easier to transform a penin-sula into an island or turn a mountain into a molehill than to change our understanding of, say, what is to count as giving direc-tions to a stranger. Furthermore, natural processes are certainly not always calm and stable, but often violent and radically trans-formative. They may be destructive or productive, and—impor-tantly—they do not always resist human intervention.[71] As for the idea that sex is immutable and gender wholly changeable, we should at least note that transsexuals vehemently insist that it is their *gender* that is immutable, and not their sex.

Poststructuralist critics, then, tend to believe that if they can only show that the body or sex is part of discourse, then they have also shown that it is a fully historical phenomenon, situated in the

[69] Comparing Butler's account of materiality to that of Adorno, Carrie Hull concludes that 'Butler *cannot* address social and economic injustice without the addition of materialism to her paradigm' (32). Hull also shows that Butler does not distinguish between different kinds of materiality (see esp. 30).

[70] Kate Soper, *What Is Nature?* gives a good critique of such views. See esp. Ch. 4.

[71] The biologist Helen Lambert reminds us that some biological differences may in fact be changed, and that others can be compensated for by social measures (see esp. 141–5).

realm of power and politics. (This is the effect of taking all the elements in the 'good' 1990s picture of gender to be inter-changeable.) The belief is, in fact, that the first claim (the body is discursive) secures the others, for the usual poststructuralist assumption is that history, politics, power, and discourse are linked in some necessary and intrinsic way.[72] Let us grant, for the sake of the argument, that this may be true on a highly abstract, general level. Yet even so it does not follow that the claim that 'sex is as constructed as gender' thereby becomes meaningful in terms of the politics of everyday life. For we still do not know whether the body is political in the same way that Sinn Fein is political, or in the way that the stock market or Bill Clinton are political, or in some other way altogether. Nor is it clear that the mere invocation of 'history' always secures the desired connection with power and politics. One may, after all, write a fairly adequate history of gold-fish-keeping in America without getting into deep political waters.[73] The general claim that a phenomenon is perceived differently in different historical epochs is not in itself enough to tie that phenomenon to questions of power and resistance. What is missing in so much poststructuralist theory is some awareness of the *specific ways* in which the body may be political and histori-cal and discursive, and so on.

After so many attempts to prove that sex is as discursive as gender, that is to say to prove that 'the distinction between sex and gender turns out to be no distinction at all', as Butler puts it (*Gender Trouble* 7), it is disconcerting to discover that poststruc-turalists still insist that it is politically important, first, to distin-guish between male and masculine, female and feminine, and, second, to accept that these terms vary freely in relation to each

[72] Teresa Ebert claims that for Butler power enters into a list of inter-changeable terms: 'through a series of tropic slippages, *power is materiality is discourse is citationality is performativity*' (214).

[73] For the record, I am not claiming that goldfish-keeping could never be politically significant under any historical conditions. Ecological activists might, for all I know, make a very good case for its world-historical consequences. My point is rather that there is a kind of history that isn't always political, or is only ambiguously or innocuously political, or, perhaps, political in an insignificant and uninteresting way. If the goldfish example offends, one might substitute another.

other.[74] In *Gender Trouble* Butler considers male drag shows to be subversive of social gender norms. But, as she herself stresses, any politically or socially subversive effects of male drag shows depend on the contrast ('gender dissonance') between male bodies (sex) and feminine clothes and behaviour (gender). It appears that the original 1960s sex/gender distinction is, after all, quite essential to Butler's political case.[75]

The same tendency to return to the 1960s distinction between sex and gender for political effect is apparent in Butler's discussion of a case where a group of scientists decided to categorize an XX individual as male:

> The task of distinguishing sex from gender becomes all the more difficult once we understand that gendered meanings frame the hypothesis and the reasoning of those biomedical inquiries that seek to establish 'sex' for us as it is prior to the cultural meanings that it acquires. Indeed, the task is even more complicated when we realize that the language of biology participates in other kinds of languages and reproduces that cultural sedimentation in the objects it purports to discover and neutrally describe.
>
> Is it not a purely cultural convention to which [the scientists] refer when they decide that an anatomically ambiguous XX individual is male, a convention that takes genitalia to be the definitive 'sign' of sex? (*Gender Trouble* 109).[76]

[74] 'When the constructed status of gender is theorized as radically independent of sex, gender itself becomes a free-floating artifice, with the consequence that *man* and *masculine* might just as easily signify a female body as a male one, and *woman* and *feminine* a male body as easily as a female one' (Butler, *Gender Trouble* 6).

[75] The usual distinction between sex and gender is clearly marked and categorized as politically radical in Butler's account of drag: 'The performance of drag plays upon the distinction between the anatomy of the performer and the gender that is being performed. But we are actually in the presence of three contingent dimensions of significant corporeality: anatomical sex, gender identity, and gender performance ... the performance suggests a dissonance not only between sex and performance, but sex and gender, and gender and performance' (*Gender Trouble* 137).

[76] See also Butler's conclusion concerning this example: 'The desire to determine sex once and for all, and to determine it as one sex rather than the other, thus seems to issue from the social organization of sexual reproduction through the construction of the clear and unequivocal identities and positions of sexed bodies with respect to each other' (*Gender Trouble* 110).

On the one hand Butler's point is that these scientists produce their understanding of sex by reference to cultural conventions of gender; on the other, she seems to imply that there is something scandalous, oppressive, and heterosexist about this.[77] But what else would someone who believes that sex is the effect of gender, of 'regulatory discourses' expect? If sex is and must be an effect of social norms, the scientists simply could not behave any differently. But if, on the other hand, sex (nature) is to be strictly distinguished from gender (cultural norms), then they have indeed behaved objectionably, by imposing their own ideology on scientific research. There is no need to become a 'radical linguistic constructivist' to reach this conclusion: Simone de Beauvoir as well as Gayle Rubin would have been perfectly capable of producing a succinct critique of sexist scientific practices.[78] Insofar as poststructuralist work on sex and gender denounces the 1960s understanding of sex and gender while relying on the same distinction for political effects, it is deeply incoherent.

Gender, Performativity, Subjectivity

Perhaps the most famous claim in poststructuralist understanding of sex and gender is Judith Butler's contention that gender is performative (see *Gender Trouble* 25, 141). Sometimes this has been taken to mean that we are all constantly performing our gender, in a way that produces either sex or gender identity, or both. At other times critics speak of the 'performance of gender' and actually mean performances on stage or screen. Expressions such as

[77] Butler introduces the case by quoting feminist researchers who have attacked these scientists for displaying 'cultural prejudice [and] gendered assumptions about sex', adding—somewhat confusingly, but clearly critically— that 'the [scientists'] concentration on the "master gene" suggests that femaleness ought to be understood as the presence [*sic!*] or absence of maleness or, at best the presence of a passivity that, in man, would invariably be active' (*Gender Trouble* 108 and 109).

[78] In fact, feminists from Ruth Bleier (*Science and Gender*) to Evelyn Fox Keller (*Reflections on Gender and Science*) and Sandra Harding (*The Science Question in Feminism*), just to mention a few, have done fundamental work on sexism in science precisely by drawing on the usual sex/gender distinction. Harding and O'Barr (eds.), *Sex and Scientific Inquiry* remains a valuable starting point for further inquiry into feminist critiques of science.

'gender performativity' or just 'performativity' abound in contemporary literary criticism and theory, and innumerable confusing claims have been made about the relationship between 'performativity' and the work of J. L. Austin on the one hand and Jacques Derrida on the other.[79] I shall not venture into this theoretical wilderness. Nor will I spend any time wondering what 'gender' means in this context (social norms? personal identity? the compulsory internalization of norms?). Instead I shall work from the assumption that when a critic speaks of 'gender performativity' she intends to oppose 'gender essentialism'; that against the being of sex, she is asserting the doing of gender. To say that one performs one's gender is to say that gender is an act, and not a thing.[80] As Judith Butler acknowledges, this is an idea that has close affinities with Sartre and Beauvoir's thought. For the French existentialists, our acts do indeed define us, we are what we do.[81] There is a sense, then, in which 'gender performativity' is a 1990s way of speaking of how we fashion ourselves through our acts and choices. On this interpretation, the claim that we all perform our gender might mean, for example, that when a man behaves in ways that are socially acceptable for men, then he feels more convinced than ever that he is a 'real' man. It might also mean that if the man behaves in idiosyncratic ways, he helps to transform our previous understanding of how men behave. More generally, we might conclude that 'gender performativity' means that when most people behave according to certain gender norms, this ensures that the norms are maintained and reinforced. On this interpretation, Judith Butler inherits Simone de Beauvoir's understanding of how sexual difference is produced. The important difference is that Butler translates Beauvoir's anti-essentialism into the conceptual register of sex and gender. To

[79] See Sedgwick, 'Queer Performativity' 1. For an incisive critique of the poststructuralist reading of J. L. Austin, see Timothy Gould, 'The Unhappy Performative'. Poststructuralists usually draw on Derrida's reading of Austin in *Limited Inc.* For a philosophical critique of Derrida's reading of Austin, see Cavell, *A Pitch of Philosophy*, Ch. 2.

[80] See Sedgwick, 'Queer Performativity' 2.

[81] See Butler, *Gender Trouble* 112 for the recognition that for Beauvoir woman is a 'becoming'.

speak about gender as something we *do*, rather than as something we *are*, may not be an entirely new idea, but it is a good one, and I have no difficulty in understanding its appeal.[82]

Unfortunately, from my point of view, Judith Butler struggles to free herself from her existentialist heritage. She would resist my interpretation of performativity on the grounds that it presupposes a 'doer behind the deed', an agent who actually makes choices. Shifting her ground from Sartre to Foucault, Butler insists that 'Gender is performative insofar as it is the effect of a regulatory regime of gender differences in which genders are divided and hierarchized under constraint. ... There is no subject who precedes or enacts this repetition of norms.'[83] Whatever we make of this, it is clear that gender performativity is a term designed to ensure that we don't think of identity and subjectivity as something that precedes social norms. But why do we have to make a choice between a 'discursive' and 'prediscursive' subject? Beauvoir, for one, would resist the dichotomy proposed by Butler. Lived experience, she would say, is an open-ended, ongoing interaction between the subject and the world, where each term continuously constructs the other.

In spite of her attempts to free herself from identity politics, it appears that, for Butler, the question of gender remains intrinsically bound up with the question of identity. In fact, poststructuralists regularly denounce any belief in a 'coherent inner self' or in 'coherent categories called women and men' as theoretically unsound and politically reactionary.[84] According to some critics, if we think of the self as coherent, stable, or in any way unified, we will fall back into the bad picture of sex, and therefore somehow become unable to resist racism and capitalism. Politically speaking,

---

[82] In the USA, West and Zimmerman's essay 'Doing Gender' made a similar point in 1987.

[83] 'Critically Queer' 21. Butler continues in this way: 'performativity is a matter of reiterating or repeating the norms by which one is constituted: it is not a radical fabrication of the gendered self. It is a compulsory production of prior and subjectivating norms, ones which cannot be thrown off at will, but which work, animate, and constrain the gendered subject, and which are also the resources from which resistance, subversion, displacement are to be forged' ('Critically Queer' 21–2). This essay was reprinted in *Bodies That Matter* 223–42.

[84] The quotations come from Haraway, 'Gender' 135, 147.

these are puzzling claims, since the whole liberal tradition and indeed the Marxist humanist tradition, with their antediluvian views on individual agency, freedom, and choice, were quite capable of fighting racism, sexism, and capitalism before post-structuralism came along.

On the theoretical level it is necessary to ask whether different pictures of subjectivity and identity actually have any necessary relationship with different theories of sex and gender. The answer seems to be yes in only one case, that of the pervasive picture of sex. Brooks and Geddes and Thomson imagine that a woman is saturated through and through by her womanness. In this picture a woman is reduced to nothing but sexual difference ('a giant ovum', Beauvoir writes). There seems to be no opportunity here for thinking that a woman's social class, race, nationality, or age might profoundly affect her way of being a woman. The poststructuralist critics are right, therefore, to assume that biological determinism is intrinsically bound up with a stable, unitary, coherent, fixed, immobile (and so on) picture of subjectivity. What they overlook is that no particular understanding of subjectivity or identity follows from the fact of *denying* that biological facts justify social norms. Beauvoir and Carol Gilligan both reject biological determinism, but they have very different views of subjectivity and consciousness. To Beauvoir consciousness is not a unified, coherent, and stable entity; yet Gilligan, who carefully distinguishes between sex and gender in the 1960s way, seems to imagine the female subject in much the same terms as traditional liberal humanists do.[85]

Liberation, Subversion—Same Thing?

Poststructuralists usually consider emancipation and liberation unfortunate Enlightenment terms, and believe that Foucault's denunciation of the 'repressive hypothesis' about sex shows that we can never speak of oppression and liberation without revealing that we actually believe in a true human nature shackled and bound by social norms. For them, anyone speaking of women's liberation must believe that it consists in letting our true, essential sexual

[85] For the existentialist understanding of consciousness, see Howells. See also Gilligan.

nature shine forth unfettered by social norms. Yet feminists ranging from Simone de Beauvoir to Juliet Mitchell have believed that
oppression is a concrete historical situation that it is in our interest
to change. Once the unfair, unjust, and exploitative conditions in
question have been eliminated, it is quite justified to speak of liberation: no metaphysics about true nature needs to be implied.

Poststructuralist theorists of sex and gender, however, prefer to
think in terms of *subversion* of dominant social norms. Since we
cannot escape power, we can only undermine it from within. For
this reason they have often invoked the male drag artist as a
particularly subversive figure. By parodying dominant gender
norms, he shows them up as conventional and artificial, and thus
enables us to maintain a critical or ironic distance to them. Unlike
Gayle Rubin, poststructuralists do not explicitly dream of a society without gender; rather, they seem to hope that greater freedom or justice or happiness will arise when we are able freely to
mix and match socially normative concepts of masculinity and
femininity as we like. Perhaps the idea is that this will eventually
so weaken the impact of the dominant social norms that gender
might ultimately wither away after all. Politically, the hopes and
aspirations of Simone de Beauvoir, Gayle Rubin, and the poststructuralist theorists of sex and gender do not seem to be all that
different. It would seem that we all wish for a society unmarred by
repressive norms legislating politically correct sexuality and
gender behaviour for women and men. Poststructuralists have yet
to show how their politics (as opposed to their theory) differ from
that of their feminist predecessors.

Imprisoned in their own theoretical framework, poststructuralist theorists of sex and gender have largely forgotten that the
distinction was supposed to carry out a specific task, namely that
of opposing biological determinism (which includes the essentialism and heterosexism produced by the pervasive picture of
sex). On my analysis, poststructuralists have yet to show what
questions concerning materiality, reference, essence, realism,
nominalism, and the inside and outside of discourse have to do
with bodies, sex, or gender, or with biology and social norms. In
short, I find poststructuralist work on sex and gender to be
obscure, theoreticist, plagued by internal contradictions, mired

in unnecessary philosophical and theoretical elaborations, and dependent on the 1960s sex/gender distinction for political effect.[86] As for the positive objectives that the poststructuralists wish to achieve, Simone de Beauvoir achieved them first, and with considerably greater philosophical elegance, clarity, and wit.

IV. 'THE BODY IS A SITUATION': SIMONE DE BEAUVOIR

The body is not a thing, it is a *situation*: it is our grasp on the world and a sketch of our projects.

Simone de Beauvoir, 1949

The Body as an Object and the Body as a Situation

'The body is a situation', Simone de Beauvoir writes in *The Second Sex*. I now want to show that this is not only a completely original contribution to feminist theory, but a powerful and sophisticated alternative to contemporary sex and gender theories. Let me stress that Beauvoir's claim is that the body *is* a situation. Some critics have taken this to mean that 'the physical capacities of either sex gain meaning only when placed in a cultural and historical context'.[87] But this is to miss the point, to reduce Beauvoir's claim that the body *is* a situation back to the more familiar idea that the body is always *in* a situation. For Beauvoir these are different claims, equally important and equally true, but not reducible to one another.[88] For Beauvoir, the body

[86] 'Theoreticism' refers to the belief that theoretical correctness somehow guarantees political correctness.

[87] I am quoting Julie Ward. Her sentence continues as follows: 'this, I argue, is what Beauvoir means by saying that the body is to be seen as a *situation*' (225).

[88] My assumption is that I do not need to explain the claim that the body is *in* a situation all that thoroughly, since most feminists are familiar with this kind of argument. What requires investigation, is the claim that the body *is* a situation. In this section I shall therefore emphasize the phenomenological philosophy that underpins Beauvoir's claim. As I will try to make clear in the text, it should nevertheless be understood throughout that, for Beauvoir as for Merleau-Ponty, the phenomenological experience of the body is always historically situated, always engaged in interaction with ideologies and other social practices. In *Sex and Existence* Lundgren-Gothlin makes the case for Beauvoir's historical understanding of 'situation' with great clarity.

perceived as a situation is deeply related to the individual woman's (or man's) subjectivity.[89]

In the first chapter of *The Second Sex* Simone de Beauvoir asks what a woman is. In the next chapter she turns her attention to attempts to answer by pointing to women's biological and anatomical differences from men. This chapter has been severely criticized by contemporary feminists: 'in turning (apparently at Sartre's suggestion) to an examination of the biological differences between the sexes, [Beauvoir] adopts something of an essentialist view of biology', one critic writes (Evans 61–2). Nothing could be further from the truth. There is no evidence that Sartre directed Beauvoir to write about biology. Moreover, it is in the chapter on biology that she first claims that the sexed body is a situation. In fact, this is a claim specifically designed to *refute* the kind of biological determinism espoused by scientists such as Brooks and Geddes and Thomson. This is how the chapter begins:

> Woman? [*La femme?*] Very simple, say the fanciers of simple formulas: she is a womb, an ovary; she is a female [*femelle*]—this word is sufficient to define her. In the mouth of a man the epithet *female* [*femelle*] has the sound of an insult, yet he is not ashamed of his animal nature; on the contrary, he is proud if someone says of him: 'He is a male!' The term 'female' [*femelle*] is derogatory not because it grounds [*enracine*] woman in nature, but because it imprisons her in her sex; and if this sex seems to man to be contemptible and inimical even in harmless animals, it is because of the uneasy hostility stirred up in him by woman. Nevertheless he wishes to find in biology a justification for this sentiment. The word *female* [*femelle*] brings up in his mind a saraband of imagery— a vast, round ovum engulfs and castrates the agile spermatozoon; the monstrous and swollen termite queen rules over the enslaved males; the female praying mantis and the spider, satiated with love, crush and devour their partners . . . (*SS* 3; *DSa* 35; TA).

This passage may seem puzzling to some readers. Why does Beauvoir leap to the conclusion that to be called a female must be an insult? Why does the word female conjure up in her mind

---

[89] I want to signal here that in *The Second Sex* Beauvoir also defines the body as *background*. See Ch. 2, below for a discussion of this understanding of the body.

pictures of insatiable and monstrous termites and spiders? In English, this does sound somewhat exaggerated; in French, the passage depends for its effect on the distinction between *femme* and *femelle*, a distinction that is not fully conveyed by the words *woman* and *female*. Although both the English *female* and the French *femelle* designate 'the sex which can bear offspring, or produce eggs', *female* refers to 'women, girls, and animals', as opposed to *femelle*, which refers exclusively to animals: its meaning is 'she-animal', not 'human female'. Precisely because of its association with she-animals, *femelle* is regularly used as a pejorative term for woman. In French, Beauvoir's point is clear: by refusing to reduce the woman (*femme*) to the she-animal (*femelle*), she takes a strong stance against the misogynist ideology which can only picture a woman as a monstrous ovum. Her imagery is a send-up of the pervasive picture of sex.

Beauvoir in fact discusses many of the theses put forward by Brooks and Geddes and Thomson, usually without quoting any particular source for them. Janet Sayers writes that Geddes and Thomson's book was quickly translated into French, and that their arguments turn up in A. J. E. Fouillée's *Tempérament et caractère selon les individus, les sexes et les races* from 1895 (see Sayers 41). Beauvoir comments directly on Fouillée's theses:

> In his book *Le tempérament et le caractère*, Alfred Fouillée undertakes to found his definition of woman *in toto* upon the ovum and that of man upon the spermatozoon; and a number of supposedly profound theories rest upon this play of doubtful analogies. It is a question to what philosophy of nature these dubious ideas pertain; not to the laws of heredity, certainly, for, according to these laws, men and women alike develop from an ovum and a sperm. I can only suppose that in such misty minds there still float shreds of the old philosophy of the Middle Ages which taught that the cosmos is an exact reflection of a microcosm—the ovum is imagined to be a female homunculus, the woman a giant ovum . . . (*SS* 14; *DSa* 47–8; TA).

After refuting the claims put forward by biological determinists, Beauvoir describes the facts of female sexual and reproductive development.[90] Overall, she concludes that women's role in the

---

[90] She tends to interpret them from a Hegelian perspective. For two serious, but divergent, accounts of Beauvoir's understanding of Hegel, see Lundgren-Gothlin, *Sex and Existence*, esp. 53–82, and Bauer, esp. Chs. 3–6.

reproduction of the species is more onerous, more time-consuming, and more dangerous than men's. A man can father a hundred children without any physical damage to himself, a woman cannot even have ten children without running considerable risks of lasting physical impairment and even death. For Beauvoir, such biological facts are 'extremely important. In the history of woman they play a part of the first rank and constitute an essential element in her situation' (*SS* 32; *DSa* 71). Her conclusions are nevertheless strikingly different from those of Brooks and Geddes and Thomson:

> But I deny that [the biological facts] establish for her a fixed and inevitable destiny. They are insufficient for setting up a hierarchy of the sexes; they fail to explain why woman is the Other; they do not condemn her to remain in this subordinate role for ever (*SS* 32–3; *DSa* 71).

How can Beauvoir maintain both that biology is extremely important to women's situation and that it is not destiny? To answer this question, we need to consider Beauvoir's existentialist understanding of what a human being is:

> But man is defined as a being who is not given, who makes himself what he is. As Merleau-Ponty very justly puts it, man is not a natural species; he is a historical idea. Woman is not a fixed reality, but rather a becoming, and it is in her becoming that she should be compared with man; that is to say her *possibilities* should be defined. . . . [A]s viewed in the perspective that I am adopting— that of Heidegger, Sartre, and Merleau-Ponty— . . . the body is not a thing, it is a *situation*: it is our grasp on the world and a sketch [*esquisse*] of our projects (*SS* 34; *DSa* 73; TA)[91]

To say that 'woman is not a fixed reality' is to say that as human beings (and unlike animals) women are always in the process of

---

[91] The published English translation of the last sentence is particularly egregious: '[Le corps] est notre prise sur le monde et l'esquisse de nos projets', Beauvoir writes. '[The body] is the instrument of our grasp upon the world, a limiting factor for our projects', Parshley translates, thereby introducing (1) the wholly erroneous idea of the body as an *instrument* for a grasp, rather than as the 'grasp [*prise*]' itself; and (2) the idea of the body as a *limitation*, as something that necessarily hampers our projects. Both thoughts correspond to the traditional picture of a consciousness inhabiting the body, but this, precisely, is the picture Beauvoir wants to resist.

making themselves what they are. We give meaning to our lives by our actions. Only death puts an end to the creation of meaning. As the famous existentialist slogan has it: 'Existence precedes essence'. For Beauvoir and Merleau-Ponty, human transcendence—human freedom—is always incarnated, that is to say that it always presents itself in the shape of a human body. My body is a situation, but it is a fundamental kind of situation, in that it founds my experience of myself and the world. This is a situation that always enters my lived experience. This is why the body can never be just brute matter to me. Only the dead body is a thing, but when I am dead I am lost to the world, and the world is lost to me: 'The body is our general medium for having a world', Merleau-Ponty writes (*Phenomenology* 146).

I just used the term *lived experience*. This is a central existentialist concept. The situation is not coextensive with lived experience, nor reducible to it. In many ways 'lived experience' designates the whole of a person's subjectivity. More particularly the term describes the way an individual makes sense of her situation and actions. Because the concept also comprises my freedom, my lived experience is not wholly determined by the various situations I may be a part of. Rather lived experience is, as it were, sedimented over time through my interactions with the world, and thus itself becomes part of my situatedness.

Beauvoir and Merleau-Ponty do not deny that there is anything object-like about my body.[92] It is quite possible to study it scientifically, to measure it, to predict how it will react to antibiotics, and so on. Both Beauvoir and Merleau-Ponty are happy to accept scientific data in their analyses of the body. Yet, for them, scientific methodology cannot yield a valid philosophy of human existence.

---

[92] Sara Heinämaa's useful account of Beauvoir's view of the body stresses that Simone de Beauvoir's phenomenological understanding of the body falls outside the parameters of the sex/gender distinction, since it doesn't consider the body as an object (see 'Woman—Nature, Product, Style'). Following Sonia Kruks's lead, Heinämaa also reminds us of Merleau-Ponty's importance for Beauvoir, who actually reviewed the *Phenomenology of Perception* in the second issue of *Les temps modernes* in Nov. 1945. See Kruks, 'Simone de Beauvoir: Between Sartre and Merleau-Ponty'; Kruks, 'Simone de Beauvoir: Teaching Sartre about Freedom'; and Heinämaa, 'What Is a Woman?', as well as 'Woman—Nature, Product, Style'.

In *Phenomenology of Perception*, Merleau-Ponty denounces what he calls the 'objective' way of looking at the world, exemplified by science on the one hand and common sense on the other. In turning the world into an object, the 'objective' perspective represses the fact that human consciousness is part of every human experience:

> Obsessed with being, and forgetful of the perspectivism of my experience, I henceforth treat it as an object and deduce it from a relationship between objects. I regard my body, which is my point of view upon the world, as one of the objects of that world. My recent awareness of my gaze as a means of knowledge I now repress, and treat my eyes as bits of matter. . . . I now refer to my body only as an idea. . . . Thus 'objective' thought . . . is formed—being that of common sense and of science—which finally causes us to lose contact with perceptual experience, of which it is nevertheless the outcome and the natural sequel (70–1).

By placing 'objective' in inverted commas, Merleau-Ponty indicates that *he* doesn't believe that the scientific (or the common-sensical) point of view is 'objective' in the positivist sense of bearing no trace of the human consciousness that produced it. On the contrary, even scientific research presupposes human experience:

> I am not the outcome or the meeting-point of numerous causal agencies which determine my bodily or psychological make-up. I cannot conceive myself as nothing but a bit of the world, a mere object of biological, psychological or sociological investigation. I cannot shut myself up within the realm of science. All my knowledge of the world, even my scientific knowledge, is gained from my own particular point of view, or from some experience of the world without which the symbols of science would be meaningless. . . . Scientific points of view, according to which my existence is a moment of the world's, are always both naive and at the same time dishonest, because they take for granted, without explicitly mentioning it, the other point of view, namely that of consciousness, through which from the outset a world forms itself round me and begins to exist for me (viii–ix).

To say that science presupposes a human perspective is not to reject its insights about the human body, but rather to reject scientism, positivism, empiricism, and other would-be 'objectivist' world-views. This is why Merleau-Ponty feels free to draw copiously on psychological and biological research concerning perception and brain functioning.

The body, then, does not carry its meaning on its surface. It is not a thing, but a situation. In *Being and Nothingness* Sartre claims that all human beings are always situated—*en situation*, as he puts it. The concept of the *situation* deserves a more thorough discussion than I can give it here. Sartre devotes over a hundred pages to it in *Being and Nothingness*. Merleau-Ponty understands it, after Sartre, as an irreducible category between subjectivity and objectivity. For Sartre, Beauvoir, and Merleau-Ponty, the concept of the situation is crucial, since they need it in order to avoid dividing lived experience up in the traditional subject/object opposition.[93] For Sartre my class, my place, my race, my nationality, my body, my past, my position, and my relationship to others are so many different situations.[94] To claim that the body *is* a situation is not the same thing as to say that it is placed *within* some other situation. The body both is a situation *and* is placed within other situations. For Sartre, a situation is a structural relationship between our projects (our freedom) and the world (which includes our bodies). If I want to climb a crag, my situation is my project as it exists in the encounter with the brute facticity of the crag. In this view, the crag alone is not a situation. My situation is not *outside* me, it does not relate to me as an object to a subject; it is a synthesis of facticity and freedom. If your project is to climb, and my project is to enjoy the mountain views, then the very same crag would present itself to you as being easy or difficult to scale, and to me as 'imposing' or 'unremarkable'. Faced with the same crag, our situations would be different because our projects are different. We are always in a situation, but the situation is always part of us.

To claim that the body is a situation is to acknowledge that the meaning of a woman's body is bound up with the way she uses her freedom. For Beauvoir, our freedom is not absolute,

---

[93] For an illuminating discussion of the successes and failures of the concept in the works of these writers, see Kruks, *Situation.*

[94] See *Being and Nothingness* 619–707; *L'être et le néant* 538–612.

but situated. Other situations as well as our particular lived experience will influence our projects, which in turn will shape our experience of the body. In this way, each woman's experience of her body is bound up with her projects in the world. There are innumerable different ways of living with one's specific bodily potential as a woman. I may devote myself to mountain climbing, become a ballet dancer, a model, a nurse, or a nun. I may have lots of sexual relations or none at all, have five children or none, or I may discover that such choices are not mine to make.

Many critics of Beauvoir would disagree with my analysis. In their view, Beauvoir sees the female reproductive body as inherently oppressive. In an interesting essay on Beauvoir and Hegel, Catriona Mackenzie considers that Beauvoir's understanding of the body forces us to accept the conclusion that 'the reproductive body must be denied' (156). I do not want to contest the idea that Beauvoir herself was highly ambivalent about mothers, motherhood, and pregnancy. In my view, almost all her texts, including *The Second Sex*, are haunted by a destructive mother imago.[95] Yet whenever Beauvoir's unconscious horror of the mother surfaces, far from spelling out the inner logic of her argument it places her understanding of the body as a situation in contradiction with itself. For the logic of her argument is that greater freedom will produce new ways of being a woman, new ways of experiencing the possibilities of a woman's body, not that women will for ever be slaves to the inherently oppressive experience of childbearing. At the end of *The Second Sex* Beauvoir writes: 'Once again, in order to explain her limitations it is woman's situation that must be invoked and not a mysterious essence; thus the future remains largely open. . . . The free woman is just being born' (*SS* 714–15; *DSb* 640–1). In a non-sexist future, women's freedom will lead to changes we cannot even imagine: 'New relations of flesh and sentiment of which we have no conception will arise between the sexes' (*SS* 730; *DSb* 661). Beauvoir's belief in social and individual

---

[95] I discuss the negative mother imago in Beauvoir's texts at length in my *Simone de Beauvoir* (see esp. Chs. 4, 6, and 8).

transformation is the logical outcome of the double claim that the body *is* a situation and that it always is *in* a situation, not of the belief that women will always be oppressed by their reproductive capacities.[96]

Some critics gloss Beauvoir's claim that the body is a situation by saying that for her, 'the body is a social construction'.[97] Without a clearer understanding of what 'social construction' means I can't say whether this is a helpful formulation. If 'social construction' is no more than convenient shorthand for 'non-essentialist', then Beauvoir's understanding of the body as a situation counts as 'constructionist'. Insofar as Beauvoir's understanding of situation includes the freedom of the subject, it clashes with the extreme determinism of some contemporary ideas of how 'social construction' works. When it comes to the body, 'social construction' is a nebulous concept which there is no reason to prefer to Beauvoir's precisely defined and highly productive concept of situation.

When Beauvoir writes that the body is not a thing, but a situation, she means that the body-in-the-world that we are, is an embodied intentional relationship to the world.[98] Understood as a situation in its own right, the body places us in the middle of many other situations. Our subjectivity is always embodied, but our bodies do not only bear the mark of sex. In *Black Skin, White Masks* (1952) Frantz Fanon analyses race as a bodily situation, drawing on exactly the same concepts as Beauvoir, and in

[96] In her well-known essay 'French Feminism Revisited' Gayatri Spivak rightly stresses that 'Beauvoir sees the Mother as a situation' (*Outside* 149). In fact, most of the chapters of the second volume of *The Second Sex* are devoted to a different situation. Thus the chapter entitled 'The Mother' describes different women's reactions to the situation of motherhood, the chapter entitled 'The Married Woman' discusses different ways of living the experience of marriage, and so on.

[97] I am quoting Julie Ward's valuable essay on 'Beauvoir's Two Senses of Body' (231).

[98] In her valuable essay 'Throwing Like a Girl', Iris Marion Young combines Merleau-Ponty and Beauvoir's analysis of the body to explore a certain 'feminine' style of orienting the body in space. Echoing Beauvoir, Young stresses that a woman under patriarchy often ends up living her body *as* a thing (see esp. 150).

Phenomenology of Perception Merleau-Ponty discusses class as a historical and bodily situation (see 442–50).[99]

'The body is to be compared, not to a physical object, but rather to a work of art', Merleau-Ponty writes (*Phenomenology* 150). Perceived as part of lived experience, the body is a style of being, an intonation, a specific way of being present in the world, but it does not for that reason cease to be an object with its own specific physical properties. Considered as a situation, the body encompasses both the objective and the subjective aspects of experience. To Merleau-Ponty and Beauvoir, the body is our perspective on the world, and at the same time that body is engaged in a dialectical interaction with its surroundings, that is to say with all the other situations in which the body is placed. The way we experience—live—our bodies is shaped by this interaction. The body is a historical sedimentation of our way of living in the world, and of the world's way of living with us.[100]

The body matters to Simone de Beauvoir. If I have to negotiate the world in a crippled body or sick body I am not going to have the same experience of the world or of myself as if I had a healthy or particularly athletic body. Nor will the world react to me in the way it would if I had a different body.[101] To deny this is to be guilty

[99] The achievement of Simone de Beauvoir consists in having shown that bodily sexual difference makes the body a potentially different situation for men and women. (I write 'potentially different' because Beauvoir does not believe that sexual differences always and everywhere matter more than other situations: she does not have a pervasive picture of sex.) Unfortunately neither Fanon (who writes after her) nor Merleau-Ponty (who writes before her) manage to discuss sexual difference as a situation that interacts with that of race and class. For a brief comparison of Fanon and Beauvoir, see my *Simone de Beauvoir*, Ch. 7.

[100] As we have seen, Beauvoir's understanding of the body is explicitly and obviously phenomenological. I am therefore struck by the fact that Elizabeth Grosz, who in *Volatile Bodies* devotes a whole chapter to Merleau-Ponty, in the subsection entitled 'Feminist Phenomenology?' makes no reference at all to Simone de Beauvoir (103–7).

[101] The medievalist Caroline Bynum complains that feminists nowadays reduce the body to sexual difference: 'an extraordinarily large amount of [the] recent discussion of the body is in fact a discussion of sex and gender'. One recent book on theology and the body, she notes, 'devotes only about seventeen pages to what was surely, in earlier times, theology's major preoccupation with bodies: suffering and death' (5). As my examples show, Beauvoir's understanding of the body would not lead to this problem.

of idealist subjectivism. To assume that the meaning of a sick or a healthy body is written on its surface, that it is and will be the same for all human beings, is to fall prey to empiricism or what Merleau-Ponty calls 'objectivism'.[102] As Fanon has shown, the same logic applies to the difference between a black body and a white body.

Although our biology is fundamental to the way we live in the world, biological facts alone give us no grounds for concluding anything at all about the *meaning* and *value* they will have for the individual and for society. At the same time, however, biological facts cannot be placed outside the realm of meaning. For Beauvoir and Merleau-Ponty, the human body is fundamentally *ambiguous*: it is subject at once to natural laws and to the human production of meaning, and it can never be reduced to either one of these elements. Because the body is neither pure nature nor pure meaning, neither empiricism nor idealism will ever be able to grasp the specific nature of human existence. When Merleau-Ponty claims that 'Man is a historical idea' he is not trying to disavow nature, but rather to expand our understanding of what nature is. Instead of accepting the scientistic and empiricist concept of nature, he wants to stress that nature also belongs to the order of meaning. 'Man is a historical idea' means that our nature is to be historical. As Merleau-Ponty goes on to say:

> Everything is both manufactured and natural in man, as it were, in the sense that there is not a word, not a form of behaviour which does not owe something to purely biological being—and which at the same time does not elude the simplicity of animal life, and cause forms of vital behaviour to deviate from their pre-ordained direction, through a sort of *leakage* and through a genius for ambiguity which might serve to define man (189).

Following Merleau-Ponty and Sartre, Beauvoir repeatedly stresses that biological facts cannot ground human values:

[102] Merleau-Ponty's discussion of 'objective' thought occurs in the context of his effort to put shortcomings of subjectivism as well as of objectivism behind him: 'We cannot remain in this dilemma of having to fail to understand either the subject or the object. We must discover the origin of the object at the very center of our experience; we must describe the emergence of being and we must understand how, paradoxically, there is *for us* an *in-itself* (*Phenomenology* 71).

But in truth a society is not a species; for it is in society that the species realises itself as existence—transcending itself toward the world and toward the future. Its ways and customs cannot be deduced from biology, for individuals are never abandoned to their nature; rather they obey that second nature which is custom, in which the desires and fears that express their ontological attitude are reflected.[103] It is not merely as a body, but rather as a body subject to taboos, to laws, that the subject becomes conscious of himself and attains fulfillment [*s'accomplit*]—it is with reference to certain values that he valorizes himself. To repeat once more: physiology cannot ground any values; rather, the facts of biology take on the values that the existent bestows upon them (*SS* 36; *DSa* 76; TA).

Beauvoir makes a number of claims amounting to a flat rejection of the theses of the biological determinists:

(1) sex is not pervasive: a woman is not a giant ovum;
(2) biology (science) cannot justify social norms;
(3) social norms are not the expression of biological facts;
(4) social hierarchy (subjection, oppression) can never be explained or justified by biology.

Beauvoir's rejection of biological determinism resembles Gayle Rubin's distinction between gender as social norms and sex as the concrete human body. Beauvoir's understanding of individual subjectivity, on the other hand, is vastly different from sex and gender theories. First of all, it never occurs to her that an individual human being can be divided into a natural and a cultural part, in the way suggested by the sex/gender distinction. Merleau-Ponty actually spells this point out with particular clarity when he writes that 'It is impossible to superimpose on man a lower layer of behaviour which one chooses to call "natural", followed by a manufactured cultural or spiritual world' (189). That Beauvoir shares this point of view becomes clear in the very last lines of her chapter on biology:

Thus we shall have to view the facts of biology in the light of an ontological, economic, social and psychological context. The

---

[103] In French: *leur attitude ontologique*. The English text, unfortunately, translates this as 'their essential nature', thus giving rise to many misunderstandings.

enslavement of the female to the species and the limitations of her various powers are extremely important facts; the body of woman is one of the essential elements in her situation in the world. But that body is not enough to define her; it does not gain lived reality [*réalité vécue*] unless it is taken on [*assumé*] by consciousness through activities and in the bosom of a society. Biology is not enough to give an answer to the question that is before us: why is woman the *Other*? We need to find out how nature has been taken up [*reprise*] in her throughout the course of history; we need to find out what humanity has made of the human female [*la femelle humaine*] (*SS* 37; *DSa* 77; TA).[104]

In this passage Beauvoir makes the following claims: (1) biological facts only take on meaning when they are situated within economic, social, and psychological contexts; (2) biological facts are nevertheless important elements in women's situation; (3) biological facts alone cannot define a woman; (4) the body alone does not define a woman, on the contrary, she needs to make it her own, turn it into 'lived reality',[105] a process that is always accomplished in interaction with the woman's socially situated, conscious choices and activities; and (5) biology cannot explain the social subordination of women.

When Beauvoir writes, 'But that body is not enough to define her,' she means to reject the biological determinist theories of

[104] This passage sounds very different in Parshley's translation. Failing to grasp Beauvoir's syntax and philosophical vocabulary, he translates 'Mais ce n'est pas non plus lui [le corps] qui suffit à la définir, il n'a de réalité vécue qu'en tant qu'assumé par la conscience à travers des actions et au sein d'une société' as 'But that body is not enough to define her as a woman; there is no true living reality except as manifested by the conscious individual through activities and in the bosom of society'. It is clear that Parshley reads Beauvoir's 'il [ce corps] n'a de réalité' as 'il n'y a de réalité', and doesn't understand the idea that consciousness must 'shoulder' or 'take on' the body for it to become part of lived experience. The last sentence in French contains the phrase 'savoir comment en elle la nature a été reprise au cours de l'histoire'. This gets translated as 'discover how the nature of woman has been affected throughout the course of history'. No wonder so many Anglophone readers of *The Second Sex* have felt that Beauvoir's understanding of the body is incoherent, or worse.

[105] Let me note that although Beauvoir here uses the expression *réalité vécue*, elsewhere she writes about *expérience vécue*: the body gains lived reality when it becomes (part of) lived experience.

sexual difference she has spent most of the chapter discussing. The formulation 'not enough' signals that she also means to reject purely idealist constructions of what a woman is. The female body is a necessary part of the definition of 'woman', but to take it to be sufficient to define the meaning of the word is to fall back into 'objectivism'. The difference between the body considered as a situation and the body considered as an object is not homologous with that between sex and gender. We are, rather, dealing with two different *perspectives* on the body: the empiricist or scientistic perspective on the one hand, and the phenomenological on the other. The implication is that we have to choose between them. The one cannot somehow be added on to the other without forcing us into an unsatisfactory see-saw movement between empiricism and idealism, or between objectivism and subjectivism. As Merleau-Ponty reminds us, it makes no sense to think of human beings as consisting of two superimposed layers, one which we choose to call 'natural' and another that we consider 'cultural' or 'spiritual'. For Beauvoir and Merleau-Ponty, then, the body perceived as an object is *not* the ground on which the body as a situation is constructed; a woman is *not* the sum of the 'objective' and the situational perspective on the body. For Beauvoir, a woman defines herself through the way she lives her embodied situation in the world, or in other words, through the way in which she makes something of what the world makes of her. The process of making and being made is open-ended: it only ends with death. In the analysis of lived experience, the sex/gender distinction simply *does not apply*.[106] I shall now go on to show that the opposition between 'essentialism' and 'constructionism' that has plagued contemporary feminist theory in the 1980s and 1990s does not apply either.

One Is Not Born a Woman: Biology and Lived Experience

'One is not born, but rather becomes, a woman', Beauvoir writes. Many contemporary feminists have assumed that this means that Beauvoir is opposing sex to gender, or biological essence to social

---

[106] On this point, I agree completely with Sara Heinämaa (see 'Woman— Nature, Product, Style').

construction. This is not the case. Anyone who tries to read *The Second Sex* through the lens of the sex/gender distinction is bound to misunderstand Beauvoir. Judith Butler's 1986 commentary on Beauvoir's famous sentence is a good example of such a misreading:

> 'One is not born, but rather becomes, a woman'—Simone de Beauvoir's formulation distinguishes sex from gender and suggests that gender is an aspect of identity gradually acquired. The distinction between sex and gender has been crucial to the long-standing feminist effort to debunk the claim that anatomy is destiny; *sex* is understood to be the invariant, anatomically distinct, and factic aspects of the female body, whereas *gender* is the cultural meaning and form that that body acquires, the variable modes of that body's acculturation. . . . Moreover, if the distinction is consistently applied, it becomes unclear whether being a given sex has any necessary consequence for becoming a given gender. The presumption of a causal or mimetic relation between sex and gender is undermined. . . . At its limit, then, the sex/gender distinction implies a radical heteronomy of natural bodies and constructed genders with the consequence that 'being' female and 'being' a woman are two very different sorts of being. This last insight, I would suggest, is the distinguished contribution of Simone de Beauvoir's formulation, 'one is not born, but rather becomes, a woman' ('Sex and Gender' 35).

In this passage, Butler shows herself to be an extremely acute reader of Beauvoir's phenomenological feminism, but her close affinities with Beauvoir are, as it were, derailed by Butler's fundamental commitment to the sex/gender distinction. Beauvoir's view would presumably be that the category of 'sex' is scientistic, and therefore useless as an explanation of what a woman is. From a Beauvoirean perspective, then, the trouble with the sex/gender distinction is that it upholds the 'objective' or 'scientific' view of the body as the ground on which gender is developed. To consider the body as a situation, on the other hand, is to refuse to break it down into an 'objective' and a 'subjective' component; we don't first consider it scientifically, and then add cultural experience. For Butler in 1986, sex or the body is an object, for Beauvoir 'sex' could only be seen as the philosophically misguided act of perceiving the body as an object.[107]

Rejecting biological determinism (anatomy is destiny), Butler denies that the objectively described ('factic') body gives rise to values. On this point, she follows Beauvoir. When Butler conceives of gender as a category that does *not include* the body, however, she loses touch with Beauvoir's category of 'lived experience'.[108] As a result, she is left with only one way of conceptualizing the body, namely as sex. In order to avoid biological determinism, Butler is then forced to claim that a woman is gender, and that the category of gender varies freely in relation to a narrowly scientistic understanding of sex. In Butler's picture of sex and gender, sex becomes the inaccessible ground of gender, gender becomes completely disembodied, and the body itself is divorced from all meaning.

For Beauvoir, on the other hand, the body is a situation, and as such, a crucial part of lived experience. Just as the world constantly makes me, I constantly make myself the woman I am. As we have seen, a situation is not an 'external' structure that imposes itself on the individual subject, but rather an irreducible amalgam of the freedom (projects) of that subject and the conditions in which that freedom finds itself. The body as a situation is the concrete body experienced as meaningful, and socially and historically situated. It is *this* concept of the body that disappears entirely from Butler's account of sex and gender.

---

[107] As Mary McIntosh has pointed out, Butler's use of the word 'gender' in relation to a number of French thinkers (including, I should add, Beauvoir and Wittig) is not very helpful: 'I find Butler's use of the sex/gender distinction confusing. This distinction . . . does not sit well with any of the French work that Butler engages with. Those writers in the French tradition who have problematized the category of "woman" have not used the term gender. What they have done is to question whether the biological category "woman" has any stable social significance, not to question the biological category as such' (McIntosh 114).

[108] Heinämaa's 'What Is a Woman?' convincingly demonstrates that Judith Butler misreads Beauvoir by reading her through the lens of the traditional understanding of sex and gender. Her 'Woman—Nature, Product, Style' argues that Beauvoir's phenomenological understanding of the body cannot be reduced to the common feminist sex/gender distinction. If she means that the sex/gender distinction is not at work *inside* Beauvoir's concepts of 'lived experience' or 'body as situation', I agree with her.

Butler returns to Beauvoir's famous sentence in *Gender Trouble* (1990). She writes that 'it follows that *woman* itself is a term in process, a becoming, a constructing that cannot rightfully be said to originate or to end' (*Gender Trouble* 33). This strikes me as a good interpretation of Beauvoir's view. But then Butler continues:

> As an ongoing discursive practice, it [the term *woman*] is open to intervention and resignification. Even when gender seems to congeal into the most reified forms, the 'congealing' is itself an insistent and insidious practice, sustained and regulated by various social means. It is, for Beauvoir, never possible finally to become a woman, as if there were a *telos* that governs the process of acculturation and construction. Gender is the repeated stylization of the body, a set of repeated acts within a highly rigid regulatory frame that congeal over time to produce the appearance of substance, of a natural sort of being (*Gender Trouble* 33).

The slippage from Beauvoir's 'woman' to Butler's 'gender' is obvious. Here Butler leaps from the thought that for Beauvoir, a woman is always becoming, always in the process of making herself what she is, to the rather different idea that, for Beauvoir, a woman must therefore be *gender*, that is to say, an 'ongoing discursive practice', a continuous production of a 'congealed' social form.[109] Butler and Beauvoir are both anti-essentialist. But whereas Beauvoir works with a non-normative understanding of what a woman is, Butler thinks of a woman as the ongoing production of a congealed ideological construct. For Butler a woman is gender, and gender is simply an effect of an oppressive social power structure. In short, Butler's concept of gender does not encompass the concrete, historical and experiencing body. This is a particularly clear example of the way in which Butler inherits Gayle Rubin's understanding of gender as an intrinsically oppressive social construct.[110]

Whereas Butler finds oppressive social norms at work in the

[109] We might note that for Beauvoir, a woman is not a particularly incomplete term: if a woman is in continuous process, it is because *all* human beings are. Since nothing (with the exception of death), could count as 'completion' for an existentialist, the claim that all human beings are 'incomplete' doesn't actually have much force.

[110] See my discussion of Rubin's work in Sect. II, above.

very concept of woman, Beauvoir takes the female body as a non-normative starting point for her phenomenological analysis of what a woman is. By 'non-normative' I mean that Beauvoir considers that only the study of concrete cases—of lived experience—will tell us exactly what it means to be a woman in a given context. For her it is impossible to derive the definition of 'woman' from an account of social norms alone, just as it is impossible to derive the definition of 'woman' from an account of biological facts alone. Butler's understanding of gender as an effect of power ends up reducing 'woman' to 'power'. This is why it becomes impossible for her and her followers to imagine that the word 'woman' could ever be used in ways that fail to reproduce oppressive power structures. In such an analysis 'power' is opposed to 'sex' or 'the body' and the result is a theory of 'woman' that is structurally similar to the transcendental idealism Beauvoir and Merleau-Ponty want to avoid. Or in other words, for Butler 'power' functions as the secret principle of all meaning, just as 'spirit' does for an idealist philosopher. In short, taking woman to mean gender, Butler thinks of the female body as sex, and assumes that there is a radical divorce between sex and woman/gender. It is *this* move that effectively exiles sex from history and society in Butler's work. However much Butler analyses women and men, she will never believe herself to be saying anything at all about sex, or about the body. For Beauvoir women exist, for Butler they must be deconstructed.[111]

As a result of her understanding of sex, Butler ends up arguing that Beauvoir thinks that anyone—regardless of whether they have a penis or not—can become a woman. This is simply not the case. For Beauvoir, a woman is someone with a female body from beginning to end, from the moment she is born until the moment she dies, but that body is her situation, not her destiny.

---

[111] Butler's belief that 'woman' or 'women' must be deconstructed is everywhere apparent: 'the category of women does not become useless through deconstruction, but becomes one . . . which stands a chance of being opened up, indeed of coming to signify in ways that none of us can predict in advance', she writes in *Bodies* (28–9). Beauvoir would say that because we define ourselves through our existence, all human beings are in principle unpredictable as long as they live. Only death deprives us of the possibility of change.

For Beauvoir people with female bodies do not have to fulfil any special requirements to be considered women. They do not have to conform either to sexist stereotypes, or to feminist ideals of womanhood. However bizarrely a woman may behave, Beauvoir would not dream of denying her the name of woman. The logic of Butler's argument, on the other hand, implies that someone who does not behave according to the dominant 'regulatory discourse(s)' for femininity, is not a woman. To behave like a woman comes to mean 'to behave like an effect of patriarchal power'. In this way the term 'woman' is surrendered to the patriarchal powers feminists wish to oppose. The fact that Beauvoir refuses to hand the concept of 'woman' over to the opposition, is precisely what makes *The Second Sex* such a liberating read. Here, finally, is a book that does not require women somehow to prove that they are 'real' women, to prove that they can conform to someone else's criteria for what a woman should be like.

I want to bring out the implications of Beauvoir's views by turning to the passage where she makes her most famous claim:

> One is not born, but rather becomes, a woman [*femme*]. No biological, psychological, or economic destiny defines the figure that the human female [*la femelle humaine*] acquires in society; it is civilization as a whole that develops this product, intermediate between male and eunuch, which one calls feminine [*féminin*]. Only the mediation of another [*autrui*] can establish an individual as an *Other*. In so far as he exists for himself, the child would not be able to understand himself as sexually differentiated. In girls as in boys the body is first of all the radiation of a subjectivity, the instrument that accomplishes the comprehension of the world: it is through the eyes, the hands, and not through the sexual parts that children apprehend the universe (*SS* 267; *Dsb* 13; TA).

In this passage, Beauvoir is not distinguishing between sex and gender but between *femme* and *femelle*, between human and animal, between the world of values and meaning (lived experience) and the scientific account of our biology (the 'objective' view of the body). The female of the human species, Beauvoir claims, cannot be understood simply as a natural kind, as a *femelle*; it is by virtue of being *human* that she is a product of civilization. In Beauvoir's reminder that a child explores the world with her whole body, and not with the sexual parts alone, we find another echo of her refusal to consider a woman a giant ovum or a monstrous vagina. If sex is not pervasive, sexual difference does not saturate a woman through and through. Rather, our lived experience encompasses bodily sexual difference, but it is also built up by many other things that per se have nothing to do with sexual difference.

If a little girl reads a book about birds, this is not in itself a sexed or gendered activity: any child can read about birds. The beauty of Beauvoir's theory is that she does not have to claim that the reading takes place in a disembodied space. She would insist on the fact that the situation of the reading is the little girl's body. Even if the girl's experience of reading initially is no different from that of her little brother, depending on the social context there is a greater or smaller chance that the gaze of the Other will fall differently on the spectacle of a little girl reading as opposed to the spectacle of a little boy reading. Some girls may not be treated differently from boys in such a context, but others will, and from such different experiences the girls' different relationship to boys and books will be forged.

'One is not born, but rather becomes, a woman': the woman that I have become is clearly not just sex. To think so, is to fall back on the pervasive picture of sex. A pervasive picture of gender, on the other hand, would be no better. The woman I have become is more than just gender, she is a fully embodied human being whose being cannot be reduced to her sexual difference, be it natural or cultural. I have said that for Beauvoir only people with female bodies become women. Writing in 1949, she does not mention sex-change operations. There is fascinating work to be done on the question of what Beauvoir's phenomenological perspective would have to say about the lived experience of transsexuals (see Section V, below, for some discussion of this.) Here I shall just note that nothing in Beauvoir's view commits her to claiming that there are no unclear cases, or that no human baby was ever miscategorized at birth, and thus brought up to become a woman regardless of its XY chromosomes. To repeat a point I have made before: the existence of hard cases does not necessarily change our perception of the easy ones.

Beauvoir does not deny that our biology fundamentally shapes the human world. But to say so is not to reduce social life to biological facts. It means, rather, that as long as technology has not made the usual method of human reproduction obsolete, the biological requirements of pregnancy, childbirth, and childcare will have to be accommodated within any social structure. In this sense, sex is different from both race and class. We can very well imagine societies in which race and class no longer exist as social categories, but it is impossible to imagine a society that has ceased to acknowledge that human babies are helpless little creatures. It follows from Beauvoir's analysis that although our biology forces us to organize human societies with child-rearing in mind, it does not impose any *specific* way of doing this.[112] There is nothing to prevent us from placing an extremely high or an extremely low social value on the task. We may assign it to any social group we like, make it the task exclusively of people with brown eyes, or of people between the ages of 40 and 50, or of anyone living in Manchester or Minnesota. What we may *not* do, is to claim that it follows from the fact that women give birth that they should therefore spend twenty years of their lives doing nothing but child-rearing. One might just as well claim that since men impregnate women, they should spend the rest of their lives looking after their offspring. Although our biology places certain limitations on culture, our specific cultural arrangements cannot be read off from our biology.

For Beauvoir, then, the question is not how someone of any sex becomes a woman, but what values, norms, and demands the female human being—precisely because she is female—comes up against in her encounter with the Other (society). In order to understand what it means for the individual woman to encounter the Other, we must investigate her concrete lived experience. It is no coincidence that the sentence 'One is not born, but rather becomes, a woman' introduces the volume of *The Second Sex* that bears the title 'Lived Experience'.

---

[112] Terry Eagleton puts a similar point very nicely: 'It is important to see . . . that we are not "cultural" rather than "natural" creatures, but cultural beings by virtue of our nature, which is to say by virtue of the sorts of bodies we have and the kind of world to which they belong' (*Illusions* 72–3).

Sex and Gender in Beauvoir?

In her pioneering essay on gender, Donna Haraway writes that 'Despite important differences, all the modern feminist meanings of gender have roots in Simone de Beauvoir's claim that "one is not born a woman" ' (131).[113] This can be a misleading statement unless one is firmly aware of what the differences are. Although no feminist draws a clearer line between biology and social norms than Simone de Beauvoir, the concepts of sex and gender cannot be superimposed on her categories. Given the vast proliferation of 'gender theory' in contemporary feminism, gender itself has become a concept that defies easy definition.[114] The word is nevertheless mainly used in two different ways: to refer to 'sexual stereotypes' or 'dominant gender norms', or to an individual's qualities and ways of being ('gender identity'). The figures below summarize the difference between various sex/gender theories and Beauvoir's categories:

(1960s:)

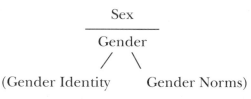

Sex
———
Gender

(Gender Identity   Gender Norms)

The mainstream model of sex and gender corresponds neatly to nature and culture, biology and social norms. Beauvoir's categories, on the other hand, cannot be reduced to such binary opposites:

(Beauvoir:)

> Body as object
> Body as situation
> Lived experience (subjectivity)
> Myths of femininity (ideology; norms)
> Sex (the fact of being a man or a woman)

---

[113] See also Haraway 133 and 147–8.

[114] In a talk entitled 'Disembodying Race and Gender' given at Duke University in Mar. 1996, Sally Haslanger made an interesting contribution to a clarifying analysis of gender and race.

To Beauvoir, the category of the body perceived as an object is 'objectivist' and 'scientistic'. For this reason this category resembles the 1960s understanding of sex. We have seen that Beauvoir rejects this category as a useless starting point for any attempt to understand what a woman is. To consider the body as a situation, on the other hand, is to consider both the fact of having a specific kind of body and the meaning that concrete body has for the situated individual. This is not the equivalent of either sex or gender. The same is true for 'lived experience' which encompasses our experience of all kinds of situations (race, class, nationality, etc.), and is a far more wide-ranging concept than the highly psychologizing concept of gender identity. Beauvoir's 'myths of femininity' closely resemble the concept of gender stereotypes or norms.[115] Roland Barthes uses the same meaning of 'myth' in *Mythologies*. I take this to be an entirely social category, with strong family resemblances to the Marxist concept of ideology. When Gayle Rubin writes that she wishes for a society without gender, I assume that she means a society without oppressive stereotypes of femininity and masculinity, not a society without the lived experience of sexual difference. In short, Beauvoir's concepts are capable of drawing more nuanced and precise distinctions than the sex/gender distinction can provide.

A comparison of the two sets of categories also reveals that the 1960s concept that is most foreign to Beauvoir's thought is that of gender identity. In *The Second Sex*, Beauvoir never discusses identity because she thinks of the individual's subjectivity as interwoven with the conditions in which she lives. To analyse lived experience is to take as one's starting point the experiencing subject, understood as always situated, always embodied, but also as always having a dimension of freedom. Subjectivity is neither a thing nor an inner, emotional world; it is, rather, our way of being in the world. Thus there can be no 'identity' divorced from the world the subject is experiencing. To speak of a generalized 'gender identity' is to impose a reifying or objectifying closure on

---

[115] This category requires some updating. We would probably want to add 'and masculinity', and explore its relationship to a concept such as ideology. The title of the first volume of *The Second Sex* is 'Les faits et les mythes': 'Facts and Myths'.

our steadily changing and fluctuating experience of ourselves in the world. If we use the words 'femininity' and 'masculinity' to designate anything other than sex-based stereotypes, we may find that we have locked ourselves into precisely such a reified concept of gender.[116]

Beauvoir believes that the fact of being born with a female body starts a process which will have specific, yet unforeseeable consequences. Each woman will make something out of what the world makes out of her: this phrase captures at once a sense of limitations and a sense of freedom. To Beauvoir the relationship between one's body and one's subjectivity is neither necessary nor arbitrary, but contingent.[117] If we want to understand what a woman is, generalizations about sexual difference will never be enough, whether this is understood in terms of sex, gender or both. Instead Beauvoir invites us to study the varieties of women's lived experience. One aspect of that lived experience will be the way in which the individual woman encounters, internalizes, or rejects dominant gender norms. But this encounter is always inflected by the woman's situation, and that means by her personal and idiosyncratic history as this is interwoven with other historical situations such as her age, race, class, and nationality, and the particular political conflicts in which she may be involved.

Beauvoir's conceptual distinctions are more nuanced and carry out more work than the usual feminist distinction between sex and gender, and they do their work with greater finesse and sophistication. Rejecting the pervasive picture of sex, Beauvoir does not reduce the *femme* to the *femelle*, does not consider that a woman can

---

[116] I return to this point in some detail at the end of this essay.

[117] Moira Gatens's excellent essay on sex and gender makes the point that a psychoanalytic understanding of the body casts the relationship between the body and the psyche as contingent: 'it is also clear that there is a contingent, though not arbitrary, relation between the male body and masculinity and the female body and femininity. To claim this is neither biologism nor essentialism but is rather to acknowledge the importance of complex and ubiquitous networks of signification to the historically, psychologically and culturally variable ways of being a man or a woman' (*Imaginary Bodies* 13). This contrasts with the widespread poststructuralist belief that if something isn't necessary, then it must be arbitrary. (I have also noticed, in some recent theoretical contexts, a confusing tendency to take the word 'contingent' to *mean* 'arbitrary'.)

only be defined within the narrow semantic register of sex, sexuality, or sexual difference. For Beauvoir, a woman is a human being as much as she is a woman: women too embody humanity. Because Beauvoir's theory denies that biological differences justify social norms, there is no risk of biological determinism. By considering the body as a situation, *The Second Sex* lays the groundwork for a thoroughly historical understanding of the body, one that steers clear of the Scylla of empiricism as well as the Charybdis of idealism. By stressing the oppressive function of sexual ideology and social norms, *The Second Sex* develops a devastating critique of sexism. By stressing the fact that women's freedom and agency only rarely disappear entirely, even under severely oppressive conditions, Beauvoir produces a powerful vision of liberation: Beauvoir's women are victims of sexism, but potential revolutionaries too. Her feminism, like that of Gayle Rubin, is emancipatory. By accepting that bodily differences of all kinds contribute to the meaning of our lived experience, Beauvoir indicates that she has a proper respect for biology and other sciences of the body: she is not against science, but against scientism. Beauvoir's account of woman as an open-ended becoming gives us the tools we need to dismantle every reifying gender theory. In short, because it rejects both biological determinism and the limiting distinction between sex and gender, *The Second Sex* provides a brilliant starting point for future feminist investigations of the body, agency, and freedom.

V DOES IT MAKE A DIFFERENCE? SEX, GENDER, AND THE LAW

In the law a constant stream of actual cases, more novel and more tortuous than the mere imagination could contrive, are brought up for decision—that is, formulae for docketing them must somehow be found.

J. L. Austin, 1956[118]

Nothing will help us more to get clear on a subject than 'cases [imagined] with vividness and fullness', J. L. Austin writes (198). In

[118] The quotation comes from the essay with the wonderful title 'A Plea for Excuses' (186).

the last main section of this essay I want to ask what a discussion of concrete cases can tell us about the body, sex, and gender. I shall use as my examples a few cases that have been brought forward by two feminist lawyers working on sex and gender, namely Mary Ann Case who takes a 1960s view of gender, and Katherine Franke who works with the poststructuralist picture of sex.[119] Their discussions will be contrasted with my own, Beauvoir-inspired perspective.

As American legal theorists Case and Franke have to propose solutions that will work with the wording of current US law. Their project is to show how the law can be made to yield a fair treatment of women and sexual minorities. Whatever their own views on sexual difference may be, their essays would not be taken seriously by other lawyers if they failed to remain responsive to the way American law is currently practised and understood. I am not bound by such concerns. In drawing attention to some of the theoretical and political implications of Case and Franke's analyses of sex and gender in the law, I am implicitly commenting on the way US law makes feminists think about sexual difference.

How would the law have to change to take account of a Beauvoirean feminist perspective? This is a fascinating question, but it is not one that I have the competence to answer. The answer would in any case be different in different legal systems. At one point below I question employers' right to fire or promote whoever they want. American law might find it harder to accommodate such ideas than the law in, say, Scandinavia, which traditionally has provided quite extensive protection of workers' rights.[120] My thoughts about a few legal cases are no more than an invitation to a conversation. Further discussion, whether of the same cases, or of different cases in different contexts, would be an immensely helpful contribution to the project of developing a feminist theory inspired by *The Second Sex.*

---

[119] Although Franke does discuss gender to some extent, Case does not focus on sex. I am grateful to Professor Katharine Bartlett at Duke Law School for drawing my attention to the essays by Franke and Case, and also for helping me to see more clearly what feminist legal theorists (as opposed to an ordinary feminist theorist such as myself) try to do.

[120] On this point, Katharine Bartlett's comments on a draft of this paper were immensely helpful to me.

Discrimination on the Basis of Sex

US anti-discrimination law states that it is unlawful to discriminate against someone 'on the basis of sex'. Here the word sex is used in its traditional pre-1960s sense: it means 'because of being a man or woman'. The law is intended to protect us from discrimination based solely on our *status* as male or female. 'What was decided among the prehistoric Protozoa cannot be annulled by Act of Parliament', Geddes and Thomson wrote (267). It seems almost too obvious to mention, but the very fact of *having* legislation outlawing sex discrimination means that the law is not committed to biological determinism. If someone wanted to fire me from my job at Duke University on the grounds that my female biology makes me unsuited to intellectual work, Geddes and Thomson would not object to the principle of it, but contemporary US law most certainly would. The introduction of anti-sex-discrimination legislation in the United States represented a major victory for feminists who deny that biology grounds social norms.[121]

The traditional sense of sex invoked by US law is not necessarily complicit with sexual conservatism. In the traditional sense, sex does not mean just chromosomal and hormonal sexual differences, it means the fact of being a man or a woman. '[I]t is fatal for anyone who writes to think of their sex', Virginia Woolf writes (*Room* 99). For Woolf as for Beauvoir it is self-evident that men and women are always situated in a particular time and place. Used in this sense, sex does not necessarily refer to some ahistorical entity. It does not prevent us from denying that biology grounds social norms, nor does it commit us to any particular view of what a man or a woman is. As Simone de Beauvoir's usage shows, the traditional meaning of sex does not oblige us to define a woman as someone who is female, feminine, and heterosexual. More open than the 1960s understanding of the term, the traditional meaning of sex has the advantage of not forcing us to classify every ordinary action or

---

[121] The question of whether the courts accept *some* biologically based generalizations about women and men remains open. Katherine Franke writes: 'We have inherited a jurisprudence of sexual equality that seeks to distinguish, as its primary function, inaccurate myths about sexual identity from true—and therefore prepolitical—characteristics of sex that are factually significant' (29).

quality as belonging either to sex or to gender. If I lose my job because I am a woman it would in most cases be a complete waste of time to try to decide whether I lost my job because of my sex or because of my gender.

Among US lawyers there is currently some confusion of usage concerning sex and gender. Although the majority of courts speak of discrimination on the basis of *sex*, the US Supreme Court Justice Ruth Bader Ginsburg usually speaks of discrimination on the basis of *gender*. For her, this is not a conceptual distinction, but a matter of convenience:

> [Ginsburg] stopped talking about sex discrimination years ago. . . .
> [S]he explained that a secretary once told her, 'I'm typing all these briefs and articles for you and the word sex, sex, sex, is on every page. Don't you know those nine men [on the Supreme Court], they hear that word and their first association is not the way you want them to be thinking? Why don't you use the word "gender"? It is a grammatical term and it will ward off distracting associations'.[122]

When she says 'gender', Ginsburg in fact means sex in the traditional sense. Many legislators now follow her example. Thus the Pentagon's 'Don't ask, don't tell' policy on homosexuality states that it will discharge members of the military who marry or attempt to marry 'someone of the same gender'.[123] In the United States, this usage is becoming increasingly accepted in everyday life, where all sorts of forms and questionnaires routinely require us to tick the box for male or female gender. Everyday references to gender to mean 'sex' or 'the fact of being a man or a woman' are now too numerous to count.[124] Ginsburg's secretary surely

[122] An interview with Justice Ginsburg, as quoted by Case (10).

[123] 'Sexual orientation will not be a bar to service unless manifested by homosexual conduct. The military will discharge members who engage in homosexual conduct, defined as a homosexual act, a statement that the member is homosexual or bisexual, or a marriage or attempted marriage to someone of the same gender' (quoted in Parker and Sedgwick, 'Introduction' 5).

[124] One recent handbook on non-sexist usage summarizes this usage as follows: 'The terms *sex* and *gender* . . . are often used synonymously in contemporary writing to denote biological femaleness or maleness (with *gender* seen by some as merely a way to avoid the word *sex*, which also designates, of course, sexual intercourse and related activities)' (Frank and Treichler 10).

provides the major explanation for this: in the latest puritanical backlash, the very word 'sex' appears to have gained pornographic connotations. Insofar as the new usage simply substitutes 'gender' for 'sex' in the traditional sense, it does not owe much to the feminist understanding of the sex/gender distinction.[125] Just as one cannot assume that someone who refers to a person's 'sex' means to espouse biological essentialism, one cannot assume, either, that someone who refers to a person's 'gender' means to reject biological determinism.

The question of what sex or gender means in US courts is complicated by the fact that one of Justice Ginsburg's more conservative colleagues on the Supreme Court, Justice Antonin Scalia, insists on distinguishing between sex and gender. In a 1994 minority opinion Scalia wrote:

> Throughout this opinion, I shall refer to the issue as sex discrimination rather than (as the Court does) gender discrimination. The word 'gender' has acquired the new and useful connotation of cultural and attitudinal characteristics (as opposed to physical characteristics) distinctive to the sexes. That is to say, gender is to sex as feminine is to female and masculine to male.[126]

The case in question was one where the prosecution in a paternity suit had used peremptory challenges to eliminate men from the jury. Scalia's point was that the case should be considered one of sex (and not gender) discrimination because it did not involve 'peremptory strikes exercised on the basis of femininity and masculinity (as far as it appears, effeminate men did not survive the prosecution's peremptories)'.[127] Any teacher of women's studies might agree. Scalia's discovery of the sex/gender distinction nevertheless produces new legal ambiguities. Does he believe that the law makes it illegal to discriminate on the basis of *gender* as well as of sex? Does he still think of sex as the fact of being a man or a woman? Or would he accept that sex means chromosomes

---

[125] Some speakers may of course have a vague idea that gender somehow is a 'more feminist' *word* than sex, but this does not necessarily change the way they use it. See also my discussion of Joan Scott's use of the word gender in Sect. III, above.

[126] Quoted in Franke 9 (also in Case 12).

[127] Scalia, quoted in Case 12.

and hormones and nothing else? To judge from the example Scalia gives—*men* were struck off the jury regardless of their *gender*—I would say he still assumes that sex means 'the fact of being a man or a woman', but the text does not explicitly address the issue.[128] The fact that such questions of interpretation arise all the way up to the US Supreme Court, shows that the question of what exactly sex discrimination means is far from settled.

Poststructuralism, Sex Discrimination, and the Sex of Transsexuals

Katherine Franke is a poststructuralist feminist lawyer. Her essay on why the law should not distinguish between sex and gender is based on the assumption that sex means 'body parts' or 'chromosomes' and that such things are entirely natural, completely outside society and culture.[129] She declares that it is oppressive and essentialist to 'conceive of sex biologically—to carve up the population into two different kinds of people' (92). Since sex is natural, whereas all discriminatory practices per definition are social, there is no such thing as *sex* discrimination:

> When women are denied employment, for instance, it is not because the discriminator is thinking 'a Y chromosome is necessary in order to perform this kind of work.' Only in very rare cases can sex discrimination be reduced to a question of body parts (36).

If *sex* discrimination does not exist, there is no point in distinguishing between sex and gender. What there is, and what the law should recognize, Franke claims, is *gender* discrimination.

In order to fend off the 'ludicrous' and 'absurd' idea that there is a biological foundation to sex discrimination, Franke denies that biological facts are relevant to any human activity whatsoever.[130] To her, any acknowledgment of biological sexual differences *must* give

---

[128] According to both Franke and Case, Scalia's opinion does not spell out his views on discrimination on the basis of gender (see Case 12; Franke 9–10).

[129] Attributing her own interpretation of sex to Scalia, Franke takes him to mean that 'gender-based distinctions are *not* what "discrimination on the basis of sex" was intended to reach' (9–10). Franke cites no evidence in support of her interpretation that Scalia intends to exclude gender. Mary Anne Case does not think that Scalia's distinction is necessarily ominous (see Case 4).

[130] See Franke 31 ('absurdity'); 40 ('indeed almost ludicrous').

rise to socially oppressive norms. Sexual equality jurisprudence in America, she writes, has accepted 'a fundamental belief in the truth of biological sexual difference' (3), and is therefore contradictory. 'How can the Court at once tolerate sexual differentiation and proscribe sexual discrimination?', Franke asks (31). The alternative is to think of biological differences as an '*effect* of normative gender ideology' (2).[131] In her poststructuralist recoil from the bad picture of sex, she recommends that we proceed as if bodies did not exist. Bodies should simply 'drop out of' the legal picture.[132]

There is an obvious tension between Franke's unproblematic use of the words women and men, and her resolute denial that the population consists of two biologically different kinds of people, namely women and men. At times she appears simultaneously to deny and affirm that sexism consists in the oppression of women just because they are (biological) women:

> Women who are sexually harassed in the workplace do not experience discriminatory harm because of their biology but because of the manner in which sex is used to exploit a relationship of power between victim and harasser. This relationship of power is based either upon supervisor/subordinate roles or upon cultural gender roles which encourage men to use sex to subordinate women. Biology has absolutely nothing to do with either one of these material grounds for workplace sexual harassment (91).

Franke is making two fundamental assumptions. First, that sex *must* mean biology, which must mean essence, nature, and ground, which can have nothing to do with social practices; and, second, that a 'man' or a 'woman' is nothing but gender. Women and men are best understood not as bodies, but as the 'congealed ideological constructs' conjured up by Judith Butler. The question of why we persist in thinking in terms of two sexes and not one or ten remains unexplored.

---

[131] 'Ultimately', Franke writes, 'there is no principled way to distinguish sex from gender, and concomitantly, sexual differentiation from sexual discrimination' (5). She also writes that 'By accepting [biological sexual differences], equality jurisprudence reifies as foundational *fact* that which is really an *effect* of normative gender ideology' (2).

[132] '[E]quality jurisprudence must abandon its reliance upon a biological definition of sexual identity and sex discrimination and instead . . . adopt a more behavioral or performative conception of sex' (8).

Franke's attitude to the sex/gender distinction is as inconsistent as that of other poststructuralists. Although the title of her essay claims that the 'central mistake of sex discrimination law [is] the disaggregation of sex from gender' (1), she is not actually against distinguishing between sex and gender at all. What she is against, is the belief that sex *determines* gender, and what she explicitly wants to escape is the 'death grip that *unifies* sex and gender' (90; my emphasis). Hers is a case against the pervasive picture of sex, and against biological determinism, but not against the distinction between sex and gender. In practice, Franke distinguishes between male and masculine, female and feminine, and even hails as 'revolutionary' the attempt to create 'the cultural conditions for masculinity to be separated from maleness and be remapped onto the female body' (87). This is the equivalent of Judith Butler's celebration of the subversive potential of men in drag.[133] When pushed to make a concrete political or legal claim, the poststructuralist theorist finds herself returning to the 1960s distinction between sex and gender that she otherwise denounces. When Mary Ann Case denounces 'gender conformity', which she defines as the belief that one's gender and one's sexual orientation *must* correspond to one's sex, she is saying exactly the same thing as Franke when she criticizes the belief that sex determines gender.[134] On this point, then, Franke's political argument is exactly the same as that of just about every other contemporary feminist.

Much of Franke's essay is devoted to extensive discussion of the dilemmas of transsexuals.[135] In the case known as *Ulane* v. *Eastern Airlines* (1984 and 1985), the plaintiff had been hired as a male pilot by Eastern Airlines. Here is Franke's account of the case:

> Ulane later took a leave of absence to undergo sexual reassignment surgery and was fired by Eastern when she returned to work as a woman. She then filed a Title VII [employment-related] sex discrimination action against her employer, alleging that she 'was fired by Eastern Airlines for no reason other than the fact that she ceased being a male and became a female' (Franke 33).

[133] This claim is made in the context of a discussion of Shannon Faulkner's brief attendance at the Citadel. I shall return to this case below.

[134] I discuss Case's views below.

[135] Franke prefers to speak of 'transgendered people' (see 32–3 n. 130).

The court dismissed Ulane's claim, reasoning that

> it is unlawful to discriminate against women because they are
> women, and against men because they are men. . . . [E]ven if one
> believes that a woman can be so easily created from what remains
> of a man, that does not decide this case. If Eastern had considered
> Ulane to be female and had discriminated against her because she
> was female . . . then the argument might be made that Title VII
> applied (cited in Franke 33).

Franke does not provide a clear discussion of this case, but the drift
of her argument is that the court was wrong to dismiss Ulane's
claim, and in particular wrong not to accept that Ulane had become
a woman: '[on a foundational level, they all [all courts] embrace an
essentially biological definition of the two sexual categories' (35).

But, as the court indicated, Ulane's problem would not necessarily have been solved if the court had thought of her as a woman,
rather than as a strangely equipped man. She wasn't fired, one
might argue, because of her *status* as male or female, but because
she had undergone a sex-change operation (i.e. because of something she had *done*, rather than something she *was*). To this one
might object that the fact of submitting to surgery is virtually part
of the definition of the term 'transsexual'. It may seem just as plausible to claim that Ulane was dismissed for *being* a transsexual as to
say that she was dismissed for *having* a sex-change operation. This
argument implicitly recommends that transsexuals should be
considered neither male or female, but a third (or third and
fourth) sex. The court seems to have recognized this option, since
it adds that 'if the term "sex" . . . is to mean more than biological
male and biological female, the new definition must come from
Congress' (cited in Franke 33). As US law currently stands, however,
there is no protection for transsexuals qua transsexuals.[136]

Many transsexuals, however, do not want to be recognized *as*
transsexuals. What they want is to have their *new* sex recognized
by the law.[137] This seems to be Franke's view too. Let us assume for

---

[136] So far at least, nothing indicates that US law, or indeed any country's law,
has developed a coherent doctrine concerning sex change (see Rogers).

[137] An increasing number of transsexuals disagree with this, however. Sandy
Stone and Kate Bornstein both make powerful cases for their right to be recognized as *transsexual women*.

the moment that Ulane's sex was not in doubt, and that all parties agreed to consider her a bona fide woman. In order to get protection under the law, Ulane would then have had to show that she was fired because of being a woman. But if she was fired not for *being* a woman, but for the *act* of changing her sex in order to *become* one, general recognition of her new sex would still not advance her case. What I am trying to show is that if we believe that transsexuals should be protected under sex discrimination law, there is no need first to dismiss the belief that there are biological differences between men and women. After all, transsexuals themselves go to painful lengths to acquire the sex organs of the 'target sex'.[138] Rather than denouncing the belief in biological sex differences, Franke ought to denounce the belief that the very fact of wanting a sex-change operation is a symptom of the kind of mental instability that makes one unsuitable for a responsible job.

Let us suspend legal and political disbelief for a moment, and assume that US legislators had just happily voted to amend current Title VII (employment related) law to the effect that nobody should be discriminated against 'because of his sex *or because of changing his sex*'.[139] Depending on the circumstances of her case, the new wording might have saved the unfortunate Ulane. The new wording does not require us to reject the traditional meaning of sex, or to accept that sex is an effect of the performance of gender. Nor does the distinction between sex and gender come up. In this case, there is no necessary link between our political aim (recognition of the rights of transsexuals) and

---

[138] Some poststructuralists have concluded that it follows that drag artists are radical and transsexuals are conservative, or, in somewhat attenuated terms, that drag artists are 'queer' (they unsettle categories), whereas transsexuals risk turning themselves into 'essentialists'. In an essay on Leslie Feinberg's fine novel *Stone Butch Blues,* Jay Prosser writes: '[In *Stone Butch Blues*] becoming fully one sex is mythicized as rightful and crucially inextricable from transsexual identity; the trope of a gendered home structures the transsexual story. In spite of the difference of its story line, *Stone Butch Blues* participates in this transsexual version of the narrative of gendered belonging and becoming which it can't quite give up in a distinctly unqueer fashion. . . . Transsexuality is a narrative of essentialist constructionism . . .' (491).

[139] I use 'his' here, because that is the wording of the law.

our beliefs about biological facts. In the case of *Ulane* v. *Eastern Airlines*, poststructuralist theory seems to make no difference at all.

But Franke is not mainly concerned with transsexuals filing Title VII cases. Her most detailed discussion of the situation of transsexuals focuses on cases involving marriage, divorce, and alimony. Her principal case is the famous British case known as *Corbett* v. *Corbett* (1971), concerning the marriage between Arthur Corbett, who had at times considered himself a male transvestite, and April Ashley, a male-to-female transsexual. They courted each other for three years, and were married in Gibraltar in September 1963. '[T]hey separated after only fourteen days', Franke writes, 'in part because Corbett was unable fully to consummate the marriage' (44).[140] Corbett challenged the legal validity of the marriage. The main question to be decided was whether April Ashley was a woman at the time of the marriage. If she was not, the marriage was never valid, and no divorce would be necessary; if she was, usual divorce proceedings would have to be undertaken.[141]

To make a long story short: in 1971 Judge Ormrod ruled that April Ashley was born male, and that subsequent surgery and hormone treatment failed to change this fact.[142] Franke denounces this as 'biological essentialism' (50), and at the end of her paper she concludes that 'Ultimately, sexual equality jurisprudence must abandon its reliance upon biology in favor of an underlying fundamental right to determine gender independent of biological sex' (99). Taken in the poststructuralist spirit in which it is written, this means that courts should accept that someone's gender *is* their sex, that the performance of gender produces sex, and that no biological facts can override this

---

[140] Franke adds her own analysis of what destroyed the relationship of this couple: 'And so the couple split, the normalizing and liberalizing effect of the institution of marriage having destroyed the fantasy that had made the relationship initially so powerful for both parties' (44).

[141] Needless to say, the court and all the parties in this 1960s case took for granted that a married couple had to be of different sex.

[142] 'The correct criteria for "womanness" should be "the chromosomal, gonadal and genital tests. . . . [But] the greater weight would probably be given to the genital criteria than to the other two"' (Franke 46).

conclusion. Applied to the case of *Corbett* v. *Corbett*, it follows that because April Ashley 'performed her gender' to perfection, the court should accept that she was a woman. (According to the medical experts in the case, Ashley had 'remarkably good' female genitals, and there was no physical impediment to full penetration.) Franke's argument assumes that the claim that gender is performative secures the conclusion that transsexuals should *always* be legally recognized as being their 'target sex'.

To accept that anyone who performs femininity is a woman, is to blur the difference between a woman who performs femininity, a man (drag artist or cross-dresser) who does it, and a transsexual who has changed his or her body in order to achieve a more convincing 'performance'. Is the 'gender' performed really the same in each case? Even if we assume that these three people all perform the same script (which is by no means a foregone conclusion), does a different body really make no difference at all as to the effect of the performance? Fortunately there is no need to make a final decision about the performativity or otherwise of sex and gender in order to accept the claim that male-to-female transsexuals should be legally recognized as women. All that is required is that we deny that biology grounds social norms. It is neither politically reactionary nor philosophically inconsistent to believe both that a male-to-female transsexual remains a biological male *and* that this is no reason to deny 'him' the legal right to be reclassified as a woman. This would be in keeping both with Gayle Rubin's wish to get rid of social gender norms, and with Beauvoir's emphasis on women's (and men's) freedom to define their sex as they please.

Some judges—including Judge Ormrod—have decided that whatever some people get up to with their bodies, the sex assigned at birth remains the only sex of the person unless there is evidence that a mistake has been made. This corresponds exactly to the views of some feminist and lesbian activists, particularly with regard to male-to-female transsexuals who claim that they are lesbians and wish to participate in lesbian women-only organizations and meetings. Some lesbians are adamant that the male-to-female transsexual remains a male, who insofar as he is trying to infiltrate lesbian organizations, is no better than a fifth columnist, an agent of homophobic patriarchy.[143] In all these cases the question at stake is the same: when deciding what sex someone is, how much importance are we to attach to genital surgery and hormone treatment—to body parts—and how much to a person's lived experience?

Some courts have decided that while individuals have a legitimate right to have their wish to *pass* as a man or a woman accepted by society, and so allow transsexuals to change their first names and get a new driver's licence, it doesn't follow that they actually *have changed* their biological sex. They cannot marry a 'same-sex' partner, or change their birth certificates.[144] Many transsexuals consider that this produces a completely absurd situation, since the same person now has documents declaring him or her to be male in some cases and female in others. I imagine that many judges and radical lesbians would agree with Franke that what is needed is a clear-cut decision about the person's sex, whether this is taken to be based on biology or performativity. But this is not an obvious conclusion.

Let us imagine that I wake up tomorrow with a fully male body, but with exactly the same memories and life experiences as I have today. Would I then be a man? First of all, we need to note that this question is formulated in a way that tempts us to think that there must be something deeply mysterious and difficult about the answer, that to find an answer requires some special insight into what it means to *be* a man or a woman, in some *deep* sense. The belief is that no ordinary considerations could possibly help us to answer the question.[145] Moreover, we may be inclined to

---

[143] See e.g. Janice Raymond, *The Transsexual Empire* and Christine Burton, 'Golden Threads'. For vociferous counterarguments, from a broadly poststructuralist perspective, see Sandy Stone, 'The Empire Strikes Back', and Kate Bornstein, *Gender Outlaw*. Leslie Feinberg's interesting new book *Transgender Warrior* shows discontent with the poststructuralist paradigm, and lack of certainty about possible alternatives.

[144] Franke quotes one decision that granted a petition to change an obviously male name to a female one, but then added that 'the order shall not be used or relied upon by petitioner as any evidence or judicial determination that the sex of the petitioner has in fact been changed' (54).

[145] My analysis here is inspired by Martin Stone's 'Focusing the Law'. Drawing on Wittgenstein, Stone shows that the temptation to invest certain questions or expressions with a mysterious strangeness leads us away from the ordinary and everyday and towards metaphysics (see esp. 44–57).

think that the question has to be settled once and for all by a clear yes or no. This is where Simone de Beauvoir teaches us to think differently. As she points out, it is the Other who assigns my sex to me. We cannot determine someone's sex in abstraction from any human situation. If I lived in perfect isolation from all other human beings, I would never even know what sex I was.

If we assume, for the sake of the argument, that my new male body was perfect, right down to the XY chromosomes, to insist that I was still simply a woman would be somewhat odd.[146] It is not enough to think of oneself as a woman in order to become one. Like most of us, Beauvoir would presumably take someone with a male body to be a man, unless she had good reason to think otherwise. Confronted with my case, she would, I imagine, agree that my brand-new male body represented a radical change of situation for me. The unsuspecting world would see nothing but a man wherever I turned up, and I would be treated accordingly. If, from old habit, I still tried to use the women's toilets, for instance, I would surely be shown the door. Under the circumstances, it is difficult to see that there would be anything wrong in this. For the purpose of using public toilets I would definitely be a man. (This is not to claim that the current sex segregation of public toilet facilities should be maintained for ever.) A different situation might produce a different answer to the question of what my sex was. If I were asked to speak at a women-only conference, it would seem unfair to exclude me on the grounds that I no longer was a woman. Should all my female experiences and work on feminist theory count for nothing just because I had woken up to find myself equipped with a penis? And what if some committee needed expertise on sex changes? Would I not be perfectly entitled to claim that I was an ex-woman, a member of the select group of people who have changed their sex? Over time my new situation would affect my general sense of identity. I

---

[146] This is precisely the problem that confronts the protagonist of Angela Carter's profound novel *The Passion of New Eve* (1977). Having been transformed into a perfect woman, Evelyn/Eve has to learn through experience what it might mean to be a woman in different situations. At the end of the novel, Eve has become a woman, and for Carter that means no more and no less mythological than any other incarnation of femininity.

would steadily gain more male experiences, yet for a very long time (and possibly always), I would have to consider the answer to the question of which sex I belonged to, as relatively open to variation.

On my reading of feminist theory, poststructuralists and other sex/gender feminists have failed to address the question of transsexuals adequately because they have no concept of the body as a situation, or of lived experience, and because they tend to look for one final answer to the question of what sex a transsexual is. Moreover, because they tend to understand sex as a matter of a few narrowly defined biological criteria, they forget that the meaning of the words man and woman is produced in concrete human situations. That is, feminists and transsexuals have overlooked the fact that what counts as being a woman for the purpose of marriage is not necessarily the same thing as what counts as being a woman for the purpose of participating in a lesbian activist group. To ask courts to have a clear-cut, all-purpose 'line' on sex changes is to ask them *not* to engage in new interpretations of the purpose of the different human institutions and practices which are brought into conflict by the arrival of transsexuals. I can't see how this could be in the interest either of feminists or of transsexuals.

All this, of course, leaves the question of whether April Ashley should be considered a man or a woman at the time of her marriage to Arthur Corbett unresolved. The fact is that I find it extremely difficult to come up with an answer. A closer reading of the case nevertheless provides some revealing information. First of all, Judge Ormrod stresses over and over again that he is only concerned with determining the sex of April Ashley for the purposes of marriage: 'The question then becomes', he writes, 'what is meant by the word "woman" in the context of a marriage, for I am not concerned to determine the "legal sex" of the respondent at large' (106).[147] Judge Ormrod, in my view, is clearly right to frame his decision in this narrow way. By asking 'what is April Ashley's sex for the purposes of marriage?' he helps us to see that the ideological difficulties arising from his decision have

[147] The legal reference to this British case is *Corbett* v. *Corbett* [1971]: 83–119.

little to do with the way he thinks about sex, and rather more to do with the way he thinks about marriage. Let us accept that a British court in 1971 had to define marriage as a relationship between a man and a woman. But even given this assumption, Judge Ormrod's understanding of what matters in a marriage is, to say the least, contentious. 'Marriage is a relationship which depends on sex and not on gender', he writes (107):

> Having regard to the essentially hetero-sexual character of the relationship which is called marriage, the criteria [of April Ashley's sex] must, in my judgment, be biological, for even the most extreme degree of transsexualism in a male or the most severe hormonal imbalance which can exist in a person with male chromosomes, male gonads and male genitalia cannot reproduce a person who is naturally capable of performing the essential role of a woman in marriage (106).

This raises the delicate question of exactly what the 'essential role of a woman in marriage' is, and what the difference between performing it 'naturally' or in some other way might be. My impression is that Judge Ormrod takes the fundamental purpose of marriage to be procreation. In order to procreate one needs a real vagina, as opposed to 'an artificial cavity': 'When such a cavity has been constructed in a male, the difference between sexual intercourse using it and anal or intra-crural intercourse is, in my judgment, to be measured in centimetres' (107). But if the decisive criterion for being a woman for the purposes of marriage is the ability to be able to reproduce 'naturally', then infertile or post-menopausal women, or women born without a vagina do not qualify as women for the purposes of marriage. A question mark must also be raised about women who get married without the slightest intention of having children. If we take Judge Ormrod's understanding of marriage to imply, at the very least, the requirement that there has to be vaginal sexual intercourse, whether it has a chance of leading to reproduction or not, then married couples who prefer not to indulge in this activity, for one reason or another, also need to ask themselves whether they are genuinely married.

Judge Ormrod took a view of marriage consonant with that of the Catholic Church. He would not have needed to wait for the gay marriage debates of the 1990s to find alternative views. In his 1643 tract on divorce, Milton writes: 'God in the first ordaining of marriage taught us to what end he did it, in words expressly implying the apt and cheerful conversation of man with woman, to comfort and refresh him against the evil of solitary life, not mentioning the purpose of generation till afterwards, as being but a secondary end in dignity ...' (183). Although Milton's editors note that 'conversation' in 1643 signified intimacy and/or cohabitation, I think Milton is saying that there is no intimacy, and therefore no marriage, without loving and joyful conversation between the spouses. As Ibsen's *A Doll's House* (1879) teaches us, if the criterion for a genuine marriage were 'apt and cheerful conversation', then few could claim to be married. When Nora discovers that she has never really known her husband, that Thorvald is not the hero she took him to be, she says: 'In that moment I realized that for eight years I have been living here with a strange man, and that I have had three children—. Oh, I can't bear to think of it! I could tear myself to bits and pieces' (85; my translation). Nora's conclusion is that regardless of their lawfully wedded legal status, and regardless of the fact that they have fulfilled the injunction to procreate, the two of them have never actually been married at all. Her famous exit line insists precisely on this point. She would only ever come back, she says, if 'our life together could become a marriage' (86). If we want to determine whether April Ashley was a woman for the purposes of marriage, we may want to leave questions of identity and essence behind and instead ask what it might mean to be married in contemporary Western society.

Against Femininity: Gender, Stereotypes, and Feminist Politics

Mary Ann Case's thoughtful analysis of gender and the law provides an exemplary starting point for further exploration of feminist gender theory. Case's essay 'Disaggregating Gender from Sex and Sexual Orientation: The Effeminate Man in the Law and Feminist Jurisprudence' is interesting both because it brings the concept of gender to bear on legal cases, and because it uses the concept in a way that is representative for feminist theory and criticism in the United States.[148]

Case's main concern is the fate of traditionally feminine qualities in present-day society. '[W]omen in this society are . . . moving closer to the masculine standard, and . . . are rewarded for so doing', she writes (29). Current interpretation of the law has permitted discrimination against the 'stereotypically feminine, especially when manifested by men, but also when manifested by women' (3). This amounts to permitting *gender* discrimination (as opposed to *sex* discrimination), that is to say discrimination that favours the 'masculine over the feminine rather than the male over the female' (33). Case shows that courts consistently favour employers who refuse to hire or promote someone who is too 'feminine', whether that person is male or female. It follows that both feminine women and effeminate men have a hard time making their Title VII claims heard. Because many courts confuse gender (effeminacy) and sexual orientation or desire (homosexuality), effeminate men suffer doubly from the present law.[149] Although the law may protect us against gender discrimination, it extends no such protection to homosexuals. A man fired because he wears an earring to work may have standing to claim sex discrimination, but if the same man also turns out to be gay he may have no recourse. In keeping with the feminist wish to analyse sexuality as an issue separate from gender and sex, Case concludes that we need a separate law for claims based on sexual orientation.

It is against this background that Case turns to her major case study: *Price Waterhouse* v. *Hopkins* (1989). This is a rather unusual case, in that it expands the standards for what is to count as discrimination on the basis of sex. So far, it has only rarely been taken as a precedent by other courts. In 1982 Ann Hopkins sued

---

[148] When it comes to gender, Franke agrees with Case's analysis whenever they discuss the same case. I therefore make no further reference to Franke's essay in this section.

[149] 'Thus, discriminating against the effeminate man may be overdetermined, and effeminacy conflated with gayness' (54).—Case tends to use 'feminine' about women and 'effeminate' about men. I am not sure how to take this usage.

the accounting firm of Price Waterhouse for not promoting her to a partnership on the grounds that she did not behave in a feminine fashion. Case writes:

> Ann Hopkins was the only woman among eighty-eight persons considered for partnership. . . . She had at that point worked at the firm for five years, and she had 'generated more business for Price Waterhouse' and 'billed more hours than any of the other candidates under consideration' that year. The Policy Board . . . recommended that Ann Hopkins's candidacy be placed on hold. . . . Both her supporters and her detractors in the partnership, as well as her clients, described Hopkins as manifesting stereotypically masculine qualities, for better and for worse. She was praised for, among other things, a 'strong character, independence and integrity', 'decisiveness, broadmindedness, and intellectual clarity' and for being 'extremely competent, intelligent', 'strong and forthright, very productive, energetic and creative' (41–2).

Other partners took a different view of the same aspects of Hopkins's personality:

> One partner described her as 'macho'; another suggested that she 'overcompensated for being a woman'; a third advised her to take 'a course at charm school.' Several partners criticized her use of profanity; in response, one partner suggested that those partners objected to her swearing only 'because it's a lady using foul language' . . . [T]he man who . . . bore responsibility for explaining to Hopkins the reasons for the Policy Board's decision . . . delivered the *coup de grace:* in order to improve her chances for partnership, [he] advised, Hopkins should 'walk more femininely, talk more femininely, dress more femininely, wear make-up, have her hair styled, and wear jewelry' (42).

In 1989 the Supreme Court found that to refuse to promote a 'masculine' woman accountant unless she became more 'feminine' was prohibited sex discrimination. Justice Brennan wrote for the majority: 'As for the legal relevance of sex stereotyping, we are beyond the day when an employer could evaluate employees by insisting they matched the stereotype associated with their group' (quoted by Case 95).

According to Case, Ann Hopkins was not refused promotion because of her sex, but because of her gender. *Hopkins* shows that

the courts accept that sex discrimination includes gender discrimination. Case concludes that there is no need to add the word 'and
gender' to existing sex discrimination law (see Case 4). Yet she still
finds a problem in *Price Waterhouse* v. *Hopkins*. The court seems to
have accepted that Hopkins needed to display stereotypically
'masculine' traits in order to do well at her job; the 'gendering' of
the job was not questioned at all.[150] Would a traditionally feminine
woman have recourse under the law if she were fired for not being
aggressive *enough*? '[A]n unquestioning acceptance of the current
gendered requirements for most jobs hurts women', Case writes.
(46). At first glance, her point seems valuable. If putting 'masculine' job requirements in place enables employers to fire traditionally 'feminine' women, then feminists should surely demand
that the employers demonstrate why 'feminine' qualities will not
be just as effective when it comes to getting the job done.

The more I consider Case's arguments, however, the more her
understanding of gender (an understanding US law no doubt
obliges her to work with) appears problematic to me. As we have
seen, Case herself characterizes the following list of Hopkins's
qualities as 'masculine': strong character, independence,
integrity, decisiveness, broad-mindedness, intellectual clarity,
extreme competence, intelligence, strength, forthrightness,
productivity, energy, and creativity.[151] But all of my women friends
display some or all of these traits, and it has never occurred to me
to consider them 'masculine' for all that. (I don't think of them
as 'feminine' either.) Why does Case concur in labelling all these
characteristics masculine? Does she want to challenge job descriptions that require decisiveness, intellectual clarity, energy, and
creativity on the grounds that traditionally feminine women have
none of these qualities?

When Case speaks of gender, she usually means sex-based

---

[150] Part of the reason why Hopkins won her case was actually that the firm
placed her in an impossible double bind: she was effectively asked to tread an
impossibly narrow line between being masculine enough to do her job well and
feminine enough to conform to some of the partners' aesthetic requirements of
a woman.

[151] See the quotation from Case 41–2 given above. I have rewritten some of
the adjectives as nouns, and removed superfluous conjunctions.

stereotypes. Her admirable research provides expert guidance on what these are. Drawing on the so-called Bem Sex-Role Inventory (BSRI), Case lists a number of adjectives that psychologists and other researchers regularly consider coded masculine and feminine in contemporary American culture:[152]

MASCULINE	FEMININE
aggressive	affectionate
ambitious	cheerful
analytical	childlike
assertive	compassionate
athletic	flatterable
competitive	gentle
dominant	gullible
forceful	loyal
independent	sensitive
individualistic	shy
self-reliant	soft-spoken
self-sufficient	sympathetic
strong	tender
	understanding
	warm
	yielding

Another 'femininity scale' lists the following items:

FEMININITY
emotional
gentle
kind
understanding
warm
able to devote oneself completely to others
helpful to others
aware of others' feelings.

No wonder that Case concludes that 'There can be, I would contend, a world of difference between being female and being

---

[152] See Case 12, including n. 20.

feminine' (11).[153] Adamantly opposed to 'gender conformity', Case insists that we should not expect sex to determine gender or sexual orientation.[154] Among feminists of all persuasions today this is a completely uncontroversial position.[155] To a Beauvoirean feminist, however, Case's *conclusion* is not uncontroversial at all. Her aim is to 'focus attention on the reasons why the feminine might have been devalued in both women and men . . . to protect what is valuable about the traditionally feminine without essentializing it, limiting it to women, or limiting women to it' (105). I take this to require that we *show* what is valuable about traditional femininity. In order to do so we need some general criteria for what is to count as 'valuable'. It would also seem arbitrary to refuse to assess traditional masculinity according to the same criteria, first because we might find something valuable there too, and second because we can't very well let traditional stereotypes of femininity determine what phenomena feminists should investigate. If we decide that it is valuable to be 'helpful to others' (just to take one item from the femininity scale), then it surely must be valuable for men as well as for women.

If we grant these claims, then the question of why we would still want to label the fact of being 'helpful to others' *feminine* becomes urgent. If we still intend to call qualities such as 'tenderness', 'warmth', and 'loyalty' feminine, how do we expect to get rid of the idea that they have or ought to have some special connection with women? If we believe that such qualities have no intrinsic or necessary, but only an ideological, connection with women or female bodies, what reason do feminists have for continuing to call them feminine? Would this not imply that sex determines gender after all? (This is where the spectre of 'gender conformity' returns to haunt us.)

[153] The preceding scale is quoted by Case as the 'femininity scale' of Spence, Helmreich and Stapps's 1974 Personal Attributes Questionnaire (PAQ). See Case 13 and n. 24.

[154] Judith Butler's critique of the belief that there must be 'coherence and continuity among sex, gender, sexual practice and desire' is entirely in keeping with Case's critique of 'gender conformity' (see *Gender Trouble* 17).

[155] As I have shown above, Katherine Franke is utterly in agreement with the critique of 'gender conformity', and the same, I imagine, would be true for Simone de Beauvoir.

Even if we make every effort to distinguish between female and feminine, sex and gender, the problem does not go away. Let us say that I declare that to me, 'feminine characteristics' only mean those characteristics conventionally categorized as feminine, not an eternal feminine essence. This amounts to saying that, ultimately, the word feminine has no necessary relation to the word female.[156] I obviously have the right to define my terms any way I want, but I ought not to be surprised if people fail to get my point. The problem is that once I have said that 'feminine' does not *have* *to* mean 'pertaining to women', or 'associated with females', it becomes difficult to explain what it *is* supposed to mean. If I speak of a 'feminine mind', and stress (*a*) that both men and women can have this kind of mind, and (*b*) that in a just world women will not have it more often than men, then what exactly am I talking about? Why can't I just *say* 'a subtle mind', 'a forceful mind', or whatever it was that I meant? The only useful answer is that when I say a 'feminine mind' I am referring to some stereotype attributed to women by a certain social group at a certain time. To make myself understood, I shall have to specify what the relevant associations to the word are. A retired woman officer interviewed on National Public Radio about what it was like to join the US Army in 1957 told the journalist: 'I didn't mind when they said I couldn't do this or that because I was too short, or because my eyesight was not good enough, but I always protested when they said I couldn't do something because I was a woman, or because they didn't have enough lavatories.'[157] This woman drew exactly the same distinction I am trying to draw between unwarranted generalizations about women and attention to individual specificity. Like Simone de Beauvoir this woman demonstrates that one does not need to imagine that only people situated entirely beyond sexism, in a space outside our common sexist history, could possibly manage to break the hold of sexist ways of speaking.

[156] Feminists have made a similar criticism of the claim put forward by some Lacanians, namely that the phallus has absolutely nothing to do with the penis. 'Why call it phallus, then?' is the logical reply. To my mind the Lacanians who accept that the phallus does have *something* to do with the penis are on stronger ground than those who don't.

[157] I heard this interview on Sunday 18 Oct. 1997.

If I say 'a woman's mind' or a 'womanly mind' the same questions arise as in the case of 'a feminine mind'. On the other hand, none of this implies that I shouldn't use the word *woman* when I need it. I can happily speak of Simone de Beauvoir as an intellectual *woman*, and of her 'femaleness' or 'femininity' (*féminité* in French, *kvinnelighet* in Norwegian) when I mean the simple fact of being a woman, not some phenomenon that is taken to be an inexorable consequence of this fact. The word 'woman' (or 'women') does not commit me to any specific view as to what women should be like. The problems only start if, like so many critics, we feel compelled to refer to Beauvoir's 'masculine intelligence' or 'feminine anxiety'. The term 'male-identified' is just as ideologically loaded, since it too implies that Beauvoir fails to live up to some stereotypical standard of femininity. But why should feminists want to uphold *any* standard of femininity? There are many good reasons to criticize Beauvoir. But such criticism can only be effective if it formulates specific charges: in my own book on Beauvoir I have claimed, among other things, that she idealizes men; that her fear and loathing of her own mother resurfaces in her theory; that she generalizes more than her own theory would seem to allow her to do; that her use of the concept of 'immanence' is philosophically unsatisfactory. To replace such specific criticisms by general references to Beauvoir's failure or success in conforming to more or less elaborate notions of femininity and masculinity is to contribute to the production of sexist ideology.

'Feminine' and 'masculine' are excellent terms of critique, but I would hesitate to use them positively, to take them as guidelines for my own work. So far at least, it looks as if even the most unsexist search for 'femininity' in literature, film, or other cultural phenomena ends up producing fairly predictable clichés. Seen in the light of such considerations the psychoanalytic concept of femininity becomes terribly difficult to categorize. Should I consider it simply as another reified ideological generalization? Or is it a serious attempt to understand what it might mean to be a woman in the modern world? As Freud himself puts it: 'It is essential to understand clearly that the concepts of "masculine" and "feminine", whose meaning seems so unambiguous to ordinary people, are among the most confused that occur in science' (*Three Essays, SE* 7: 219 n). What phenomenon is a psychoanalyst trying to account for when she speaks about femininity? To what question is 'femininity' the answer? Can all psychoanalytic theorizing about femininity be written off as so much ideological nonsense? Or is that an unfair generalization? There are clear parallels between Freud's case histories and Beauvoir's phenomenological descriptions in *The Second Sex* of the situation of married women, young girls, prostitutes, and so on. Would it be true to say that psychoanalytic theory is simply trying to understand and describe the psychological effects of living in the world in a female body? If so, is the body a situation for Freud as for Beauvoir? But in that case, how general are psychoanalytic accounts of femininity supposed to be? Are they examples of phenomenological descriptions or normative moralizing? And what are we to make of the many different psychoanalytic accounts of femininity, not least those produced by women analysts from Karen Horney, Joan Rivière, and Helene Deutsch to Juliet Mitchell, Françoise Dolto, and Julia Kristeva? Any feminist reassessment of psychoanalytic theory will require answers to such questions, and all I am capable of saying here is that the task of providing them will not be easy.

Beauvoir's denunciation of femininity as a patriarchal concept is a critique of ideology. As such it is still as valid as when it was written. Regardless of whether we believe that masculinity and femininity are manifestations of deep sexual essences or the products of dazzling discursive performances, the very fact of continuing to label qualities and behaviours as 'masculine' and 'feminine' will foster sex-based stereotypes. In *this* context the essence/construction or sex/gender opposition is irrelevant.[158] What I am criticizing here, then, is the belief that the sex/gender

---

[158] French and Norwegian do not have two words for 'feminine': *kvinnelig* and *féminin* mean both 'female' and 'feminine'. Feminists who generalize about *féminité* or *kvinnelighet* encounter exactly the same problems as those who generalize about femininity. The difference is that the speaker cannot assume that the very word she uses automatically signals opposition to biological determinism. This may either make her more careful to specify exactly what she means, or completely oblivious to the whole question.

distinction somehow protects us against oppressive generalizations about sexual difference. The only thing it is designed to
protect us against is biological determinism. This it does quite
efficiently. In contemporary English, feminists are right to think
that although a 'female mind' and a 'feminine mind' may refer to
exactly the same awful beliefs, the two expressions *may* still signal
a different attitude to biology.[159] Oppressive generalizations,
however, are not only produced by the likes of Geddes and
Thomson. Contemporary feminist gender theory runs a close
second when it comes to contributing to our general stock of
nonsensical ideas about 'femininity'.

Here is one example. The Virginia Military Institute (VMI) and
the Citadel are two state-funded military-style American colleges
that until 1996 steadfastly refused to admit women. When they
were sued by rejected female candidates, both schools proposed
to set up new, parallel institutions for women. These would offer
a more 'feminine' leadership training, which although different
in style, would be equal in quality to the training received by the
men. In 1996 the US Supreme Court decided that the proposed
parallel institutions for women did not offer equal educational
opportunities. The schools would have to admit women or lose
their state funding. Case, who was writing before this opinion was
handed down, considers that it would be acceptable to open up
the VMI and the Citadel to members of either sex 'who are appropriately gendered, thus both masculine men and masculine
women could attend VMI or the Citadel, while [the parallel insti-
tutions] could admit those of both sexes more suited to or
attracted by a more feminine approach' (105). She is surely right
to say that this would be compatible with current US law. My question, which Case may not be free to address in the context of a
legal essay, is whether this really is desirable feminist politics.

Imagine a scenario in which two schools specializing in 'leadership' are open to both sexes. One school provides a stereotypically 'masculine' education, the other a stereotypically 'feminine'

---

[159] Many speakers of English do not try to distinguish between female and
feminine. In order to find out what words such as feminine and female mean in
a given case, we need to analyse the whole speech act that produced them (to
consider what was said when, to paraphrase J. L. Austin).

education. At the same time, young men and women are classi-
fied as being either 'gendered masculine' or 'gendered feminine'. As a result of the classification they will be encouraged to
apply to the relevant institution. It is difficult to understand why
this will not reinforce stereotypes of femininity and masculinity.
Do feminists really want to strengthen the belief that the world
contains only two, clearly separable styles of gendered behaviour?
(In my experience, even under patriarchy most men and women
do not conform to one of two gender stereotypes.) What is feminist about having a system of feminine schools training people of
both sexes to become kind and helpful to others, and masculine
schools training them to become aggressive, dominant, and
competitive? Do we want *anyone* to be trained in any of these ways?
How could such institutions avoid reifying and perpetuating the
very sex-based stereotypes feminists have argued against for
centuries?

For more than twenty years now feminist theorists have characterized women as relational, caring, and nurturing; as
mumbling and incoherent; or as always seething with feminist
rage, just to mention a few well-known leitmotifs. Since nothing
distinguishes them from traditional stereotypes, such 'gender
theories' are all too easy to appropriate for sexist purposes. Carol
Gilligan's research opposing a masculine 'ethics of justice' to a
feminine 'ethics of care' is a good example of this. In the cases
against the Citadel and VMI her research was used by the *defence*,
in spite of Gilligan's protestations that she in no way intended
her research to support all-male institutions.[160] The American
broadcasting network NBC drew on the same kind of theories
when it planned its condescending, vacuous, and self-styled
'feminine' coverage of the 1996 Summer Olympics. Specially
designed to appeal to women, the resulting programming was
long on tear-jerking profiles of athletes overcoming everything
from cancer to criminal grandparents, and short on actual sports

[160] Case is sensitive to the problems raised by Gilligan's theories, but, again,
considers that as long as one stresses that one speaks of gender and not sex
(masculine and not male), this is not a serious obstacle to agreeing with Gilligan,
who did file a brief *against* the all-male schools, protesting against the way they
used her research (see Case 98 and n. 345 and 346).

coverage.[161] I hope that the feminist future does not lie with gender stereotypes, however influential they may currently be.

So what is the alternative? Let me suggest that we reconsider Simone de Beauvoir's distinction between detrimental social norms ('myths') incarnated in other people and in institutions, and the individual human being's lived experience. Case writes that she does not 'have as a normative goal the preservation of gender any more than its abolition'.[162] Here it is not clear what gender means: is it stereotypes or lived experience? The same ambiguity runs through all contemporary 'gender theories'. Feminists want to get rid of stereotypes, but nobody has ever proposed giving up lived experience. Sexist ideology attempts to reduce our lived experience to two simple sex-based categories. Beauvoir teaches us that to accept such categorization is alienating and destructive of freedom.[163]

The accountancy firm Price Waterhouse wanted Ann Hopkins to go to 'charm school' before making her a partner. The US Supreme Court found that this was unacceptable, and rightly so. Under contemporary social conditions I have no doubt that male partners in an accountancy firm would be far more likely to require a potential female colleague to be charming than a man. In the social context where the requirement was made, 'charm' was indeed gendered feminine. Yet it is also true that in present-day society 'charm' is not in fact a characteristic that is unique to women, nor one that somehow makes a man less masculine were he to display it. Feminists are not well advised to encourage the belief that there is something particularly feminine about charm. Instead of protecting stereotypically feminine values we should argue that to require an *accountant* to be charming is an irrelevant job requirement, regardless of the sex of the accountant.

---

[161] In a scathing *New Yorker* review of NBC's coverage, David Remnick writes: 'In fact, the NBC creed does not depart so much in spirit from a range of feminist theories about differences in gender and narrative' (27). Then follow references to Carol Gilligan, Tania Modleski, and Hélène Cixous (27–8).

[162] Case 76 n. 258.

[163] For a more thorough analysis of Beauvoir's concept of alienation, see ch. 6 of my *Simone de Beauvoir*.

Case proposes a strategy in which feminists ask the courts to protect traditionally feminine qualities in men as well as women. To my mind this will have the reactionary effect of forcing more courts, and more people generally, to classify more actions and behaviours as either masculine and feminine. In the attempt to avoid gender stereotyping we will produce more of it. In employment cases, it seems that feminists can only escape this vicious circle by proposing that we should be protected under the law against employers who fire *anyone* (man, woman, gay, heterosexual, transsexual, black, white, working class, disabled, and so on) for reasons that have nothing to do with the requirements of the job. Instead of protecting traditional femininity just because it happens to be traditional femininity, feminists should challenge all unreasonable job requirements. (I realize that US law such as it is today may not allow this.) I agree with Case that it is difficult to believe that an accountant really needs to be 'aggressive' and 'abrasive' to get her job done, I just don't think it will advance our case to harp on the idea that to be aggressive and abrasive is 'unfeminine'. Nor should we go along with the idea that any quality that is not feminine must be masculine. The world is full of more interesting adjectives.

It is by no means certain that it makes sense to try to separate Hopkins's gender from her sex. Feminists have known for years that the same qualities are perceived differently in men and women.[164] It is impossible to categorize any specific quality as masculine or feminine without 'objectifying' it, Beauvoir would say. To imagine that I can determine what counts as feminine in isolation from any particular human situation, is to reify 'femininity'. This is why the lists of 'gender characteristics' quoted above look so absurd. When I meet a charming man or a charming woman, I am incapable of separating the quality of their charm from the fact that the charm comes from a man or a woman. In itself charm is neither feminine nor masculine, neither female nor male. This is what Beauvoir means when she says that the body—the sexually different

---

[164] Case is very well aware of this: 'The same degree of masculinity and femininity is read quite differently in a man and in a woman, as Ann Hopkins learned to her cost' (23).

body—is a fundamental human situation. The meaning of my charm cannot be determined by reference to my body alone, but nor can it be assessed without taking my body into account.[165] The problem with so many contemporary gender theories is that they take a number of qualities that, at best, have been associated with a specific group of women at a specific time and turn them into reified stereotypes, in effect creating new social norms for women to be oppressed by. No wonder such theories are eagerly seized upon by sexists looking for simple solutions to difficult questions.

Because it can refer to 'social stereotypes' or 'dominant gender norms' as well as to an individual's qualities and ways of being, the very word gender lends itself to such reification, in a way that Simone de Beauvoir's distinction between 'lived experience' and 'myths' does not. Ultimately, I think we should follow Gayle Rubin's suggestion and stop thinking in terms of gender altogether. To me, that means trying to produce a society without sexist ideology or gender norms, without oppressive myths of masculinity and femininity. It does not mean that we should stop thinking of the sexually different human body as a fundamental situation that tends to leave its trace on the meaning of our words and actions.[166] The old choice between sameness and difference does not apply here. *The Second Sex* doesn't ask us to choose between a society with or without sexual difference but between one with or without sex-based oppression.

AFTERWORD: THE POINT OF THEORY

In this paper I have asked whether the sex/gender distinction is helpful to a project shared by most contemporary feminist theorists, namely the wish to elaborate a concrete, historically

---

[165] As discussed above (Sect. IV), *within* the category of the body as a situation, or the category of lived experience, Beauvoir does not distinguish between sex and gender.

[166] 'Beauvoir's final message is that sexual difference should be eradicated and women must become like men', Tina Chanter writes (76). That such a good reader of Irigaray can be such a bad reader of Beauvoir indicates that like so many other contemporary feminists, Chanter does not take Beauvoir seriously as a philosopher.

grounded and socially situated understanding of what it means to have a human body. I have shown that the distinction usually dissolves into a scientistic understanding of 'sex' and an idealist understanding of 'gender', and that although poststructuralist sex and gender theorists strive to overcome this problem, they remain caught in the see-saw between scientism and idealism set up by their own understanding of the distinction. By turning to the phenomenological approach of Merleau-Ponty and Beauvoir, I hope to have shown that there are ways to answer the question 'What is a woman?' that escape the constraints both of the sex/gender distinction and the essence/construction opposition. By reflecting on what it means to say that the body is a situation, I have shown that for Beauvoir the question of what a woman is can never have just one answer. *The Second Sex* shows us that what it means to be called a woman, or to call oneself a woman, is a question that cannot be settled once and for all.[167] There is, then, no reason to believe that the word woman is always inherently metaphysical or essentialist. 'In a *large* class of cases . . . the meaning of a word is its use' (*PI* §43).

Poststructuralist theorists declare that the relationship between sex and gender is arbitrary, usually because they see this as the only alternative to the idea that sex necessarily determines gender. Against this, I have claimed that the best defence against biological determinism is to deny that biology grounds or justifies social norms. If we consistently deny this, we do not have to assume that the idea that there are only two sexes must be steeped in sexism and heterosexism. This is not to deny that invocations of nature usually come wrapped up in sexist or heterosexist ideology. To show that ideology is at work in such contexts remains a necessary feminist task. But to claim that sexist and heterosexist ideology often seeks to justify its claims by naturalizing them—by representing social relations as if they were given in nature—is precisely to assume that there is nothing in nature that actually justifies the ideological claims of biological determinists. To be even more precise: my argument is *not* that there is nothing in

---

[167] I investigate some situations in which Beauvoir calls herself a woman, or imagines being called one by others in Ch. 2, below.

nature (i.e. that we have to deny the existence of biological facts), but that whatever there is in nature (whatever facts we may discover about human biology and genetic structure) is never going to justify any *particular* social arrangement. Even if we assume that there are only two sexes, this is no reason not to construct a society with three or five or ten genders, or indeed without gender at all. Or in other words, on my understanding of what the biological facts are, we can never get rid of sex, but we can certainly hope to produce societies that either multiply or eliminate gender. This, precisely, is the logical consequence of denying that biology justifies social norms. The power of the sex/gender distinction is that it is one way of saying precisely this. What the sex/gender distinction does not provide, however, is a good theory of subjectivity or a useful understanding of the body.

Instead of speaking in terms of sex and gender, I have found it useful to speak in terms of bodies and subjectivity. What Merleau-Ponty and Beauvoir show is that the relationship between body and subjectivity is neither necessary nor arbitrary, but contingent. For these thinkers the body is fundamentally ambiguous, neither simply subject to the natural laws of cause and effect that science might uncover, nor simply an effect of consciousness (or of power, ideology, or regulatory discourses, for that matter). When Merleau-Ponty writes that 'man is a historical idea and not a natural species', he does not mean to say that human bodies are not natural at all, but rather that our nature is to be historical beings. His project is to expand our understanding of nature, to wrench it away from the deadening hand of positivism and scientism by showing that in so far as the human body is concerned, one can draw no clear-cut line between that which belongs to the realm of nature and that which belongs to the realm of meaning. This is what he means when he speaks of the *ambiguity* of human existence. On this account, the human body is neither sex nor gender, neither nature nor culture. To say that my subjectivity stands in a contingent relationship to my body is to acknowledge that my body will significantly influence both what society—others—make of me, and the kind of choices I will make in response to the Other's image of me, but it is also to acknowledge that no specific form of subjectivity is ever a necessary consequence of having a particular body.

No theory of bodies and subjectivity is of any use if it does not yield significant understanding of concrete cases. To challenge the ideas in this essay, it would be useful to see if they would help to understand transsexuality. Transsexuals are usually defined as persons who feel that their sex does not correspond to their gender, and who wish to undergo hormone treatment and surgery in order to align their sex with their gender. As I have shown, the sex/gender distinction was first invented by medical personnel working with transsexuals and intersexed persons. The distinction emerged in the 1950s and early 1960s in response to the new medical technologies developed after World War II (hormone treatment, new and improved techniques of plastic surgery). Thus the very existence of the concept of the 'transsexual' depends on a distinction I think is useless for the understanding of lived experience. What would happen if one tried to understand transsexuality in completely different terms?

This is a more contentious question than it might seem. For the very language of sex and gender is a language that implies that sex is a matter of body parts, and that gender is 'everything else'. This language produces a picture of human bodies and subjectivity that makes it appear meaningful to call a certain number of medical procedures a sex change. Many transsexuals fear that unless one accepts the standard definitions of sex and gender and also believes that the relationship between sex and gender is absolutely arbitrary, it will become impossible to justify their demand for surgical transformation of the body. My critique of the sex/gender distinction, on the other hand, makes the very meaning of the term *sex change* problematic. When the sex/gender distinction disappears, it is no longer obvious what one desires when one desires a sex change. It does not follow, of course, that so-called sex-change operations are unjustified. What their purpose and meaning might be, would precisely be the subject of a phenomenological account of transsexuality.

The method such an account would employ would have much in common with Simone de Beauvoir's method in *The Second Sex*. One would have to study historical and legal material in order to establish what social norms and expectations transsexuals encounter, read fiction and watch films to discover something about the cultural signification of sex changes, and examine medical material in order to understand what interventions a sex change requires, and what the medical consequences actually are. Psychoanalytic and psychiatric case studies would be central to the project. Perhaps most important of all would be autobiographies, memoirs, and other texts written by transsexuals, as well as interviews and conversations with them. It goes without saying that the differences between transsexuals, transvestites, and other transgendered people would need to be taken into account. Such an investigation might help explain why it is that the number of people who want to change their sex is steadily increasing. If one could understand what the wish to become a woman represents for someone who started out in life as a man, one would perhaps also understand why it is that so many women never wish to change their sex. In short, a serious attempt to understand the transsexual's project and situation in the world would provide a deeper understanding than a purely theoretical essay like this one of what it means to claim that the sexed body is a situation.

I just mentioned psychoanalytic theory and case studies as a valuable source of insight about transsexuality. Among transsexuals, however, there is considerable hostility towards psychoanalysis. I suspect that some transsexuals' worries are based on the fact that, like existentialism, psychoanalysis has no use for the sex/gender distinction. The fear is that any psychoanalytic account of the desire to change one's sex *must* lead to the conclusion that transsexuality is a psychiatric condition, and that all that is required to make the transsexual 'normal' is a good bout of analytic therapy. I don't think this is necessarily the case.[168] In general, transsexual arguments against psychoanalysis are similar to feminist arguments against psychoanalysis, and I shall not go into them here.

---

[168] Even Catherine Millot, a French psychoanalyst highly sceptical of the transsexual's claim to have a firm and non-contradictory gender identity, does not doubt that surgical interventions can have psychological effects: 'Gabriel's [Gabriel is the pseudonym of a female-to-male transsexual] operations seem in any case to have modified his subjective position. . . . The possibility of intervention in the real having effects on the symbolic plane cannot be excluded' (135–6).

Just as I have not engaged with psychoanalysis in this paper, I have not discussed sexuality in the sense of sexual desire or sexual orientation. This is because I consider the relationship between the body and sexuality to be as contingent as the rest. Neither heterosexuality nor homosexuality is inscribed in the structure of our bodies. Even if scientists were to find the infamous 'gay gene', it would not follow that everyone who had it would choose the same sexual practices, or that sexuality would have the same meaning for them. This is what Merleau-Ponty means when he says that the body—including our genes and chromosomes—is fundamentally ambiguous. Precisely because Beauvoir stresses over and over again that biology provides no foundation for social norms, her understanding of the body provides no justification for sexual bigotry and oppressive gender norms.

Since heterosexism and homophobia are the effects of social norms for sexuality and sexual practices, it makes a great deal of sense to consider such questions under the rubric of 'gender', as long as we are aware that 'gender' here means 'social norms', 'ideology', 'power', or 'regulatory discourses', and that such terms do not tell us all that much about bodies. That an individual's encounter with such social norms has consequences for the way she will experience her body and for the kind of subjectivity she will develop is precisely Beauvoir's and Merleau-Ponty's point. But their point is also that different individuals will respond in different ways to the same coercive pressure. Freud could have said the same thing. To put this in Beauvoir's terms: although social norms concerning sex and sexuality are of crucial importance to the formation of a given person's subjectivity, an account of such norms and regulations will not in itself explain that person's lived experience. We are continuously making something of what the world continuously makes of us: our subjectivity is always a becoming that neither precedes nor follows from the encounter with the Other.

When Beauvoir says 'I am a woman', she is not saying that she is a creature that in every respect conforms to the dominant gender norms of her society. She is making the verb signify existence, and existence is always a becoming, a process that only comes to an end in death. To say that existence precedes essence is not to say that it replaces or obliterates it. 'I am a woman' also means 'There are women in the world, and I am one of them'.[169] Given that existence precedes essence, however, the fact that I am a woman does not tell you what kind of a woman I am. Stereotyping of any kind is incompatible with Beauvoir's under-standing of what a woman is. The opposition between identity and difference is not central to Beauvoir's feminism; the concepts of freedom, alienation, and oppression are. Beauvoir's funda-mental value is not identity, but freedom, and for Beauvoir free-dom is a universal value: if it is good for women and feminists, it is because it is good for everyone.

In my discussion of poststructuralist sex and gender theory I have not been trying to contest the political aims of the theorists in question: my argument is, on the contrary, that those aims appear to be compatible with those of non-poststructuralist femi-nists from Beauvoir to Rubin. For this very reason it becomes important to challenge the theoreticism of poststructuralist femi-nist theory, that is to say the belief that certain theoretical posi-tions function as guarantees of one's radical political credentials. The poststructuralist theorists who appear to believe that a general account of meaning or reference (interpretivism, real-ism, nominalism, etc.) *must* have a necessary set of political impli-cations have yet to make a convincing case for their claims. They also have yet to show why questions of materiality and the inside and outside of discourse must be settled in the correct way in order to enable us to make politically acceptable claims about bodies, sex, and gender. The attempt to lay down theoretical requirements for what politically 'good' theory *must* look like regardless of the actual situation in which one is trying to inter-vene, is idealist and metaphysical to the core.

The point of doing a critical analysis of some of the presuppo-sitions of poststructuralist thinking about sex, gender, and the body is to free us (I mean anyone who has ever been caught up in it, including myself) from a theoretical picture that tells us how things *must* be, and so blinds us to alternative ways of thinking. One such picture is the idea that we *must* think in terms of the

---

[169] I return to this claim in Ch. 2, below.

sex/gender distinction as soon as we are interested in questions of sexual difference. What I have done here is to show that in the case of a question that truly matters to me, namely 'What is a woman?', there are good reasons to consider alternatives to the sex/gender distinction. I have not tried to lay down some *other* set of requirements for how things must be. In particular, I have not suggested—and I do not think—that the sex/gender distinction is always useless. On the contrary, I think it is useful when it comes to opposing biological determinism à la Geddes and Thomson, for example. Others may be able to show that it also excels in other, specific contexts.

For Wittgenstein, the role of philosophy is to be therapeutic, to produce a diagnosis of the theoretical pictures that hold us captive, not in order to refute them, but in order to make us aware of other options: 'A *picture* held us captive. And we could not get outside it, for it lay in our language and language seemed to repeat it to us inexorably' (*PI* §115). The aim of his own thought is to reach 'perspicuous representation [*übersichtliche Darstellung*]' (*PI* §122). Once we see things clearly, Wittgenstein believes, all specifically philosophical problems fall away. 'For the clarity that we are aiming at is indeed complete clarity. But this simply means that the philosophical problems should completely disappear' (*PI* §133). Here it may be useful to recall that Wittgenstein thinks of a philosophical problem as a question that arises when we are lost in a kind of linguistic fog. What characterizes such questions is that they have no satisfactory answer because they have no clear meaning (see *PI* §5). Wittgenstein pictures the clearing of the fog as an intellectual liberation: we are released from the linguistic shackles that hold us captive. There is no loss here, since all that has disappeared is nonsense. Once we manage to escape from the picture that held us captive, we are released from the futile task of trying to answer questions that can have no answers because they do not make sense. Rather than solving the problem we struggled with, Wittgenstein's therapy makes it fall away. We see, as it were, that the problem was the way we posed the problem. Once we realize this, it is pointless to remain obsessed with the old problem. We find that we are free to ask new questions. To anyone who has experienced the effects of

psychoanalysis, Wittgenstein's account of how philosophical therapy works will sound quite familiar.

Yet Wittgenstein does not believe that the fog can be cleared
once and for all. New situations and new confusions will always
arise. There will always be a need for philosophical therapy. This
means that in the very act of asking a new question we risk
succumbing to new confusions, to lock ourselves up in new
prison-houses of language. The task is always to try to produce
language that makes sense as opposed to what Wittgenstein calls
'language on holiday', that is to say, language that does no work
for us (see *PI* §38).[170] The way I understand Wittgenstein, this task
is at once intellectual and ethical; it is always with us; it can never
be done once and for all. Serious intellectual work would seem to
have much in common with housework.[171]

It would be nice if 'feminist theory' could eventually come to
mean a kind of thought that seeks to dispel confusions concerning bodies, sex, sexuality, sexual difference, and the power relations between and among women and men, heterosexuals and
homosexuals. Such theory would aim to release us from the metaphysical pictures that hold us captive, and so return our words to
the sphere of the ordinary, that is to say the sphere in which our
political and personal struggles actually take place. 'What *we* do is
to bring words back from their metaphysical to their everyday
use' (*PI* §116). Such a course of philosophical therapy would help
feminist critics and theorists not to get lost in meaningless questions and pointless arguments, and enable us instead to raise
genuine questions about things that really matter.

---

[170] Specialized languages—those of chemistry and infinitesimal calculus, for
example—are part of ordinary language. Such languages are to be pictured as
'suburbs of our language', Wittgenstein writes in a passage where he likens our
language to an 'ancient city': 'a maze of little streets and squares, of old and new
houses, and of houses with additions from various periods; and this surrounded
by a multitude of new boroughs with straight regular streets and uniform
houses' (*PI* §18). I discuss the meaning of 'ordinary language' more fully in Ch.
2, below.

[171] New paths seem to have led me back to an old idea. In the introduction
to my *Simone de Beauvoir* I also compare my intellectual approach to housework
(see 8).

'I Am a Woman':
The Personal and the Philosophical

If any individual—Samuel Pepys or Jean-Jacques Rousseau,
mediocre or exceptional—reveals himself with sincerity,
almost everyone is called into question. It is impossible to
shed light on one's own life without at some point illuminating the life of others.

Simone de Beauvoir[1]

All the philosopher, this kind of philosopher, can do is to
express, as fully as he can, his world, and attract our undivided attention to our own.

Stanley Cavell[2]

INTRODUCTION

'I now tend to think that theory itself, at least as it is usually prac-
ticed, may be one of the patriarchal gestures women *and* men
ought to avoid', Jane Tompkins writes in 'Me and My Shadow',
her controversial defence of the inclusion of the personal in
literary criticism (122). I am writing this essay because I am a
woman and a feminist who has written and intends to continue
to write theory. If I were to accept Jane Tompkins's view, I would
have to give up writing theory altogether.[3] 'But Tompkins is just

I am grateful to Stanley Cavell for his generous response to this essay. Terry
Eagleton, Hazel Rowley, Kate Soper, Martin Stone, and Lisa Van Alstyne also
provided valuable last minute feedback.

[1] I have translated Beauvoir's 'tout le monde, plus ou moins, se trouve mis
en jeu' as 'almost everyone is called into question' (*PL* 10; *FA* 1; TA).

[2] 'Aesthetic Problems of Modern Philosophy', in *Must We* 96.

[3] The title of this essay is 'The Personal and the Philosophical'. It could just
as well have been called 'The Personal and the Theoretical'. The former is more
suitable for the second half dealing with Simone de Beauvoir, the latter would

an anti-intellectual', some would surely say, 'why do you want to take her so seriously?'

Tompkins's point of view cannot be dismissed out of hand. In different ways and different formulations, her worries about the oppressive effects of theory are shared by a large number of literary critics. Postmodern theory declares that all knowledge is situated or 'located', tied to specific subject positions, imbricated in particular contexts of power, subversion, and resistance.[4] Summarizing the dominant trend, David Simpson writes that the 'contemporary notion [is] that all knowledge claims must be accompanied by or seen as consisting in a rhetoric of speaking personally and saying where one is coming from' (78). Most critics link the demand for subjectivity to a general postmodern scepticism about claims to objective knowledge. Given the postmodern understanding of what knowledge is, how can I pretend to make 'objective' or 'universal' statements? How can I possibly imagine that I am speaking for anyone but myself? On the other hand there is no such thing as a theoretical statement that does not lay claim to general validity. The claim that 'knowledge is always situated' is itself as universalizing and generalizing as the claim that 'knowledge is never situated'. The universalism of theory is not undermined by producing theory that universalizes the local, the specific, and the subjective. This essay is an attempt to think through the relationship between the personal (subjectivity) and theory. I hope that this investigation will help me to find a way to write theory without neglecting or repressing the claims of the personal, the local, and the specific, but also without dismissing or diminishing the claims of the impersonal, the objective, and the universal.

---

fit the first half better. For the purposes of my project in this essay, there is no important distinction to be drawn between the two terms. I think of what I write as 'theory'. At the same time, a lot of the texts I am inspired by and learn from, not least those of Simone de Beauvoir, are conventionally known as 'philosophy'.

4 I use the term 'postmodern theory' fairly loosely. I just mean various kinds of recent theories that tend to stress that knowledge is local, specific, subjective, relative, and so on.

The questions of subjectivity and the locatedness of knowledge are central in the postmodern tradition. Yet postmodern theory generalizes as much as the theories it wishes to supplant. Moreover, much contemporary theory often gives the impression of preaching to the converted. Descartes, who starts from first principles, is more fun to read, not to mention a genuine Enlightenment thinker such as Rousseau with all his universalist pronunciations. Such texts invite passionate reactions, comments, and critical discussion in a way that much recent theory often does not. Reading the section devoted to Sophie in *Émile*, for example, everyone in my class instantly understood why it inspired Mary Wollstonecraft to write *Vindication of the Rights of Woman*. Our own reactions to Rousseau helped us not only to get something out of his text, but to read Wollstonecraft's writing with deeper understanding as well. What characterizes both Rousseau and Wollstonecraft is their passionate engagement in the questions they explore. Engagement is always personal. If there is no engagement in the writing, it is difficult to produce engagement in the reader, and without engagement there is usually little thought and no political commitment. If one wants to find out how to write theory in a way that acknowledges the claims of the personal, questions about philosophical or theoretical tone, style, and voice are going to be as important as questions about 'speaking position' or 'location' or 'where one is coming from'.

Like other theorists, I have no wish to write in a way that is falsely universalizing, exclusionary, arrogant, and domineering. Yet the fact remains that it is impossible to write theory without generalizing and universalizing. Is it possible to write theory in a way that overcomes the apparent conflict between the general and the particular, the third person and the first person? How do I write theory in a personal voice? How do I write theory without losing myself and alienating my readers in the process?

Because my focus is on theory, I am not going to discuss interesting recent attempts to produce new kinds of personal memoirs and intellectual autobiographies such as my colleague Alice Kaplan's *French Lessons* or Deborah McDowell's *Leaving Pipe*

Shop.[5] And although theory is produced in all kinds of disciplines, I am going to stick to a loosely defined field stretching from literary theory to philosophy.[6] This may sound unduly conservative. Am I not imprisoning myself in traditional disciplinary thinking? Have I no understanding of the need to cross and break up generic and disciplinary boundaries? Do I really believe that there is no 'theory' in an autobiography? Think of St Augustine! Clearly, literary and autobiographical work offer thoughtful analyses of philosophical and theoretical questions. I regularly teach Ibsen's *A Doll's House* alongside Hegel on women and Milton on divorce, precisely because each text, regardless of genre, is at work on the same set of problems. This can be done,

---

   5 I see Carolyn Steedman's *Landscape for a Good Woman* as a more explicitly theoretical kind of book than the two I mention here. I want to acknowledge the importance of Steedman's attempt to write on the margins of autobiography, history, and psychoanalysis in order to understand the factors that shaped her own life and that of her mother. Her book was an inspiration for my very different attempt to understand the making of Simone de Beauvoir as an intellectual woman. My question in this essay, however, is not about the making of subjectivity, but about the writing of theory.

   6 Different disciplinary starting points tend to produce somewhat different questions, and a different sense of what counts as relevant answers. On one level, the anthropologist Ruth Behar's account of her difficult relationship to 'scientific' writing has much in common with Jane Tompkins's frustrations with literary theory (see Behar, *Translated* 330–1). On another level, however, Behar's 'vulnerable writing', defined as writing in which she tries to 'make my emotions part of my ethnography' (*Vulnerable* 18) cannot be properly understood without paying attention to the fact that Behar starts from the discipline of anthropology, which she describes as 'this business of humans observing other humans in order to write about them' (*Vulnerable* 5). Literary criticism and theory work on texts, not other people. A literary critic is not a 'participant observer' and the question of 'how women are to make other women the subjects of their gaze without objectifying them and thus ultimately betraying them' does not arise in the same way for a literary critic as for an anthropologist (*Vulnerable* 28). For Jane Tompkins to include her emotions in literary criticism is not necessarily the same gesture as for Ruth Behar to do so in her book on the life of a Mexican street peddler (see ch. 17 of *Translated* 320–42). To me, the most striking difference is the fact that Behar does not worry about 'theory', but about 'science', 'neutral observation', and 'impersonality'. On the other hand, both Tompkins and Behar agree that to be personal is to be autobiographical and particularly to reveal one's own emotions. A more thorough comparison of Tompkins and Behar might yield interesting insights about the difference that disciplinarity makes. I am grateful to Kathy Rudy for bringing Behar's work to my attention.

however, without making any claims as to whether *Phenomenology of Spirit* and *A Doll's House* break disciplinary boundaries or established generic divisions.

My main example in this essay will be Simone de Beauvoir's *The Second Sex*, which in itself is a perfect example of interdisciplinarity, a text that breaks down a host of generic boundaries as it freely moves to and from literature, memoirs, sociology, psychoanalysis, medicine, biology, history, art, and philosophy. Yet at the same time it is a marvellous attempt to write philosophy in a new key, an attempt so revolutionary that in the fifty years since its publication it has only recently come to be accepted (and then only in some quarters) *as* philosophy. If we are to break boundaries and undermine the existing *doxa*, we will surely do so not by proclamation but, like Simone de Beauvoir, as a result of asking questions that turn out to have no traditional disciplinary answer.[7]

Finally, I should say that there is nothing intrinsically feminist about the question of how to write theory in an intellectual situation marked by various forms of postmodern scepticism about knowledge. But, as Simone de Beauvoir might have said, it is significant that I, who happen to be a feminist, raise it. In contemporary theory feminists brought the question of the relationship between subjectivity and knowledge to the forefront of intellectual debate well before it became a fashionable postmodern issue. In this essay I shall frequently be drawing on feminist examples, simply because they readily come to mind. I also hope that the questions I raise will inspire others to consider whether my analyses are relevant in their own fields of interest.[8]

This essay falls in two main sections. Section II reads the first few pages of *The Second Sex* as an example of writing that is both personal and philosophical. Section I takes a closer look at contemporary accounts of the personal and the theoretical. I

---

[7] See Ch. 4 below, for Bourdieu's definition of *doxa*.

[8] As I was reading a review of books on the pedagogy of mathematics, I discovered that a number of the questions I raise in this essay (When does it make sense to 'get personal'? When is it relevant to stress location or subject position? When does personal anecdote and narrative deepen our understanding of a subject and when does it not?) appear to be relevant to ongoing debates about the teaching of mathematics in the USA. Only a maths teacher could tell me whether this is a superficial impression (see Gardner, 'The New New Math').

shall start by returning to 'Me and My Shadow', to find out what Jane Tompkins thinks the personal is, and what it has to do with the theoretical.

I. CONTEMPORARY THEORY

'All Alone and Feeling Blue'

Picking up a volume by Félix Guattari, Tompkins quickly puts it down in disgust. To her, the text exemplifies male theory speech. 'I find this language incredibly alienating', she writes. 'What strikes me now is the incredibly distancing effect of this language. It is totally abstract and impersonal' (131). Tompkins is angry with men for belittling women, and with theorists for belittling emotion:

> The disdain for popular psychology and for words like 'love' and 'giving' is part of the police action that academic intellectuals wage ceaselessly against feeling, against women, against what is personal. The ridiculing of the 'touchy-feely', of the 'Mickey Mouse', of the sentimental . . . belongs to the tradition Alison Jaggar rightly characterized as founding knowledge in the denial of emotion. It is looking down on women, with whom feelings are associated, and on the activities with which women are identified: mother, nurse, teacher, social worker, volunteer. So for a while I can't talk about epistemology. I can't deal with the philosophical bases of feminist literary criticisms. . . . I have to deal with the trashing of emotion, and with my anger against it (138).

According to this view, to engage in academic intellectualizing is to trash emotions and reject the 'touchy-feely', the sentimental, and, by association, women.[9] For Tompkins, the personal means above all the emotional and the sentimental, but also the private. Splitting herself in two, the professional critic and the private person ('me and my shadow'), she describes the latter as someone who 'talks on the telephone a lot to her friends, has seen psychiatrists, likes cappuccino, worries about the state of her soul. Her father is ill right now, and one of her friends recently

---

[9] As examples of off-putting theoretical writing, Tompkins quotes two philosophers and one literary critic (Guattari, Foucault, and Harold Bloom).

committed suicide' (122). Tompkins's plea for a 'personal criticism' is a plea for a criticism that would allow her to talk about herself and to identify with the experience of others:

> I think readers want to know about each other. Sometimes, when a writer introduces some personal bit of story into an essay, I can hardly contain my pleasure. I love writers who write about their own experience. I feel I am being nourished by them, that I'm being allowed to enter into a personal relationship with them. That I can match my own experience up with theirs, feel cousin to them, and say, yes, that's how it is (123).[10]

So Tompkins includes information about 'herself as a person', sitting at her desk writing the essay we are reading:

> Most of all, I don't know how to enter the debate [about epistemology] without leaving everything else behind—the birds outside my window, my grief over Janice, just myself as a person sitting here in stockinged feet, a little bit chilly because the windows are open, and thinking about going to the bathroom. But not going yet (126).

> This is what I want you to see. A person sitting in stockinged feet looking out of her window—a floor to ceiling rectangle filled with green, with one red leaf. The season poised, sunny and chill, ready to rush down the incline into autumn. But perfect and still. Not going yet (128).

I first read 'Me and My Shadow' in a manuscript version given to me by Jane Tompkins in the autumn of 1987, when I was visiting Duke University for the first time and had just started to think about my book on Simone de Beauvoir. Jane had been very welcoming to me. She and I had gone to yoga classes together. We also shared an interest in meditation. But this essay confounded me. Suddenly it was as if we were living on different intellectual planets. I felt that Jane was telling me that what I wanted to do—to think clearly about questions considered theoretical—was patriarchal to the core, and that there was no way for a woman to think theoretically without excluding her body, her emotions, her experiences. I felt that Jane was telling me that

---

[10] Tompkins later abandoned criticism for autobiography. In her memoir *A Life in School* she explains why.

systematic thought is and always will be the enemy of emotion, that there is no way of writing theory without producing alienation in oneself and others, and, in particular, that women (let alone feminists) who love theory are alienated, male-identified, and necessarily oppressive of other women. And so, to my dismay, Jane's essay made me feel that there was an unbridgeable gulf between us, that just as I could not understand why she wanted to set up such an absolute divide between thought and feelings, she could never understand my passion for theory, or for Simone de Beauvoir for that matter.

Jane Tompkins's delight in reading about the experience of others is based on the assumption that she will recognize her own in it, to be able to exclaim: 'yes, that's how it is'. But could she really recognize herself in Simone de Beauvoir's experience of falling in love with philosophy at the age of 16? In *Memoirs of a Dutiful Daughter*, Beauvoir tells us that even the boring and unadventurous philosophy lessons dispensed by the abbé Trécourt at her very Catholic girls' school allowed her to catch a glimpse of a different world, to realize that philosophy had the power to challenge everything she had been taught in her pious childhood, and everything she thought she knew about herself:

> the world of the grown-ups was no longer self-evident; it had another side, an underside, doubt was creeping in: if one went even further, what would be left? We did not, of course, go very far, but it was already quite extraordinary, after twelve years of dogmatism, to find a discipline that asked questions, and asked them of *me*. For suddenly my own self, hitherto only spoken of in commonplaces, was being challenged [*mise en cause*]. My consciousness— where did it come from? Where did it get its powers? . . . Henri Poincaré's speculations on the relativity of space and time and measurements plunged me into endless meditations. I was moved by the pages where he evoked man passing through a blind universe: only a flash, but a flash that is everything! For a long time I was haunted by the image of this great fire blazing in the dark.[11]

---

[11] This passage comes from *MJF* (219–20). I am providing my own translation (see *MDD* 157–8 for the highly inadequate published translation). Over and over again I discover that even otherwise acceptable English translations of Beauvoir's works fall apart as soon as she starts using a philosophical vocabulary.

The young Simone de Beauvoir was deeply moved by the power of philosophy. It stirred her imagination, and allowed her to hope for liberation from her stifling Catholic environment. It didn't occur to her to consider Poincaré's speculations alien or irrelevant to her own concerns. She *was* that flash blazing in the dark: to her, philosophy was poetry. Beauvoir never lost the sense that philosophy was magical and poetic, and had the power to help her understand her own life. 'In truth there is no divorce between philosophy and life', she noted in 1948, as she was busy writing *The Second Sex* (*L'existentialisme et la sagesse des nations*, 12). Throughout the 1930s and the 1940s Beauvoir wrote in cafés where she also met her friends and lovers and conducted her professional life. The way she organized her everyday life reinforced her sense that life and philosophy were interconnected. In Beauvoir's writing, her philosophical imagination is constantly at work on material from ordinary life, turning everyday life into philosophy in *The Second Sex*, and showing us the philosophical significance of lived experience in *Memoirs of a Dutiful Daughter*.[12]

The young Simone's experience of the power, poetry, and personal challenge of philosophy is at odds with Jane Tompkins's experience of theory as repressive, alienating, and misogynist. Tompkins recommends that women turn their backs on the very theory Beauvoir delights in. According to her analysis, Beauvoir's passion for philosophy does not count as a genuine feeling, but rather as a sign of her alienated identification with male values. Paradoxically, Tompkins's respect for her own personal experience prevents her from respecting that of her illustrious predecessor. Locked into their different experiences Jane and Simone are stuck: there is, apparently, no possibility of further communication. In *Getting Personal*, Nancy Miller writes: ' "Just me and my shadow, walkin' down the avenue." The next line of the song goes, "Me and my shadow, all alone and feeling blue." But is the personal critic necessarily alone, immured in isolation?' (23). This is an excellent question. As long as the advocates of

---

[12] Francis Jeanson's reading of *Memoirs of a Dutiful Daughter* remains a masterly elucidation of the way in which the text embodies philosophy. An important excerpt of Jeanson's book is now available in English, in Elizabeth Fallaize (ed.), *Simone de Beauvoir: A Critical Reader*.

personal criticism turn self-contained individual experience into the linchpin of truth and reality, the answer is yes.[13] Cut off from dialogue, immured in her own experience, the personal critic will indeed be 'all alone and feeling blue'. Finding herself, the personal critic loses her connectedness to others.

Tompkins longs for the concrete and the everyday. Yet her defence of the personal remains as general and abstract as the theory she is attacking. For does it really make sense to claim that theory—all theory—is inherently oppressive, male, alienating, and so on? Are not the effects of theory dependent on what the theory says, who reads it, and in what context? In the section of her essay where she discusses some examples of theoretical writing, namely texts by Guattari, Foucault, Harold Bloom, and Jessica Benjamin, Tompkins herself recognizes that the effects of theory are enormously varied. Jessica Benjamin's essay on erotic domination is the only one to catch her imagination. On closer inspection, however, it turns out to be a theoretical essay without any personal narrative or self-revealing glimpses of the author. So, Tompkins muses, perhaps Guattari just adores reading sentences containing the words machine, structure, and determination, excitedly muttering 'Great stuff. Juicy, terrific', to himself as he goes (134):

> I will concede the point. What is personal is completely a function of what is perceived as personal. And what is perceived as personal by men, or rather, what is gripping, significant, 'juicy', is different from what is felt to be that way by women. For what we are really talking about is not the personal as such, what we are talking about is what is important, answers one's needs, strikes one as immediately *interesting*. For women, the personal is such a category (134).

The right to define what is to count as interesting has always been fought over in the academy. Bourdieu would call it the struggle for distinction, and Tompkins is right to say that some

---

[13] Nancy Miller answers no: 'I would rather argue that this mode of criticism, far from being turned in on itself . . . is on the contrary, to bring back an old-fashioned word: engaged' (24). I agree that engagement is personal, but all personal writing is not necessarily *politically* engaged. Unfortunately, Miller chooses not to pursue her wonderful intuition about the loneliness of the personal critic any further.

people use their power to impose their own interests on others. That 'theory' has been used in this way in the American academy over the past two or three decades is clearly true. Yet there are two conflicting meanings of 'personal' at work here. If we use the word 'personal' to describe *whatever* we find interesting (so that if I am passionate about machines, or theory, then machines, or theory, are 'personal' to me), then the personal can't be of greater immediate interest and relevance for women than for men. In fact, on this definition the personal doesn't even have to be personal. Tompkins's argument, after all, is that the problem for women in academia is that men, precisely because they feel passionately interested in Guattari, or Foucault, or Harold Bloom, display a chilling disdain for women and the emotions associated with them. If, on the other hand, we stick to the definitions operative everywhere else in the essay, namely that in scholarly (literary and theoretical) texts, the personal means (1) emotion and sentiment, or (2) autobiographical information, or (3) any reference to actual persons, concrete situations, and everyday life, then the claim that the personal is always of particular interest to women is simply too sweeping to be true.

Tompkins's essay does seem to be thoroughly anti-intellectual. It casts me—and Simone de Beauvoir, and any other woman who loves theory and philosophy—as some kind of intellectual police force waging war against everything she passionately wishes to include in her own writing. Beauvoir and I become the twin incarnations of death-dealing, male-identified theoretical alienation. 'Me and My Shadow' is a very angry text: 'The rage I feel inside me now is the distillation of forty-six years. It has had a long time to simmer, to harden, to become adamantine, a black slab that glows in the dark', she writes (137). For a long time I simply could not deal with this essay. Although I felt deeply challenged by Tompkins's views, I had no idea how to respond to such anger. Back in 1987 I just put the essay aside, probably disappointing her by giving her no response at all.

Yet 'Me and My Shadow' stayed with me. For although I was truly upset at the way the essay seemed to want to block women from access to theory and philosophy, I actually agreed that Jane Tompkins had identified a major problem in contemporary theory, namely the tendency to produce alienating, obfuscating, and off-putting language. And I also *almost* agreed with her point about emotions. I would say that emotional responses to texts, whether literary or theoretical, are good starting points for further investigation, in which we go on to work hard to widen and deepen the emotional response through deeper understanding. By deepening our thought we can also deepen our feelings. To respond emotionally to a text is to care about it. If the response is boredom, that is also an emotion, and usually signals disengagement from the text. As such it is as analysable as rage or delight. Some texts deserve an enraged or a bored response, others do not: the intellectual challenge is to show why or why not. If a student feels enraged by Rousseau's treatment of Sophie, she can go on to find out what it is in the text that makes her react that way, what the alternatives might have been, how other people reacted at the time and how they react now, and so on.

Where I disagreed with Tompkins was in the assumption that serious and systematic thought somehow must block access to genuine emotions, so that the two become mortal enemies. The alienation I too detect in quite a lot of contemporary theory is not absent from certain kinds of autobiographical criticism. Instead of alienating oneself in a theoretical vocabulary, or in a picture of oneself as a Great Theorist, one alienates oneself in a picture of oneself as a Uniquely Interesting Human Being. (Simone de Beauvoir's analysis of narcissism in *The Second Sex* is pertinent here.) The two forms of alienation can be equally effective in making the reader wonder why she should bother to read another sentence of this kind of material.[14] Although Tompkins's solution

[14] The anthropologist Ruth Behar recommends 'vulnerable' writing, that is to say writing that reveals the anthropologist's own emotions, in ways that reminds me of Tompkins. Yet she also worries about the limits of the practice: 'Even I, a practitioner of vulnerable writing, am sometimes at a loss to say how much emotion is bearable within academic settings,' Behar writes (*Vulnerable* 17). Then she tells the story of a colleague's heart-rending paper which started out as ethnography but ended with the woman's own experience of being beaten by a former husband. Behar writes: 'When my colleague had finished speaking, a terrible silence, like a dark storm cloud, descended upon everyone. A part of me wished the cavern in the middle of the room would open up and swallow us all, so we wouldn't have to speak' (*Vulnerable* 17). This story is food for thought.

(to turn her back on theory) was wrong, I thought, her sense that there was a problem was right. There *is* something wrong with the way a lot of theory is written these days. An increasing number of intellectual women from different disciplines tell me that they have given up reading feminist theory because it seems obscure, abstruse, and removed from their interests and experiences. Such common experiences cannot all be due to the limitations of the readers.

Changing social conditions explain some aspects of the problem. Without a powerful women's movement, feminist intellectuals no longer have a strong sense of constituency. Writing for the narrower audience of the academy, the feminist intellectual is justified in using a more specialized language than she might have done in the 1970s. But this is not all there is to it. Nowadays even highly educated women who take a strong interest in feminism, tell me they can't bear to labour through another obscure and theory-laden book on the subject. Some such complaints may well be motivated by laziness or anti-intellectual prejudice, and have no claim to be taken seriously. Moreover, many books are justifiably written for specialists in narrow fields: it would be ridiculous to complain about obscurity just because I don't instantly understand the language in a book devoted to medieval theology, or to the finer points of the philosophy of Quine, or Deleuze for that matter. In any case, the problem of obscurity can't be reduced to a question of specialist vocabularies. Carefully defined terms used stringently are per definition not unclear, however difficult and specialized they may be. It is impossible to assess the effects of a theoretical style without asking who the theory is addressed to, and what it actually is about. There can be no question of setting up some general rule for *the* correct way to write theory.[15]

The problem of off-putting obscurity arises most urgently in the case of theory that wishes to make a political or cultural

What exactly went wrong in the seminar presentation? Why was silence—the wish not to engage in conversation—the dominant response? When (under what circumstances) is 'vulnerability'—in this case, heart-rending emotional openness—neither useful nor productive?

[15] Different subject matter usually gives rise to somewhat different style or tone, even in texts written by the same author at roughly the same time.

difference in the world beyond the academy, but which is written in such a way that it fails to reach more than a highly specialized and elite audience. Theory does not have to be ponderous to read. Some contemporary US feminists, such as Elaine Showalter, Camille Paglia, and Catharine MacKinnon are capable of writing with admirable wit and sharpness of style.[16] Historically, many of the most intellectually challenging thinkers in the Western tradition have displayed great mastery of style (just think of Plato, Rousseau, Thoreau, Nietzsche, and Freud) without ceasing to present serious problems of interpretation and understanding. An aspiration to clarity is not going to keep genuine difficulty out of a text. In his wonderful study of Mallarmé, Malcolm Bowie shows that difficulty and obscurity are two different things. This distinction is as useful for someone who wishes to defend difficult poetry or difficult theory against anti-intellectual attacks as it is for someone who wishes to make theory as readable as it can hope to be, given its subject matter.[17] In the higher reaches of academia

---

[16] These examples are symptomatically marginal to feminist theory. Some would say that Elaine Showalter is not a theorist at all, others would call Paglia an anti-feminist, and some fervently pray that MacKinnon would stop referring to herself as a feminist.

[17] Entitled *Mallarmé and the Art of Being Difficult*, Bowie's delicious epigraph comes from Mozart and Da Ponte's *Così fan tutte:* 'Cara semplicità, quanto mi piaci!' Bowie reminds us that there are many different ways of being difficult: 'Mallarmé's poems are difficult in different ways and at different levels of intensity. Certain of them are difficult to come at, to get meaning from, but yield to pressure. . . . [O]ther poems have difficulty at their centre, being concerned with open metaphysical questions. . . . Such poems are centred upon difficulties which are the product of an intended and scrupulous indecision on the poet's part' (ix–x).

In the same way, there are many different ways of producing theoretical obscurity: among the more common methods we find vagueness of thought and imprecision of language. In recent theoretical writing I have been struck by the obscurity produced by an excessive generality of reference to other theorists. A statement may be secured by a reference to 'Foucault's theory of discursivity', for instance. But Foucault's understanding of discourse and discursivity is not simple and straightforward, and has given rise to different interpretations. Given that different readers probably have quite different ideas of what Foucault actually means by discursivity, the theoretical point the author is trying to secure by the reference may either be dramatically misunderstood or perceived as a puzzling non sequitur by many readers. Another way of formulating this problem is to say that such writers of theory too readily assume that their readers will be exactly like themselves.

there is nevertheless a tendency to assume that the clearer (or the more elegant) the writing, the less intellectually challenging it must be.[18]

Asking for clarification of an obscure theoretical claim, I have quite often been told that I fail to appreciate the deliberate opacity of the text and, moreover, that my wish to understand what is and what is not being claimed amounts to a wish for 'transparent language'. This amounts to telling me that I am guilty of an epistemological sin. To want language to be transparent is to subscribe to a simplistic realist thesis about the relationship between language and the world, to turn language into a mere window on to the world so that the less it is noticed the better. To ask for 'transparent language', then, is to ask language to efface itself as a living, material structure. This is indeed a grievously problematic request, but luckily one that has nothing to do with a wish for clarity. Just as there is a difference between difficulty and obscurity, clarity and transparency are not synonymous. To put a difficult thought with some clarity and precision is not going to make it any simpler or less challenging than it actually is. Rather, it will make intellectual difficulties and problems more salient and more pressing than if they are masked by a mess of imprecision and approximations. Wittgenstein's *Philosophical Investigations*, to give a fairly extreme example, shows that writing

[18] In her influential essay 'The Race for Theory', first published in 1987, the same year as 'Me and My Shadow', Barbara Christian eloquently complains about the aridity of theoretical language in terms very similar to those of Jane Tompkins: 'as a student of literature', Christian writes, 'I am appalled by the sheer ugliness of the language, its lack of clarity, its unnecessarily complicated sentence constructions, its lack of pleasurableness, its alienating quality' (230). But Christian does not write in order to recommend a turn to the personal, but in order to defend her wish to reach an audience that differs from the standard academic audience. The connection between intended readership and theoretical style is obvious, and lends itself to a Bourdieuian analysis of the quest for symbolic capital. Bourdieu, however, is an implacable theorist: every attempt to write theory in a more simple way, he would surely say, is going to be taken more seriously if it comes from a writer who already has accumulated much theoretical capital than if it comes from someone who hasn't. The same is true for the turn to autobiographical writing among academics: graduate students usually do not have enough symbolic capital to attempt it. Interesting studies could be done on these matters.

striving for clarity of thought and simplicity of style is not synonymous with intellectual banality and lack of interpretative challenge. Freud's very different style demonstrates exactly the same
thing. As Einstein is supposed to have said: 'Everything should be
made as simple as possible, but not simpler.'

'Me and My Shadow' teaches us that there is a profound
connection between the question of the personal and the question of style. This is its most important, yet curiously undeveloped,
insight. Finding the right diagnosis, Tompkins proposes the
wrong cure. In this essay I shall try to show that we do not have to
give up on theory to avoid alienating obfuscation in academic
work, and that we do not have to choose between the personal
and the theoretical. The personal is not the enemy of serious
thought. To imply that it is, is to reinforce the very dichotomy that
Jane Tompkins experiences as a painful split in her own life. To
expand on Beauvoir: there is no necessary divorce between life
and philosophy, between the personal and the theoretical,
between feelings and thought.[19]

To the many contemporary critics who have acknowledged the
importance of the personal because they consider self-consciously
subjective expression to offer an escape from the twin horrors of
objectivity and universalism, Beauvoir's position must appear
unconvincing. Would she also say that there is no necessary
divorce between the first person and the third person, between
speaking *as* and speaking *for*? Isn't she herself a typical example
of the universalizing Enlightenment tradition that the turn to the
personal is trying to undermine? Such questions will be discussed
in Section II of this essay. In what remains of Section I, I shall
examine some further issues arising out of the contemporary
debates about the personal. Throughout I try to show that the
term 'the personal' has different meanings for different critics.

The discussions in Section I are intended to prepare the
ground for Section II, where I turn to my main task, namely to
show through a close study of Beauvoir's philosophical style

[19] In an essay written in 1988, that is to say shortly after reading 'Me and My
Shadow', I try to show, with the help of Freud, that the intellectual is shot
through with emotion and desire. See 'Patriarchal Thought and the Drive for
Knowledge' (Ch. 7 below).

exactly how she uses herself (her own subjectivity) in order to produce a philosophical analysis of women's condition. The purpose of this exercise is to show that Beauvoir has a profound contribution to make to contemporary debates about the relationship between the personal and the theoretical. Her philosophical style, I claim, can show us a way (not the way) to write theory without losing ourselves or our connectedness to others.[20]

Ad Feminam: *The Argument for Location and Its Excesses*

Painting a rosy picture of the personal, Jane Tompkins thinks of it as warm, emotional, loving, giving, autobiographical, embodied, and concrete. Unfortunately, however, there are less pleasant ways of 'getting personal', to quote Nancy Miller's delightfully ambiguous phrase. It would seem that many critics believe, much like Jane Tompkins, that because the personal has been undervalued in academia, it is now time to privilege it. Unlike Tompkins, however, some of these critics do not believe that we have to choose between the personal and the theoretical, declaring instead that the two always 'go together'. Although this sometimes leads to sympathetic analyses of the factors that contribute to the production of someone's beliefs, it is on the strength of this claim that some critics proceed to reduce an intellectual argument to its personal components, as if the personal circumstances of an intellectual claim were always more important than the claim itself. They are in fact making use of a classical rhetorical strategy, namely the *ad feminam* argument.

According to the OED, the phrase *ad hominem* means 'to the man' or 'to the person'; an *ad hominem* argument is 'directed to

---

[20] My wish to show the relevance of Beauvoir to problems in contemporary feminist theory makes my project similar to that of Nancy Bauer, who in her important work on Simone de Beauvoir also shows how Beauvoir teaches contemporary feminist theory a new method of philosophical appropriation. The difference is that Bauer shows what we can learn from Beauvoir's inventive and imaginative relationship to the works of other philosophers (particularly Hegel, but also Sartre and Descartes), whereas I want to show what her way of writing teaches us about how to use oneself in the writing of theory. In Bauer's discussion of Beauvoir's relationship to Descartes, our two projects intersect more closely than elsewhere.

the individual, personal; appealing to feeling not reason'. Developed to assist the male participants in Greek and Roman public and political life, classical rhetoric never coined the term *ad feminam* to describe arguments directed 'to the woman'. To argue *ad feminam* or *ad hominem* is to attack the person who makes the argument one detests, rather than the argument itself, usually in order to move the audience, to stir their passions against this abhorrent person. In a court of law or in political debate such arguments have their uses, but they are hardly philosophically or logically respectable. Traditionally the quintessentially sexist form of the *ad feminam* argument has been the dismissive 'you say that because you are a woman'. The point of the argument is to discredit the speaker, not to engage in debate with her. The effect is to make the person attacked feel as if nobody listened to what she actually said. The attacker, on the other hand, has to be suspected of having run out of better arguments: in intellectual circles the *ad feminam* attack is usually one of last resort and brings no credit to its user. In reviews it is always used negatively, as a point of criticism of the author who engages in it.[21] Thus the *ad feminam* argument usually backfires: instead of discrediting one's opponent, one manages only to discredit oneself.

In contemporary academia the recent emphasis on the personal has nevertheless led to some confusion about what exactly is to count as an *ad feminam* argument.[22] For if we are

[21] I have only ever seen the actual phrase *ad feminam* or *ad hominem* argument used with negative connotations, but I suppose one might imagine a positive version of the practice, if not of the phrase: 'I will support whatever *she* is saying because her subject position is one that I wish to support,' might be a form of *ad feminam* praise (but the formulation '*ad feminam* praise' sounds odd). Although humanly nicer, the argument is as intellectually vacuous as the *ad feminam* attack.

[22] Nancy Miller's use of the phrase *ad feminam* is representatively ambiguous. Referring to 'attacks on academic feminism', she writes: 'What should we make of this published violence against feminist ideology in general and individual critics in particular (ad feminam)?' (*Getting Personal* x). Here it is not clear from the context whether the attacks took the form of arguments against some named person's views ('Jane Smith's critique of essentialism is derivative, or insufficiently argued, for the following reasons'), or whether they took the form of saying something like 'Jane Smith's critique of essentialism is entirely due to her wish to remain on good terms with the feminist Mafia that currently runs our

justified in thinking that the speaker's subject position and social location affects his or her understanding of the world, surely it cannot be unjustified to point out that since so-and-so actually is a white, heterosexual, bourgeois male, his views exhibit traces of his male privilege? In the same way, wouldn't it be quite fair to tell me that I am criticizing Judith Butler's account of the sex/gender distinction (see Chapter 1, above) just because I am heterosexual and she is not? Or perhaps I am dissatisfied with Butler's account of sex and gender just because I am Norwegian and she is not? If our views are indeed influenced by our 'location', then such questions cannot be easily dismissed. In practice, I think most of us can tell the difference between an *ad feminam* argument and a serious investigation of 'location' or 'context' or 'speaking position', yet in the present intellectual climate it sometimes becomes difficult to justify one's sense that there is a difference. I shall nevertheless try to do so here.

I shall start by considering two examples of *ad feminam* argumentation and its effects. Hostile reductions of her philosophical and political positions to her personal circumstances have been extremely common in the critical reception of Simone de Beauvoir. Instead of discussing the meaning and implications of (say) her claim that the highest human value is freedom, or that the French war in Algeria was a deeply unjust and shameful colonialist venture, critics endlessly focus on her private, personal, and emotional motivations for saying so. Insisting that Beauvoir only says this or that because she was trying to please Sartre, because she was male-identified, because she was a sexually licentious woman living in sin, or because she hated her bourgeois parents, they try to dismiss her views without engaging with them. The strategy is deeply sexist: the point is to convey that whatever passes for thought in this woman is really only the symptoms of her frustrated sexuality, her neurotic emotional life, her desperate dependence on a man, or her hostility to other women. In my book on Beauvoir I described the effects of the strategy as follows:

---

universities/the influence of her lesbian lover/her vicious and unfeminine careerism'. According to the usual definition, the latter would certainly qualify as an *ad feminam* attack, the former not.

the hostile critics' favourite strategy is to personalize the issues, to reduce the book to the woman: their aim is clearly to discredit her as a speaker, not to enter into debate with her. These critics are out to cast doubts on Beauvoir's right to produce any kind of public discourse. By discrediting her status as a speaker, they intend to preclude any further discussion of what she actually says (75).

[P]olitically motivated critiques of Beauvoir contain surprisingly little discussion of politics and much apparently pointless dwelling on her personality and private life. . . . The intended effect is to depoliticize her by presenting her political choices not as the outcome of careful reflection on the issues at stake, but as the inexplicable *élans* of an overemotional or even hysterical woman. Having reduced their opponent to a neurotic woman, such hostile critics avoid having to reveal—and defend—their own politics, let alone their own personal problems (81).

In short, the main effects of the strategy are to discredit the woman as a speaker, to cast doubt on her right to participate in the conversation, to dispense the hostile critics from having to take the woman's thought seriously, and to protect the critics from inquiry into their own neuroses and blind spots.

Let me move on to the second example. If I permit myself to criticize, however mildly, a point in a visiting feminist speaker's talk I may be told that I have failed to be 'supportive'.[23] Insofar as this comment is based on the assumption that intellectual disagreement is always 'unsupportive' (unhelpful? unproductive? irrelevant?), it is in itself problematic. But let us take the worst case scenario. Let us assume that I am someone who generally goes around feeling vicious and spiteful, full of hostility towards every feminist theorist in the world except myself. Let us further assume that my public question after the talk was uttered in a provocatively hostile tone. In short, let us assume that I am a person sadly lacking in humanity, love, and forbearance. Let us then note that so far no mention has been made of the argument of the visiting feminist nor of the content of my response to her. The statement has been reduced to the speech act, or rather, to

---

[23] I am not implying that feminists engage in hostile uses of the personal more than other academics. Readers might want to consult their own experience for other examples.

one particular circumstance of the speech act, namely the personality of the speaker. Whatever was actually said has disappeared from view. Moreover, further discussion is now impossible. The diagnosis of my personality has taken the place of intellectual exchange.

Once I recognize that I have miserably failed to be 'supportive' (or 'sisterly' for that matter), all I can do is to find a therapist, turn to religion or whatever else it takes to turn myself into a better person. What I cannot do, is to come back to the theoretical point I originally made, for the accusation of 'unsupportiveness' has now thoroughly discredited me. The accusation turns out to be a version of the *ad feminam* attack. Branded as a hostile and unloving woman I have apparently lost my right to participate in feminist intellectual debate. (At this point it ought to be obvious that it does not matter in the least whether I actually did intervene in the discussion out of hostility. The point is to impute disreputable motivations, not to describe them accurately.) By speaking up for 'supportiveness', moreover, my interlocutors imply that their own psychiatric or sisterly credentials are above suspicion. The hostile reduction of the theoretical to the personal dissolves into anti-intellectualism and velvet-gloved censorship (if all critical statements will be taken as evidence of one's spiteful nature, one may be excused for thinking that it is better to say nothing at all). Blocking intellectual dialogue, this particular turn to the personal yet again leaves us 'all alone and feeling blue'. To stress the point: the main problem with *ad feminam* argumentation is that it locks us into our variously discredited subject positions and so makes productive intellectual exchange impossible.[24]

Whereas my first example, that of hostile uses of the personal against Simone de Beauvoir, seems clearly reprehensible, it is not at all clear what goes wrong in the second case. It is not even clear *that* anything goes wrong. Should I not be prepared to accept the accusation of 'unsupportiveness' as a fair interpretation of, say, the effect of my remarks? Let me stress that the remark 'That was unsupportive' does not have to be an *ad feminam* attack. It can be

---

[24] I realize that I have focused entirely on *ad feminam* argumentation of a diagnostic or clinical kind. There are others, but they will have to be left for another day.

offered as part of a discussion of when—under what circumstances—it is right for feminists to disagree in public, for instance.
I may say that in a sexist society, to take another intellectual
woman seriously enough to want to engage in discussion with her
is politically more valuable than to shut up for fear of producing
an 'unsupportive' effect.[25] My interlocutors may want to point out
that although there is some value in this, I forget that in the
specific situation at hand, there was a potential major donor to
the women's studies programme present, well known for her
dislike of disagreement. One possible outcome of such a discussion is that I acknowledge that I misjudged the situation.[26] This is
a fair enough debate to have, and it is not *ad feminam* to the extent
that it no longer necessarily tries to discredit me as a speaker, yet
it still counts as a derailing of any discussion concerned with the
visiting speaker's paper. The question my interlocutors have to
weigh is under what circumstances it is worth doing that.

Nothing is less contentious among US literary critics today
than the claim that someone's race, class, sex, sexuality, nationality, and individual experiences (of sexual abuse, rape, and racism,
but also other, more innocuous experiences) affect his or her
understanding of the world. As Linda Alcoff puts it in a frequently
quoted phrase, the general assumption is that 'a speaker's location is epistemically salient' (7). Yet, in the cases I just described,
this assumption—one that I share—appears to breed a disastrously reductive anti-intellectual stance. How do we prevent a
proper concern for speaking position from degenerating into *ad
feminam* argumentation? It may help to describe *ad feminam* arguments as *reductive* and *irrelevant* deployment of the argument for

---

[25] From a slightly different angle, namely the problems of speaking for
others, Linda Alcoff produces a thoughtful critique of the 'retreat response', the
decision to say nothing for fear of being ideologically incorrect: 'But surely it is
both morally and politically objectionable to structure one's actions around the
desire to avoid criticism . . . In some cases perhaps the motivation is not so much
to avoid criticism as to avoid errors, and the person believes that the only way to
avoid errors is to avoid all speaking for others. However, errors are unavoidable
in theoretical inquiry as well as political struggle, and moreover they often make
contributions' (22).

[26] This is one way to claim responsibility for one's words. See Alcoff for
further discussion of what it might mean to take responsibility for what one says.

'location' (by which I mean the claim that the location of the
speaker matters for the meaning of the speech act). Then the
question becomes more concrete: what do we need to do to avoid
reductionism and irrelevance?

Since every theory can be used reductively, no theory can be
rejected simply on the grounds that some of its practitioners are
reductionists. Ultimately, the only antidote against reductionism
is sound judgement. Reductionisms nevertheless do different
things to different theories. Linda Alcoff provides a fairly poststructuralist analysis of the reductionism that concerns us here:

> [It] involves a retrograde, metaphysically insupportable essential-
> ism that assumes one can read the truth and meaning of what one
> says straight from the discursive context. . . . Such a reductionist
> theory might, for example, reduce evaluation to a political assess-
> ment of the speaker's location, where that location is seen as an
> insurmountable essence that fixes one, as if one's feet are super-
> glued to a spot on the sidewalk (16).

What has gone wrong, in Alcoff's view, is that a general assumption of 'epistemic salience' has been essentialized and made
absolute: 'To say that location *bears* on meaning and truth is not
the same as saying that location *determines* meaning and truth,'
she writes (16). Location and positionality should be understood
as multiple and shifting, not as a given essence. Furthermore,
Alcoff argues, we should not claim that a given speaking position
always has the *same* effects: 'we need to analyse the probable or
actual effects of the words on the discursive and material context.
One cannot simply look at the location of the speaker or her
credentials to speak, nor can one look merely at the propositional
contents of the speech; one must also look at where the speech
goes and what it does there' (26).

Offered as a protection against reductionism, these are useful
reminders. But there is nothing here to guard against irrelevance.
Must we always look at 'where the speech goes'?[27] Do we really, as
Alcoff also puts it, in each and every case have to 'analyse the

---

[27] I think Alcoff underestimates the difficulty of knowing 'where the speech
goes'. Sartre's *What Is Literature?* contains thoughtful considerations on this
subject.

probable or actual effects of the words on the discursive and material context' (27)? In spite of her sensitive and thoughtful discussion of the problems attending her position, Alcoff wants to hang on to the claim that 'there is no possibility of rendering positionality, location, or context irrelevant to content' (14). Yet even the briefest of considerations of contemporary critical practice shows that we don't in fact always analyse the location and circumstances of the speaker we are concerned with, nor do we always engage in discussion of our own speaking position before saying something. Simone de Beauvoir reads Hegel in order to fashion her own, highly original understanding of women's oppression, and never lets the fact that Hegel was a bourgeois, sexist, white male stop her.[28] Luce Irigaray and Judith Butler both return to Plato in order to discuss sex and gender without even mentioning the effect of his speech acts in Greek fifth-century BC society, and without saying anything about their own 'location'.[29]

Ought these women to have spent lots of time uncovering the effects of Plato's or Hegel's interventions in their own time and society? Should they not, at the very least, have discussed the potential effects of rereading Plato in their own time and society? If one thinks that location is *always relevant*, the answer has to be yes. But then these theorists' freedom to use a text for their own creative purposes would be severely curtailed. Most of us became intellectuals because we felt challenged and inspired by writing and ideas. Because we read with an eye to what we can use and what we need in our own situation, there is no reason why we should always have to reconstruct the historical location of the original speech act, or indeed offer up our own autobiography as a preface to everything we say. The insistence that location and speaking position is *always* relevant, or that it is always incumbent on the speaker to guard against malignant consequences of her speech act, magnifies the speaker's powers, encourages her to take a paranoid stance towards her audience, and, however paradoxically, also casts the reader or

---

[28] See Bauer and Lundgren-Gothlin, *Sex and Existence* for divergent analyses of Beauvoir's appropriation of Hegel. The question of how successful Beauvoir's use of Hegel is remains a fascinating topic of discussion.

[29] I am thinking of the title essay in Butler's *Bodies that Matter* and the long last section devoted to Plato in Irigaray's *Speculum of the Other Woman*.

listener as nothing but a passive victim of the speaker's discursive violence.[30] On this model, the writer becomes too powerful and the reader too unfree. Thus the theory radically underestimates the fact that a speech act is also an *encounter* between a speaker and a listener or a writer and a reader.

This may sound too idealist, too oblivious of differences in power between speakers and listeners. Alcoff is right to stress that 'Certain contexts and locations are allied with structures of oppression, and certain others are allied with resistance to oppression. Therefore all are not politically equal, and, given that politics is connected to truth, all are not epistemically equal' (15). In cases where the powerful speak to the powerless, the picture of master speaker and victimized listener is more relevant than in cases where the powerful or the powerless speak among themselves. All speech acts do not take place in situations of unambiguous domination. The fact that some do is no reason to claim that we must *always* analyse the location and position of an utterance. Even when a speech act does take place in a situation of domination, this is not always the most important thing to say about it. One still needs to give some reasons for such claims, not simply postulate them as obviously true.

If we admit that there is such a thing as utterly irrelevant invocations of personal circumstances, we have invalidated the claim that analysis of 'location' and 'speaking position' is always relevant. It does not follow that knowledge is not situated, but neither does it follow that it isn't. If all knowledge is always situated, the statement cancels all the way through. It simply means that no statement is any less situated than any other. If this is so (and I am not here out to deny such claims), then it follows that the claim that all knowledge is situated tells us nothing at all about when—under what circumstances—we should *raise* the question of location. In my view, only

[30] Joyce Trebilcot, for example, thinks that any attempt to persuade anyone of anything at all is an act of violence. In an essay arguing against trying to persuade others to accept one's own beliefs, she writes: 'the term "persuasion" must be construed broadly so as to include not only argument and discussion but also other forms of deliberately influencing people's beliefs, such as various kinds of reward and punishment (e.g., bribery, blackmail), the inducement of conversion experiences, and so on' (5).

when there is something problematic about the speech act do we need to analyse it more fully. Problems may arise at any time in a statement's lifetime: the fact that so far nobody to my knowledge has found anything problematic about Judith Butler's lack of interest in ancient Greek society, doesn't mean that the question could not arise under future, as yet unforeseen, circumstances. But it is neither possible nor desirable to produce theoretical prescriptions intended to guard against all possible future eventualities. The demand that we *always* examine 'location' is one such prescription.

Once a problem of interpretation or evaluation has arisen, however, we do need to look to who is speaking, what was said, to whom it was said, under what circumstances it was said, and so on. This is where I feel inspired to draw on J. L Austin's remark that in order to solve questions about meaning we need to examine 'what we should say when, what words we should use in what situation' ('Plea' 182). It is incumbent on the person who wishes to raise the question of 'location' to show why it is relevant, that is, first to show what problem of evaluation or meaning has arisen, and then to show that her investigation of 'what we should say when' helps to resolve the issue. The fact that so many speech acts appear to be felicitous—that they do *not* go wrong, misfire, or backfire—is of great theoretical interest. We do not need a theory of language or speech acts geared only to emergencies, crises, and conflicts. Although such theories heighten literary critics' sense of excitement, it leaves us resourceless in front of the ordinary and the unremarkable, so that we will have nothing to say about the many felicitous speech acts we all engage in every day. The only way out—and one frequently taken—is to insist that these too are in fact *always* the sites of failure, crisis, and melodramatic intensities, and if we don't notice it, it is because we are enslaved to dominant ideology, blinded by false consciousness, or incapable of resisting the master discourse. I find this implausible.[31]

---

[31] The question I am raising here and in the previous paragraph is really one that goes to the core of the difference between a Wittgensteinian and a Derridean account of language, and this paper is not the place to discuss it further. I am much indebted to Martin Stone's lectures on Derrida and Wittgenstein at The School of Criticism and Theory at Cornell in the summer of 1997 for clarifying the issues at stake.

I am now in a position to answer my own questions about the white heterosexual male or the reasons why I am dissatisfied with Butler's understanding of sex and gender. The idea that my reading of Butler could be adequately explained by the fact that I am Norwegian or heterosexual or whatever else, is utterly preposterous, a clear case of *ad feminam* argumentation. The same is true for the assumption that because someone is a heterosexual, white male his views can be discarded without further consideration. There is a world of difference between finding patterns of misogyny and racism in a text and using the author's personal characteristics to dispense oneself from the hard work of reading. If someone engages with Chapter 1 in this book and carefully establishes that there are patterns of heterosexism or Norwegian nationalism in it, then I cannot complain about unfair rhetorical strategies. Once this has been shown, however, the question of why I of all people have such attitudes no longer appears all that interesting or relevant.[32]

In short, any claim about motivations, intentions, or general bias based on subject position that appears to be unsupported by a fair-minded reading of the text in question is irrelevant to intellectual work. To me, the worst aspects of *ad feminam* argumentation remain its cavalier disinterest in serious thought and its attempt to discredit the speaker, and so to block further discussion.

Against Impersonality and Objectivity

As we have seen, in 'Me and My Shadow' the personal is pictured as concrete, embodied, emotional, warm, feeling, and autobiographical. Theory on the other hand is pictured as impersonal, and to Tompkins that means unfeeling, cool, objective, distanced, disembodied, and abstract. The personal, moreover, gets linked to concrete, sensuous, pleasurable language; the theoretical to an obscure, abstruse, and unpleasant aridity of style. In contemporary theory, the distinction between speaking for oneself—speaking *as*

[32] The writer's project largely determines what is relevant: if someone—God forbid!—had decided to write a biography of me, then the question of my motivations and intentions and how I came to have them might be highly relevant.

the person one is—and speaking *for* (in the place of, on behalf of) others often gets mapped on to this set of binary opposites. It is generally assumed that speaking for others is a bad thing. By the late 1990s the idea that some kind of turn to the personal will rescue us from arrogant impersonality, discriminatory objectivity, and imperialist universalization appears to have congealed into established academic *doxa* among literary critics.

In October 1996 the *PMLA*, the journal of the Modern Language Association of America, devoted a special issue to 'The Place of the Personal in Scholarship'. In this issue there is a general 'Forum' where twenty-six different letter-writers discuss the question of the personal. Reading through these letters is an illuminating exercise. Whatever their individual disagreements about what the personal is, the writers are overwhelmingly in agreement about what it is not. With striking consistency the contributions cast 'objectivity' and 'universality' as the twin dragons to be slain by the knights of the personal.

Some contributors focus exclusively on the opposition between a free, playful expression of self and a rigid search for objectivity. The wish to mask the personal or the self stems from a scientistic need to 'make literary studies respectable, objective, and scientific', one contributor writes (1147).[33] 'We are, willy-nilly, personal', he declares: 'Let's go with it, then. Let's enjoy it. Let's chuck the pretensions to infallibility customary to our profession and have some fun' (1147). Later on he also enjoins us to 'be creative' since in this postmodern age we cannot pretend to be objective. Aspirations to objectivity only reveal our pretensions to infallibility. Against such dour scientism is pitted an upbeat, free-wheeling spirit of creative personalities playfully expressing themselves. Many writers echo the idea that 'scholarly prose, like imaginative literature, is inevitably personal' (1147).

I imagine that anyone influenced by psychoanalysis (as I am) would agree that our desires and unconscious investment reveal themselves in all our speech acts, and often where we least expect it. Yet psychoanalysis is not the theoretical source of the recent

---

[33] All unattributed quotes come from the 'Forum' section of *PMLA* 111/5 (Oct. 1996), 1146–96.

turn to the personal, and for good reason. The psychoanalytic claim is that there is always someone who writes, and that the writer always leaves traces of her subjectivity in her work. Since this is equally true for *Critique of Pure Reason* and 'Me and My Shadow', we can conclude that whatever present-day postmodern academics want from the personal, it is not adequately explained by invoking the psychoanalytic understanding of subjectivity and desire. The idea expressed in many of the letters in the *PMLA* Forum is that because there is subjectivity in everything, then nothing is objective. This is a kind of 'pan-subjectivism', akin to the pan-sexualism that Freud always strenuously rejected. Such 'pan-subjectivism' overlooks the difference between claiming, as psychoanalysis does, that there is subjectivity in every belief, and claiming that every belief is purely subjective.

What is excluded from the *PMLA* Forum is any serious examination of the meaning of 'objectivity'. Imprisoned in a binary opposition with the personal, objectivity becomes the villain of the piece. It would seem that most contributors think the word is always used to mean something like the point of view of a pure clinical gaze situated outside every human context. On such a definition, clearly, nobody is objective, and to pretend that one is, is just to indulge in fantasy. But this is not the only possible meaning of the word. Even today, literary critics can be overheard saying things like 'The Dean gave a fairly objective account of the troubles in our department', or—more likely—hotly disputing the Dean's account on the grounds that it was *not* objective. In both cases, objectivity seems to have a potentially valuable and realizable meaning. This meaning is absent from every recent discussion of the personal that I have seen: in the *PMLA* Forum, for example, objectivity (and impersonality) is consistently reduced to being the repudiated and rejected Other of the personal. There is also a striking absence of nuanced views. Caught in a binary taxonomy of their own making, the *PMLA* Forum participants tend to believe that there are only two options: to admit to being subjective (good) or to pretend to be objective (bad). Underlying this binary grid, quite obviously, is the belief that objectivity does not exist, or rather, that the word objectivity can be given no useful meaning.

A frequent move is to tie the refusal of objectivity to a refusal to speak for others, on the grounds that the repudiated desire for universality is an ethically disreputable attempt to silence others: 'When we invoke objectivity and universality, we appeal to power and mystify our personal investments so as to speak for everyone. In doing so, we silence those who cannot make similar appeals' (1147). No contributor challenges the opposition produced here between the personal and the universal or objective, although some wish that the two could go together: 'Objectivity must be allowed as part of the personal', one person writes (1148). On the understanding of objectivity evident in the *PMLA* Forum, however, it is hard to see how this could happen.

Others attempt to deconstruct the opposition between the personal and the objective and/or universal by declaring that everything is personal, only to resurrect it as an opposition between knowledge and ignorance, between those who know they are speaking personally and proudly say so, and those who either don't know how personal they are or deliberately pass their subjective and situated utterances off as universal: 'What worries me is not scholarship that seems narrowly personal but rather scholarship where the personal does not recognize itself as such and thus passes for the universal' (1150). Objectivity, understood as impersonal, scientistic, and oppressive of difference, has no defenders: 'The writer who believes in the possibility of objectivity will not be on the lookout for bias and will do nothing to correct for it, thereby increasing the likelihood that the analysis will be compromised by it. . . . Scholars who don't reveal their participation in interactions they analyse risk the appearance of hiding it' (1152).

A somewhat different approach is taken by those who wish to align the personal with the literary, with the use of the first person singular, and with the everyday. Some think of narrative—either any narrative, or only narratives about real as opposed to fictional persons—as personal. Others are slightly more restrictive, and think of the personal much in the same terms as Nancy Miller who defines it as 'an explicitly autobiographical performance within the act of criticism' (*Getting Personal* 1). Such critics often see the turn to the personal as a way to escape the arrogance and

authoritarianism that according to them invariably accompanies
the deployment of theory. In the *PMLA* Forum, one writer feels
that by adding some 'quasi-confessional' material to his work of
criticism, he is escaping from the professional posturing that is
rife within the discourse of theory today. He overcomes his fear of
acknowledging that there are things he doesn't know, of not
being up to scratch theoretically, by turning to the personal:

> The most valuable way we can personalize, hence humanize, the
> teacher–student relationship, I suspect, is not to make our lives an
> open book but something altogether more self-exposing: to offer
> up our thought processes as a kind of open text from which
> students can learn that it is all right to say: 'I don't know', 'I don't
> understand', 'Help me out' (1153).

For this writer, the personal is a pedagogical tool, opposed to
forbidding theoretical arrogance and displays of mastery. In this
he again sounds very similar to Nancy Miller, who in a happy
phrase says that the unveiling of her own lack of mastery in class
is a feminist strategy designed to undermine the 'standard
peacock model of graduate teaching, designed to dazzle the hens'
(*Getting Personal* 41). Countered by confession, theoretical arrogance and one-upmanship will crumble, or so the personal critic
hopes.

The personal is also conceived of as closer to 'real life', and is
often invoked as a means to bridge the gap between scholarship
and the 'world beyond the page' (1158), yet strangely enough
nobody explicitly claims that the personal is the political. Only
one contributor bemoans the fact that the current adherents of
the personal have forgotten the original meaning of the phrase.
While we once used to claim that the personal is the political,
meaning that personal experience was 'part of a larger system of
(gender) ideology', nowadays the phrase 'has come to mean that
the personal is all there is of the political', she writes (1166).

A few contributors do have some worries about personal criticism. Yet, although the Forum is divided into two sections, the
first entitled 'The Inevitability of the Personal' (seventeen
contributors) and the other 'Problems with Personal Criticism'
(nine contributors), there isn't actually much of a difference

between them. Most of the contributors to the second section also stress the virtues of the personal while offering up some reservations. One critic in the first section lists a number of dangers, but thinks they can be overcome. On his danger list are shameless self-indulgence, irrelevance, offering a personal reason for overlooking the obvious, being so entranced with the personal genesis of a theory that one forgets the obligation to mention contrary evidence. Finally, he warns against the potential arrogance of the personal: 'the foregrounding of personal testimony may turn out to be nothing more than an appeal to another kind of authority: my conclusions must be true because I believe them' (1160). Another contributor also stresses the potential authoritarianism and self-enclosure of the personal:

> Perhaps the most immediate concern with the personal in scholarship—or at least the one that seems most troublesome—is related to rebuttal, dialogue, and other interactions in knowledge production. While some may argue that scholarship is not an equal interaction but a genre of communication that intends to silence other voices, the collegial, collective, and communal process of producing, evaluating, and disseminating knowledge is necessary to intellectual activity. The personal seemingly stifles this process by silencing the judgments and critiques of others (1166).

Arrogance, in fact, appears to be the only quality which ends up on both sides of the divide between the personal and the impersonal. Theoretical arguments are taken to be arrogant because they intimidate and silence others, but the same thing is said about expressions of personal experience. The general wish not to silence others appears to express the most widely shared ideal among US literary critics, namely the wish to construct situations in which everyone is equally free to participate in the intellectual (or social or political) conversation. As we shall see, this is an ideal shared by Simone de Beauvoir.

One writer sees the current turn to the autobiographical as a symptom of the *loss* of meaningful individuality: 'Our critics speak personally not for a real self but for a self conceived as representative of an approved ideology, race, or sexual preference—self-stereotyped as subaltern postdeconstructionist, a black male lesbian, and so on' (1164). What emerges here is the difference between the personal understood as any aspect of subjectivity, including quite factual aspects, and the personal taken to mean something like a truly individual perspective on the world.

Finally, some contributors link the turn to the personal to the academic star system. Only a very established critic can permit herself to 'get personal'. 'Call it a matter of class', one critic writes: 'I'm reminded of a colleague who met her dissertation advisor at the convention. He said he was organizing a national conference on subalternity. I asked why he didn't offer her a place. "I'm too subaltern to be subaltern," she replied. She meant she doesn't teach at a distinguished university and hasn't published enough' (1168). In order to indulge in the luxury of the personal, one needs to have tenure, and preferably the power and prestige that may make people interested in one's experiences. In my experience (to get right down to it), the personal in the sense of the autobiographical is not (yet) an option for graduate students, whereas the personal in the sense of 'saying where one is coming from' and indulging in the obligatory denunciations of universality and objectivity has become more or less compulsory for them.

What conclusions can be drawn from the views of the twenty-six contributors to the *PMLA* Forum on the personal? There is a major difference between those who consider that nothing short of autobiographical narrative will do, and those who consider the personal to mean any trace of subjectivity in a text. For some, the statement 'I am a Chinese American woman' is personal, for others Jane Tompkins's descriptions of the weather and her liking for cappuccino are what is required. Others again wish for something like the expression of a person's uniquely individual outlook on the world. Some think that only the first person singular is personal, others see the self or subjectivity transfusing the scholar's text whether she knows it or not. If she doesn't know it, she is a universalizing dinosaur, if she does, she must explicitly signal the fact, or she will become a treacherous purveyor of the universal anyway. Among these critics there is no willingness to grant that even when she does not explicitly say so, a writer might still realize that she is writing as a person, and even as a writing subject situated in history.

When it comes to determining what is to count as 'personal' writing, Anne Fernald's interesting paper on Virginia Woolf and the essay adds some relevant points to the debate in the *PMLA*. Placing the contemporary turn to the personal in its historical context, Fernald reminds us that the tradition of essay-writing from Montaigne to Virginia Woolf embodies the best personal writing Western culture has ever produced. Compared to the works of such forebears, contemporary academics' struggles to get personal appear singularly unimpressive to Fernald. For her, the personal means that which bears the stamp of a unique individual's thought, and not just a generic expression of subject position. The point of writing personally is to convey serious thought in a better and more accessible form than one otherwise could have managed: 'when the personal is brought to the service of an idea, it becomes the most persuasive criticism there is' (187).

Persuasively showing that the mere use of the first person singular or autobiographical narrative is not enough to produce an impression of personal thought, Fernald argues that in contemporary academia the turn to the personal often amounts to a set of not so hidden appeals to the reader to like and admire the writer: 'The problem is [the writer's] desperate desire for us to care for and approve of her and to believe that her interest in her topic is heartfelt', she writes, before adding the *coup de grâce*: 'As to our liking her, no one, in person or in print, has ever come to be liked by pleading for us to like her' (183). For Fernald, Virginia Woolf's essays represent the antithesis to such posturing: 'Woolf tells us something about herself to help bring into focus the complexity of the idea, the seriousness with which she approaches the topic, not because she wants us to like her' (177).

As far as I can see, the *PMLA* Forum contributors tend to agree that the politics of the turn to the personal is to be found in its undermining of discourses of arrogance, mastery, impersonality, objectivity, and universality, in short discourses redolent of the vices usually attributed to theory and philosophy. In this way, the personal does become the political, but only because a certain theory declares that this is the theoretically correct way to undermine the authoritarian universalism of theory. This leaves us with the question of how to write theory at all, a question I will return to in Section II.

Impersonality and Objectivity: Take Two

What struck me most of all in the special issue of the *PMLA* was that nobody seemed to think that subjectivity can become a prison-house from which a few moments of impersonality could offer a delightful respite. Anne Fernald is the only recent critic I have read who makes the point: 'Woolf makes thinking seem personal in part by creating an argument passionately committed to securing "the greatest release of all . . . which is freedom to think of things in themselves" ' (172).[34] As we shall see, Simone de Beauvoir shares Virginia Woolf's sense that one of the major strategies of sexism is to imprison women in their subjectivity, thereby severely curtailing their freedom to transcend the narrow confines patriarchy has prepared for them. Creativity requires the freedom to escape the given, the familiar, and the known as well as the freedom to return to it. Psychoanalytic theory offers us the thought that insofar as we are shackled and bound by our neuroses, the impersonality of the analyst's voice will help us to relate more freely to the world and less compulsively to ourselves. Here, however, the impersonal does not mean the unfeeling or the unsympathetic, it means the fact that the analysand doesn't know anything about the analyst as a person. Contemporary literary critics, however, appear utterly impervious to such ideas: in the late 1990s the impersonal and the objective have overwhelmingly bad press, at least among American critics.

The philosophical ground for the turn to the personal and the rejection of objectivity is the idea that knowledge is 'situated'. A famous feminist version of the claim is that knowledge—all knowledge—is gendered, that 'women's ways of knowing' are different from men's or, in the full-blown version, that 'women's experiences constitute a different view of reality, an entirely different "ontology" or way of going about making sense of the

---

[34] Fernald is quoting Woolf in *A Room of One's Own*. She also reminds us of T. S. Eliot's unfashionable plea for impersonality in 'Tradition and the Individual Talent'.

world' (Stanley and Wise 117). In her wonderful essay 'Knowing
Tornadoes and Other Things', Cora Diamond distinguishes
between strong versions and weak versions of this claim.[35] The
strong version is the one just quoted. Weaker versions will claim,
less dramatically, that in our patriarchal society child development, for instance, will produce

> men who in their mature thought separate subject and object, or
> mind and body, or who think in terms of what belongs to individ-
> uals as such rather than what belongs to them by virtue of webs of
> relationships, as so on. . . . The intellectual structures we find in
> the sciences and in our theorizing about knowledge are suppos-
> edly rooted in the way men shape their identity in the context of
> our child-rearing practices (Diamond 1003).

Diamond points out that both the weak and the strong argument
proceed from 'theories about how a pervasive masculine bias can
or must characterize knowledge in our society' (1004). The alternative, Diamond notes, is to start from what she calls 'epidemio-
logical data', to begin by 'looking at different bodies of
knowledge, bodies of knowledge with different characteristics,
associated with different populations' (1003). 'Whether experience shows something about the world or about the experiencer
depends, and we learn on what, in different contexts, it does
depend', Diamond adds (1006).

Taking her own advice, Diamond goes on to analyse specific
examples of knowledge. First there is the particular scientific
model of knowledge exemplified by meteorology. I will quote
Diamond's description of this at some length, since it seems to
exemplify exactly what postmodern critics deplore the most,
namely the scientific, objective, mode of knowledge:

> The person seeking scientific knowledge of tornadoes, the meteo-
> rologist, can properly ignore all the rich full experience that one
> might get by actual direct experience of a tornado. Science seeks the
> laws governing tornadoes; it does not seek to convey *what it is like* to
> be in a tornado. . . . [I]n the case of the tornado, if you the meteo-
> rologist want an accurate account of the changes in wind-speed and

---

[35] I shall give a fairly detailed summary of Diamond's arguments because I
have the impression that her essay is little known both among feminist theorists
and among literary critics.

direction during the tornado, you do not if you can help it want to rely on the actual experience of people in the tornado's path, what it felt or looked like to them, but rather, if possible, on instruments, because people who have gone through the tornado will exaggerate in their accounts; their accounts will be affected by their emotions and will lack accuracy. The kind of experience relevant to scientific knowledge of tornadoes will be the experience of looking at the output of sophisticated and carefully designed measuring instruments (1006–7).

This model of knowledge, Diamond shows, is fine for tornadoes. Used to study phenomena such as pregnancy or sexuality, however, it leads to the assumption that 'just as you the scientist do not need to consider people's experience of tornadoes, you do not need to consider women's experience of pregnancy' (1007). She then shows that on the tornado model, it is not only women's experiences that fail to qualify as knowledge (their understanding of their lives is *mere* experience, that of their doctors is knowledge), but also the experience of animal trainers:

> when the trainers' experience with dogs or horses is treated by scientists as irrelevant to genuine knowledge, this is precisely because there is in that experience, and in their expression of it, their love of animals. The scientific view is not that sentimentality may distort one's experience . . . it is the far stronger and deeply questionable view that the experience of the person who loves animals reveals only that person's own emotional state (1008).

The fact that the animal trainers whose knowledge is discounted by scientists are often men working in the police force and the army, shows that the tornado model of knowledge is not necessarily gendered, at least not in any simple way.

The tornado model of knowledge is impersonal, Diamond writes, in the sense that the data obtained 'can be compared to the data of others; one's hypotheses can be evaluated by anyone. . . . The ways scientific knowledge is built up detach it from people's particular traits like their maleness' (1010). Diamond stresses that just as there are many different styles of knowledge, there are different sorts of impersonal knowledge. Think of the kind of knowledge one obtains when asking a 'travel agent for information about plane schedules to Detroit. One hopes for a correct answer, the answer one could get from *any* competent travel agent' (1010).

Diamond's point is at once simple and powerful:

> Techniques of impersonal knowledge may themselves be in the service of all sorts of good or bad individual or social projects. The availability, that is, of facts that bear no stamp on them of who, what sort of person, came to those facts, got them into the body of knowledge, serves all sorts of further ends (1011).

It follows that it is actually immensely useful for revolutionaries to have impersonal knowledge lying around. This is precisely the kind of knowledge that can be picked up and put into the service of projects quite different from those which originally motivated the development of that knowledge in the first place. Terry Eagleton once remarked that to discard objectivity is also to discard conflict.[36] Instead of the common terrain necessary to any struggle over different interests and claims, one gets bland consensualism, which works to gloss over conflict in the manner of the most naturalizing ideology.

Diamond finally shows that the kind of knowledge tourists regularly ask for (what is in the soup? where is the post office? is it handmade?) may well be impersonal and objective, but nevertheless 'serves some people's ends much more than those of others. . . . What the right answer is to "Where is the post office?" is independent of the particular person who answers, but there being practice in handling such questions is useful to tourists rather than natives' (1011). To Diamond, this means that 'Knowledge that is impersonal in the sense of being relatively abstract and detached from experience may not be at all impersonal, in the second sense, in that it is tied to the aims of some people rather than others' (1012). Some knowledge is actually gender-free, impersonal and neutral (Diamond's example is $7 + 5 = 12$). Once we recognize this, we can go on to ask whose projects this knowledge serves.

This is a question which will have different answers in different cases. One of the valuable insights emerging from a reading of Cora Diamond's unjustly neglected essay is that impersonal

---

[36]   Private communication.

knowledge—the tornado model—may be put to feminist as well as to non-feminist use. Simone de Beauvoir and Virginia Woolf both thought that knowledge of our actual conditions of life would make the struggle against injustice easier, not more difficult. Audre Lorde agreed. Quoting Simone de Beauvoir, Lorde writes: 'It is in the knowledge of the genuine conditions of our lives that we must draw our strength to live and our reasons for acting' ('Master's Tools' 113). It is precisely because some kinds of knowledge are impersonal in the sense of not bearing the mark of the individual person(s) who first discovered them, that they are available to anyone who needs them. On the other hand, the knowledge of children in a good children's book is personal, Diamond shows. The author's knowledge of children is embodied in the book she wrote for them. It cannot just be picked up and used by someone else without losing some or all of its original features. To reject 'impersonal' or 'objective' knowledge is to reject a mode of knowledge that potentially can be made more democratically available to all than 'personal' knowledge, which per definition remains tied to the person who developed it.

Discussing the reception of *The Second Sex*, Beauvoir writes that it was precisely the objectivity of her tone that irritated her sexist opponents:

> A wild cry of rage, the revolt of a wounded soul—that they could have accepted with a moved and pitying condescension; since they could not pardon me my objectivity, they feigned a disbelief in it. For example I attacked a phrase of Claude Mauriac's because it illustrated the arrogance of the First Sex. 'What has she got against me?' he wanted to know. Nothing; I had nothing against anything except the words I was quoting. It is strange that so many intellectuals should refuse to believe in intellectual passions. (*FC* 200; *FCa* 264; TA)

Beauvoir's irritation at Claude Mauriac's personalizing (*ad hominem*) interpretation of her critique of his writing, as well as her defence of intellectual passions, are timely reminders of the limitations of the personal. Even more important is the fact that the contemporary tendency to bundle objectivity and impersonality together is not shared by Beauvoir. Although she thinks of

The Second Sex as an objective account of women's condition, she doesn't think of it as impersonal in the 'tornado model' sense. The kind of knowledge we find in it does bear the mark of its writer, but this is not enough to deny the text its claim to objectivity. Beauvoir, in short, makes an assumption similar to that of Cora Diamond, namely that the meaning of the word 'objective' is not going to be the same in a philosophical or feminist essay and in meteorology. In the introduction to *The Second Sex* Beauvoir writes:

> But it is doubtless impossible to approach any human problem with a mind free from bias. The way in which questions are put, the points of view assumed, presuppose a hierarchy of interests; all properties [*qualités*] cover [*enveloppe*] values, and there is no so-called objective description which does not imply an ethical background.[37] Rather than attempt to conceal principles more or less definitely implied, it is better to state them openly at the beginning. Then one will not have to specify on every page in just what sense one uses such words as *superior, inferior, better, worse, progress, reaction,* and the like (*SS* xxxiv; *DSa* 30; TA).

For Beauvoir, then, one achieves greater objectivity by stating one's general principles openly, and not by describing what one is wearing at the time of writing.

Instead of worrying about whether a certain insight is 'impersonal' because we assume that it therefore *must* be masculinist and falsely universalizing, we would be better off asking whether the mode of knowledge employed is suitable for the case at hand, and whose purposes the information thus gathered serves. It follows from Diamond's analysis, I think, that we need to ask the same questions of modes of knowledge considered to be 'personal'. Are we engaged in discussing a question where personal insights are relevant and useful? Whose interests does the deployment of the personal serve in the case at hand? Only in this way can we hope to account for the very different effects and purposes to which the personal is put by American TV talk show

---

[37] The French formulation is 'qui ne s'enlève sur un arrière-plan éthique' (30). In Sect. II below, I discuss Beauvoir's use of the expression *s'enlever sur* (*un fond*) at length.

hosts on the one hand and by Virginia Woolf in *A Room of One's Own* on the other.[38]

I shall end this discussion of the difficulties that arise from an uncritical embrace of the personal and the subjective and an equally uncritical dismissal of the impersonal and the objective by turning to Roland Barthes's classical analysis of ideological uses of personal information about writers. We have already seen that some critics find it highly desirable to include in their critical texts information about the writer's person, particularly in the form of autobiographical passages. We have also seen that one or two voices worry about the links between such autobiographical performances and the academic star system. There are in fact striking similarities between a certain form of 'autobiographical performance' in criticism and celebrity journalism.[39] The kind of details Jane Tompkins (and she is far from the only one) considers relevant and pleasurable to present for our consumption is that she is wearing stockings, that she has a famous husband who is into epistemology, that she likes cappuccino, is thinking about going to the bathroom, and that she lives in North Carolina. These are precisely the kind of details Roland Barthes picks up on in his acerbic and very funny piece on 'The Writer on Holiday' collected in that genuinely popular, political, and personal book of criticism called *Mythologies*.[40] This is how Barthes starts his short essay:

[38] To mention some examples of different uses of the personal: in his thoughtful essay on the academic star system David Shumway distinguishes between autobiograpy used 'to make an academic argument' and autobiography used by marginal or oppressed groups to 'establish communal identity' (97). Charles Altieri also stresses 'fostering community' as one function of the critics' turn to autohiography (58, 66).

[39] The connection between the recent turn to the personal and the culture of TV talk shows has been pointed out by many critics: 'the autobiographical move afoot in scholarly writing today is part of a larger trend that I call the Phil Donahue syndrome: the multiplication of talk shows, audience participation shows, call-in shows, and so on, featuring guests who bare it all, figuratively and sometimes literally, before a fascinated audience. Are academics suddenly admitting they have emotions and entrails and genitals, that they have hit their wives, or have to go to the bathroom, or prefer anal sex for the same reasons as the folks on TV, whatever those reasons?' Candace Lang writes (44).

[40] I am grateful to Richard Moran for reminding me to reread Barthes's text.

> Gide was reading Bossuet while going down the Congo. This posture sums up rather well the ideal of our writers 'on holiday', as photographed by *Le Figaro*: to add to mere leisure the prestige of a vocation which nothing can stop or degrade (29).

Barthes's errand is to show that bourgeois French culture in the 1950s represented writers as divine creatures, endowed with a different essence from other workers. When a worker goes on holiday he is nothing but a simple holidaymaker, whereas a writer is always and everywhere a writer. Whenever the writer goes on holiday, the newspaper marvels, he still reads and writes. 'And he who does nothing confesses it as truly paradoxical behaviour, an avant-garde exploit, which only someone of exceptional independence can afford to flaunt' (30). The result is to produce a mystified image of the writer as a deified, sacralized creature, eternally in thrall to his Muse, his divine source of inspiration:

> Thus the function of the man of letters is to human labour rather as ambrosia is to bread: a miraculous, eternal substance, which condescends to take a social form so that its prestigious difference is better grasped. All this prepares one for the same idea of the writers as a superman, as a kind of intrinsically different being . . . (30).

The very representation of the writer's prosaic, everyday existence serves to reinforce this mythological and mystifying picture of what a writer is:

> this myth of 'literary holidays' is seen to spread very far, much farther than summer: the techniques of contemporary journalism are devoted more and more to presenting the writer as a prosaic figure. But one would be very wrong to take this as an attempt to demystify. Quite the contrary. True, it may seem touching, and even flattering, that I, a mere reader, should participate, thanks to such confidences, in the daily life of a race selected by genius. I would no doubt feel that a world was blissfully fraternal, in which newspapers told me that a certain great writer wears blue pyjamas, and a certain young novelist has a liking for 'pretty girls, *reblochon* cheese and lavender-honey'. . . .
>
> To endow the writer publicly with a good fleshly body, to reveal that he likes dry white wine and underdone steak is to make even more miraculous for me, and of a more divine essence, the products of his art (31).

Barthes's analysis presupposes that someone else does the writing. Yet the writer who gives interviews while on holiday participates in the mystifying cult of his own divine essence. If we are to follow Barthes, the academics who indulge in the kind of 'autobiographical performances' where they tell us what they are wearing when they are writing, what kind of food they like, and so on are in fact mythologizing themselves. Since nothing is less unusual than the fact of having a human body that eats, drinks, has sex and wears clothes, such information can only be interesting on the assumption that although we all do these things, it is truly surprising that a *literary critic* should do so. A more narcissistic version would go: although we all know that *other* literary critics do these things, what is truly surprising is that this *particular* literary critic does it. The assumption is that there is something about this specific person, or about the class of people known as literary critics, that is so extraordinary, so godlike as to warrant such exhibitions. As Barthes puts it, 'By having holidays, he displays the sign of his being human; but the god remains, one is a writer as Louis XIV was king, even on the commode' (30).

Barthes's mythologies are intended as a critique of the kind of ideology that seeks to represent as natural that which in fact is socially produced. For Barthes, then, what is reprehensible here is the attempt to represent ordinary human activities as extraordinary simply because a certain social category of people carry them out. But this is not an argument against including ordinary actions and circumstances in theoretical texts. On the contrary, Barthes's scathing critique of more or less self-mythologizing pretentiousness gives us all the more reason to try to write about the ordinary and the everyday in non-mythologizing ways.

Some Preliminary Conclusions

Speaking in the first person about one's own experience easily blocks further discussion. Instead of acknowledging the presence of others, we isolate ourselves, ending up 'all alone and feeling blue'. The insertion of autobiographical performances in literary criticism does not always make the writer vulnerable, since it can just as easily turn into a narcissistic and self-mythologizing performance. As

Anne Fernald shows, only when the personal is in the service of original thought, as in the case of Virginia Woolf, do we experience it as illuminating rather than embarrassing. In my view, the claim that every speech act has something personal in it is true, but precisely for that reason it does not justify explicitly autobiographical writing any more or less than it justifies haughtily impersonal performances. In short, the effects of the personal will depend—on the context, on what the personal is taken to mean in any given case, and on the interests the personal performance is supposed to serve. I have also tried to show that the much maligned impersonality can be experienced as liberating. Just as there are different ways of being personal, there are different ways of being impersonal, and for different purposes. Poetic impersonality, accurate train tables or flight schedules and Diamond's tornado model of knowledge are a few examples of such different ways. The postmodern quest for the personal is a theory-generated attempt to escape from the bad effects of theory, and as such bears all the hallmarks of theoreticism: it is overgeneral, prescriptive, and impervious to experiences running counter to the theory.[41]

Here it must nevertheless be acknowledged that there are at least two routes to the personal. In the case of Jane Tompkins the motivation appears to be classically humanist. This is why she perceives *all* theory as alienating; for her, the goal is to reach her own true humanity, to let her own emotions and feelings shine forth unfettered by theoretical obstruction. Although the end result in many ways is quite similar to, say, the autobiographical performances of Nancy Miller and Jane Gallop, the motivation that drives their turn to the personal appears to be grounded in postmodern considerations concerning the subjectivity of knowledge.[42] This also seems to be the case for just about all the

[41] Insofar as the wish to write autobiographically is theory-driven, the 'person' or 'subject' produced is going to conform to whatever theory the critic prefers. Charles Altieri makes a similar point when he claims that Jane Tompkins's dwelling on her wish to go to the bathroom is 'driven by theoretical considerations about how to write personally, and motivated not by communication but by desires to stage the self for certain effects' (67 n. 3).

[42] I am thinking of Miller's *Getting Personal* and Gallop's *Thinking Through the Body* and *Feminist Accused of Sexual Harassment*.

contributors to the *PMLA* Forum. The true sign of this is the fact that such critics do not, like Jane Tompkins, reject *all* theory. They reject *bad* theory, usually conveniently generalized under the label 'Enlightenment theory'.

The rhetorical move which consists in declaring that what follows is said by a white male bourgeois heterosexual, or by a black lesbian working-class woman usually does not work. Unless there is something in the text that somehow exemplifies what it means to speak as this or that type of subject, one might just as well not bother. As Linda Alcoff puts it, 'Simple unanalyzed disclaimers do not improve on this familiar situation [of oppression] and may even make it worse to the extent that by offering such information the speaker may feel even more authorized to speak and be accorded more authority by his peers' (25).[43]

Attempts to produce autobiographical anecdotes as part of the theoretical text are often quite embarrassing to read. As Wendy Lesser remarks, 'We may at times be embarrassed *by* [the essay-writer], but we should never feel embarrassed *for* him' (quoted in Fernald 171). Autobiographical material can liven up a text, but only if the reader is convinced of the relevance and interest of the material. Even if the narrative included is relevant, there is another question that matters even more: what is the power of the story? Can it function as an example, as a specific case study? Does it challenge us to think further for ourselves? Or does it just invite us to like and admire the author? As I will discuss at length in relation to Simone de Beauvoir, the power of thought developed through careful examination of a particular case can be immense. But the more powerful the thought, the less it matters whether the case is autobiographical or biographical, personal or impersonal, true or fictional.

As for Jane Tompkins's claim that theory prevents us from expressing our emotions, there is some truth in that, at least if she means that one can't write theory and at the same time focus exclusively on one's own rage or elation. At some point there will have to be some widening of perspective, some attempt to universalize, or

---

[43] Alcoff is referring to people in a privileged position. I think the criteria of relevance and power or interest applies to all attempts to 'get personal' or to invoke location.

the experiences described will not be theory. (Raw, courageous autobiography is a wonderful thing to write, but my question throughout this essay is not how to write a good autobiography but how to write good theory.) Although theorists from Darwin to Freud have taken emotions utterly seriously, and although every theoretical inquiry is fuelled by emotion, desire, sexuality, childhood traumas, and so on, once we have pointed out that this is the case, we really shall have to get on with the theoretical inquiry our subjectivity has impelled us to undertake. Whether or not we tell our readers all about the personal motivations for undertaking the work they are reading is a matter of judgement: the criteria of power and relevance still apply.

Cora Diamond's analysis of different modes of knowledge is based on a fundamental methodological stance. To her, very general theoretical arguments purporting to demonstrate that masculine bias *must* exist are unconvincing (see 1004). It is not that she doubts that such bias exists, the question is rather how to demonstrate in a convincing way that it does. As we have seen, Diamond recommends that if we want to find out whether knowledge—some specific kind of knowledge—is gender-biased, we should actually analyse different forms of knowledge. I share Diamond's distrust of arguments about bias and exclusion derived from highly general and abstract theoretical claims. They always take the form of assuming that if the claim is right, then such and such a phenomenon simply *must* be sexist, racist, or whatever. Once this conclusion has been established, no amount of experience to the contrary can prevail. No wonder that the number of musts and shoulds in contemporary theoretical prose is astonishingly high.[44]

Against such theoreticism I too would recommend analysis of the concrete phenomena that interest us. This is the only way to get away from the horrifying grid of binary oppositions that

---

[44] Nina Baym's 1987 essay entitled 'The Madwoman and her Languages: Why I Don't Do Feminist Theory' picks up on this linguistic symptom: ' "she must . . . she must . . . she must." If that *she* is *me*, somebody (once again) is telling me what I "*must*" do to be a true woman, and that somebody is asserting (not incidentally) her own monopoly on truth as she does so. I've been here before' (61 n. 32).

structure so much contemporary theoretical debate on the question of subjectivity and the personal. In this essay I am neither denying nor asserting that the impersonal must be masculinist or exclusionary, or whatever. Instead I am trying to show that there are all kinds of situations and contexts in which the simplistic assumption that the personal = good and impersonal = bad don't hold. At the same time, it is evident that the opposite and equally simplistic assumption (the impersonal = good, the personal = bad) doesn't hold either. Freed from this picture of how things *must* be, we can emerge from the straitjacket of binary oppositions and move into a world in which we might find more than two intellectual alternatives to choose from.

Now, finally, we are in a position to see that the problem with the postmodern turn to the personal is that it is derived from a highly general theory about knowledge (knowledge is always situated; to say so is always necessary and important; claims to objective knowledge are always just a way of imposing the interests of the dominant class or group; and so on). In their style and mode of writing, postmodern theories tend to be as generalizing and universalizing as the Enlightenment theory they oppose (as if there were such a thing as *one* monolithic Enlightenment theory, any more than there is *one* postmodern theory). This kind of theory generates the belief that if we always claim to be speaking *as* the singular individuals we are, then this *must* make our texts less arrogant, less universalizing, less domineering, more properly situated, and perhaps also more capable of reaching out to others.

I have tried to show through numerous examples that such assumptions are by no means generally true. In my discussion of *ad feminam* argumentation, I stress that the turn to the personal needs to be justified by showing what problem it solves. In the same way, I have tried to show that one cannot assume that any attempt to turn to the impersonal is a universalist, patriarchal plot. The analysis of the particular case—of the individual speech act—will tell us whether this is a likely explanation. What I am warning about here, is the tendency to let theoretical parameters block our openness to conflicting and contradictory evidence. If all I ever seek are cases that confirm my theory, the likelihood is that I will find them, but at what intellectual cost?[45]

So what are we left with? In my view, two closely related problems require further examination. The first is: how do I manage to undo the idea that the third person is always exclusionary, always oppressive, always opposed to the first person, or in other words, the belief that the only alternatives we have are either speaking *as* or speaking *for*? At this stage I suspect that such a very limiting way of looking at speech acts may be another one of those pictures that 'hold us captive', as Wittgenstein would say, but I have not shown that this is so. Linda Alcoff makes some very useful points about the difficulty of keeping the first and third person separate, but she does not propose any alternative ways of framing the question.[46] Are there any? The second, related, question is: how do I manage to write in a way that manages to make strong theoretical claims without falling into the trap of overgeneralizing? Theory cannot relinquish its wish to make claims that are valid for others without ceasing to be theory. What I need now

---

[45] Some readers will surely notice that I have said nothing about the 'subject' in this discussion of the turn to the personal. Some defenders of the personal think in terms of a traditional humanist subject, others don't. I find that the question of how the individual critic figures the subject is of very limited interest in this context. It certainly seems to make no difference to their recommendations as to when to 'get personal', for instance. Thus Pamela Caughie criticizes Linda Alcoff for not consistently deconstructing the 'I' (see 'Let It Pass'). Although Caughie declares that she herself knows that her subjectivity is an effect of her own discursive performance (and so on), as far as I can tell, Caughie uses the word 'I' in exactly the same way as Alcoff. It seems to me that what Caughie is asking for—and in this she is by no means alone—is some kind of preliminary metaphysical statement about the nature of 'the subject', after which we continue to use language in exactly the same way as before.

[46] I should add that Alcoff thinks that in some situations it is better to speak for (on behalf of) others than to remain silent. Her insistence on concrete analysis of specific speech acts is very similar to mine. The difference between our analyses is that I don't subscribe to the general idea that we *must* always investigate location, or that impersonal and objective knowledge *must* be sexist, racist, or otherwise oppressive in every case. Alcoff proposes specific analysis as a way to attenuate the consequences of her general theoretical stance, whereas I propose it as a starting point for further discussion. I imagine that in many cases we might reach exactly the same conclusions about the meaning and effects of a given speech act.

is to find a different model, some other path to insight. In short, I need a case study of sufficient power and relevance to advance my understanding of these questions. It is at this juncture that I turn to Simone de Beauvoir and *The Second Sex*.

II. THE SECOND SEX

Introduction

In order to try to answer some of the questions I have raised, I want to study Simone de Beauvoir's philosophical style by taking a close look at the beginning of *The Second Sex*. I shall focus on the first five pages, or the first three paragraphs of the text, starting from the beginning and continuing until Beauvoir reaches her justly famous conclusion that woman is the Other.[47] I should perhaps say, by way of warning, that what follows is an extremely long and detailed close reading of a short excerpt from a philosophical text. The inspiration and energy to undertake such a reading come from my overwhelming frustration that Simone de Beauvoir in general is still not being seriously read among feminist and other theorists.[48]

By philosophical style I mean the way Beauvoir thinks: how she constructs an argument, what kind of examples she uses, how she chooses to express an idea, what kind of vocabulary she draws on, what tone she uses. The word 'style', from the Greek *stulos* (column), is used to describe the difference between a Doric and an Ionic column, or 'the characteristic manner of literary expression of a particular writer, school, a period, etc.'. Style also designates 'a manner of speaking or conversing'. In such contexts, style is often opposed to content: style becomes the manner but not the substance, the clothing that dresses the man, but not the man himself. Style can also refer to a specific person's way of being in

---

[47] I am referring to the first three paragraphs in the two-volume French Folio edition of *Le deuxième sexe* (*DSa* 11–15). In the American 1989 Vintage edition this corresponds to the first *six* paragraphs, or the first four pages (*SS* xix–xxii).

[48] Obviously, I don't mean to include the increasing number of scholars specializing in Beauvoir studies among those who fail to read her works in sufficient detail.

the world: 'a mode or manner of living or behaving; a person's bearing or demeanour'. Taken in this sense, the form/content opposition is not necessarily in play; we have arrived at Buffon's 'Le style est l'homme même' ('the style is the person', to paraphrase a little).

The word 'method' has interesting affinities to style, and comes from the Greek *methodos*, a word produced by combining *meta* (with, after) with *hodos* (way). When I say that I want to study the *way* Beauvoir thinks, etymologically speaking this means that I want to consider her method. Unlike style, however, method can mean 'systematic arrangement, order', or 'order in thinking or expressing thoughts'. A method is often taken to be an underlying plan or grid that can be uncovered and abstracted from the finished work. In this sense, method comes to mean something like a set of general principles for how to go about things. But method can also mean a 'mode of procedure; a (defined or systematic) way of doing a thing in accordance with a particular theory or as associated with a particular theory or as associated with a particular person'. To speak of Beauvoir's method in this latter sense would simply be to speak of a way of thinking associated with her person, and with existentialist philosophy. When method is used in this sense, philosophical method and philosophical style become virtually interchangeable terms. The kind of inquiry I want to undertake here is situated precisely on the level where method shades into style, or in other words: when philosophy shades into literary criticism.

Insofar as the concept of style still tends to conjure up binaries such as style/substance, surface/depth, and form/content, I should say that these terms do not have to be seen as mutually exclusive. To read *for* style is not necessarily to read *against* content: these two terms do not always operate on different sides of a divide. To read for philosophical style is to ask *how* something is being said without in the least neglecting or ignoring *what* is being said. Fundamentally intertwined, form and content, style and substance (or whatever terms we prefer) collaborate in the production of meaning. It is confusing and unhelpful to pit them against each other. Style is therefore not well understood if one thinks of it as a surface which either conceals or conveys the real meaning lurking in the depths beneath the rhetorical effects. The *what* is not 'deeper' than the *how:* they are both right there, in our words.

One final introductory note: I do not mean to imply that Beauvoir's style is uniform and unvarying throughout *The Second Sex*. What I am claiming is that the pages I am about to analyse are characteristic of her thought at its best. I will show that Beauvoir arrives at the claim that woman is the Other not through metaphysical speculation but through analysis of expressions and anecdotes from everyday life. I will also show that her argument gains much of its impressive power from the way she uses herself as a philosophical case study, or in other words, from the way in which she makes the personal do philosophical work for her. It will also emerge from my reading that Beauvoir's way of writing philosophy has strong affinities with ordinary language philosophy, particularly with the work of Stanley Cavell. When these affinities are brought out, Beauvoir's work gains new dimensions, not least when it comes to the question that interests me here, namely what Beauvoir's philosophical style can teach us about the personal and the philosophical.

The Style is the Philosopher

To convey more concretely what I mean by 'philosophical style' and what difference style can make, I will start by briefly comparing the beginning of *The Second Sex* to the beginning of another influential feminist text, Luce Irigaray's *Speculum of the Other Woman*. Both books start by raising the question of femininity, yet the first few lines in each text immediately reveal interesting differences in philosophical style. This is how *The Second Sex* begins:

> I have hesitated for a long time to write a book on woman. The subject is irritating, especially to women; and it is not new. The quarrel over feminism has spilt enough ink, and now it is more or less over: let's talk no more about it. It is still talked about, however. It seems that all the voluminous nonsense uttered during the last century has done little to illuminate the problem. After all, is there a problem? And if so, what is it? Are there women, really? Most assuredly the theory of the eternal feminine still has its adherents

who will whisper in your ear: 'Even in Russia women still are *women*'; and other well informed persons—sometimes the very same—say with a sigh: 'Woman is losing her way, woman is lost.' We [*on*] no longer know if women still exist, if they will always exist, whether or not it is desirable that they should, what place they occupy in this world, what place they should occupy in it. 'Where are the women?' an ephemeral magazine recently asked. But first: what is a woman? (*SS* xix; *DSa* 12; TA).[49]

'I' is the first word of *The Second Sex*. 'J'ai longtemps hésité à écrire un livre sur la femme', Beauvoir writes.[50] In this way she introduces herself firmly yet unobtrusively as the author of her own text. To my ears, this does not sound like a phenomenological or metaphysical I, but like the everyday I of the person who is writing the philosophical text we are about to read.[51] A few pages later we will learn that there is nothing easy or self-evident about this woman's claim to philosophical authority and authorship, yet here, at the outset, Beauvoir chooses to write as if it goes without saying that she has the right to start her essay by saying I in such an unremarkable way.

In the passage quoted the dominant pronouns are I and we, but the French *on* also makes an appearance. The characteristic value of *on* is that it always includes the speaker: according to context it may be translated either as 'one' or 'we'. The text is also punctuated by a number of questions that appear to be addressing the

[49] The usual problems with the English translation of *The Second Sex* are everywhere apparent in the first few pages. I amend the translation as necessary. In English the last sentence of this quotation appears as the first sentence in the second paragraph of the text. In French, on the other hand, the first three pages constitute one long paragraph.

[50] In Parshley's translation the first sentence reads: 'For a long time I have hesitated to write a book on woman'. This loses the effect Beauvoir creates by starting her book with 'I'.

[51] Some readers may still want to challenge the idea that *The Second Sex is* a philosophical text. By now, however, the depth and intensity of Beauvoir's philosophical engagement has surely been established beyond doubt. Texts such as Le Dœuff, *Hipparchia's Choice*; Kruks, *Situation*; Lundgren-Gothlin, *Sex*; Bergoffen; Vintges; and the still unpublished work by Bauer all demonstrate the philosophical interest of Beauvoir's great essay. The question of what it may mean to take Beauvoir seriously as an original philosopher, however, is far from settled. Bauer in particular asks pertinent questions about how to read Beauvoir once we have agreed that she is to be read as a philosopher.

reader. These are not necessarily rhetorical questions, in the sense that they do not always take for granted that everyone knows what the right answer is.[52] By asking 'is there a problem?' Beauvoir encourages the reader to consider for herself whether she thinks there is a problem, what she thinks a woman is, and whether she thinks these are good questions. Initially, at least, Beauvoir's text presents itself as an invitation to the reader to make up her own mind about the questions it is exploring.

There is also a great deal of irony in the text. Beauvoir's dead-pan quotation of silly ideas about women is an attempt to send up the 'mythologies' of everyday life, to use Roland Barthes's expression. But her irony is not entirely dismissive: the fact that there are misguided believers in the eternal feminine helps Beauvoir to demonstrate that the question of what a woman is and what her role in the world should be, is far from settled. The initial 'let's talk no more about it' is countered by evidence that nonsensical ideas about women still prevail. By claiming that the very same connoisseurs declare both that the eternal feminine never disappears and that woman is lost, Beauvoir reveals the confusion of sexist thought. By being ironical about the confusion of others, Beauvoir justifies the writing of *The Second Sex* by presenting it as an exercise in lucidity. Towards the end of the introduction, she makes this point explicitly: 'It is striking', she writes, 'that everything women write [*l'ensemble de la littérature féminine*] these days is animated less by a wish to demand our rights than by an effort toward lucidity. As we emerge from an era of wild polemics, this book is offered as one attempt among others to analyse our position' (*SS* xxxiii–xxxiv; *DSa* 29–30; TA).[53] For Beauvoir, the lucidity

---

[52] The OED defines a 'rhetorical question' as one that is 'asked not for information but to produce effect'. The example given is *who cares?* for *nobody cares*. Much more could be said about rhetorical questions, but this is not the place to do so.

[53] Parshley's curiously biased translation of the phrase *l'ensemble de la littérature féminine* is 'books by women on women'. And in the last sentence quoted, Beauvoir writes: 'ce livre est une tentative parmi d'autres pour faire le point'. Parshley's translation here is even more bizarre: 'this book is offered as one attempt among others to confirm that statement [about the lucidity of women's writing]'. Admittedly, *faire le point* is difficult to translate well. The expression is nautical in origins, and originally meant to find one's bearings, to find out

and objectivity of philosophy permit her to overcome and undo sexist ideology.[54]

Irony is a matter of tone: either we hear it or we don't. The more subtle the irony, the more it tends to split the audience between those who get it and those who don't. Among the readers who do get it, moreover, there are usually some who don't particularly enjoy the experience. For irony is a rhetorical manœuvre which can make the very act of understanding the author's point feel invasive and contaminating. To get the irony of a text, the reader has to be able to imagine the author's point of view, if only for the briefest moment. Resisting readers hear the irony, but resent not only its ideological point, but the very fact that they have been made to see what the world looks like from a politically alien point of view. Feminists exposed to sexist irony have ample experience of what it feels like to be caught in this rhetorical trap. As the French reception of the book showed, sexist readers of *The Second Sex* reacted with fury to Beauvoir's unerring targeting of their cherished beliefs in the eternal feminine. Whatever its fate among actual readers, irony is an invitation to the reader to share the writer's critical attitude to the object of the irony. It is up to the reader to notice the invitation, to decide whether to accept or decline it, whether to smile in delighted recognition or groan in exasperated resentment. However we react, to listen for irony is to listen for the attitude of the speaking subject. Like Beauvoir's use of 'I' and 'we', her irony also signals her presence in the text.

Turning now to *Speculum of the Other Woman*, we notice that Irigaray starts her book not by asserting her own subjectivity, but by masking her voice:

---

where one is on the map. It is commonly used to mean 'produce an overview', 'produce an analysis', and could very well be translated as 'to take stock'. *Le point sur . . .* means something like 'an overview of the relevant issues concerning . . .'. This meaning is echoed in the title of the French political magazine *Le point.*

[54] This does not mean that she thinks one can be objective in the sense of producing value-free descriptions. See pp. 159–60, above for a brief discussion of her understanding of objectivity and impersonality. In *The Second Sex* this discussion follows directly after the passage about lucidity quoted here.

'Ladies and Gentlemen ... Throughout history people have knocked their heads against the riddle of the nature of femininity—... Nor will *you* have escaped worrying over this problem— those of you who are men; to those of you who are women this will not apply—you are yourselves the problem.'[55]

So it would be a case of you men speaking among yourselves about woman, who cannot be involved in hearing or producing a discourse that concerns the *riddle*, the logogriph she represents for you. The enigma that is woman will therefore constitute the *target*, the *object*, the *stake*, of a masculine discourse, of a debate among men, which would not consult her, would not concern her. Which, ultimately, she is not supposed to know anything about (*Speculum* 13).

In the first sentence, Irigaray ventriloquizes or mimics the voice of Freud. The dominant pronoun in Freud's original text is the plural you (*vous*), and so it is in the paragraph following the Freud quotation, in which Irigaray muses on Freud's text. While Freud's 'you' addresses first men and then women, Irigaray's 'you' is defined as male. Although it erases all explicit markings of the subject position of the speaker, the impassioned opening passage of *Speculum* leaves the reader in little doubt about where Irigaray is and what her views are. In fact, Irigaray's ironic use of quotations focuses attention on the attitude of the speaker. After reading Irigaray's first paragraph the reader is bound to ask whether she is expected to agree with Freud or challenge him. The next paragraph tells her exactly what to think. Just as Beauvoir quotes the believers in the eternal feminine, Irigaray quotes Freud. Simply by quoting him, she produces a certain distance between the reader and Freud; and by being ironical about the quote she invites the reader to share her attitude, to hear Freud's words in the same way as she does. To quote someone is a speech act like any other: the responsibility for the quotation lies with the speaker. To quote someone ironically, moreover, is certainly not to efface one's own voice; on the contrary, it is to lay bare one's trust in that voice.

[55] At this point a footnote in the text, in French as well as in English, signals that Irigaray is quoting Freud's fictive lecture on femininity from *New Lectures on Psycho-Analysis*.

Beauvoir and Irigaray both trust that their own tone will convey their point. Irigaray's constant use of ironic quotations—her famous mimicry—is an invitation to the reader to share the speaker's attitude and evaluations.[56] In *Speculum*, Irigaray's Plotinus chapter ('Une mère de glace') is a wonderful example of this.[57] Located near the middle of the book, the chapter is composed entirely of quotations, without a single word of commentary. Irigaray is gambling on the idea that having read so far, the reader will be so immersed in her arguments, so used to her tone, her way of quoting male thinkers ironically, that no more commentary is necessary. The gamble pays off, I think. By the time they reach the Plotinus chapter most readers of *Speculum of the Other Woman* are ready to read him in the way Irigaray herself would have done it, thus taking a chapter composed entirely of quotations to be a critique, not a simple report or summary.[58] Thus, in an act of astonishing rhetorical brilliance, Irigaray manages to convey her critique of Plotinus by relying almost entirely on tone.[59]

Beauvoir's and Irigaray's styles both emphasize the question of who is speaking, and more particularly, the question of whether women have the right to speak the language of philosophy. Clearly Beauvoir's existentialist and Irigaray's psychoanalytic approach lead them to raise similar questions about subjectivity. Yet, at the same time, the difference between Irigaray's emphatic 'you' and Beauvoir's unassuming 'I' indicates that the two women

[56] Naomi Schor defines Irigaray's mimesis (*mimétisme*) as follows: '[It has] been widely and correctly interpreted as describing a parodic mode of discourse designed to deconstruct the discourse of misogyny through effects of amplification and rearticulation that work, in Mary Ann Doane's words, to "enact a defamiliarized version of femininity" ' ('This Essentialism' 53).

[57] The Plotinus chapter has the same title both in the French and English. In French the title contains two puns, on *mère/mer* (mother/ocean) and the double meaning of *glace* (ice/mirror). Irigaray signals by an initial footnote that Plotinus is being quoted (see *Speculum* 168–79; *Spéculum* 210–26).

[58] As with other uses of irony, Irigaray's irony will not only create a split between readers who read the chapter ironically and those who don't, but also between the readers who gladly join in the critique of Plotinus, and those who resist doing so, although they full well understand that they are intended to.

[59] 'Almost', because the selection of the quotations and their organization also helps to produce the desired effect.

will respond differently to the question of sexual difference. By placing her own everyday 'I' on the philosophical scene, Beauvoir indicates that she thinks of the ordinary and the everyday as integral to her philosophical project of analysing women's situation. Irigaray's masking of the speaking subject, on the other hand, seeks to foreground the thought that a woman under patriarchy is doomed to mimicry, not least when she wants to write philosophy. To my ears, however, there is a great deal of tension between Irigaray's evident trust in the power of her own tone of voice, and her belief that as a woman writing under patriarchy she will somehow never find her own words. In Irigaray the ordinary plays no philosophical role. Unlike Beauvoir, Irigaray doesn't quote gossip and hearsay or ephemeral student publications. In short, Beauvoir's and Irigaray's different attitudes towards the use of the first person singular and the ordinary and everyday are symptomatic of their different understanding of what philosophy is, how it should be written, and in what voice women can speak of or to the philosophical tradition.

What this brief comparison shows is that a writer's philosophical style reveals a great deal about her philosophical purpose and attitude. Whatever rhetorical strategies a writer uses, it is always possible to detect in them traces of her subjectivity.[60] Read in this way, philosophical style becomes a record of subjectivity.

'What Is a Woman?' Beauvoir's Rejection of Essentialism and Nominalism

On the first page of *The Second Sex* Beauvoir asks 'What is a woman?' Her answer is an ironic expression of exasperation with sexist replies to the question:

> All agree in recognizing the fact that females [*des femelles*] exist in the human species, today as always they make up about one half of humanity.[61] And yet we are told that 'femininity is in danger'; we are exhorted to 'be women, remain women, become women'.

[60] It does not follow, of course, that we always *have* to read for the writer's subjectivity. We still need to show why it is relevant and important to do so in a particular case.

[61] I discuss Beauvoir's distinction between *femelle* and *femme* in Ch. 1, above.

> Therefore every female human being is not necessarily a woman; to be so considered she must share in that mysterious and threatened reality known as femininity. Is this attribute something secreted by the ovaries? Or is it fixed in a Platonic heaven?[62] Is a rustling petticoat enough to bring it down to earth? (*SS* xix; *DSa* 11–12; TA).

What makes this passage ironic is Beauvoir's pretence of taking absurd ideas seriously by bringing philosophical logic to bear on them. The series of questions that closes the passage are intended at once to make us laugh at the confusions of sexist common sense and to show that philosophical reason will help us to break the hold of such everyday mythologies. Like Descartes, Beauvoir considers reason an instrument of liberation available to everyone.[63]

Precisely because she believes that she has as good a grasp on reason as everyone else, Beauvoir refuses to accept uncritically whatever philosophers have had to say about women. Essentialist thinkers get short shrift: 'In the times of St. Thomas [femininity] was considered an essence as certainly defined as the somniferous virtue of the poppy', she writes. 'But conceptualism has lost ground', she continues, so that today femininity is considered by biologists and social scientists to be the effect of a *situation*. The conclusion is clear: 'If today femininity no longer exists, then it never existed' (*SS* xix; *DSa* 12).[64]

---

[62] '[Est-elle] figée au fond d'un ciel platonicien?', Beauvoir writes, obviously assuming that her readers instantly will grasp the reference to Platonic essences. Parshley's translation rewrites and expands the point, probably in the belief that without explicit help, American readers might miss the reference: 'Or is it a Platonic essence, a product of the philosophical imagination?'

[63] Nancy Bauer provides a thoughtful discussion of Beauvoir's philosophical relationship to Descartes: 'the routine condemnations of Descartes in the feminist philosophical literature overlook what is productively radical about the Cartesian method of doubt. In these aspects, this method [is]—not accidentally—exactly that employed by Beauvoir in *The Second Sex*. Far from wishing to assimilate Beauvoir and Descartes on every count, however, I will argue that the different *motivations* underlying each thinker's inquiry decisively separate them. Specifically, whereas Descartes' goal is to provide a firm foundation for the sciences, Beauvoir wants to write truthfully about herself . . .' (60).

[64] Beauvoir develops the notion of situation at great length in *The Second Sex*. I discuss it in some detail in Ch. 1, above.

The next question follows logically: 'But does the word *woman*, then, have no content?' (*SS* xx; *DSa* 12; TA). Enlightenment thinkers, rationalists, and nominalists would say that it doesn't, Beauvoir writes. For them, women are 'merely the human beings arbitrarily designated by the name *woman*' (*SS* xx; *DSa* 12). At this point, Beauvoir chooses to give an example. American women are particularly inclined to agree with such mistaken views, she writes, producing Dorothy Parker as her evidence: 'I cannot be just to books which treat of woman as woman. . . . My idea is that all of us, men as well as women, should be regarded as human beings', Parker writes, at least according to Beauvoir (*SS* xx; *DSa* 12).[65] This kind of humanism is instantly dismissed: 'But nominalism is a rather inadequate doctrine', she continues, 'and the antifeminists have had no trouble in showing that women simply *are not* men:

> Surely woman is, like man, a human being; but such an assertion is abstract. The fact is that every concrete human being is always in a specific situation [*spécifiquement situé*].[66] To refuse to accept such notions as the eternal feminine, the black soul, the Jewish character, is not to deny that Jews, Negroes, women exist today—this denial does not represent a liberation for those concerned, but rather an inauthentic flight. Clearly, no woman can without bad faith pretend to be situated beyond her sex (*SS* xx; *DSa* 13; TA).[67]

[65] Here it becomes clear that Beauvoir does not imagine that she is writing for an audience of American readers.

[66] This passage reminds me of Sartre's 1946 text *Réflexions sur la question juive* (translated as *Anti-Semite and Jew*) where he criticizes 'the tendency that we have noted in many democrats who wish purely and simply to suppress the Jew in favour of the *man*. But *man* does not exist: there are Jews, Protestants, Catholics; there are Frenchmen, Englishmen, Germans; there are white, black, and yellow people' (175; my translation).

[67] Disastrously, the last sentence is omitted in Parshley's translation. This omission is particularly galling since it deprives the English-language reader of evidence that Beauvoir does not at all think of sexual difference as something to be avoided or denied. The rest of his translation of this passage is also full of philosophical howlers. When Beauvoir declares that every human being is always in a specific situation, Parshley has her say that 'every concrete human being is always a singular, separate individual'. When she claims that to deny that women, Jews, and blacks exist is not a liberation, but an 'inauthentic flight', Parshley has her say that it is a 'flight from reality', thus losing the reference to bad faith that is implied in the adjective *inauthentique*.

What Beauvoir attacks here is both the post-Enlightenment humanism which hopes to make all differences disappear by insisting on our common humanity ('we are all human beings'), and the nominalist idea that sex and/or gender are nothing but the effects of discourse, an arbitrarily applied signifier. Both types of argument lose sight of the fact that women exist in the world. To pretend to be beyond one's sex or race is to be in bad faith. At this point, Beauvoir produces three examples supplementing the quote from Dorothy Parker. The first concerns a woman writer who didn't want her photograph in a series of pictures devoted to women writers, but wanted it to be included among the pictures of famous male writers. In order to achieve this, she used the influence of her husband. The second is about a young, frail Trotskyite woman who wanted to get into a fist fight at a political meeting because she was in love with a young activist and wanted to be his equal. Finally, there is a quick reference to the 'attitude of defiance' that American women are stuck in. According to Beauvoir, American women refuse to accept the fact that they are women, and in so doing show that they are obsessed by that very fact.

The most significant thing about these examples is that they are there at all. That the inclusion of three everyday examples and a quote from a book review by a middlebrow woman writer is a significant stylistic feature in a book of philosophy is obvious. In comparison, there are no such examples in Irigaray's *Speculum of the Other Woman*, and only two in Judith Butler's *Gender Trouble*.[68] Taken from

[68] If I have overlooked examples in *Speculum*, I hope someone will correct me. In *Gender Trouble* I may also have missed some cases. The two I have in mind are, first, the example concerning the scientists who decided to classify a person with XX chromosomes and anatomically ambiguous genitalia as male (see *Gender Trouble* 106–11), and, second, the various references to male drag shows, used as examples of the destabilizing and subversive effects of playing gender against sex.

My point is not that one approach is intrinsically preferable to another, but rather that a theorists' use or non-use of examples is revealing of her philosophical stance. Different kinds of theory tend to generate different attitudes to examples. The highly abstract and generalizing nature of much poststructuralist theory is bound to produce the feeling that examples are irrelevant to the argument at hand. The paucity of examples then reinforces the impression that the text is overgeneralizing. Beauvoir's existentialism, on the other hand, cannot proceed without analysis of concrete cases. I shall return to the question of the value and effect of examples, particularly anecdotes.

her own observations, from stories her friends have told her, from the literary gossip in Paris, and from a book review that Beauvoir probably read on her trip to America in 1947, Beauvoir's examples are strikingly ordinary and unpretentious. This fact alone has surely contributed to the belief that a book based on such evidence cannot possibly be taken seriously as philosophy.

Since Beauvoir's use of examples in this passage is such a significant aspect of her philosophical style, I shall study them in some detail. First of all, I suspect that the quote attributed to Dorothy Parker is made up from memory, and misattributed to boot. Here is the context of Beauvoir's reference to Parker:

> American women, in particular, are prepared to think that there is no longer any place for woman as such; if a backward individual still takes herself for a woman, her friends advise her to be psychoanalyzed and thus get rid of this obsession. In regard to a work, *Modern Woman: The Lost Sex*, which, incidentally, is highly irritating, Dorothy Parker has written: 'I cannot be just to books which treat of woman as woman. ... My idea is that all of us, men as well as women, should be regarded as human beings'. But nominalism is a rather inadequate doctrine, and the antifeminists have had no trouble in showing that women simply *are not* men (*SS* xx; *DSa* 12–13; TA).

Beauvoir is notoriously inaccurate in her references, and she has a particularly infuriating tendency to get names and titles wrong.[69] I was not entirely surprised, therefore, to discover that in spite of considerable effort, I could not trace the quote attributed to Dorothy Parker. The book Parker is supposed to have reviewed, and which Beauvoir seems to have read, since she says it is 'highly irritating', is Ferdinand Lundberg and Marynia Farnham's controversial, sexist, and deeply essentialist *Modern Woman: The Lost Sex*, which was published in New York in January 1947.[70] The

[69] In the French text, the title of the book is given as *Modern Woman: A Lost Sex*.

[70] The major point of *Modern Woman* is that women in 1947 fail to have orgasms because they do not devote themselves entirely to husband and children. To work outside the home is to give in to masculine strivings. The ideal woman is totally feminine; to try to combine femininity and masculinity is impossible: 'The plain fact is that increasingly we are observing the masculinization of women and with it enormously dangerous consequences to the home, the children (if any) dependent on it, and to the ability of the woman, as well as her

standard bibliography of Dorothy Parker's work shows that Parker did not write book reviews in 1947. Nor does she seem to have written anything else of relevance to the theme.[71]

Beauvoir arrived in New York on 25 January and left for Paris on 17 May 1947. *America Day by Day* shows that she read American newspapers, magazines, and literary and political journals avidly throughout her stay.[72] There were a number of prominent reviews of *Modern Woman: The Lost Sex* in the spring of 1947, some of which Beauvoir is bound to have seen. In fact, it probably was one of the first American books to come to her attention during her trip to the United States. *Modern Woman* was negatively reviewed by Margaret Mead in the *New York Times* on 26 January, the day after Beauvoir's arrival in New York. I can't imagine that Beauvoir failed to run out to buy the leading American newspaper on the first day of her stay, a day which she spent walking around Manhattan, according to the account of it in *America Day by Day*. Nor can I imagine that she skipped a review of a book so relevant to her own work on *The Second Sex*, which she was in the middle of writing when she left for the United States. *Modern Woman* instantly became highly controversial, not least among American intellectuals. Mary McCarthy, whom Beauvoir met several times that spring, published the most brilliant and by far the funniest review of the book ('Tyranny of the Orgasm') in the *New Leader* on 5 April. But neither Mead nor McCarthy make the point that Beauvoir attributes to Parker.

---

husband, to obtain sexual gratification' (235). This kind of thing goes on for 500 pages. The book may well be one of the examples Beauvoir has in mind when she criticizes the tendency to think in terms of 'femininity' and 'masculinity'.

[71] My source here is Randall Calhoun, *Dorothy Parker: A Bio-Bibliography*. This book is not totally reliable. (Parker's story 'Song of the Shirt, 1941' is listed as appearing in the *New Yorker* in 1947, in spite of the fact that it appeared, as the title indicates, in 1941.) I nevertheless find it hard to believe that Calhoun would have overlooked a review of a widely noticed and much debated book.

[72] Already on 5 Feb. she writes: 'During this first week I had been too enchanted by my discovery of New York to be depressed by my reading of the daily and weekly papers, but this morning all the anger and fear I had suppressed make my heart heavy' (*L'Amérique* 61, my translation; see *America* 41 for the English translation). As this book was going to press, Carol Cosman's excellent new translation was published. Page references are to this edition, far superior to the old 1953 translation.

Although I couldn't find anything by Dorothy Parker that even remotely connected her to *Modern Woman: The Lost Sex*, there is a connection of sorts between Parker and the book. On 22 February 1947 Marynia Farnham, New York psychoanalyst and co-author of *Modern Woman*, wrote an article on women's writing in *The Saturday Review of Literature* entitled 'The Pen and the Distaff'. This was the lead article of the week, and prominently featured three photographs of women writers on the first page. The first of these was of Dorothy Parker, with the caption 'Dorothy Parker, defying attempts at pigeon-holing, has something of a corner on unrelieved hostility toward both sexes' (7). This sentence is repeated in the text. Farnham sees Parker as an exception to her general rule, which is that most women writers display an 'intense hostility to men' (29). It is of course more than possible that Beauvoir read something by Parker that I haven't been able to find.[73] In the absence of more relevant evidence, however, Farnham's article does establish a connection between *Modern Woman* and Parker that might explain Beauvoir's misattribution.

Farnham's article would have struck Beauvoir, an *agrégée* in philosophy, with particular force, since the photograph under that of Dorothy Parker is of Ayn Rand, with the caption 'Ayn Rand, of "The Fountainhead", and another non-categorite, shows a rare preoccupation with a philosophical problem'.[74] The text running next to this picture confidently states that history, politics, and economics are a man's world, and then continues: 'Philosophy finds us in like case. There is no woman's name in the philosophical roster. The indication would appear that women have little interest in the problems of man's relation to the moral world' (7). This is Farnham's conclusion:

> [Women] leave aside with barely a nod the broad abstractions, the great struggles of man's spirit with the material or moral world. They do not strive with logic. Theirs is the immediate, the sensed and intuitively known, the deeply felt, the life of the heart. These

[73] All credit for the laborious research that went into the question of what Parker did or did not write in 1947 goes to my research assistant, Virginia Tuma.

[74] For the sake of completion, the third photograph is of Lillian Smith, with the caption 'Lillian Smith consistently displays an equally rare concern with a social disaster' (Farnham 7).

things fit neatly into what is known and observed about the essentially feminine which remains much unchanged—the intimate, personal, immediate, and intuitive (30).

Other reviews of *Modern Woman* do make the point that Beauvoir attributes to Parker, but not in exactly the same words. Thus Dorothy Van Doren, reviewing in the *New York Herald Tribune Weekly Book Review* on 9 February, writes that she found the book 'deeply disturbing' because she cannot accept that 'man, including woman . . . should be categorized, reproached and stigmatized solely on the performance of his or her reproductive system', and then concludes that the book misses out on the 'most exquisite and complex [organ in man], the one which cannot be seen by mortal eye. It is what makes man a man' (16). Van Doren's insistence on the invisible but essential humanity that makes 'man, including woman' a man, is a strong candidate for Beauvoir's criticism of humanist nominalism. The fact that her first name is Dorothy is one reason why Beauvoir might have thought of Dorothy Parker in this context.[75]

Beauvoir's analysis does not depend on the historical accuracy of her reference. Even if Dorothy Parker never said what Beauvoir thinks she said, there is plenty of evidence that this kind of nominalism was common in America at the time. As I have shown, there is also evidence that it was a common reaction to Lundberg and Farnham's book. What Beauvoir requires to make her argument stick is an example, whether made-up or not, that the reader will accept as illuminating of the problem at stake. (I shall return to the question of why Beauvoir's examples do not need to be empirically true.)

Beauvoir's next three examples are intended to exemplify and expand on her rejection of nominalism. They follow the claim that 'no woman can without bad faith pretend to be situated beyond her sex'. The first case is that of the well-known woman writer:

[75] Reviewing in the *New Republic* on 10 Feb. 1947, Frederic Wertham rejects *Modern Woman* on similar grounds: 'After all, most of what we know about women and their share of the suffering in the world is universally human and not specifically female. This book dehumanizes the whole question and treats women in a way that is belittling, unfair and fundamentally untrue' (38).

Some years ago a well-known woman writer refused to permit her portrait to appear in a series of photographs especially devoted to women writers; she wished to be counted among the men, but in order to gain this privilege she made use of her husband's influence. Women who assert that they are men lay claim none the less to consideration and respect from men (*SS* xx; *DSa* 13; TA).

I have an idea that Beauvoir has Colette in mind. But I can't prove it, since I haven't been able to find the 'series of photographs' in question.[76] This story seems to me to be typical of a certain French kind of intellectual gossip, and as such it is not necessarily more accurate than the Dorothy Parker reference. Again, the point is not whether we believe that Colette or any other well-known woman writer in France did this, but whether we believe that some woman in such a position might have done something like this.

The next example concerns the young Trotskyite: 'I recall also a young Trotskyite standing on a platform at a boisterous meeting and getting ready to use her fists, in spite of her evident fragility', Beauvoir writes. 'She was denying her feminine weakness; but it was for love of a militant male whose equal she wished to be' (*SS* xx; *DSa* 13). Here Beauvoir presents the example as a personal recollection. And in this case, she remembers accurately. The young Trotskyite alluded to here is the French writer and lifelong socialist activist Colette Audry (1906–90), who was Beauvoir's colleague at the *lycée* Jeanne d'Arc in Rouen from 1932 to 1936, and who remained a lifelong friend and supporter of Beauvoir and Sartre. Audry's book of memoirs, *La statue* (1983), shows that Beauvoir became a good friend to her in 1932, precisely at a time when Audry was struggling with an impossible and contradictory passion for another young Trotskyite.

> [In 1936] I already had four years of politics behind me, all burdened, illuminated, shaken by a happy and unhappy love affair, which I could not finish, and which I don't want to write about. . . . My friend was only two years older than me, but he had entered into politics seven or eight years before me, and mathematics had prepared him to move easily among economic facts. Thus I found myself yet again in the situation of a student, a situation I no longer

---

[76] Perhaps a Colette scholar can put me right.

wanted. . . . Above all, I obscurely felt that to be in such a situation with a man placed me in great danger. I rejected it furiously. This was deep-rooted weakness of character or plain stupidity. Because I was a woman I despaired of my strength, I despaired of ever controlling the situation, and I would not admit it. . . . To put an end to the story: I did have the love, but I lost the man. It is enough to say that thirty years later neither of the two had forgotten—what one calls forgetting. That matters in a life, after all.

As I was going through this difficult time, I was not reduced to my own resources. One morning in October 1932, a young woman with blue eyes came up to me in the teachers' room and wanted to get acquainted. It was the recently arrived Mlle de Beauvoir (*Statue* 206–7).

Finally, there is the reference to the American women: 'The clenched attitude of defiance of American women proves that they are haunted by a sense of their femininity' (*SS* xx; *DSa* 13; TA).[77] This is Beauvoir's own assessment of women's condition in America. Her thought is that although American women insist that they are 'men', their endless defiance and bitter recriminations reveal their sense of being at a disadvantage because they are women. This is a theme Beauvoir had recently developed in *America Day by Day*:

That American women are not really on a tranquil equal footing with men is proved by their attitude of protest [*revendication*] and defiance. They despise, and often rightly so, the servility of Frenchwomen, always ready to smile at their men and to put up with their moods, but the clenched tension they display on the pedestal masks the same amount of weakness. Whether they are docile or demanding, the man remains king: he is the essential, woman the inessential; the praying mantis is the antithesis of the submissive servant girl in the harem, but both depend on the male. The Hegelian dialectic of master and slave is confirmed in this domain, too: the woman who wants to be an idol is really subject to her worshippers. Her whole life is consumed in ensnaring the man and keeping him subject to her law (*L'Amérique* 453–4; my translation).[78]

---

[77] 'L'attitude de défi dans laquelle se crispent les Américaines . . .'. The difficulty is to render *se crisper* adequately. The verb represents a clenching or contraction of muscles, but is also linked to nervous tension and irritation.

[78] The new published English translation may be consulted in *America* 330–1.

In this example, then, Beauvoir's Hegelian analysis of the power relation between the sexes that was to become one of the main themes of *The Second Sex* is explicitly linked to a comparison between France and the United States. This example shows how important Beauvoir's American experiences were to the writing of *The Second Sex*. It is also striking to note that the page devoted to a denunciation of humanist nominalism is framed by references to American women who refuse to believe they are women.

In the first paragraph of *The Second Sex*, then, essentialism is linked to the canonical fathers of philosophy, exemplified by Thomas Aquinas and Plato, whereas nominalism is represented as a contemporary American phenomenon. The examples make it resplendently clear that Beauvoir has no intention of following either line of thought. After reading Beauvoir's account of America in 1947, contemporary postmodern nominalism in America starts to look like the historical heir to the discredited humanist nominalism of the postwar period. Both types of nominalism claim—for different reasons, to be sure—that it is a mistake to believe that one is a woman. It would be interesting to know more about the social and historical conditions that make such views appear particularly plausible to important groups of American intellectuals. Beauvoir's much underrated *America Day by Day* would be a good place to start looking for an answer.

I have already said that Beauvoir's examples are ordinary and unpretentious. What strikes me now, after investigating them more closely, is how steeped they are in women's writing and women's experiences. In my more or less frustrating search for the sources of Beauvoir's examples, I found myself reading Colette, Mary McCarthy, Margaret Mead, Colette Audry, Dorothy Van Doren, Marynia Farnham, Dorothy Parker, and many others. The depth of Beauvoir's engagement with women's lives and writing is evident in these examples. The fact that she includes them in the introduction to a philosophical essay is brave, and already tells us that what we are about to read is not philosophy as it always was practised, but philosophy in a new key, one in which women are included right from the start. The common accusation that Beauvoir is a 'male-identified' philosopher in *The Second Sex* could not be more unfair.

By the end of the first paragraph of her text, Beauvoir has dismissed essentialism and nominalism, that is to say, the two most common answers to the question 'What is a woman?' The fact that she so easily rejects positions that contemporary feminist theorists still feel deeply engaged by should make us wonder what her alternative is. Does she know something we don't?[79] The passage that closes the paragraph and also functions as the conclusion drawn from the examples concerning women who believe they can situate themselves beyond their sex, already indicates what direction she is heading in:

> In truth, to go for a walk with one's eyes open is enough to demonstrate that humanity is divided into two categories of individuals whose clothes, faces, bodies, smiles, gaits, interests, and occupations are manifestly different. Perhaps these differences are superficial, perhaps they are destined to disappear. What is certain is that at the moment it is stunningly evident that they exist (*SS* xx–xxi; *DSa* 13; TA).

There is a powerful reference to Descartes in the last sentence. Beauvoir's search for the one thing that is beyond doubt, the one thing that she can take for granted, the one thing on which she can ground her philosophical inquiry, has led her to the claim that what is *certain* is that for the moment women exist *avec une éclatante évidence*, as she puts it.[80] What she takes to be incontrovertibly true about women is the fact of their existence.[81]

Beauvoir, like other existentialists, believed that 'existence precedes essence'. This means that each concrete human being is involved in an open-ended process in which she constantly makes something of what the world makes of her (I discuss this further

[79] In Chapter 1, above, I attempt to explain why Beauvoir's understanding of the body as a situation is neither essentialist nor nominalist.

[80] My attempt at a literal translation is not wonderful. *Une éclatante évidence* can also be used to indicate that something is a blatant fact; *se rendre à l'évidence* means 'to yield to the facts; to acknowledge that one is in the wrong'.

[81] Nancy Bauer traces Beauvoir's rewriting of Descartes, focusing on Beauvoir's 'I am a woman' as a commentary to and rewriting of Descartes's 'I think therefore I am'. Bauer brilliantly establishes that Beauvoir's 'What is a woman?' is to be 'read as an attempt to displace Descartes' "What is a man?" ' (62).

in Chapter 1, above). 'It is enough to go for a walk with one's eyes open', she writes. Perhaps she lifted her head from her café table to look out at the Boulevard Saint Germain as she wrote those words. A busy street in Paris will more or less instantly yield up examples of every one of the sexual differences listed by Beauvoir. What one discovers when one wanders down the Boulevard Saint Germain keeping one's eyes open are not eternal essences or historical constants, but the fact that in Paris in 1949 there are two kinds of human beings who mark their differences by their 'clothes, faces, bodies, smiles, gaits, interests, and occupations'. The idea is not that the meaning of these differences is self-evident, but that whatever they mean—and this is going to be the subject of Beauvoir's inquiry—nobody in their right mind will deny that they exist in Paris at that moment in history.

What Beauvoir is saying here is that she wants to take the fact of women's concrete existence as the starting point for her philosophizing. In so doing she shows herself as a true existentialist. Existentialism was born in 1932 when Raymond Aron told Sartre that if he started reading phenomenology he would be able to make philosophy out of an apricot cocktail. As Beauvoir tells it, the three of them were drinking apricot cocktails at the Bec de Gaz in the Rue Montparnasse when Aron said, pointing to his glass: ' "You see, my dear school friend, if you are a phenomenologist, you can talk about this cocktail and make philosophy out of it!" Sartre almost turned pale with emotion. Here was just the thing he had been longing to achieve for years—to describe objects just as he saw and touched them, and to make philosophy out of it' (*PL* 135; *FA* 156, TA).

The concrete sexual differences that surround her in everyday life are to Beauvoir in 1949 what the apricot cocktail was to Sartre in 1932. Beginning with sexual differences as she finds them, Beauvoir's project is to uncover the significance of these differences for the human beings shaped by them. Thus the thought that Beauvoir denies sexual difference, or has no philosophy of sexual difference, ubiquitous in recent feminist theory, finds no support in her text. Luce Irigaray is often mentioned as an example of a feminist who theorizes sexual difference, in contrast to

Beauvoir who dismally fails to do so. I now believe that this mistaken contrast is best understood as the result of the critics' failure to grasp *The Second Sex as* theory or *as* philosophy (as the case may be). By this I mean that the critics' understanding of what theory is, or what 'theorizing' should look like, prevents them from seeing that Beauvoir is 'doing theory' on every page of her book.

In the French text, the first five pages of *The Second Sex* consist of only three paragraphs: the first runs for almost three pages and the third for about two pages. The two long paragraphs are symmetrically distributed around a brief transitional paragraph that ends by repeating the question 'What is a woman?'. By its very brevity this paragraph stands out from the rest of the text and marks a self-conscious transition from Beauvoir's ironic critique of second rate philosophy and sexist common sense to her own, original thought. It is significant that the transitional paragraph, which I shall quote in full, takes the form of a highly logical 'if . . . then' sentence. Again Beauvoir shows that philosophical reason—impersonal logic and objectivity—can be a powerful resource for those who wish to emerge from ideological confusion and get back to fundamental questions:

> If her functioning as a female [*femelle*] is not enough to define woman, if we refuse also to explain her through the 'eternal feminine', and if nevertheless we admit, even if it is only provisionally, that there are women on earth, then we must ask ourselves: what is a woman? (*SS* xx–xxi; *DSa* 13; TA)

'I Am a Woman': The Body as Background

We have now reached the crucial third paragraph of *The Second Sex*. Covering only two pages in the French text, this paragraph is a landmark in feminist thought. At the beginning Beauvoir starts by declaring 'I am a woman', at the end she affirms for the first time that woman is the Other. How does she get from a declaration about herself to a general claim about all women? And in what way do these claims answer the question about what a woman is? This is how she begins:

The very act of stating the problem at once suggests to me a first answer.[82] It is significant that I raise it. A man would never think of writing a book on the specific [*singulière*] situation of males in the human race.[83] But if I want to define myself, I must first of all declare: 'I am a woman'; this truth is the background from which all further claims will stand out [*cette vérité constitue le fond sur lequel s'enlèvera toute autre affirmation*].[84] A man never begins by affirming that he is [*par se poser comme*] an individual of a certain sex: that he is a man goes without saying (*SS* xxi; *DSa* 14; TA).

Some feminist theorists would probably feel that Beauvoir here turns her back on the real problem. Perhaps, they might say, she unconsciously realizes that the very fact of uttering the question 'What is a woman?' is to condemn oneself to metaphysical essentialism. Since she doesn't wish to take up an essentialist position, the argument might go, she abandons the terrain of theory for that of autobiography: confession takes the place of analysis. This is why, they might say, Beauvoir never succeeds in *theorizing* sexual difference, as opposed to simply gathering more or less positivist information about it. Needless to say, I think this is to leap to conclusions, and fairly predictable conclusions at that. I want to suggest instead that if we allow ourselves to be patient with this passage, it will emerge as the cornerstone of a truly original effort to think beyond the narrow choice between theory and autobiography, beyond the

---

[82] 'L'énoncé même du problème me suggère aussitôt une première réponse'. There are several translation problems here. The first and most common meaning of *énoncé* is *énonciation* or *déclaration*. Yet the expression *l'énoncé du problème* usually means the terms, or the exact formulation, of a problem. Linguistically, after Benveniste, *l'énoncé* has come to mean the statement as opposed to *l'énonciation*, the utterance, the act of making the statement. Given that Benveniste only published this distinction after 1949, it is probably not relevant here. For once I agree with Parshley, and opt for the most common meaning, namely 'the act of saying or declaring something'.

Parshley translates *une première réponse* as 'a preliminary answer'. I don't think the answer given here is preliminary in the sense of being a preface or a preamble to a more substantial answer to come. Rather, I think it is the first of two answers of equal weight. (The second answer given in this paragraph to 'What is a woman?' is 'Woman is the Other'.)

[83] Beauvoir writes: 'la situation singulière qu'occupent dans l'humanité les mâles'. At this point she inserts a footnote stating that the Kinsey report only deals with male sexual behaviour, which is something else entirely.

[84] I will return to the translation of this significant phrase.

dichotomy between the first and the third person that irks so many contemporary critics, and, not least, beyond the opposition between essentialism and nominalism.

This passage is offered as a response to the question 'What is a woman?' The first thing Beauvoir does is to investigate the speech act of the original question. Who is likely to ask what a woman is? In what situation would they ask such a question? Her first discovery is that sexual difference manifests itself in her very interest in the question. (She has, after all, just declared that it is enough to go for a walk with one's eyes open to discover that men and women have different interests.) The composition of the passage is strikingly symmetrical. Twice a statement about herself is countered by a sentence about what a man would do or say (*I* raise the question; *a man* would never ask; *I* must declare; *a man* never begins). The structure produces a strong contrast: not, as one might have expected, between 'woman' and 'man', but between 'I' and 'man'.

Beauvoir here realizes that she is writing in a situation where, unlike male writers, she is forced to define herself as a sexed being; where she has no choice but to fill the empty shifter 'I' with her sexual difference. The first 'I' in the book ('I have hesitated for a long time to write a book on woman') was casual. It took itself for granted, without any philosophical ado. This 'I' ('I am a woman'; 'I must define myself', etc.) is showing signs of political and philosophical tension. In this sentence the idea that woman is the Other is already close. 'But if I want to define myself, I must first of all declare: "I am a woman"; this truth is the background from which all further claims will stand out [*cette vérité constitue le fond sur lequel s'enlèvera toute autre affirmation*]'.

The language here is crucial. In French *s'enlever sur un fond* is a somewhat unusual turn of phrase, particularly in this context. *Se détacher* would have been the more obvious choice, since *Le Petit Robert* defines it as 'to appear clearly as if standing out against a background'. In general, *détacher* always has connotations of visual separation, clarity, clear-cut contours, and so is often used about a colour or shape set off against a different background colour of some sort. If Beauvoir chooses to write *s'enlever* and not *se détacher*, it is presumably because she wishes to bring out a different nuance. Many of the most common meanings of *enlever* are obviously unsuitable for the context: Beauvoir does not appear to be thinking of kidnapping and ravishing, of stain-removing, or of something being taken away. One of the primary meanings of *enlever*, however, is 'to lift upwards' (*en + lever*), and so *enlevure* has come to be a technical term for sculptural relief. In English 'relief' may be used about visual as well as tactile effects (relief maps use colours and shading to indicate elevations and depressions); in French, however, *enlevure* is always tactile; an *enlevure* is something I should be able to feel in the dark. I don't mean to exaggerate the differences between these words: sculptural relief is visible too, and if I am in a landscape I could touch the church in the foreground as well as the trees in the background, yet the different sensory emphasis of these two words is obvious.

The image Beauvoir has in mind is now available. The fact that she is a woman is the truth which constitutes the background from which all further claims will stand out in relief, she writes. There are two facts here: first, it is a fact that she is a woman, second, it is a fact that whenever she wants to define herself, she is obliged to draw attention to the first fact. Beauvoir considers the fact of being a woman as the background against which the woman's speech acts stand out. The word 'claim' or 'assertion' (*affirmation*) indicates that she is speaking about her own intellectual undertaking: to write a book about women. Like all other acts, my speech acts define me, an existentialist would say. If I am a woman, my claims are inevitably going to be taken to stand out from the background of my sex. This means that, however hard I try to define myself through what I am saying and doing (through my self-assertions), my interlocutors will try to reduce my assertions to my sex. My struggle for existence will be met by their insistence on essence. I take Beauvoir to experience a sense of consternation at this discovery, to strongly wish for things to be otherwise.

There is a further complication in the sentence. In French, the verb is in the simple future tense (*s'enlèvera*). The published English translation uses the word *must*: 'on this truth must be based all further discussion', Parshley writes. This could give the impression that Beauvoir thinks that this is a desirable state of affairs, perhaps even that she thinks that the fact of being a woman always *ought* or *should* be taken into account. But Parshley here overlooks some common nuances of the French future tense. 'Tu ne sortiras pas' usually carries connotations such as 'you are not allowed to go out', or 'I predict that you will not manage to get yourself out of the house'. There is often a nuance of command, i.e. of being subjected to someone else's power, or of inescapable destiny ('under no circumstances will you be able to escape this fate'). Beauvoir is not in fact saying that the background of sex *must* be kept in mind whenever a woman speaks, nor is she saying that it *ought* to be or *should* be kept in mind: she is saying that it *will* be kept in mind whether the woman likes it or not, and whether it is relevant or irrelevant to whatever she is asserting. In other words, the meaning of the sentence is that whenever a woman speaks, there is no way the fact of her sex is *not* going to be taken into account.

This is contrasted to the situation of human males, who will not automatically be taken to speak against the background of a sexed—male—body whenever they open their mouths. As Nancy Bauer has shown, just by saying that she is a woman, Beauvoir indicates that she rejects the Cartesian body/mind split:

> It turns out . . . that the first thing Beauvoir has to say about herself is that she is a woman. This means that unlike Descartes Beauvoir begins with a fundamental investment in the significance of her body, so that her thinking will not be able to accommodate a Cartesian mind–body split. Furthermore, since her inquiry is rooted in a sense of herself as being an instance of the generic concept 'woman' a certain Cartesian threat of solipsism is avoided from the start: to call herself a woman is to start with the idea that other beings like her exist—that is, other beings who are called, or call themselves, women (60).

Beauvoir writes: 'A man never begins by affirming that he is an individual of a certain sex; that he is a man goes without saying'. What is being begun here is a piece of writing, most probably a philosophical essay. Beauvoir is claiming that because she is a woman and not a man everything she says ('asserts' or 'claims') in *The Second Sex* is going to be related to the fact that she has a female body. The reception of her book in France certainly proved her point.[85]

But there is more. For Beauvoir's sentence 'But if I wish to define myself, I must first of all say: "I am a woman"; this truth is the background from which all further claims will stand out', sets up a strong intertextual link to a passage in the preface to Merleau-Ponty's *Phenomenology of Perception*:

> Perception is not the science of the world, it is not even an act, a deliberate taking up of a position; it is the background [*fond*] from which all acts stand out [*se détachent*], and is presupposed by them. The world is not an object such that I have in my possession the law of its making; it is the natural setting of, and field for, all my thoughts and all my explicit perception (x–xi).

Merleau-Ponty writes this in a context where he wants to explain that the body gives us our perceptions, and that without perceptions there is no world. The body is at once what we are and the medium through which we are able to have a world. Speaking of bodily perception Merleau-Ponty uses the same imagery of foreground and background as Beauvoir when she speaks of the fact of having a female body. For Merleau-Ponty the body is the necessary background for everything I do, and everything I do has the perceiving body as its obvious presupposition. This background is something like a general (not particular or individualized) condition enabling human agency and subjectivity to come into being. By speaking of background and foreground Merleau-Ponty means to warn against scientistic or positivist reductionism. A background is not the meaning or essence of whatever takes place in the foreground: the natural processes of the body cannot in themselves explain the acts and thoughts of human beings. On the other hand, the specific background that the body is cannot be thought away or denied, or presumed to have no effects on the foreground. Against Kantian idealism and scientistic positivism,

---

[85] Summarizing the reception of *The Second Sex* in *Force of Circumstance*, Beauvoir writes: 'Unsatisfied, frigid, priapic, nymphomaniac, lesbian, a hundred times aborted, I was everything, even a clandestine mother ... But that even [François] Mauriac joined in! He wrote to one of the contributors to *Les Temps Modernes*: "Your boss's vagina no longer has any secrets for me" '(197; *FCa* 260–1; TA).

Merleau-Ponty sets phenomenological materialism, one might say.[86]

To consider the body as a background is to allow that its importance for our projects and sense of identity is variable. Merleau-Ponty's visual metaphor (*se détacher*) makes me think of theatre and of landscapes. In a play, the background—the backdrop—is sometimes crucial to the understanding of the actors' words and gestures, whereas at other times a relentless focus on the background would be quite misplaced. Let us imagine a building placed against a dramatic landscape. If it is the building I wish to study, the landscape is a simple background to which I need pay no attention at all. If it is the landscape, however, the building may either be considered as a part of it, or be disregarded. The background is always there, but its meaning is far from given.

Beauvoir's tactile metaphor has slightly different connotations. The relief on a sculpture may be admired for its own sake, but it is usually quite difficult to focus on the relief without paying any attention to the sculpture it is a part of. The case of the sculpture produces a more integral unity between foreground and background than the case of the backdrop on a stage or the landscape behind an Italian church. The difference in metaphors signals a difference in emphasis. Choosing *s'enlever* rather than *se détacher*, Beauvoir deliberately uses an image that makes it somewhat more difficult to focus on the foreground without taking the background into account than Merleau-Ponty's *se détacher*. Her metaphor takes sexism into account; Merleau-Ponty's does not. By seeing the sexed body as a background which the woman is *obliged* to foreground whenever she is asked to define herself, Beauvoir indicates that for a woman living under patriarchy, the body is a far more inescapable fact than it is for a man. Whatever the woman says, she will have her body—her female sex—taken into account. We should note that this may or may not be what the woman wants. By thinking in terms of foreground and background Beauvoir avoids implying that women's words can be reduced to their bodies.

---

[86] For further discussion of Merleau-Ponty's and Beauvoir's critique of scientism and positivism, see Ch. 1, above.

In Chapter 1 I spent some time discussing Beauvoir's understanding of the body as a situation, as a fundamental part of
lived experience. What is the difference between the body
understood as a situation and the body understood as background? In Beauvoir's sentence, the body considered as a background is represented as a body perceived by the Other. The
presence of the Other is implied in the attempt to define
oneself (one rarely finds it necessary to declare 'I am a woman'
to oneself), and it is explicitly there in the claim that this act of
definition is the result of submission to an external obligation.
The concept of situation also presupposes that there are others
in the world and that we interact with them. But it is not a
concept that applies exclusively to the body. The body is a situation, but so is the fact of going to high school, or being
married. The body as a situation is the body as experienced by
the human subject, the body as interwoven with the projects of
that subject. Perceived as a general background for my existence, on the other hand, the body precedes and enables
perception and experience. While the body as situation presupposes agency in the subject, the body as background enables
such agency to come into being. At least this is the impression
I get from reading Merleau-Ponty. It seems to me that Beauvoir
in this sentence uses the idea of the body as a background a
little differently, that she quite consciously chooses to imagine
the acting and situated body as a background. This becomes
quite clear when she goes on to discuss the 'assertions' coming
from the woman involved in an abstract discussion with a man.
The actual, physical female body sitting there at the café table
discussing philosophy is both a situation for the woman who is
talking, and a background to her words for the man who is talking to her.

The same expression—to stand out in relief from a background—also turns up in the introduction to the second volume
of *The Second Sex*, entitled 'L'expérience vécue' ('Lived
Experience'). In this brief text Beauvoir writes that women are
starting to assert their independence. This doesn't happen without difficulty, however, for 'virile prestige' is far from extinct. In
order to understand what it means to modern women to assert

their independence, it is important to study 'women's traditional destiny'. Then she finishes the introduction as follows:

> I shall seek to describe how woman learns her condition, how she experiences it, in what kind of universe she is confined, what forms of escape she is allowed to have. Only then will we understand what problems arise for women who, inheriting a heavy past, strive to forge a new future. When I use the words 'woman', 'feminine' or 'female',[87] I evidently refer to no archetype, no changeless essence; after most of my claims [*mes affirmations*] the reader should understand 'in the present state of education and custom'. The point here is not to proclaim eternal truths, but rather to describe the common background [*fond*] from which every particular female existence stands out [*sur lequel s'enlève toute existence féminine singulière*] (*SS* xxxvi; *DSb* 9; TA).[88]

The second volume of *The Second Sex* is divided into four main sections entitled 'Formation', 'Situation', 'Justifications', and 'Towards Liberation'. This volume has given rise to much criticism, usually on the grounds that Beauvoir generalizes from an unrepresentative sample, that she takes the French experiences of her mother's generation and those of her own to be representative of women everywhere. It is also often assumed that she thinks that the situations she describes are such that no woman can transcend them. Thus her critique of motherhood or bourgeois marriage is often taken to mean that no individual woman could ever realize herself as an authentically free person within these institutions. If this were the case, Beauvoir would be an extreme determinist. On the other hand it has also been assumed that Beauvoir is a radical voluntarist, an idealist who thinks that women, just by an act of will, can throw off the sexist yoke and realize themselves, that they have only themselves to blame if they fail to rid themselves of their bad faith. If this were the case,

---

[87] Beauvoir writes: *les mots 'femme' ou 'féminin'*. In order to stress that the French *féminin* can refer to sex as well as to gender, I have chosen to translate it as 'feminine or female'. See Ch. 1, above, for a thorough discussion of sex, gender, and *The Second Sex*.

[88] Compare H. M. Parshley's translation: 'It is not our concern here to proclaim eternal verities, but rather to describe the common basis that underlies every individual feminine existence.'

Beauvoir would have no reason to claim that institutions and ideology ('myths') oppress women.

The play between foreground and background proposed by Beauvoir avoids reductionism and essentialism (the individual woman in the foreground cannot be reduced to the general historical situation which is her background) while still enabling us to grasp the historical factors that influence and shape the choices of individual women. In *The Second Sex* Beauvoir tries to produce a historical analysis of women's condition. A historical analysis cannot be all-inclusive or universal in the sense of reaching a level of abstraction that might hold for all women in all countries at all times. In order to have any analytic and historical power at all it needs to be specific and particular. Even if we think that Beauvoir is wrong to deal with women 'in the present state of education and custom [in France]', all we could do to correct her would be to propose that she deal with some other group instead. Since no such group is going to be more or less universal than any other, this would not make the analysis more or less representative of women's condition than the one Beauvoir proposes.[89]

Beauvoir does not attempt to describe or predict what any individual woman will make of the conditions in which she is brought up. Her own life was extremely unusual for a woman in mid-century France, yet she fully believed that it was informed and shaped by the traditional background she describes in *The Second Sex*. Describing her discovery of patriarchal mythology, she writes: 'it was a revelation to me: this world was a masculine world, my childhood had been nourished by myths forged by men, and I hadn't reacted to them in at all the same way I should have done if I had been a boy' (*FC* 103, *FCa* 136; TA). Beauvoir's fundamental understanding of subjectivity is based on the assumption that we continuously make something of what the world makes of us. The 'background' she is describing and analysing in the second volume of *The Second Sex* tells us what the world wants to make of women. She also includes many case studies and innumerable examples in which she shows what women, responding to this

[89] I return to the question of exemplarity and representation in the next section, 'My Spade is Turned', below.

situation, make of what the world makes of them. The very fact that Beauvoir quite often dwells on exceptional women demonstrates that she does not take her description of the general historical and social background to be invalidated when she moves the focus to a specific case in the foreground, however exceptional it might be.

Finally, Beauvoir's sentence—'this truth is the background . . .'—allows for two different political interpretations. On the one hand, she may be taken to mean that in a sexist society (such as Paris in 1949) a woman's claims will always be heard with reference to her body, but that in a non-sexist society this will no longer be the case. On the other hand, however, she may be saying that although sexism insists on reading a woman's books against the background of her sex, in a non-sexist society the same thing will happen to men as well. Here, in a nutshell, we find encapsulated the feminist conflict between a certain understanding of equality and a certain understanding of difference.[90] Is Beauvoir saying that the aim of feminism is to make sexual difference irrelevant, that we should all be treated just as the human beings we are? Or is she saying that the aim of feminism is to show that sexual difference is relevant at all times and in every social and personal situation?[91]

First, it is crucial to note that Beauvoir's sentence refuses to embrace either interpretation. There is no sign that what she *really* means is one or the other. Second, it appears that neither interpretation corresponds to the logic of Beauvoir's text. For the first interpretation (that sexual difference is irrelevant) sounds like an echo of the humanist nominalism she explicitly rejected just one page earlier: 'Clearly, no woman can without bad faith pretend to be situated beyond her sex'. The second interpretation (that

[90] See my discussion of the unsatisfactory opposition between a feminism of equality and a feminism of difference in 'Is Anatomy Destiny?' (Ch. 8, below).

[91] There are strong parallels between this claim and the idea, discussed in Sect. I of this essay, that 'location' is always relevant for the understanding of every speech act. I want to stress that I am not trying to *deny* that sex or location are always relevant: I am, rather, trying to shift the argument towards a different question, namely the question of when (under what circumstances) it is worth while *saying something* about sex or location.

sexual difference is always of fundamental importance) is no more convincing, for it makes sexual difference appear absolute (or essential) by assuming that there can be no situation in which it is *not* a significant factor, and this is a view that clashes with the existentialist belief that existence precedes essence.

By thinking of the body as a background, Beauvoir avoids both interpretations. To say that the sexed body is the inevitable background for all our acts, is at once to claim that it is always a *potential* source of meaning, and to *deny* that it always holds the key to the meaning of a woman's acts. Sculptural relief cannot always be understood by referring it back to the surface from which it stands out. Sometimes we need to understand the relief itself; at other times we want to consider how the relief affects the sculpture as a whole, and vice versa. In yet other cases, we want to see the whole sculpture as part of some larger context. In short, the sex of a body is always there, but it is not always the most important fact about that body. The dying body or the body in pain is not necessarily grasped primarily in terms of sexual difference. If I am trying to learn Chinese, this is evidently an act that I undertake on the background of my sexed body, but the relevance of saying so is not always obvious. If, on the other hand, I am trying to get pregnant, this is a project that certainly foregrounds my sexed body. More complex cases will arise from women's participation in different sports, or in other physical activities.

It follows from Beauvoir's analysis that in some situations the fact of sex will be less important than the fact of class or race; in other situations it will not. There can be no question of giving *one* of these factors general, overarching priority. The old debates about whether class-based exploitation or sex-based oppression are 'primary', never yielded a convincing answer. They were in fact doomed to failure precisely because they sought a general answer, one that would establish the correct hierarchy of oppressions once and for all. One does not get out of this problem, incidentally, by denying that there are hierarchies of oppression. In Spain in 1936, for example, it was more important for Republicans of both sexes to fight against fascism than against sexism (this is not to say that the Spanish Republicans were not sexist). In other cases there may be no hierarchy: fighting for women's right to education may be as useful for socialism as it is for feminism. In yet other cases, sex will be the dominant form of oppression, hierarchically more important than class-based oppression. This is surely the case in Afghanistan, where women without male family members die because the Taliban will not allow them to see a doctor without a brother or a husband present.

I take Beauvoir to be saying that women's oppression consists in the compulsory foregrounding of the female body at all times, whether it is relevant or irrelevant to the task at hand. But sexism also consists in preventing women from foregrounding the female body when they want it to be significant. (A Beauvoirean feminist would be critical of anti-sex and anti-pornography feminism.) In a scene of flirtation or seduction, for example, a woman may want to foreground her body. Thus Françoise in *L'invitée* (*She Came to Stay*) intensely wants Gerbert to notice her sexed body, to notice her as a woman. On the other hand, it can be annoying and painful to be interpellated as a sexed body when one is immersed in a project that has nothing to do with one's sex. The same logic holds for the raced body. To be cast as a representative of one's race when one is immersed in a project in which this is an entirely irrelevant element, can be painful and humiliating. A cartoon that appeared in the *New Yorker* is a perfect illustration of the point:

Frantz Fanon brilliantly captures the sense of fragmentation and dislocation that arises from the experience of being reduced to one's raced body against one's will. In a passage in *Black Skin, White Masks* he describes walking down the street in a French city, passing a white woman and her little daughter on his way. I quote the scene at length because it so perfectly conveys Fanon's pain and alienation, his sense that the gaze of the white man imprisons him in his subjectivity, a subjectivity that is reduced to the fact of his black skin:

> 'Look, a Negro!' It was an external stimulus that flicked over me as I passed by. I made a tight smile.
> 'Look, a Negro!' It was true. It amused me.
> 'Look, a Negro!' The circle was drawing a bit tighter. I made no secret of my amusement.
> 'Mama, see the Negro! I'm frightened!' Frightened! Frightened! Now they were beginning to be afraid of me. I made up my mind to laugh myself to tears, but laughter had become impossible (112).

> I was responsible at the same time for my body, for my race, for my ancestors. I subjected myself to an objective examination, I discovered my blackness, my ethnic characteristics; and I was battered down by tom-toms, cannibalism, intellectual deficiency, fetishism, racial defects, slave-ships, and above all else, above all: 'Sho' good eatin'.
> On that day, completely dislocated, unable to be abroad with the other, the white man, who unmercifully imprisoned me, I took myself far off from my own presence, far indeed, and made myself an object. What else could it be for me but an amputation, an excision, a hemorrhage that spattered my whole body with black blood? But I did not want this revision, this thematization. All I wanted was to be a man among other men. I wanted to come lithe and young into a world that was ours and to help to build it together (112–13).

There are situations in which we freely choose to be recognized as sexed or raced bodies, where that recognition is exactly what we need and want. Identity politics starts with such identity-affirming situations, but unfortunately goes on to base a general politics on them, thus forgetting that there are other situations in which we do not want to be defined by our sexed and raced bodies, situations in which we wish that body to be no more than the insignificant background to our main activity. As we are about to see, Beauvoir herself gives a marvellous example of just such a situation when she discusses the case of an abstract conversation where a man says to her: 'you say that because you are a woman'. Although this experience may be far less painful for the intellectual woman than the experience of racism was for Fanon, the juxtaposition of the two situations reveal that similar mechanisms of oppression are at work in the encounter between the raced and the sexed body and the Other.[92]

I am tempted to say: in certain situations I want to be considered as an intellectual, and not as an intellectual woman. Yet I do not say it. For this statement is not exactly right. I now realize that there is something in our language that makes it exceptionally hard to express what I do wish to say. It is far too easy to take my original impulse (to call myself an intellectual, rather than an intellectual woman) to mean that in some situations I wish to *deny* that I am a woman, and so to accuse me of being one of the humanist nominalists pretending to be situated beyond my sex. But I do not wish to claim that my body does not exist, or that I am not a woman. Beauvoir helps me to put it more clearly: In certain situations I wish my female body to be considered as the insignificant background of my claims or acts. This is not the same thing as to say that I wish my body to disappear or to be transformed into a male body. My wish does not represent an attempt to escape my particularity, to be considered as a neuter, or as some kind of universalized human being. It represents, rather, a wish to deny that the fact of being a woman is of any particular relevance to my understanding of trigonometry or my capacity to compose symphonies or think ethically.

Ever since feminism became part of public life, some women writers and painters (and so on) have felt that feminism is an ideology that locks women up in their particularized female subjectivity. Opposing such versions of feminism, they have

---

[92] I am not claiming that Fanon and Beauvoir understand racism and sexism in exactly parallel terms. For a brief comparison of the two writers, see ch. 8 of my *Simone de Beauvoir*.

refused to be called 'women writers' and 'women painters'. Feminists have usually agreed that there is something anti-feminist about such a refusal to call oneself a woman, often responding by accusing such women of being male-identified and sadly lacking in solidarity with their sex. But the fact is that women are right to refuse attempts to make their subjectivity out to be coextensive with their femininity. We have no reason to accept attempts to imprison us in our 'femininity', whether such attempts originate in sexist or in feminist thought. The problem arises when some women assume that the only way to escape imprisonment in one's sex is to deny that sex altogether, and so actually give in to temptation to say: 'I am a writer, not a woman writer.' In this way they only manage to foreground their claim to universality at the cost of sacrificing their femininity (here the word simply means their 'femaleness'). They forget, a Beauvoirean might say, that the sexed body is both a background and a situation, and as such not a phenomenon that can simply be disavowed.

For I also wish to acknowledge that I probably do read Kant or Kierkegaard in ways I would not have done had I been a man. Yet the fact that I read as the woman I am is no reason to deprive me of my right to be considered an intellectual. *Must* I always refer to myself as an 'intellectual woman'? Men who read Kant and Kierkegaard in ways they would not have done had they been women, usually refer to themselves as intellectuals or philosophers, not as 'intellectual men' or 'male philosophers'. This fact does not lead people to accuse them of denying or repressing their masculinity, or to consider them 'female-identified'. In sexist ideology, men can be self-evidently male and self-evidently intellectual at the same time. This is why the phrase 'an intellectual man' sounds quite odd whereas 'an intellectual woman' sounds quite normal. Beauvoir's feminist goal is to produce a society in which women will gain access to the universal *as women*, not as fake men nor as some impossibly neutered beings.

In a sexist society women often find themselves in situations where they are obliged to make a 'choice' between being imprisoned in their femininity or having to disavow it altogether. That sexist ideologies and practices produce this alienating split in women's subjectivity is Beauvoir's most fundamental point in *The*

Second Sex. For her, both alternatives are equally sexist and equally alienating.[93] Because male subjectivity is not 'hailed' ('interpellated') in this way, this alienating 'choice' in fact defines women's situation under patriarchy. So insidious is this ideology that much feminist theory, whether willingly or not, has ended up espousing one alternative or the other. The amount of time feminists have spent worrying about women's 'equality' or 'difference' is a symptom of the success of this ideological trap. A genuinely feminist position would refuse either option, and insist, rather, that women should not have to choose between calling themselves women and calling themselves writers (or intellectuals, or painters, or composers). It remains an important feminist task to show that this way of thinking of female subjectivity produces an impossible ideological dilemma for women. By now I hope it is obvious that when I refuse to accept the terms of this 'choice', then it does not follow that I really wish to be a man.

To put this differently: it does not go without saying that what a woman does or says is always expressive of 'the woman in her'. Yet at the same time, it is undoubtedly true that whatever a woman does or says is done by a woman. It is because both claims are true that we get so confused about what 'femininity' actually means. What is admirable about Beauvoir's understanding of what a woman is, is precisely her capacity to convey this doubleness without reducing it to one or the other of its components, without acquiescing in it, and also without choosing one of the two equally unsatisfactory theories of what a woman is ('a woman is just a human being' *versus* 'a woman is always just a woman').

By considering the body as a background Beauvoir at once affirms that sexual difference is a fact of fundamental philosophical and social importance *and* that it is not necessarily the most important fact about a human being. Because she pictures the sexed body as the phenomenological background (not the content, essence, or meaning) against which a woman's choices and acts will be foregrounded, these are not contradictory claims. As I will now go on to show, Beauvoir's formulation also reveals

[93] I discuss Beauvoir's analysis of this dilemma below, in my reading of the intellectual conversation where the man says to the woman 'You think that because you are a woman'.

that her fundamental feminist project is to find a way of thinking about sexual difference which steers clear of the Scylla of having to eliminate her sexed subjectivity and the Charybdis of finding herself imprisoned in it.

'You Say That Because You Are a Woman'

I shall now continue reading the third paragraph of *The Second Sex*. In this section I will show that Beauvoir's philosophical style in *The Second Sex* has much in common with that of ordinary language philosophy. This in itself is an interesting observation with implications that ought to be studied in far greater depth than I can do here. My goal here is to show that when Beauvoir's analysis of women and sexism is read in the light of ordinary language philosophy, it gains new and important dimensions.

The text gathers pace after Beauvoir's self-definition. It is as if the realization that whenever she wants to define herself she *has* to say 'I am a woman' precipitates a host of path-breaking insights. In the next sentence she produces another reflection on 'what we should say when'. 'A man never begins', she writes, 'by affirming that he is an individual of a certain sex; that he is a man goes without saying' (*SS* xxi; *DSa* 14; TA). Beauvoir's first insight after her self-definition, then, is that there are situations in which a woman would say something, and a man would say nothing, and that one such situation is the situation of a woman about to undertake a philosophical investigation. A woman who wants to do philosophy, she realizes, has to make painfully explicit that which ordinarily goes without saying. This is also what philosophers who proceed from everyday language take the task of philosophy to be. What is striking in Beauvoir's text, however, is that she is led to this insight by thinking about what it means to her to have to define herself as a woman. Her insight arises both because she has had to place her own subjectivity in the text, and because she has had the intellectual resourcefulness to make that very fact a subject for philosophical reflection. Coming to an explicit awareness of the way her own subjectivity is bound up with her thinking, Beauvoir discovers a way of doing philosophy in which the personal and the philosophical are intrinsically linked.

It is because Beauvoir has to say 'I am a woman' at the beginning of *The Second Sex* that she ends up extending and expanding her philosophical method in the direction of the autobiographical and the linguistic (I mean in the direction of asking what we should say when). This is where *The Second Sex* differs most dramatically from *Being and Nothingness*. By using such strategies Beauvoir becomes a different kind of philosopher to Sartre, who never starts by declaring that he is a man, because he doesn't have to. Without signalling the fact as such, Beauvoir makes a decisive shift in her philosophical style, both in relation to previous philosophers and in relation to her own earlier essays.[94] Stanley Cavell writes: 'One requirement of new philosophical answers is that they elicit a new source of philosophical interest, or elicit this old interest in a new way. Which is perhaps only a way of affirming that a change of *style* in philosophy is a profound change, and itself a subject of philosophical investigation' ('Austin at Criticism' 102).

In her considerations of what she would say as opposed to what a man would say, Beauvoir shows that the question of 'what we should say when' does not have to presuppose the invocation of a falsely universalized 'we', a 'we' arrogantly pretending to know the ways of language much better than anyone else. To 'examine what we should say when' is to imagine 'what words we should use in what situations', Austin writes ('Plea' 182). To take for granted that a given situation must have a male speaker (or a white speaker, or a bourgeois speaker) is as philosophically flawed as to imagine that any other aspect of the speech act necessarily goes without saying.

In order to prevent some common misunderstandings, I will explain briefly what I take the appeal to ordinary language, to 'what we should say when', to imply and not to imply. For Cavell, an appeal to 'what we should say when' is not an appeal to expertise or superior knowledge. On the contrary, if I want to take issue with your understanding of a certain situation, I must first be able

---

[94] My sense is that Beauvoir's philosophical style in *The Second Sex* is different from her style in *Pyrrhus et Cinéas* and *An Ethics of Ambiguity*. But this is not certain: more work would be required to show whether or how far this intuition is right.

to understand the way the world looks to you. My critique cannot come from the outside, and certainly not from above:

> Understanding from inside a view you are undertaking to criticize is sound enough practice whatever the issue. But in the philosophy which proceeds from ordinary language, understanding from inside is methodologically fundamental. Because the way you must rely upon yourself as a source of what is said when, demands that you grant full title to others as sources of that data—not out of politeness, but because the nature of the claim you make for yourself is repudiated without that acknowledgment: it is a claim that no one knows better than you whether and when a thing is said, and if this is not to be taken as a claim to expertise (a way of taking it which repudiates it) then it must be understood to mean that you know no better than others what you claim to know (Cavell, 'Knowing and Acknowledging' 239–40).

The ordinary language philosopher has no monopoly on meaning. No speaker of the language can meaningfully be thought of as more or less a speaker of it than anyone else.[95] Wittgenstein's 'the meaning of a word is its use' means that to be a speaker of the language is to contribute to its meanings. By the act of using words, we necessarily contribute to their meaning. 'What is normative is exactly ordinary use itself', Cavell writes ('Must' 21).[96] The idea that certain concepts wield a social power

[95] Nancy Bauer thinks in very similar terms when she writes: 'In answering "I am" to the question "What is a woman?" [Beauvoir] means not to distinguish herself but, to the contrary, to count herself a member of a group comprising at least half of the human race' (55).

[96] This sentence has been much misunderstood. Let me quote Cavell's own comment on it in 'The Politics of Interpretation': 'When in the title essay of *Must We Mean What We Say?* I come out with the assertion that "what is normative is exactly ordinary use itself," it is with a certain air of triumph, and what I felt (still feel) I was triumphing in was not the affirmation of a distinction between ordinary and some other kind of language; on the contrary, I felt I was winning freedom from such distinctions between the normative and the ordinary' (38). This explanation is offered in the context of a discussion of Stanley Fish's reading of Austin, where Fish claims that for Austin literary language is opposed to ordinary language. Fish believes that 'ordinary language' is a term that 'designates a kind of language that "merely" presents or mirrors facts independently of any consideration of value, interest, perspective, purpose, and so on' ('How Ordinary is Ordinary Language?' 97). As far as I can see, nothing could be further from Austin and Cavell's understanding of what ordinary

denied to others is not incompatible with this thought. The existence of evil and exploitative social systems does not invalidate Wittgenstein's recognition that all speakers of the language participate in the production of meaning. If anything, Wittgenstein's thought gives us a justification for resisting attempts to silence some speakers and impose the voices of others. To say that the meaning of a word is its use is not, either, to imply that there is only one use of any given word. The very fact that there is continuous struggle over meaning (think of words such as *queer, woman, democracy, equality, freedom*) shows that different uses not only exist but sometimes give rise to violently conflicting meanings. If the meaning of a word is its use, such conflicts are part of the meaning of the word.

An appeal to ordinary usage, then, is not an appeal to dominant ideology or a passive submission to 'regulatory discourses'. Let me quote Cavell again:

> An appeal to what we should ordinarily say does not constitute a defense of ordinary beliefs or common sense. . . . Proceeding from what is ordinarily said puts a philosopher no closer to ordinary 'beliefs' than to the 'beliefs' or theses of any opposing philosophy,

---

language is (see also Fish, 'How to Do Things with Austin and Searle'). On my reading of Wittgenstein and Cavell, the only thing ordinary or everyday uses of language are opposed to, are metaphysical uses of language, which Wittgenstein sees as cases when 'language goes on holiday' (*PI* §38), i.e. cases when language is doing no useful work at all.

The other reason why Cavell's statement about the normativity of ordinary language is so often misunderstood, has to do with the question of what 'normative' means. In our postmodern intellectual climate it is often taken to mean *ideologically* normative. But that is not Cavell's point. He means normative in the sense of having meaning at all. The word 'glass' is normative in the sense that in most cases when I say 'Could you give me a glass, please?' you will—most astonishingly—hand one to me. Nevertheless, there is always the possibility that in some particular case you will think that I mean something else. As Wittgenstein reminds us: '[Even] an ostensive definition can be variously interpreted in *every* case' (*PI* §28). But the existence of difficult cases does not make the easy ones go away. Cavell is not trying to say that a word only has one, normative use. Ordinary language philosophy is precisely engaged in analysis of what makes some speech acts felicitous and others not. This is not the place to go into these questions. The purpose of this footnote is simply to indicate that some common objections to the words 'ordinary language' and 'normative' are not well founded.

e.g., skepticism. In all cases his problem is to discover the specific plight of mind and circumstance within which a human being gives voice to his condition ('Knowing and Acknowledging' 240).[97]

On Cavell's understanding of the ordinary and the everyday, the ordinary is the arena where human struggle takes place. Murder and mayhem, revolution and resistance are as much part of the ordinary as successful communication and felicitous speech acts. The fact that we all experience misunderstandings or conflicts with distressing regularity surely makes that clear. Feminist analysis of sexism and the oppression of women is usually located within the sphere of the ordinary. The point made by Cavell and others is that we cannot even have struggle and disagreement unless we speak to each other on the basis of some common understanding (a shared practice) of what counts as political conflict or disagreement. If there is no such shared practice, we would not understand each other sufficiently to disagree: 'If a lion could talk, we could not understand him', Wittgenstein writes (*PI*, p. 223).

By examining two different situations—one in which a man begins a work of philosophy and one in which a woman does so— Beauvoir demonstrates that there are cases where the sex of the speaker has decisive influence on what 'we' would say, so that there cannot be any question of what 'we' would say' in general, if 'in general means 'without regard to sex'. This insight immediately leads to the realization that the two sexes do not, in fact, stand in a symmetrical relation to each other. The way we do or do not use the expressions 'I am a man' and 'I am a woman' shows that when it comes to philosophical writing, there is no

---

[97] Some critics believe that Wittgenstein or ordinary language philosophy *must* be conservative. This obviously deserves further discussion. Here I can just say that I would not be interested in this way of thinking about meaning if I thought such critics were right. In *Sexual/Textual Politics* I quote Vološinov who writes 'differently oriented accents intersect in every ideological sign. Sign becomes an arena of class struggle' (157). I still agree with this. It is important to note that Vološinov writes 'every *ideological* sign', not '*every* sign'. I take Vološinov to mean that we have to be able to *show* that a sign is ideological and also be able to analyse the different social interests that struggle over its use in a particular case. To me, this is compatible with Wittgenstein's fundamental understanding of meaning.

reciprocity between 'man' and 'woman'. A man, in other words, cannot stake his subjectivity in philosophy by saying 'I am a man', since this is a statement that has not been considered *subjective* by male philosophers.[98]

Beauvoir goes on to develop this insight. It is only on bureaucratic forms, she writes (her examples are marriage certificates and identity papers), that the terms male and female appear to have equal weight.[99] The two sexes cannot be compared to two electrical poles:

> the man represents both the positive and the neutral, so much so that one says 'man' [*les hommes*] in French to designate human beings; here the specific meaning of the word *vir* has been assimilated to the general meaning of the word *homo*.[100] Woman appears as the negative, with the result that every determination is ascribed to her as a limitation, without reciprocity (*SS* xxi; *DSa* 14, TA).

It follows that under patriarchy it does not really matter *how* one defines woman, for whatever qualities one ascribes to her, they will appear as negative in relation to the qualities of men. This is the fundamental reason why Beauvoir consistently refuses to engage in definitions of femininity.

At this point, Beauvoir packs the text with examples. Falsely symmetrical bureaucratic papers, genuinely symmetrical electric poles, and examples of what one would say in French and Latin follow on the heels of the analysis of her own speech act. The

---

[98] It was only after the feminist analysis pioneered by Beauvoir had become widely accepted that some men started to think of male subjectivity as sexed and particular.

[99] Beauvoir writes *masculin* and *féminin*. I think she means the fact of being a man or of being a woman, and translate 'male' and 'female'.

[100] Parshley omits the reference to what one says in French, which is philosophically unfortunate, but understandable since one says the same thing in English. He also omits the last part of the sentence (from 'here the specific meaning of *vir*' to the end) altogether. In his translation this sentence reads: 'man represents both the positive and the neutral, as is indicated by the common use of man to designate human beings in general . . .'. The effect is to conceal Beauvoir's use of linguistic examples to make her case, and to transform her reference to the French language into a falsely universalizing claim implicitly based on French and English, but not necessarily on other languages (in Norwegian, for example, the word for a human being (*menneske*) is not the same as the word for man (*mann*)).

result is an analysis of sexism (it turns woman into a relative being, the negative of man) which was to be shared by just about every feminist in the second half of this century. At this point, with no further transition, she goes on to tell an apparently auto-biographical story which the reader initially takes to be one more example of the tendency to cast women as relative beings. That the story does more work than that starts to become apparent when we read the comments that Beauvoir attaches to it:

> I have sometimes been annoyed, in the middle of an abstract discussion, at hearing men say to me: 'You think this or that because you are a woman'; but I knew that my only defence would be to reply: 'I think it because it is true,' thereby removing [*éliminant*] my subjectivity.[101] It would be out of the question to retort: 'And you think the contrary because you are a man', for it is understood that the fact of being a man is no peculiarity.[102] A man is in

[101] Parshley translates *éliminant par là ma subjectivité* as 'thereby removing my subjective self from the argument'. But he also translates Beauvoir's 'je savais que ma seule défense, c'était de répondre' as a straightforward present tense sentence: 'but I *know* that my only defence *is* to reply' (my emphases). My understanding of the French is that Beauvoir tells us about a comment she has heard several times in the past, specifically in a past which still has effects in the present moment (this is the effect of the perfect tense: *je me suis agacée parfois*). Parshley is right to expect a present tense continuation. But that doesn't come. Instead we get a slightly odd imperfect tense. The imperfect has strong descriptive and evocative powers, it presents the past action from the inside, telling us 'this is what it used to feel like'. It can also indicate something that would (habitually) happen over an indefinite period in the past. It is as if Beauvoir first remembers that she has often been annoyed at the sentence 'you think that because you are a woman'. Then she continues by evoking fully what she felt and thought on those repeated occasions: 'je savais que ma seule défense c'était de répondre'. The next phrase continues in the same way; 'il n'était pas question de répliquer'.

The next phrase has to be translated 'it would be out of the question to retort'. To write 'it *was* out of the question' would make it sound as if Beauvoir were talking of one, specific occasion. In the same way, and for the same reason, I translate the first sentence as 'I knew that my only defence would be to reply'. The French, to my ear, is ambiguous as to whether Beauvoir ever actually used this defence. She could have said it, or she could simply be reporting the analysis that would go through her head at these occasions, namely that if she were to say something to this idiot, then this is what the situation would oblige her to say. I shall return to the possibility of remaining silent in the face of the man's claim.

[102] In this and the previous sentence the French text sets up a nice opposition between *répondre* (reply) and *répliquer* (retort), which indicates the difference in tone that Beauvoir has in mind here. Parshley translates both verbs as 'reply'.

the right in being a man; it is the woman who is in the wrong. In fact, just as for the ancients there was an absolute vertical with reference to which the oblique was defined, there is an absolute human type, namely the male.[103] Woman has ovaries, a uterus; there we have [*voilà*] the particular circumstances that imprison her [*l'enferment*] in her subjectivity; one often says that she thinks with her glands. In his grandiosity man forgets that his anatomy also includes hormones, and testicles. He thinks of his body as a direct and normal connection [*relation*] with the world which he believes that he apprehends objectively, while he considers the woman's body to be weighed down by everything specific to it: an obstacle, a prison (*SS* xxi–xxii; *DSa* 14–15, TA).[104]

Why does Beauvoir think that her only option is to reply 'I say it because it is true'? Let me stress that she thinks of this as her only option *for a reply*. To know that this is the only option is not necessarily to choose to take it up. She may decide to turn on her heel and walk off, or in some other way signify that she chooses to remain silent. What such a silence might mean, will be discussed later.[105] This passage tells us that if she were to reply to the man, then this is what she would say, not with a sense of pleasure or jubilation, but with a heavy sense of being forced to choose what might possibly be (in her eyes) the lesser of two distinct evils. Because she is a woman, the man's 'You think that because you are a woman', places her in an impossible situation. She can't very well deny that she is a woman, since that truth is the 'background from which all further claims will stand out', but she cannot, either, accept the man's claim, for instance by saying that 'of course I think this because I am a woman'. There are two reasons

[103] Parshley translates *le type masculin* as 'the masculine [type]', even in a context where it is a question of the male body with its testicles and hormones.

[104] This passage contains a number of terms emphasizing the fact that the woman is being turned into the particular as opposed to the man, who is perceived as universal. Since it is difficult to translate these without losing some of the philosophical overtones, I signal the original French in square brackets here:

being a man is no peculiarity [*n'est pas une singularité*];

Woman has ovaries, a uterus; there we have the particular circumstances [*voilà des conditions singulières*];

weighed down by everything specific to it [*tout ce qui le spécifie*].

[105] I am deeply grateful to Stanley Cavell for suggesting this example.

for this. First, it is not possible for her to relativize the man in the same way that he relativizes her: he doesn't think of himself as engaging his subjectivity in the discussion, or even if he does, he doesn't think of that subjectivity as having anything to do with his male body, and doesn't realize, therefore, that he is a *man* engaging in an intellectual conversation.[106] For this reason he would not understand what the retort 'and you think the contrary because you are a man' would imply: he would simply see it as a sign that the woman had given up trying to come up with 'proper' intellectual arguments to support her views. In this situation it does not help the woman to be as well or better educated as her interlocutor, or to have a superior or equally prestigious social position: it is the specific fact of her being a woman that is mobilized to undercut her arguments.

In other words, in a situation where the woman is defined as deviant in relation to an absolute, any reminders that his interlocutor actually is female will make the man experience what she says as relative, insignificant, and untrue. It is to save her intellectual integrity that Beauvoir has to 'remove her subjectivity', and it is precisely the fact of having to do that, that makes the situation unfair, unequal, and ultimately oppressive to her. To make her 'remove her subjectivity' is to choke her voice.[107] This is why the question of choosing silence as an alternative to this reply becomes so complicated. The man's comment is already an aggressive attempt to silence her. Were she to choose to remain silent, she would have to find some way of showing that *this* silence is *her own* silence. This is not exactly an easy task. (So perhaps turning on her heels?) In this context it is deeply significant that Beauvoir's 'I am a woman' *precedes* the anecdote: if she hadn't

---

[106] As mentioned before: this was surely a very likely scenario in France in 1949. In the 1990s some men will think differently. To explore such a different situation is precisely to follow up Beauvoir's invitation to consider her example in the light of our own lives. See also my discussion of disagreement on the following pages.

[107] For Beauvoir this is an act of oppression. In *Pyrrhus et Cinéas* (1944) she writes that the primary condition of freedom is to 'be allowed to appeal. I shall therefore fight against those who want to choke my voice, prevent me from expressing myself, prevent me from being' (113; my translation). I shall return to this quotation at the end of this essay.

established her subjectivity in the text precisely by placing that utterance before all the others, before telling us the story, she might not have been able to see that the man's arrogant 'You think that because you are a woman' amounts to an attempt to exclude her from philosophy.

Beauvoir complains that the man forces her to *eliminate* her subjectivity. But she also complains that the man's belief that the woman's body is somehow more limiting, more particular than his own, *imprisons* the woman in her subjectivity. In 1949, Beauvoir states, proudly and with much philosophical energy: 'I am a woman'. In 1931, however, she thought differently: 'I did not think of myself as a "woman": I was *me*', she writes in *The Prime of Life* (*PL* 62; *FA* 73). There is no reason to believe that she had stopped thinking 'I am me' in 1949. The difference is that she no longer believes that the statement 'I am a woman' is incompatible with the statement 'I am me'. Beauvoir, then, wants neither to eliminate her subjectivity, nor to be imprisoned in it; she wants to understand herself as a woman, without losing her sense of freedom (transcendence).[108] This is why she dismisses both essentialism and nominalism at the beginning of *The Second Sex*: we might say that while the former seeks to imprison women in their specific subjectivity, the latter seeks to divest them of it entirely. Beauvoir's feminist project is a sustained attempt to define a different perspective, one that firmly distances itself from both alternatives.

From a Beauvoirean perspective the problem with being imprisoned in one's subjectivity is that it implies that one *is* a woman in an essentialist sense. If one wholeheartedly believes that one *is* a woman in this sense, one is alienated and in bad faith. (This would be true whether the person in question had a female body, was a male-to-female transsexual, or someone with a male body living, dressing, and loving like a woman. To be alienated is to identify with the Other's image of what a woman is by attempting to freeze one's subjectivity into the desired picture,

---

[108]   Kate Soper writes that Beauvoir attempts to encompass 'two contrary but equally compelling assertions of identity: "I am a woman" and "I simply am" '. Beauvoir's whole work, Soper adds, is 'the sustained expression . . . of this "woman–person" doublet' (*Troubled Pleasures* 176).

thus denying freedom by turning existence into essence.[109]) The person who takes herself to *be* a woman in this sense, loses her claim to universality—to be someone capable of speaking the truth—because her thought is now imagined to be pervaded by her femininity. This is why Beauvoir has to refuse to be imprisoned in her subjectivity.

To have to eliminate her subjectivity is no better, however. For then the woman is also alienated, this time either into an absurd picture of a general human being without sex, or into the picture of a man. (This is the option she would in effect be resigning herself to take up were she to say 'I say it because it is true'.) Losing touch with her subjectivity, she has to cut herself off from her own lived experience in the very act of philosophizing. Beauvoir is not about to accept an invitation to turn herself into a travesty in this way. Yet she can't just accept the man's alternative, accept that she says what she says because she is a woman, because the situation here described is one in which the man has just demonstrated his intellectual bankruptcy by having recourse to an *ad feminam* argument. One cannot win a debate with an opponent who sinks to such levels by responding in kind. So Beauvoir chooses to assert the truth of her claims instead. (She

[109] Rather than insisting that they are a man or a woman, some transgendered people insist that they are *neither* one or the other sex. Alice Myers, a woman—I mean woman in the usual physical sense—portrayed in Melanie Thernstrom's 1998 article 'Sexuality 101' is a case in point. An undergraduate at Harvard, Alice has changed her name to Alex, lives in the male dorm, has a girlfriend, but has had no hormone treatment or surgery. Alex accepts that he is female, and declares not that he is a man, but that he is *not* a woman. Alex doesn't want to call himself a woman because he does not want to do what women are conventionally supposed to do: 'You have to be constantly fighting society: I'm still a woman even though I'm sleeping with women. I'm still a woman even though I don't know how to cook and I hate wearing dresses. . . . It's so much easier for me to say "Screw it, I'm not a woman" and try to do what I want to do' (100). On this evidence it looks as if Alex's image of what a woman is, is alienated (fixed, other-imposed) in Beauvoir's sense of the word. Instead of identifying with a certain cultural image of femininity, however, Alex appears to build his identity on the denial of the same image.

In a presentation at the 1998 Chicago Humanities Festival, the well-known transgender activist Kate Bornstein stressed, in a very different way, that she considers herself neither male nor female.

does not, however, *deny* that her views have anything to do with the fact of being a woman.) Her response is a subtle hint—probably altogether missed by the man—that she wishes to claim her own particularity *without* abdicating her claim to speak with the ambition of the universal (i.e. to claim that what she is saying is true).

To spell out the implications: if the philosophical institution seeks to eliminate women's subjectivity, women (and that includes Beauvoir) simply cannot be philosophers. Or to be more precise: if a woman is barred from including her subjectivity in philosophy (in 'abstract conversations'), she cannot become the kind of philosopher who has to stake her subjectivity in her judgements. If, under such conditions, a woman *still* insists on becoming a philosopher, her only options would be to do mathematical logic, or various forms of positivist philosophy (i.e. to choose forms of work that do not draw on the thinker's subjectivity to any great extent), or, alternatively, to masquerade as a man, to persuade herself that she is 'just a human being', just like all her male colleagues. But since her male colleagues' maleness is not philosophically problematic to them, the woman philosopher who thinks she is 'just a human being' will from the outset be prevented from having recourse in her thought to the full range of her own experiences, whereas her male colleagues will not be prevented from doing so by their sex.[110] This means that although she may well produce serious work, she risks missing out on those exhilarating moments when one's thought truly seems to illuminate one's experience and vice versa, the moments when one finally recognizes that '*this* is how it is with me'. Without such moments, many of us surely would not feel much satisfaction in intellectual work at all. (I take the longing for such moments of human and intellectual satisfaction to be what gives Jane Tompkins's 'Me and My Shadow' its energy and interest.) For Beauvoir to say that there is no divorce between philosophy and

---

[110]   The male philosopher's social class or race may interfere with his thought in somewhat similar ways. The question of sexuality or sexual desire, however, appears to be somewhat different. The tradition of male homosexuals claiming philosophy as their own stretches from Socrates to Foucault and beyond. There is work to be done on the reasons for this.

life, then, is to say that philosophy has to be a place where women's subjectivity is considered just as universal as men's. It is not least in *this* sense that Beauvoir's defiant 'I am a woman' becomes the truth which provides the background for everything she goes on to say in *The Second Sex*.

If we now move from the philosophical claims developed in Beauvoir's anecdote to its methodological and stylistic implications, the first thing to note is that she chooses to make her point through the telling of a story. This procedure is remarkably consonant with that of ordinary language philosophers: 'The appeal to "what we should say if . . ." requires that we imagine an example or story, sometimes one more or less similar to events which may happen any day, sometimes one unlike anything we have known', Stanley Cavell writes ('Aesthetic Problems' 95). In fact, Beauvoir is not only telling us a story, she is telling us a story about a conversation, consisting entirely of considerations of what a man and what a woman might say in a certain situation. The dialogue is the form or the genre closest to the heart of the kind of philosophy that proceeds from ordinary language.

According to Austin, the point of telling stories is to imagine concrete situations where it becomes possible to see whether we agree or disagree about what we should say in such a situation:

> no situation . . . is ever 'completely' described. The more we imagine the situation in detail, with a background of story—and it is worth employing the most idiosyncratic or, sometimes, boring means to stimulate and to discipline our wretched imaginations   the less we find we disagree about what we should say. Nevertheless, *sometimes* we do ultimately disagree . . . ('Plea' 184).

For Austin, then, disagreement is essential to the procedures of ordinary language philosophy: 'A disagreement as to what we should say is not to be shied off, but to be pounced upon: for the explanation of it can hardly fail to be illuminating' ('Plea' 184). Cavell expands the point:

> if we find we disagree about what we should say, it would make no obvious sense to attempt to confirm or disconfirm one or other of our responses by collecting data to show which of us is in fact

right.[111] What we should do is either (*a*) try to determine why we disagree (perhaps we are imagining the story differently)—just as, if we agree in response we will, when we start philosophizing about this fact, want to know why we agree, what it shows about our concepts; or (*b*) we will, if the disagreement cannot be explained, either find some explanation for *that*, or else discard the example. Disagreement is not disconfirming: it is as much a datum for philosophizing as agreement is ('Aesthetic Problems' 95).

Beauvoir's anecdote is an exceptionally good invitation to the dialogic process both Austin and Cavell see as constitutive of philosophy. 'I knew that my only defence would be to reply: "I think it because it is true" ', she writes. Many feminists in the 1990s would strongly disagree, insisting that they would *never* say, let alone be tempted to say, 'I think it because it is true' in the situation Beauvoir describes. Many of my students report that they would want to say: 'Of course I think this because I am a woman', adding 'and you think the contrary because you are a man', for good measure. I imagine that theorists as different as Luce Irigaray and Carol Gilligan might be inclined to agree with my students. Yet further discussion usually reveals that my students have made a number of presuppositions about the situation that Beauvoir most likely did not make. When I ask for some concrete examples of situations in which they would say 'of course I think so because I am a woman', it turns out that most of them overlook Beauvoir's reference to the 'abstract conversation'. Some take the man's reply to be an appeal to expertise. This is not a bad idea: in some situations, surely, the fact of being a woman (of having been brought up as a woman) bestows special insight. One student once suggested the following example: 'Of course I made wonderful suggestions about the table decorations. I think so well about these things because I am a woman.' Or in a different version: perhaps it makes sense to say that 'you say that the

---

[111]   This is another reason why appeals to 'what we should say' are not appeals to expertise in the sense of knowledge of facts about language (see above, 208–9). Elsewhere Cavell writes: 'When the philosopher who proceeds from ordinary language tells us, "You can't say such-and-such", what he means is that you cannot say that *here* and communicate *this* situation to others, or understand it for yourself' ('Must' 21).

department will vote against this proposal because you are a woman', meaning 'because you have been trained as a woman in this culture, you have a unique insight into the emotional dynamics of faculty meetings'.

But this raises the question of the tone in which 'you say this because you are a woman' is spoken. As Cavell puts it, 'saying something is never *merely* saying something, but is saying something with a certain tune and a proper cue and while executing the appropriate business' ('Must' 33). If the man's phrase is to be interpreted as an invitation to the woman to admit expertise, the assumption is that the man is quite admiring in his tone. 'You say that because you are a woman' then becomes similar to something like 'You say that because you are a plumber', spoken on a tone of admiration or pleasure at the insight the other person has just produced. Beauvoir's story, not least the word 'retort', indicates that she felt irritation. Here we may suspect that she is excessively sensitive, a shrinking intellectual violet, or overly paranoid ('all men are out to get me'), but for the sake of the argument I will assume that her experience of irritation is a reasonable response to something in the man's remark. If so, it is likely to be a response to aggression or condescension. It is, of course, still possible to retort 'Indeed I say it because I am a woman', but now the tone of the reply is likely to be hostile, not proud or satisfied. At this point, in fact, both interlocutors would be angrily trading *ad feminam* and *ad hominem* arguments. The price one pays for this is to lose sight of the original 'abstract conversation' for ever. This is why Beauvoir replies 'I say it because it is true', but it is also why she doesn't say it without noting the loss of her subjectivity

This discussion only opens the questions produced by Beauvoir's anecdote. In my teaching I have found that encouragements to imagine different situations and different examples, to imagine what Irigaray or Gilligan or Spivak might say, or to consider what we should say if the man in question was Frantz Fanon and not just any white Frenchman with philosophical ambitions, are immensely helpful in bringing out differences in different theorists' understanding of what a woman is and how sexism works. Different situations will produce different responses. What I have tried to do here is to indicate what motivates Beauvoir's temptation to reply 'I say it because it is true'.

But, someone might want to say, you have basically just told us that nothing can count as a counterargument to Beauvoir: every disagreement just confirms the brilliance of her method. This is what Cavell says about the best way of arguing against a claim based on ordinary language:

> I take it to be a phenomenological fact about philosophizing from everyday language that one feels empirical evidence about one's language to be irrelevant to one's claims.[112] If such philosophizing is to be understood, then that fact about it must be understood. I am not saying that evidence about how (other) people speak can never make an ordinary language philosopher withdraw his typical claims; but I find it important that the most characteristic pressure against him is applied by producing or deepening an example which shows him that *he* would not say what he says 'we' say ('Aesthetic Problems' 95).

The most telling argument against Beauvoir's anecdote, then, would be one that showed that given her own understanding of the social relations between men and women, *she* would not feel 'I say it because it is true' to be the best available response. I have not been able to produce such an argument. It certainly doesn't follow that nobody else could, but the fact that I can't is one reason why I think this anecdote is such a brilliant invitation to consider what it means to be a woman in a sexist world.

It follows from Cavell's analysis that even if we found evidence conclusively proving that every other woman in France in 1949 would say something different from Beauvoir in this situation, then this would neither prove nor disprove her claim about what *she* would say. Rather, such evidence would be important because it would give rise to analysis of the reasons for the differences. Since each woman's response is as valid as every other woman's (this is one implication of what it means to say that we are all speakers of the language), the point is to understand what motivates different

---

[112] This is yet another version of the fundamental idea that philosophy based on ordinary language is not a positivist science, that the point is not to gather statistics, or to appeal to one's own supreme expertise. The point, rather, is to invite the reader to think about what *she* would say.

responses, not to make Beauvoir toe the majority line (or vice versa). As Cavell puts it, 'one sample does not refute or disconfirm another; if two are in disagreement they vie with one another for the same confirmation' (*Claim* 19).

This is why it doesn't make sense to claim that Beauvoir's anecdote is 'exclusionary', for example because it doesn't stage a conversation between a black woman and a white man, doesn't represent an Indian woman or an American woman, and so on. No anecdote or story can represent a universal subject. All one can do is to place a concrete, particular subject on the linguistic stage. Beauvoir's anecdote succeeds if it helps its readers to reach a description of sexism that not only makes sense to those who read it, but invites them to think up new examples or new responses for themselves. If a woman in India or in South Africa or in Norway can show that there are presuppositions in the anecdote that Beauvoir has not noticed, presuppositions that would make one see that other ways of responding would make more sense, this is precisely to participate in the process of building a better analysis of what it means to be a woman, and of sexism. This is why Austin is right to say that disagreements are reasons for rejoicing. We should not forget, however, that some disagreements are so profound that all further conversation comes to a halt. There are cases where even after exhaustive effort we simply do not understand each other at all. These are the situations, as Wittgenstein puts it, when 'I have exhausted the justifications [and] have reached bedrock, and my spade is turned' (*PI* §217). The question is whether the man's 'You say that because you are a woman' produces such a situation. I shall return to this.

There is another sense in which empirical evidence is irrelevant to the procedures of the ordinary language philosopher. The example or story produced does not need to be empirically true. Even when I tell a story in the first person singular ('I have sometimes become annoyed in the middle of an abstract discussion . . .'), it doesn't matter whether I tell the truth. There is actually good reason to doubt the veracity of Beauvoir's anecdote. In *Force of Circumstance* she writes, with specific reference to the genesis of *The Second Sex*:

> I realized that the first question to come up was: What has it meant
> to me to be a woman? At first I thought I could dispose of that
> pretty quickly. I had never had any feeling of inferiority, no one
> had ever said to me: 'You think that way because you're a woman';
> my femaleness had never been irksome to me in any way (*FC* 103;
> *FCa* 136; TA).

Obviously, when it comes to the question of whether anyone
actually ever said to her 'you think that because you are a
woman', Beauvoir flatly contradicts herself. In her essay she
claims it sometimes happens, in her memoirs she claims it never
happened. Empirical research might establish the truth of the
matter. My guess is that Beauvoir told the truth in *The Second Sex*
and lied in her autobiography, but this is of no importance here,
since it makes no difference to the force of her argument
whether her story is empirically true or not. If an entirely fictive
story is found to be powerful when it comes to producing a careful analysis of some question, then it is philosophically useful and
valuable. It is in this sense that 'one feels empirical evidence
about one's language to be irrelevant to one's claims', as Cavell
puts it.[113]

The passage I have quoted here is followed by half a page of
quotations from Aristotle, Aquinas, Genesis, Bossuet, Michelet,
and Benda which all confirm Beauvoir's claim that for traditional
male philosophers 'Humanity is male [*mâle*] and man defines
woman not in herself but as relative to him; she is not regarded as
an autonomous being' (*SS* xxii; *DSa* 15). It is at the end of this
page—which is also the end of the third paragraph of *The Second
Sex*—that Beauvoir sums up her findings, and for the first time
uses the word 'Other' about women:

---

[113] Beauvoir's use of anecdote seems to be different from the use of anecdote
among new historicists. According to Joel Fineman's influential essay 'The
History of the Anecdote', the anecdote is the 'narration of a singular event', and
as such it is 'the literary form or genre that uniquely refers to the real' (67). For
a philosopher such as Beauvoir, the 'reality effect' of the anecdote does not seem
to be all that crucial. Fineman has historical anecdotes, such as those used by
Stephen Greenblatt, in mind. Beauvoir's and Greenblatt's apparently different
uses of anecdote are precisely an example of philosophical disagreement which
could give rise to new insights (about the nature of anecdotes, or existentialism
and New Historicism) if pursued further.

[Woman] is nothing but what the man decrees; thus she is called 'the sex', which means that she appears essentially to the male [*mâle*] as a sexed [*sexué*] being: since she is sex to him, she must be sex absolutely. She is defined and differentiated in relation to man and not he in relation to her; she is the inessential confronting [*en face de*] the essential. He is the Subject, he is the Absolute: she is the Other (*SS* xxii; *DSa* 15; TA).

What got Beauvoir to this point? What evidence has she produced for the claim that woman is the Other? In the first two paragraphs she refers to everyday life (her own and that of her friends), casual reading, literary gossip, common sense, and some mistaken philosophical beliefs. In the third paragraph, she adds extensive analysis of speech acts and linguistic examples (the final paragraph contains another one, namely the reference to the fact that women are called 'the sex [*le sexe*]'). Equally important is her reliance on evidence from her own experience of being a woman, including the feeling of irritation that the encounter with sexist attitudes sometimes produces. Finally, the importance given to the conversation with the man embodies Beauvoir's ambition to produce a world in which a woman's subjectivity is not taken to be either more or less particular or more or less subjective than anyone else's.

There is one striking difference between the preceding text and this rousing finale, which starts with the reference to Aristotle and goes on to invoke a whole list of other philosophers. So far Beauvoir has hardly named any philosophers at all, except extremely briefly in the first paragraph where she dismisses essentialism and nominalism. In that context the only philosophers mentioned by name are Plato and Aquinas, and even there Plato is referred to only by the adjective 'Platonic'. Here, however, she suddenly produces a long list of philosophical names, and then ends the paragraph with a long footnote challenging the views of one of her contemporary philosophical colleagues in France, namely Emmanuel Lévinas. It is as if the analysis of the anecdote of the woman in an intellectual conversation has made her feel free to engage with the philosophical tradition, to use it for her own purposes, and so finally express her distaste for sexist philosophy, however important and influential the philosopher in question may be. (Her first quote comes from Aristotle, who claims that woman is woman in virtue of a certain lack of qualities.) After this paragraph Beauvoir continues with a fairly scholarly discussion of the category of the Other in religion, anthropology, history, and philosophy, which I shall not go into here. It is as if the work carried out in these first pages of *The Second Sex* has enabled her to find her own voice even in relation to traditional philosophical material.

The footnote attached to the last sentence in the text ('she is the Other') is interesting. Here Beauvoir quotes Lévinas's essay *Le temps et l'autre* and says that like all the other philosophers she has just mentioned, Lévinas too writes from the point of view of a man: 'It is striking that he deliberately adopts a man's point of view without signalling the reciprocity of subject and object. When he writes that woman is mystery, he implies that she is mystery for man. Thus a description that presents itself as objective is in fact an affirmation of male [*masculin*] privilege' (*SS* xxii; *DSa* 16; TA).[114] The fact that she ends by launching into a debate with a contemporary French colleague shows that she now has found a voice that she thinks will hold, even in 'abstract discussion'. I read the footnote in which she engages in discussion with Lévinas as an embodiment of Beauvoir's hope that she will no longer need either to eliminate her subjectivity or to imprison herself in it during philosophical conversations. The fact that in this footnote she makes a perfectly clear, perfectly philosophical, but also perfectly feminist point tells us something about what voice Beauvoir's use of herself as a philosophical case study has enabled her to find.

'My Spade is Turned': Exemplarity, Failure, and Freedom

I have reached the end of the first three paragraphs of *The Second Sex*, and I have almost finished my analysis of Beauvoir's philosophical style. In the previous section I showed that Beauvoir

---

[114] My Lévinasian friends think that Beauvoir is unfair to Lévinas here. All they need to do to substantiate this is to show that Lévinas in fact does not write as if it goes without saying that the subject is male, and, more particularly, that he never implies that woman is more of a mystery for man than he is to her.

stakes her subjectivity in her philosophy by using herself—her own experience—as an example, and that her method is dialogical, so that the anecdote about the abstract conversation can be read as an invitation to try to find ourselves in Beauvoir's words. If we can't do that, our disagreement is as philosophically valuable as our agreement. Beauvoir, then, is neither simply speaking as herself without pretensions to represent anyone else (as if that were possible), nor simply speaking for (in the place of, on behalf of) others. She is, rather, staking her own subjectivity in an attempt to speak *to* the other.

Two sets of questions arise from this analysis. First, there is the question of exemplarity. Isn't there something arrogant about using oneself as an example? Isn't this another way of saying that Beauvoir is generalizing from the particular case? And doesn't this resurrect all the problems attached to the attempt to speak for others? Then there is the question of disagreement. So far I have taken it to be entirely productive. But isn't my analysis of Beauvoir's dialogic method far too sanguine, far too confident in something like the fundamental good will of human nature? What happens when the dialogue breaks down? When we have nothing more to say to each other? These are the problems I shall discuss in this last section, which will be followed by a brief conclusion in which I say something about what my reading of the first pages of *The Second Sex* has taught me about the contemporary turn to the personal.

Exemplarity

What does it mean to turn one's own experience into a philosophical example? I have said that the ordinary language philosopher does not claim to know better than anyone else what we should say when. To speak is to participate in the production of meaning. What I mean by my words will be taken as partly constitutive of what the words mean in the language. Fundamentally, it follows from this that my usage exemplifies the meaning of a word as well as anyone else's usage. To put this in another register: because I am a human being I am as good an example of a human being as you are. By making myself exemplary I am assuming that I am no better and no worse than anyone else. To put myself forward as exemplary, then, I do not need to place myself above anyone else. It is in this sense that *any one of us* can pretend to be representative of us all, put ourselves forward as representative or exemplary of what *we* might say.

I just put this argument in Wittgensteinian or Cavellian terms, a language which Beauvoir does not use. In *Pyrrhus and Cinéas*, an essay on the ethics of freedom first published in 1944, she herself formulates very similar thoughts in existentialist terms.[115] In this text, Beauvoir stresses that language and writing (among other acts in the world) are *appeals* to the other. 'Language is an appeal to the freedom of the other, because the sign only becomes sign when it is grasped [*ressaisit*] by a consciousness', she writes (*PC* 104).[116] What the writer wants, is the other's free and unconstrained response: 'I can only appeal to the other's freedom, not force it [*non la contraindre*]' (*PC* 112). The other remains free to respond or not respond to my appeals, however pressing, charming, or enticing they may be. If Beauvoir were to take the view that she knows better than anyone else what a woman is, she would, in her own vocabulary, be imagining that her knowledge and her experiences enable her to 'transcend the other'. If I imagine that my freedom transcends the other's freedom I cast her as limited and finite, as a thing, not as a transcendence. In short, I imagine the other as a lesser being than myself. A narcissist or a vain person might be satisfied with the adulation of such objectified others, Beauvoir writes, but such satisfaction is worthless, for as soon as I imagine that the other is not free, her response loses its value: 'The moment the other appears limited or finite to me, the place he creates for me on earth is as contingent and vain as he is' (*PC* 99). For Beauvoir, then, to write philosophy is to appeal to an other imagined to be

---

[115] I do not think of *Pyrrhus et Cinéas* as an unproblematic work. But I do think that Beauvoir's analysis of freedom, generosity, and the appeal to the other in this text was deeply influential on Sartre's *What Is Literature?* (1947) and that these views always remained fundamental to Beauvoir's understanding of writing. In *The Philosophy of Simone de Beauvoir* Debra Bergoffen has a useful chapter on *Pyrrhus et Cinéas* (45–71). All translations of *Pyrrhus et Cinéas* are mine.

[116] See also *PC* 95 for an example concerning books.

as free and responsible as she is.[117] The man in the abstract conversation has failed to see the woman as free in this sense. He draws the boundaries of the woman's consciousness, or to put it in ultra-existentialist terms, he imagines that he transcends her transcendence.

At this point someone will surely say that since it is obvious that all human beings are not equally free, Beauvoir's philosophy is pure idealism, and conservative or apolitical idealism at that. Beauvoir's concept of freedom deserves much more detailed discussion, but that will have to be the subject of another paper. Let me just briefly say that in *Pyrrhus et Cinéas* she distinguishes between two types of freedom, namely freedom as transcendence (as the existential condition of human beings, this is in principle the same for everyone) and concrete freedom (the social, political, material conditions in which each human being finds herself, and which clearly vary immensely). This is how Beauvoir summarizes the distinction in *The Prime of Life*:

> [In *Pyrrhus et Cinéas*] I distinguished two separate aspects of freedom. It is first the very modality of existence, which willy-nilly, in one way or another, takes up [*reprend à son compte*] all that comes to it from the outside; this internal movement is indivisible, and thus a totality for each individual. On the other hand, the concrete possibilities open to people are unequal. Some have access only to a small part of all those that are available to mankind as a whole, and all their efforts only bring them closer to the platform from which the most privileged are departing. Their transcendence thus loses itself in the collective and takes on the appearance of immanence. In more favourable situations, however, the project becomes a genuine going beyond the given [*dépassement*]; it builds a new future. An activity is good when it aims to conquer for oneself and for others such privileged positions: when it aims to free freedom (*PL* 459; *FA* 628; TA).

Precisely because my acts require the response of free beings, Beauvoir writes, I need to want (and work for) 'health, knowledge,

---

[117] Eva Lundgren-Gothlin has done fundamental work on the concept of the appeal (*l'appel*) in Beauvoir's texts. She is the first to have developed an analysis of what it means when Beauvoir calls female sexual desire an 'appeal to the other' in *The Second Sex*. Some of Lundgren-Gothlin's work on the appeal is forthcoming in English, in the essay entitled 'Simone de Beauvoir, Jean-Paul Sartre, Ethics, Desire and Ambiguity'.

well-being and leisure for all human beings, so that thcir freedom is not consumed in the effort to fight illness, ignorance and poverty' (*PC* 115).[118] When it comes to the concrete situation of writing philosophy or theory, then, Beauvoir would consider it unethical to write in ways that revealed that she did not take the other's existential freedom (to respond in whatever way he or she pleases to her text, including not reading it at all) as seriously as her own. Contemporary critics who unanimously agree that it is unethical to write in ways that silence others, appear to agree. Furthermore, on the existential and ethical level, nobody is more or less free than anyone else. To imagine otherwise is to objectify and diminish the other, to imply that some human beings are less exemplary than others. For this reason, it is a cause for outrage for Beauvoir that some people have far greater concrete freedom, far more extensive opportunities, than others.

Beauvoir formulates an answer to the question of what a woman is by putting forward her own experience as 'exemplary' or 'representative' of the experience of women. Although the terms 'exemplary' and 'representative' are not synonymous, there is an intimate connection between them. To represent can mean to stand for or speak for others. To exemplify is to be a particular instance of the general. If I find the courage to make an example of myself, I am doing so in the hope that it will be recognized that my experience is an illuminating instance of a more general state of affairs. But as soon as I make any claim at all about any state of affairs, I am saying something about what the world looks like to me. However much I stake my subjectivity in them, such claims are in their very nature going to be general. Whether I say 'it is raining' or 'woman is the Other', I am speaking for others, inviting them to see if they can find themselves—their own experiences, their own world-view—in such claims, hoping that they will be able to do so, but also knowing that they may not. This is what happens when Beauvoir attempts to find out what a woman is.

The difference I want to get at here is the difference between

---

[118] Beauvoir's distinction, in 1944, between existential and concrete freedom represents a clear departure from Sartre's *Being and Nothingness* (1943), in which there is no concept of concrete freedom.

speaking for others in a way which leaves no space for them to respond, or in a way that attempts to coerce a specific response: such ways of speaking would not be good faith appeals to the freedom of the other; they would be monologic and not dialogic. The other is not imagined to be as free as the speaker is. (The man in the abstract conversation provides a good example of this attitude.) This contrasts with attempts to speak for others by addressing them (appealing to them) in the hope of a response. This difference is erased by the simplistic insistence that to speak *for* is always to silence the other. If I speak out on behalf of someone else, I am usually not preventing them from speaking too. The difference turns on two elements: the presence or absence of a stance of superiority in the speaker, and the presence or absence of a dialogic attitude. If the other to whom I am speaking is imagined to be someone who knows less than I do about the meaning of words or the question of being human, or someone whose existential freedom is less extensive or less important than mine, I am not asking for the other's free response, but for adulation and thoughtless admiration. Contemporary critics are right to see such condescension as a form of discursive violence, as an attempt to silence or belittle the other. To determine whether such a stance is at work in a text, careful analysis is required. It is simply not enough to pick a 'we' or a 'they' out of context and claim that a text containing such rhetorical features must be 'exclusionary' or otherwise belittling of others.[119]

[119] This sounds a little abstract. To give an example: Elizabeth Spelman's discussion of 'exclusionism' in feminist theory has a tendency to do this. Spelman writes: ' "We need to hear the many voices of women." . . . Who are "we" here, what is the need, and what will the hearing involve? "We" are of course those who have been heard from, who have been calling the shots in feminism, who now recognize a need that can only be satisfied by hearing from other women' (163). I would have thought that there are many cases in which the 'we' in a sentence such as 'We need to hear the many voices of women' could refer to the writer *and* anyone who reads the text, or to anyone at all with an interest in feminist theory.
In *Sexual/Textual Politics* I deliberately wrote: 'recent work on Third World Women has much to teach us' (86). Some critics took the bait and upbraided me for excluding Third World women from my arguments. But 'us' in this sentence can refer to anyone at all with an interest in feminist theory, including women from the so-called Third World. It is not enough simply to be Nigerian or

To see one's own experience as exemplary, as an instance of a more general case, is not the same as to generalize from a particular case. While it is possible to do the latter without putting one's own subjectivity on the line, it is quite impossible to do the former without staking oneself in one's claims.[120] 'The problem of the critic, as of the artist', Cavell writes, 'is not to discount his subjectivity, but to include it; not to overcome it in agreement, but to master it in exemplary ways' ('Aesthetic Problems' 94). If my subjectivity—my experience—is to be of any use in my criticism or my philosophy, Cavell seems to say, I have to be able to make it exemplary. Otherwise it will remain staunchly particular, and so of no interest to anybody but myself. To make it exemplary is to show what light it can shed on a general question, not to claim that it is itself general, that it in some mysterious way already subsumes that of others.

By turning myself into an example in a way which does not assume that I know better than anyone else what the meaning of my experience is, I deprive myself of the feeling of invulnerability that an inner conviction of narcissistic superiority could provide. Such speech makes me vulnerable, regardless of what it is about. Unlike Ruth Behar, I don't think that 'vulnerable' speech needs to be about emotions or feelings or even about concrete autobiographical experiences. The sense of vulnerability, or risking one's whole being in one's writing, can be just as overwhelming for someone who puts forward an intellectual analysis in which she

---

Norwegian to understand one's own condition. Recent work on Nigerian or Norwegian women will have much to teach women who live in those countries, just as recent work on women in the US ought to be illuminating to women born and bred in the US. None of this implies that the 'recent work' in question should be listened to in a particularly subservient way: it will be a starting point for response, discussion, and criticism just like any other work. Nor does the statement imply that all women in all situations will learn the same things from the 'recent work' in question. To leap to such assumptions is precisely to produce the false generalizations the critics in question usually wish to avoid.

[120] In my book on Beauvoir, I approach the question of the personal in philosophy towards the end of ch. 5. But there I fail to understand the difference between using oneself as an example and generalizing from the particular case (see 146–7 for a discussion which in some ways now appears as an early attempt to write the present essay).

has drawn on her whole experience, and used all her intellectual and emotional powers, as for someone who publishes the rawest of autobiographies. Because my writing is an appeal to the other's freedom, I cannot coerce or control the other's response. Writing done in good faith (this means writing for which the writer is ready to take responsibility) is therefore intrinsically risky, whether or not I reveal autobiographical details about myself in the text. As Cavell puts it in a different context, 'To speak for yourself . . . means risking the rebuff . . . of those for whom you claimed to be speaking; and it means risking having to rebuff . . . those who claimed to be speaking for you' (*Claim* 27).

In whatever mode it occurs, it takes courage to turn oneself into an example. This is, I think, what Cavell means when he speaks of the difficulties of *finding one's voice*. Since we all are equally representative of humanity, why should I take it upon myself to say something? Surely there is an unbearable arrogance here. Why speak if you are no better than anyone else? (This kind of question comes right out of my non-bourgeois Norwegian childhood, where the first cultural commandment was 'don't believe there's anything special about you'.[121]) What is liberating about Cavell's view is that he makes it clear that one really doesn't need to be special in any way to have the right to speak: 'Who beside myself could give me the authority to speak for us? . . . [W]e are each in a position to give ourselves the right, take it from ourselves, as it were', he writes (*Pitch* 9). To speak is the birthright of any human being. Yet, even when this realization sinks in, I still need to find the courage to go ahead and make a spectacle (an example) of myself, my values, my judgements, my skills.

The moment Beauvoir writes the first word of *The Second Sex*, she enacts what Cavell in *A Pitch of Philosophy* has called the 'systematic arrogation of voice, or the arrogant assumption of the right to speak for others' (viii). Cavell's *arrogation* deliberately mixes 'arrogance' with 'arrogate' (to claim unduly, to attribute unjustly). In so far as I am speaking when others are not, there is

---

[121] Norwegians and Danes will recognize a very free translation of *Janteloven*'s first commandment: 'Du skal ikke tro at du *er* noe'.

always something undue, unfair, and unjust about it. By arrogating the voice of philosophy to herself, Beauvoir is taking, as Cavell
says about Austin and Wittgenstein, 'what [she does and says] to
be representative or exemplary of the human condition as such.
In this way [she] interpret[s] philosophy's arrogance as the arrogation of the right to speak for us' (*Pitch* 8). For Cavell, the writing of theory or philosophy necessarily passes through such a
moment of arrogation. In contrast, contemporary critics who
worry about 'speaking *for*', sometimes appear to believe that it is
possible to speak *without* such a moment of arrogation. But there
is always someone who is not speaking. Even the most well-intentioned attack on 'exclusionary' writing is written in the presence
of someone else's silence.

The moment she says 'I am a woman' Beauvoir makes her pitch
to the reader. Arrogating voice to herself, she challenges the
reader to think about the experiences she puts forward. The arrogance in her claim lies in the fact that she dares to speak at all,
that she arrogates to herself the right to speak. But there is
another form of arrogance here too, an ambitious wish to make
us all agree with her, regardless of our own specific positions in
the world. In 1949, for a woman to stake her right to philosophy—
her right to be taken seriously as a philosopher—on the statement 'I am a woman' was wildly ambitious. No wonder, perhaps,
that Beauvoir spent so much time later on trying to divert attention from her immodest claim, by insisting that *The Second Sex*
should not be given the name of philosophy.[122]

To 'arrogate voice' to oneself as a thinker or critic, then, has
nothing to do with dictating to others what they should think. It
means, rather, to claim for oneself the right to appeal to the
judgement of others: 'All the philosopher, this kind of philosopher, can do is to express, as fully as he can, his world, and attract
our undivided attention to our own,' Cavell writes ('Aesthetic
Problems' 96). The first epigraph to this essay is taken from the
introduction to the second volume of Beauvoir's autobiography,

---

[122] Michèle Le Dœuff has called Beauvoir a 'tremendously well-hidden
philosopher' (*Hipparchia's Choice* 139). Beauvoir herself kept giving interviews
insisting that Sartre was the original philosopher, not she (see ch. 1 'Second
Only to Sartre' in my *Simone de Beauvoir* for further discussion of this theme).

where she wonders how to defend her wish to write about herself at considerable length. Her justification is that if a person reveals herself with sincerity, it doesn't matter whether that person is remarkable or unremarkable. If there is honest self-examination, just about everyone will have something at stake in the text: 'It is impossible to shed light on one's own life without at some point illuminating the life of others', Beauvoir notes (*PL* 10; *FA* 1; TA). When Beauvoir writes about herself, then, it is not out of a sense of superiority to others. Any life can be as exemplary as any other life. Obituaries are a case in point. We read obituaries of people we have never heard of precisely because they invite us to think about what we ourselves have done with our lives, what we could still do with them, and so, ultimately, about what it is possible to make out of a human life, and how the world shapes that making.

In *The Second Sex* Beauvoir finds her voice by representing her world—which, as she just has made very clear, is a woman's world—as honestly as she can. It is by trying to understand her own situation as fully as she can that she will be able to inspire me, her reader, into examining my own condition. What I have been trying to show in this paper is that her writing in the beginning of *The Second Sex* is uniquely powerful as philosophy *because* it is fully marked by Beauvoir's own subjectivity. The difference between the Beauvoir who feels tempted to answer 'I say it because it is true' to the man in the abstract discussion, and the Beauvoir who writes *The Second Sex* is that whereas the former would have been obliged to eliminate her subjectivity, the latter has refused to do so. As Stanley Cavell puts it, this woman has eliminated her defensiveness.[123] Nor is the woman who writes *The Second Sex* a prisoner of her female subjectivity. In these pages Beauvoir's *voice* shows that she speaks as the woman and philosopher she is, neither more nor less. If we now understand what this means, we also understand why she does not need constantly to preface her claims with 'in my view', or 'speaking as a white French bourgeois woman'.

A somewhat different form of arrogance still remains to be discussed. That is Beauvoir's outrageous ambition to speak for all.

---

[123] Private communication in response to an advanced draft of this paper.

Cavell considers that ordinary language philosophy has much in common with aesthetic judgements, which according to Kant are judgements in which we aspire to speak with a 'universal voice'. Throughout this essay I have argued that Beauvoir's particular kind of philosophy is illuminated by comparisons with ordinary language philosophy such as Cavell understands it. So also in this case. Cavell takes Kant to mean that in making aesthetic judgements we are not simply making gratuitous remarks about our own personal tastes, but aiming to achieve universal agreement: ideally we would like everybody else to come to see what we see. The hope of agreement constitutes the aspiration towards the universal. It is in order to be as convincing as possible that critics of various kinds engage in rational argument, in building our 'patterns of support', as Cavell labels them ('Aesthetic Problems' 94). To say that they do this in the *hope* of agreement, however, is not to claim that such agreement will ever be reached. Even more important, perhaps, is the fact that, as Cavell puts it, 'even were agreement in fact to emerge, our judgments, so far as aesthetic, would remain essentially as subjective, in [Kant's] sense, as they ever were' ('Aesthetic Problems' 94).

In the text of *The Second Sex* the anecdote about the abstract discussion is intended as an illustration to Beauvoir's claim that whenever 'woman' is defined, it is as a limitation. But it also resonates with her own defiant 'I am a woman', and so reveals the enormous ambition that informs her project. Beauvoir's aim is nothing short of revolutionary: she wants to produce the dramatic changes necessary to *make* the statement 'I am a woman' appear as something else than a limitation, to place woman in a reciprocal relationship to man. And now it is possible to see why her 'arrogation of voice' is a necessary part of this project. For how can we ever achieve reciprocity between men and women if women are denied the right to speak for all, to speak with the ambition of the universal, to speak in the outrageous hope that we will all agree with them, a right that men have considered unproblematically theirs for so many centuries? For women to gain the right to speak for all is, as a matter of course, also to gain the right to be philosophers, the right to define themselves at once as women and as lovers of wisdom and seekers of truth. It is no coincidence that throughout *The Second Sex* Beauvoir insists that one of the worst effects of sexism is that it excludes women from the universal at every turn.[124]

If the ambition to reach the universal can be understood as speaking in the hope of encountering agreement, and if at the same time the fundamental strategy of the ordinary language philosopher or the literary critic may be characterized as an appeal to the subjectivity of the other, an appeal that occurs in the very act of staking one's own subjectivity in one's claims, then the arrogance of Beauvoir's 'I am a woman' consists precisely in the fact that she *arrogates to herself the right to speak as the woman she is with the ambition of the universal.* In so doing she exemplifies the kind of freedom *The Second Sex* is about.

Failure and Freedom

Beauvoir's ambition is to make the other see what she sees. The reception history of *The Second Sex* shows that she was remarkably successful in this enterprise. But in some cases the attempt at making the other see what we see fails. These are not only cases where we disagree, but cases where we don't even start to see what the other sees. What would happen if we imagine that Beauvoir is addressing the sentence 'I am a woman; this truth is the background from which all further claims will stand out' not to essentialists (as I basically did in my reading of the sentence) but to a nominalist who is also an epistemological sceptic? The problem Beauvoir would face then is not how to avoid essentialism, but how to convince the other that there are women and that she is one of them.

Beauvoir's syntax gives prominence to her truth claim. 'I am a woman' is the *truth* that forms the unavoidable background for

---

[124] By this she means that sexist thought deprives women of the chance to make their own experience exemplary, and blocks them from having the ambition or hope that their experience might one day come to speak for all. See e.g. Beauvoir's discussion of Hegel's notion of the universal in ethics and the prosecution, sometime in the 1890s, of two little girls who had been put to work in a brothel (*SS* 612–17; *DSb* 503–8). Naomi Schor's 'French Feminism is a Universalism' is a useful overview of different kinds of universalism in French feminist theory.

everything she will go on to say. In what way are we to take this? Is Beauvoir inviting us to consider 'I am a woman' as an empirical hypothesis to be verified by a checking of pre-existing facts? In so far as she is trying to answer the question of what a woman is, this seems rather to beg the question. Moreover, an existentialist philosopher would hardly take the view that objective facts somehow speak for themselves. It is highly unlikely that Beauvoir's 'I am a woman' represents a concession to objectivism or empiricism. On the other hand, the weight of the word 'truth' precludes subjectivist interpretations: Beauvoir is not saying that although it is her private opinion that she is a woman, you may be equally justified in thinking that she is a man, a child, or a Martian. Clearly, she would like us all to agree that the claim is true. But how would she go about convincing the sceptic?

Just because you say you are a woman, the sceptic might say, it doesn't follow that you are one. (In fact, this is a response one doesn't have to be an epistemological sceptic to share.) You might be psychotic (think of Freud's Schreber), or you might be a pre-operative male-to-female transsexual. In Jenny Livingston's documentary *Paris is Burning*, for example, both Octavia St Laurent and Venus Xtravaganza refer to themselves as women. Venus Xtravaganza may have died because someone took her too literally.[125] Just as Descartes worried that the figures whose hats and coats he saw in the street below him might turn out to be automata and not human beings, I might worry that although you are in every respect the physical incarnation of a highly attractive woman, you may still be a monstrous alien from outer space (this is the theme of innumerable films, including the relatively recent *Species* movies). Or perhaps I don't even suspect that although you have a perfect female body, you are in fact an outrageously sexist and selfish man who has just been forcibly sex-changed by a gang of Mother-worshipping female terrorists (this is the fate of Angela Carter's protagonist in *The Passion of New Eve*). These are the familiar questions of philosophical scepticism, and as everyone knows who has ever been caught up in

---

[125] See Judith Butler, 'Gender Is Burning', esp. 128–37 for an interesting discussion of Jenny Livingston's film.

them, there is no way to satisfy this kind of doubt by appeals to empirical facts.[126]

In the context of such doubt, the autobiographical form of Beauvoir's sentence ('I am a woman' as opposed to 'there are women') is not coincidental. It is as if Beauvoir wants to convey something she has learned from experience. Trying to make the epistemological sceptic understand that she is a woman, Beauvoir is in a position similar to that of Shylock in *The Merchant of Venice* trying to convince hostile Christians that a Jew is a human being just like them:

> Hath not a Jew eyes? Hath not a Jew hands, organs, dimensions, senses, affections, passions; fed with the same food, hurt with the same weapons, subject to the same diseases, healed by the same means, warmed and cooled by the same winter and summer as a Christian is? If you prick us do we not bleed? If you tickle us do we not laugh? If you poison us do we not die? And if you wrong us shall we not revenge? (III. i. 54–62).

There is helplessness, exasperation, and eloquence in Shylock's speech. The emphasis on the most material of human attributes, the body, is striking. Yet none of this moved his Christian opponents. For how can one *prove* by argument alone, even by arguments that place all the stress on the body, that one is a human being, or a woman for that matter?[127]

In a famous incident in 1858 Sojourner Truth's right to speak in the name of enslaved women was challenged by pro-slavery men, who claimed that she wasn't a woman because she had a male voice (the reference to Truth's voice is particularly symbolic here, I think). 'Denying the womanliness of women speaking in public was a familiar ploy', Nell Irvin Painter writes: 'Hostile audiences questioned the sexual identity of American women preachers like Harriet Livermore, of lecturers like the antislavery poet Frances Ellen Watkins Harper, and of actresses like Rachel, the great French tragedian' (139). In response to the challenge,

---

[126] I am inspired to say this by my reading of Cavell's 'Austin and Examples' in *The Claim of Reason* 49–64.

[127] Judith Butler's struggle to prove by rational argument alone that the body is material may be considered a parallel case (see my discussion of Butler's understanding of the body in Ch. 1, above).

Sojourner Truth bared her breasts and taunted the racist men by saying that many white babies had sucked these breasts and grown up to become far more manly than these hecklers, and then asked if they too wanted to suck (see Painter 139). Truth's chances of success were no better and no worse than Shylock's. The naked breasts or the body that bleeds when pricked will not overcome the fundamental doubt of the sceptic.[128] Even in the most convincing of cases there is always the possibility that Descartes so richly acknowledges, namely that my perception of your body is caused by some evil spirit, a malevolent devil intent on playing tricks on me.

Beauvoir's 'I am a woman' can be made to sound both as the fairly level-headed beginning of a conversation, and as the exasperated end point of the same conversation hours later. If we place Beauvoir in the company of Shylock and Sojourner Truth, then 'I am a woman' becomes a last ditch appeal to the other: 'Don't you *see* that I am a woman?' or 'What will it take for you to realize that I am a woman?', are possible glosses here. If we imagine that the sentence is the end of a long and futile conversation, a certain feeling of helplessness may be apparent in Beauvoir's voice. For how can she convince her interlocutors that she is a woman if they can find no way out of their fundamental scepticism?

At this point—where I imagine Beauvoir throwing up her

---

[128] Deborah McDowell discusses white feminists' use of the figure of Sojourner Truth to represent black women or black feminists in 'Transferences' (see esp. 158–63). I am using her famous statement here to exemplify a specific epistemological dilemma. In this case, Sojourner Truth represents all women asked to prove that they are women (not just black women, since the hecklers don't seem to have doubted that Soujourner Truth was black). I suppose one could say that I am choosing to foreground Truth's sex, and in so doing, I am placing her race in the background. The implication is not that race always has to be considered the background of sex. (In the case of Fanon (see above, 203) I foreground his race, not his sex.) McDowell writes that 'Truth's declarative question—"Ain't I a Woman"—might be read as "political" and "epistemological" simultaneously (159). This is obviously right. But what aspect (these two or others) of Truth's speech act to foreground is not given once and for all: the reason for turning to her experience will determine the interpretation given of her famous statement. Those reasons are themselves open to criticism. There are bad reasons as well as good reasons for using a given example.

hands in despair at ever being able to communicate her sense
that she is a woman to her interlocutor—I am reminded of
Stanley Cavell's discussion of the peculiar feelings of exasperation
and helplessness that arise when discussions between a positivist
analytic philosopher and a philosopher proceeding from ordinary language reach an impasse:

> The positivist grits his teeth when he hears an analysis given out as
> a logical one which is so painfully remote from formality, so obvi-
> ously a question of how you happen to feel at the moment, so
> psychological; the philosopher who proceeds from everyday
> language stares back helplessly, asking, 'Don't you feel the differ-
> ence? Listen: you *must* see it.' Surely, both know what the other
> knows, and each thinks the other is perverse, or irrelevant, or
> worse ('Aesthetic Problems' 90).

There is the same sense of impasse, of having reached bedrock, at
the bottom of some aesthetic disagreements: 'It is essential to
making an aesthetic judgment', Cavell writes, 'that at some point
we be prepared to say in its support: don't you see, don't you hear,
don't you dig? The best critic will know the best points. Because
if you do not see *something*, without explanation, then there is
nothing further to discuss' ('Aesthetic Problems' 93). Addressed
to the sceptic, Beauvoir's 'I am a woman' takes on the same status
as sentences such as: 'Can't you hear the desolation in this line?'
or 'Don't you see that this painting treats light in a different way
from that one?'

Efforts at agreement must end somewhere. The sceptic may
never agree that Beauvoir is a woman, just as she may never agree
that we know that there is a tomato on the table. Even after the
best and most genuine effort we may still fail to see what the other
sees. In the end, when all attempts to find agreement have failed,
thinkers of Beauvoir's and Cavell's kind must stake their claims on
their own experience. Cavell writes: 'At some point, the critic will
have to say: This is what I see. Reasons—at definite points, for
definite reasons, in different circumstances—come to an end'
('Aesthetic Problems' 93). Cavell is here alluding to
Wittgenstein's famous comment 'If I have exhausted the justifications I have reached bedrock, and my spade is turned. Then I am
inclined to say: "This is simply what I do" ' (*PI* §217).

Wittgenstein's image is arresting: when it is impossible to dig any further, when productive labour comes to an end, then there is nothing left but to say 'This is what I do'. It should be noted that he does not necessarily say this: he reports, rather, that he is *inclined* to say this. The parallel to Beauvoir's 'I knew that my only defence would be to say . . .' is quite striking. What Wittgenstein does not say or do is equally revealing: he does not, for example, lift up the spade and hit his interlocutor over the head with it. Nor does he continue to hack furiously away with the bent spade. Rather, he recognizes bedrock when he hits it. Whether or not he actually says 'This is what I do', the inclination to say so is an acknowledgement of the nature of bedrock, an acknowledgement that bedrock is the kind of thing that no amount of spadework will ever make a dent in. Wittgenstein's attitude here is quite gentle, without being in the least submissive. 'This is what I do' and the silence that follows are restful and utterly non-defensive. They indicate that Wittgenstein accepts that the other will never see what he sees, understand what he is doing. He is not prepared to go any further: he will neither use violence, nor keep battering away at the other. What he will do, however, is to take his stand on the value of his own view. He is *not* saying 'This is what I have been doing, but now that I realize that you are unable to see it in the way I do, I will stop doing it.' Had he said something like that, he would have let the other's inability (however well founded) to see what he sees determine his own perception; in Beauvoir's terms this would be tantamount to alienating his own subjectivity into an image projected by the other. In the abstract conversation, Beauvoir is, as it were, searching for a path towards this kind of non-defiant silence.[129] The whole of *The Second Sex* is an attempt to explain why it is so much harder for a woman than for a man to find this path.

Leaning on his bent spade, Wittgenstein demonstrates respect for the other's difference, for the other's right to continue to see what he sees. If the sceptic simply cannot see that there are women in the world and that Beauvoir is one of them ('It may

---

[129] I want to acknowledge that it was Stanley Cavell's extremely apt comments on a draft of this paper that helped me to bring out the value of the silence—the non-defensiveness—in these cases.

look like that, but how do I know these are not just appearances, induced by evil demons or regulatory discourses?'), then Beauvoir's spade will also be turned. She cannot continue to insist for ever. In this context, saying 'This is what I do' means acknowledging that the sceptic will not be able to share her perspective, without taking this as a reason to abandon her own project. Instead she will continue to show what the world looks like from the point of view of a person who takes herself to be a woman, in the hope that others will come to see what she sees. In the case of the abstract conversation, we might hope, then, that a woman could find a silence accompanied not by aggression but a sense of restful self-respect, a knowledge that the resistance and aggression of this other is no longer enough to eliminate her subjectivity.

The case Wittgenstein has in mind when he finds that he has to say 'This is what I do' is a philosophical conversation, in which both parties have made a serious good faith effort to understand the source of their divergence, but which nevertheless failed. This parallels Beauvoir's understanding of the ideal conditions of intellectual dialogue, namely that I should be free to speak and that you should be free to respond:

> First I must be allowed to appeal. I shall therefore fight against those who want to choke my voice, prevent me from expressing myself, prevent me from being. . . . Then I need to have before me human beings who are free *for me*, who can respond to my appeal (*PC* 113).[130]

To choke someone's voice is to deprive them of their fundamental freedom to speak, to participate in human decision making. A writer needs the response of the reader. If her response is to be worth anything, however, it must be freely given. (This is why Beauvoir considers both reading and writing to be acts of generosity.) For this reason I shall have to fight not only against those who attempt to choke my voice, but also against those who attempt to choke your voice. If, as I have tried to show, the beginning of *The*

---

[130] Eva Lundgren-Gothlin's 'Simone de Beauvoir, Jean-Paul Sartre' uses this quotation. The connection that Beauvoir makes here between *appeal* and *voice* brings out the parallels between her philosophy and that of Cavell.

Second Sex is an invitation to the other to consider her own experience in response to the text, it now becomes apparent that such an invitation presupposes Beauvoir's commitment to the other's freedom as well as to her own.

Intellectual exchanges nevertheless take place in all kinds of situations. The restful non-defiant and self-respecting silence arising after (or instead of) Wittgenstein's 'This is what I do' will not necessarily arise in other situations. Ruth Behar's story about the woman who ended a presentation by telling about the husband who beat her, also produced silence.[131] In that case, the silence was one of deep embarrassment, a sense that nothing can count as a valid academic response to such experiences. I may also remain silent in response to your appeal because I have resolved to fight it with all my might, and find that my best strategy involves a refusal to talk to you. Silence in the face of the other's appeal, Beauvoir writes, may also be a sign of indifference or icy contempt:

> If we fight against a project, we choose to appear as an obstacle in relation to it. There are projects which simply are of no concern to us; we envisage with indifference the judgments where they are expressed. . . . It happens that my disdain covers not a particular project but a whole human being. Then it is the global project of his being that we refuse and fight against. In that case disdain becomes contempt. I am indifferent to every opinion of those I despise. . . . True contempt is silence: contempt takes away even the wish to contradict and our sense of outrage [*scandale*] (*PC* 106–7).

To Beauvoir there is nothing intrinsically wrong with contempt: the meaning and value of my contempt will depend on the situation in which it occurs. In the same way, indifference in relation to the other's project is sometimes an appropriate and sometimes an inappropriate response. The value of this passage is that it encourages us to think of the many different ways of being silent. Whether my silence is caused by self-respect, exhaustion, opposition, indifference, or contempt it still represents a response to the other's appeal (as Beauvoir would put it), or, as Cavell would put

---

[131] See n. 14, above.

it, a form of acknowledgement of the other's presence.[132] For these thinkers, once an appeal has been expressed, whatever we do (including callous disregard or violent suppression) is a response to it, and that response is our responsibility. (Here we should remember that the man's 'You say that because you are a woman' is not an appeal in Beauvoir's sense of the word, since his intervention clearly shows that he doesn't imagine the woman to be as free as he is.)

To conclude: *The Second Sex* is an appeal to the reader's freedom. By arrogating voice to herself, by staking her own subjectivity in her claims, and by taking herself to be neither more nor less capable of philosophy than the reader whom she is addressing, Simone de Beauvoir shows us how to write personally and philosophically at the same time, without abandoning the outrageous ambition of speaking for all and without silencing the other.

III. SOME CONCLUDING THOUGHTS

In the introduction to this essay, I wrote that I wanted to see if I could find a way to write theory without neglecting or repressing the claims of the personal, but also without dismissing or diminishing the claims of the impersonal, the objective, and the universal. Have I succeeded? By reading *The Second Sex* I have discovered that to write theory in a way that does not neglect the personal entails, among other things, finding a voice of one's own and a way to write that acknowledges the presence of others. It also entails being able to stake one's own experience (subjectivity) in one's general claims, and to do so in a way that addresses the other's freedom.

---

[132] In his fabulous essay on *King Lear*, Cavell writes: 'Whether or not we are acknowledging others is not a matter of choice, any more than accepting the presence of the world is a matter of choosing to see or not to see it. Some persons sometimes are capable of certain blindnesses or deafnesses toward others; but, for example, avoidance of the presence of others is not blindness or deafness to their claim upon us; it is as conclusive an acknowledgment that they are present as murdering them would be' ('Avoidance' 332).

In this essay I place dialogue, exchange, conversation, engagement, and response at the heart of intellectual life.[133] It is not a coincidence, I think, that my engagement with Beauvoir takes the form of extremely attentive close reading. Beauvoir herself thinks of reading as a generous engagement of one's own freedom in the encounter with the other. In a different way, this essay is also a response to the work of Stanley Cavell. Although my main concern is with Beauvoir, I hope that the very fact of placing Beauvoir and Cavell in each other's company sheds new light on both of them. Finally, in the most obvious way the whole of this essay is my belated response to Jane Tompkins's 'Me and My Shadow'. Finding a way to address her concerns without abandoning my own took eleven years.

There is no all-purpose recipe for 'personal' writing of theory here. There are innumerable ways of fulfilling the criteria I arrive at in the last two sections. *The Second Sex* itself certainly does not lend itself to imitation. If I set out to write *like* Beauvoir, I would be denying the lessons I claim to have learned from her. In particular, I would have overlooked the vast differences between her situation and mine, between her audience and the one I can hope for, and of course, between our different experiences. Identifying with Beauvoir, imitating her style, I would only succeed in alienating myself, just as surely as if I identified with some other model for theoretical or personal writing. What Beauvoir teaches me, is that regardless of the mode or style of my writing (theory or autobiography) I have to find a voice of my own, even if the voice I find is a voice that in every way is unlike hers. What Cavell in particular helps me to see, is that the personal is not something given, it is a task (Beauvoir would surely say a 'project'); the personal is not a possession, but something to be learned and refined.[134]

How does Section II of this essay illuminate Section I? Working on Beauvoir's philosophical style I have found myself thinking about the ordinary, the concrete, and the everyday, about situations and

---

[133] The attitude I explore here has considerable implications for one's way of teaching, whether on the graduate or undergraduate level.

[134] This sentence is based on Cavell's expressions, in a personal communication.

examples, about staking one's subjectivity in one's claims, about dialogue and response, about the difficulty of finding a voice, about generosity, responsibility, and freedom, and a host of other things, too: what it means to be a woman, to have a female body, what it means for a woman to write philosophy; and how style and tone matter to philosophical and theoretical writing. Set against such concerns, contemporary debates about the personal and the theoretical have come to look conceptually impoverished to me. All too often current discussions turn out to be based either on the idea that we *must* choose between 'speaking for' or 'speaking as', between writing personally or writing theoretically, between the personal and the impersonal, and between subjectivity and objectivity; or on the equally lame idea that we don't have to choose at all since the two (meaning, the two parts of the same binary oppositions) always go together. The problem is not that the old binary grid is always wrong or mistaken. I have no objection to using words like 'personal' and 'impersonal' and so on. The problem is that it makes us believe that no alternatives are available (except the predictable and to my mind boring deconstruction of the very same binary grid). What I have tried to do is to show that there are alternatives to the binary straitjacket. Investigation of other examples will surely produce other alternatives. I am struck by the fact that theories that make such enormous claims for the virtues of location in practice rarely demonstrate anything like attentive interest in specific cases or situations. In contrast, I have tried to show by example that close attention to a particular case (in this case the beginning of *The Second Sex*) can produce serious theoretical insights.

Working on Beauvoir has also taught me that there is no one way of 'getting personal'. The effects of autobiographical material or emotionally painful revelations in scholarly writing will vary as much as the effects of the most impersonal and objective prose. General claims for the 'vulnerability' or 'openness' of this or that form of writing are hollow. The same rhetorical or thematic elements may have widely varying effects in different contexts, as any literary critic knows. In the same way there is no such thing as one monolithic form of 'theory-writing' which is bound always to have oppressive and silencing effects. Nor can one assume that 'writing personally' always has a set of predictable political effects that 'writing impersonally' somehow does not have. As Cora Diamond might have put it, such effects will depend.

Some theoretical writing is execrable, but so is some so-called 'personal' writing. Explicitly autobiographical and emotional writing can be genuinely open and revealing or just as 'silencing'—just as closed off to engagement from others—as the most arrogantly impersonal prose. A friend of mine who has written both theoretical and autobiographical material once told me that when she wrote theory she didn't think about the reader, but when she wrote more personal work she did. No wonder that she thought that her personal work was far more lively, better written, and more interesting. Beauvoir thinks that all kinds of writing, including theory and philosophy, are appeals to the reader, whether the writer knows it or not. My friend's experience indicates that the tone and style of the finished text will depend a great deal on the writer's own understanding of what she is doing.

Contemporary debates about the personal and the philosophical have been productive for scholars who wish to write in autobiographical ways. In the 1990s, autobiographical and other kinds of personal writing have definitely become more acceptable within the American academy, if not necessarily elsewhere.[135] On the other hand, the limited conceptual range and the fairly anti-intellectual tenor of some of the more common arguments have made the same debates quite unproductive for anyone who really wants to write theory and philosophy. As a result it has been all too easy for theorists and philosophers to turn their back on the important questions about the role of the theorist's or philosopher's subjectivity and about writing style raised by critics such as Jane

[135] I do not mean to give the impression that personal writing only takes place in the USA. In some other countries that I know of, explicitly feminist forms of personal writing have been developed. I am thinking of the 'memory work' pioneered by Frigga Haug in Germany which links work on individual memory with theories of oppression and exploitation (see esp. Haug's *Female Sexualization*). In 1994, the Swedish sociologist Karin Widerberg published a much discussed book in Norway entitled *Kunnskapens kjønn* ('The Sex of Knowledge') inspired by Frigga Haug's work. Haug and Widerberg both see 'memory work' as a way to develop and continue the insights of the feminist consciousness raising groups of the 1960s and early 1970s.

Tompkins. The result has been that theory-writing has proceeded with business as usual, and that 'confessionalism' or 'personal writing' has become an academic subgenre like any other without influence on that other subgenre known as 'theory'. To me, this is an indication that unless the personal critic is willing to engage in genuine dialogue with people who do take theory seriously, she will not be able to show why they should care about her point of view. Turning one's back on theory, as Jane Tompkins recommends, will only make one end up 'all alone and feeling blue'.

The anxiety of excluding others has been prominent in the turn away from theory and towards the personal, and in many arguments about location. The worry is that by speaking or writing theoretically, I will falsely subsume the point of view of others under my own. In the frequent expressions of this anxiety I hear a recurring fantasy: the fantasy of being able to speak in a way that would genuinely be all-inclusive. What this fantasy denies (or tries to forget) is that the very moment of speaking (or writing) is a moment of *arrogation of voice*, as Cavell puts it (see above, 233–4). Cavell speaks of an arrogation of voice because he recognizes that each one of us is different from others, and that each of us is separated from all other human beings. (In this he is very much like Lacan.) To deny the moment of arrogation—the moment of injustice, of unfoundedness—in the act of writing, is to wish for a kind of imaginary non-separation from the other. The fantasy is one of merger, in which one would not have the problem of separating one's own voice from that of others, so that, ultimately, it would not matter who was speaking. Denouncing every attempt to arrogate voice to oneself as a denial of voice to others, the critic of 'speaking for' may be attempting to cure her own guilt feelings about speaking and writing at all. (If I understand this fantasy, it is because I have come to realize that I have at some point shared it.)

I don't mean to say that every critique of 'exclusionism' is based on guilt feelings about the writer's own arrogation of voice. Some such critiques are entirely valuable and necessary. My point, rather, is that the usual catch-all critique of 'exclusionism' is far too simple and unspecific, and particularly, that it often confuses the question of arrogation of voice (to which there is no alternative) with questions of style, tone, contents, and address (here the potential choices and effects are endlessly varied and variable). Critics of 'exclusionism' need to establish more specific criteria, ask more specific questions, and—above all—read more carefully if they want to produce genuinely important critiques of *The Second Sex* or any other text.

Our speaking—even the most deep-felt critique of 'exclusionism'—is never justified by anything but our own wish to speak: 'Who beside myself could give me the authority to speak for us?' Cavell writes (*Pitch* 9). There is something arrogant and something unjust about writing anything at all. How can I write when my mother, who never got more than seven years of primary education, cannot? How can I justify my arrogation of voice? How can anyone? If we do decide to write, it is pointless to consume ourselves in guilt about the 'exclusionary' effects of writing per se. The question, therefore, is not how to justify writing anything at all, but rather what one aims to do with one's writing. I can spend my life feeling guilty about having more opportunities to express myself than my mother ever had, or I can try to write in a way that may inspire more women (and perhaps some men, too) to find a theoretical voice of their own. This is not a revolutionary act. It will not turn society upside down, at least not in the short term. It does not make up for the inexpressive life my highly intelligent mother has had to lead. Because I understand that nothing can make up for that, I have found the courage to write about things that matter to me in the hope that they will also matter to others.

PART II

APPROPRIATING THEORY:
BOURDIEU AND FREUD

Introduction

The essays in this part represent my abiding interest in Freud and my more recent interest in the cultural sociology of Pierre Bourdieu. The first three essays on and around Freud date from the 1980s, the two on Bourdieu from the 1990s. The last essay on Freud, 'Is Anatomy Destiny?', was written in 1998.

I started to study Bourdieu in the late 1980s. Initially, my main purpose was to understand Bourdieu and his collaborators' work on the French intellectual field well enough to be able to see whether it would throw any light on the situation of Simone de Beauvoir. The essay called 'Appropriating Bourdieu' (Chapter 3) is relatively unusual in that it emphasizes Bourdieu as a theorist of subjectivity. I see in Bourdieu a theorist who helps us to understand what it might mean to speak of a social unconscious. But I also feel that Bourdieu's attention to the details of everyday life, to the ways in which we dress, walk, or decorate our living spaces is immensely valuable to anyone who really wishes to understand human cultural practices. Feminists have often pointed out that women's ordinary work and women's everyday practices usually fall outside the parameters of traditional cultural research. Bourdieu shows us one way to approach the seemingly insignificant, the most ordinary aspects of our everyday lives.

'Appropriating Bourdieu' was first published in *New Literary History* in 1991, and earlier drafts were presented at the Commonwealth Center for Cultural Change at the University of Virginia, on the kind invitation of Ralph Cohen. Drawing on most of the work Bourdieu had published by 1990, the essay is an effort to assess the value of a Bourdieuian approach for contemporary feminist theory and criticism. In my book on Simone de Beauvoir, particularly in the first three chapters, my own Bourdieuian inspiration is evident in the kind of questions I ask and the kind of evidence I feel is relevant in answering them. The question of how to use or not to use Bourdieu is also central in 'The Challenge of the Particular Case: Bourdieu's Sociology of Culture and Literary

Criticism', an essay written in 1997 on the invitation of Marshall Brown, editor of *MLQ* (Chapter 4). In this essay I consider some ways in which literary critics in the United States have approached Bourdieu, and situate him as one among a lineage of theorists who understand the subject as the subject of praxis. The essay pays special attention to Bourdieu's major study of Flaubert and other literary and cultural topics, *The Rules of Art* (first published in French in 1992).

In the essays collected here I try to bring a feminist consciousness to bear on both Freud and Bourdieu. By using the word 'appropriation' I mean to say that I am not considering Freud or Bourdieu feminists, but that I do think that feminist intellectuals can benefit enormously from taking their work seriously. Some feminists have questioned the value of using so-called 'male' theory for feminist purposes. 'The master's tools will never dismantle the master's house' is a slogan one often hears.[1] I have to confess that I have never understood why they will not. It seems to me that a sledgehammer is a sledgehammer, and that the question is who wields it to what purpose. An intellectually interesting theory is not exactly a sledgehammer, though.[2] One can't reduce the work of Freud or Bourdieu to a set of instruments or tools lying around ready to be picked up by anyone. This is why any feminist appropriation of their work is bound to be critical as well as properly appreciative. To say this is simply to state the obvious: no self-respecting intellectual, whether feminist or not, is going to declare that she is happy *un*critically to accept the words of some master or other. When I read Beauvoir I appropriate her work for my purposes in much the same way as when I read Freud or Bourdieu. The difference is that Beauvoir explicitly speaks to my feminist concerns, whereas Freud and Bourdieu on the whole do

[1] The formulation is Audre Lorde's. It is the title of a powerful critique of feminist racism, presented at a panel devoted to the personal and the political at a 1979 conference. Although the formulation about the master's tools puzzles me, the essay's plea for feminists to attend to the concrete differences between women, to get to know the actual conditions under which women live, is quite wonderful, and still relevant.

[2] The more 'impersonal' a work of knowledge is, the more it is like a set of tools ready to be picked up by anyone, I think. See my discussion of Diamond in Ch. 2, above.

not. Here the work of appropriation becomes more complex, since I have to *make* these thinkers address my own questions before I can start assessing the value of doing so.[3]

Elizabeth Grosz has voiced a more sophisticated objection to the idea of appropriating non-feminist theory for feminist purposes. Specifically addressing the question of whether Freud is usable for feminist and lesbian purposes, she writes:

> It seems to me that one must be aware of a certain 'ethics' of read-
> ing, an ethics of the appropriation and use of discourses. One
> cannot simply buy into a theoretical system (especially one as
> complex and as systematically conceived, in spite of its inconsis-
> tencies, as psychoanalysis) without at the same time accepting its
> basic implications and founding assumptions. I am not here
> suggesting that one must always read Freud with the view to accept-
> ing it all, but rather, that when one uses a discourse for one's own
> purposes it is never entirely clear which of its implications or
> assumptions are incompatible with one's own. Problematic impli-
> cations cannot be contained and prevented from infiltrating those
> considered unproblematic ('Labors of Love' 289).

I have some difficulties understanding why one can *never* get clear on whether certain Freudian assumptions are incompatible with one's own. Perhaps Grosz means to say that, ultimately, we never fully understand all possible implications of our own words. New interpretations may always arise in different times and places. Because this is obviously true for all uses of language, it is no argu-ment against any specific instance of language use. If we are deal-ing with a particular case, it is surely not impossible to reach clarity on whether there is a contradiction between the feminist's own principles and Freud's, or on whether, perhaps, we are faced with a genuinely ambiguous case, one in which it is difficult indeed to say whether incoherences exist or how important they may be.

If Grosz were right in her scepticism about appropriation of non-feminist theories, then feminists would be barred from seri-ous exploration of almost the whole of the Western intellectual heritage. Historically, however, genuinely revolutionary cultural

[3] For a wonderful account of what appropriation might mean in a philo-sophical context, see Bauer.

work has always taken as its starting point the tradition it wants to transform. Mary Wollstonecraft was deeply inspired and deeply challenged by Rousseau and the French Revolution. *A Vindication of the Rights of Woman* is no less revolutionary for all that. Marx turned Hegel on his head, Simone de Beauvoir found a feminist voice by reading Hegel and Sartre. The works of Wollstonecraft, Marx, and Beauvoir may all be characterized as powerful appropriations of theory not intended for the particular use to which it was put.

Elizabeth Grosz rejects feminist appropriations of Freud, Marx, and Foucault by saying: 'it is not clear what the long-term benefits are of continuing to prop up or support a discourse which has well-recognized problems' ('Labors of Love' 287). But of course it is not clear: the intellectual task is to *make* it clear in each case. Or, alternatively, we could try to show what other intellectual approach might be used instead. Grosz might prefer to do the latter. But even the alternative is going to come from somewhere. If I turn to Beauvoir, I find myself confronted with Descartes, Kant, Hegel, Sartre, and Merleau-Ponty as well. All intellectual works carry the marks of their time, their tradition, and their situation. All intellectual statements, whether by Aristotle or Plato or Woolf and Beauvoir, require rethinking in new circumstances. We always read with an eye to what we need and what we can use. What other way is there? Intellectual life *is* appropriation.

In Chapter 5, 'The Missing Mother: René Girard's Oedipal Rivalries', I use Freud to show that René Girard's theory of 'mimetic desire' has sexist and heterosexist implications. My conclusion is that there are no strong reasons for feminists to turn to Girard's desiring triangles, particularly not when other alternatives, such as psychoanalysis, are readily available. This essay, originally written while I was visiting Cornell as an unemployed Ph.D. in the autumn of 1980, is a kind of companion piece to my *Dora* essay 'Representation of Patriarchy: Sexuality and Epistemology in Freud's *Dora*' (Chapter 6). Although it did not appear until 1983, I wrote the Girard essay and the *Dora* essay at the same time, finishing them both in the winter of 1980/1. My *Dora* essay, which has been much anthologized, has been taken by some as an outright attack on Freud. Even today I can't quite see that it is. It is after all Freud himself who shows us how to produce a fundamental critique of his own practice in this famous case. Using Freud to think against the Freud of the Dora case, I show that Freudian psychoanalysis has genuinely critical value for feminists. Although Freud's treatment of Dora has not got much to recommend it as therapy goes, my essay is nothing if not a piece of psychoanalytic criticism. Considering the enormous number of feminist essays on Freud's *Dora*, I should perhaps say that what I take to be original about my paper is that it demonstrates that the case study is written in a way that highlights the struggle for knowledge between the two protagonists. This insight allows me to show that in this case study the question of desire is bound up with the questions of power and knowledge.

The second to last essay in this part, 'Patriarchal Thought and the Drive for Knowledge' (Chapter 7) was written in 1987/8, just as I was starting work on my Beauvoir book and getting more interested in Bourdieu. What strikes me today is that this essay raises problems that remained with me for the next ten years. The question I actually wanted to write on at the time, was Freud's famous statement 'Anatomy is destiny', surely a crucial one for any attempt at feminist appropriation of Freud. At the time, however, I found myself quite incapable of doing something interesting with the topic, and turned instead to another subject of abiding interest to me: that of the interaction between desire and knowledge. The emphasis on Freud's understanding of the body as a starting point for thought and emotions shows the direction I wanted my understanding of the Freudian body to take. It was only after working through Beauvoir's and Merleau-Ponty's understanding of the body (see Chapter 1, above), that I finally felt able to work out a satisfying answer—or rather, the beginning of an answer—to the question of whether Freud thinks anatomy is destiny. At the invitation of Peter Brooks, I wrote the essay 'Is Anatomy Destiny?' for the conference called 'Whose Freud?' held at Yale in April 1998. The version included here, as Chapter 8, is the expanded version, prepared for the proceedings from that conference. The intellectual affinities between this chapter and Chapter 1 are strong and, I think, obvious (the concern with biological determinism, the questioning of the category of femininity, and so on).

'Patriarchal Thought and the Drive for Knowledge' also questions whether reason and emotion, intellect and affect, must be perceived as binary opposites. The impetus to write about this, I now realize, probably came from my encounter with Jane Tompkins's plea for a personal criticism, 'Me and My Shadow', in the autumn of 1987. This essay is therefore also the precursor of my work on the relationship between the personal and the philosophical (see Chapter 2, above). Although I have always liked 'Patriarchal Thought', I have never thought of it as more important or more productive than some of my other essays. As I am putting this collection together, however, I realize how much of my more recent work turns out to be anticipated by it. Although I think its analysis of the Freudian concept of 'epistemophilia' or the 'drive for knowledge' is still both interesting and useful, I now also see that the essay is a little fractured, that it bears marks of being caught between past and future work. Whether I knew it or not, the essay occupies a crucial position in my intellectual trajectory. Perhaps there are personal reasons for this as well: it was written in January and February of 1988, immediately after my return to England from my first visit to Duke University and just as I was deciding whether to move to America or stay in Europe.

But 'Patriarchal Thought and the Drive for Knowledge' is interesting to me for another reason as well. Before publishing it in the collection edited by Teresa Brennan entitled *Between Feminism and Psychoanalysis* in 1989, I gave it as a lecture at the School of Criticism and Theory at Dartmouth in 1988. Some years later, I discovered that this particular lecture was singled out, in a book appropriately entitled *Conflicts in Feminism*, as an example of unacceptable 'trashing' of other feminists' work:

> [Her] paper was built on what appeared to me and to others as the trashing of other feminists' work. The paper summarized, erroneously, and dismissed, as naive, a range of complex and influential feminist theoretical work for an audience that took these summaries to be 'useful'. All that to lead up to the 'correct' answer which was Freud.[4] As I listened to that talk, I realized that this had become a pervasive move, that there is now a way of building a

---

[4] At this point a footnote in the text signals that the paper in question was mine.

career on trashing feminist work (Hirsch, in Gallop, Hirsch, and Miller 350).

This somewhat harsh judgement of my lecture was interesting to me for several reasons. It reminded me of some of the reactions to *Sexual/Textual Politics*, which a number of American feminists also seemed to find too harshly critical of other women. It made me think about the apparent difference between my own views and those of some of my American feminist colleagues when it comes to deciding what constitutes relevant and reasonable criticism of other intellectuals and what does not. The difference in sensibilities between someone of my Norwegian and British intellectual background and my colleagues trained in the USA appears in sharp focus when I consider my reactions to Marianne Hirsch's comments.

First of all, I feel that Marianne Hirsch here engages in a sound 'trashing' of her own. What I find difficult in her account is not the fact that she has problems with my arguments, nor that she chooses to say so in public. Engagement with ideas is what intellectual life is about. To have one's work discussed in public is usually every intellectual's dream. The power of good work is not going to be diminished by severe testing: it might even come to shine forth more strongly as a consequence. What bothers me is that Hirsch does not attempt to provide any intellectual justification for her assessment. My views are simply said to be 'erroneous', and it is just assumed that Freud can't possibly be the 'correct' answer to anything. What the paper was about is not mentioned, nor is there any mention of what feminist work was 'trashed', or of the fact that some feminist work (that of Le Dœuff) was highly praised. Hirsch thus appears to believe that just to say that some feminist work is less useful than some of Freud's work when it comes to answering a specific question (in this case: how do we escape the idea that the emotions and the intellect are separate and opposing entities?), is evidence of unacceptably unfeminist behaviour.

This is troublesome. Feminist intellectuals cannot possibly believe that no feminist work ever deserves critique. Indeed, Hirsch's reaction to my talk proves the opposite. It is impossible to advance feminist intellectual work without engaging with other feminists. But in order to do so, one must take them seriously. That is to say, one has to engage critically with their ideas, as opposed to reducing the ideas to the person.[5] I can't help noting that I am also said to be 'building a career' on trashing other feminist's work. Well, maybe. But even if it could be shown to everyone's satisfaction that I did indeed have such a shallow and negative professional (as opposed to intellectual) agenda, it would not absolve my critics from showing what is wrong with the essay in question. There is a trace of an *ad feminam* argument here, which I find particularly worrying in a feminist context.[6] In my view, feminists do each other a service by producing serious and searching critiques of the foundations of feminist work. As Teresa Ebert puts it in *Ludic Feminism and After*: 'Such critical engagements [as that of Moi in 'Patriarchal Thought'] are not only politically valid but also, I would argue, quite important for the intellectual and political vitality of feminism. Why then such distress over critique?' (3–4).[7]

If one thinks of a critique of feminist work as a speech act like any other, the exact meaning of the speech act will depend on who is speaking and in what particular context that person is speaking. But to say this is not to agree that the meaning of the statement can be reduced to the person of the speaker. The state-ment—the *énoncé* as Benveniste would call it—still contributes to the meaning. Even if we think we understand why someone makes a specific claim in a particular context, that claim must still be examined on its merits. (I develop this argument in Chapter 2, above.)

---

[5] My work on the reception of Simone de Beauvoir only served to reaffirm my conviction that in a sexist society intellectual women need above all to be taken seriously as intellectuals if they are to be heard. See esp. Ch. 3 in my *Simone de Beauvoir*.

[6] Some of the American critics of *Sexual/Textual Politics* engaged in quite vicious *ad feminam* attacks on me. Perhaps that is why I am particularly allergic to the strategy. But an *ad feminam* or *ad hominem* argument is still a bad argu-ment.

[7] Ebert comments: 'We thus need to ask why critique, when aimed at other feminists, is misrecognized as trashing, as uncourteous demolition. What is at stake in this misreading, and can critique be understood in more productive terms?' (4).

There are, of course, political contexts in which a feminist would not want to engage in public criticism of another feminist. But contemporary US academia is not always such a context, it seems to me. By engaging in a public critique of my paper Hirsch appears to agree with this assessment. In general, Hirsch's reaction to my talk, and my reaction to her reaction, reveal two apparently different attitudes to the intellectual and political value of critique in feminist criticism and theory, and possibly also two different assessments of the political climate in 1988. But other differences are also at stake. Rereading the conversation between Marianne Hirsch, Jane Gallop, and Nancy K. Miller where the remark about 'trashing' occurs, I become aware of a wholly different set of fears and anxieties. In the editors' introductory note to the conversation, the editors (Marianne Hirsch and Evelyn Fox Keller) write: 'The fact that Gallop had both criticized Hirsch and Miller and had managed nevertheless to continue her friendship with them, gave this conversation its promise' (349). This saddens me. For now it looks as if it is only to be expected that intellectual disagreement is incompatible with friendship. Exceptions to this rule are so rare as to deserve applause. Perhaps I am reluctant to accept this because of my experiences in Britain in the 1980s where pleasurable intellectual friendships regularly took the form of intense intellectual disagreements starting inside the seminar room and carrying over into the pub afterwards.

Elsewhere in the conversation the question of emotional needs and professional power comes up. I'll quote a passage which starts with Marianne Hirsch responding to Jane Gallop's critique of some of her own and Nancy Miller's work:

> **Marianne:** ... One of the responses we had to your piece ... was precisely this feeling that you were exposing us to 'them' in some way. You were exposing problems in the big arena out there where what we needed was protection and mutual support—the appearance, at least, of a united front.
> **Jane:** This reminds me of books like *Sexual/Textual Politics*. It may have hurt people's feelings, but it doesn't seem to me that the people Moi was writing about who were very powerful in the scene are any less powerful because of her work.
> **Marianne:** It is not that someone like Elaine Showalter is less powerful in the profession as a result of her critics, but it is that

Showalter's work is now read by a lot of people through the
critiques and therefore dismissed (Gallop, Hirsch, and Miller 362).

There is an interesting, and unsettling, mixture of the emotional,
the professional, and the intellectual here. Feminist critics obviously need support. But why is it always assumed that it is not
supportive to produce a serious response to someone's intellectual work? And if it is emotional support that is sought, is the
arena of professional publications, conferences, and so on, really
the place to look for it? As for professional support, feminist critics should obviously have as much of it as anyone else. The problem in the market-driven US intellectual field is that intellectual
evaluation—job letters and tenure letters—so often is pressed
into professional service. But professional support is not the same
thing as intellectual agreement. I may very well consider you a
superb critic, think of you as the best possible candidate for the
job in my department, and strongly support you for it, without in
the least agreeing with your interpretation of Lacan and Foucault.
When Jane Gallop points out that Elaine Showalter still has
professional power, Hirsch points out that, as a result of my work,
she has lost intellectual influence.[8] But if that is so, it may be
because the critiques (mine, among others) actually did seem
intellectually convincing to many. To accept an argument after
careful judgement is hardly unethical. Hirsch's answer implies
that a *real* engagement with Showalter (as if her critics had not
tried to produce precisely that) would of necessity lead to a positive assessment of her work, yet we are given no reasons for this
assumption.

There is something unsatisfying about the haphazard amalgam
of the emotional, the professional, the political, and the intellectual that appears in the round-table discussion I have been quoting here. It leaves feminists with too many ways of complaining
about a bad review, and makes it too easy to accuse the reviewer
of being emotionally unsupportive, damaging for the feminist

---

[8] In 1998, when she was president of the MLA, Elaine Showalter herself, in
an interview in *Lingua Franca*, says that she was 'very shaken by Toril Moi's book.
. . . It's been a widely influential book, and a lot of people formed their views of
me from it. I felt I had been rendered obsolete in a single stroke' (34).

writer's career, and politically reactionary. All this may very well be true, and if it is, it ought to be pointed out. But what happened to the question of whether the bad review was intellectually valid? Not every critical review is spiteful, vindictive, and self-serving. Surely not all feminist books are masterpieces. When Simone de Beauvoir was asked whether one ought to criticize women as severely as men, she answered: 'I think one must be able to say, "No, that won't do! Write something else, try and do better. Set higher standards for yourselves! Being a woman is not enough" ' (*Simone de Beauvoir Today* 117).[9] Being a feminist is not enough either. As for the essay that provoked the accusation of 'trashing', I collect it here and commend it to the reader's judgement.

[9] This quote and the sentence leading in to it are taken from the preface to *Sexual/Textual Politics* (xiv).

3

Appropriating Bourdieu: Feminist Theory and Pierre Bourdieu's Sociology of Culture (1990)

FEMINISM AS CRITIQUE

Feminist theory is critical theory; feminist critique is therefore necessarily political. In making this claim I draw on the Marxist concept of 'critique', succinctly summarized by Kate Soper as a theoretical exercise which, by 'explaining the source in reality of the cognitive shortcomings of the theory under attack, call[s] for changes in the reality itself' ('Feminism' 199). In this sense, Soper writes, feminist critique comes to echo critical theory as developed by the Frankfurt School with its emphasis on 'argued justification for concrete, emancipatory practice' ('Feminism' 199).[1] This is clearly an ambitious aim, which would require me to situate Pierre Bourdieu's social theory in relation to the specific

I am grateful to Pierre Bourdieu for his encouragement in my struggle to develop a productive feminist perspective on his theories, and to Craig Calhoun for valuable bibliographical information. I would also like to thank Penny Boumelha, Terry Eagleton, Jonathan Freedman, Ian Glenn, John Guillory, Diana Knight, and Janet Wolff for their careful critical responses to various drafts of this essay. My work was much helped by the incisive discussions of early versions of this paper presented at the Commonwealth Center for Cultural Change at the University of Virginia and at the Graduate Conference of the English Department at the University of Houston in the spring of 1990. I am also deeply grateful for the critical feedback I received from my lectures and seminars on Bourdieu in Perth, Melbourne, Sydney and Brisbane in May and June 1990: my Australian interlocutors enabled me at long last to finish this paper. Finally, I would like to thank Ralph and Libby Cohen for their intellectual generosity and friendliness.

[1]   For another discussion of feminism as critique see Benhabib and Cornell.

French social formation which produced it. Such analysis would require substantial empirical research: there is no space for such an undertaking in this context.

I have therefore called this paper 'Appropriating Bourdieu'. By 'appropriation' I understand a critical assessment of a given theory formation with a view to taking it over and using it for feminist purposes.[2] Appropriation, then, is theoretically somewhat more modest than a full-scale critique, and has a relatively well-defined concrete purpose. Neither 'appropriation' nor 'critique' rely on the idea of a transcendental vantage point from which to scrutinize the theory formation in question. Unlike the Enlightenment concept of 'criticism', the concept of 'critique' as used here is immanent and dialectical. My proposal of 'appropriation' and 'critique' as key feminist activities is intended to contest the idea that feminists are doomed to be victimized by what is sometimes called 'male' theory. If I prefer to use terms such as 'patriarchal' and 'feminist' rather than 'male' and 'female', it is precisely because I believe that as feminists we struggle to *transform* the cultural traditions of which we are the contradictory products.

WHY BOURDIEU?

Since the 1960s the French sociologist Pierre Bourdieu, professor of sociology at the Collège de France and Directeur d'études at the École des Hautes Études en Sciences Sociales in Paris, has published over twenty books on anthropology, cultural sociology, language, and literature. Only recently, however, has he found an audience outside the social sciences in the English-speaking world. One of the reasons for such relatively belated interdisciplinary interest is surely the fact that his resolutely sociological and historical thought, which owes far more to classical French sociology, structuralism, and even Marxism than to any later intellectual movements,[3] could find little resonance in a theoretical space

---

[2] I first tried to develop the concept of appropriation in a paper reprinted under the title 'Feminist, Female, Feminine'.

[3] I am not arguing that Bourdieu is a Marxist. For his critique of certain forms of traditional Marxism see 'The Social Space and the Genesis of Groups'.

dominated, in the humanities at least, by poststructuralism and postmodernism. Today, however, there is a renewed interest in the social and historical determinants of cultural production. The fact that Bourdieu has always devoted much space to problems pertaining to literature, language, and aesthetics makes his work particularly promising terrain for literary critics.[4]

In a recent paper, the British cultural sociologist Janet Wolff puts the case for a more sociological approach to feminist criticism: 'it is only with a systematic analysis of sexual divisions in society, of the social relations of cultural production, and of the relationship between textuality, gender and social structure', she writes, 'that feminist literary criticism will really be adequate to its object'.[5] I agree with Wolff that feminist criticism would do well to develop a more sophisticated understanding of the social aspects of cultural production.[6] Bourdieu's sociology of culture, I would argue, is promising terrain for feminists precisely because it

[4] See e.g. 'Flaubert's Point of View' and *Ce que parler veut dire*, as well as *Distinction*. See also 'Sartre', and the closely related work on Sartre and *Les temps modernes* by one of Bourdieu's students, Anna Boschetti. In this introductory context I would also like to mention Bourdieu's inaugural lecture at the Collège de France, 'A Lecture on the Lecture' and the collection of short essays entitled *Choses dites* as accessible and readable examples of his cultural criticism. A selection of essays from *Choses dites*, along with Bourdieu's inaugural lecture, have now been published in English under the title *In Other Words: Essays Towards a Reflexive Sociology*. New readers of Bourdieu's social theory should perhaps start with this volume and then go on to *Outline of a Theory of Practice, Sociology in Question*, 'Le marché des biens symboliques', 'The Production of Belief', 'Champ du pouvoir', and at least the first few sections of *Distinction*. They might then turn to *The Logic of Practice* and *The State Nobility*. Yvette Delsaut has produced a full bibliography of Bourdieu's work up to and including 1988, a bibliography now readily available in English (see *In Other Words* 199–218). Loïc J. D. Wacquant has conducted, edited, and annotated a series of interviews with Bourdieu under the title *An Invitation to Reflexive Sociology*. This book provides by far the most pedagogical, accurate, and accessible introduction to Bourdieu's work in English.

[5] I am quoting from the English manuscript version of her paper 'Texts and Institutions: Problems of Feminist Criticism'. In the French published version, 'Textes et institutions', the quote can be found on 181. The published English version can be found in Wolff's collection of essays *Feminine Sentences*.

[6] Bourdieu does not provide the only theoretical inspiration for such work. The whole tradition of British cultural criticism from Raymond Williams to the Birmingham school would be another obvious source of such inspiration.

allows us to produce highly concrete and specific analyses of the social determinants of the literary *énonciation*. This is not to say that such determinants are the only ones that we need to consider, nor that feminist critics should not concern themselves with the *énoncé*, or the actual statement itself.[7] Again I agree with Janet Wolff who holds that feminist criticism fails in its political and literary task if it does not study literature both at the level of texts and at the level of institutions and social processes. I should perhaps add that just as it is absurd to try to reduce the *énoncé* to the *énonciation* (for instance by claiming that every statement can be fully explained by one's so-called 'speaking position'), it is equally absurd to treat texts as if they were not the complex products of a historically and socially situated *act* of utterance, the *énonciation*.

If I am interested in Bourdieu, then, it is not because I believe that his theories of the social construction of conceptual categories, including that of 'woman', somehow makes all other theory formations superfluous. There can be no question of abandoning Freud for Bourdieu, for instance. Nor can we afford to neglect textual theories in favour of sociology or psychology. I do not wish, either, to reduce the work of the French sociologist to a simple tool for literary critics. For Bourdieu also has considerable theoretical relevance for feminism. In this paper, for instance, I hope to show that a Bourdieuian approach enables us to reconceptualize gender as a social category in a way which undercuts the traditional essentialist/non-essentialist divide.

Bourdieu's *general* theories of the reproduction of cultural and social power are not per se radically new and original. Many of his most cherished themes have also been studied by others. To some, his general theory of power may seem less original than that of a Marx or a Foucault; his account of the way in which individual subjects come to internalize and identify with dominant social institutions or structures may read like an echo of Gramsci's theory of hegemony; and his theory of social power and its ideological effects may seem less challenging than those of the

---

7 For Émile Benveniste's original definition of the terms *énoncé* and *énonciation*, see his 'Les relations du temps' and 'L'appareil formel'.

Frankfurt School.[8] For me, on the other hand, Bourdieu's originality is to be found in his development of what one might call a *microtheory* of social power.[9] Where Gramsci will give us a general theory of the imposition of hegemony, Bourdieu will show exactly *how* one can analyse teachers' comments on student papers, rules for examinations, and students' choices of different subjects in order to trace the specific and practical construction and implementation of a hegemonic ideology. Many feminists claim that gender is socially constructed. It is not difficult to make such a sweeping statement. The problem is to determine what kind of specific consequences such a claim may have. It is at this point that I find Bourdieu's sociological theories particularly useful. For a feminist, another great advantage of Bourdieu's microtheoretical approach is that it allows us to incorporate the most mundane details of everyday life in our analyses, or in other words: Bourdieu makes sociological theory out of *everything*.

Refusing to accept the distinction between 'high' or 'significant' and 'low' or 'insignificant' matters, Bourdieu will analyse various ways of chewing one's food, different forms of dressing, musical tastes ranging from a predilection for 'Home on the Range' to a liking for John Cage, home decoration, the kind of friends one has and the films one likes to see, and the way a student may feel when talking to her professor. In one sense, then, some of my interest in Bourdieu is grounded in my basic conviction that much of what patriarchal minds like to trivialize as *gossip*, and as women's gossip at that, is in fact socially significant. But it is one thing to make such a claim, quite another to make a convincing case for it. After reading Bourdieu I now feel confident that it *is* possible to link the humdrum details of everyday life to a more general social analysis of power. This in itself ought to make his approach attractive for feminists looking for a mode

---

[8] My claim, then, is not that Bourdieu somehow supersedes or transcends these other theories. In order to fully grasp the relative strengths and limitations of Bourdieu's theories, one would need to produce a careful reading of his works in relation to the whole tradition of Western Marxism on the one hand, and to French sociology and ethnology on the other: such an appraisal is not my purpose here.

[9] This specific formulation was first coined by Terry Eagleton.

of social analysis which seeks to undo or overcome the traditional individual/social or private/public divide. Again it may be necessary to stress that I am not arguing that Bourdieu is the only thinker to take a theoretical interest in everyday life. What I am arguing, however, is that I know of no other theory formation which allows us to make highly complex, yet quite concrete and specific, links between, say, my fascination with Simone de Beauvoir, my tendency to eat fish in restaurants, and my specific position in a given social field.

It nevertheless remains true that until very recently Bourdieu himself has not had much to say about women.[10] This means that the place of gender in his thought is somewhat undertheorized. A feminist approaching Bourdieu must necessarily ask whether his major concepts can simply be applied to gender or whether they require rethinking and restructuring in order to become usable for her purposes. She will also have to raise the question of social change. Are Bourdieu's theories, with their insistence on the way in which social agents internalize dominant social values, capable of theorizing change? Is Bourdieu implying that social power structures *always* win out? That *amor fati*—love your destiny—is an appropriate motto for every socially determined act? Crucial for feminists and socialists alike, these questions will be considered below.

FIELD, *HABITUS*, LEGITIMACY, SYMBOLIC VIOLENCE

At this point it is necessary to introduce some of Bourdieu's key concepts. Two of his most fundamental terms, *field* (*champ*) and *habitus*, are deeply interdependent. A field may be defined as a competitive system of social relations which functions according to its own specific logic or rules. 'By "field" ' Bourdieu writes, 'I mean an area, a playing field [*espace de jeu*], a field of objective

---

[10] This is not to say that Bourdieu systematically ignores the question of women in earlier works. There are sustained and interesting discussions of the position of women in Bourdieu and Passeron, *The Inheritors* (1964; trans. 1979) and *La reproduction* (1970), and in Bourdieu, *Distinction* (1979; trans. 1984) and *The Logic of Practice* (1980; trans. 1990).

relations among individuals or institutions competing for the same stakes' (*Sociology in Question* 133). In principle, a field is simply any social system which can be shown to function according to such a logic.

But if the field is a competitive structure, or perhaps more accurately a site of struggle or a battlefield, what is at stake? Generally speaking, any agent in the field may be assumed to seek maximum power and dominance within it. The aim is to *rule* the field, to become the instance which has the power to confer or withdraw *legitimacy* from other participants in the game. Bourdieu defines *legitimacy* as follows: 'An institution, or an action, or a usage is legitimate when it is dominant but not recognized as such [*méconnu comme tel*], in other words tacitly recognized' (*Sociology in Question* 70). Such a position of dominance is achieved by amassing the maximum amount of the specific kind of symbolic capital current in the field. In his pioneering article of 1966, 'Champ intellectuel et projet créateur', Bourdieu presents a striking analysis of the interrelations between the writer's project and the structures of the intellectual field. The intellectual field, he argues, is relatively autonomous in relation to the whole social field, and generates its own type of legitimacy. This is not to say that the social field is not present within the intellectual field, but rather that it is present only as a *representation* of itself, a representation, moreover, which is not imported from outside, but produced from within the intellectual field itself.

The intellectual and educational field, like any other such, have their own specific mechanisms of selection and consecration. Intellectual legitimacy as a symbolic value is produced by the field itself, and may be defined as that which is *recognized*—or in Bourdieu's terms, *consecrated*—by the field at any given time. In order to achieve legitimacy, the agents in the field have recourse to many and varied strategies. These strategies, however, are rarely if ever perceived as such by the agents themselves. Instead, each field generates its own specific *habitus*, which Bourdieu defines as 'a system of dispositions attuned to [the] game [of the field]' (*Sociology in Question* 18). 'For a field to work', he writes, 'there must be stakes, and people ready to play the game, equipped with the habitus which enables them to know and recognize the immanent laws of the game, the stakes and so on' (110). *Habitus*, then, may be seen as the totality of general *dispositions* acquired through practical experience in the field. At one level, then, *habitus* is practical sense (*sens pratique*). In some ways, *habitus* may be compared to what educationalists have called the 'silent curriculum': those norms and values that are inculcated through the very forms of classroom interaction, rather than through any explicit teaching project. For Bourdieu, however, *habitus* is an active, generative set of unformulated dispositions, not a store of passive knowledge. At one point he even uses the term 'cultural unconscious' to explain his concept of a cultural *habitus* ('Champ intellectuel et projet créateur' 902).

As the internalized set of tacit rules governing strategies and practices in the field, the *habitus* of a field is destined to remain unarticulated. Insofar as the field cannot function without its specific *habitus*, any field is necessarily structured by a series of *unspoken* and *unspeakable* rules for what can legitimately be said— or perceived—within the field. In this sense, Bourdieu writes, the whole field functions as a form of *censorship* (see *Sociology in Question* 90–3). Within the field, every discourse is *euphemistic* in the sense that it has to observe the correct *forms*, legislated by the field, or risk exclusion as nonsense (in the case of the intellectual field, excluded discourses would tend to be cast as stupid or naive).

If the field as a whole, however, functions as a form of censorship, every discourse within the field becomes at once an enactment and an effect of *symbolic violence*. This is so because a field is a particular structure of distribution of a specific kind of capital. The right to speak, *legitimacy*, is invested in those agents recognized by the field as powerful possessors of capital. Such individuals become spokespersons for the *doxa*, and struggle to relegate challengers to their position as *heterodox*, as lacking in capital, as individuals whom one cannot *credit* with the right to speak. The powerful possessors of symbolic capital become the wielders of symbolic power, and thus of symbolic violence. But given the fact that all agents in the field to some extent share the same *habitus*, such richly endowed agents' right to power is implicitly *recognized* by all, and not least by those who aspire one day to oust them from their thrones. That different factions within the (battle)field fight to the bitter end over politics, aesthetics, or theory does not mean that they do not to some extent share the same *habitus*: in the very act of engaging in battle, they mutually and silently demonstrate their recognition of the rules of the game. It does not follow, as far as I can see, that they will all play the game *in the same way*. The different positions of different players in the field will require different strategies. To the extent that different agents have different social backgrounds (they may come from different geographical regions, be of different class, gender, or race, and so on), their *habitus* cannot be identical.

The same thing goes for legitimacy as for 'distinction' (distinction, after all, is nothing but *legitimate taste*). The whole point of the process of imposing legitimacy is to reach a point where the categories of power and distinction merge. Legitimacy (or distinction) is only truly achieved when it is no longer possible to tell whether dominance has been achieved *as a result of* distinction or whether in fact the dominant agent simply appears to be distinguished *because* he (more rarely she) is dominant (see *Distinction* 92).

In *The Logic of Practice*, Bourdieu defines symbolic violence as 'soft' violence, or as 'violence censored, euphemized, that is, misrecognizable, recognized violence [*méconnaissable et reconnue*]' (126). One has recourse to symbolic violence when open or direct violence (such as economic violence, for instance) is impossible. It is important to realize that symbolic violence is *legitimate*, and therefore literally unrecognizable as violence. If explicit ideological or material struggle between groups or classes develops, such as class conflict or the feminist struggle, symbolic violence may be unmasked and recognized for what it is. In the very moment it is recognized, however, it can no longer function as *symbolic* violence (see *The Logic of Practice* 303, n.18). Insofar as they tend to deny the importance of economic structures, precapitalist societies, Bourdieu argues, make widespread use of symbolic violence. In late capitalist societies, on the other hand, symbolic violence flourishes not so much in the general social field as in the domains of art and culture, perceived as sacred refuges for disinterested values in a hostile, sordid world dominated by economic production (see *The Logic of Practice* 133–4).

EDUCATION AND THE REPRODUCTION OF POWER

For Bourdieu, the educational system is one of the principal agents of symbolic violence in modern democracies.[11] It is also a pivotal factor in the construction of each individual's *habitus*. In *The State Nobility* he studies the way in which the imposition of social power in the educational system is linked to the transmission or reproduction of power in other social spheres.[12] The function of the educational system, Bourdieu argues, is above all to produce the necessary social *belief* in the *legitimacy* of currently dominant power structures, or in other words, to make us believe that our rulers are ruling us by virtue of their qualifications and achievements rather than by virtue of their noble birth or connections. The coveted diploma or exam paper becomes a token of *social magic*, the emblem of a transformational exercise which truly changes the essence of the chosen elite.[13] To claim that

[11] It is important to stress that Bourdieu's work is based on the French educational system. This is a system which is ostensibly egalitarian and meritocratic in a way which is not true for, say, the British educational system with its more clear-cut class-based divisions between public schools and state schools. Some of Bourdieu's conclusions about the discriminatory and oppressive nature of the French educational system may come as a surprise to the French, while in Britain the very same points may seem rather obvious, precisely because the British educational system does not mask its symbolic violence as well as the French.

[12] For other works on education and the intellectual field in France, see Bourdieu and Passeron, *The Inheritors* and *La reproduction*, Bourdieu's own *Homo Academicus* and 'Epreuve scolaire', and Bourdieu and Saint-Martin, 'Les catégories de l'entendement professoral' (the last two papers are now revised and included in *The State Nobility*). See also the closely related work by Boschetti, Charle, and Fabiani.

[13] As mentioned above (n. 11), Bourdieu's work on the social power of the tokens of educational capital is based on empirical research in France. In other countries certain educational diplomas do not necessarily carry such high social prestige as in France. This does not mean that the educational systems of other nations are not crucial to the reproduction of social power: what remains to be studied is precisely how the educational system interacts with other social institutions and structures in different countries. There is no reason why Bourdieu's general point about *social magic*—the socially sanctioned belief in the value of certain tokens and insignia—should not be deployed in contexts quite different from those of the French educational system.

something is an effect of social magic, Bourdieu reminds us, is not of course to say that it is illusory or unreal:

> One must be noble to act nobly, but one would cease to be noble if one did not act nobly. In other words, social magic has very real effects. Assigning someone to a group of superior essence (noblemen as opposed to commoners, men as opposed to women, educated as opposed to uneducated, etc.) causes that person to undergo a subjective transformation that contributes to bringing about a real transformation likely to bring him closer to the assigned definition (*State Nobility* 112).

The fact that distinguished products of the educational system are distinguished as a result of the social *belief* in their distinction, then, does not mean that they do not in fact also possess some objective competence (the ability to read Greek, solve complex equations, or whatever). Such competence, however, has very little to do with the nature of the tasks they will be called upon to perform as, say, managing directors of important companies or members of politically powerful commissions. The fact that the educational system necessarily produces some competence without for that matter ceasing to exercise social magic is a phenomenon Bourdieu labels the 'ambiguity of competence'. This ambiguity, then, is precisely what enables the educational system to make such an efficient or *convincing* contribution to the legitimization and naturalization of power.

The reproduction of power, however, is not merely an effect of education. On the contrary, the evidence produced by Bourdieu would seem to indicate that whereas the educational system has an indispensable role to play as one of the most important agents of legitimate symbolic violence, social agents rich in political and economic power know how to overcome the educational hurdle if they have to. If persons from disadvantaged social groups require all the educational capital they can obtain if they are to advance in society, members of more favoured classes can get further on less educational capital, simply because they have access to large amounts of other kinds of capital.

Bourdieu convincingly shows how the educational system favours the bourgeoisie even in its most intrinsically academic exercises. The consequences are ominous: students lacking in cultural capital (for instance those of modest social origins) tend to fare badly at a very early stage in their educational careers. According to Bourdieu there is an almost perfect homology between the class position of the individual pupil and their teachers' intellectual judgements of them. Defined as failures, these students *become* failures in precisely the same way as the distinguished students *become* distinguished.

When it comes to measuring social success in later life, however, Bourdieu chillingly demonstrates how a certain lack of educational capital can be compensated for by the possession of other forms of capital. Money and political power (i.e. economic and political capital in Bourdieu's terms) are obviously important here. But in *The State Nobility* he also places much emphasis on a new concept, that of *social capital*. Social capital is defined as 'relational power', that is to say the number of culturally, economically, or politically useful relations accumulated by a given person. In France it would seem that the 'great' bourgeois families maintain or reproduce their social standing by relying on extensive networks of family members with large amounts of capital in different fields. Thus one family may comprise outstanding medical doctors, powerful bankers, influential politicians, and perhaps an important artist, writer, or professor. In this way the family as an extended group can be said to have heavy symbolic investments safely spread across the whole social field. This was also true for the great noble families under the *ancien régime*, and, as Bourdieu dryly remarks, this is why even a revolution tends to have little impact on the fortunes of such family networks. Persons from this kind of background can be shown regularly to achieve higher positions of power in relation to their educational capital than members of less favoured social groups. Or in other words: a star pupil at the École Polytechnique who is also the son of a prominent politician is far more likely to become the president of an important bank than an equally successful student at the École Polytechnique whose father happens to be a mere worker, schoolteacher, or engineer.

And if the son or daughter of the prominent banker somehow fails to get into the Polytechnique, there are other, less prestigious but 'classy' educational establishments, such as the new breed of private schools focusing on business and management, which compensate for their lack of intellectual prestige by their upmarket, 'modern' image. For the offspring of the privileged, such 'little' schools (as opposed to the 'great', intellectually highly prestigious state schools such as the École Normale, the Polytechnique, and so on) produce an educational cachet which allows them to aspire, after all, to positions of a certain economic or political power. For the sons and daughters of the less favoured classes, however, such schools hold little promise. Again, the social logic at work is the same: if capital is what it takes to produce more capital, an agent lacking in social capital at the outset will not benefit greatly from a relatively non-prestigious ('low-capital') education.

The ideological role of the educational system, then, is to make it *appear* as if positions of leadership and power are distributed according to merit. The existence in every educational institution of a tiny percentage of what Bourdieu likes to call 'miraculous exceptions' (*des miraculés*—educationally highly successful members of disadvantaged groups) is precisely what allows us to believe that the system is egalitarian and meritocratic after all.[14] For Bourdieu, then, the widespread democratic belief in education as a passport to freedom and success is no more than a myth: the myth of the *école libératrice* is the new 'opium of the people'.

DOXA, ORTHODOXY, HETERODOXY, AND CHANGE

Taste or *judgement* are the heavy artillery of symbolic violence. In *Distinction*, Bourdieu denounces the 'terrorism [of] the peremptory verdicts which, in the name of taste, condemn to ridicule, indignity, shame, silence . . . men and women who simply fall short, in the eyes of their judges, of the right way of being and doing' (511):

---

[14] This still leaves the problem of where the *miraculés* come from. In *The Inheritors* Bourdieu and Passeron point to specific and exceptional constellations in the family of the successful student from the peasantry as one element that may explain the relatively successful educational career of the individual in question. This is clearly not all there is to be said about such a matter. Bourdieu, himself a *miraculé*, would seem to be well placed to produce a fuller analysis of the question.

[There is terrorism] in the symbolic violence through which the dominant groups endeavor to impose their own life-style, and which abounds in the glossy weekly magazines: 'Conforama is the Guy Lux of furniture,' says *Le Nouvel Observateur*, which will never tell you that the *Nouvel Obs* is the Club Méditerranée of culture.[15] There is terrorism in all such remarks, flashes of self-interested lucidity sparked off by class hatred or contempt (511).

These are not the comments of a man who believes in the inevitability of the status quo: *Distinction* is nothing if not a work of *critique*, a theoretical intervention which assumes that the very fact of exposing the foundations of bourgeois aesthetics will contribute to its transformation.[16] In order to discover how Bourdieu would argue this case, it is necessary to turn to an earlier work, *Outline of a Theory of Practice*. For Bourdieu, 'every established order tends to produce . . . the naturalization of its own arbitrariness' (164). In a highly traditional, and relatively stable and undifferentiated, society, this process is so successful as to make the 'natural and social world [appear] as self-evident' (164). Such self-evidence is what Bourdieu calls *doxa*. *Doxa* is to be distinguished from *orthodoxy* (the effort to defend the *doxa*), as well as from *heterodoxy* (the effort to challenge the *doxa*) in so far as these two positions more or less explicitly recognize the possibility of different arrangements. To defend the 'natural' is necessarily to admit that it is no longer self-evident.

A 'doxic' society is one in which the 'established cosmological and political order is perceived not as arbitrary, i.e. as one possible order among others, but as a self-evident and natural order which goes without saying and therefore goes unquestioned' (166). Or to put it differently, this is a society in which everybody has a perfect *sense of limits* (see 164). In such a society there is no

[15] Here Bourdieu uses exactly the same rhetorical strategy against *Le nouvel observateur*. I take it that the difference is that Bourdieu is not in a position of power in relation to *Le nouvel observateur*. His ironic echoing of their rhetoric can thus be read as a denunciation, not as a celebration of the strategy. I have previously argued that in some cases Luce Irigaray's ironic use of mimicry functions in a similar way (see *Sexual/Textual Politics* 140).

[16] In his paper 'Habitus, Field of Power, and Capital' Craig Calhoun also argues that Bourdieu's theory should be seen as critical theory in the tradition of the Frankfurt School.

place for opinion in the liberal sense of the word, or as Bourdieu puts it: 'what is essential *goes without saying because it comes without saying*: the tradition is silent, not least about itself as tradition' (167). In such a society, then, there is no space for change or transformation. Entirely doxic, social power rules without opposition: this is a universe in which the very question of legitimacy does not even arise.

What, then, does it take for critique—and thus for change—to enter the social space? On this point Bourdieu is recognizably *marxisant*: the condition of possibility for a critical discourse which would bring 'the undiscussed into discussion', he writes, is an 'objective crisis, which, in breaking the immediate fit between the subjective structures and the objective structures, destroys self-evidence practically' (168–9). '[T]he would-be most radical critique always has the limits that are assigned to it by the objective conditions', he continues: 'Crisis is a necessary condition for a questioning of doxa but is not in itself a sufficient condition for the production of a critical discourse' (169).

Crisis, then, is necessary for critique to develop, and crisis is always a matter of *praxis*. The class struggle is the obvious example of such a crisis, but it is not the only one: other social groups, such as women or ethnic minorities, or the old or the young, may also constitute themselves as social agents challenging specific power structures. The reason why crisis alone is not sufficient to trigger critical discourse is obvious: only the dominated classes or groups have an objective interest in 'pushing back the limits of *doxa* and exposing the arbitrariness of the taken for granted', as Bourdieu puts it (169). The dominant classes, on the other hand, will take up their position as orthodox defenders of the integrity of the *doxa*. The emergence of a critical discourse becomes a stake in the very social struggle which at once enables and limits it.

For Bourdieu, crises also provoke a redefinition of experience, giving rise to new forms of language. When the everyday order is challenged by an insurgent group, hitherto *unspoken* or *private* experience suddenly finds itself expressed in public, with dramatic consequences:

> 'Private' experiences undergo nothing less than a *change of state* when they recognize themselves in the *public objectivity* of an already

constituted discourse, the objective sign of their recognition of their right to be spoken and to be spoken publicly: 'Words wreak havoc,' says Sartre, 'when they find a name for what had up to then been lived namelessly.' Because any language that can command attention is an 'authorized language', invested with the authority of a group, the things it designates are not simply expressed but also authorized and legitimated. This is true not only of establishment language but also of the heretical discourses which draw their legitimacy and authority from the very groups over which they exert their power and which they literally produce by expressing them: they derive their power from their capacity to *objectify* unformulated experiences, to make them public—a step on the road to officialization and legitimation—and, when the occasion arises, to manifest and reinforce their concordance (170–1).

This account of the way in which previously dominated experience is legitimated and constituted qua experience in the very act of being given public utterance, strikes me as a particularly useful theorization of feminist practice with its emphasis on constructing a language expressing women's experience. On this theory, to study feminist discourse is to situate it in relation to the structures of the field in which it arises. A truly critical (that is to say, *anti-doxic*) account of feminism, then, would be one which also reflects on the social conditions of possibility of feminist discourse. Or in other words: feminism as critique must also be a critique of feminism.

In this way, the would-be critic of the *doxa* finds herself obliged to reflect on the conditions which produce her as a speaker. As an intellectual, her position becomes particularly ambiguous, insofar as her social or political critique necessarily also finds itself caught up in the mechanisms and strategies—the *habitus*—of the intellectual field she is in. Bourdieu's own role as an intellectual setting out to describe and explicate the tacit rules of the intellectual game is of course no exception. Any effort to make a specific analysis public—to objectify it, as Bourdieu puts it—must include the speaker (see also *Distinction* 12).

But such 'objectification' of one's own position can never be complete. If the intellectual field itself constitutes the 'site of objectification, the unseen standpoint, the blind spot of all theories' (*Distinction* 511), it follows, Bourdieu adds, that 'scientific work on [such an] object is inseparable from work on the working subject'

(*Distinction* 511). In this way the cultural sociologist finds herself in a position analogous to that of the psychoanalyst, that is to say, not as one who has managed to jettison her own unconscious, or who is free from blind spots, but rather as somebody who can be expected to recognize the strategies of the unconscious for what they are when they manifest themselves. 'Sociology is rarely more akin to social psychoanalysis than when it confronts an object like taste', Bourdieu writes in *Distinction* (11). And for Bourdieu as for Freud, the way to change goes through a verbalization and analysis of the unspoken and repressed rules that govern our behaviour. The point to be remembered, however, is that such discourse itself is the product of the very crisis it seeks to resolve.

Change, then, is not impossible in Bourdieu's scheme of things: symbolic violence is not the only form of violence in society. Insofar as symbolic violence is deeply doxic, it may be challenged on precisely the same grounds and in the same ways as the *doxa*. But social change is grounded in practice, in the objective conditions of everyday life. In this context the revolutionary role of intellectuals is bound to be relatively limited. Insofar as intellectuals may contribute to change through the production of discourse, they can only do so when the social structure they inhabit is in an explicit or implicit state of conflict. The very fact of producing a critical discourse, however, helps to *legitimize* the experience which directly or indirectly has contributed to producing the critique in the first place.[17] In this way, I take it, critical discourses do not simply remain derivative or marginal in relation to the material and practical conditions which enable them to come into existence, but come to produce material and practical effects in their own right. This is why such discourses, in their limited way, can be seen as transformative of practice.

THE SOCIAL CONSTRUCTION OF GENDER

What, then, can Bourdieu's sociology of culture add to a feminist analysis of social power structures? Recently, in an effort to show

---

[17] I should make it clear that I am not arguing that such legitimizing expressions of experience must always take the form of intellectual discourse.

that his own approach can expand beyond class, Bourdieu has turned to the question of the social construction of gender. In principle, such a turn ought not to surprise us. As Rogers Brubaker has shown, Bourdieu's concept of 'class' is so indistinct as to be applicable to any social group whose members share a certain number of material and social conditions, and thus also develop a common *habitus*. In an unpublished paper from 1989 entitled 'La construction sociale du sexe', Bourdieu starts from the assumption that men and women do in fact constitute two such social groups, and then proceeds to analyse the social relations between men and women in exactly the same terms as any other set of social relations between a dominant and a dominated class. This analysis is expanded and developed in 'La domination masculine', published in September 1990.[18] In 1990, for the first time, Bourdieu's journal, *Actes de la recherche en sciences sociales*, devoted two special issues to questions of sexual difference.[19] Questions of patriarchal power and the social construction of gender would therefore seem finally to be acknowledged as central issues for Bourdieu's sociological enterprise.

For Bourdieu the sexual division of human beings into two fundamental categories is a thoroughly arbitrary cultural construction. For him, sexism—like racism—is an essentialism: 'It [sexism] aims to ascribe historically produced social differences to a biological nature functioning like an essence from which every actual act in life will be implacably deduced' ('Domination' 12). Such essentialism is politically nefarious insofar as it is invoked to *predict* and thus to *control* the behaviour of every member of a given social group. On this point, then, Bourdieu's analysis rejoins that of many socialist or materialist feminists over the past two decades.

---

[18] In fact, I have consulted three different papers by Bourdieu dealing specifically with gender. First there is the full-length unpublished 1989 manuscript entitled 'La construction sociale du sexe' (50 pp.). A somewhat rewritten excerpt from this paper appeared in English in 1989 under the title 'He Whose Word Is Law'. Then there is Bourdieu's 1990 essay published in *Actes de la recherche en sciences sociales*, entitled 'La domination masculine'. Bourdièu's book entitled *La domination masculine*, was published in Paris in the autumn of 1998.

[19] *Actes de la recherche en sciences sociales* 83 and 84 (June and Sept. 1990).

The invocation of biology as the 'root' or 'cause' of any specific social practice is deeply suspect to Bourdieu. To believe that the so-called biological 'facts' of reproduction, for instance, are the *causes* of the sexual division of labour, which hands 'important' tasks to men and 'low' or 'menial' tasks to women, is precisely to be in the grip of phallocentric thought. Far from ruling our social life, Bourdieu writes, our perceptions of the biology of reproduction are the *effects* of the thoroughly arbitrary social construction of gender divisions which they are supposed to legitimate and explain (see 'Domination' 14).

While the invocation of biology allows the social construction of sexual difference to appear motivated or 'natural', its real function is to mask the true, socially produced power relations between the sexes, to present social gender divisions as *doxic*, that is to say, as that which cannot be questioned. For Bourdieu, then, sexual oppression is above all an effect of *symbolic violence*. As such, the traditional relationship between the sexes is structured by a *habitus* which makes male power appear legitimate even to women.[20] Insofar as symbolic violence works, it produces women who share the very same *habitus* which serves to oppress them. In a wholly doxic society, women as social agents will freely choose the social destiny which they cannot in any case expect to escape: *amor fati* or 'self-confirming prophecy' are terms Bourdieu uses to describe the position of such women.

To produce a gender *habitus* requires an extremely elaborate social process of education or *Bildung*. For Bourdieu, an important aspect of this process is the inscription of social power relations on the body: our *habitus* is at once produced and expressed through our movements, gestures, facial expressions, manners, ways of walking, and ways of looking at the world. The socially produced body is thus necessarily also a political body, or rather an embodied politics. Thus even such basic activities as teaching children how to move, dress, and eat are thoroughly political, in that they impose on them an unspoken understanding of legitimate ways to (re)present their body to themselves and others.

---

[20] It is, of course, impossible to use the term *habitus* without raising the question of the social conditions which gave rise to it (see 'Domination' 11).

The body—and its apparel such as clothing, gestures, make-up, and so on—becomes a kind of constant reminder (*un pense-bête*) of sociosexual power relations.

It follows from Bourdieu's understanding of the social effects of gender divisions that the dominant group—in this case men—do not escape the burdens of their own domination. Through a reading of the episode in Virginia Woolf's *To the Lighthouse* where Mrs Ramsay overhears Mr Ramsay's monologic recitation of 'The Charge of the Light Brigade' and pities him for his childish preoccupations with intellectual prestige and his masculine delusions of grandeur, Bourdieu makes the point that the sexual division of labour assigns to men the most prestigious and therefore the most serious games. This is certainly true, but it is hardly news to feminists.[21] Bourdieu's own formulation is nevertheless striking: men, he says, are socialized to *take serious games seriously*.[22] According to Bourdieu this has a series of unpleasant side effects for the men themselves, effects which may be qualified as the *noblesse oblige syndrome*.

Only an outsider, or perhaps somebody lacking in legitimacy

---

[21] In a 1993 essay in *Nouvelles questions féministes*, Françoise Armengaud accuses Bourdieu of having stolen the ideas of French materialist or ('radical') feminists such as Christine Delphy, Colette Guillaumin, Nicole-Claude Mathieu, and Michèle Le Dœuff. In my view the problem could just as well be that Bourdieu has behaved like any 'distinguished' male intellectual and set out to write about feminist theory without ever bothering to read his French feminist colleagues. In the same way he completely fails to acknowledge that his own analysis of patriarchal domination echoes that of Simone de Beauvoir (and Simone de Beauvoir is a major source of inspiration for the theorists mentioned by Armengaud). As I say repeatedly in the text, Bourdieu's general understanding of women's oppression is hardly original or new to anyone vaguely familiar with feminist thought in this century. My point, however, is that whatever we think about Bourdieu's own lack of feminist credentials, the concepts he develops (*habitus*, field, symbolic capital, distinction, and so on) remain deeply useful for certain kinds of feminist projects. I am grateful to Christina Angelfors for sending me a copy of Armengaud's paper.

[22] This formulation is taken from 'La construction sociale du sexe' (37). This specific turn of phrase has been left out of 'La domination masculine'. The argument nevertheless remains the same. It is also expressed in 'He Whose Word Is Law', where Bourdieu writes that the 'specific process of socialization of which they [men] are the products inclines them to take seriously those games that the social world constitutes as being serious, and to "play them seriously" ' (13).

within the dominant group, can expect to see through what Bourdieu calls the 'masculine illusion'—the illusion of self-importance. But this is not a *necessary* effect of marginalization; on the contrary, only exceptional agents who somehow find themselves in a position relatively free from various forms of dependence can expect to get away with the superb irony of a Virginia Woolf. Thus women who laugh at male self-importance in university seminars may find themselves constructed not as lucid critics of male ridicule, but as frivolous females incapable of understanding truly serious thought. And to say that a construction prevails is to say that it becomes a social fact with real effects for those agents' careers. In some circumstances, then, female laughter may be an excellent instrument of critique, and in other instances quite counterproductive.

The example of Virginia Woolf would seem to demonstrate that critique and change may occur even within fairly traditional social structures of gender. What, then, does it take to change dominant gender relations, to undo *la dominance masculine*? Given the fact that patriarchal power[23] would seem to be universal, it is exceptionally hard to 'denaturalize', Bourdieu writes, since such critical unmasking tends to come about as the result of the historical encounter with other ways of life (see 'Domination' 7). It is striking—and somewhat surprising—to notice how close Bourdieu's analysis on this point comes to that of Simone de Beauvoir in *The Second Sex*. Like Bourdieu, Beauvoir sees male domination as a universally existing social phenomenon, and as such particularly likely to be mistaken for nature:

> Throughout history [women] have always been subordinated to men; their dependency is not the result of an event or a change— it was not something that *occurred*. It is in part because it does not

---

[23] I use the terms *patriarchal* or *masculinist* power or domination as synonyms to Bourdieu's *domination masculine*. It is well known that the term *masculin* in French may correspond either to 'male' or to 'masculine' in English. It is clear that what Bourdieu has in mind is domination by males, but it is equally clear that for him it is unthinkable to posit such a domination without at the same time positing the concomitant social construction of masculinity and so-called masculine values. When I use the term 'patriarchy' I do not mean to indicate any specific social theory of patriarchal rule. For me, the term is equivalent to the idea of 'domination by men'.

have [*échappe à*] the accidental character of a historical fact that otherness in this case appears as an absolute. A situation created over time can be abolished at some other time, as the Negroes of Haiti and others have proved; but it seems that a natural condition is beyond the possibility of change. In truth, however, nature is no more immutably given than is historical reality. If woman discovers that she is the inessential which never returns to the essential, it is because she herself fails to take charge of this return (*SS* xxiv–xxv; *DSa* 18; TA).

Focusing on women's complicity in their own oppression, Beauvoir here raises a question more recent feminist theory often has sought to avoid. For Beauvoir, there can be no liberation until women themselves cease to reproduce the power mechanisms that confine them to their place. In spite of her own valiant efforts to construct a *social* understanding of the female condition, Beauvoir overestimates the ease with which change may be accomplished. Nowhere is her tendencies towards existentialist voluntarism with its characteristic underestimation of the effect of social and psychological structures more apparent than in her profound belief that, in 1949, she and other professionally trained women of her own generation had already 'won the game' (*SS* xxxiii; *DSa* 29).[24]

Bourdieu, on the other hand, certainly does not underestimate the difficulties of breaking loose of patriarchal shackles. It follows from his theory that the effects of symbolic violence do not necessarily disappear even if social conditions change. Here Simone de Beauvoir's own life furnishes an excellent illustration of his point. Earning her own living, leading a life independent of social conventions, and believing in her own freedom, Beauvoir nevertheless displays the most painful conflicts and contradictions when it comes to asserting emotional autonomy or intellectual independence in relation to Sartre. While such difficulties may well be analysed from a psychoanalytic perspective, they should also—simultaneously—be grasped as the *political* effects of the socially constructed *habitus* of a bourgeois woman brought up in Paris in the 1910s and 1920s. There can be no doubt, either, that Bourdieu is right to point to the powerful and lasting effects of

[24] 'En gros, nous avons gagné la partie', she writes in French (*DSa* 29).

the social construction of our body as well as our subjectivity. One cannot 'liberate the victims of symbolic violence by decree', he writes ('Domination' 12).

In its insistence on the way in which women's *habitus* is produced by the symbolic violence that oppresses them, Bourdieu's analysis in 'La domination masculine' comes across as somewhat bleak, or even despondent. What is required to effectuate change, according to Bourdieu, is 'collective action which sets out to organize a *symbolic struggle* capable of *questioning* practically every tacit presupposition of the phallonarcissistic vision of the world' ('Domination' 30). This is certainly true, but in my view, it is precisely what the feminist movement has been striving to do for the past few decades. Luckily we are not today in a position where we have to *start* this struggle afresh. If Bourdieu's analysis of gender in 'La domination masculine' ends up sounding such a gloomy note, it is not least because the bulk of his empirical material is taken from his own fieldwork in Kabylia in the late 1950s and early 1960s. Judging from his evidence, it would appear that at that time, Kabylia was indeed a near-doxic society in so far as gender relations were concerned. While Bourdieu is probably right to claim that such a society may reveal more clearly than others the way in which gender comes to be *experienced* (and not just *represented*) as natural, his reliance on his Kabyle material makes him underestimate, in my view, the level of crisis we are experiencing in gender relations today. On his own theory, such social crisis produces the conditions for social change on a scale unthinkable in a more doxic situation.

In contemporary society, then, the position of women—and of men—in relation to social power is far more complex and contradictory than Bourdieu would seem fully to acknowledge.[25] Such

[25] Bourdieu does insist, however, that there is always space for 'cognitive struggle' over the meaning of the world ('Domination' 15). The paradox is, according to Bourdieu, that when or if the dominated group applies the schemes of dominant thought *to their own situation*, they cannot fail to expose the logic of that thought. The question is, I suppose, whether they themselves always realize the political implications of their own insights. But Bourdieu also points out that even the closest-knit mythical categories of sexual difference leave a space for reinterpretation *within the very same schemes of thought*. Let us assume that if patriarchal thought holds that men are superior because they have

complexity is precisely what allows for questioning of received notions: in my view, current gender relations are by no means tacitly and unquestioningly accepted, or in other words, they are by no means entirely doxic. In many areas of social life today, there is an outspoken and ferocious battle between what Bourdieu would call the orthodox and the heterodox. This is not to say that social change takes place at a uniform pace in all social fields. If there is explicit struggle over the received order of things in one field, it does not follow that the same absence of natural or doxic gender differences dominates in others. This complex social situation is, in my view, at once a problem and a source of great strength for the feminist project of social transformation.

For contemporary feminist theory the strength of Bourdieu's analysis is perhaps not so much his specific analysis of the social relations between the sexes—the *effects* described by him are, after all, fairly well known—as the fact that he manages to eschew the traditional essentialist/anti-essentialist divide. Firmly anti-essentialist, Bourdieu's analysis does not lose sight of the fact that if women are socially constructed as women, that means that they *are* women. Or to put it in the terms of current theoretical debates within feminism: *sexual differences are neither essences nor simple signifiers, neither a matter of realism nor of nominalism, but a matter of social practice.* Sexual differences or sexual identities, then, cannot simply be deconstructed away: real social change is required to empty these categories of current meanings. This is not to say that the deconstruction of sexual metaphysics is not a useful activity in the struggle against patriarchy: it is rather to indicate that only

---

penises, women might counter that *they* are superior because they have breasts. In such an exchange there is no challenge to the fundamental structure of patriarchal thought, yet that very thought gives space for conflict, even on its own terms. The problem with this account, as it appears in 'La domination masculine', is that Bourdieu does not sufficiently elaborate his understanding of the nature of male power in society. If it is seamlessly efficient in its imposition of symbolic violence, it would seem to be difficult ever to get out of it. If it isn't, we need to know more about the gaps and contradictions in its mode of operation, which may provide the space for critique and resistance. A more complex theory of ideology and its relations to the contradictions of power might be helpful here. For a truly complex understanding of ideology, see Terry Eagleton, *Ideology: An Introduction*.

the existence of a social crisis—a power struggle—on the level of gender can enable such a potentially critical activity to take place in the first place.

BOURDIEU AND FEMINIST THEORY: GENDER, *HABITUS*, AND SOCIAL MAGIC

Bourdieu's analysis of the oppression of women as a matter of *habitus* and symbolic violence would seem logically to presuppose the idea of a *field*. If gender has a *habitus*, there must, surely, be a field (*champ*) in which this *habitus* can come into play. But how can one conceptualize a field of gender? In her thoughtful essay 'Gender and Symbolic Violence' Beate Krais argues that the concept of *habitus* is crucial for feminism, and leaves out any mention of the concept of field.[26] It is true that gender seems never to operate separately from all other fields. But it does not seem impossible to argue that gender might be theorized in much the same way as social class, that is to say that we might claim that—like class—gender *is* part of a field, but that this field is the general social field, rather than any specific field of gender.

Sociologically speaking, gender would seem to behave in an unusually *relational* way. There seems to be no limits to its chameleonlike capacity for change in value and importance according to its specific social context. One of the advantages of Bourdieu's theory is that it not only insists on the social construction of gender, but that it permits us to seize the immense *variability* of gender as a social factor. But if we assume that gender is a particularly *combinatory* social category, one that infiltrates and influences every other category, it would precisely seem to have much in common with the concept of *social class* in Bourdieu's own theories. All his analyses of education, art, and taste tend to show the influence of social class on the *habitus* of individual agents. Yet he never studies social class as a 'pure' field in its own

---

[26] In the manuscript version of her essay Krais explictly stated that she would not discuss field, since it is impossible to isolate a 'distinctive field where gender is of special relevance' (6). This sentence does not appear in the published version.

right. Nor does he ever talk about 'class capital'. Rather it would seem that class is part of what he sometimes calls the 'whole social field': that which underpins or structures all other fields. This 'whole social field' may then be imported into another field as a field-specific *representation* of itself (see 'Champ intellectuel et projet créateur').[27]

Such a conceptualization of gender is not unproblematic. It does not, for instance, resolve the general problem of the relationship between gender and class. The question of whether *race* can be theorized in such terms would also require further investigation. Bourdieu's own discussions of gender sometimes, but by no means always, occur in contexts where it is assumed that class is a 'more fundamental' social category (this would for instance seem to be the case in *Distinction*). In 'La domination masculine', however, he explicitly states that 'male domination constitutes the paradigm (and often the model and stake) of all domination' (30–1). It nevertheless does not follow that male power is always the most central power relation at stake in every social situation. My own tentative view is that we may try to see both class and gender as belonging to the 'whole social field' without specifying a fixed and unchangeable hierarchy between them. The advantage of such an approach is that it enables us to escape a futile dogmatism which would declare the absolute primacy of class over gender or of gender over class.[28] Instead we might be able to seize the complex *variability* of these social factors as well as the way in which they influence and modify each other in different social contexts.

A field is a space structured by competition and exchange, and thus behaves much like a market. If, as the very term 'symbolic capital' implies, the 'whole social field' is assumed to behave according to a logic of exchange, a Marxist might argue that this in itself is an ideological analysis of social relations, one which

---

[27] I have not been able to discover a sustained account of the *precise* relationship of social fields to the 'whole social field'. The way in which specific fields relate to each other and to the general social field strikes me as somewhat undertheorized in Bourdieu's work.

[28] Perhaps a similar move might be productive when it comes to theorizing race as well.

presupposes something like a Hobbesian view of human self-interest as the prime mover of social relations. This is not necessarily a theory compatible with current feminist ideals for social interaction. On the other hand, it must be said that feminists have never been reluctant to analyse current gender-arrangements in terms of interests and benefits.[29]

Leaving these questions aside, I would now like to turn to the productive implications of theorizing gender in Bourdieuian terms. In Western democracies sexual oppression tends to take the form of *symbolic violence*. As we have seen, in times of social crisis symbolic violence ceases to function as such and is replaced by more overt forms of violence. In this sense the increase in physical violence against women since the emergence of the new women's movement signals the fact that gender relations now are constantly in crisis.

The imposition of femaleness on women (or in other words, the gendering of women as socially female) can be seen as another example of *social magic*.[30] This is why Simone de Beauvoir is quite correct to insist on the fact that one isn't born a woman, one becomes one. As we have seen, social magic is a socially sanctioned act which attributes an essence to individual agents, who then struggle to become what in fact they already are declared to be. In other words: to cast women as women is precisely to *produce* them as women. From a social perspective, without this categorizing and defining act of symbolic violence, women would simply not *be* women. Theorized in this way, the category of woman is neither an essence nor an indeterminate set of fluctuating signifiers, but a socially imposed definition with real effects. Like all other social categories, the category of woman therefore at once *masquerades as* and *is* an essence. While

[29] Much more work needs to be done on this subject. Many more problems than the ones I touch on here are raised by Bourdieu's field theory. Some of these are discussed in Thompson, Lamont, Craig Calhoun, and in Garnham and Williams. The implications of these debates for feminism remain to be discussed.

[30] Bourdieu would seem to agree. In 'La domination masculine' he stresses both the crucial role of social violence when it comes to upholding male power (see 11), and the process of *symbolic consecration* essential to the reproduction of such 'mythico-ritual' systems (see 15).

it is necessary to deconstruct the ideological category of woman, it should be remembered that such deconstruction remains politically toothless unless it also demonstrates the *social* interests at stake in the construction of this or any other 'social essence'.

The difference between a feminist appropriation of Bourdieu and certain other forms of materialist feminism is not, of course, the emphasis on gender as a socially constructed category, but the fact that a Bourdieuian perspective also assumes that gender is always a socially *variable* entity, one which carries different amounts of symbolic capital in different contexts. Insofar as gender never appears in a 'pure' field of its own, there is no such thing as pure 'gender capital'. The capital at stake is always the symbolic capital relevant for the specific field under examination. We may nevertheless start from the assumption that under current social conditions and in most contexts maleness functions as positive and femaleness as negative symbolic capital.

In order to illustrate some of the concrete consequences of these positions, I will use the case of Simone de Beauvoir to provide a few cursory examples. When analysing the social position and *habitus* of one particular woman it is easy to overestimate the effects of one specific social factor such as femaleness, or to ascribe to gender alone the effects of a much more complex and interconnected web of factors such as sex, class, race, and age (see *Distinction* 105–6). This amounts to saying that although social agents are undoubtedly always gendered, one cannot always assume that *gender* is the most relevant factor in play in a given social situation. But insofar as gender is implicated in all other social fields, it is always in principle a relevant factor in all social analysis: one can therefore never discard it without further examination. If feminists sometimes are guilty of overemphasizing gender to the detriment of other factors, then, this is a venial sin compared to the massive repression of gender routinely carried out by the great majority of workers in every intellectual discipline.

In the case of Simone de Beauvoir, it would seem that we are dealing with a particularly suitable subject for a gender-based analysis. Born into a middle-class Parisian family, Beauvoir grew up in circumstances very similar to those of her male friends, colleagues, and competitors at the time. The *only* obvious social stigma from which she suffers in the educational and intellectual fields of her day is that of femaleness. When analysing certain tensions and contradictions in her discourse, then, it is therefore not unreasonable to ascribe them to the fact of her femaleness. In the case of other French women writers, however, the analysis of the impact of gender would be far more complex. I am thinking of Christiane Rochefort, born into the Parisian working class, or Marguerite Duras, growing up as a 'poor white' in a French colony, or, at the other end of the social scale, of Marguerite Yourcenar, an aristocrat of independent means.

A feminist analysis of the impact of gender on a woman's discourse and consciousness must also bear in mind that to be a member of a disadvantaged minority within a given institution or field in no way guarantees that one will develop a revolutionary or oppositional consciousness. On the contrary: ostensibly egalitarian institutions tend to breed consent rather than opposition, *particularly* among the *miraculés*—the miraculous exceptions. For the paradox is that members of minority groups who do succeed in such a system are at least as likely to identify with it as the enabling cause of their own success as to turn against its unjust distribution of symbolic capital. In this way, for instance, the very fact that Simone de Beauvoir was a brilliant student, combined with the fact that she met with very little overt institutional discrimination at any point in her career, would certainly dispose her to identify with the intellectual values of the system, rather than to revolt against them. Such implicit intellectual solidarity with the dominant French educational institutions of her time can in fact be traced in the very texture of her style and rhetoric.

Bourdieuian categories are always relational, always determined by their fluctuating relationship to other categories. One interesting consequence of this is that we cannot assume that femaleness will carry equal amounts of negative capital throughout a woman's life or in all social fields. Socially speaking, then, it follows that sometimes a woman is a woman and sometimes she is much less so. In some contexts, 'femaleness' may even be converted from a liability to an advantage. If black women are more likely than black men to complete college education in the

United States, for instance, it amounts to saying that considered in relation to blackness (in a racist society blackness is another form of negative capital) femaleness in the field of education would seem to carry more positive educational capital than maleness.

In general, the impact of femaleness as negative capital may be assumed to decline in direct proportion to the amount of other forms of symbolic capital amassed. Or to put it the other way round: although a woman rich in symbolic capital may lose *some* legitimacy because of her gender, she still has more than enough capital left to make her impact on the field. In the case of exceptionally high amounts of symbolic (and economic) capital, femaleness may play a very small part indeed. In sociological terms such cases are so rare as to be negligible. For literary critics, however, it is not an entirely irrelevant problematic, since until recently the very fact of being a non-neglected woman writer was so rare as to turn the author into a *miraculée* almost per definition.[31] The works of such women cannot be read in the same way as those of writers lacking in symbolic capital. Their relationship to the works of more or less legitimate male colleagues will also be different from that of their less well-endowed sisters.

When it comes to explaining why it is that some exceptional women writers manage to accumulate more symbolic capital than others, Bourdieu's concept of *social capital* becomes particularly interesting. As we have seen, social capital is defined as relational capital, or in other words, the power and advantages one gains from having a network of 'contacts' as well as a series of other, more personal or intimate personal relations. Social capital helps its possessor to develop and increase other forms of capital, and may greatly enhance his or her chances of achieving legitimacy in a given field.

By the early 1950s, Simone de Beauvoir had developed considerable social capital in addition to the intellectual capital she had accumulated through her education and early career. At this

[31] There is also the complicated problem of the difference in a writer's status in her own life and after her death. It would be anachronistic to assume that Stendhal, to give an obvious example, carried as much literary capital in his own lifetime as he does in ours.

stage, then, her gender does not produce the same effects as, say, in 1943, when she was an unknown philosophy teacher publishing her very first novel. A social agent as richly endowed in intellectual and social capital as Beauvoir was in the 1950s will not suffer the most usual effects of gender discrimination in the intellectual field: she will not be silenced, ignored, or relegated to subservient positions in the contexts where she appears. Paradoxically, it is the very fact that such a woman has become *impossible to ignore* that inspires some of the more outrageous sexist attacks on such women. Some patriarchal souls, and particularly those whose own position in the field is threatened in some way or other, find the very thought of a female *monstre sacré* extremely hard to swallow. The very intensity of the sexist onslaughts on Beauvoir in the later parts of her life, then, could be read as the *effects* of her legitimacy, rather than as serious threats to that legitimacy.[32] Needless to say, such a reading of sexist responses would not be at all appropriate if applied to the younger, less prestigious Beauvoir, or indeed to other young, unknown women writers without conspicuous amounts of cultural or social capital.

The concept of social capital also allows us to grasp the *social* significance of Beauvoir's relationship to Sartre. Beauvoir often said that she did not owe her post-war success to Sartre. Although it is true that he never used his influence to further her projects, the very fact of being his companion enabled her quickly to gain access to important institutional contexts (including those of Gallimard and *Les temps modernes*) and thus to wield a considerable amount of symbolic power in the cultural field. It is not unfair to point out that without Sartre she would not have gained access to these contexts quite so easily. To my mind, then, there can be no doubt that, at least from about 1943 onwards, Beauvoir's relationship with Sartre significantly increased her social capital,

---

[32] The virulence of sexist attacks on Beauvoir in the 1970s and 1980s, however, is not necessarily an effect of legitimacy. The emergence of the women's movement made it impossible to ignore the fact that relations between the sexes were in a state of crisis. In France, the appearance of the women's movement in the early 1970s led to a predictable intensification of *explicit* struggle between the sexes. One sign of this struggle is that the general level of sexist invectives in newspaper and magazine articles increases.

and thus helped her to maximize her intellectual and literary capital.

It should be noted that there is nothing gender-specific about Sartre's role here. Traditionally women have performed exactly the same kind of service for men. This is particularly obvious if one looks for instance at the role of society hostesses and literary salons in the late nineteenth and early twentieth centuries.[33] In this case women exceptionally well endowed with social capital would put it at the disposal of aspiring young artists or writers from undistinguished social origins. As a result, their intellectual or artistic careers would be significantly advanced. Social capital is above all a matter of personal relations. Since some personal relations are sexual and intimate as well as social, it follows that aspiring artists of both sexes risk squandering their artistic capital by loving unwisely. From a purely social point of view, outstanding female intellectuals have often loved very wisely indeed: think of George Eliot, Virginia Woolf, or indeed of Simone de Beauvoir.[34]

An analysis of gender as a socially variable effect of social magic has obvious implications for feminist theory. Insofar as the accent is placed firmly on social practice, and on the shifting social relations between gender and other fields, this is a truly non-essentialist, yet historically and socially concrete, analysis of the shifting significance of gender. To say that Simone de Beauvoir was a woman, then, is no longer to invoke a rather static or predictable social category, but invite a highly flexible analysis of a variable and often contradictory network of relations. Such an analysis cannot remain on the level of generalities: it must engage with specific social institutions and practices, and it must show precisely how these factors influence the intellectual choices and strategies of the writer in question. The attraction of Pierre Bourdieu's sociology of culture is that it may help us to do precisely that.

[33] I am grateful to Pierre Bourdieu for suggesting this example.

[34] I am not at all arguing that these women *only* achieved social capital through their social relations, only that the social capital obtained through marriage or stable liaisons may have helped them to maximize other forms of symbolic capital more rapidly and efficiently than they could have done without these relationships.

READING WITH BOURDIEU

I have argued that Pierre Bourdieu's sociology of culture may be of considerable use to literary and/or cultural critics. Yet my claim is not that Bourdieuian theory provides us with new models of narrativity or a better understanding of rhetoric or tropology than current textual theories. On the contrary: insofar as his is not a theory of textuality at all, a *purely* Bourdieuian reading is unthinkable.[35] What his analyses may help us to see, however, is the way in which certain texts enter into field-related intertextual relations with other texts. Once we have perceived these relations, we may then go on to use them to produce new readings of the texts in question.

To be consistent, such a Bourdieuian strategy must of course also be applied to Bourdieu's own works. At first glance, at least, his texts would seem to situate themselves in intertextual relations above all to the work of Sartre and of Derrida. In the early 1950s when Bourdieu started studying philosophy, Sartre was *the* dominant French philosopher. Derrida, on the other hand was Bourdieu's fellow student (his *petit camarade*, as it were) at the École Normale Supérieure. The intertextual links between Bourdieu's work and that of Sartre are numerous, but perhaps best illustrated in Bourdieu's enduring concern with Flaubert. In some ways it is tempting to say that Bourdieu's whole project may be seen as an effort to do what Sartre could not do in *L'Idiot de la famille*: provide an exhaustive analysis of every social and individual determinant of agency and subjectivity. Bourdieu's implicit polemics against Derridean aesthetics is nowhere more obvious than in *Distinction*, but can also be traced in his persistent effort to vindicate empirical methods of research against what he would call the *unscientific* textual idealism of dominant trends in French philosophy.

But, one may ask, what are the *effects* of such analyses on what many take to be the primary task of the literary critic—that of

[35] It may be necessary to add that I am using a fairly narrow definition of 'textual' theory: I am referring to the vast body of work dealing with narratology, genre, rhetoric, figures, tropes, and so forth.

reading texts? A simple example from my own experience may help to provide a concrete answer to this question. In *Sexual/Textual Politics* I devote considerable space to a discussion of Hélène Cixous's highly influential essay 'The Laugh of the Medusa'. At the time of writing (1984) I was perfectly well aware of the fact that the French text of that essay was originally published in a special issue of the literary magazine *L'Arc* devoted to Simone de Beauvoir. It is difficult to overlook the fact that there is a photograph of Simone de Beauvoir on the cover, and that the issue opens with an interview with Jean-Paul Sartre conducted by Simone de Beauvoir herself. Yet I utterly failed to grasp the implications of the discursive and institutional aspects of Cixous's *énonciation*. The significant point that escaped me is the fact that in 'The Laugh of the Medusa' there is not a single reference to Simone de Beauvoir. Now, it is true that this issue of *L'Arc* is entitled *Simone de Beauvoir et la lutte des femmes*, and that several other essays deal with various topics concerning the situation of women in France without mentioning Simone de Beauvoir by name.[36] Apart from 'The Laugh of the Medusa', however, every one of the essays in this issue is consonant with Beauvoir's own feminist positions. 'The Laugh of the Medusa' is also the only essay to deal with women's writing, a field in which Beauvoir after all has a certain claim to fame.

Today I would not hesitate to analyse this phenomenon as an effort to snub Beauvoir, a deliberate challenge to the doyenne of French feminism, and, more specifically, as Cixous's bid for power—*legitimacy*—within the field of French feminism. Implicitly casting Beauvoir as *orthodox*, Cixous's defiant exclusion of the author of *She Came to Stay* and *The Second Sex* signals her need to erase a figure she perceives as the powerful and censorious origin of her own discourse.

---

[36] The editors, Bernard Pingaud and Catherine Clément, explain that for political reasons Simone de Beauvoir herself chose to be 'une parmi d'autres, une femme entre autres, anonyme' (1). Given the title, layout, and contents of this special issue, this anonymity is somewhat illusory. I have already mentioned the cover photograph and the initial interview where Beauvoir makes Sartre discuss his views on women. There is also a discussion between Simone de Beauvoir and several other militant feminists, and a series of essays on various aspects of women's situation, including an essay by Sylvie Le Bon (Beauvoir's close friend, later her adoptive daughter) on *The Second Sex*.

Drawing on Bourdieu's work on French intellectual styles, I also think one can show that in the very act of denouncing the rhetoric of male-dominated French philosophy (which is that of Beauvoir in *The Second Sex*, for instance), Cixous displays a range of the very same rhetorical strategies (silencing of the opposition, tendentious summary of unnamed opponents' views, generalizing from one's own particular experience, and so on). This is not surprising: Cixous's own bid for legitimacy cannot succeed were she to jettison *all* the hallmarks of the field she is in. Given her rhetoric, that field can now be defined as that of the French intellectual field in general, not simply that of French feminism. In this context it is easy to show that in 1975 it is Cixous, not Beauvoir, who most masterfully displays the strategies and moves likely to be defined as 'high' or 'canonical' in the French intellectual field.[37] This is no doubt an important reason why 'The Laugh of the Medusa' produced such a powerful impact in 1975, and thus did so much to secure the prestige of its author, at the direct expense, I would argue, of that of Simone de Beauvoir. Drawing on Bourdieuian categories, then, it is possible to show that the rhetoric of Cixous's brilliant essay more or less unwittingly enters into conflict with her explicit message of generosity, openness, and receptivity to the text of the other writer/woman.

What then, is the status of these observations on Cixous's essay? In my view, they all, including my comments on the significance of certain rhetorical moves typical of French philosophy, contribute to an understanding of the *énonciation* of 'The Laugh of the Medusa'. As argued above, however, the *énoncé* can never simply be reduced to the *énonciation*. While the latter certainly constrains the former, this constraint is best envisaged as a horizon or limit to what is *speakable*, rather than as a set of unmediated reflections to be faithfully reproduced in the *énoncé*. The *énoncé*, then, must necessarily still be read in ways which may not be directly related to the position of the speaker.

As a *reader* of 'The Laugh of the Medusa', I might go on to use my Bourdieuian insights to produce an intertextual reading of

---

[37] For a discussion of Beauvoir's relative lack of distinction in the French intellectual field, or what one might call her 'petit bourgeois appeal,' see ch. 2 in my *Simone de Beauvoir*, esp. 68–72.

Cixous's essay with *The Second Sex*. My hypothesis would be that a careful reading of the texts—perhaps one drawing on psychoanalytic as well as deconstructive strategies—would show that the obliterated figure of the powerful mother is a problem not only for Beauvoir, but for Cixous as well. No doubt the Oedipal mother Cixous seeks to displace has many names: what I am arguing here is that one of them is that of Simone de Beauvoir.

Such a reading is not the only desirable reading of 'The Laugh of the Medusa' nor indeed of *The Second Sex*. It does not, for instance, oblige me to reject my own theoretical analysis of Cixous's text in *Sexual/Textual Politics*. Moreover, one may also produce elegant intertextual readings of these two texts without having read Bourdieu. The problem for *any* intertextual reading, however, is to counter the charge of arbitrariness. Paradoxically, it is precisely because there is, in principle, no limit to the number of possible intertexts to any given text, that it becomes necessary explicitly to justify one's choice of any *particular* intertext. In the case of Cixous and Beauvoir, then, the advantage of a Bourdieuian approach is, first, to provide us with a series of insights about the relations between Hélène Cixous and the feminist and intellectual fields in France, and between 'The Laugh of the Medusa' and *The Second Sex*. It also enables us to note and interpret a series of formal, rhetorical moves in the texts (the presence or absence of footnotes, quotations, and certain names, for instance) as recognizable power bids in a specific intellectual field. And, finally, such an approach provides a reply to the question of *why* one should juxtapose these specific texts in the first place and *why* such an intertextual reading should be considered relevant and interesting. I am old fashioned enough to believe that such questions still matter.

4

The Challenge of the Particular Case: Bourdieu's Sociology of Culture and Literary Criticism
(1997)

This essay started out as a commentary on the other essays in the December 1997 special issue of *Modern Language Quarterly* (*MLQ*) entitled *Pierre Bourdieu and Literary History*, edited by Marshall Brown. After reading the rich and varied contributions, I realized that only one question stayed with me: what is the use of Pierre Bourdieu's sociology of culture for contemporary literary criticism? Or in other words, how can Bourdieu's sociological method benefit the practice of literary critics? I gave up the idea of writing a conventional commentary and decided to think about this question instead. For the answer is not obvious. As John Guillory points out in 'Bourdieu's Refusal', his outstanding contribution to the *MLQ* issue, Bourdieu has yet to be seriously received by literary critics in the United States. Even the essays in the *MLQ* issue reveal that there is something in Bourdieu's sociology of culture that resists the usual strategies of literary critics. Guillory's analysis brings out one misunderstanding, namely, the one that consists in seeing him as a determinist. Guillory shows that at the heart of much American literary and cultural criticism is a tendency to understand social change in voluntarist terms, and that this voluntarism then produces its own negative other in the form of 'determinism'. According to Guillory, this voluntarism prevents US critics from seeing that Bourdieu's project is an effort to understand the play of freedom *and* necessity in human

I want to thank Julia Hell for her response to a draft of this essay. I also want to thank Marshall Brown for his meticulous reading and excellent editorial suggestions.

lives, to elaborate an understanding of human action which avoids having to make the sterile choice between voluntarism and determinism in the first place.

In my view, the difficulty that Bourdieu represents for literary critics has to do with the fact that he inherits a philosophical tradition that remains poorly understood in US literary criticism. On my reading of his works, Bourdieu takes his place among the group of twentieth-century thinkers that includes Freud, Heidegger, Sartre, Beauvoir, Merleau-Ponty, J. L. Austin, and Wittgenstein.[1] These thinkers share, among other things, a painstaking attentiveness to the particular case, a wish to take the concrete manifestations of human behaviour as the starting point of thought. Freud develops psychoanalysis from his work with patients. His case studies as well as his essays on interpretation always start with the particular symptom, the particular dream or slip of the tongue. Sartre analyses the different philosophical implications of downhill skiing and water-skiing, and Beauvoir uncovers the Manichaean metaphysics of housework. Merleau-Ponty investigates the way the sexual body is experienced, Austin worries about shooting donkeys by accident or by mistake (no wonder that he refers to his speech act analysis as 'linguistic phenomenology'), and Wittgenstein shows us over and over again that the only way to recover from philosophical nonsense is to bring our words back into their contexts of significant use: 'What *we* do is to bring words back from their metaphysical to their everyday use'.[2] When Bourdieu investigates the way people chew

---

[1] In 'To Follow a Rule' Charles Taylor makes a similar point when he distinguishes between philosophies that consider the subject primarily as a 'monologic' subject of representation, and philosophies such as those of Heidegger, Merleau-Ponty, and Wittgenstein that consider the subject as an embodied agent of practices.

[2] In this paragraph I have the following sources in mind: Sigmund Freud and Joseph Breuer, *Studies on Hysteria*; Freud, *The Interpretation of Dreams*; Freud, *The Psychopathology of Everyday Life*. Sartre discusses skiing and sliding in *Being and Nothingness* 742–7; Beauvoir uncovers the philosophy of housework in *SS* 448–57; Merleau-Ponty discusses the sexual body in pt. 1, ch. 5 of *Phenomenology of Perception* 154–73; Austin wonders about the shooting of donkeys in 'A Plea for Excuses' 185, and uses the expression 'linguistic phenomenology' in the same essay (182). The passage quoted by Wittgenstein comes from *PI* §116, whereas the expression 'context of significant use' is inspired by Wittgenstein, *Tractatus*

their food, the way they look at photographs, and the way their exam results affect their way of being in the world, he is following in the footsteps of these distinguished predecessors.

For these thinkers, the concrete example is not a secondary illustration of a general rule. It is the place where thought happens, where theoretical questions get raised, elaborated, and answered. To understand Wittgenstein is to understand that words removed from every language game, from every conceivable context of significant use, are neither 'right' nor 'wrong', neither 'true' nor 'false', but simply empty. In the same way, French phenomenology (Sartre, Beauvoir, Merleau-Ponty) sets out to make philosophy emerge from the study of the concrete case. Thus Sartre's great unfinished work, the 3,000-page-long study of Flaubert, begins: '*The Family Idiot* is the continuation of *Questions of Method*. Its subject: what can one know about a human being today? It seems to me that one can only answer this question by the study of a concrete case: what do we know—for example—about Gustave Flaubert?'3

Pierre Bourdieu's major investigation of a concrete literary case is precisely an investigation of Flaubert. Anyone who wants to understand what a Bourdieuian analysis of literature and the literary field might look like should consider his method in *The Rules of Art*, which contains the great study of Flaubert and *L'Éducation sentimentale*.4 It is no coincidence that *The Rules of Art* is replete

---

Logico-Philosophicus §3. 326: 'In order to recognize a symbol by its sign we must observe how it is used with a sense'; and §3. 328: 'If a sign is *useless*, it is meaningless.' 'Context of significant use' is my understanding of what a language game is (cf. *PI* §23 and §24). My understanding of Wittgenstein is deeply indebted to Martin Stone, esp. to his seminar on Wittgenstein at Duke University in the spring of 1997.

³ Jean-Paul Sartre, *L'idiot de la famille: Gustave Flaubert de 1821 à 1857* 1: 7. My translation.

⁴ William Paulson's 'The Market of Printed Goods' contains extensive discussions of the book. Let me just add a few remarks about Bourdieu's method. He first collects as much information as he can about the social origins and positions of all the players in the French literary and/or cultural field at the time. Bourdieu's analyses of social positions pay detailed attention to location in space: the geographical origins of individual agents as well as their specific placement within the social space of Paris are always of interest to Bourdieu, who himself grew up in the south-western French province of Béarn as the son of a postman. Elaborating a painstakingly detailed social map of the agents represented in

with references to Sartre; indeed, the section titled 'Questions of Method', deliberately echoes his separately published 'introduction' to *The Family Idiot*. *The Rules of Art* also include a brief, sardonic, and highly significant commentary on Sartre, entitled 'The Total Intellectual and the Illusion of the Omnipotence of Thought'.[5] Bourdieu's analysis is that Sartre, by operating in the fields of philosophy, literature, and criticism, and by founding a literary and political review, *Les temps modernes*, concentrated in his hands all the kinds of intellectual capital available to a post-war intellectual in France.

In the early 1950s, in other words, Sartre was the incarnation of distinction in the French intellectual field. At the time, the young Bourdieu, an ambitious student of philosophy at the École Normale Supérieure (ENS), the leading educational institution in France, could hardly avoid pitting himself against him. Jacques Derrida, Bourdieu's classmate, chose the same project. To this day the two remain rivals for distinction in the French intellectual field. Because they were at the ENS together, the rivalry is particularly intense and deeply encoded in their texts. One reason, then, why Bourdieu feels compelled to criticize Derrida's aesthetic in *Distinction* (see Jonathan Loesberg's 'Bourdieu's Derrida's Kant'), is that in the 1970s when that book was written, both Bourdieu and Derrida were powerful young masters, eager to claim the regal mantle left behind by Sartre.

Although both Derrida and Bourdieu were out to destroy Sartre, they chose different strategies. Until May 1968, the most prestigious discipline in France had undoubtedly been philosophy. But in the

---

L'Éducation Sentimentale, he concludes that the novel, among other things, contains Flaubert's analysis of his own position as a writer. *Habitus* is always discussed in relation to placement in the field, and the battle for symbolic capital is always understood in terms of concrete competition for specific stakes. The social analysis of aesthetics contained in *The Rules of Art* echoes and develops the remarks on Derrida's and Kant's aesthetics at the end of *Distinction* (discussed by Jonathan Loesberg in 'Bourdieu's Derrida's Kant').

5 This is a revised version of the obituary of Sartre that Bourdieu published in the *London Review of Books* in 1980. See Pierre Bourdieu, *The Rules of Art*, 209–13. V. Y. Mudimbe has also discussed the importance of Sartre for *The Rules of Art*.

1970s it began to lose its grasp on the French educational institutions. In a radical move, Bourdieu attempted to enthrone sociology as the new 'queen of the disciplines'. If this bold attempt succeeded, then it would simply follow that even the best philosopher would be considered less impressive than the best sociologist; in one stroke, Bourdieu would triumph over Derrida as well as Sartre. Derrida, on the other hand, seems to have counted on keeping philosophy the supremely distinguished discipline in the French cultural field. (In the 1970s and 1980s, Derrida, significantly enough, was active in various movements that aimed to preserve the status of philosophy in French *lycées* and universities.) His strategy was to claim the role as master-philosopher, the revolutionary inheritor of the Western philosophical tradition, by producing a philosophy in which Sartre figured, implicitly and explicitly, as an antediluvian humanist essentialist, unworthy of serious philosophical attention, and Bourdieuian sociology as a deliberately negated absence.[6]

In the United States, literary criticism is still dominated by poststructuralism and its aftermath. With the possible exception of Heidegger (as read by deconstructionists) and Freud (mostly as read by Lacanians), none of the thinkers I mention above is 'hot' in US literary criticism and theory today, which amounts to saying that the tradition in which I situate Bourdieu is not poststructuralist at all. As Charles Taylor has pointed out, the major preoccupation of Merleau-Ponty or Wittgenstein, is not with the subject as subject of representation, but as a subject 'engaged in practices, as a being who acts in and on a world' (49). To put it in existentialist terms: Sartre, Beauvoir, Freud, Wittgenstein, and Bourdieu all set out to understand human beings as embodied creatures trying to make something of what the world makes of them. This is Sartre's project in *The Family Idiot* and Beauvoir's in her autobiographies.[7]

The dialectical tension in the turn of phrase, 'to make something

---

[6] Derrida's *Of Spirit: Heidegger and the Question*, for example, is among other things a hidden polemic against Bourdieu's *The Political Ontology of Martin Heidegger*.

[7] In a more modest way, it is also my project in *Simone de Beauvoir: The Making of an Intellectual Woman*.

of what the world makes of us', is endlessly echoed in Bourdieu's rhetorical elaborations on the theme of *amor fati*, the ways in which we are led to choose our destiny or to 'love our fate' so as to make choices which further strengthen the social patterns that conditioned those choices in the first place. The theme of *amor fati* is not to be taken as a form of determinism. In *The State Nobility*, for example, Bourdieu studies the way in which the imposition of social power in the educational system is linked to the transmission or reproduction of power in other social spheres. The main function of the educational system, he argues, is above all to produce the necessary social belief in the legitimacy of currently dominant power structures. The coveted diploma or exam paper becomes a token of *social magic*, the emblem of a transformational exercise which truly changes the essence of the chosen elite. Social magic has real, material effects:

> One must be noble to act nobly, but one would cease to be noble if one did not act nobly. In other words, social magic has very real effects. Assigning someone to a group of superior essence (noblemen as opposed to commoners, men as opposed to women, educated as opposed to uneducated, etc.) causes that person to undergo a subjective transformation that contributes to bringing about a real transformation likely to bring him closer to the assigned definition (*State Nobility* 112).[8]

Social magic helps produce love of one's destiny. Students who have been consecrated as budding geniuses by being accepted at the ENS, for instance, are thereby enjoined to develop the tastes and strategies (the *habitus*) that will make it possible for them to live up to the role of 'genius' now bestowed upon them, such as a genuine taste for obscure art movies, Japanese theatre, or the finer points of Kant's philosophy. The fact is that a large number of them do develop precisely such tastes. Yet this is still a matter of choice. They do not all develop strictly the same tastes. Nor do all students at the École Normale uniformly obey the mandate to behave as 'proper' geniuses. For reasons that Bourdieu thinks it is possible to explore, some fail to, or refuse to, conform. Some develop tastes of

---

[8] This quotation also appears in Ch 3. The paragraph preceding this quotation in this paper is an edited version of the passage leading up to the same quotation in Ch. 3 (see pp. 273–4).

resistance, others choose strategies that make them marginal to the field that initially consecrated them. Jean-Paul Sartre and Paul Nizan went to the same prestigious Parisian *lycée*, and were class-mates at the ENS in the late 1920s, yet while Sartre adored his time at the school, Nizan hated it. Both were consecrated inheritors of French intellectual capital: only one of them fully accepted his role.[9] The theme of *amor fati* explains how it is that we so often honestly and authentically choose the tastes and strategies that correspond to our position in the social field, but it doesn't imply that we all inevitably and without exception end up loving our destinies.

Against the attempt to grasp and hold both sides of the formula-tion 'what we make of what the world makes of us'—our freedom as well as the necessity that constrains it—poststructuralist literary crit-icism invariably posits a series of binary oppositions: subject or object, activity or passivity, voluntarism or determinism, freedom or necessity. Their fatal penchant for binary oppositions effectively prevents poststructuralists from grasping the project of the philoso-phers of agency or praxis that I have mentioned here.[10] Currently, these philosophers are less prestigious and therefore more unfamil-iar among American literary critics than, say, Barthes, Derrida, Foucault, Lacan, Deleuze, Irigaray, Kristeva, and so on. Or in other words, poststructuralism is the 'normal science' of contemporary literary criticism. In the intense struggle for symbolic capital that is so characteristic of American academia, a graduate student inspired by Beauvoir will easily come to be seen as less 'theoretically sophisti-cated' (i.e. endowed with less symbolic capital) than one inspired by Irigaray. In the current job market the disincentive for graduate students to break with the dominant *doxa* is enormous.[11] I take it

---

[9] I discuss the ENS, Sartre, Nizan, and others in ch. 2 of my *Simone de Beauvoir* (see esp. 54–62).

[10] Although Marx is arguably the greatest philosopher of human *praxis*, I have left the Marxist tradition out of my account. Not because I think it is irrel-evant (on the contrary!), but because my understanding of the similarities and differences between, say, Marx and Freud, Marx and Sartre, and Marx and Bourdieu is not (yet) sufficiently developed.

[11] I analyse Beauvoir's lack of distinction in the *French* intellectual field in ch. 2 of my *Simone de Beauvoir.* In my view, she has higher prestige in the American academic field, yet even in the USA existentialism is hardly theoretically presti-gious at the moment.

that this illustrates one of the things Bourdieu has in mind when he claims that 'a field functions as a censorship' (*Sociology in Question* 91).

In this intellectual context it becomes hard for literary critics to read and use Bourdieu. First of all, in North American literary criticism, poststructuralism quickly got enmeshed with the legacy of New Criticism. The erasure of the writing subject promoted by the New Critics was eagerly continued by American deconstruction. As practised by Paul de Man and his disciples, close reading gained philosophical cachet, but remained fundamentally alien to any attempt to see language as a form of human praxis. All the philosophers I mention above are philosophers of subjectivity understood as an embodied locus of action and choice. A literary theory based on their insights will have to take the form of a concrete, historically grounded speech act theory. For such a theory there can be no question of bracketing off the speaking subject and its audience from the sphere of the close reading. As J. L. Austin puts it: if we want to find out what an utterance means, we should ask 'what we should say when', that is, picture a concrete speech act where it might make sense to use the expression in question.[12]

Insofar as it is almost impossible to base a strategy of disembodied and decontextualized close readings on Bourdieu's sociology of culture, he is unlikely to be widely adopted by US literary critics. Bourdieu grounds any literary analysis on an immense mass of social and cultural data. As Elizabeth Harries puts it in 'Out in Left Field':

> [Bourdieu's] microtheories of social power are always based on precise, detailed examinations of the things people do and say and write and even eat. What we need is a similar 'thick description' of the cultural field of the 1780s and 90s—a description that takes account of all the practices (prefaces, footnotes, dedications, earnings, sales, quarrels, silences) that were part of the struggle for cultural power and prestige (473).

---

[12] In 'A Plea for Excuses' Austin writes: 'When we examine what we should say when, what words we should use in what situations, we are looking again not merely at words (or "meanings", whatever they may be) but also at the realities we use the words to talk about: we are using a sharpened awareness of words to sharpen our perception of, though not as the final arbiter of, the phenomena' (182).

This requirement produces huge problems for critics studying American or British literature. There is no existing body of Bourdieuian analyses of the relevant fields or institutions. Only the most intensive research can rectify this situation. To gather the relevant data for a thoroughly Bourdieuian analysis of a text, a writer, or a specific cultural field, is extremely time-consuming. In order to produce his remarkable investigation of *L'Éducation sentimentale*, for example, Bourdieu mobilized a huge team of researchers, and it still took him over ten years to get to the point where he could publish *The Rules of Art*. Without this kind of data, however, the 'thick' phenomenological and sociological descriptions that Bourdieuian sociology promises literary criticism simply cannot be produced.

My own limited experience bears this out. In chapter 2 of my *Simone de Beauvoir: The Making of an Intellectual Woman* I set out to produce a very limited Bourdieuian analysis of Beauvoir as an intellectual woman. I don't think I would even have attempted the project if I had not been working on French intellectual institutions richly documented by Bourdieu and his fellow researchers. They had already elucidated the meaning of the *agrégation* examination, the pecking order of intellectual disciplines at the time, the status of philosophy in the cultural field, and so on. Yet, in spite of the fact that so much material was available, I still had to put in huge amounts of research just to uncover basic facts about Beauvoir's position in the French educational field. I discovered, for example, that Beauvoir was only the ninth woman in France to pass the prestigious *agrégation* in philosophy. That she herself never mentions this struck me as significant. Eventually my research into the signification of her education and exam results enabled me to grasp some of the determinants that led Beauvoir to cast herself as 'second only to Sartre'. There was, for instance, her decision to study philosophy in the first place. What did it mean for a woman to do so at the time? In order to find out, I needed to discover what it meant for men as well. What intellectual habits did she pick up as a student? How did they mark her subsequent writing? To follow a Bourdieuian strategy in the attempt to answer these questions means locating Beauvoir among her contemporaries, discovering how philosophy was taught at the time, finding out what other people thought about philosophy and literature, getting clear on what the positions of those other people were in the intellectual and educational fields at the time, what stakes they were competing for, and so on. The effort involved in producing just one chapter studying Beauvoir from a somewhat Bourdieuian perspective taught me not to undertake such projects lightly.[13]

Two factors, then, shape the reception of Bourdieu in the US literary academy: (1) the relative absence of the concrete data that Bourdieuian sociology of culture requires; and (2) the towering presence of the poststructuralist *doxa*. In this situation, the US literary critics who nevertheless want to use Bourdieu face two dangers. The first is that they will turn one or two favourite Bourdieuian terms into the loosely defined 'themes' of a close reading. The second is that they will take Bourdieu's sociology to be just another poststructuralist 'theory'.

The problem with the 'thematic' approach to Bourdieu is that it tends to proceed without any of the specific data that alone enable Bourdieuian sociology of culture to provide the rich, concrete grounding of aesthetic phenomena that so many literary critics wish to develop. The literary critic is thus doomed to produce more or less impressionistic readings of the representation of social themes in the literary text, or of the competition for prestige in literary history. But as Harries warns us, as long as we do not know, for example, what sort of rewards ('stakes') were available in the relevant field and who had the power to distribute them, such speculations remain idle.

The thematic method also tends to select one of the three major Bourdieuian terms—*habitus* or 'field' or 'symbolic capital' (the latter is sometimes simply translated into 'distinction')—and then go on to use it without further reference to the other terms. On my reading of Bourdieu, however, the only way to understand the concept of symbolic capital is to link it to a specific cultural field. Only a field can grant symbolic capital. The name of the symbolic capital current in a field changes with the field: the

[13] My preparatory work for this chapter also produced a more general essay on Bourdieu. See Ch. 3, above, 'Appropriating Bourdieu: Feminist Theory and Pierre Bourdieu's Sociology of Culture'.

educational field grants educational capital, the intellectual field intellectual capital, and so on. The question of the exchange value of different forms of symbolic capital arises every time an agent attempts to move from one field to another. What constitutes a field is the fact that there are agents who compete for specific stakes. 'A field defines itself by (among other things) defining specific stakes and interests, which are irreducible to the stakes and interests specific to other fields (you can't make a philosopher compete for the prizes that interest a geographer) and which are not perceived by someone who has not been shaped to enter that field' (*Sociology in Question* 72). The field-specific competition generates its own specific *habitus* in agents competing for field-specific symbolic capital. To remove these concepts from each other's company and from any actual social and human context is to miss the close, concrete relationship between subjectivity, institutions, and social field that constitutes the original and powerful intellectual contribution of Bourdieu's sociology of culture to contemporary thought. The 'thematic' use of Bourdieu can bring to light previously unnoticed aspects of literary texts or of literary history. There is no reason to stop drawing on Bourdieu for such purposes. My point is simply that, however interesting or relevant such analyses may be, they turn Bourdieu into just another furnisher of themes for close reading. What is lacking in such readings is the most distinctive and original aspect of Bourdieu's work, namely his sociological method.

The second approach usually consists in discussing Bourdieu in terms that are central to poststructuralism, but not necessarily to Bourdieu. The poststructuralist binary oppositions return: the question becomes whether Bourdieu is determinist or voluntarist, essentialist or anti-essentialist, whether he sees subjects as active or passive, or whether he reverts to Enlightenment humanism. But given such a starting point, the critic will almost inevitably either happily demonstrate that Bourdieu can in fact be turned into a poststructuralist, or take him to task for not quite managing to become one. In this way, even well-intentioned critics end up taking a more negative view of Bourdieu than they may have intended. Guillory's incisive analysis demonstrates how the terms in which the debate is framed contribute to the relative non-reception of Bourdieu among literary critics in the United States.

Even the most cursory account of Bourdieu must try to apply its own insights to a concrete case, or it will fail to grasp Bourdieu's intellectual project. In my view one should not exaggerate Bourdieu's intellectual debt to Wittgenstein. Yet Bourdieu is Wittgensteinian in the sense that he knows that his theories make no sense outside the language games to which they belong. If we remove Bourdieu's concepts from every specific context of significant use, we will never be able to do anything interesting, or even remotely relevant, with them.

5

The Missing Mother:
René Girard's Oedipal Rivalries
(1980)

In the female prison
There are seventy-five women
And what wouldn't I give if I were there
But that old triangle
Goes jingle-jangle
All along the banks of the Royal Canal.

(Dominic Behan)

Since the publication in 1961 of *Deceit, Desire, and the Novel: Self and Other in Literary Structure* (trans. 1965) René Girard has tirelessly expanded and expounded his theory of triangular or mimetic desire. In this first book he claimed that triangular desire was the key to a true understanding of the novels of authors like Cervantes, Stendhal, Dostoevsky, and Proust. In his next major theoretical work, *Violence and the Sacred* (1972; trans. 1977) he transported his triangle into the fields of anthropology and religion. Girard now maintained that triangular desire could explain all sacrificial rituals and religious beliefs concerning victims and scapegoats. At the end of *Violence and the Sacred* he promised further developments of his theory, and he did not fail us: in 1978 he published, in French, *Things Hidden Since the Foundation of the World*.[1] Here Girard read the Old and the New Testament in the light of his theories and also sought to prove that his understanding of the nature of desire is considerably superior to Freud's. By this point, he was laying claim to total and universal validity for his theories:

[1] In the original version of this essay I referred to the French text, *Des choses cachées depuis la fondation du monde*. The translations were my own. I now refer to the English translation, *Things Hidden Since the Foundation of the World*, which appeared in 1987.

We will see now that not only the prohibition but also ritual and ultimately the whole structure of religion can be traced back to the mechanism of acquisitive mimesis. A complete theory of human culture will be elaborated, beginning with this single principle (*Things Hidden* 18).

I shall argue here that such claims cannot in fact be validated. My main contention is that Girard's theory of mimetic desire cannot account for women's desire.[2] Any claims to universal validity for his theory must therefore be abandoned. Through a reading of Girard's theoretical works I will try to show that women's desire is in fact absent from his works, and that the reason for this absence is to be found in Girard's exclusion of the mother from the Oedipal triangle, an exclusion which can only be maintained at a high theoretical cost: Girard has to posit heterosexuality as an inborn instinct in human beings in order to save his reading of the Oedipus complex.

In a style itself prodigal with hieratic and authoritarian gestures ('The truth is that . . .'; 'All we have to do to account for every-thing . . .') Girard states that all desire is appropriative and medi-ated. The subject can only desire an object insofar as another subject already desires the same object. All desire is an imitation of the rival's desire and therefore mimetic. Girard himself puts it in this way:

> In all the varieties of desire examined by us, we have encountered not only a subject and an object but a third person as well: the rival. It is the rival who should be accorded the dominant role. . . . The subject desires the object because the rival desires it. . . . The rival, then, serves as a model for the subject, not only in regard to such secondary matters as style and opinions but also, and more essentially, in regard to desires. . . . We must understand that desire

[2] In the original version of this essay I wrote 'feminine desire'. I think that was because I wanted to signal that I wasn't speaking of women's essential or inherent desire. In fact, however, the specific distinction between 'feminine' and 'female' that this usage depends on, is irrelevant in relation to my critique of Girard's theories. For what my essay shows is that Girard cannot account for the fact that *women* desire, whatever the object of their desire may be: whether that desire is conceptualized as essential or constructed makes no difference to my case. See Ch. 1, above, 'What Is a Woman?' for a more careful discussion of words such as 'woman', 'female' and 'feminine'.

itself is essentially mimetic, directed toward an object desired by the model. . . . Thus, mimesis coupled with desire leads automatically to conflict (*Violence* 145–6).

The competition between subject and rival soon overshadows the subject's mediated desire for the object. The importance of the mediator increases as he approaches the subject, and the importance of object decreases correspondingly. Before long the subject is caught up in an intense and ambivalent relationship with the rival/model. The object recedes more and more into the background, and is presently declared superfluous:

> JMO [Jean-Marie Oughourlian]: What strikes me about all you have been saying is that there is no longer any object. Everything comes down to the relationships between the mimetic rivals, each of which is model and disciple to the other. . . .
> RG [René Girard]: . . . Desire becomes detached from the object, bit by bit, and attaches itself to the model. This development is accompanied by a marked aggravation of the symptoms (*Things Hidden* 310–11).

The conflictual relationship between subject and rival would lead to endless violence if society did not manage to curb the expression of mimetic conflict. This, in effect, is the role of religion. Girard maintains that all sacrificial rites, all choice of scapegoats, are designed to prevent social violence. Violence is thus an inherent part of the sacred; the very function of the sacred is to procure socially acceptable outlets for mimetic violence.

Mimetic rivalry between subject and model increases as the difference between them diminishes; the model then becomes the subject's *double*, and the mimetic violence grows in intensity. In order to halt this circle of violence a victim who is *different* from the rivalling subjects/mediators, a scapegoat, must be chosen. Precisely because the scapegoat is *different* it can break the unending circle of mimetic rivalry between near-identical doubles. This choice of a scapegoat is expressed in two stages. Girard writes:

> All sacrificial rites are based on two substitutions. The first is provided by generative violence, which substitutes a single victim for all the members of the community. The second, the only strictly ritualistic substitution, is that of a victim [*une victime sacrifiable*] for the surrogate victim. As we know, it is essential that the

victim [*les catégories sacrifiables*] be drawn from outside the community. The surrogate victim, by contrast, is a member of the community (*Violence* 269).

The sacrificial mechanism consists in finding an outlet for the mimetic violence outside the community, thereby providing the basis for a stable and peaceful society.

SEXISM AND LITERARY CRITICISM

Girard admits to almost having succumbed to the 'neo-Marxian and Lukácsian temptation embodied in the late and lamented Lucien Goldmann, for whom mimetic desire was the monopoly of a specific literary genre, the novel, belonging to a historically dated milieu' ('An Interview with René Girard', *Double Business* 200). And Girard's mimetic hero is in effect strikingly influenced by Goldmann's 'problematic' hero, searching for authentic value in a world where it has been lost and degraded.

In *Deceit, Desire, and the Novel*, however, Girard seems more interested in subverting Goldmann's project than in imitating him. Whereas Goldmann sought to situate Lukácsian categories in a historical and material context, Girard rejects this historical perspective and thus effectively undoes Goldmann's historicization of Lukács. In its return to the early Lukács Girard's work is more reminiscent of the idealist typological categories of *The Theory of the Novel* than of *The Hidden God*. It is indeed significant that Girard defines Goldmann as the 'Lukácsian temptation': he himself succumbs to that temptation by absolutizing the historically relative gender-roles of his sexual triangles.

Already in *Deceit, Desire, and the Novel* it would seem that for Girard the desiring subject is always male, and that so is the rival, whereas the object is female. Throughout Girard's work this male-male-female constellation recurs as an absolute, ahistorical structure. The following passage is typical:

> The subject does not want to win the girl decisively; if he did, he would lose the mediator and he would lose all interest in the girl. The mediator must not win too decisively either; if he did, the subject would go on desiring intensely but the risk of being permanently

excluded would be too great. No resolution of the deadlock is really satisfactory. The only tolerable situation is for the rivalry to go on. The triangle must endure ('Nietzsche, Wagner and Dostoevski', *Double Business* 66).

Since full possession of the object implies the absence of all rivalry, the subject can never be satisfied. The subject's desire is sustained by the rival and disappears with 'him'. Because the triangle must endure Don Juan becomes the desired rival, the rival par excellence:

If the subject desires a particular woman rather than another one, this is because of the flattering attentions of which she is the object. And this attention is all the more flattering, it gives the sexual object all the more value in the eyes of the subject, if it is directed to her by a greater expert in the matter, a person who appears as invincible in the erotic field, for instance what one would call a 'ladies' man'. . . . This attention is necessarily 'ambivalent', since it comprises both the exasperation provoked by the obstacle and the admiration and even veneration provoked by the Don Juan's prowess (*Things Hidden* 339–40; TA).

In *Deceit, Desire, and the Novel* Girard claims that only the truly great novelists (Cervantes, Stendhal, Flaubert, Proust, Dostoevsky) have discovered and understood the true nature of desire, that is to say that all desire is mimetic and mediated. This claim makes it almost impossible to criticize Girard's thesis, since novels that do not display mimetic desire can easily be judged 'not great' and thus discounted as a falsification of the theory. It is evident that for Girard, women have not produced many great texts. The only novel written by a woman that he mentions is Mme de Lafayette's *La princesse de Clèves*, which is treated in a very perfunctory manner.

The best way of countering Girard's readings in *Deceit, Desire, and the Novel*, then, is to meet him on his own terrain, by commenting on a text that he himself alludes to in a positive way. In his chapter on how great novels end, Girard claims that the conclusion of Tolstoy's *Anna Karenina* parallels that of *The Red and the Black*, *The Brothers Karamazov*, *Crime and Punishment*, and *Time Regained*. According to Girard, all 'great' novels end in the same way: the vision of the subject/hero ('subject' is here used in the traditional sense of protagonist) becomes identical with the vision of the novelist. Confronted with death, both discover the true meaning of life, the falsity and hypocrisy of mimetic desire, and recognize the value and nature of a direct, transcendental, and vertical desire for God.

The only way one can possibly maintain this reading of the conclusion of *Anna Karenina* is by assuming that Levin is its main subject (protagonist). Levin does indeed find transcendental desire (God) in the last few chapters, but even so the parallel with the other novels is halting. Levin is depicted precisely as untainted by mimetic desire. He is no Julien Sorel or Marcel. Levin's love for Kitty is presented by the text as entirely unmediated by any rival; Levin loves her before Vronsky starts courting her, and continues to love her afterwards in much the same way. There is no trace of an intensification of his desire for Kitty after he learns about the existence of a rival/obstacle. Levin is not at all caught up in fierce mimetic rivalry with Vronsky; on the contrary, they hardly meet throughout the novel, and never think of each other in particularly intense fashion. The passionate, violent, and ambivalent circulation of desire that Girard describes between the subject and the rival is absent between Vronsky and Levin.

The glaring insufficiency of Girard's reading of *Anna Karenina* lies in the fact that Girard implicitly assumes that Levin, and not Anna, is the principal subject in the novel. It never occurs to Girard that Don Quixote should not be the subject of *Don Quixote*, or Emma of *Madame Bovary*. But Anna's desire for Vronsky does not at all correspond to Julien Sorel's desire for Mathilde. There is nothing calculating about Anna's desire; all she can gain from it is loss of social recognition. Indeed, this would seem to be a general characteristic of women's desire in these 'great' novels: it invariably leads them to social ruin, whereas the mediated desire Girard describes in men is mediated precisely because male erotic desires are calculated to lead to social gain. Anna's death, of course, in no way constitutes the clear, tranquil recognition of the necessity for reconciliation with God that Girard insists on finding everywhere else in 'great' literature.

Girard avoids dealing with women as subjects in literature,

except for Emma Bovary. But Emma's desire is a cause of 'external' mediation (the rival is never in direct contact with the subject), parallel to Don Quixote's rivalry with Amadis and the books of chivalry. As such, it does not fall in the same category as the other novels mentioned, which all depict 'internal' mediation, that is, when the subject and the rival confront each other within the novel.

The absence of female subjects is puzzling not least because Girard claims that his theory of desire is equally valid for women and men: 'One of the advantages of this genesis [of desire] by rivalry is that it occurs in an absolutely symmetrical way in both sexes. In other words, any form of sexual rivalry is homosexual in structure, with women as well as with men . . .' (*Things Hidden* 337). Reviewing Cesar Bandera's *Mímesis conflictiva* Ciriaco Morón-Arroyo points out, albeit in a peculiarly reluctant and uncertain manner, that Girard's theory is unable to account for women as agents:

> Why should the stories of Cardenio and the curious impertinent be approached from the couples Cardenio-Fernando, and Anselmo-Lotario only? This approach casts women merely as objects of the conflicting desires; from this angle the theory is illuminating. But is it not legitimate to look at the story from the side of the women, as subjects who are the tragic victims? Whom do the women imitate and desire? . . . In this case, it seems to me, the scheme of mimetic desire fails. But my view of these stories from the side of the women may be prompted by a hypercritical, conflictive desire to expose the apparent weaknesses of the theory (83).

The curious volte-face of Moron-Arroyo's last sentence may signify an understandable reluctance to criticize a theory on what might seem to be purely political—feminist—grounds. In this case the reluctance is not, however, justified: Girard himself quite explicitly stresses the fact that mimetic desire must essentially be taken to mean 'masculine' desire. In *Violence and the Sacred* he wonders why it is that women seem to have such a predominant role in the cult of Dionysus. His answer is that this must be an example of what he calls 'a secondary mythological displacement':

> an effort to exonerate from the accusation of violence, not mankind as a whole, but adult males [*non pas aux hommes en general*

. . . mais aux adultes du sexe masculin], who have the greatest need to forget their role in the crisis because, in fact, they must have been largely responsible for it. They alone risk plunging the community into the chaos of reciprocal violence (*Violence* 139).

One should note the distinction Girard is forced to draw here between *les hommes en général* and *les adultes du sexe masculin*. As soon as his text has to accommodate the presence of women, its language cracks open to reveal what it strives to conceal: the subsumption of women under the category of 'man'. Elaborating on this point, Girard continues in the same vein:

> The role played by women in the religious and cultural structure of a society—or rather, the minor importance of that role [*ou plutôt ... leur absence de rôle*]—is graphically illustrated by the social framework [*plan*] prevailing in certain South American villages—in those of Bororo, for example (*Violence* 140).[3]

Girard then attacks certain anthropologists who have taken the physical layout of the Bororo village to express the superiority of women:

> In fact, far from attesting to women's importance [*la puissance supérieure des femmes*], [the immobility of the women] suggests that women are only passive spectators at a masculine tragicomedy. . . . The physical structure [*plan*] of the Bororo village seems to reflect the centrifugal inclinations of its weakest inhabitants, the women, by making the center an exclusively masculine preserve. This inclination is universal (*Violence* 140).

Unrestrained mimetic desire leads to violence and disruption—*la crise sacrificielle.*

> The *sacrificial crisis*, that is, the disappearance of the sacrificial rites, coincides with the disappearance of the difference between impure violence and purifying violence. When this difference has been effaced, purification is no longer possible and impure, contagious, reciprocal violence spreads throughout the community (*Violence* 49).

Logically enough, Girard stresses that among the effects of the sacrificial crisis is the feminization of men and the masculinization of women, or in other words, a certain levelling of sexual difference.

---

[3] Somehow the English version seems more polite to women than the French original.

For Girard such minimization of differences indicates the collapse of social norms; the incipient disappearance of sexual difference is just one of many signs of crisis in a society. But when one discovers that he also claims that his own theory of desire allows us to jettison the 'far too absolute concept of sexual difference' (*Things Hidden* 337), the reader is left wondering how it is possible to distinguish so easily between the Scylla of the disappearance of sexual difference and the Charybdis of the too absolute conception of it.

OEDIPUS, FREUD, AND GIRARD

Girard is irresistibly fascinated by the Oedipus complex. With the exception of the Holy Trinity Freud's triangle is so evidently the main competitor to Girard's, that Girard simply cannot leave it alone; the fascinating and ambivalent circulation of desire between René and Sigmund never quite comes to an end. Girard constantly claims superiority over Freud. In *Things Hidden* this is voiced not only by Girard himself, but also by his two interlocutors, Jean Marie Oughourlian and Guy Lefort, conveniently set up to articulate views which might have proved less palatable coming from the author himself. Indeed, Lefort's contributions to the book seem largely to consist in voicing the most unembarrassed flattery of Girard himself:

> once you realize the superior effectiveness of the mimetic principle—that it is a simpler, more intelligible and more effective way of generating everything that Freud seeks to relate to his Oedipus without really succeeding—you cannot fail to wonder about the reason for its belated appearance and for the incredible vogue that the Oedipus complex has enjoyed and continues to enjoy (*Things Hidden* 354; TA).

Girard himself underscores Lefort's statement:

> The Oedipal scheme is absolutely incapable of fulfilling the function that its inventor has assigned to it: to generate all the possible triangular configurations that structure the erotic relationships of the mentally ill or, indeed, the plots of literary works, be they comic or tragic, plays or novels (*Things Hidden* 355–6; TA).

It is clear by this point that what Freud cannot do is exactly what Girard can do for him. Girard particularly enjoys 'refuting' the

Oedipus complex through Freud's account of it in his 1928 essay 'Dostoevsky and Parricide':

> In his article Freud summarizes the Oedipal doctrine. The small child sees his father as a rival and desires to kill him, but he manages to repress this desire. On the one hand he fears 'castration' and on the other he maintains a certain 'affection' for the father who was initially the model. This 'affection', it seems to me, constitutes a particularly weak link in Freudian reasoning ('The Underground Critic,' *Double Business* 50).

Girard's chief argument against the Oedipus complex is that he simply cannot believe that it accounts for any affection towards the father. 'The more I adopt Freud's reasoning, the closer I move to the heart of his subject, the more ardently I say *yes* to patricide and incest, the more I want to say *no* to this affection, to see it as a vestige of an outdated mode of thought' (*Double Business* 51). In *Things Hidden* Girard further attacks the notion of the little boy's desire for the father, insisting that this really is the most absurd of Freud's theories: 'a passive homosexual desire for the father, a wish to be desired by the father as a homosexual object! . . . The unconscious has a very broad back in psychoanalysis, but this homosexual desire of the small infant for his father is quite a heavy weight, even for the broadest of backs' (*Things Hidden* 362–3).

THE MISSING MOTHER

'The main difference between the mediation principle and psychoanalysis', Girard writes, 'is that, for Freud, the desire for the mother is intrinsic' ('Nietzsche, Wagner and Dostoevski', *Double Business*, 67). This belief—that Freud just assumes that the child will desire the mother—is a cornerstone in Girard's analysis of Freud. Insisting that *all* desire is mimetic and mediated, Girard's final 'refutation' of the Oedipus complex labours hard to deny that there can be a fundamental desire for the mother:[4]

---

[4] Greenberg makes the same point when she writes that 'The very elements which make the Oedipus myth so useful in the discussion of male sexuality tend to deny the importance of the woman, since she acquires meaning only as the symbol of the father's power' (303).

Freud does not understand that the mediator's desire is the essential factor in the desirability of the woman. The subject needs the desire of his rival to sustain and to legitimize his own desire. In Oedipal terms, this would mean that the son wants the father's desire to sustain and legitimate his desire for the mother. If there is one thing the Oedipus complex will not allow, it is certainly that. It would mean that the mother is not desired 'for herself', that she has no independent value of her own, that she is desired primarily as an object for the father. In addition, it would mean that the father is not the incarnation of the law against incest. The two pillars of the Oedipus edifice crash to the ground ('Nietzsche, Wagner and Dostoevski', *Double Business* 67).

Girard here actually seems to be *proud* of having shown that the mother (the woman) cannot possibly be desired for 'herself'. Her whole value resides in her status as an object for the father. This, of course, is the logical implication of Girard's triangular theory.[5] Both in *Things Hidden* (see 352–3) and in his chapter on Freud and the Oedipus complex in *Violence and the Sacred*, Girard rejects the suggestion that the child should desire the mother. But it is precisely in this *escamotage* of the mother that the flaw in his own theory can be detected. For he has apparently not discovered that the Oedipus is the situation, for Freud, in which sexual differentiation *begins*. The Oedipus complex enables Freud to *account* for sexual difference. Since Girard cannot account for it at all, he has consequently to deny its existence. To be concerned with sexual difference, he believes, is reactionary. The luckless Guy Lefort is again manipulated as a mouthpiece for this rather striking view: 'We perhaps ought to explain that by criticizing Freud's notion of "bisexuality" we are not just carrying out a rearguard action in favour of sexual difference' (*Things Hidden* 367).

If Girard manages to lose the mother somewhere in his discussions of the Oedipal triangle, it is largely because he refrains from all mention of the pre-Oedipal stage, that is to say the stage preceding sexual difference. If we are to believe Girard, the child

---

[5] The same logic operates in his account of narcissism, which Sarah Kofman has brilliantly interrogated in her article 'The Narcissistic Woman: Freud and Girard', which first appeared in English in *Diacritics* (Fall 1980). The whole of Kofman's *The Enigma of Woman* was published in English in 1985. The section on Freud and Girard is here entitled 'Narcissistic Woman'.

is born directly into the Oedipal conflict. He never alludes to the first years of the child's wholly mother-dependent development (still the dominant—if socially determined—practice), the period when all its desires take her as their object, and when the very existence of the father will go unrecognized.

Mimetic desire, however, is automatic and indiscriminate:

> [The automatic mechanism of mimetic desire] is already at work before the beginning, by virtue of the fact that the subject is parasitic on an already formed desire, and that he constitutes the third corner of the triangle and not the first, as the implicit solipsism of the archetypal conception quite wrongly imagines (*Des choses cachées* 380).[6]

If we are to believe Girard here, it would follow that any newborn child would automatically imitate the desire of the only person to whom it is closely related, namely the mother. Yet Girard himself does not seem to be aware of these implications. He totally ignores the pre-Oedipal stage, and for good reasons. For if we apply his own mimetic theory to the pre-Oedipal stage, the weaknesses of the theory are clearly exposed. If we suppose, on a Girardian scheme, that the infant assumes its place as a rival to the mother's already existing desire for the father, it follows that the baby girl will imitate her desire—and *so will the baby boy*. If Girard's mimetic theory is applied to the pre-Oedipal stage, then, one finds oneself obliged to posit the woman's desire as original: the mother's desire becomes paradigmatic of all desire. This stands in stark contradiction to Girard's own positing of men's desire as normative, and—I have to say—it is also totally improbable. Given that, still according to Girard, the first mimetic triangle in one's existence has the power to generate later ones, the

---

[6] This passage has been substantially altered in the English edition, which René Girard himself revised before it was published in 1987. The point I want to make in this section of my paper was based on the original French text. For comparison I give the revised English text here: 'The triangle of rivalry is always around precisely because the rivalry is never Oedipal in the Freudian sense. If the subject truly inherited his desire from his own past, he could not so readily adopt the desire of another model and so make up the third tip of the triangle, rather than the first one, as the archetypal conception in its implicit solipsism would have us believe' (*Things Hidden* 358).

application of the mimetic principle to pre-Oedipality forces us to conclude that all males would be homosexual, as a consequence of their initial imitation of the mother's desire for the father.

Since Girard's 'simple and intelligible' mimetic principle does not theorize object changes, the only way out of this logical aporia is to declare, as Girard in fact does, that heterosexuality is an inborn instinct in all human beings:

> any form of sexual rivalry is homosexual in structure, with women as well as with men—at least for as long as the object remains hetero-sexual, that is to say, remains the object prescribed by the instinctual structures inherited from animal life (*Things Hidden* 337).

Here indeed is the crucial precondition for the smooth functioning of the mimetic principle. In order to preserve his structures intact, Girard is forced to assume that humankind is instinctually heterosexual. On the one hand he claims that 'Sexuality is indeed controlled by rivalry' (*Things Hidden* 343); on the other hand he is obliged to argue that heterosexuality already informs the *first* object-choice of the baby. Since half the human race—women—are excluded as objects from the start, Girard in fact implies that the subject chooses both its rival and its object: but in that case, following Girard's own logic, the desire for the object is no longer mimetic at all.

I have shown that if Girard applied his own theories to the pre-Oedipal child—here understood as a child who does not yet have a sexual identity—he would be constrained not only to posit the desire of the woman (the mother) as original, but also to declare heterosexuality innate. Girard's silence on the subject of the pre-Oedipal child is only made credible by the assumption that every child is born with a clear notion of sexual identity (of being a boy or a girl) and with an equally clear heterosexual structure of desire. I take this to be a fatal flaw in this proud, patriarchal, and oppressively monolithic theory.

INSTINCTUAL HETEROSEXUALITY AND HOMOSEXUALITY: GIRARD AND FREUD

Girard's theory is oddly paradoxical: explicitly stating that all desire is heterosexual, it does not hesitate to posit rivalry as the essential condition for desire. All rivalry then logically becomes homosexual, and Girard gives far more attention to the love/hate liaison between rivals than to the subject/object relationship. Firmly denying the existence of 'a direct homosexual drive', he nevertheless insists that a same sex rival is indispensable:

> In all these triangles, the goal is less to wrench the loved one from the mediator than to receive her from him and to share her with him. The presence of the rival is indispensable. . . . Why? Is there a direct homosexual drive, as Freud believes? There is nothing of the sort. . . . The rival is needed because his desire alone can confer on the girl whatever value she has in the eyes of the subject. If the rival disappears, this value will also disappear ('Nietzsche, Wagner and Dostoevski', *Double Business* 67).

When Girard insists that it is necessary for a man to receive the beloved woman from another man, this is strangely reminiscent of Luce Irigaray's reading of sexual relations under patriarchy. For Irigaray, heterosexual relations serve only to mask the real libidinal impulse: homosexual relations between men. For her, all sexual relations are *hom(m)osexuelles*: women are merchandise exchanged between men as tokens of their—the men's—love for each other. From this point of view Girard may perhaps be said to give an accurate description of male desire under patriarchy, but his repression of the mother renders him incapable even of seeing the desire of women.

Girard proudly claims that mimetic desire has managed to eliminate 'the false difference between homosexual and hetero-sexual eroticism' (*Things Hidden* 337). Strongly stressing the utilitary nature of mimetic desire, he once more implicitly postu-lates its heterosexual character:

> Only one genesis is needed, since the exasperation of the vicious circle that constitutes the relationship with the mediator accounts perfectly for the varying degrees of fascination vis-à-vis the rival and for the gradual shift away from the heterosexual object to the rival and model of the same sex. Before he is an object, the homo-sexual partner is a rival ('Nietzsche, Wagner and Dostoevski', *Double Business* 67–8).

This is clearly an untenable position, not least when it is compared with Freud's conception of desire as anaclitic. Girard assumes that heterosexuality is 'prescribed by our instinctual apparatus inherited from animal life', that is to say that the object-choice is instinctually given. The Freudian model of the sexual drive as anaclitic to (leaning on or propped against) the instinctual biological need, as for instance hunger, leads Jean Laplanche to conclude that 'sexuality does not have, from the beginning, a real object':

> On the one hand there is from the beginning an object, but . . . on the other hand sexuality does not have, from the beginning, a real object. It should be understood that the real object, milk, was the object of the function, which is virtually preordained to the world of satisfaction. Such is the real object which has been lost, but the object linked to the auto-erotic turn, the breast—become a fantasmatic breast—is, for its part, the object of the sexual drive. Thus the sexual object is not identical to the object of the function, but displaced in relation to it; they are in a relation of essential contiguity which leads us to slide almost indifferently from one to other, from milk to the breast as its symbol (19–20).

Laplanche also demonstrates how the loss of this first object contributes to making later objects relatively contingent. In some ways, Girard's own theory of desire would seem to support the notion of the cathected object as contingent. When he speaks of the 'mechanical character of primary imitation' (*Things Hidden* 295) or about the 'mimetic disease', one is left with the indelible impression that the object of desire has considerably less significance than the fact that somebody else (man or woman) desires it too. This, however, is immediately contradicted by Girard's own insistence elsewhere on the heterosexuality of the object-choice.

That Girard should reject Freud's concept of pre-Oedipal desire is in one sense remarkable, since Freud's theory actually implies that the child's desire at this very early stage is essentially mediated or mimetic. Jean Laplanche, for instance, convincingly shows that Freudian desire in no way is 'intrinsic' in the way Girard thinks it is. Laplanche points out that the erotogenic zones are exactly those zones of the body where the exchange from biological instinct to sexual drive takes place, the mouth being the most evident example:

> This zone of exchange is also a zone for care, namely the particular and attentive care provided by the mother. These zones, then,

attract the first erotogenic manoeuvers from the adult. An even more significant factor, if we introduce the subjectivity of the first 'partner': these zones focalize *parental fantasies* and above all *maternal fantasies*, so that we may say, in what is barely a metaphor, that they are points through which is *introduced into the child that alien internal entity* which is, properly speaking, the *sexual excitation* (Laplanche 24).

The baby is seen here as opening up for and internalizing the mother's fantasies in a way with which Girard might well agree. The baby's desire for the mother, in Freud's account, can now hardly be said to be 'intrinsic'; Girard has merely misread the Freudian text.

THE ANXIETY OF INFLUENCE

Why is it, one must ask, that Girard so insistently misreads and rejects Freudian theory throughout his writings? One answer, it would seem, is that Girard, in his valiant effort to avoid all confrontation with the Mother, is impelled all the more starkly to confront the alternative parental figure. Freud is Girard's haunting rival, daunting double, and castrating father. As Hayden White shrewdly has written: 'It is no accident that mirroring, doubling, repetition and displacement are crucial concepts in Girard's critical economy. His enemies are mirror images of himself' (7). Indeed, Girard's relation to Freud emerges as a classic case of Harold Bloom's *tessera*, or 'completion and antithesis' (see Bloom 49–73). Working within a Freudian sphere of discourse, attending to the same questions as Freud himself, Girard makes the excessively ambitious claim that only his own reading of (for example) the Oedipus triangle is the true and correct one. The precursor's error, as so often, is simply to have been the precursor:

> Except for writers, Freud was the first one to observe this type of configuration [the mimetic triangle] and to attempt a scientific interpretation of it. Thus he could not fail to do so better than anyone before; but it is easy to show that, in spite of his very great merits, he did not come up with the right interpretation, nor did he even observe the triangular operation properly ('Nietzsche, Wagner and Dostoevski', *Double Business* 66).

It is no accident that the sexism of Girard's works should be coupled with a generally reactionary outlook. He believes that all struggle for liberation is doomed to failure: 'The more people think that they are realizing the Utopias dreamed up by their desire—in other words, the more they embrace ideologies of liberation—the more they will in fact be working to reinforce the competitive world that is stifling them' (*Things Hidden* 286). The true object of desire is God; if the religious dimension disappears from society, society will sink back into unlimited mimetic violence. Behind the assumptions which structure Girard's sexual triangulation can be discerned the shape of another mystifying Trinity.

6

Representation of Patriarchy: Sexuality and Epistemology in Freud's Dora *(1981)*

Over the past few years Freud's account of his treatment of the 18-year-old Dora has provoked many feminists to take up their pen, in anger or fascination. Dora had for some time suffered from various hysterical symptoms (nervous cough, loss of voice, migraine, depression, and what Freud calls 'hysterical unsociability' and *taedium vitae*), but it was not until the autumn of 1900, when her parents found a suicide note from her, that Dora's father sent her to Freud for treatment. Freud's case history reveals much about the situation of a young woman from the Viennese bourgeoisie at the turn of the century. Dora's psychological problems can easily be linked to her social background. She has very little, if any, scope for independent activity, is strictly guarded by her family, and feels under considerable pressure from her father. She believes (and Freud agrees that she is right) that she is being used as a pawn in a game between her father and Herr K., the husband of her father's mistress. The father wants to exchange Dora for Frau K. ('if I get your wife, you get my daughter'), so as to be able to carry on his affair with Frau K. undisturbed. Dora claims that her father only sent her to psychiatric treatment because he hoped that she would be 'cured' into giving up her opposition to her father's affair with Frau K., accept her

The main sources of this essay were oral: it would never have been written were it not for the invaluable insights I gained both from Neil Hertz's seminars on 'Freud and Literature' at Cornell University in the Fall semester of 1980, and from the extremely inspiring discussions in the 'Women's Group on Psychoanalysis' at Cornell that same autumn.

role as a victim of the male power game, and take Herr K. as her lover.

Freud, then, becomes the person who is to help Dora handle this difficult situation. But Freud himself is the first to admit that his treatment of Dora was a failure. Freud has his own explanations of this failure, but these are not wholly convincing. Feminists have been quick to point out that the reasons for Freud's failure are clearly sexist: Freud is authoritarian, a willing participant in the male power game conducted between Dora's father and Herr K., and at no time turns to consider Dora's own experience of the events. That Freud's analysis fails because of its inherent sexism is the common feminist conclusion.

But *Dora* is a complex text, and feminists have stressed quite different points in their reading of it. Hélène Cixous and Catherine Clément discuss the political potential of hysteria in their book *The Newly Born Woman* and agree that Dora's hysteria developed as a form of protest, a silent revolt against male power. They differ, however, as I shall show later, in their evaluation of the importance of hysteria as a political weapon. Cixous and Clément do not discuss in any detail the interaction between Freud and Dora, but Hélène Cixous returned to this theme in 1976, when she published her play *Portrait de Dora*.[1] Here Dora's story is represented in dreamlike sequences from Dora's own viewpoint. Cixous plays skilfully with Freud's text: she quotes, distorts, and displaces the 'father-text' with great formal mastery. This technique enables her to create new interpretations of Dora's symptoms in a playful exposure of Freud's limitations.

Jacqueline Rose's article 'Dora: Fragment of an Analysis' differs considerably from these two French texts. Rose sees *Dora* as a text which focuses with particular acuteness on the problem of the representation of femininity and discusses several modern French psychoanalytic theories of femininity (particularly Michèle Montrelay and Luce Irigaray in relation to Lacan). She concludes by rejecting that simplistic reading of *Dora* which would see Dora the woman opposed to and oppressed by Freud the man.

---

[1] This play was translated by Sarah Burd in *Diacritics* in 1983. Another translation, by Anita Burrows, was published in *Benmussa Directs* in 1979.

According to Rose, *Dora* reveals how Freud's concept of the feminine was incomplete and contradictory, thus delineating a major problem in psychoanalytic theory: its inability to account for the feminine. A valuable contribution to a feminist reading of psychoanalysis, Rose's essay is nonetheless silent on its political consequences.

The same is true of Suzanne Gearhart's 'The Scene of Psychoanalysis: The Unanswered Questions of Dora'. Gearhart reads *Dora* principally through Lacan's and Irigaray's discussion of Dora's case, arguing that the central problem of the text is 'the symbolic status of the father'. According to Gearhart, *Dora* must be seen as Freud's 'interrogation of the principle of paternity'; it is in the correct understanding of the text's handling of this problem that we will find the key to the ultimate explanation of Dora's illness and also the basis of the identity of Freud and his work (114). Gearhart's highly sophisticated reading of *Dora* shows that the status of the father in *Dora* is problematical, and the father himself made marginal, because Freud wants to avoid the central insight that the (Lacanian) Imaginary and Symbolic realms are fundamentally complicit. Theoretically valuable though this essay is, it fails to indicate the consequences of its reading of *Dora* for a feminist approach to psychoanalysis.

Maria Ramas's long study of *Dora*, 'Freud's Dora, Dora's Hysteria: The Negation of a Woman's Rebellion', is the most accessible article on *Dora* to date. Whereas Rose and Gearhart use a sophisticated theoretical vocabulary, Ramas writes in a lucid, low-key style. But her inquiry advances little beyond a scrupulous, somewhat tedious résumé of Freud's text. Ramas argues that 'Ida's' problem (Ramas uses Dora's real name, Ida Bauer, throughout her text) was her unconscious belief that 'femininity, bondage and debasement were synonymous' (502).[2] Since Freud unconsciously shared this belief, she claims, he could only reinforce Dora's problem rather than free her from them. This, at least, is a traditional feminist reading: it implies that Dora could escape her hysteria only through feminist conciousness-raising—

---

[2] The reference is to the original text of Ramas's essay, published in *Feminist Studies*. An abridged version appears in Bernheimer and Kahane.

that if she could stop equating femininity with bondage she would be liberated. But it is also a fairly partial and superficial account, failing to encompass many controversial areas of Freud's text. Despite one brief reference to Jacqueline Rose's article, Ramas seems to find the status of the term 'femininity' in the text quite unproblematical; she unquestioningly accepts Freud's automatic reduction of oral sex to fellatio (a point I shall return to later), and does not notice many of Freud's more eccentric concerns in the case study. Qualifying her own essay as pure 'feminist polemics', Ramas suggests that further study of *Dora* would lead beyond feminism: 'If this were Freud's story, we would have to go beyond feminist polemics and search for the sources of the negative countertransference—the unanalyzed part of Freud—that brought the analysis to an abrupt end' (504).[3]

I believe that it is precisely through an exploration of the 'unanalyzed part of Freud' that we may uncover the relations between sexual politics and psychoanalytical theory in *Dora,* and therefore also in Freud's works in general. In my reading of *Dora* I want to show that neither Rose's and Gearhart's depoliticized theorizing nor Ramas's rather simplistic idea of 'feminist polemics' will really do. Feminists must neither reject theoretical discussion as 'beyond feminist polemics' nor forget the ideological context of theory.

FRAGMENT OR WHOLE?

The first version of *Dora* was written in 1901. Freud entitled it 'Dreams and Hysteria' and had the greatest ambitions for the text: this was his first great case history, and it was to continue and develop the work presented in *The Interpretation of Dreams,* published in the previous year. But Freud recalled *Dora* from his publisher and curiously enough delayed publication until 1905, the year of the *Three Essays on Sexuality.* Why would Freud hesitate for more than four years before deciding to publish *Dora?*

---

[3] Maria Ramas cut this passage from the version published in Bernheimer and Kahane. The quote appears in the full version published in *Feminist Studies* 500.

According to Jacqueline Rose, this hesitation may have been because *Dora* was written in the period between the theory of the unconscious, developed in *The Interpretation of Dreams,* and the theory of sexuality, first expressed in the *Three Essays. Dora* would then mark the transition between these two theories, and Freud's hesitation in publishing the text suggests the theoretical hesitation within it. Jacqueline Rose may well be right in this supposition: it is at any rate evident that among Freud's texts *Dora* marks an unusual degree of uncertainty, doubt, and ambiguity.

This uncertainty is already revealed in the title of the work: the true title is not *Dora,* but 'Fragment of an Analysis of a Case of Hysteria'. Freud lists three reasons for calling his text a fragment. First, the *analytic results* are fragmentary both because Dora interrupted the treatment before it was completed and because Freud did not write up the case history until after the treatment was over. The only exceptions to this are Dora's two dreams, which Freud took down immediately. The text we are reading, in other words, is constructed from fragmentary notes and Freud's fragmentary memory. Secondly, Freud insists on the fact that he has only given an account of the (incomplete) analytic *results* and not at all of the *process* of interpretation—that is to say Freud wilfully withholds the *technique of the analytic work.* To describe the analytic technique, Freud argues, would have led to 'nothing but hopeless confusion' (*SE* 7: 13). Finally, Freud stresses that no *one* case history can provide the answer to *all* the problems presented by hysteria: all case histories are in this sense incomplete answers to the problem they set out to solve.

It is of course perfectly normal to state, as Freud does here, the limitations of one's project in the preface to the finished work, but Freud does more than that. In his 'Prefatory Remarks' to *Dora,* Freud seems positively obsessed with the incomplete status of his text. He returns to the subject again and again, either to excuse the fact that he is presenting a fragment or to express his longings for a *complete* text after all. His 'Prefatory Remarks' oscillate constantly between the theme of fragmentation and the notion of totality.

These two themes, however, are not presented as straight opposites. Having expressed his regrets that the case history was incomplete, he writes: 'But its short-comings are connected with the

very circumstances which have made its publication possible. . . .
I should not have known how to deal with the material involved
in the history of a treatment which had lasted, perhaps, for a
whole year' (*SE* 7: 11). Freud here totally undermines any notion
of a fundamental opposition between fragment and whole: it
would have been impossible to write down a *complete* case history.
The fragment can be presented as a complete book; the complete
case history could not. Nevertheless, Freud insists on the fact that
the fragment *lacks* something:

> In the face of the incompleteness of my analytic results, I had no
> choice but to follow the example of those discoverers whose good
> fortune it is to bring to the light of day after their long burial the
> priceless though mutilated relics of antiquity. I have restored what
> is missing, taking the best models known to me from other analy-
> ses; but like a conscientious archaeologist, I have not omitted to
> mention in each case where the authentic parts end and my
> construction begins (*SE* 7: 12).

Once again, Freud candidly admits that his results are incomplete—only to claim in the same breath that he has 'restored what
is missing'. Freud's metaphors in this context are significant.
Dora's story is compared to the 'priceless though mutilated relics
of antiquity', and Freud himself figures as an archaeologist,
digging the relics out from the earth. His claim here is that when
he adds something to the 'mutilated relics', completeness is established *malgré tout*. But this new completeness is after all not quite
complete. On the same page as the above quotation, Freud writes
that the psychoanalytic technique (which he jealously retains for
himself) does not by its nature lend itself to the creation of
complete sequences: 'everything that has to do with the clearing-
up of a particular symptom emerges piecemeal, woven into various contexts, and distributed over widely separated periods of
time' (*SE* 7: 12). The 'completeness' achieved by Freud's supplementary conjectures is doubly incomplete: it consists of Dora's
story (the 'mutilated relics of antiquity'), to which Freud's own
assumptions have been added. But Dora's story is not only a fragment: it is a fragment composed of information that has emerged
'piecemeal, woven into various contexts, and distributed over
widely separated periods of time'. We must assume that it is Freud

himself who has imposed a fictional coherence on Dora's story, in order to render the narrative readable. But Dora's story is in turn only one part of the finished work entitled 'Fragment of an Analysis of a Case of Hysteria'. The other part is supplemented by Freud. In itself Dora's story is too fragmentary; it is readable only when Freud supplies the necessary supplement. But that supplement is based on Freud's experience from other cases of hysteria, cases that must have been constructed in the same way as Dora's: by information provided 'piecemeal, over widely separated periods of time'. The fragment depends on the supplement, which depends on other fragments depending on other supplements, and so on ad infinitum.

We are, in other words, surprisingly close to Jacques Derrida's theories of the production of meaning as *différance*. According to Derrida, meaning can never be seized as presence: it is always deferred, constantly displaced on to the next element in the series, in a chain of signification that has no end, no transcendental signified that might provide the final anchorpoint for the production of sense. This, need one say, is not Freud's own *conscious* theory: he clings to his dream of 'complete elucidation' (*SE* 7: 24), refusing to acknowledge that according to his own account of the status of the *Dora* text, completeness is an unattainable illusion. Even when he insists strongly on the fragmentary status of his text, he always implies that completeness is within reach. He can, for instance, write that 'if the work had been continued, we should no doubt have obtained the fullest possible enlightenment upon every particular of the case' (*SE* 7: 12). Freud's text oscillates endlessly between his desire for complete insight or knowledge, and an unconscious realization (or fear) of the fragmentary, deferring status of knowledge itself.

TRANSFERENCE AND COUNTERTRANSFERENCE

We have seen that in his 'Prefatory Remarks' Freud discloses that 'Dora's story' *is* largely 'Freud's story': he is the author, the one who has conjured a complete work from these analytic fragments. This in itself should alert the reader eager to discover Dora's own view of her case to the dangers of taking Freud's words too much for granted. His account of the analysis of Dora must instead be scanned with the utmost suspicion.

The better part of the 'Postscript' is devoted to a discussion of the reasons why the analysis of Dora was at least in part a failure. Freud's main explanation is that he failed to discover the importance of the *tranference* for the analysis; he did not discover in time that Dora was transferring the emotions she felt for Herr K. on to Freud himself. Psychoanalytic theory holds that transference is normal in the course of analysis, that it consists in the patient's transferring emotions for some other person on to the analyst, and that if the analyst, unaware of the transference, cannot counteract it, the analysis will in consequence go awry.

Freud adds this information in this 'Postscript'. But if we are to grasp what is being acted out between Freud and Dora, it is important to keep in mind from the outset this transference on Dora's part from Herr K. to Freud. Transference, however, is something the patient does to the analyst. Freud does not mention at all the opposite phenomenon, *countertransference*, which consists in the analyst's transferring his or her own unconscious emotions onto the patient. Jacques Lacan has discussed precisely this problem in *Dora* in an article entitled 'Intervention on Transference'. According to Lacan, Freud unconsciously identifies with Herr K. in his relationship to Dora, which makes him (Freud) far too interested in Dora's alleged love for Herr K. and effectively blind to any other explanation of her problems. Thus the countertransference contributes decisively to the failure of Dora's analysis.

The fact of transference and countertransference between Freud and Dora considerably complicates the task of the *Dora* reader. Freud's attempts to posit himself as the neutral, scientific observer who is merely noting down his observations and reflections can no longer be accepted. The archaeologist must be suspected of having mutilated the relics he finds. We must remember that Freud's version of the case is not only coloured by his own unconscious countertransference, but also by the fact that he signally fails to notice the transference in Dora, and therefore systematically misinterprets her transference symptoms throughout the text. This, oddly, is something the reader is not told until he/she gets to the 'Postscript'.

Freud's interpretation of Dora's case can be summarized as follows. Dora develops hysterical symptoms because she represses sexual desire. But her case has an added, Oedipal dimension: one must suppose that Dora originally desired her father, but since her father disappointed her by starting an affair with Frau K., Dora now pretends to hate him. Herr K. represents the father for Dora, particularly because he is also Frau K.'s husband. Dora's repression of her sexual desire for Herr K. is therefore at once a hysterical reaction (repression of sexual desire) *and* an Oedipal reaction (rejection of the father through rejection of Herr K.). Based on this interpretation, Freud's treatment of Dora consists in repeated attempts to get her to admit her repressed desire for Herr K., a 'confession' Dora resists as best she can.

We have already seen that, according to Lacan, the analysis failed because of Freud's unconscious identification with Herr K. Since Dora is at the same time identifying Freud with Herr K., the result is inevitably that she must experience Freud's insistence on the necessity of acknowledging her desire for Herr K. as a repetition of Herr K.'s attempt to elicit sexual favours from her. In the end she rejects Freud in the same way she rejected Herr K.—by giving him two weeks' notice. Herr K. had earlier had an affair with the governess of his children, and Dora felt greatly insulted at being courted like a servant by the same man. Her revenge is to treat both Freud and Herr K. as servants in return.

But Freud's incessant identification with Herr K., the rejected lover, leads to other interesting aspects of the text. One of the most important episodes in the study is Freud's interpretation of Herr K.'s attempt to kiss Dora, then 14, after having tricked her into being alone with him in his office. Freud writes that

> [Herr K.] suddenly clasped the girl to him and pressed a kiss upon her lips. This was surely just the situation to call up a distinct feeling of sexual excitement in a girl of fourteen who had never before been approached. But Dora had at that moment a violent feeling of disgust, tore herself free from the man, and hurried past him to the staircase and from there to the street door (*SE* 7: 28).

At this moment in the text Freud is completely in the grip of his countertransference: he must at all costs emphasize that Dora's reaction was abnormal, and writes that 'the behaviour of this child of fourteen was already entirely and completely hysterical' (*SE* 7: 28). Her reaction was hysterical because she was already repressing sexual desire: 'Instead of the genital sensation which would certainly have been felt by a healthy girl in such circumstances, Dora was overcome by . . . disgust' (*SE* 7: 29). It is, of course, resplendently clear to any scientific observer that any normal girl of 14 would be overwhelmed by desire when a middle-aged man 'suddenly clasps her to him' in a lonely spot.

Freud then links Dora's feeling of disgust to *oral* impulses, and goes on to interpret as a 'displacement' Dora's statement that she clearly felt the pressure from the upper part of Herr K.'s body against her own. What she really felt, according to Freud, and what aroused such strong oral disgust, was the pressure of Herr K.'s erect penis. This unmentionable organ was then repressed, and the feeling of pressure displaced from the lower to the upper part of the body. The oral disgust is then related to Dora's habit of thumbsucking as a child, and Freud connects the oral satisfaction resulting from this habit to Dora's nervous cough. He interprets the cough (irritation of oral cavity and throat) as a revealing symptom of Dora's sexual fantasies: she must be fantasizing a scene where sexual satisfaction is obtained by using the mouth (*per os*, as Freud puts it) (*SE* 7: 48), and this scene is one that takes place between Frau K. and Dora's father.

Having said as much, Freud spends the next few pages defending himself against accusations of using too foul a language with his patients. These passages could be read as betraying a certain degree of unconscious tension in Freud himself, but it is enough to point out here that he argues his way from exhortations to tolerance to the high social status of 'the perversion which is the most repellent to us, the sensual love of a man for a man' (*SE* 7: 50) in ancient Greece, before returning to Dora's oral fantasy and making it plain that what he had in mind was fellatio, or 'sucking at the male organ' (*SE* 7: 51). It would not be difficult to detect in Freud a defensive reaction-formation in this context, since on the next page he feels compelled to allude to 'this excessively repulsive and perverted phantasy of sucking at a penis' (*SE* 7: 52). It is little wonder that he feels the need to defend himself against the idea of fellatio, since it is more than probable that the fantasy exists, not in Dora's mind, but in his alone. Freud has informed us that Dora's father was impotent, and assumes this to be the basis of Dora's 'repulsive and perverted phantasy'. According to Freud, the father cannot manage penetration, so Frau K. must perform fellatio instead. But as Lacan has pointed out, this argument reveals an astonishing lack of logic on Freud's part. In the case of male impotence, the man is obviously much more likely, *faute de mieux*, to perform cunnilingus. As Lacan writes: 'everyone knows that cunnilingus is the artifice most commonly adopted by "men of means" whose powers begin to abandon them'.[4] It is in this logical flaw that Freud's countertransference is seen at its strongest. The illogicality reveals his own unconscious wish for gratification, a gratification Freud's unconscious alter ego, Herr K., might obtain if only Dora would admit her desire for him.

Freud's countertransference blinds him to the possibility that Dora's hysteria may be due to the repression of desire, not for Herr K., but for his wife, Frau K. A fatal lack of insight into the transferential process prevents Freud from discovering Dora's homosexuality early enough. Dora's condition as a victim of male dominance here becomes starkly visible. She is not only a pawn in the game between Herr K. and her father; her doctor joins the male team and untiringly tries to ascribe to her desires she does not have and to ignore the ones she does have.

PATRIARCHAL PREJUDICES

Freud's oppressive influence on Dora does not, however, stem only from the countertransference. There are also more general ideological tendencies to sexism at work in his text. Freud, for instance, systematically refuses to consider female sexuality as an

---

[4] Rose's translation, in Bernheimer and Kahane 98. Lacan writes: '[C]hacun sait que le *cunnilingus* est l'artifice le plus communément adopté par les "messieurs fortunés" que leurs forces commencent d'abandonner' (*Écrits* 221).

active, independent drive. Again and again he exhorts Dora to accept herself as an object for Herr K. Every time Dora reveals active sexual desires, Freud interprets them away, either by assuming that Dora is expressing masculine identification (when she fantasizes about female genitals, Freud instantly assumes that she wants to penetrate them) or by supposing that she desires to be penetrated by the male (Dora's desire for Frau K. is interpreted as her desire to be in Frau K.'s place in order to gain access to Herr K.). His position is self-contradictory: he is one of the first to acknowledge the existence of sexual desire in women, and at the same time he renders himself incapable of seeing it as more than the impulse to become passive recipients for male desire. Lacan assumes precisely the same attitude when he states that the problem for Dora (and all women) is 'fundamentally that of accepting herself as an object of desire for the man' and that this is the reason for Dora's adoration of Frau K.[5]

Feminists cannot help feeling relieved when Dora finally dismisses Freud like another servant. It is tempting to read Dora's hysterical symptoms, as do Cixous and Clément, as a silent revolt against male power over women's bodies and women's language. But at the same time it is disconcerting to see how inefficient Dora's revolt turned out to be. Felix Deutsch describes Dora's tragic destiny in an article written in 1957. She continued to develop various hysterical symptoms, made life unbearable for her family, and grew to resemble her mother (whom Freud dismissed as a typical case of 'housewife psychosis'). According to Deutsch, Dora tortured her husband throughout their marriage; he concluded that 'her marriage had served only to cover up her distaste of men' (*SE* 7: 166). Dora suffers continuously from psychosomatic constipation, and dies from cancer of the colon. Deutsch concludes that 'Her death . . . seemed a blessing to those who were close to her. She had been, as my informant phrased it, one of the most repulsive hysterics he had ever met' (*SE* 7: 167).

It may be gratifying to see the young, proud Dora as a radiant example of feminine revolt (as does Cixous); but we should not

---

[5] Rose's translation, in Bernheimer and Kahane 99. Lacan writes: 's'accepter comme objet du désir de l'homme' (*Écrits* 222).

forget the image of the old, nagging, whining, and complaining Dora she later becomes, achieving nothing. Hysteria is not, *pace* Hélène Cixous, the incarnation of the revolt of women forced to silence, but rather a declaration of defeat, the realization that there is no other way out. Hysteria is, as Catherine Clément perceives, a cry for help when defeat becomes real, when the woman sees that she is efficiently gagged and chained to her feminine role.

Now if the hysterical woman is gagged and chained, Freud posits himself as her liberator. And if the emancipatory project of psychoanalysis fails in the case of Dora, it is because Freud the liberator happens also to be, objectively, on the side of oppression. He is a male in patriarchal society, and moreover not just any male, but an educated bourgeois male, incarnating *malgré lui* patriarchal values. His own emancipatory project profoundly conflicts with his political and social role as an oppressor of women.

The most telling instance of this deeply unconscious patriarchal ideology in *Dora* is to be found in Freud's obsession with the sources of his patient's sexual information. After stressing the impossibility of tracing the sources of Dora's sexual information (*SE* 7: 31), Freud nevertheless continually returns to the subject, suggesting alternately that the source may have been books belonging to a former governess (*SE* 7: 36), Mantegazza's *Physiology of Love* (*SE* 7: 62), or an encyclopedia (*SE* 7: 100). He finally realizes that there must have been an *oral* source of information, in addition to the avid reading of forbidden books, then sees, extremely belatedly, that the oral source must have been none other than the beloved Frau K.

The one hypothesis that Freud does not entertain is that the source of oral information may have been Dora's mother—the mother who is traditionally charged with the sexual education of the daughters. This omission is wholly symptomatic of Freud's treatment of Dora's mother. Although he indicates Dora's identification with her mother (*SE* 7: 75), he nevertheless strongly insists that Dora had withdrawn completely from her mother's influence (*SE* 7: 23). Dora's apparent hatred of her mother is mobilized as evidence for this view.

But Freud ought to know better than to accept a daughter's hatred of her mother as an inevitable consequence of the mother's objective unlikeableness ('housewife's psychosis'). Even his own Oedipal explanation of Dora's rejection of Herr K. should contribute to a clearer understanding of the mother's importance for Dora. Oedipally speaking, Dora would be seen as the mother's rival in that competition for the father's love, but this rivalry also implies the necessity of identifying with the mother: the daughter must become like the mother in order to be loved by the father. Freud notes that Dora is behaving like a jealous wife, and that this behaviour shows that 'she was clearly putting herself in her mother's place' (*SE* 7: 56), but he draws no further conclusions from these observations. He also points out that Dora identifies with Frau K., her father's mistress, but is still quite content to situate her mainly in relation to her father and Herr K. He fails to see that Dora is caught in an ambivalent relationship to her mother and an idealizing and identifying relationship to Frau K., the other mother figure in this text. Freud's patriarchal prejudices force him to ignore relationships between women and instead centre all his attention on relationships with men. This grievous underestimation of the importance of other women for Dora's psychic development contributes decisively to the failure of the analysis and the cure—not least in that it makes Freud unaware of the *pre-Oedipal* causes for Dora's hysteria. Maria Ramas writes: 'By Freud's own admission, the deepest level of meaning of hysterical symptoms is not a thwarted desire for the father, but a breakthrough of the prohibited desire for the mother' (498).

SEXUALITY AND EPISTEMOLOGY

Freud's peculiar interest in the sources of Dora's sexual information does not, however, merely reveal that for as long as possible he avoids considering oral relations between women as such a source; it also indicates that Freud overestimates the importance of this question. There is nothing in Dora's story to indicate that a successful analysis depends on the elucidation of this peripheral problem. Why then would Freud be so obsessed by these sources of knowledge?

First, because he himself desires total knowledge: his aim is nothing less than the *complete elucidation* of Dora, despite his insistence on the fragmentary nature of his material. The absence of information on this one subject is thus tormenting, since it so obviously ruins the dream of completeness. But such a desire for total, absolute knowledge exposes a fundamental assumption in Freud's epistemology. Knowledge for Freud is a finished, closed whole. Possession of knowledge means possession of power. Freud, the doctor, is curiously proud of his hermeneutical capacities. After having interpreted Dora's fingering of her little purse as an admission of infantile masturbation, he writes with evident satisfaction:

> When I set myself the task of bringing to light what human beings keep hidden within them, not by the compelling power of hypnosis, but by observing what they say and what they show, I thought the task was a harder one than it really is. He that has eyes to see and ears to hear may convince himself that no mortal can keep a secret. If his lips are silent, he chatters with his finger tips; betrayal oozes out of him at every pore. And thus the task of making conscious the most hidden recesses of the mind is one which it is quite possible to accomplish (*SE* 7: 77–8).

Freud in other words possesses powers more compelling than those of hypnosis. He is the one who discloses and unlocks secrets; he is Oedipus solving the Sphinx's riddle. But like Oedipus he is ravaged by a terrible anxiety: the fear of castration. If Freud cannot solve Dora's riddle, the unconscious punishment for this failure will be castration. In this struggle for the possession of knowledge, a knowledge which is power, Dora reveals herself both as Freud's alter ego and as his rival. She possesses the secret Freud is trying to discover. At this point we must suspect Freud of countertransference to Dora: he identifies with the hysterical Dora in the search for information about sexual matters. Freud has his own secret, as Dora has hers: the analytic technique, which, as we have seen, cannot be exposed without causing 'total confusion'. Freud jealously keeps his secret, as Dora keeps hers: her homosexual desire for Frau K.

But since Dora is a woman, and a rather formidable one at that, a young lady who hitherto has had only scorn for the incompetent (and, surely, impotent) doctors who have treated her so far, she becomes a threatening rival for Freud. If he does not win the fight for knowledge, he will also be revealed as incompetent/impotent, his compelling powers will be reduced to nothing, he will be castrated. If Dora wins the knowledge game, her model for knowledge will emerge victorious, and Freud's own model will be destroyed. Freud here finds himself between Scylla and Charybdis: if he identifies with Dora in the search for knowledge, he becomes a woman, that is to say, castrated. But if he chooses to cast her as his rival, he *must* win out, or the punishment will be castration.

The last point (that the punishment in case of defeat will be castration) requires further explanation. We have seen that Dora's sources of knowledge have been characterized as female, oral, and scattered. Freud, on the contrary, presents his knowledge as something which creates a unitary whole. In both cases we are discussing sexual knowledge. But Freud's own paradigmatic example of the desire for sexual knowledge is sexual curiosity in children, and Freud's most important text on this topic is *Little Hans*. When the reader moves from *Dora* to *Little Hans*, she is struck by the remarkable difference in tone between the two texts. The 5-year-old little Hans, straining to understand the mysteries of sexuality, is strongly encouraged in his epistemophilia, or drive for knowledge.[6] Freud never ceases to express his admiration for the intelligence of the little boy, in such laudatory statements as 'Here the little boy was displaying a really unusual degree of clarity' (*SE* 10: 44), or 'little Hans had by a bold stroke taken the conduct of the analysis into his own hands. By means of a brilliant symptomatic act . . .' (*SE* 10: 86). This tone is far removed from Freud's stern admonitions of Dora, his continuous *et tu quoque* ripostes to her interpretation of her own situation.

Why this differential treatment? It is arguable that in *Little Hans* Freud equates the desire for knowledge and the construction of theories with the desire to discover the role of the penis in procreation. The penis, in other words, becomes the

---

[6] The phrase 'epistemophilic instinct' appears in James Strachey's translation of *The Rat Man* (*SE* 10: 245).

epistemological object par excellence for Freud. But if this is so, knowledge and theory must be conceptualized as whole, rounded, finished—just like the penis. Little Hans becomes in this sense a penis for Freud. He is both a pleasurable object to be studied, a source of excitation and enthusiasm, *and* Freud's double: a budding sexual theoretician emerging to confirm Freud's own epistemological activities. But where Little Hans confirms, Dora threatens. Her knowledge cannot be conceptualized as a whole; it is dispersed and has been assembled piecemeal from feminine sources. Dora's epistemological model becomes the female genitals, which in Freud's vision emerge as unfinished, diffuse, and fragmentary; they cannot add up to a complete whole and must therefore be perceived as castrated genitals. If Freud were to accept Dora's epistemological model, it would be tantamount to rejecting the penis as the principal symbol for human desire for knowledge, which again would mean accepting castration.

Freud's masculine psyche therefore perceives Dora as more fundamentally threatening than he can consciously express. Instead, his fear of epistemological castration manifests itself in various disguises: in his obsessive desire to discover the sources of Dora's knowledge, and in his oddly intense discussion of the fragmentary status of the *Dora* text. To admit that there are holes in one's knowledge is tantamount to transforming the penis to a hole, that is to say, to transforming the man into a woman. Holes, empty spaces, open areas are at all cost to be avoided; and with this in mind we can discern further layers of meaning in the passage quoted earlier:

> In the face of the incompleteness of my analytic results, I had no choice but to follow the example of those discoverers whose good fortune it is to bring to the light of day after their long burial the priceless though mutilated relics of antiquity. I have restored what is missing (*SE* 7: 12).

'The priceless though mutilated relics of antiquity' are not only Dora's story: they are Dora herself, her genitals, and the feminine epistemological model. Freud makes sure that the message here is clear: 'mutilated' is his usual way of describing the effect of castration, and 'priceless' also means just what it says: price-less, without value.[7] For how can there be value when the valuable piece has been cut off? The relics are mutilated, the penis has been cut.[8] Freud's task is therefore momentous: he must 'restore what is missing'; his penis must fill the epistemological hole represented by Dora.

But such a task can only be performed by one who possesses what is missing. And this is precisely what Freud occasionally doubts in his text: the fear of castration is also the fear of discovering that one has already been castrated. Freud's hesitation in *Dora* between insisting on completeness and admitting fragmentary status indicates that in his text the penis is playing a kind of *fort-da* game with its author (now you have it, now you don't).[9] Freud's book about Dora is the narrative of an intense power struggle between two protagonists—a struggle in which the male character's virility is at stake, and in which he by no means always has the upper hand.

When Dora dismisses Freud like a servant, she paradoxically rescues him from further epistemological insecurity. He is left, then, the master of the *writing* of Dora. And even though his text bears the scars of the struggle between him and his victim, it is a victorious Freud who publishes it. Dora dismissed him, but Freud

[7] Some friends have asked me whether this interpretation would hold in German. They are right to ask. It is quite impossible to make an analysis of unconscious associations stick unless it is based on the language the author actually wrote in. At the time of writing I checked my reading of *Dora* against Freud's German, but since I didn't find any reason to change my interpretations, I didn't supply any German quotations. On this specific point, I probably ought to have done so. So here it is: in German Freud writes 'die unschätzbaren wenn auch verstümmelten Reste des Altertums' (*Studienausgabe* 6: 92). The point I make in English depends on the suffix '-less'. In German the prefix 'un-' would seem to function in the same way. *Schätzbar* means valuable or estimable. The verb *schätzen* means to value, to appreciate. So if 'priceless' produces associations to 'price-LESS', then *unschätzbaren* produces associations to *UN-schätzbaren*, that is to say 'not valuable' or 'not estimable'.

[8] Freud always assumes that castration means the cutting off of the penis. This is quite odd; not so much because real castration usually consists in the cutting off of the testicles, but because he nowhere discusses the discrepancy between his own definition of castration and the actual practice.

[9] The *fort-da* game is the game in which the child, by rejecting and retrieving a toy, enacts the absence and presence of the mother. *Fort-da* means roughly 'gone—here'.

got his revenge: Dora was the name Freud's own sister, Rosa, had foisted on her maid in place of her real one, which also was Rosa (*Psychopathology of Everyday Life, SE* 6: 241). So Ida Bauer, in a bitter historical irony, was made famous under the name of a servant after all.

Freud's epistemology is clearly phallocentric. The male is the bearer of knowledge; he alone has the power to penetrate woman and text, woman's role is to let herself be penetrated by such truth. Such epistemological phallocentrism is by no means specifically Freudian; on the contrary, it has so far enjoyed universal sway in our patriarchal civilization, and one could hardly expect Freud to emerge untouched by it. It is politically important, however, to point out that this pathological division of knowledge into masculine totality and feminine fragment is totally mystifying and mythological. There is absolutely no evidence for the actual existence of two such gender-determined sorts of knowledge, to be conceptualized as parallel to the shapes of human genitals. Dora can be perceived as the bearer of feminine epistemology in the study only because Freud selected her as his opponent in a war over cognition, creating her as his symbolic antagonist. To champion Dora's 'feminine values' means meekly accepting Freud's own definitions of masculine and feminine. Power always creates its own definitions, and this is particularly true of the distinctions between masculine and feminine constructed by patriarchal society. Nowhere is patriarchal ideology to be seen more clearly than in the definition of the feminine as the negative of the masculine—and this is precisely how Freud defines Dora and the 'feminine' epistemology she is supposed to represent.

To undermine this phallocentric epistemology means to expose its lack of natural foundation. In the case of *Dora*, however, we have been able to do this only because of Freud's own theories of femininity and sexuality. The attack upon phallocentrism must come from within, since there can be no outside, no space where true femininity, untainted by patriarchy, can be kept intact for us to discover. We can only destroy the mythical and mystifying constructions of patriarchy by using its own weapons. We have no others.

7

Patriarchal Thought and the Drive for Knowledge
(1988)

FEMINISM, SCIENCE, AND PHILOSOPHY

Feminists have long criticized a phenomenon variously labelled 'male science', 'male theory', or 'male rationality', arguing that such forms of structured thought are inextricably linked with traditional sexualized—and sexist—categories of dominance and oppression. The subject/object division, for instance, essential to certain conceptions of objectivity, is cast as homologous with the male/female opposition. Science, philosophy, rationality—call it what you like—constantly re-enacts the Cartesian mind/body divide in its most basic methodological moves, so feminists claim. Always and everywhere the rational, active, masculine intellect operates on the passive, objectified, feminized body. To be intellectual—to think?—under patriarchy, the argument goes, is willynilly to take up a position marked as masculine. If one doesn't, one has no option but to embrace the other side of the tedious series of homologous patriarchal oppositions, where irrationality and thoughtlessness is equated with femininity, the body, object-being, emotionality, and so on. In this paper I want first to examine certain problematic aspects in current feminist critiques of the subject/object and mind/body split, and then to sketch out a somewhat different approach to these problems.

The most influential arguments against 'male science' have been put forward by Evelyn Fox Keller. Drawing on Keller's critique in her own reading of Descartes, Susan Bordo extends

I am grateful to Parveen Adams, Teresa Brennan, and Jane Tompkins for their comments on earlier versions of this paper, and to Vigdis Songe Møller for philosophical inspiration and feminist solidarity.

her arguments to philosophy and the humanities in general. Keller's main enemy is the concept of 'objectivity', which she sees as the ruling ideological paradigm of the natural sciences. In her pioneering article 'Gender and Science', first published in 1978, she first outlines her critique of 'male science'. According to Keller, scientific ideology divides the world into 'two parts—the knower (mind) and the knowable (nature)' (190), and insists that the relation between 'knower and known is one of distance and separation . . . that between a subject and object radically divided' (191). Having divided the world, patriarchal ideology *genders* the two halves. Nature, objectified and oppressed, is female, whereas knowledge is characterized as male:

> the characterization of both the scientific mind and its modes of access to knowledge as masculine is indeed significant. Masculine here connotes, as it so often does, autonomy, separation and distance. It connotes a radical rejection of any commingling of subject and object, which are, it now appears, quite consistently identified as male and female (191).

Scientific objectivity, then, may best be characterized as the result of the unflinching enforcement of such gendered distance between male knower and female known. Such ideology, Keller claims, excludes women from science by casting them as 'non-objective', as 'non-knowers'. Feminists, Keller argues, must refuse to accept this male vision of the subject/object division. Instead, Keller proposes a 'commingling' of the two, or an empathetic 'feeling' for the object, where the object is no longer reified, but respected in its integrity. Such empathy can only be achieved if *feeling* is allowed a place within science, not relegated to a space outside it.

So far, there is no reason to disagree with Keller. Her critique of dominant forms of Cartesian rationalism is inspiring; her denunciation of the logic of domination and objectification at work in the ideology of science timely. I particularly warm to the idea of undoing the split between reason and emotion: Keller is surely right to assume that such a change will make science—or intellectual work in general—more accessible and more attractive for many women. Apparently, my only doubt concerns a trivial matter of language: her decision to label the new mode of knowledge (which will include feeling) 'female'. If, as I take it, the new mode of thought is superior to traditional ways, why should we not claim it as universal—simply as *the* way to do science? Why imply that this new mode somehow is less suitable for males? Nor would I want to call traditional science 'male'—why not 'patriarchal'? Just as all women are not feminist, not all males are patriarchal.

Pondering these differences in vocabulary, however, I realize that they are not coincidental, and that Keller's predilection for the terms 'male' and 'female' is closely bound up with her espousal of Nancy Chodorow's deeply influential feminist rewriting of non-Kleinian object-relations theory in *The Reproduction of Mothering*.[1] Keller's project is first to analyse and criticize dominant notions of science and objectivity, and then to study the 'processes by which the capacity for scientific thought develops, and the ways in which those processes are intertwined with emotional and sexual development' ('Gender' 191–2), which for her means turning to Chodorow's account of the development of female and male personality structures. This theory is too well known to be repeated here.

Chodorow-inspired philosophy of science, however, goes something like this. First there is the original, blissful unity between mother and child. Then comes the inevitable separation which makes little boys lose touch with the maternal body for ever, but luckily makes little girls more permeable, more open to merging with the world. Male science is structured on the male experience of separation and autonomy, which not only severs it from true communion with nature, but also leads it to adopt a language of conquest, power, and domination in its dealings with the world. This situation makes it harder for women to become scientists or intellectuals, since they will have to do violence to their female nature, their need for contact and communion, if they are to

---

[1] Although Chodorow notes that object-relations theory has been less popular in the USA than in Europe, it is significant that the theories of the object-relations school she uses may overlap with those of the American ego-psychology school. Despite manifest differences (the ego-psychologists are biologistic, Chodorow is not) both schools stress adaptation as an aim of psychoanalysis, privilege external reality, and neglect psychical reality. Both discount Klein's theory because it is not based on external reality.

follow the paths of male science or male philosophy. The feminist solution is to work for a transformation of male science by demanding that the female virtues of empathy and understanding, often called 'female modes of knowing', be included in the scientific enterprise. Such an inclusion would also put an end to science as a domineering, power-mongering enterprise. True science or true philosophy re-creates the lost unity between the knower and the known.

Keller's vocabulary of 'male' and 'female' signals her Chodorovian belief in fundamental sexual differences in male and female personality structures. In its consistent promotion of 'female' relatedness and 'male' separateness, Chodorow's deep-seated cultural (as opposed to biological) essentialism reintroduces age-old patriarchal beliefs in a specific female nature pitted against an equally specific male nature. Chodorow, Keller, Gilligan, Bordo, *et al.* come to stand as exponents of a psychosocial variety of 'difference feminism'. The root of their essentialism can be located in Chodorow's unproblematic use of non-Kleinian object-relations theory for feminist purposes. And this is not the only problem with such theory: in my (Freud- and Lacan-inspired) opinion non-Kleinian object-relations theory does not take the unconscious sufficiently into account, mistakenly rejects Freud's theory of drives as pure biologism, fails to theorize the difficult construction of subjectivity and sexual difference, neglects the contradictory and self-defeating nature of sexuality as theorized by Freud, and ends up idealizing the pre-Oedipal mother–child relationship without being able to offer a coherent account of the role of the father, the Law, or repression in the construction of the subject

The consequences for feminism are, among other things, an essentialist and quasi-biologist belief in fixed gender-identities (Chodorow will unproblematically discuss gender differences in the pre-Oedipal period), and the failure to theorize resistance, disruption, and failure of identity, a failure which leads Chodorow to assume that ideologically suspect gender roles *always* succeed in imposing themselves on the human subject. Such theories cannot account for disruption, exceptions, or 'unsuccessful' socialization. Chodorow, for instance, simply abandons the question of women who choose *not* to 'reproduce mothering', just as Keller or Bordo can say nothing at all about male philosophers who do not conform to their idea of 'male objectivity'. But surely a series of male thinkers from Marx, Nietzsche, and Freud to Heidegger, Wittgenstein, and Derrida have suggested deeply anti-rationalist, anti-philosophical critiques of the Cartesian subject/object or body/mind division? Perhaps we are to think of them as 'female' philosophers? But if so, why are they never discussed by Keller and her followers?

But let us return to Keller's main problematics: the question of the 'commingling' of subject and object ('Gender' 191), which goes hand in hand with the 'interaction between emotional and cognitive experience' (*Reflections* 116). Unfortunately, the Chodorovian rejection of the theory of the drives deprives Keller of *any* discourse of the body. While 'affective' and 'cognitive' structures are supposed to meet, mind and body go unmentioned. Leaving the problem of the body aside, it is hard to understand exactly what kind of union of subject and object Keller has in mind. Terms such as 'mediation' and 'interaction' ('Feminism' 238 and 242) remain vague. Susan Bordo, drawing on Keller, Gilligan, and Chodorow, writes approvingly about the 'natural foundation for knowledge, not in detachment and distance, but in closeness, connectedness, and empathy' (263), and nostalgically evokes the 'medieval sense of relatedness to the world', which she sees as the 'interpenetrations, through meanings and associations, of self and world' (257). Perhaps the best account of the ideal relationship between subject and object comes in Keller's outline of ideal, adult maturity: 'Ultimately, however, both sense of self and of other become sufficiently secure to permit momentary relaxation of the boundary between—without, that is, threatening the loss of either' ('Gender' 194).

I take this to mean that the distance between subject and object is to be momentarily abolished, that is to say that the two are to merge or commune without losing their self-identity. But in its paradoxical insistence on a unity *containing* self-identity untransformed, Keller's vision of communion can only reassert the original subject/object division. In many ways the whole discourse of empathy is neither new nor particularly feminist, but rather an unwitting repetition of 'male' Romanticism. Romantic poets and philosophers sought precisely to overcome the subject/object division by advocating some form of communion between subject and object. Logically speaking, there are only two possible forms of such communion: either the object engulfs the subject, in which case there is nobody around to do the communing; or the subject engulfs the object, thereby radically destroying it as other. There is of course a sense in which the Chodorovian account of 'male' science presents us with a third solution: the image of a transcendental, *lost* unity (the original, symbiotic relationship between mother and child) to be *re-established* through 'female' empathy. As paradoxical and prone to fissures as any other 'unity' of different self-identities, such a strategy can be no more than a fantasy dissolution of a real problematics.

Drawing on her critique of the scientific 'objectification' of nature, Keller denounces modern science as essentially an enterprise of domination and mastery. In 'Feminism and Science' she claims that science has only two options: control and domination (both expressions of 'masculine' aggression) over nature or 'ecstatic communion' with it (242). But just as the child's attempt to impose control and order on its world cannot be equated with exploitative domination, it is singularly unhelpful to see all forms of intellectual mastery simply as aggressive control and domination. To be consistent, Keller's denunciation of all possible forms of mastery would logically have to include the rejection, not only of rapacious exploitation of natural resources, nuclear weapons, and dictatorship, but of agriculture, housebuilding, and bicycling as well.

For me, then, the problem with Keller's and Bordo's Chodorovian analysis of gender and science and philosophy is not only its cultural essentialism, but the fact that the solution proposed ('commingling', 'union' of subject and object) remains curiously timid and flawed. If the 'union' proposed reinforces the separate identities of subject and object, their grand vision of 'female science' promises no more than a certain elasticity of boundaries between separate, self-identical essences. There is no attempt here to question the logic that underpins patriarchal metaphysics, or to contest the very meaning of terms such as masculine/feminine, reason/emotion, and so on. Keller's and Bordo's timidity contrasts sharply with Hélène Cixous's deconstructive onslaught on the very same oppositions:

> Where is she?
> Activity/passivity
> Sun/Moon
> Culture/Nature
> Day/Night
>
> Father/Mother
>
> Head/Heart
> Intelligible/Palpable
> Logos/Pathos.
> Form, convex, step, advance, semen, progress.
> Matter, concave, ground—where steps are taken, holding- and dumping-ground.
>
> Man
> Woman
>
> . . .
>
> [A]ll these pairs of oppositions are *couples* . . . Theory of culture, theory of society, symbolic systems in general—art, religion, family, language—it is all developed while bringing the same schemes to light. And the movement whereby each opposition is set up to make sense is the movement through which the couple is destroyed. A universal battlefield. Each time, a war is let loose. Death is always at work.[2]

By focusing on the inevitable struggle, the warring relationship between such hierarchical oppositions, Cixous at once signals that the battle between the sexes insinuates itself in the very structure of the sign, and that in the case of such binary oppositions, the sexual struggle is bound up with the effort to deconstruct phallogocentric logic. By reversing and displacing the oppositions at stake, Cixous seeks to show that every opposition entails repression, violence, and death. The deconstructive move is not to *abolish* oppositions, or to deny that such signifiers exist, but rather to trace the way in which each signifier contaminates and subverts the meaning of the others. Such an approach *opens* the sign up,

---

[2] Cixous, 'Sorties', in Cixous and Clément, *The Newly Born Woman*.

insists that its meaning is always deferred, never fully present to itself. In its questioning of the metaphysics of presence and identity, deconstruction offers a more radical solution to the problem of subject and object raised by Keller and Bordo. The problem is, of course, that deconstructive logic undermines all forms of essentialism, including the Chodorovian belief in 'self-identity' or 'female identity'. Paradoxically, then, the very psychological theory which enables Keller and Bordo to launch their research into the problem of knowledge in the first place, in the end radically prevents them from breaking out of the straitjacket of patriarchal binary thought.

THE STRUCTURES OF KNOWLEDGE: MICHÈLE LE DŒUFF

If Keller's analysis of knowledge and femininity turns out to be somewhat disappointing, it may be because it remains trapped by the categories of the scientific ideology it sets out to read. Perhaps one way around this problem is to approach the problem from a slightly different angle. Examining not so much the ideology of knowledge as the way in which that ideology is produced by the very structures of knowledge, the French feminist philosopher Michèle Le Dœuff raises two questions: what is there in the structure of knowledge itself that lends itself to patriarchal ideologization?[3] And what is the alternative for feminists? In her excellent and wide-ranging essay 'Women and Philosophy' (first published in 1976), she opens up the question of the relationship between feminism, femininity, and philosophy. Although Le Dœuff adheres to the term 'philosophy', her critique of philosophy may be read as a general critique of so-called 'male science' or 'male theory' as well.

[3] Since this essay was first written (in 1988), Michèle Le Dœuff's work has become much better known in the English-speaking world. 'Women and Philosophy' is included in Moi, *French Feminist Thought*. The collection of philosophical essays, *L'imaginaire philosophique*, in which 'Women and Philosophy' originally appeared, was translated as *The Philosophical Imaginary* in 1989, and Le Dœuff's full-scale discussion of the relationship between women and philosophy, *L'Étude et le rouet: des femmes, de la philosophie* etc. appeared in English as *Hipparchia's Choice* in 1991. In 1998, Le Dœuff published *Le sexe du savoir*, her long-awaited analysis of sexism in science, philosophy, and culture.

Focusing on the double problem of the empirical exclusion of women and the theoretical repression of femininity in Western philosophy, Le Dœuff argues that traditional Western philosophy exhibits a striking contradiction at its centre. On the one hand, philosophy is an activity based on the recognition of *lack*: philosophy, in other words, exists because there is something that *remains to be thought*. On the other hand, philosophy also works from the imaginary assumption that the knowledge produced by philosophy creates completion, that its aim is to construct a flawless structure *without lack*. The paradoxical truth is that for this school of thought, perfect philosophy would simply cease to be philosophy at all.

Confronted with this fundamental contradiction, woman is caught in a double bind and found doubly wanting. First, woman (the singular here denotes the imaginary, universal fantasy of woman entertained by philosophy) is perceived as lacking the phallus. According to the patriarchal imagination, what a woman needs is a man, not philosophy. If a woman declares that she too feels the philosophical lack, her desire for knowledge can only be a compensation for her primary sexual frustration. On this logic, then, the thinking woman necessarily becomes synonymous with the bluestocking, the frustrated spinster of patriarchal ideology: the female lack is never *truly* a philosophical lack. In other words, the woman is always suspected of not being able to think simply because she is taken to suffer from the *wrong* lack.

On the other hand, woman is also deemed incapable of philosophy, that is to say of rational thought, because of her self-sufficient plenitude. Here there is no question of her lack or her castration, rather, she becomes the very emblem of narcissistic self-sufficiency. On this logic, women cannot think because they suffer no lack at all: they are complacent, cow-like, content, or *plant-like* as Hegel prefers to put it:

> Women may be capable of education, but they are not made for the more advanced sciences, for philosophy and certain forms of artistic production which require universality. Women may have ideas, taste, and elegance, but they do not have the ideal. The difference between men and women is like that between animals and plants; men correspond to animals, while women correspond to plants because their life is more a placid unfolding, the principle of which

is the undetermined unity of feeling. When women hold the helm of government, the state is at once in jeopardy, because women regulate their actions not by the demands of universality, but by arbitrary inclinations and opinions.[4]

Woman is an inferior thinker, in other words, not because of her lack, but because of her lack of a lack. Whether woman is thought of as a whole or a hole, she is perceived as lacking in philosophy, that is to say as irrational.

By positing woman as the symbol of lack and negativity, Western philosophy turns her into the ground of its own existence: by her very inferiority she guarantees the superiority of philosophy. In this way the idea of 'woman' as defective becomes a defence against the thinking male subject's potentially devastating insight into his own lack. Historically, such strategies have not only been used against women, but also against 'primitive tribes', 'slaves', 'blacks', 'children', 'Jews', 'Moslems', and so on.

The fact that philosophy presents woman as that which relentlessly undermines man's rational endeavours, is not an ideological coincidence. It is the very structure of scientific thought which here is revealed. Le Dœuff insists that a discipline can only exist insofar as it can define itself *against* something else: in the same way, rational discourse can only know itself as rational by positing some irrational *outside* excluded from its own territory. Philosophical discourse is structurally obliged to assume that there is also a *different, non-rational knowledge,* of which it can know nothing. This illicit, mysterious, and threatening knowledge becomes a nameless undefined object of exclusion, only capable of metaphorical description. Thus, Le Dœuff claims, the 'man/woman difference is invoked or conscripted to signify the general opposition between definite and indefinite, that is to say validated/excluded' (*Philosophical Imaginary* 115). Philosophy itself creates its own inner enemy: femininity becomes the necessary support and signifier of rationality, operating within it as an eternal shadow that cannot be dialectically absorbed, neither obliterated nor fully assumed by the discipline.

---

[4] Cf. Hegel, *Philosophy of Right*, para. 166, Zusatz, tr. Knox; trans. modified by Le Dœuff (see *Philosophical Imaginary* 109).

Unlike some French feminists, Le Dœuff scornfully rejects this fantasmatic image of femininity:

> women (real women) have no reason to be concerned by that femininity. We are constantly being *confronted* with that image, but we do not have to recognize ourselves in it . . . As soon as we regard this femininity as a fantasy-product of conflicts within a field of reason that has been assimilated to masculinity, we can no longer set any store by liberating its voice. We will not talk pidgin to please the colonialists (*Philosophical Imaginary* 116).

For Le Dœuff only a philosophy aware of its own open and unfinished nature can hope to avoid being caught in the sterile dichotomy between reason and unreason, masculinity and femininity. A philosophy or a science conscious of its own lack, abandoning any hope of achieving that magic, imaginary closure, would be able to think through its own relationship to exclusion, instead of becoming its unwitting victim and perpetrator. This is not to say, of course, that such a self-reflexive inclusiveness would lead to the *end* of exclusion: as Le Dœuff shows, no structured thought is possible without it.

KNOWLEDGE AS ANALYTICAL DIALOGUE

There can be no doubt, then, that even the most radical new construction of knowledge will produce new forms of closure, new boundaries, and new exclusions. The advantage of Le Dœuff's account is that it allows us to analyse and deconstruct the opposition between inside and outside which structures knowledge itself. In this respect, Le Dœuff's deconstruction of the boundaries between knowledge and non-knowledge is not only reminiscent of Derrida,[5] but of the very specific dialogic situation created by psychoanalytic practice. Perhaps the analytic situation may be seen as a different model of structuring knowledge, one that forces us steadily to reflect on the points of exclusion, repression, and blockage in our own discursive constructions?

---

[5] I am not implying that Le Dœuff is directly influenced by Derrida. Le Dœuff herself emphasizes that her theoretical inspiration on this point comes from her intensive study of the plays of Bertolt Brecht.

At one level, Freudian psychoanalysis can be characterized as an effort to open up and extend the field of rational knowledge. Unlike Charcot, who chose to exhibit his hysterical patients in a gesture of dominance, Freud decided to listen to them: psychoanalysis is born in the encounter between the hysterical woman and the positivist man of science. It is in this reversal of the traditional roles of subject and object, of speaker and listener, that Freud more or less unwittingly opens the way for a new understanding of human knowledge. But the psychoanalytical situation is shot through with paradoxes and difficulty. For if Freud's (and Breuer's) act of listening represents an effort to *include* the irrational discourse of femininity in the realm of science, it also embodies their hope of *extending* their own rational understanding of psychic phenomena. *Grasping* the logic of the unconscious, they want to make it accessible to reason. In Joseph Breuer's listening to Anna O there is at once a colonizing, rational impulse and a revolutionary effort to let female madness speak to male science.

When the colonizing impulse gains the upper hand, psychoanalysis runs the risk of obliterating the language of the irrational and the unconscious, repressing the threatening presence of the feminine in the process. There can be no doubt that such an imperialist tendency runs right through Freud's own writings, surfacing for instance in his treatment of Dora. But there is also in his texts a will to let the madwoman speak, to consider *her* discourse as one ruled by its own logic, to accept the logic of another scene. As long as this contradictory project is in place, the discourse of the hysteric continues to unsettle and disturb the smooth positivist logic of the man of science. Inscribing the madwoman's discourse into science, Freud unknowingly starts a process that will transform the very notions of scientificity that he believed in.

But if the analytical situation radically questions the split between active subject and passive object denounced by Keller, it is not simply because the doctor here turns listener (that would be a simple reversal and nothing more), but because the analytical session engages both analyst and patient in *transference* and *countertransference*. If transference in analysis can be roughly defined as the process whereby the patient transfers earlier traumas and reactions, whether real or imaginary, on to the analyst, countertransference may be characterized as the analyst's more or less unconscious reactions to the discourse of the patient, or rather to the transference of the patient. Transference and countertransference engage analyst and analysand in a complex, differential set of interactions, which may literally 'make or break' the analysis. The truth of the analysis, its power to cure, is the discursive construction of this transferential network. Transference and countertransference turn the analytic session into a space where the two participants encounter each other in the place of the Other, in language.[6]

Emphasizing and developing the methodological and theoretical implications of Freud's analytical practice, Jacques Lacan sees the Freudian discovery of the unconscious as a discovery of a new form of *participatory* reading:

> [Freud's] first interest was in hysteria . . . He spent a lot of time listening, and while he was listening, there resulted something paradoxical, a *reading*. It was while listening to hysterics that he *read* that there was an unconscious. That is, something he could only construct, and in which he himself was implicated; he was implicated in it in the sense that, to his great astonishment, he noticed that he could not avoid participating in what the hysteric was telling him, and that he felt affected by it (Felman 22–3).

Caught in a web of transference and countertransference, the psychoanalytic reading, or the psychoanalytic construction, is, as Shoshana Felman points out, 'essentially, constitutively dialogic' (23). Such dialogue, however, is not enclosed in a simple dualism: for Lacan, the fact that analysis is constructed in language implies that analytic dialogue is essentially *triangular*. Felman writes: '[It] is not a dialogue between two egos, it is not reducible to a dual relationship between *two* terms, but is constituted by a third term that is the meeting point in language . . . a linguistic, signifying meeting place that is the locus of . . . insight' (56). For Lacan, Freudian reflexivity, Freudian dialogue, unsettles and undoes any

---

[6] For further information on transference and countertransference see Laplanche and Pontalis. For a brilliant discussion of transference as rhetorical trope, see Chase.

clear-cut oppositions between subject and object, self and other. Felman draws out the implications of this point:

> By shifting and undercutting the clear-cut polarities between subject and object, self and other, inside and outside, analyst and analysand, consciousness and the unconscious, the new Freudian reflexivity substitutes for all traditional binary, symmetrical conceptual oppositions—that is, substitutes for the very foundations of Western metaphysics—a new mode of interfering heterogeneity. This new reflexive mode—instituted by Freud's way of listening to the discourse of the hysteric and which Lacan will call 'the inmixture of the subjects' (*Écrits* 415)—divides the subjects differently, in such a way that they are neither entirely distinguished, separate from each other, nor, correlatively, entirely totalizable but, rather, interfering from within and in one another (61).

There is, then, in the psychoanalytic situation a model of knowledge which at once radically questions and displaces traditional notions of subject/object relationships and deconstructs the firm boundaries between knowledge and non-knowledge. As this situation of knowledge offers no firmly established binary opposites, it cannot be gendered as either masculine or feminine, thereby offering us a chance to escape the patriarchal tyranny of thought by sexual analogy. As feminists in search of new ways to think about objectivity, knowledge, and modes of intellectual activity, we can ill afford to neglect the model offered by psychoanalysis.

EPISTEMOPHILIA OR THE DRIVE FOR KNOWLEDGE

If the psychoanalytic situation offers an interesting model of knowledge, it has little to say to Evelyn Fox Keller's interest in the genesis of knowledge or cognition. If I am unhappy with Keller's Chodorovian account of the origins of knowledge, it is first and foremost because it posits *separate* systems of emotion and cognition from the start (see 'Gender' 192, 193, 195, 197, and 203). But this is precisely the problem that needs to be solved. We should also bear in mind the way in which the reason/emotion (or head/heart) split is deeply bound up with the mind/body division (needless to say, both oppositions are read through the male/female paradigm). Feminism needs a theory of knowledge which undoes and displaces *both* dualisms, not one that in a mistaken fear of biologism rejects all efforts to include the body in thought. I now want to argue that the Freudian theory of *epistemophilia*, or the drive for knowledge, provides us with a first outline of such a theory.

For Freud the drive for knowledge, often manifested as curiosity, informs all forms of human knowledge production, including intellectual work. The desire to construct intellectual hypotheses, to obtain knowledge, and to engage in philosophical speculation, Freud claims, can be traced back to the little child's insatiable curiosity about sexuality. Often reacting to the unwelcome birth of a sibling, the child wants to know where babies come from. The question of sexual relations or what 'it means to be married' is associated with this quest for origins. So strong is the desire for knowledge that Freud calls it a drive (or 'instinct' as the *Standard Edition* has it):

> This instinct cannot be counted among the elementary instinctual components, nor can it be classed as exclusively belonging to sexuality. Its activity corresponds on the one hand to a sublimated manner of obtaining mastery, while on the other hand it makes use of the energy of scopophilia. Its relations to sexual life, however, are of particular importance, since we have learnt from psycho-analysis that the instinct for knowledge in children is attracted unexpectedly early and intensively to sexual problems and is in fact possibly first aroused by them (*Three Essays*, SE 7: 194).

An ambiguous force, the drive for knowledge is uneasily poised on the dividing line between anal mastery, sadism, and voyeurism and sublimated cultural creativity. In a later (1913) essay on obsessional neuroses Freud emphasizes the sadistic aspect:

> we often gain an impression that the instinct for knowledge can actually take the place of sadism in the mechanism of obsessional neurosis. Indeed it is at bottom a sublimated off-shoot of the instinct of mastery exalted into something intellectual, and its repudiation in the form of doubt plays a large part in the picture of obsessional neurosis ('Disposition', SE 12: 324).

Surfacing in the anal phase, the drive for mastery signals the child's need to dominate itself and its world (starting with its bowel movements). Sadism and masochism are, respectively, the active and passive forms of this drive.[7]

Consistently emphasizing the ingenuity and perceptivity of children's theory formations, Freud is never tempted to discard them as irrational fantasies. However muddled, they always contain a kernel of truth—they are, in other words, prototypes of adult, rational operations: 'the sexual theories of children . . . are reflections of their own sexual constitution, and . . . in spite of their grotesque errors the theories show more understanding of sexual processes than one would have given their creators credit for' (*Three Essays, SE* 7: 196). The inquisitive child is nevertheless always disappointed in its intellectual explorations. The truth about sexual intercourse is not to be had, or cannot be properly understood by the child because of its own physical immaturity. 'There are', Freud writes, 'two elements that remain undiscovered by the sexual researches of children: the fertilizing role of semen and the existence of the female sexual orifice—the same elements, incidentally, in which the infantile organization is itself undeveloped' (*SE* 7: 197). If this frustration is deeply felt by the child it may lead to permanent injury to the drive for knowledge.

As a consequence of the unduly repressive child-rearing practices brought to bear on little girls, this tragic destiny is more often imposed on women, Freud argues in his 1908 paper ' "Civilized" Sexual Morality and Modern Nervous Illness':

> [Women's] upbringing forbids their concerning themselves intellectually with sexual problems though they nevertheless feel extremely curious about them, and frightens them by condemning such curiosity as unwomanly and as a sign of a sinful disposition. In this way they are scared away from *any* form of thinking, and knowledge loses its value for them . . . I do not believe that women's 'physiological feeble-mindedness' is to be explained by a biological opposition between intellectual work and sexual activity . . . I think that the undoubted intellectual inferiority of so many women can rather be traced back to the inhibition of thought necessitated by sexual suppression (*SE* 9: 198–9).

---

[7] For an outstanding discussion of Freud's endless hesitations over what comes first, sadism *or* masochism, see Laplanche. On psychoanalytic theories of masochism, see Adams.

This passage stands in marked contrast to Freud's own disapproval of Dora's attempts to gain sexual knowledge. Strongly encouraging childish sexual theory, both the *Three Essays* and '"Civilized" Morality' passage are much more reminiscent of Freud's analysis of Little Hans than of Dora. If we take a closer look at the chronology of these papers, the discrepancy between Freud's treatment of Dora and that of Little Hans comes across not simply as one of sexist denial of knowledge to women, but one of a marked development *away* from an early, patriarchal disapproval of sexual curiosity in females towards a later, more liberal view. The point to notice here is that although he did not publish *Dora* until 1905, Freud actually analysed her in 1900 or 1901, and wrote up the case story in 1901. In the period leading up to 1905 and the publication of the *Three Essays* with their positive view of epistemophilia, it seems likely that Freud fundamentally revised his views on sexual curiosity, now explicitly linking it with intellectual development. ' "Civilized" Morality' from 1908 and *Little Hans* from 1909 only continue and expand on this trend, which culminates in the 1910 paper on Leonardo da Vinci.

Whatever the fate of the child's early sexual researches, Freud insists, its solitary quest for knowledge opens up a gap between it and its environment. 'The sexual researches of these early years of childhood are always carried out in solitude', Freud writes. 'They constitute a first step towards taking an independent attitude in the world, and imply a high degree of alienation of the child from the people in his environment who formerly enjoyed his complete confidence' (*Three Essays*, SE 7: 197). The seeds of intellectual life are sown in the solitary brooding of a child who suspects its parents of deliberately hiding secrets of vital importance to its existence. No wonder, then, that Freud in later years compared philosophical speculation to paranoid delusions (see, for instance, *Totem and Taboo*, SE 13: 73).

In his 1910 essay on Leonardo da Vinci, Freud argues that after the initial repression of the period of infantile sexual researches, the drive for research has 'three distinct possible vicissitudes open to it' (*SE* 11: 79). In Freud's account, then, there is no 'normal' development and no 'deviations' from the norm: the three paths are simply possible 'turns' where none is more 'normal' than the others. In the case of the first 'vicissitude' curiosity remains inhibited for the rest of the subject's life. Such a person, presumably, will not become an intellectual. In the second case the intellect resists repression, without being able to free itself from the repressed association between thought and sexuality. In this case, Freud writes, the 'suppressed sexual activities of research return from the unconscious in the form of compulsive brooding, naturally in a distorted and unfree form, but sufficiently powerful to sexualize thinking itself and to color intellectual operations with the pleasure and anxiety that belong to sexual processes proper' (*SE* 11: 80). In such individuals, the frustration of the early infantile explorations is repeated in endless brooding over problems that remain permanently unresolved: the orgasmic solution never comes.

Finally, there is the case of the fully sublimated intellectual drive, where the libido is not repressed but simply diverted to a new aim. The diversion of libido means that for the truly sublimated intellectual research becomes to a large extent a substitute for sexual satisfaction. Given the absence of repression, his or her compulsive epistemophilic drive remains free of neurosis and therefore 'operate[s] freely in the service of intellectual interest', as Freud puts it (*SE* 11: 80). Obviously destined to bolster his own ego as well as to explain Leonardo da Vinci's life and work, Freud's powerful idealization of intellectual life nevertheless has the merit of including childhood sexuality as an element in the highest intellectual endeavours.

KNOWLEDGE, SUBLIMATION, THE BODY, AND THE DRIVES

But what exactly does it mean to say that intellectual pursuits are sublimations? And what are the implications of linking the production of theory to childhood sexuality? Is this not just another wildly reductive view of knowledge? Whatever else it may be, sublimation is *not* the same thing as repression. Notoriously vague and undertheorized, the concept of sublimation is normally defined as a diversion of sexual energy to new, culturally acceptable aims. This new aim is no longer sexual, Freud claims, but 'psychically related to the first aim' (' "Civilized" Morality', *SE* 9: 187).

It remains unclear whether the new aim is anaclitic (metonymically linked) to the first (as seems to be the case in the Leonardo essay), or whether there is some other relationship between them. The first of these relationships would be analogous to that between the body and the drives.

But what exactly is the role of the drives in Freud's theory of epistemophilia? First of all, the drive for knowledge, or the capacity for intellectual speculation, is set in motion by the child's frustration at the arrival of a new baby (or other frustrations of its narcissistic fantasies of omnipotence). The intellectual activity itself sets the child apart from its surroundings, emphasizing for the first time its loneliness and its incapacity to understand the world into which it has been thrown. If rational thought is the result of the child's effort to *overcome* frustration, rational inquiry only succeeds in the end in producing an even more overwhelming—and alienating—sense of impotence and disenchantment. So deep is the frustration created by the exercise of the child's intellectual faculties that it threatens to obliterate curiosity for ever. Intellectual labour, then, is not only the *result* of frustration: in its very powerlessness it is also the *source* of its own frustration. The desire for rational knowledge, or indeed the pursuit of philosophy, is a self-defeating drive for imaginary satisfaction.

Like sexuality, then, rationality is its own frustration. In his 1912 paper 'On the Universal Tendency to Debasement in the Sphere of Love' Freud explicitly formulates the idea that 'something in the nature of the sexual instinct itself is unfavorable to the realization of complete satisfaction' (*SE* 11: 188–9). In the same way, something in the nature of human rationality is unfavourable to its own unfolding. This 'something', in both cases, is the human body.

For Freud, the drives take the human body as their point of departure: oral, anal, and genital drives develop because of the physical functions of these parts of the human body. This is not to say that the drive is *identical* to the original biological need, or that it can be *reduced* back to it. Freud explains that the drive is 'anaclitic' to the body, a spin-off from the physical function, neither identical with nor reducible to the biological need that set it in motion in the first place. The Freudian body is perceived as the limiting *horizon* of our thought and our discourse, not as its inherent identity or essential meaning. In this way, Freudianism is a materialism, but not, as is often argued, a form of biologism.[8] The body limits and frustrates the drives: the desire for total sexual satisfaction, or for complete epistemological mastery, can be no more than a fantasy of the Imaginary. The human body, whether male or female, is constructed under the sign of castration: it is always suffering, always already mutilated.

This is not to deny the fact that the full, 'Oedipal' castration complex posits the subjects differently in relation to the phallus, and thus also constructs sexual difference. It is, however, to indicate that for Freud the roots of rationality are to be found in the first narcissistic wound, one that is situated in the pre-Oedipal space where sexual difference does not yet apply. (A full examination of sexual difference and the construction of knowledge, and of the psychoanalytic deconstruction of the 'subject supposed to know' would require a separate paper.) Intellectual labour, then, is the spin-off of our original effort to understand how this incomplete and limited body came to be, our defence against the narcissistic wound imposed by the arrival of other bodies on our scene. The presence of the body produces the drag in our discourse and the muddle in our thoughts. And this meddling body is always already libidinal.

Self-defeating, always frustrated by the limitations of the body, the Freudian drive for knowledge is structurally incapable of achieving total insight or perfect mastery: the philosopher's dream of self-contained plenitude is here unmasked as the imaginary fantasy it is. Freudian theory posits the drive for knowledge (epistemophilia) as crucially bound to the body and sexuality. If reason is always already shot through with the energy of the drives, the body, and desire, to be intellectual can no longer be theorized simply as the 'opposite' of being emotional or passionate. Evelyn Fox Keller is right to turn to

---

[8] For an excellent account of the 'anaclitic' relationship between the drives and the body, see Laplanche.

psychoanalysis for valuable inspiration for her battle against patriarchal ideology in science, and much work remains to be done in the field pioneered, however differently, by Keller and Le Dœuff. I see my own contribution simply as an effort to indicate that an anti-essentialist feminist philosophy of science stands to gain rather more from Freud and Lacan than from Winnicott and American ego-psychology.

8

Is Anatomy Destiny?
Freud and Biological Determinism

This paper is a response to the question of the place of psycho-analysis in contemporary culture. In modern feminism debates pitting cultural against biological causation have played an important role. Such debates have also arisen in relation to research in biotechnology, neurobiology, sociobiology, and ethnomethodology. I think it could be shown that Freud thinks of the body in terms that undermine the opposition between natural causation and cultural meanings that has been with us since Kant first distinguished between the realm of necessity and the realm of freedom. If this is right, then Freud does have a philosophically original contribution to make to contemporary debates about the relationship between body and mind, nature and nurture, genetic inheritance and social construction. I want here to take a first step towards this larger argument by raising a question that has been important to feminists: Is Freud a biological determinist?

Biological determinists believe that social norms are or ought to be grounded on biological facts. They also believe that no amount of social change will change the fundamental biological nature of human beings. As the late nineteenth-century determinists Geddes and Thomson put it: 'What was decided among the prehistoric Protozoa cannot be annulled by Act of Parliament (267).[1] Many biological determinists believe that biological facts express themselves in the social roles prevalent in their own society, and

I want to thank Peter Brooks for inviting me to participate in the 'Whose Freud?' conference, which took place at Yale University in April 1998. This paper is a substantially revised and expanded version of the presentation I gave at the conference. I also want to thank David Paletz and Hazel Rowley for commenting on different drafts of this paper.
  [1] I discuss biological determinism in general and the work of Geddes and Thomson and W. K. Brooks in particular in Ch. 1, above, 'What Is a Woman?'.

that any change would lead to a disastrous incapacity to reproduce. This was the view of W. K. Brooks, a professor of biology at Johns Hopkins in the 1880s:

> The positions which women already occupy in society and the duties which they perform are, in the main, what they should be if our view is correct; and any attempt to improve the condition of women by ignoring or obliterating the intellectual differences between them and men must result in disaster to the race (263).

Freud's views on women have often been taken to be consonant with this. Given that Freud studied medicine at a time when determinism was widespread and started his scientific career in the late 1870s with research on the physiology of eels, it would hardly be surprising were we to find traces of it in his work. Read against this historical background, Freud's famous phrase 'Anatomy is destiny' appears to clinch the case. If he can say such a thing, he must be a biological determinist. No single sentence of Freud's has been more troublesome to feminists. Sooner or later, anyone who believes that Freud was not in fact a biological determinist will have to explain why this sentence does not undermine their claim. Usually this is done by writing it off as a casual witticism, not compatible with Freud's more thoughtful comments on the body. I don't think that argument is good enough. After all, Freud was sufficiently content with the formulation to use it twice, twelve years apart. The phrase 'Anatomy is destiny' first appears in 1912, in his essay called 'On the Universal Tendency to Debasement in the Sphere of Love', and again in the 1924 paper on 'The Dissolution of the Oedipus Complex'. Unless there is evidence to the contrary, the assumption must be that Freud actually meant what he said. The question to be answered is: What exactly *did* Freud mean when he claimed that anatomy is destiny?[2]

---

[2] A fuller investigation of the status of the body in Freudian theory would have to consider many more texts by Freud. Of immediate relevance are the 1925 essay called 'Some Psychical Consequences of the Anatomical Distinction between the Sexes', the 1920 case study entitled 'Case of Homosexuality in a Woman' (1920), *Three Essays on the Theory of Sexuality* (1905), and the unpublished 'Project for a Scientific Psychology' (1895), as well as all the texts dealing with femininity.

THE MEANING OF DESTINY

What Freud actually wrote was not, of course, 'Anatomy is destiny', but rather, 'die Anatomie ist das Schicksal'.[3] There are some differences between the German *Schicksal* and the English *destiny*. *Schicksal* can be translated either as 'fate' or as 'destiny'. In English, 'destiny' is linked to words like 'destination': the idea is that a certain outcome is bound to occur, regardless of human attempts to intervene. Oedipus will kill his father and marry his mother, whatever his own wishes and inclinations might be. According to the OED, destiny means 'predetermined events; what is destined to happen to person, country, etc.; power that foreordains, invincible necessity'. The difference between destiny and fate is that whereas fate more often is negative, associated with death and destruction, destiny can be quite positive. One can have a magnificent destiny, but hardly a magnificent fate. Both words nevertheless carry connotations of preordination and inevitability.

The German word *Schicksal* is more imbued with metaphysical gloom than the English word 'destiny'. In her extensive analysis of the cultural meanings of different words for fate and destiny in different European languages, Anna Wierzbicka writes that *Schicksal* has a 'pessimistic orientation' (80), that it has connotations of something 'inevitable, superhuman and awesome' (84), and that it 'suggest[s] a mysterious and other-worldly power' (84).[4] In contrast, the English 'destiny' has a less awesome and more upbeat ring, and the English 'fate' comes across as more unambiguously fatal than *Schicksal.*

---

[3] 'Über die allgemeinste Erniedrigung des Liebeslebens', *Studienausgabe* 5: 209.

[4] While Wierzbicka's treatise is truly fascinating in its attempt to convey the different feel of apparently similar words in different languages, I should say that I find her analysis of the English 'fate' and 'destiny' less subtle than the rest. According to her, destiny cannot mean something bad and inevitable, and therefore the more pessimistic meanings of *Schicksal* should never be translated as destiny (see 93). She also believes that in the usage of this century, at least, the English words destiny and fate are free of metaphysical implications (see 93), and that they have empiricist or positivistic overtones (see 93–4). I am very grateful to Professor Robert A. Paul for kindly sending me a copy of Wierzbicka's text.

In 1915 Freud did give the word *Schicksal* great prominence, by putting it in the title of his important paper 'Triebe und Triebschicksale', which literally means 'Drives and the Destinies of Drives'.[5] It is striking to note that he chose to put the word in the plural, thereby making it quite obvious that he did not intend to write a paper about 'the one inexorable fate' or 'the inevitable and unescapable outcome' of drives. Translating the title as 'Instincts and their Vicissitudes', James Strachey, the editor of *The Standard Edition*, shows himself to be sensitive to Freud's main point, which is to show that drives are subjected to transformation by three different 'polarities', each functioning more or less independently in relation to the other two.[6] Whatever happens to the drive—the outcome of the different and varying pressure of these factors—is what Freud calls its *Schicksal*. To translate this as 'destiny', Strachey recognizes, would be to provoke quite the wrong associations in English-speaking readers.[7]

In *Freud and Man's Soul,* his scorching critique of the translation of *The Standard Edition,* Bruno Bettelheim, who considers that both 'Instinct' and 'Vicissitudes' utterly fail to convey Freud's thought, comments: 'It is true that both "fate" and "destiny" carry the implication of inevitability, which neither the German *Schicksale* nor the English "vicissitudes" does. And Freud certainly

---

[5] I am grateful to Judith Butler for reminding me of this important example of Freud's use of the word *Schicksal.*

[6] This is how Freud summarizes his findings in 'Instincts and Their Vicissitudes' ('Triebe und Triebsschicksale'): 'We may sum up by saying that the essential feature in the vicissitudes undergone by instincts [*die Triebschicksale*] lies in *the subjection of the instinctual impulses to the influences of the three great polarities that dominate mental life.* Of these three polarities we might describe that of activity–passivity as the *biological,* that of ego–external world as the *real,* and finally that of pleasure–unpleasure as the *economic* polarity' (*SE* 14: 140, all emphases in the original). We note that Freud here sees biology, understood as activity–passivity (in itself hardly a common understanding of biology), as only one among several factors working on the drives. It is very difficult to see how this could be evidence of biological determinism.

[7] The debate about whether 'instinct' is a good translation of *Trieb* belongs in another context. See Bruno Bettelheim's *Freud and Man's Soul* 103–7 for a scorching critique of 'instinct' and a convincing defence of 'drive'. It is interesting to note that even the first English translation of the paper, made in 1925 by C. M. Baines, used the title 'Instincts and their Vicissitudes'.

did not mean that there is any inevitability inherent in the changes our inner drives are subject to. But if the translators rejected "fate" because of its implication of immutability, they could have used "change" or "mutability" instead. They could, for example, have translated the title as "Drives and Their Mutability" ' (105). The very fact that Bettelheim can propose to translate *Schicksale* as *mutability* shows that the range of meanings clustering around the word in Freud's work hardly add up to conclusive evidence of determinism or a belief in predestination. The meaning of the phrase 'Anatomy is destiny', however, cannot be settled simply by examining dictionary definitions or by looking at how Freud uses the word *Schicksal* in other contexts. The question now is what meaning the sentence acquires in the two contexts where Freud actually uses it.

'ATROPOS, THE INEXORABLE'

I have said that *Schicksal* can be translated either as destiny or as fate. In its most traditional, mythological sense, 'fate' is linked to the three fates (in Greek: the *moira*), the three goddesses of destiny. Fate has thus come to mean the 'impersonal power by which events are determined'. Freud himself mentions the three fates or *moira* in the 1913 essay entitled 'The Theme of the Three Caskets', where he suggests that the three caskets that occur in so many fairy tales stand for, among other things, the three fates. Hesiod represents them as three old women spinning the thread of life: Klotho ('the spinner') held the distaff, Lachesis ('the apportioner') drew off the thread, and Atropos ('the inflexible') cut it short. Freud focuses on the third sister, the Goddess of Death, whom he calls 'Atropos, the inexorable' (*SE* 12: 296).

The mythological meaning of destiny or fate foregrounded by Freud himself is death. We are all inexorably subject to death because we have human bodies. The fact that all human beings without exception are destined to die has enormous consequences for every human practice and every social institution, as well as for our own lived experience. Yet nobody seems to believe that to say so constitutes politically unacceptable biological determinism, or that it is evidence of an attempt to situate human existence outside history or discourse. My point here is simple: it is often assumed that when Freud says that 'Anatomy is destiny' he must mean that certain features of our anatomy lead to an inexorable fate, that whatever the individual subject does, he or she cannot escape the predestined outcome dictated by anatomy. It is also usually assumed that any thought along these lines is bound to be evidence of biological determinism and sexism. Yet if Freud were saying that the fact of having a human body destines us to death, this would at once be a true description of a biological fact and a statement devoid of politically controversial implications. In this context, the word destiny does refer to Kant's necessity, to the iron law of natural cause and effect, yet *this* natural necessity does not abolish freedom. Or rather, the meaning we usually give to the word freedom is not such that it is undermined or voided by the fact of death. (Simone de Beauvoir, to mention one feminist explicitly opposed to biological determinism, would go even further: for her death is the very condition of human freedom.[8])

'TO VARY A SAYING OF NAPOLEON'S'

When Freud writes 'Anatomy is destiny', the idea that the human body destines us to death may linger in the air. Yet this is most likely not the meaning he had uppermost in his mind when he wrote the sentence. In the two passages I am considering here, 'anatomy' refers to the specific configuration or structure of the human body, not just the body in its widest, biological generality. Let me return to Freud's texts. The most striking thing about the saying is the fact that in both passages, in 1924 as well as in 1912, Freud introduces it as a self-conscious twist on a 'well-known' saying of Napoleon's:

> 'One might say here, varying a well-known saying by the great Napoleon: "Anatomy is destiny" ' (1912).

> '"Anatomy is Destiny," to vary a saying of Napoleon's' (1924).

---

[8] Beauvoir's novel *All Men Are Mortal* (*Tous les hommes sont mortels*, 1946) portrays an immortal man slowly succumbing to debilitating depression because his immortality deprives his projects of all meaning.

The fact that neither Freud nor James Strachey, the meticulous editor of the *Standard Edition* of Freud's works in English, supply a reference to what Napoleon actually said suggests that at the time the saying must have been well known in the German and the English-speaking world. This is hardly the case today.[9]

Freud, an avid reader of the German classics, is referring to a conversation that took place between Napoleon and Goethe in Weimar in September 1808. According to Goethe's account in his 'Autobiographische Einzelheiten', the subject of the conversation was literature and theatre:

> Then he got to the destiny plays, of which he disapproved.[10] They had belonged to a dark age. 'What does one want destiny for now?', he said. 'Politics is destiny' (my translation).

> So kam er auch auf die Schicksalsstücke, die er mißbilligte. Sie hätten einer dunklern Zeit angehört: 'Was', sagte er, 'will man jetzt mit dem Schicksal, die Politik ist das Schicksal' (546).

When Freud writes 'Anatomy is destiny', he explicitly intends us to recall Napoleon's 'Politics is destiny'.[11] Napoleon, the most powerful man in the world at the time, scoffs at destiny. Power is destiny, he says. But this puts the meaning of destiny under pressure. For the victorious armies of Napoleon invading Europe irrevocably shaped the lives of millions, and many of those who starved and died in the Napoleonic wars must have thought that

---

[9] Before writing this paper I had no idea what Napoleon said, and nor did any of the friends and colleagues I asked about it. My efficient and creative research assistant, Christian Thorne, found the reference for me. Much to my surprise he reported that it was very easy. All that was required was to look up 'Anatomy is destiny' in a dictionary of quotations. The dictionary provides the page reference to Goethe's text. If it is this easy to find out what Freud's reference is, why hasn't it been more widely discussed by psychoanalytic and feminist critics concerned with Freud's phrase?

[10] The destiny plays (*die Schicksalsstücke*) were Gothic melodramas, popular at the end of the 18th cent.

[11] Here it has to be acknowledged that since Goethe and Napoleon must have been speaking French together, what Napoleon in all probability actually said was 'la politique est le destin'. But this can have no bearing on the question of what Freud meant, since he is quoting Goethe's German text. Nothing indicates that Freud particularly wanted his readers to think of the French language in this context.

such suffering was their fate. Yet Napoleon's armies were neither
the agents of divine intervention nor the ineluctable effects of the
laws of nature. Napoleon, the self-made man par excellence, is
not saying that he too is the mere plaything of politics. He makes
politics. If anything, Napoleon sounds a positively Nietzschean
theme here: in a world dominated by power, we either grasp the
opportunity to forge our own destiny or succumb to the slave
morality of Christianity. What some weak souls experience as the
blow of fate, is actually the work of other, more energetic personalities.

Flaubert captures the irony implicit in Napoleon's point of view
perfectly in his account of the last words of the broken Charles
Bovary: 'No, I am no longer angry with you', he says to Rodolphe,
Emma's first lover. The passage continues:

> He even added a grand phrase, the first he had ever uttered:
> 'It was the fault of fate!'
> Rodolphe, who had directed this fate, found him very meek for a
> man in his situation, comic even and a little despicable (my trans-
> lation).

> — Non, je ne vous en veux plus!
> Il ajouta même un grand mot, le seul qu'il ait jamais dit:
> — C'est la faute de la fatalité!
> Rodolphe, qui avait conduit cette fatalité, le trouva bien débon-
> naire pour un homme dans sa situation, comique même et un peu
> vil (*Madame Bovary* 410).

What the dying Charles Bovary in his pathetic last words takes to
be fate, Rodolphe knows to be the work of human agency.
Flaubert's irony recalls Napoleon's: to invoke fate is to be termi-
nally deluded. Yet Napoleon is not saying that destiny does not
exist, he is saying that it is politics. What makes Napoleon's *grand
mot* so difficult is that it makes the meaning of 'destiny' opaque.
Napoleon challenges us to consider what 'destiny' might mean in
a world where the mythological meaning (the oracles, prophe-
cies, oaths, and curses of the melodramatic *Schicksalsstücke*) no
longer make sense. Freud's grand phrase resonates with the
complexity and irony of Napoleon's original saying. A slightly
tongue-in-cheek invocation of Napoleon's 'Politics is destiny',
Freud's 'Anatomy is destiny' invites us to think about what

'destiny' might mean in a modern, demythologized world. Just as Napoleon did not mean to say that politics belongs to a sphere unreachable by human agency, Freud probably did not mean to say that the *Diktats* of anatomy inexorably override human agency and choice.

1912: ANATOMY AND HUMAN SEXUALITY

Turning now to the contexts in which Freud's 'Anatomy is destiny' occurs, the first and most striking thing to be noted, is that in 1912 he uses it to back up a claim about sexuality in general, whereas in 1924 the same phrase is invoked to make a point about sexual difference. I will start by looking at the 1912 paper. Here is the phrase quoted in its context (I apologize for quoting at such length, but if we are to grasp Freud's thought here we have to read his words carefully):

> The excremental is all too intimately and inseparably bound up with the sexual; the position of the genitals—*inter urinas et faeces*—remains the decisive and unchanging factor. **One might say here, varying a well-known saying of the great Napoleon: 'Anatomy is destiny.'** The genitals themselves have not taken part in the development of the human body in the direction of beauty: they have remained animal, and thus love, too, has remained in essence just as animal as it ever was. The instincts of love are hard to educate; education of them achieves now too much, now too little. What civilization aims at making out of them seems unattainable except at the price of a sensible loss of pleasure; the persistence of the impulses that could not be made use of can be detected in sexual activity in the form of non-satisfaction.
>
> Thus we may perhaps be forced to become reconciled to the idea that it is quite impossible to adjust the claims of the sexual instincts to the demands of civilization; that in consequence of its cultural development renunciation and suffering, as well as the danger of extinction in the remotest future, cannot be avoided by the human race. This gloomy prognosis rests, it is true, on the single conjecture that the non-satisfaction that goes with civilization is the necessary consequence of certain peculiarities which the sexual instinct has assumed under the pressure of culture. The very incapacity of the sexual instinct to yield complete satisfaction as soon as it submits to the first demands of civilization becomes

the source, however, of the noblest cultural achievements which are brought into being by ever more extensive sublimation of its instinctual components. For what motive would men have for putting sexual instinctual forces to other uses if, by any distribution of those forces, they could obtain fully satisfying pleasure? ('Debasement', *SE* 11: 189–90; my emphasis in bold).

These paragraphs are written in order to back up a claim just made in the previous paragraph. What is at stake here is nothing less than one of Freud's most famous and most important claims about sexuality:

It is my belief that, however strange it may sound, we must reckon with the possibility that something in the nature of the sexual instinct itself is unfavourable to the realization of complete satisfaction ('Debasement', *SE* 11: 188–9).

Much loved by deconstructionists and other postmodern readers of Freud, this sentence is central to the psychoanalytic understanding of sexuality. Freud is here sounding a warning to all those who wish to believe that it is possible simply to 'liberate' human sexuality from the shackles of repression. Sexuality is not a strong libidinous stream forced to deviate from its original, inborn, and healthy course by the repressive forces of civilization. Rather, Freud is saying, there is no such thing as pure or unthwarted human sexuality. Even in the most benign social setting, conflict and displacement will be inherent in all forms of human sexual expression. None of this means that all human beings are likely to be equally sexually conflicted, or sexually conflicted in exactly the same way, in this or in any other society.

In the part of the 1912 essay just preceding the quoted passage, Freud gives two reasons for the peculiarly self-thwarting nature of sexuality. First, he explains, there is the fact that any adult object choice is 'never any longer the original object but only a surrogate for it' (*SE* 11: 189). (The original love object is the mother or the father.) This, he adds, often leads to the choice of 'an endless series of substitutive objects none of which . . . brings full satisfaction' (*SE* 11: 189). Second, there is the fact that the sexual drive has had to repress a number of its original components. The most important of these is the coprophiliac aspects of the drive. A coprophiliac, we may recall, is someone who exhibits an undue interest in faeces and defecation. Although we quickly learn to repress our coprophilic tendencies, they still lurk in a more or less remote corner of our psyche. This sets up a conflict: our civilized superego tells us to love what is clean, pure, and beautiful, whereas our lower instincts still take an interest in the ugly, the dark, and the dirty. This, Freud stresses, is an effect of our anatomy: 'The excremental is all too intimately bound up with the sexual; the position of the genitals—*inter urinas et faeces*—remains the decisive and unchanging factor. One might say here, varying a well-known saying of the great Napoleon: "Anatomy is destiny" ' (*SE* 11: 189).

On the evidence of the quoted passages, it would seem that if anatomy is destiny, it is destiny in a peculiar way: what anatomy—the fact that the genitals are located where they are—seems to guarantee, without fail, is psychic conflict. Yet Freud is very explicit that it is the fact of human civilization—the fact that every known human society socializes its children—that makes such psychic conflict inevitable. Freud always stressed that because the human baby is born prematurely—he means, born in a state of helplessness, before it can manage on its own—it is destined to interact with others.[12] Or in other words, our biology destines us to become social beings. Freud's thought here is strikingly similar to that of Merleau-Ponty who declares that: 'Man is a historical idea, and not a natural species' (*Phenomenology* 170). Merleau-Ponty is not trying to deny that the body is natural, his point is rather that it is our nature to be historical beings, just as Freud seems to be saying that it is our nature to be social creatures.[13]

This passage makes it clear that anatomy only becomes destiny in the necessary and inevitable process of bringing up children. (The word translated as 'education' in the English text is *Erziehung*, which means upbringing in a wide sense, not just formal education.) It should be clear, moreover, that Freud is not suggesting that all human beings will experience sexuality in the same way, or have the same sexual conflicts and problems. After

[12] Freud also thought that infantile helplessness was the psychical origin of religious ideas (see *The Future of an Illusion*, 1927).

[13] I discuss Merleau-Ponty's view in relation to that of Simone de Beauvoir in Ch. 1, above, 'What Is a Woman?'.

all, Dora, Little Hans, and the Rat Man, three patients whose case studies were published by Freud well before 1912, had spectacularly different symptoms. The passage shows that anatomy is only one element that contributes to our psychic conflicts. Insofar as we all share the same bodily structure, however, it may be said to constitute something like the inescapable background of our choices and acts.[14]

The meaning of Freud's 'Anatomy is destiny' seems to be that our anatomy and our biological needs will make psychic conflict inevitable. Just as we all have to die, we will all suffer from psychic conflicts. For Freud, there is no such thing as conflict-free, unambivalent human sexuality, or a homogenous, unconflicted human psyche. This is hardly a theory that denies human freedom and agency or overlooks the difference between human beings. Freud neither believes that all psychic conflicts will be of the same kind or have the same degree of severity, nor that it is impossible to free oneself from the more severe effects of psychic conflict through psychoanalytic therapy and life-changing experiences.[15] Neither the specific kind of psychic conflicts that will arise, nor the meaning and importance they will acquire in any given person's life can be inferred from human anatomy.

In 1912 'Anatomy is destiny' means that the fact of having a human body is bound to have conflictual consequences for the human psyche. To say this is not at all the same thing as to say that biological facts ought to ground social norms. On my reading of their works, radical anti-determinists such as Beauvoir and Merleau-Ponty believe much the same thing. What Freud reveals here is not his biological determinism, but rather his deep-rooted pessimism about the possibility of human happiness.

---

[14] In *The Second Sex*, Simone de Beauvoir develops the idea of the sexed body as a background (she also, more famously, considers it a situation). See Ch. 1, above 'What Is a Woman?' for a discussion of the body as a situation, and Ch. 2, above, 'I Am a Woman' for a discussion of the body as background.

[15] Between 1911 and 1914, Freud wrote intensively on the technique of psychoanalytic therapy. Some of his best known papers on analytic practice, including his first sustained discussions of transference, date from this period (see the section entitled 'Papers on Technique', *SE* 12).

1924: THE FEMINIST DEMAND

In the 1924 essay entitled 'The Dissolution of the Oedipus Complex', the phrase 'Anatomy is destiny' is placed in a very different context. The question is no longer about human sexuality in general, but about sexual difference. Freud has just explained how the Oedipus complex is commonly overcome by little boys. Again I am obliged to quote at length:

> The process which has been described refers, as has been expressly said, to male children only. How does the corresponding development take place in little girls?
>
> At this point our material—for some incomprehensible reason—becomes far more obscure and full of gaps. The female sex, too, develops an Oedipus complex, a super-ego and a latency period. May we also attribute a phallic organization and a castration complex to it? The answer is in the affirmative; but these things cannot be the same as they are in boys. Here the feminist demand for equal rights for the sexes does not take us far, for the morphological distinction is bound to find expression in differences of psychical development. **'Anatomy is Destiny,' to vary a saying of Napoleon's.** The little girl's clitoris behaves just like a penis to begin with; but, when she makes a comparison with a playfellow of the other sex, she perceives that she has 'come off badly' and she feels this as a wrong done to her and as a ground for inferiority. For a while still she consoles herself with the expectation that later on, when she grows older, she will acquire just as big an appendage as the boy's. Here the masculinity complex of women branches off. A female child, however, does not understand her lack of a penis as being a sex character; she explains it by assuming that at some earlier date she had possessed an equally large organ and had then lost it by castration. She seems not to extend this inference from herself to other, adult females, but, entirely on the lines of the phallic phase, to regard them as possessing large and complete—that is to say, male—genitals. The essential difference thus comes about that the girl accepts castration as an accomplished fact, whereas the boy fears the possibility of its occurrence.
>
> The fear of castration being thus excluded in the little girl, a powerful motive also drops out for the setting-up of a super-ego and for the breaking-off of the infantile genital organization. In her, far more than in the boy, these changes seem to be the result of upbringing and of intimidation from outside which threatens her with a loss of love (*SE* 19: 177–8; my emphasis).

From a feminist perspective, this passage is packed with many of Freud's most dubious ideas. Here we find the image of woman as the dark continent, as an obscure and fragmented site where psychological exploration loses its way, and the belief that women regularly suffer from a 'masculinity complex' just because they do not have a penis. Here too is the conviction that the founding trauma for little girls is the experience of *seeing* the penis of their little brothers or playmates, and that little girls know themselves to be castrated. It is difficult to imagine a more incriminating context for Freud's (in)famous claim about anatomy.

In this paper I cannot discuss the extremely complex subject of what Freud's theory of femininity actually is, and what questions he thinks it answers. What I will show, however, is that whatever the trouble with Freud's understanding of women may be, the source of the problem does not necessarily have anything to do with the phrase 'Anatomy is destiny'. Let me put this more clearly: even if we assume that Freud is wrong about penis envy, and about little girls' reactions to their brother's penis, this doesn't prove that he is wrong to assume that bodily sexual differences will produce psychological differences. He may be mistaken both about what these differences actually are and how they come about, without being wrong in his underlying assumption that as a result of biological and anatomical sexual difference, *some* psychological sexual differences will arise. And none of this means that he will *have* to take a normative view of sexual difference. Even if we think that Freud does end up making normative and normalizing declarations about what a woman should be like (and I shall leave open the question of whether he does or not), this is not a compulsory consequence of the belief that in general, anatomical differences will give rise to psychological or psycho-sexual differences. The two questions I am going to focus on here, then, are fairly narrow: I want to ask whether this general assumption must be unacceptable to feminists, and whether it makes Freud a biological determinist.

It may look as if I am dragging feminism into the argument here. Why not just subsume the question of Freud's compatibility with feminism under that of biological determinism? After all, contemporary feminists detest biological determinism, so if

Freud is a biological determinist, further arguments will be moot. But here I am only following the letter of Freud's text. Let us look once more at the words that lead up to the crucial phrase:

> but these things cannot be the same as they are in boys. Here the feminist demand for equal rights for the sexes does not take us far, for the morphological distinction is bound to find expression in differences of psychical development. 'Anatomy is Destiny,' to vary a saying of Napoleon's (*SE* 19: 177).

What is it that pushes Freud to mention equal rights for the sexes in the very sentence where he sets out a theory of sexual difference? Why does he feel the need ironically to dismiss the 'feminist demand' as irrelevant to his theory? And if he thinks it is irrelevant, why bring the feminist demand into this at all?

I shall consider two possible answers. Perhaps Freud chose to address the issue of feminism because he wanted to fend off accusations of social conservatism. He may have imagined that his theory of sexual difference would be unpopular with women, who would accuse him of being a reactionary anti-feminist. This would have been an uneasy position for Freud, who always encouraged women to train as doctors and analysts, and who was liberal and radical on many social issues, particularly those concerning sexuality and sexual practices. Against such a background, the reference to the feminists' demands may be read as Freud's attempt to stress that his theory has no relevance for feminist politics at all.

On this reading, Freud's sentence ('here the feminist demand for equal rights for the sexes does not take us far') means that the feminist demand has *no bearing* on what Freud has to say about biological and psychological sexual differences. But would the reverse also be true? Would he also gladly concede that claims about biological sexual difference have no bearing on the feminist demand for equal social rights? Feminists could then proceed with their political agitation regardless of what Freud has to say about sexual difference. Compressed and unclear as it is, Freud's reference to feminism could then be read as an attempt to *deny that biological facts ground social norms.* Such a denial is the sine qua non for effective opposition to biological determinism, and it is a position shared by the great majority of feminist theorists today.

But let us consider the alternative. What if Freud does intend to dismiss the feminist demand as impossibly unrealistic? His casual juxtaposition of the feminist demand for equal rights with his own theory of sexual difference certainly makes it look as if the misguided feminists must be denying the obvious. Does Freud think that the 'feminist demand' is based on a fundamental misrecognition? That if only feminists would realize that men and women are not physically identical, they would give up their demands for equality? The major problem with this reading is that it sounds silly. Could Freud really have believed that feminists had not noticed that men have penises and women do not? Or that too much feminism would turn women into men? The term 'equal rights for the sexes' clearly situates the feminist demand on the social level. The German phrase *Gleichberechtigung der Geschlechter* also makes it clear that Freud is speaking of equal *status* or *rights*, and not about bodies.[16] Most likely, Freud was simply trying to be witty. Yet, as he would be the first to acknowledge, it is often in our lame attempts at jokes that we reveal our most important unconscious investments.

Whether Freud was trying to be funny or not, his remark is extraordinarily revealing. What is at stake here, again, is the question of the relationship between a claim about social and political rights and a claim about physiological and psychological differences. As mentioned before, biological determinists believe that biology grounds social norms, and that sooner or later, biological differences will express themselves in the form of social differences. But as soon as we deny that there is a necessary relationship between human biology and social organization, we can cheerfully accept that there are biological differences between men and women without believing that this gives us grounds for organizing society in an unjust and unegalitarian way. This was Simone de Beauvoir's view in *The Second Sex*: 'in truth a society is not a species. . . . Its ways and customs cannot be deduced from biology, for individuals are never abandoned to their nature;

---

[16] 'Die feministische Forderung nach Gleichberechtigung der Geschlechter trägt hier nicht weit, der morphologische Unterschied muß sich in Verschiedenheiten der psychischen Entwicklung aüssern' (*Studienausgabe* 5: 249). I note that Bettelheim's critique of the *SE*'s translation of *Unterschied* as 'distinction' quoted in n. 20, below, also applies here.

rather they obey that second nature which is custom, in which the desires and fears that express their ontological attitude are reflected. . . . To repeat once more: physiology cannot ground any values; rather the facts of biology take on the values that the existent bestows upon them' (*SS* 36; *DSa* 76; TA).

'Here the feminist demand for equal rights does not take us far . . .'. There is a slight but unmistakable animosity in Freud's tone here. The attempted witty aside dissolves into aggression. If we assume for a moment that my most anti-determinist reading of the passage is right, and that Freud is saying that our views on social justice are irrelevant to our understanding of biological sexual differences and, conversely, that biological sexual differences cannot ground our views on how to organize society, he is certainly not a biological determinist. Yet none of this would make him a feminist. Sexists may well be opposed to biological determinism: all they need to do is to claim that the gender ideology they wish to promote is the inevitable result of social construction, or, alternatively, of God's plan for mankind. The animosity in his tone gives me the impression that Freud wishes to castigate the feminists of his day for underestimating the psychological importance of biological sexual differences. He may also believe that the logic of the feminists' arguments lays them open to the accusation that they do want women to be like men. Although we may disagree with such an assessment of feminism in the 1920s, we should realize that this is a critique of 'equality feminism' that remains extremely common in contemporary feminist theory. Few theorists, for example, have been so frequently accused by other feminists of being 'male-identified' and of wanting women to be like men as Simone de Beauvoir, always invoked as the prime example of 'equality feminism'.[17]

I want to explain here why I think it is conceptually confusing and politically misleading to oppose a 'feminism of equality' to a 'feminism of difference', first because it is possible that Freud himself bases his offhand remark about feminism on this very confusion, and because contemporary feminist responses to

---

[17] 'Beauvoir's final message is that sexual difference should be eradicated and women must become like men', Tina Chanter writes in a book devoted to Luce Irigaray (76).

Freud tend to be influenced by this opposition. Usually, 'equality feminism' is defined as a feminism committed to the struggle for social equality between the sexes. Very often, however, the word 'social' is left out of the definition. Thus Luce Irigaray, famous for her psychoanalytically based 'difference feminism', writes that her own feminism 'has gone beyond simply a quest for equality between the sexes' (*Je, tu, nous* 11). Then she goes on to accuse certain unnamed 'equality feminists' of genocide, on the grounds that they want to eradicate sexual difference. On Irigaray's account, then, if 'equality feminists' had their way, they would be responsible for greater crimes against humanity than the Nazis:

> To demand equality as women is, it seems to me, a mistaken expression of a real objective. The demand to be equal presupposes a point of comparison. To whom or to what do women want to be equalized? To men? To a salary? To a public office? To what standard? Why not to themselves?
> . . . Women's exploitation is based upon sexual difference; its solution will come only through sexual difference. Certain modern tendencies, certain feminists of our time, make strident demands for sex to be neutralized. This neutralization, if it were possible, would mean the end of the human species. The human species is divided into *two genders* which ensure its production and reproduction. To wish to get rid of sexual difference is to call for a genocide more radical than any form of destruction there has ever been in History. What is important, on the other hand, is to define the values of belonging to a gender, valid for each of the two genders. It is vital that a culture of the sexual, as yet nonexistent, be elaborated, with each sex being respected (*Je, tu, nous* 12).

Irigaray's wildly exaggerated account brings out the fatal consequences of assuming that there is a real opposition between a feminism of equality and one of difference. She takes for granted that the word equality must either be meaningless ('equal to what?'), or it must mean biological and psychosexual 'neutralization' of both sexes. That people using the word might want a fair and just organization of society so as to ensure that no one sex is unfairly favoured over another, seems to her unthinkable. That such a social organization will have to take biological facts such as female pregnancy into account is obvious. There is no equal right to education, for instance, unless it is equally possible for teenage fathers and teenage mothers to go to school. The right to maternity leave for anyone who is pregnant and gives birth (and so far, this still means women) is unproblematically accepted as part of 'equality feminism' throughout Europe. Only on the most abstract concept of equality would it be possible to think of maternity leave as logically incompatible with the demand for social equality for women.[18]

There is some conceptual confusion here. As Rita Felski has recently reminded us, the opposite of difference is identity (or sameness), and the opposite of equality is inequality (see Felski 15). No concept of social equality that I know of requires the relevant parties to be identical. Yet this thought forms the basis for Luce Irigaray's unbridled polemics against 'equality feminism': against her own vision of a rich culture of sexual difference she posits a childless and sexless culture of identical androgynes. Given her picture one would have to be mad to wish for anything like equality between the sexes. The mythological opposition between a feminism of equality and a feminism of difference is based on an unjustified slippage between different concepts so that equality is taken to mean identity and difference is taken to be an absolute social value rather than a relational term.

Yet, someone is likely to ask, are there not real differences between the kind of feminism espoused by Simone de Beauvoir and that embraced by Luce Irigaray? How do we account for those? There are real differences between the two thinkers, but they are not well explained by positing an opposition between 'equality' and 'difference'. First of all, it is quite absurd to believe, as Luce Irigaray pretends to do, that so-called equality feminists never discovered sexual difference, or that having discovered it, they then spend the rest of their lives wishing that women were men. I don't know any feminists who deny that sexual differences exist, and I doubt that Freud knew any either. Conflicts in femi-

---

[18] Such an abstract concept of equality is quite common in the USA, where the right to maternity leave is still taken by some to constitute 'differential treatment'. One example may be found in the conservative feminist Elisabeth Fox-Genovese's book *Feminism Without Illusions*, where the argument is that 'equality feminists' are guilty of a logical mistake when they demand equal rights *and* the right to maternity leave.

nist theory arise over the origin and value of current sexual differences, not over their existence. The conflict between so-called 'equality' and 'difference' feminists have to do with their different social visions and values, not with their understanding of biological facts. As Simone de Beauvoir teaches us, our politics are justified by our values, and our values are not given in nature. As long as we deny that biology grounds social norms, no genetic or biological discovery will prevent us from founding society on values such as freedom, equality and solidarity, if that is what we wish to do. The difficult question of how concretely to implement such values in a way that upholds rather than undermines them cannot be solved by reference to an abstract principle, be it one of 'difference' or 'equality'.

The real difference between Beauvoir and Irigaray is not that one accepts psychosexual and biological sexual difference and the other does not. Beauvoir refuses to define 'woman' once and for all. In so doing she refuses to engage in what Nancy Bauer has called 'untethered metaphysics' (53). She is also highly critical of efforts to generalize (and thereby reify) any concept of 'femininity'. Since her most fundamental social and individual value is freedom, Beauvoir's feminism should rightly be referred to as a 'feminism of freedom'. Irigaray, on the other hand, does not hesitate to define woman (as the sex which is not one, excluded from the symbolic order by the specular logic of phallogocentric patriarchy) and is quite convinced that it is necessary to found a culture permeated by sexual difference such as she herself theorizes it. For her, 'difference' is a social and individual value, not simply a relational term.[19]

We now have two options: either Freud thinks that the demand for social equality between men and women conflicts with a properly psychoanalytic understanding of sexual difference, or he believes that the two have no direct bearing on each other. If the former is the case, Luce Irigaray would be his true inheritor. If the latter is the case, he might think of bodily sexual difference as something like a situation (I elaborate briefly on this concept

---

[19] The subtitle of *Je, tu, nous*, after all, is *Toward a Culture of Difference*. This book provides some revealing glimpses of Irigaray's concrete social and legal vision.

below), and he would have more in common with Beauvoir than with Irigaray. I am reluctant to settle this question here. Not because I think there is anything wrong with clear answers, but because only a more extensive investigation of Freud's texts about femininity and sexual difference would provide sufficient evidence to resolve the question. Resolving it would mean either coming down on one side or the other, or being able to specify exactly why the question of the relationship between biological sexual difference, psychological sexual difference, and social norms remains deeply ambiguous in Freud's texts.

1924: THE MORPHOLOGICAL DISTINCTION

I shall now turn to the second aspect of the sentence that occupies us here: 'for the morphological distinction is bound to find expression in differences of psychical development. "Anatomy is Destiny," to vary a saying of Napoleon's', Freud writes. The different genital configuration will express itself in psychic differences, he claims. Once the question of what this has to do with equal rights is left aside, both Beauvoir and Irigaray would agree with this view, which in itself is neither particularly new nor particularly controversial in feminist theory. The question is whether Freud believes that certain psychic differences will occur with *necessity* in *all* women and men. Another question is whether he believes that the psychological differences produced by 'morphology' also constitute some kind of *socially normative* femininity. The alternative would be to consider Freud's reference to 'destiny' as an effort to consider the genital and other sexual differences between male and female bodies as a *situation* or a *background* on which further differences may or may not develop. This would be in keeping with his use of the word in the 1912 text.

This view would claim support from the fact that both at the end of this passage, and in the 1925 paper entitled 'Some Psychical Consequences of the Anatomical Distinction between the Sexes', Freud stresses that it is her discovery of the Other, and the gaze of the other on the little girl, that sets in motion the whole process of sexual differentiation that occurs in society.[20] In his 1920 case study on 'The Psychogenesis of a Case of Homosexuality in a Woman', he writes that homosexuality is the outcome of the interaction of many different elements:

The mystery of homosexuality is ... by no means so simple as it is commonly depicted in popular expositions ... It is instead a question of three sets of characteristics, namely—

Physical sexual characters
(physical hermaphroditism)

Mental sexual characters
(masculine or feminine attitude)

Kind of object-choice

which, up to a certain point, vary independently of one another, and are met with in different individuals in manifold permutations (*SE* 18: 170).

Here Freud sounds positively postmodern. Sex and gender (physical and mental sexual characters) may vary relatively independently of one another, and sexual object-choice may vary relatively independently of sex and gender. It is difficult to see how anyone capable of writing this passage could be a biological determinist. On this evidence, it looks, rather, as if Freud thinks of the sexually different body as constantly interacting with its environment, and particularly with other people whose reactions to us are, among other things, determined by our sex (or to be precise, by the sex they think we are). In short, there are good reasons to believe that Freud never thought that biological sexual differences with necessity caused any specific psychosexual result. Freud may be using the word 'destiny' in much the same way in 1924 and in 1912.

In the most famous passage of *The Second Sex*, Simone de

[20] Bruno Bettelheim is unhappy with the English title of this essay. In German the essay is called 'Einige psychische Folgen des anatomischen Geschlechtsunterschieds'. Bettelheim writes: 'Freud discusses the consequences of the anatomical *differences* between the sexes ... but the translators speak instead of a *distinction*. ... *Webster's* discriminates between 'difference' and 'distinction' as follows: 'different, applied to things which are not alike, implies individuality (three *different* doctors) or contrast; distinct, as applied to two or more things, stresses that each has a different identity and is unmistakably separate from the others'. If 'difference' indeed stresses contrast and individuality in what is basically likeness (as the example of three different doctors implies), then it is preferable to 'distinction' in the context of this essay and its title' (97).

Beauvoir says something similar, and she is no biological determinist:

> One is not born, but rather becomes, a woman [*femme*]. No biolog-
> ical, psychological, or economic destiny defines the figure that the
> human female [*la femelle humaine*] acquires in society; it is civiliza-
> tion as a whole that develops this product, intermediate between
> male and eunuch, which one calls feminine [*féminin*]. Only the
> mediation of another [*autrui*] can establish an individual as an
> *Other*. In so far as he exists for himself, the child would not be able
> to understand himself as sexually differentiated. In girls as in boys
> the body is first of all the radiation of a subjectivity, the instrument
> that accomplishes the comprehension of the world: it is through
> the eyes, the hands, and not through the sexual parts that children
> apprehend the universe (*SS* 267; *Dsb* 13; TA).

For Beauvoir, the body is our medium for having a world in the
first place. We perceive the world through the body, and when the
world reacts to our body in a more or less ideologically oppressive
way, we react to the world. Our subjectivity is constituted through
such ongoing, open-ended interaction between ourselves and the
world. We constantly make something of what the world makes of
us. This view considers the body—and not only the sexual different body, but the sick body, the athletic body, the ageing body, the
black body, the white body, and so on—to be of fundamental
importance. It is perhaps the fundamental ingredient in the
make-up of our subjectivity. Yet subjectivity can never be reduced
to some bodily feature or other.

Unlike Freud, Beauvoir explicitly denies that any fate (*destin*)
determines what a woman is to be like. She stresses the similarities between the bodies of little girls and little boys, but she never
denies that sexual differences exist, or that they play a role in society. Otherwise, the newborn female (*la femelle humaine*) would
simply not become a woman (*une femme*). For Beauvoir as for
Freud (and Lacan, whom Beauvoir goes on to quote in the next
few pages), sexual difference is at once produced by anatomical
and biological factors and by the intervention of other people
(the Other), who cannot help but be the bearers of specific social
values.

The major difference between Beauvoir and Freud is not to be
found in their general understanding of the relationship between

the body and subjectivity. They both think it is contingent—that is, not necessary, but not arbitrary either—and they both stress the fundamental role played by others, by the agents of society or 'civilization'. The difference is that Beauvoir is far more aware of the historically relative nature of any given set of social norms than Freud. Although sexual difference will always be with us, Beauvoir sees no reason to assume that the female sexual specificity will always be perceived as more salient, more profound, more far-reaching, more socially significant than male sexual specificity.

Freud, on the contrary, has a tendency to think of male sexuality as fairly easy to investigate, and to cast female sexual difference as an unsolvable mystery, the bedrock on which both the analytic process and psychosexual research eventually founder.[21] Freud's gloomy view of femininity could not be more different from Beauvoir's political optimism, her vision of a world in which there no longer would be any social norms regulating the correct presentations of 'femininity' (or 'masculinity', for that matter). Towards the end of *The Second Sex* Beauvoir writes: 'Once again, in order to explain her limitations it is woman's situation that must be invoked and not a mysterious essence; thus the future remains largely open. . . . The free woman is just being born' (*SS* 714–15; *DSb* 640–1). Freud could not have written this. That sexual difference was taken to be mainly a question of women's difference in Freud's time is beyond dispute. Freud failed to see the historical relativity of this perception. In 1924 as at other times, he is guilty, not of biological determinism, but of a failure of political vision.

Joyce McDougall writes that psychoanalysis is a form of thought

---

[21] In his very late (1937) paper 'Analysis Terminable and Interminable' Freud writes that *the repudiation of femininity* is a biological fact, and the 'bedrock' on which the analytic process founders: 'We often have the impression that with the wish for a penis and the masculine protest we have penetrated through all the psychological strata and have reached bedrock, and that thus our activities are at an end. This is probably true, since, for the psychical field, the biological field does in fact play the part of the underlying bedrock. The repudiation of femininity can be nothing else than a biological fact, a part of the great riddle of sex' (*SE* 23: 252). This is an extremely obscure passage. In what sense is the 'repudiation of femininity' a biological fact? I quote it here simply to show how difficult it is to reach a clear understanding of Freud's theory of femininity.

that attempts to understand the psychological consequences of three universal traumas: the fact that there are Others; the fact of sexual difference; and the fact of death.[22] Freud might have said that it is our destiny to have to find a way to coexist with others, to have to take up a position in relation to sexual difference, and to face death. To say so is not evidence of biological or any other kind of determinism.

[22] McDougall writes: 'The child's discovery of the difference between the sexes is matched in traumatic quality by the earlier discovery of otherness and the later revelation of the inevitability of death. Some individuals never resolve any of these universal traumas, and all of us deny them to some degree in the deeper recesses of our minds—where we are blessedly free to be omnipotent, bisexual, and immortal!' (xv).

PART III

DESIRE AND KNOWLEDGE:
READING TEXTS OF LOVE

Introduction

The three essays in this final part are all concerned with desire
and knowledge. Theoretically, they are closely related to the
essays on Freud's *Dora* (Chapter 6) and on the drive for knowledge (Chapter 7). But these three essays also all focus on texts
that deal with love and other passionate relationships between
men and women. Two of the essays, Chapters 9 and 10, deal with
medieval texts, Andreas Capellanus's *De amore* and Thomas's
Tristan. This work goes back to the year I spent as a Hambro
Fellow at Clare Hall in Cambridge in 1981/2. At the time, I was
very interested in medieval French texts, not because I wanted to
be a medievalist, but because they really struck me as offering
wonderfully original, refreshing, and unusual perspectives on
heterosexual passion and jealousy. During that year, I drafted
early versions of both of these essays. I also translated Angela
Carter's *The Magic Toyshop* into Norwegian, read Kristeva's
Révolution du langage poétique, and wondered whether I would ever
figure out how to write anything interesting on feminist theory.
By the end of the year I had worked out the proposal for what was
to become *Sexual/Textual Politics*. My work on medieval texts could
not have been carried out without advice and help from friends
and colleagues who actually have the expertise in Medieval Latin
and Old French that I sorely lack. I hope they will find themselves
adequately acknowledged in the notes to each essay.

In Chapter 9, 'Desire in Language', which was written in 1985,
I investigate the powerful and fascinating misogyny rooted in an
intense fear of women that we find in Andreas Capellanus's
marvellous 'handbook' in courtly love, the *De amore*. Andreas's
world is full of men trying to produce seductive language to lure
women into bed. At the same time these men are desperately
worried that the woman they think they are seducing may in fact
be trying to catch them out in schemes of her own. The world of
suspicion and desire, passion and distrust conjured up by Andreas
is quite equal to that of Balzac in *La cousine Bette*. Working on the

essay, I particularly warmed to Andreas's fundamental dilemma: the only way a man hell-bent on seducing by language can find out whether the woman is out to take him to the cleaners, according to Andreas, is by talking to her, while knowing full well that a truly treacherous woman will talk a man into believing anything.

Chapter 10, 'She Died Because She Came Too Late' is a reading of Thomas's *Tristan*. Of all the *Tristan* poems, Thomas's is the most psychological, the most analytical, in fact the most Freudian: no wonder that I felt so taken by it. It is a marvellous text, one which stunningly analyses jealousy and treachery, and the longing for an absent lover, and which thinks a great deal about what love does to our knowledge of the other. My argument in this essay is specifically that Thomas's *Tristan* does not show any traces of 'gendering' knowledge. Rather the poem divides knowledge into imaginary and symbolic kinds, both of which are available to both men and women. In this way, this reading is closely connected to my general distrust of theories attempting to stereotype male and female behaviour. The essay was written up in its present form in 1989, the year after I finished 'Patriarchal Thought and the Drive for Knowledge,' and the kinship between the two essays is quite strong.

In the last chapter of the collection, I return to Simone de Beauvoir in order to take a look at one of her last fictional texts, the short story 'The Woman Destroyed'. The chapter was written in 1988, just after I had written 'Patriarchal Thought' and was starting to read Bourdieu with an eye to writing a book on Beauvoir. The question here is what it is about this harrowing chronicle of jealousy, depression, and divorce in a middle-aged woman that made so many readers read it exactly against the grain of Beauvoir's intentions. Beauvoir wanted us to be critical of her heroine Monique, whereas most readers ended up identifying with her. The question of intentions and effects that I raise here presupposes all the theories of the speaking subject that I had worked with by that time, notably Kristeva and Benveniste. I am not quite happy with my tone in this essay. I don't seem to be able to work out whether I think Beauvoir is to blame for not succeeding in making her readers read the text as she wanted them to. Today, I would spend more time discussing the question of what texts can and cannot do to readers. Today I also realize that 'The Woman Destroyed' is in fact a marvellous 'melodrama of the unknown woman', to quote Cavell's subtitle to *Contesting Tears*, and for that reason I would read it differently today, without at all wanting to renege on the reading I collect here, which remains a genuine attempt to take this often slighted short story seriously.

As I was reading through these last essays in the collection, I realized again what a pleasure it is to work on literary texts. The text I have chosen to work on here are about love, passion, jealousy, distrust, scepticism, anguish, fear, and death. There are villains, or suspected villains, heroes and heroines, and good and evil. Or at least the protagonists tend to think so. In short, there is a lot of melodrama here. As I am ending my work on this collection of essays, I find that the essays in this section contain the most genuine pointer to the work I want to do now. After almost five years of writing nothing but theory, it is time to return to literature, not in a way that leaves theory and philosophy behind, but in a way that integrates theory and philosophy with the concretion and the ordinariness of the kind of literature that I care about. As I was thinking about this, I decided to make a start by teaching a graduate course on modernity and the aesthetics of melodrama. The other day, as I finally got the reading list together, I realized that my so-called 'return to literature' (this in itself is a misleading turn of phrase, for I have never stopped teaching literature in undergraduate classes), has produced a course that will be just about equally divided between literature and philosophy. The reading list is also suspiciously full of art history, Ibsen, and Strindberg. I am curious to see what will come of this.

9

Desire in Language:
Andreas Capellanus and the Controversy of Courtly Love
(1985)

> Love is a thing of jealousy and dread.
>
> *Troilus and Criseyde* IV. 235

Composed in France in the 1180s, Andreas's treatise on love, the *De amore*, is celebrated as the first comprehensive discussion of the theory of courtly love.[1] Often hailed as the key to the understanding of a whole range of medieval texts on love from Chrétien de Troyes's *Lancelot* to Chaucer's *Troilus and Criseyde*, the *De amore* is situated at the centre of the modern debate on the nature of courtly love. Indeed, it would seem that much of this debate is little more than a conflict over the 'correct' interpretation of Andreas's text. The first section of this essay, 'Text and History: The Controversy of Courtly Love', relates the different readings of Andreas to the debate over the historical reality of the institution of courtly love in the Middle Ages, showing how this debate raises the wider question of the relations between texts and reality. Focusing on the interlocking structures of desire, knowledge, and rhetoric, the second section, 'Love, Jealousy, and Epistemology in the *De amore*', presents a new, feminist reading of Andreas's essay. Given the importance of the *De amore* for our

---

[1] My quotations are from John Jay Parry's elegant translation *The Art of Courtly Love*. Readers interested in studying the Latin original should consult the bilingual Latin/English edition, edited and translated by P. G. Walsh, entitled *Andreas Capellanus on Love*. I chose Parry's translation in the knowledge that as far as my selected quotations are concerned, there are no important disagreements between Parry and Walsh. All page references to Parry's translation are put in brackets in the text.

understanding of the ideology of courtly love, a rereading of Andreas would naturally lead to the reconsideration of other medieval love-texts as well. Such a project, however, would far exceed the scope of a single paper, and the task of rereading Chrétien or Chaucer will have to be left to others.

TEXT AND HISTORY: THE CONTROVERSY OF COURTLY LOVE

To English-speaking readers, C. S. Lewis's study *The Allegory of Love* is the book which first presented courtly love, defined as an idealization of women in the name of romantic passion, as a fundamental aspect of medieval culture. Inspired by Gaston Paris's original essay on Chrétien's *Lancelot* (*Le Chevalier de la Charrette*), Lewis gives a short and succinct summary of the main features of what he sees as a cult of love:

> Every one has heard of courtly love, and every one knows that it appears quite suddenly at the end of the eleventh century in Languedoc. . . . The sentiment, of course, is love, but love of a highly specialized sort, whose characteristics may be enumerated as Humility, Courtesy, Adultery, and the Religion of Love. The lover is always abject. Obedience to his lady's lightest wish, however whimsical, and silent acquiescence in her rebukes, however unjust, are the only virtues he dares to claim. There is a service of love closely modelled on the service which a feudal vassal owes to his lord. The lover is the lady's 'man'. . . . The poet normally addresses another man's wife, and the situation is so carelessly accepted that he seldom concerns himself much with her husband: his real enemy is the rival (2–3).

Perhaps even more influential than *The Allegory of Love*, Denis de Rougemont's *L'amour et l'occident* (1939: translated in the USA as *Passion and Society* and in the UK as *Love in the Western World*) has shaped Western belief in the existence of unpunished adulterous passion in the Middle Ages. For Rougemont, the 'great European myth of adultery', *Tristan et Yseut*, enacts the courtly code much as described by C. S. Lewis; however, far from sharing Lewis's romanticizing vision of courtly love, Rougemont deplores its idealization of the destructive and narcissistic form of desire which he labels 'Eros'. For Rougemont, only *agape*, or disinterested love in God, can elevate and purify mankind.[2] However, in spite of their otherwise opposing views, Lewis and Rougemont, both writing in the 1930s, shared the belief that 'courtly love' was an actual medieval institution which flourished in the Provence of the troubadours, and then, in the 1170s, came to dominate the love practices of the Court of Champagne, ruled at the time by the Countess Marie and her spouse, Count Henri of Champagne.

It was not until the 1960s that scholars unleashed a veritable campaign against this eroticized vision of medieval life.[3] Thus John F. Benton's minutely researched account of life at the Court of Champagne in the 1170s dealt a considerable blow to the devotees of courtly love. He concluded that there is absolutely no historical evidence that 'courtly' love was practised there at that time, nor that the famous 'courts of love', where beautiful and noble ladies gave judgements on points of erotic etiquette, ever existed ('Court of Champagne'). Later, he also came categorically to reject the value of the term 'courtly love' itself, and in doing so he focused precisely on the problem of reading Andreas's *De amore.*

> I have found the term 'courtly love' no advantage in trying to understand the theory and practice of love in medieval Europe. It is not a medieval technical term. It has no specific content. A reference to 'the rules of courtly love' is almost invariably a citation of Andreas's *De amore,* a work which I think is intentionally and humorously ambiguous about love. The study of love in the Middle Ages would be far easier if we were not impeded by a term which now inevitably confuses the issue (*Clio and Venus* 36–7).

According to Benton, then, some people's misguided ideas about courtly love stem directly from their misreading of Andreas: they have committed the cardinal sin of taking seriously a work which should be seen as no more than light-hearted fun. In other words, the ambiguous status of the concept of courtly love reflects

---

[2] In his *The Mind and Heart of Love,* Martin d'Arcy argues against Rougemont's definitions of Eros and *agape* as entirely separate and opposed concepts.

[3] Henry Ansgar Kelly states that the first full attack on this idealizing view of courtly love was presented as early as 1938 in an unpublished thesis by Donnel van de Voort at Vanderbilt University (see 21).

the ambiguous nature of the *De amore* itself. But how does Benton know that his own reading of Andreas is superior? And how is it that the text of the *De amore* supports such seemingly contradictory interpretations?

The *De amore* consists of three books addressed to a young man called Walter. The first two books instruct Walter in the art of courtly love, and seem at first glance wholly to justify C. S. Lewis's description of its conventions. The third, however, is entitled 'The Repudiation of Love', and contains not only a vehement rejection of secular love, but also reels off a list of the vices of womankind in the misogynist tradition of the Church Fathers. According to Book III, far from ennobling man, as claimed in Books I and II, man's love for woman can only pollute and destroy him. Given this apparent contradiction, it is hardly surprising that critics have presented divergent readings of Andreas's treatise. Most of these readings, however, can be summarized under four main headings:

1. *Andreas defends courtly love.* Books I and II are serious; Book III must be seen as a conventional piece of retraction only meant to save the author, a priest, from getting into trouble with the Church.
2. *Andreas holds that both the Church and the adherents of courtly love are right.* All three books are serious; Andreas is an exponent of the doctrine of 'double truth'.
3. *Andreas defends the Church and condemns courtly love.* Books I and II are ironic; Book III is serious and contains Andreas's real opinion.
4. *All three books are ironic.* Andreas has provided an entertaining, but not necessarily subversive, pastiche of scholasticism and courtly love alike.

The most famous representatives of Reading 1 are, as already mentioned, C. S. Lewis and Denis de Rougemont. Reading 2 can be found in A. J. Denomy's *The Heresy of Courtly Love.* Denomy argues that Andreas held the so-called doctrine of 'double truth', which implied that 'what Andreas teaches to be true according to nature and reason, he teaches to be false according to grace and divine authority' (39). In other words, Andreas believed that according to reason and nature, secular love is the source of all virtue, but also that according to revelation the highest good originates in God; revelation, moreover, always takes precedence over the insights provided by reason. For Denomy there is therefore no doubt that Andreas ultimately was a good Christian.[4]

The major exponent of Reading 3 is D. W. Robertson who, in his *A Preface to Chaucer*, reveals himself as a formidable opponent of courtly love. His thesis is that the 'discouragement of the pursuit of love is . . . something that runs through the whole work [*De Amore*], not something confined to the last book' (*Preface* 395). Stressing Andreas's equation of love with fear and jealousy in the first two books, Robertson argues that Book III only makes explicit the implications of the first two. As a whole, then, the *De amore* should show that the 'fear and jealousy of love constitute a miserable servitude' (447). He thus sees Andreas's treatise as a coherent attack on profane love, made in order to advocate St Augustine's doctrine of charity as the only ennobling form of love; a doctrine which also constitutes the true meaning of works as different as Chrétien de Troyes's *Lancelot* (*Le Chevalier de la Charrette*), *Tristan et Yseut*, and Chaucer's *Troilus and Criseyde*. Argued in relation to Andreas, the case may seem plausible enough. Repeated in relation to a whole series of medieval works, Robertson's plea for Augustinian theology sounds rather less convincing. Thus other critics have seriously questioned Robertson's readings. E. Talbot Donaldson, for instance, argues that Andreas cannot by any stretch of the imagination be turned into a devotee of St Augustine's:

> I do not agree with Robertson's oft-stated premise that any serious work written in the Middle Ages that does not overtly promote St Augustine's doctrine of charity will be found, on close examination, to be doing so allegorically or ironically, nor do I agree that Andreas can be made to read as a good disciple of St Augustine. Yet I agree with Robertson that Andreas is not to be understood as seriously promulgating immoral doctrine (159–60).

According to Donaldson, Andreas has 'merely adopted Ovid's theme of adulterous love and medievalized it by subjecting it to

---

[4] Denomy's reading is heavily dependent on a late dating of the *De amore*. The doctrine of 'double truth' was not widely known until the Latin translation of Averroes appeared in 1179. If the *De amore*, as Denomy argues, was composed in the 1170s, the 'double truth' claim becomes dubious. In 'André le Chaplain', Peter Dronke points out this inconsistency, but has also argued that Andreas's treatise could have been written at any time between 1174 and 1238.

scholastic analysis and by infusing it with that spiritualization of the erotic that the troubadours show' (160). Andreas simply wanted to be outrageous, Donaldson claims, and therefore also grossly exaggerated the anti-eroticism and anti-feminism of Book III: Book III, in other words, is as ironic as Books I and II (Reading 4).[5]

When it comes to the question of the historical reality of courtly love, the different readers of Andreas split neatly down the middle: critics adopting Readings 1 or 2 (that Andreas in some way can be said to be positive about the practice of courtly love) believe that courtly love was a real, historical practice, whereas critics who adopt Readings 3 or 4 (that Andreas condemns courtly love in some way) believe equally firmly that it was not. Thus Donaldson holds that 'at least a part of what is called courtly love was no more real in the Middle Ages than it had been before and has been since' (163). And Robertson, like Benton, rejects the concept entirely:

> The study of courtly love, if it belongs anywhere, should be conducted only as the subject is an aspect of nineteenth- and twentieth-century cultural history. The subject has nothing to do with the Middle Ages, and its use as a governing concept can only be an impediment to our understanding of medieval texts ('Concept' 17).

Robertson is, of course, quite right in stressing the historically determined nature of this kind of research: if 'courtly love' became a focal point of interest first in the 1930s and then again in the 1960s, this is surely not unrelated to the fact that these two decades witnessed a crisis of conventional sexual ideology and values. Similarly, my own interest in Andreas and courtly love is inspired by contemporary feminist debate on love and sexuality. The point is, surely, that there is nothing particularly unusual about this: to a careful observer all research will bear the mark of its own historical situation. But if Robertson's point can be shown

---

5 Donald R. Howard shares Donaldson's view. In his *The Three Temptations: Medieval Man In Search of the World,* he writes about the *De amore:* 'I should be inclined to . . . say that while the first two books are ironic and game-like, the last is no less so' (96). Jean Leclercq's *Monks and Love In Twelfth-Century France* takes a similar view.

to be generally true, it loses its force as a specific argument against certain readings of Andreas. The question of the historical reality of courtly practices cannot, in other words, be decided as easily as Robertson seems to believe, nor can it, *pace* Benton, be decided simply through empirical research of the Court of Champagne in the twelfth century. For Benton has taken for granted that the relationship between text and history is static and one-sided: his painstaking work is based on the implicit assumption that texts (in this case Andreas's treatise) are no more than reflections of a given reality.

Since the 1960s this kind of naive reflectionism has come in for an increasing amount of criticism, particularly from Marxist theorists (for further discussion of this problem, see Macherey; Eagleton, *Criticism and Ideology*; Jameson, *Political Unconscious*), and it is now quite possible to argue that Benton's efforts do not really tell us very much at all about the meaning of Andreas's text. But before we return to this point it may be useful to take a closer look at the function of courtly ideology in France, since this will provide us with a concrete example of the difficulty of arguing, as Benton does, a simple reflectionist case about the relations between the literary text and society.

The function of chivalry and courtliness seems to have been to provide the ruling feudal aristocracy with a legitimizing ideology. According to Marc Bloch, the twelfth century witnessed the apotheosis of feudal power in France, a power as yet unthreatened by the bourgeoisie. This stabilization of power produced a culture designed to display aristocratic superiority; the codes of courtly and chivalric behaviour seem selected precisely by virtue of their inaccessibility to the lower classes. The fundamental requirements for any exercise of courtliness were leisure and money: the time and resources necessary to woo the fair lady according to the courtly canon would only have been available to an aristocratic minority. The stress put on cleanliness (frequent use of baths, perfumed oils, etc.) as well as the need to wear beautiful and well-kept clothes also made it impossible for poor and working people to be courtly, had they wanted to be. The necessity of being generous on a large scale (giving banquets, holding tournaments, giving away precious objects) made *courtoisie* the exclusive domain of the rich; the whole chivalric code (the knight proving his worth and his love for the lady by his prowess in armed combat) would seem to be tailor-made for the feudal nobility who perceived themselves as a warrior class. Although the insistence on culture as a necessary part of the accomplishments of the courtly hero and lover (he had to be able to compose and recite poems and songs, write letters to the lady, and read suitable books with her) gave some scope for the special talents of the clergy, it also catered specifically for the other reading and writing class at the time: the aristocracy. In this context it is interesting to note that Andreas takes great care to define all clergy as belonging to the highest class of all on the grounds of their noble occupation (see 36). As far as class is concerned, this code is almost watertight: a wealthy and educated bourgeois man might have fulfilled all these requirements only to fall foul of the demand for knightly deeds. The weak link in the chain is the bourgeois woman: since a lady was not supposed to fight in heroic battle, nothing would prevent a rich and graceful *bourgeoise* from winning the favours of a man of the highest nobility. Andreas neatly solves this problem by making his two bourgeois ladies stalwart defenders of the status quo: refusing all hope of their love to their noble suitors, their discourse eloquently demonstrates the dangers of upsetting the social order, thus obligingly helping Andreas to fend off his obvious anxiety about the potentially subversive nature of passion.

In addition to its evident appeal to aristocratic exclusivity, the code of courtly love and chivalry also mobilizes a more subtle interpretation of the categories of nature and culture in order to produce its ideological impact. Fundamentally unnatural, courtly love emphasizes the cultural and spiritual values of love. Love ennobles the (male) lover, Andreas claims, it refines and reforms him through the influence of the beloved lady, presumably already a fairly ethereal being herself. Dante's Beatrice is only the most sublime in a series of spiritualized ladies in courtly literature. In Andreas's text, as in the *Chevalier de la Charrette*, the spiritualizing power of love nevertheless remains at odds with its crudely physical manifestations. Andreas seems to be uneasily aware that there is something illogical about a spiritual desire for the good and virtuous which in the end posits the same tediously physical act as the lover's highest bliss. He thus goes to great lengths to imply that there is a difference between courtly love, even if this is of a 'mixed' (i.e. sexual) kind, and straightforward, 'natural' sex: 'We say that it rarely happens that we find farmers serving in Love's court', Andreas writes, 'but naturally, like a horse or a mule, they give themselves up to the work of Venus, as nature's urgings teaches them to do' (149). Natural desire has nothing, or very little, to do with love in the courtly sense, at least according to Andreas's commentary at this stage. This, incidentally, leads him to conclude that a courtly lover (clearly not a farmer) ought simply to rape peasant women at will:

> If you should, by some chance, fall in love with some of their [peasants'] women, be careful to puff them up with lots of praise and then, when you find a convenient place, do not hesitate to take what you seek and to embrace them by force. For you can hardly soften their outward inflexibility so far that they will grant you their embraces quietly or permit you to have the solaces you desire unless first you use a little compulsion as a convenient cure for their shyness (150).

Though there is some ambiguity in Andreas's use of the word love in this passage, it would seem that the message is clear: peasants are natural creatures and must be treated as such. Intercourse with peasant women can neither refine nor ennoble the courtly lover; in fact, Andreas advises Walter to restrain his dealings with them to the utmost, presumably because such *natural* relations could seriously undermine his claim to possess a sophisticated, cultured courtliness.

This aversion to the natural life of peasants reveals the real function of courtly ideology. If, as Bloch has argued, courtly ideology can be seen as an effort to impose the more refined habits of the aristocratic ladies on the boorish feudal lords, the cultured noble lady becomes the arbiter of taste in courtly society; no wonder then that peasant women were considered their absolute antithesis. The whole point of the various courtly and chivalric exercises described in Andreas's and Chrétien's texts was to escape all comparison with villains. Signalling their cultural superiority, the 'effeminization' of the aristocracy paradoxically enough comes to signify their 'natural' right to power. It is precisely in its insistence on the 'natural' differences between rulers and ruled that courtly ideology achieved its legitimizing function, a function which operates long after the feudal aristocracy has lost its central position in society.

In his influential study of the fourteenth and fifteenth centuries, *The Waning of the Middle Ages*, J. Huizinga emphasizes the lasting influence of courtly and chivalric codes of behaviour on the aristocracy: 'Long after nobility and feudalism had ceased to be really essential factors in the state and in society', Huizinga writes, 'they continued to impress the mind as the dominant form of life' (54). This society was obsessed with courtly love:

> In no other epoch did the ideal of civilization amalgamate to such a degree with that of love. Just as scholasticism represents the grand effort of the medieval spirit to unite all philosophic thought in a single centre, so the theory of courtly love, in a less elevated sphere, tends to embrace all that appertains to the noble life (105).

In this period the courtly texts seem to precede reality, not vice versa: the courts of love which Benton could not find in the twelfth century are enacted now as an imitation of the courtly ideals of Andreas's and Chrétien's time by an aristocracy whose 'whole system of ideas was permeated by the fiction that chivalry ruled the world,' as Huizinga puts it (65).

At this point it is tempting to argue, *pace* Benton and Robertson, that *no* reading of the *De amore* (or any other courtly text) will tell us anything at all about 'reality' in the twelfth century. But this case is not altogether convincing. If, after our study of courtly ideology in the Middle Ages, we feel obliged to drop the idea that literature should be no more than a pale reflection of reality, we might want to consider the view that texts produce a reality of their own. But it does not follow that this textual reality is entirely cut off from its own historical moment of production. Rejecting the fashionable view that history is just another text and therefore cannot constitute a 'ground' of truth for other texts, Fredric Jameson suggests that 'history is not so much a text, as rather a text-to-be-(re)constructed. Better still, it is an obligation to do so, whose means and techniques are themselves historically irreversible, so that we are not at liberty to construct any historical narrative at all' ('Imaginary and Symbolic' 388). For Jameson, history is the Real in the Lacanian sense, that is to say, 'that which resists symbolization'. The Real is only available to us through language, and language can never coincide with reality; the text stands in an asymptotic relationship to history.

One of the reasons why it is extremely difficult to say just where on the asymptote a particular text is situated is that all texts, among other things, are manifestations of ideology. Ideology, of course, represents social relations, but nothing guarantees the veracity of the ideological representation: it may very well be mistaken about the real nature of its own society. In this sense, it is the very nature of the text's mistakes and omissions which most tellingly reveals its ideological preoccupations (for a full discussion of this view, see Macherey). It is thus paradoxically only through the study of the text's 'misrepresentation' of reality that we can seize its ideological dimension as that 'indispensable mapping fantasy or narrative by which the individual subject invents a "lived" relationship with collective systems', as Jameson puts it.[6] In this way we can construct the text as a map of its own ideological and psychological investments, its fears, hopes, and desires. The fact that the map never coincides with the terrain does not mean that there never was a terrain at all.

LOVE, JEALOUSY, AND EPISTEMOLOGY IN THE *DE AMORE*

In his admirable study of Proust, Leo Bersani claims that the hopelessly jealous and insecure love of a Swann or a Marcel has little in common with the nobler forms of passion represented in courtly literature:

> In the medieval courtly epics and lyrics, for example, as well as in Corneille, Rousseau and Claudel, love includes moral admiration; the lover's personality is ennobled by his passion for someone worthy of being loved. Love thus realizes and intensifies a profound harmony between the self and the world: the lover *knows*

---

[6] This formulation appears in the *Yale French Studies* version of Jameson's 'Imaginary and Symbolic' (394).

the object of his love, and his responses are governed by moral qualities he rightly perceives (98–9).

One of the purposes of this essay is to show that, at least as far as the *De amore* is concerned, such an idyllic vision of medieval passions is simply mistaken. Already in the introductory passages (chapters 1–5 of Book I) where Andreas sets out, in his best scholastic manner, to define his topic, love is the object of considerable ambivalence and hesitation:

> Love is a certain inborn suffering derived from the sight of and excessive meditation upon the beauty of the opposite sex, which causes each one to wish above all things the embraces of the other and by common desire to carry out all of love's precepts in the other's embrace (28).

Here *suffering* is presented as the essence of love: unfulfilled sexual desire never ceases to torment the (male) lover. This suffering, moreover, is 'inborn', or in other words, *natural*. In this way Andreas's treatise can be read as an effort to conceal or displace the painful naturalness of love by dressing it up in the necessary courtly trappings. This process is, however, never entirely successful: the 'inborn' suffering never disappears; love for Andreas, like desire for Freud or Lacan, is doomed to remain unsatisfied.

The sexual frustration suffered by the lover is aggravated by his constant anxiety: in one paragraph the word 'fear' occurs no less than eleven times. Or as Andreas himself puts it: 'To tell the truth, no one can number the fears of one single lover' (28). The lover's main fear is that his chosen lady will reject him, either because of rumours about their illicit love, or because she finds him insufficient or unworthy in character, behaviour or social status. There is no 'safe' position here: if the lover is poor, he fears that the lady will scorn his poverty; if he is rich, he trembles that she may despise his past parsimony. By far the greatest threat to the lover's project of conquering the lady's favours, however, is posed by his rivals: constantly agonizing in his neurotic fear of being rejected for another suitor, the lover is driven to despair by extreme jealousy.

It is always the lady who is invested with the power to make judgements of a social nature: *her* desire seems either to be non-existent or entirely cultural, inextricably caught up, as it must be, in a series of mundane considerations of wealth and social prestige. Perhaps it is from her very unnaturalness, the fact that she incarnates the cultural standards of her society, that she derives the power to ennoble and civilize her lustful lover. 'Every attempt of a lover tends towards the enjoyment of the embraces of her whom he loves', Andreas writes, 'he thinks about it continually, for he hopes that with her he may fulfill all the mandates of love . . . in the sight of a lover nothing can be compared to the act of love' (30). It is strange that this very basic drive for sexual satisfaction should have such ennobling consequences: 'O what a wonderful thing is love', enthuses Andreas, 'which makes a man shine with so many virtues and teaches everyone, no matter who he is, so many good traits of character!' (31). The paradox is that if the lover were to become as refined as his lady, he might lose the very natural desire which led him to seek her 'solaces' in the first place.

Andreas extends his definition of love by providing it with an etymological origin, apparently derived from Isidore of Seville's (false) etymology for the word *amicus*, friend:

> Love gets its name (*amor*) from the word for hook (*amus*), which means 'to capture' or 'to be captured', for he who is in love is captured in the chains of desire and wishes to capture someone else with his hook. Just as a skillful fisherman tries to attract fishes by his bait and to capture them on his crooked hook, so the man who is a captive of love tries to attract another person by his allurements and exerts all his efforts to unite two different hearts with an intangible bond, or if they are already united he tries to keep them so forever (31).

The lover here is both beast and prey; a slave bound by the chains of desire, he is at the same time a skilful fisherman trying to trick the lady into swallowing his bait. The ambiguity of the image of the lover as simultaneously fish, bait, and fisherman signals the same hesitations as in Andreas's uneasy definition of love as an inborn suffering which relentlessly forces men to seek bliss. No wonder, perhaps, that the lover's 'crooked hook' seems curiously unsuited to the delicate task of creating an 'intangible bond' between two hearts.

In spite of his expressions of admiration for the ennobling force of love, Andreas finishes off this introductory section by warning Walter that 'love, at times, does not use fair weights' (32). In fact, Andreas believes that desire is both deceitful and untrustworthy: 'Because [love] is in the habit of carrying an unjust weight in his hand, I do not have full confidence in him any more than I do in a judge whom men suspect' (32). Living then as he does in a universe filled with jealousy, fear, and deceit, Andreas's lover apparently has little choice. Since love's sufferings are inborn, he cannot escape the yoke of desire; his only option is to make the best of a bad job. Andreas therefore reluctantly agrees to instruct Walter in the art of courtly love since, as he puts it in his prefatory note, 'I know clearer than day that after you have learned the art of love your progress in it will be more cautious' (27). On the surface then, Andreas presents the *De amore* more as an emergency kit for wounded (male) lovers than as an introduction to the delights of love.

After this introduction to love, Andreas gets down to his main task, which is to teach Walter 'in what manner love may be acquired, and in how many ways' (33), and launches into eight sample dialogues organized according to the participants' class background ('A man of the middle class speaks with a woman of the same class'; 'A man of the higher nobility speaks with a woman of the simple nobility', etc.). These dialogues are, not surprisingly, obsessed with class, and particularly with the threat that desire poses to stable social structures. And, as in the introductory sections, it is the man who is tempted towards subversive action by his unruly passions, whereas the woman defends the social status quo.

The dialogues of Book I alone take up over half of Andreas's treatise, and constitute the bulk of the two books dealing with the art of love, whereas the rejection of love (Book III) apparently requires no such linguistic patterns. In fact, language is so prominent in Andreas's model of courtship that the reader, like the lady, occasionally feels submerged by the endless flow of the lover's discourse. For it is the lover who does most of the talking: the lady, although obviously capable of a quick repartee, limits her remarks to shrewd criticism of the lover's points, and hardly ever instigates a new topic of her own. The lover's lust makes him speak, and when he does so his style is rational in the extreme: every single one of Andreas's lovers attempts to *prove* to the woman that she ought to love him. However discouraging her response, the lover is prepared to go on talking until dismissed by her. It is as if this veritable deluge of passionate, scholastic argumentation could go on for ever: the lover's eloquence seems to give him pleasure for its own sake. And it is, of course, true that by the very act of speaking the lover has already achieved an important courtly aim, the elegant use of language being precisely one of the distinctions which set the upper classes apart from the common crowd. A courtly lover cannot speak like a country yokel; the lover's untiringly intellectual discourse validates his claim to *be* a lover in the first place. In spite of appearances then, desire does not necessarily precede language in Andreas's text; on the contrary, if the man's linguistic performance establishes him *as* a lover, his desire is produced *by* language and seeks its satisfaction *in* it. (It is, for instance, remarkable how little sexual success the lovers in these dialogues have in proportion to their verbal efforts: the prowess is linguistic, not erotic.)

The language which thus constitutes the lover's passion is curiously aggressive. His pleasure lies in his *mastery* of language, obtained through his neurotic ordering and scholastic subdivision of his discourse. In this sense, of course, the dramatized lovers in Andreas's dialogues give but a shadow of Andreas's own performance in the *De amore* as a whole. The lover is in love with his own eloquent lucidity: by dominating the word, he gains a phallic power that contradicts his seemingly humble stance towards his lady. This mastery is only achieved, however, by the most humble submission to the inflexible rules of scholastic rhetoric. Chained and fettered, the lover's discourse enacts his own lack of freedom, which is bearable only because it procures him at the same time the satisfaction of a certain sadistic dominance. As in Andreas's etymology of love, the lover is both master of and slave to his own discourse of desire. The effect of his aggressive verbal onslaught is that the lady in these dialogues, in spite of her vigorous replies to the lover, remains a curiously cold, distant, and enigmatic creature whose love is perceived as a capricious and unreliable entity precisely because we, as well as the lover, suspect her of having no passion at all, deprived as she is of a discursive initiative of her own.

It is perhaps for this reason that Andreas's lovers often recur to scarcely veiled threats in order to make her succumb. In the fifth dialogue the lover launches into an elaborate allegory which is supposed to prove that women who refuse to take lovers suffer horrible torments after death. The courtly lover's strategy is thus one of intimidation and verbal sadism: his language enacts his aggression (which becomes all the more menacing precisely because of its dependence on an abject surrender to the rules of discourse), and the fact that the courtly lady, unlike the peasant woman, escapes outright rape ought not to be interpreted as conclusive evidence of his respect for her.[7] In the end, the lover is not interested in the woman; his narcissistic self-display centres on his own desire, his own discursive performance.

The *De amore* does, of course, also present language as the 'hook of love' which allows the lover to attract the lady by his 'allurements' in order to create an 'intangible bond' between their hearts. There is in Andreas's treatise a deep desire for a trusting union with the other, a union which, if successful, would infinitely improve the man's character and behaviour. But as the original image of the 'hook of love' is double-edged (to be caught on the fisherman's hook is a painful and ultimately deadly business), the intermittently expressed desire for full knowledge of the partner is undercut by a whole series of rhetorical and thematic moves which indicate that true love, the blissful union of two different hearts, is an unrealizable fantasy. It is the misfortune of (male) lovers that they have to spend their lives in pursuit of such a chimera.

The fundamental scepticism of Andreas's vision emerges in his

---

[7] Andrée Kahn Blumstein, in her study of German courtly romances in the 12th and 13th cents., has also criticized the implicit patriarchal assumptions of the courtly code: ' "The courtly code" of love and most especially the idealization of women in the romance are in many respects a *covert* form of misogyny; chivalry is but one more method by which what has been called the "great patriarchal conspiracy" is perpetrated and perpetuated in our culture' (2).

treatment of jealousy. For Andreas, jealousy is the 'mother and nurse of love' (101). True jealousy, not to be confused with the possessive tyranny of a husband, consists of a triple fear:

> Now jealousy is a true emotion whereby we greatly fear that the substance of our love may be weakened by some defect in serving the desires of our beloved, and it is an anxiety lest our love may not be returned, and it is a suspicion of the beloved, but without any shameful thought (102).

In this passage we recognize the endless fears of the lover described as an essential part of love at the very outset of Andreas's treatise. The puzzling part of this passage is the reference to jealousy as an *unshameful* suspicion of the beloved. *Shameful* suspicion, according to Andreas, is that nourished by possessive husbands only interested in protecting their own dynastic interests.[8] The lover's jealous suspicion seems entirely different: perhaps it is not shameful simply because it is an integral part of love. 'He who is not jealous cannot love', Andreas comments (107). From the context, it seems clear that his jealousy is a form of fear, a generalized worry about the lady's activities and thoughts, clearly not limited (as in the case of the husband) to straightforward sexual jealousy (it is not 'shameful'). His jealousy, then, seems caused by the feeling that the lady remains *other*: however hard he tries to master her by his discourse, he will always suffer in the knowledge that her consciousness is not his. In this respect, Andreas is no different from a Marcel or a Swann. As with the Proustian lover, the beloved becomes enigmatic precisely in so far as the lover

---

[8] In an illuminating article, Erich Köhler compares the attitude towards jealousy in troubadour lyrics with Andreas's views, and shows that the seemingly opposed ideas in the two kinds of text really cover the same jealous mechanisms. According to Köhler, the *troubadours* are not particularly jealous of the husband, since he represents an established attitude towards property and social class, which they as an upwardly mobile group (the *chevalerie*) despise. Their jealousy is directed towards the whole of their peer group, all of whom are seeking social promotion through the favours of the lady. This generalized, competitive form of jealousy is then often projected onto one figure, representative of the whole group, the much-despised *lauzengier*, the *slanderer* or *flatterer*, who by divulging the secret of the poet's love destroys all possibility of exclusive communication between him and the lady.

perceives her as a secretive space which at all costs must be penetrated.

Desire, in the *De amore*, is not only a discursive enterprise but a hermeneutical challenge. The lover's happiness depends on his ability to decipher the lady's words and uncover their hidden meaning. This is surely why Andreas insists on the dialogue form: the lover is in desperate need of an introduction to the art of rhetoric which might make him a more proficient hermeneuticist, a better reader of the lady's text. But in this case it is *love* (desire) itself which requires the lover to become an expert reader. The necessity of deciphering the beloved's discourse would of course not be particularly painful if the lover could be reasonably sure of reaching the correct interpretation. If the torments of jealousy constitute, as Andreas claims, the 'very substance of love' (101), it is because they reveal the most unspeakable secret of all: that the lover *never* knows whether he has hit upon the true reading. For the jealous lover, the world is transformed into a treacherous text full of traps; since every utterance, every event, is susceptible to different, often contradictory readings, he must suspect every single word or phrase. There is no refuge from this vertiginous multiplicity of meanings; the jealous lover must live in a universe deprived of a firm ground upon which truth can rest. His raging desire for knowledge ('epistemophilia', as Freud would call it; Othello's need for the 'ocular proof') is pathetic and painful precisely because this desire can never be satisfied. The paradox is that it is the nature of jealousy itself which ensures that the jealous lover (and for Andreas all lovers are jealous) will never find a transcendental signified, a point at which his interpretations can come to rest.[9]

If we are to believe Andreas's claim that 'jealousy is the

---

[9] A modern psychiatrist has described the same phenomenon in cases of pathological jealousy: 'The desire to obtain proof of the offence is often overwhelmingly strong; it appears to be related to a need to resolve a tormenting doubt which in some cases leads to repeated attempts to extort a confession from the partner. Such patients declare this to be the only satisfaction that they demand, but the irrational nature of their request is strikingly demonstrated by the futility of the confession which is occasionally feigned by a blameless but desperate spouse' (Shepherd 690).

substance of love', this epistemophiliac drive also constitutes the essential movement of desire. The lover's need for union with the beloved represents a need for absolute insight into the innermost recesses of her mind, but her very otherness, the fact that her consciousness is not his, means that she will always escape his hermeneutical probing. The logic of his desire may thus lead him to conclude that the best way of preventing her consciousness from escaping him yet again is simply by annihilating it: however counterproductive, Othello's murder of Desdemona at least put an end to his anxiety about her behaviour. The endless fears of the jealous lover are thus accompanied by the temptation to put an end to it all by an act of sadistic violence.

Andreas's treatise is not only candidly open about the lover's jealous dilemma; it also focuses on the problem of the amorous language in this context. The problem, as Andreas sees it, is how the man can interpret the woman's words correctly (in keeping with his insistence on male lust and female impassivity, the man is of course always the reader, the woman the text to be read).

A particularly graphic example of this can be found towards the end of Book I, in the chapter entitled 'Love Got with Money'. Here Andreas discusses the dangers of dealing with women who only pretend to be in love in order to 'draw money' out of the lover. These women conceal their desire for money behind a mask of love, and Andreas mobilizes his most aggressive language in his description of their deceit: 'A woman who you know desires money in return for her love should be looked upon as a deadly enemy, and you should be careful to avoid her like a venomous animal that strikes with its tail and fawns with its mouth' (145). In an extraordinarily violent—and extraordinarily contradictory—passage, Andreas seeks to persuade both himself and Walter that if the lover were only to act early enough he might just manage to capture the sordid truth behind the lady's loving appearance:

> Therefore, my friend, you should always follow this maxim: when-
> ever you have reason to believe that a woman is interested in piling
> up the coin, be careful to avoid her in the very beginning and not
> to involve yourself at all in her snares. For if you try to fall in with
> what she says in order to find out what her real intention is, you

will find yourself foiled by your own plan, because no amount of searching will reveal how she feels and what she means to do until the leech is full of blood and leaves you only half alive with all the blood of your wealth drained off. A wise man's best efforts can hardly find out what is beneath the guile of a deceitful lady-love, for she knows how to color her frauds by so many arts and with so much cleverness that the faithful lover is rarely clever enough to see through them. The ability of a greedy woman is greater than that of the Ancient Enemy was when by his shrewdness he cleverly perverted the mind of our first parent. Therefore you should use all your cleverness to see that you are not tripped up by the snares of such a woman, because a woman of that kind does not want to love, but to revel in your wealth (147).

The grisly imagery of the woman as a venomous animal (a scorpion?), a bloodsucking leech, as more cunning than the devil, is, if anything, even more sadistic than the openly misogynist passages of Book III. The difference is that here Andreas claims that 'We do not say these things with the desire of running down honorable women' (147), whereas in Book III he allows no such distinction between good and bad women: '*no* woman ever loved a man' (200) he asserts, '*no* woman ever has enough money' (201), and so on. In Book III there are no exceptions from the rule:

> Furthermore, not only is every woman by nature a miser, but she is also envious and a slanderer of other women, greedy, a slave to her belly, inconstant, fickle in her speech, disobedient and impatient of restraint, spotted with the sin of pride and desirous of vainglory, a liar, a drunkard, a babbler, no keeper of secrets, too much given to wantonness, prone to every evil, and never loving any man in her heart (201).

The bloodsucking leech never ceases to 'drain away' her unsuspecting lover's property, an action which leaves him without any 'substance' (144). But this 'substance' is clearly more than just property: 'there is nothing so contemptible as for a man to waste his substance on the work of the flesh and the solace of Venus' (147), Andreas claims. This substance/semen also appears disguised as the man's lifeblood: 'no amount of searching will reveal how she feels and what she means to do until the leech is full of blood and leaves you only half alive with all the blood of your wealth drained off' (147). When the greedy and deceitful female vampire is done she will leave the man drained of all substance/semen/property/blood.[10]

But is Andreas's distinction between deceitful and honourable women really tenable? If we return to the passage quoted above, it is easy to see that the text is caught here in a particularly unpleasant paradox. If it is true that the greedy woman's cunning pretence of love is so convincing that even a 'wise man's best efforts' cannot find the truth located 'beneath the guile of a deceitful lady-love', the lover clearly has a problem. The deceitful woman's duplicity is even greater than the devil's, and so it follows that no amount of conversation will uncover the unpalatable truth. Andreas's only advice to Walter is therefore to avoid such women altogether. But this is far too easy a way out. If the deceitful woman's language is indistinguishable from an honest woman's, the lover will never know whether he is listening to truth or deceit. He thus finds himself caught in exactly the same trap as the jealous lover: they are both in a situation where no amount of subtle interpretation will reveal the lady's true intention. Jealousy is indeed the essence of love; and Andreas's advice to Walter really amounts to saying that he ought to avoid *all* women, given the impossibility of distinguishing between them.

Andreas conveniently represses the fact that he has unmasked a problem of general linguistic and epistemological importance (how can language convey truth?), and blames it all on the deviousness of women instead. If the deceit of language only presents us with appearances, the distinction between good and evil women necessarily collapses, and Andreas's Book III logically enough explicitly recommends a total rejection of all women. The fact that by his own analysis men's language would be equally devious and impossible to pin down to an essential truth apparently does not occur to him. Irksome as this may be to feminists,

---

[10] Several authors have discussed the psychological structures of courtly love from a psychoanalytical perspective. Richard A. Koenigsberg reads the *De amore* as a straightforward case of Oedipal desire for a mother figure; whereas Herbert Moller, in a thoughtful article, explains the love-lyrics of the troubadours as a case of infantile desire for the pre-Oedipal mother. Melvin Askew's 'Courtly Love: Neurosis as Institution' is a more superficial approach to the topic.

it is interesting to observe that in the modern debate over the 'true' meaning of the *De amore*, the critics accurately enact the problematics of the text: like hermeneutically distraught lovers, they untiringly try to decipher the sibylline utterances of the lady, who now, in a final twist of the plot, turns out to be Andreas himself.[11] There is much consolation for feminists in the thought that in the end the old misogynist has been forced to play the female lead himself.

If desire is constituted by and conducted in language, the lover is helplessly thrown from one set of deceitful appearances to another. Andreas's final solution is again rigorously logical: reject earthly love altogether and turn to God, who is Alpha and Omega, the beginning and the end, the only self-sufficient cause in the universe; in short, the transcendental signifier and signified par excellence. In the end, then, the courtly lover's constant search for the essence beneath the multiple, treacherous appearances of language is resolved: God for Andreas, like death for Lacan, is the only instance which can put a final end to the discourse of desire.

[11] My reading, then, doesn't fit any of the four kinds of reading listed above (403). I find that in all three parts of the text Andreas's view of women and of love is marked by suspicion, hostility, and fear. In this respect, Andreas's views are consistent with those of other churchmen at the time, and my reading would seem to come close to Reading 3, the one espoused by D. W. Robertson in *A Preface to Chaucer*, yet I do not find any evidence of a transcendent commitment to Augustinian charity anywhere in Andreas's account of women and love. All the four types of reading, moreover, explicitly or implicitly posit a contrast between Andreas' 'ironic' and his 'serious' views. I don't think that it is particularly helpful to read the text through the grid of the opposition between appearance and reality. This opposition is precisely the one that structures Andreas's own reading of the lady, fuelling his obsessive belief that the lady's actual words and behaviour *must* be understood as nothing but a mask of charm and courtesy covering up the monstrous reality of her being.

10

'She Died Because She Came Too Late ...':
Knowledge, Doubles, and Death in
Thomas's Tristan
(1989)

For some reason Thomas's *Tristan* (probably written between 1150 and 1165) has attracted less critical interest than the Tristan poems of, say, Gottfried or Béroul. One traditional account of the Tristan material, that of A. T. Hatto, holds that Thomas's text is lacking in 'literary' quality. For Hatto, Thomas is a 'great writer rather than a poet' ('A Note' 361), 'inferior to Gottfried and Chrétien in his appreciation of artistic economy' ('A Note' 362), and a 'rationalist' rather than an 'artist'. Indeed, Hatto concludes, while not exactly a poet, '[Thomas] was a learned man who had made the human heart and mind his subject' ('A Note' 362). Unwittingly casting Thomas as the Sigmund Freud of his time, Hatto apparently remains convinced that true *literary* merit is incompatible with an analytical or 'rationalist' cast of mind. The implication is that the

I would like to thank Sarah Beckwith and Stephen G. Nichols for their truly helpful comments on the first draft of this text. Roberta Kreuger, Lee Patterson, and Judith P. Shoaf made very useful suggestions for improvement on later drafts. I do not pretend to expertise in medieval studies. In particular I have no wish to comment on the tricky questions of the status of the various manuscript sources, their dating and relative importance. The main source of information about the missing parts of Thomas's *Tristan* is the old Norse translation made by the otherwise unknown brother Robert. The Old Norse *Saga af Tristram ok Isönd* exists in various translations. I read Alfrún Gunnlaugsdottir's Spanish version, *Tristán en el norte*. Her comments and comparisons with the extant parts of Thomas's text have been most useful to me. As for the exact date of the Saga, Sverrir Tómasson would seem to prove that it was indeed translated during the reign of Hákon Hákonsson the Old (1217–63). In preparing this essay I also found much interesting material in the following books and articles not otherwise mentioned in my text or notes: Barteau, Blakeslee, Bouchard, Bredsdorff, Curtis, Fisher, Payen, 'Ordre moral' and 'Lancelot contre Tristan', Pensom, and Tang.

literarity of literature—its so-called 'poetry'—is a unique kind of essence. As such its quality would seem to depend on its purity: to add other discourses, such as philosophy or logic, is to adulterate literariness, turning the clear waters of literary pleasure into a murky mixture of unholy substances. That such post-Kantian aesthetics have little to do with medieval practices of writing is obvious. For a modern reader, the fact that Thomas's exceptionally acute analysis of passion, desire, and knowledge necessarily transgresses nineteenth-century notions of genre, makes his texts more rather than less challenging. In order fully to appreciate Thomas's account of the problem of passion, his *Tristan* should be placed in the same textual space (*not*, of course, the same *historical* space) as the works of Stendhal, Freud, or Proust. In this essay my contribution towards such a construction of Thomas will be to indicate how his *Tristan* may be read as a remarkable analysis of the relationship between passion, death, and knowledge.

SUMMARY OF THE TEXT

It is estimated that as much as the first two-thirds of Thomas's poem may be missing, leaving us with a text focusing almost exclusively on the tragic end of passion. We first encounter the lovers in an orchard scene where Tristan decides to leave England for Britanny in order to save Yseut and himself from punishment for adultery. A later fragment dwells on Tristan's doubts and suffering in exile, culminating in his ill-fated marriage to Yseut of the White Hands. This marriage is never consummated. Accompanied by his faithful friend Kaherdin, Tristan makes two journeys back to England in various disguises to see Yseut. Meanwhile Yseut is courted by the noble Baron Cariadoc, whom she rejects. At one point Yseut's attendant Brangien, who has become Kaherdin's lover, threatens to expose Yseut's adultery to King Mark, but in fact only warns the King against Cariadoc.

The denouement takes up over half of the extant text, and requires a more detailed presentation. Tristan and Kaherdin have not been long back in Britanny from their expedition to see Yseut's *bruine* or leather corset, when an unknown knight called Tristan the Dwarf (but who is not in fact a dwarf) asks for Tristan's help in winning back his beloved lady who has been captured by the terrible Estout l'Orgueilleux Castel Fier. Promising to set out the very next morning, Tristan is accused of cowardice by Tristan the Dwarf. As for him, he says, now that he has lost the woman he loved above all else in the world, he only wants to die. The two Tristans then set out immediately. At Estout l'Orgueilleux's castle they both fight bravely against Estout and his six brothers and kill them all, but Tristan the Dwarf is mortally wounded and dies shortly thereafter, whereas Tristan himself is seriously wounded in the hip by a poisoned spear. He manages to get back to his own castle, but the poison spreads in his body, and Tristan knows that only the Queen can save him from death. He tells Kaherdin to sail at once to get the Queen and gives him forty days in which to accomplish his task. If he returns without Yseut, the ship is to carry black sails; if she is on board, the sails are to be white. Eavesdropping, Yseut of the White Hands instantly becomes enraged with jealousy, and resolves to get her revenge. Disguised as a rich merchant, Kaherdin arrives in London, and both Yseut and Brangien willingly escape with him. But first a storm and then lack of wind delay their return, and Yseut despairs of ever seeing Tristan again. Finally, on the fortieth day, the ship lies just off the coast where it can be seen from Tristan's castle, but lack of wind prevents it from landing. Yseut of the White Hands sees her chance and takes her revenge:

> Ço dit Ysolt: 'Jol sai pur veir:
> Sachez que le sigle est tut neir'
>
> (vv. 3025–6; Douce 1753–4)

And then Yseut says: 'I know the truth: the sails are quite black.'[1]

---

[1] I am quoting from Jean Charles Payen's edition of the text, *Les Tristan en vers*. All translations are my own. Line references are to Payen's edition. As Payen unfortunately gives consecutive line numbers for the whole poem, thus obscuring the various transitions from one fragment to another, I also give line references to Bartina H. Wind's edition of the Tristan fragments (*Les fragments du Tristan de Thomas*). References to Wind will be preceded by the following abbreviations:

Cam.   —   Cambridge fragment
Sn1   —   first Sneyd fragment
Douce   —   Douce fragment
Sn2   —   second Sneyd fragment.

Working on the translations, I found much help in Payen's French prose translations (in *Les Tristan en vers*) and A. T. Hatto's English prose rendering (appended to his translation of Gottfried von Strassburg).

Tristan then gives up hope and dies. The wind rises and the ship reaches port. Yseut hears of Tristan's death, rushes to his body, kisses him, and dies.

IMAGINARY KNOWLEDGE

In the first remaining plot fragment King Mark discovers the two lovers post-coitally sleeping in each other's arms in the palace orchard. Seeing his chance finally to have both of them legally punished for adultery, he sets off to get his barons to come and witness the *flagrant délit*. Tristan, however, wakes up just in time to catch a glimpse of the King. Only his own immediate departure, Tristan decides, can help both of them escape punishment and death:

> Je m'en voil aler, bele amie.
> Vos n'avez garde de la vie,
> Car ne porez estre provee . . .
> . . . Fuïr deport et querre eschil,
> Guerpir joie, siovre peril.
>
> (vv. 24–8; Cam. 24–8)

I am going away, fair love! Your life is not in danger, for they will not be able to prove anything . . . Flee pleasure and seek exile, abandon joy, follow danger.

King Mark would seem to have an ironclad case against the two lovers: here surely is the ocular proof sought by Othello's fevered imagination. Tristan's sudden exile, however, deprives the King of the evidence of his own senses. Having witnessed the scene, he finds himself unable to prove it. His vision of the lovers is thus transformed from fact to what Freud might call *psychic reality*: that which is experienced as real by the psyche, but which may or may not correspond to the historical truth.[2] On the historical or 'real'

---

[2] The background for the concept of 'psychic reality' is as follows. In 1896 Freud elaborated his so-called 'seduction theory', or the hypothesis that the cause of neurosis in all his patients might be that they had been 'seduced' or molested by their father in early childhood (see Freud, 'The Aetiology of Hysteria'). Very soon after the publication of this paper, however, Freud revised his theory. Instead of assuming that every case of hysteria was caused by real

level, Mark's adulterous vision remains indeterminate: neither fiction nor fact, it cannot serve as legal evidence. More than just a cunning strategy of deceit, Tristan's exile succeeds in radically undermining the King's reliance on visual evidence as his primary source of knowledge.

King Mark is by no means unusual in casting knowledge in visual terms. In her pioneering study of Western philosophy, *Speculum of the Other Woman*, Luce Irigaray demonstrates how thinkers from Plato to Freud have equated knowledge with vision. For Freud, for instance, the little girl as well as the little boy are expected to see the fact of sexual difference, and draw the 'obvious' conclusion that girls are lacking or deprived. But this, according to Irigaray, is a dubious move, since to see something is not the same thing as to interpret it: there can be no inherent or obvious reason why the very fact of seeing a penis should convince us of the intrinsic superiority of that organ. Starting from Freud's own analysis of the visual sense as linked to the drive for mastery or control and the desire sadistically to dominate one's object, Irigaray goes on to argue that the distance and relative abstraction involved in seeing something rather than in touching or smelling it allows the perceiving subject to believe in his or her own mastery of the visual field. Extremist versions of this theory, such as that of Sartre, one might add, go as far as explicitly to equate seeing with possessing.[3] For Irigaray, then,

---

(historically true) 'seduction', he now claimed that neurotic symptoms might also develop without such an external cause. This in no way implies that no neuroses are caused by 'seduction', but it does mean that neurotic symptoms no longer have a *necessary* link to one specific set of external facts. What matters is the child's reaction to real *or* imagined traumas: 'psychic reality' takes precedence over empirical reality. It was this shift in emphasis which enabled Freud to develop the basic theoretical positions of psychoanalysis, particularly the hypotheses of childhood sexuality and the Oedipus complex. For an impassioned defence of the original 'seduction' theory (and a disreputable attack on Freud's reasons for abandoning it) see Jeffrey Masson's controversial *The Assault on Truth: Freud's Suppression of the Seduction Theory*.

[3] See e.g. Sartre's account of knowledge as possession and rape in *Being and Nothingness*, in the section entitled '"Doing" and "Having": Possession' (635–61, esp. 638–42). In *Hipparchia's Choice* Michèle Le Dœuff gives a witty and incisive critique of Sartre's simplistic 'epistemology' in this section.

visual knowledge is the patriarchal mode of knowledge par excellence.

At one level, such a reading would seem to fit Thomas's *Tristan* well. King Mark is after all the very embodiment of law and order, the incarnation of the society he rules, the representative of the phallocentric symbolic order which persistently marginalizes women. Nothing is more logical than for the King to prefer visual evidence above all other forms. But this perspective, however convincing, overlooks one crucial point: the fact that visual evidence can never remain *private*. If King Mark sets off to get his barons, it is because he needs to have his vision duplicated by others if it is to carry any kind of legal force. Although it is true that in some discourses, such as that of Sartre, visual knowledge does remain deeply bound up with the alienating specular relations of the Imaginary, there is no need to assume that it can never be successfully triangulated and circulated within the symbolic order. Legal evidence, such as that sought by King Mark, is *socially sanctioned* vision, not simply vision. The same thing is true for scientific vision: whatever the scientist claims to have seen does not count as evidence or insight unless it can be *repeated* by others. Scientifically speaking, a once-off vision seen by one person is not knowledge, but hallucination. For all its strengths, then, Irigaray's analysis of specularity and visuality in Western culture tends to remain trapped in an imaginary problematics primarily concerned with dual relationships, which does not sufficiently account for the social dimension of the visual in the symbolic order.

In the passage studied above, then, Tristan's strategy consists above all in turning King Mark's vision into private hallucination. While the main motivation for Tristan's sudden exile is his understandable wish to save himself and Yseut from punishment and death, his departure also signals his own desire to place himself outside dominant social categories. The Sneyd fragments, set sometime during Tristan's exile in Britanny, open with a fascinating account of Tristan's doubt and hesitations about whether to marry another woman, Yseut of the White Hands. In this section a different theory of knowledge can be seen to emerge. Tristan's first complaint is that he feels *deceived* by Yseut:

> Et dit dunc: 'Ysolt, bele amie,
> Molt est diverse vostre vie:
> La nostre amur tant se desevre
> Qu'ele n'est fors pur mei decevre.
> Jo perc pur vus joie e deduit,
> E vus l'avez e jur e nuit . . .'
>
> (vv. 57–62; Sn1 5–10)

And then he says: 'Yseut, fair love, your life is very different from mine: our love is becoming so distant that it can only deceive me. I am losing joy and pleasure for you, and you have it day and night . . .'[4]

Complaining that distance and absence introduce an element of *ignorance* into his life, Tristan immediately leaps to the conclusion that ignorance and deceit amount to one and the same thing. The very fact of his distance from Yseut produces doubt, and, according to Tristan, pain is basically an effect of insufficient knowledge. The logic of his case is clear: if he could only procure himself secure knowledge of Yseut, his suffering would abate. Deprived of her presence he chooses an alternative mode of knowledge: marriage to Yseut of the White Hands. The text repeatedly emphasizes the epistemological motivation for this marriage:

> Fors qu'assaier voldrai sa vie:
> Je voil espuser la meschine
> Pur saveir l'estre a la reïne.
>
> (vv. 224–6; Sn1 172–4)

I should like to try myself how she lives. I will marry the maiden in order to learn what it is like to be the Queen.

The choice of Yseut of the White Hands is motivated at once by her beauty and her name:

---

[4] The problem in this passage is the meaning of v. 59 (Sn1 7). The verb *se desevre* would seem to imply increasing difference between the lovers. Payen translates this as 'notre amour n'est plus communion', whereas Hatto (301) has the somewhat less precise 'our love is so remote'. I have settled for the somewhat ungrammatical construction 'our love is becoming distant', in order to emphasize Tristan's feeling of increasing distance which he will try to remedy by insisting on identification and unity.

> Car Ysolt as Blanches Mains volt
> Pur belté e pur nun d'Isolt.
> Ja pur belté quë en li fust,
> Se le nun d'Isolt në oüst,
> Ne pur le nun senz la belté
> N'en oüst Tristans volenté:
> Ces dous choses qui en li sunt
> Ceste faisance emprendre font
> Qu'il volt espuser la meschine
> Pur saveir l'estre la reïne,
> Coment se puisse delitier
> Encuntre amur od sa mollier:
> Assaier le volt endreit sei
> Cum Ysolt fait envers lu rei.
>
> (vv. 249–62; Sn1 196–210)

[Tristan] wants Yseut of the White Hands because she is beautiful and because her name is Yseut. Tristan would never have desired her for her beauty had she not borne the name of Yseut; nor for the name without the beauty. These two things cause him to embark on this enterprise, that is, to marry the maiden so as to learn what it is like to be the Queen, and to find out how he can take pleasure with his wife in spite of his love. He wants to experience for himself what Yseut experiences with the King.

At this point the narrator intervenes to stress that Tristan, as so many others before him, is making a mistake. This is neither love nor anger, Thomas writes, neither vengeance nor consolation, but an uneasy mixture of both (see vv. 370–6; Sn1 318–19). Thomas for his part deplores such lack of constancy: it is the fickle desire for change at all cost that leads to such rash and unwise decisions. Tristan's marriage to another Yseut, then, is first and foremost an effect of his *identification* with the Queen. If he cannot see her, he can at least act like her. In this way he hopes to satisfy his sexual frustrations while sustaining or even intensifying his passion for the Queen. As soon as he finds himself married to Yseut of the White Hands, however, he realizes that he cannot after all make love to her:

> A sei dit: 'Coment le pois faire?
> Icest ovre m'est a contraire;
> Nequedent si m'estuit cholcher
> Cum ove ma dreite moillier'
>
> (vv. 463–6; Sn1 411–14)

'How can I do it?' he says to himself. 'This deed is repugnant to me. Nevertheless I must sleep with my lawful wife.'

What Tristan discovers here is that to *have* Yseut is not the same thing as to *be* her. Exclusively focusing on imitation, Tristan overlooks the fact of sexual difference. What he fails to realize is that the very fact of his maleness necessarily positions him differently from Yseut socially as well as sexually. However much he strives to imitate her, his difference will ensure that the result achieved is not identity but more difference. Intended to cast him as Queen Yseut in relation to King Mark, his marriage only succeeds in placing three Yseuts in his marriage bed: Yseut of the White Hands, Queen Yseut, and, of course, Tristan-who-wants-to-be-Yseut. Spectacularly absent is the phallic power of the King: Tristan's appeal, through the marriage ceremony, to the social sanction of the Law only succeeds in placing him even more firmly on the side of the imaginary, the side of narcissistic identification and desire for total dissolution in the Other.[5] No wonder he cannot find the power to have sex with Yseut of the White Hands.

Tristan is not alone in this view of knowledge. Yseut too suffers from the compulsion to repeat. After Tristan's first clandestine visit to see her, she decides to 'share his sufferings' in exile:

> Pur les granz mals qu'il ad suffert
> Qu'a privé li ad descovert,
> Pur la peine, pur la dolur,
> Que tant ad eü par s'amur,
> Pur l'anguise, pur la grevance,
> Partir volt a la penitance.

[5] Stephen G. Nichols draws my attention to the ambiguous manuscript form of v. 246 (Sn1 194), where Tristan either claims that he is getting married to a worthy woman (Yseut of the White Hands) so that *Yseut* cannot blame him for *his* infidelity, or, alternatively, that he is getting married so that *he* no longer can blame Yseut for *her* infidelity. For Wind, in her note to this line, the very grammatical ambiguity of this construction (which turns on the presence or absence of an 'l' or an apostrophe in the manuscript) shows that Thomas here is 'up against a language which did not yet lend itself to his psychological sophistication'. Wind's awareness of the psychological complexity of this passage parallels my own view of Tristan's inextricable entanglement in the very confusion of identities produced by the lovers' passion.

> Pur ço que Tristran veit languir,
> Ove sa dolur vult partir.
>
> (vv. 2013–20; Douce 741–8)

Because of the great ills which he has suffered, and which he has told her about in private, because of the pain and the sorrow which he has endured for love's sake, because of the anguish and the grief, she wants to share the penance. Because she sees Tristan languishing, she wants to share his sorrow.

Desiring to share Tristan's sufferings, she decides to wear a *bruine* next to her body at all times, except when in bed with her husband. A *bruine* (mod. French: *broigne*) seems to have been a kind of uncomfortable leather corset, constructed for penitential use, much like a hair shirt. Through a wandering minstrel, Yseut succeeds in letting Tristan know what pain she is enduring for his sake:

> Quant Tristran la novele solt
> De la roïne qu'il amout,
> Pensif en este e deshaitez:
> en sun quer ne pot estre liez
> De si la quë il ait veüe
> La bruine qu'Ysolt ot vestue
> Ne de sun dos n'ert ja ostee
> De si qu'il venge en la cuntree.
>
> (vv. 2049–56; Douce 777–84)

When Tristan receives the news of the Queen whom he loves, he becomes thoughtful and sad. In his heart he cannot be happy until he has seen the corset which Yseut is wearing and which she will not take off until he arrives in her country.

Tristan immediately sets out for a second perilous journey to England. The narrative logic here is clear: to gain *some* knowledge of the other only intensifies the desire for more. Caught in an epistemological frenzy which can find no satisfactory outcome, short of the end of all desire, the lovers' drive for imaginary knowledge sends them headlong into destruction and death.

The fact that Tristan wants to *see* the corset which remains hidden from King Mark, might suggest that Tristan here departs from the model of knowledge as identification, settling for visual knowledge instead. Perhaps he desires the exultant triumph of *seeing* that which Yseut never shows to King Mark? The narrative, however, does not bear out such a reading. When, after many dangerous adventures, Tristan and Kaherdin arrive at King Mark's palace and meet their mistresses again, we hear no more about the ostensible motivation for the journey, Yseut's corset. It is as if the sexual union of the lovers makes the visual economy of distance, mastery, distinction, and difference irrelevant.

Both Tristan and Yseut, then, tend to see knowledge as identification, imitation or repetition, not as definition, description, or deduction, nor, in a different mode, as work, transformation, or *praxis*. There is in this text an absolute contradiction between King Mark's reliance on visual knowledge and Tristan's efforts to gain knowledge through imitation or repetition. Where visual knowledge seeks to master its object, identificatory knowledge seeks to *become* that which it desires to know. Needless to say, such an imaginary epistemological project can only ever achieve paradoxical success: in the very moment the knower merges with that which is to be known, both entities are abolished as such. In this way imaginary knowledge undercuts all other forms of knowledge, blurring all boundaries and dissolving all definitions in its way. In this sense it is not knowledge at all, but *confusion*. In Latin *confundere* means to mix or to fuse together. The Old French *confondre* means to destroy as well as to discomfit, and the Old French *confus* retains the double sense of destruction and ruin on the one hand and unexpected mixture or reversal on the other. Tristan's marriage to Yseut of the White Hands highlights the effects of such destructive confusion. Marrying one woman, he behaves as if he were married to another. Having already transgressed the law of marriage by committing adultery with the Queen, he now undoes it from the other side, as it were, by refusing to have sex with his own wife. It is as if Tristan has become incapable of distinguishing between what is allowed and what is prohibited: he can no longer position himself in relation to the Law.

In Thomas's text, then, the lovers' passion is firmly anchored in the imaginary. Epistemologically speaking, Thomas insists on the destructively *confusing* effects of such a passion. Tristan's death thus becomes starkly ironic: in the end he stakes his life on visual evidence, on being able to tell black from white. Claiming that the white sails of Kaherdin's ship are black, Yseut of the White Hands coolly pays Tristan back in his own currency. If it does not even occur to Tristan to doubt her account, it is because the very fact of querying somebody's reported vision necessarily implies an effort to make that vision socially accountable. Provoking the collapse of all boundaries and distinctions, Tristan's passion strives to obliterate all differences. If, as Thomas puts it, Queen Yseut dies 'because she came too late' (v. 3124; Sn2 817), Tristan dies because he can no longer tell the difference between truth and lies.

From a feminist perspective it is important to note that nothing in the text permits us to cast the imaginary mode of knowledge as gendered in any particular way, since it is generally represented as the inevitable effect of passion *tout court*. According to Thomas, men and women are equally likely to succumb to the lures of passion. The opposition in this text is not between female and male forms of knowledge, but between the law and the imaginary. In his staging of a sophisticated encounter between these two modes of knowledge, moreover, Thomas is careful not to endorse the lovers' frenzied drive for identity: Tristan's ironic death is a warning against the dangers of casting knowing as being.[6]

'THEN THE SAME FISH MIGHT EAT US . . .':
DOUBLES AND THE DEATH DRIVE

Commenting on Tristan's decision to marry Yseut of the White Hands, Thomas says that the remedy turns out to be worse than the disease. Tristan is not alone in making such mistakes, however:

---

[6] The feminist debate on the politics of different forms of knowledge has often focused on the difference between knowledge as communion and knowledge as distance or mastery. It is sometimes assumed that the Middle Ages represent an emphasis on the former, whereas the Renaissance (Bacon, Descartes) introduces the latter. My reading of Thomas implies that medieval positions on the issue were far more complex than is sometimes argued. For further discussion of the theoretical implications of these issues see 'Patriarchal Thought and the Drive for Knowledge' (Ch. 7, above).

Pur de l'amur sei delivrer,
Pur sei oster de la dolur:
Par tant enchaï en greinur.
Issi avient a plusurs genz:
Quant ont d'amur greinurs talenz,
Anguisse, grant paine e contraire,
Tel chose funt pur euls retraire,
Pur delivrer, pur els venger
E sovent itel chose funt
Par conseil, dunt en dolur sunt.

(vv. 386–96; Sn₁ 334–44)

Trying to free himself from love, trying to rid himself of pain, he only fell into greater misery. This happens to many people: when they have the greatest erotic desire, and the greatest anguish, pain, and torment, they deliberately choose to deliver and avenge themselves by an act which intensifies their unhappiness.

As we have seen, Tristan's marriage represents an effort to set up Tristan as well as his bride as Yseut's double. The only result of Tristan's compulsion to repeat Yseut's situation, however, is what Freud would call *unpleasure*. In *Beyond the Pleasure Principle* (1920) Freud distinguishes between libidinal (sexual and self-preserving) drives ruled by the pleasure principle and those drives which, manifesting themselves in a compulsion to repeat even unpleasurable experiences, find their origin somewhere beyond the pleasure principle. The latter, Freud concludes, are more primitive, more elementary and instinctual than the libidinal ego drives. After some hesitation, he labels these highly volatile impulses the *death drives*, reserving the term *Eros*, or the *life drives*, for the libidinal drives.

Where the drives in the service of the pleasure principle seek to bind or fuse energy, the death drives seek to unbind or free energy. Where Eros seeks harmony and union, the death drive produces dissonance, disintegration, and fragmentation. The ferocious aggression of the death drive is responsible for our most murderous desires. Manifesting itself in the compulsion to repeat, the death drive must fundamentally be seen as an urge to restore the organism to an earlier state of being. Ultimately, this means that the organism will seek to return to the inorganic, to death. Where Eros seeks to produce life through the union of sexually different organisms, the death drive erases or dissolves difference in its search for stasis. Where Eros binds and builds, becoming the driving force in the construction of civilization, the death drive produces disintegration, fragmentation, and destruction.

But the relationship between Eros and death drives is not one of a simple opposition. To say that the life drives are in the service of the pleasure principle is to insist that Eros too seeks to diminish excitation, to avoid unpleasurable tension and expenditure of energy. Whereas the death drives seek to return to the inorganic, to a state of complete inertia, the life drives set out to achieve stability and a pleasurable absence of tension through the discharge or voiding of excess irritability or excitation. If Eros, then, seeks to achieve harmony through fusion or binding of excitation, this in itself is a repetition of the ultimate desire for the inanimate proper to the death drive. The organism, in Freud's phrase, always strives to 'follow its own path to death' (*Beyond the Pleasure Principle, SE* 18: 39). The various life drives, including the drives for self-preservation, self-assertion, and mastery are there to ensure that the organism finds its own appropriate mode of death, that is to say, a death that in some way repeats its own original emergence from the inanimate. If the death drives belong to the very earliest stages of primary narcissism, the life drives and the pleasure principle are products of primary narcissism as well. In this way, the life drives do not oppose the death drives, but rather work on their behalf: the collaboration of Eros is required if the organism is to find its proper path towards the end.

Towards the end of *Beyond the Pleasure Principle*, in an effort to explain why the life drives exist at all, Freud returns to the question of the origins of sexuality. For if the death drive is the earliest and most primitive of our drives, it is hard to understand why all organisms do not simply die as soon as they can, before they get entangled in the detour on the way to death imposed by Eros. If the origin of a drive is the '*need to restore an earlier state of things*', Freud writes (*SE* 18: 57), then nothing explains sexuality better than Aristophanes' account in Plato's *Symposium* of the origins of sexual desire. As we know, Plato has Aristophanes explain that originally there were three sexes, all of them double (man/man, woman/woman, man/woman), but that one day Zeus decided to cut these human beings in two, and since then each human being is driven by the need to find his or her own missing half. 'Shall we follow the hint given us by the poet-philosopher', Freud continues, 'and venture upon the hypothesis that living substance at the time of its coming to life was torn apart into small particles, which have ever since endeavored to reunite through the sexual instincts?' (*SE* 18: 58).

It is not a coincidence that Freud alludes to the founding myth of doubles and androgynes in European civilization precisely at a point where he is discussing the death drive. In his essay on 'The Uncanny' (1919), he explicitly relates the figure of the double to the death drive. The double 'appears in every shape and in every degree of development', Freud writes (*SE* 17: 234). But whatever its specific characteristics it is the result of division or splitting on the one hand and repetition on the other. Echoing Otto Rank's study *The Double*, Freud argues that if every double is not uncanny, it is because the double was originally an 'insurance against the destruction of the ego . . . probably the "immortal" soul was the first "double" of the body' (*SE* 17: 235). Produced by primary narcissism, the benign version of the double belongs to the magic world of fairy tales:

> Such ideas, however, have sprung from the soil of unbounded self-love, from the primary narcissism which dominates the mind of the child and of primitive man. But when this stage has been surmounted, the 'double' reverses its aspect. From having been an assurance of immortality, it becomes the uncanny harbinger of death (*SE* 17: 235).

Apart from the protagonists themselves, in Thomas's *Tristan* the two principal doubles are Yseut of the White Hands and Tristan the Dwarf.[7] While not particularly uncanny at first

[7] Tony Tanner argues that the existence of two Yseuts in the *Tristan* legend represents a splitting of Tristan's feelings towards the 'real' Yseut. The effect, according to Tanner, is to remove ambiguity from the tale, to cast the Queen as entirely desired, and Yseut of the White Hands as entirely undesired (30–1). But if this were the logic of the doubles in Thomas's text, we would have to assume that the two Tristans represent different aspects of Yseut's feelings for Tristan as well. This, however, makes no sense at all, both because the two Tristans do not occupy different positions in their attitudes towards love or women, and because Yseut never even meets Tristan the Dwarf. Tanner's account is sexist in so far as he unwittingly assumes that the use of doubles in the legend can be satisfactorily explained by focusing exclusively on Tristan's desire.

approach, both become harbingers and instruments of death in the course of the poem. Otto Rank succinctly summarizes the dual aspect of this kind of double:

> So it happens that the double, who personifies narcissistic self-love, becomes an unequivocal rival in sexual love; or else, originally created as a wish-defense against a dreaded eternal destruction, he reappears in superstition as the messenger of death (86).

According to Thomas, Yseut of the White Hands kills because of her jealousy: death comes about as a result of her rivalry with the other Yseut. And if Tristan the Dwarf succeeds in making Tristan set out to kill Estout l'Orgeuilleux without delay, it is because he threatens to usurp Tristan's identity as Tristan l'Amoureux— Tristan the Lover—by being even more wildly in love than Tristan himself. Taunting Tristan, Tristan the Dwarf accuses him of never having been in love, and then goes on to dwell on his own death wish:

> E vus, amis, que ren n'amez,
> Ma dolur sentir ne poez;
> Se ma dolur pusset sentir,
> Dunc vuldrïez od mei venir.
> A Deu seiez! Jo m'en irrai
> Querre Tristran quel troverai.
> N'avrai confort se n'est par lui.
> Unques si esgaré ne fui!
> E! Deus, pur quei ne pus murir
> Quant perdu ai que plus desir?
> Meuz vousisse la meie mort
> Car jo n'avrai ja nul confort,
> Ne hait, ne joie en mun corage,
> Quant perdu l'ai a tel tolage,
> La ren el mund que jo plus aim.

> (vv. 2265–79; Douce 993–1007)

And you my friend who don't love cannot understand my torment; if you could feel it, you would come with me. Adieu! I will go and seek Tristan and I will find him. I can only be helped by him. I have never been so desperate! Oh God, why can I not die when I have lost that which I desire the most? I want to die since I shall never be comforted, and never feel happiness or joy again now that this abduction has taken away the being I love most in the world.

Tristan often appears in disguise. The various *Folie de Tristan* fragments show him pretending to be mad or playing the role of the fool or the jester, at one point even turning his own name inside out, calling himself Tantris. The most significant case of disguise, however, is the episode where Tristan appears as a leper. Dressing in rags, he drinks a herbal infusion in order to achieve his transformation, with the result that his face and body swell up:

> Sun vis em fait tut eslever,
> Cum se malade fust emfler;
> Pur sei seürement covrir
> Ses pez e sé mains fait nercir:
> Tut s'apareille cum fust lazre.
>
> (vv. 1779–83; Douce 507–11)

It makes his face bloat, as if he were sick, and swell up. He swells up like a sick man. In order to be even better disguised he paints his feet and hands black, and makes himself look like a leper.

Successfully disguised, Tristan tries to approach Yseut, but is prevented from reaching her by Brangien who at this stage is angry with Yseut. Desperate and exhausted he seeks refuge under a staircase in a nearby manor house:

> Suz le degrez languist Tristrans.
> Sa mort desire e het sa vie:
> Ja ne levrad mais senz aïe.
>
> (vv. 1876–8; Douce 604–6)

Under the staircase Tristan languishes. He desires death and hates his life: he cannot even get up without help.

A few days later Tristan is discovered immobile, on the point of freezing to death. The kindly people in the manor house save him and ensure that he gets to meet Yseut after all. At no other point in the narrative, except for the denouement, does Tristan come as close to death as in this case. There is a striking similarity between this scene and that of his real death where, wounded by a poisoned spear, Tristan falls gravely ill:

> Li venims s'espant par le cors,
> Emfler le fait dedenz e fors;
> Nercist e teint, sa force pert.
>
> (vv. 2341–3; Douce 1069–71)

The venom spreads in his body and makes him swell up all over, it makes him go black and weakens him.

Tristan's wound stinks (Thomas alludes to 'la puür de la plaie' (2361; Douce 1089)), his body is swollen, his skin is black: he has become the very image of his own disguise. If the disguised Tristan in some sense can be said to be his own double, this time, in a somewhat uncanny way, the 'real' Tristan would seem to have become the double of his own double. This process of continuous splitting and doubling is best understood as being at once an effect of the 'unbinding' of energy characteristic of the death drives and another example of the epistemological confusion characteristic of Tristan's passion. In fact the process of destructive confusion can now properly be seen as another effect of the way in which the 'unbinding' of energy in the death drive dissolves differences and distinctions, making it increasingly difficult to tell appearance and reality apart. Yet from the perspective of the narrative as a whole there is a difference: huddling under his staircase Tristan was not dying from his 'leprosy', but from the cold. As in Yseut of the White Hands' final betrayal, the reality principle strikes back, punishing Tristan's cavalier disregard for socially recognizable concepts of truth by the very symptoms he once so successfully imitated. If Tristan is collapsing under his passion, nothing indicates that the narrator of the poem is in danger of following him on the path to destruction.

We have already seen that Tristan seeks to *become* Yseut and that she too seeks to merge with him. The most moving expression of Yseut's desire for Tristan comes when Yseut, caught in a storm on her way to the dying Tristan, fears for her life:

> De la meie mor ne m'est ren:
> Quant Deu la volt, jo la vul ben;
> Mais tresque vus, amis, l'orrez,
> Jo sai ben que vus en murrez.
> De tel manere est nostre amur
> Ne puis sen vus sentir dolur,
> Vus ne poez sens moi murrir,
> Ne jo sen vus ne puis perir.
>
> (vv. 2907–14; Douce 1635–42)

I do not mind dying: if God wills it, so be it. But when you, my love, hear about it, I know that you will die. Our love is like this: I cannot feel a pain which you do not share, you cannot die without me, nor can I perish without you.

Yseut's lament dwells on her desire to die in Tristan's arms and to be buried in the same coffin. If she dies at sea, however, another end must be imagined:

> Car, si jo dei neier ici,
> E vus, ce crei, devez neier:
> Uns peissuns peüt nus mangier;
> Eissi avrum par aventure
> Bels amis, une sepulture,
> Car tel hum prendre le purra
> Ki nos cors i reconuistra,
> E fra en puis si grant honur
> Cume covient a nostre amur.
>
> (vv. 2926–34; Douce 1654–62)

For if I must drown here, then I believe that you too will drown. Then the same fish might eat us and in that way, my love, we will by good fortune get the same grave. For perhaps a man will catch it and recognize our bodies and do them the great honour that befits our love.

Yseut's striking image of the two drowned lovers entwined in the belly of the great 'fish' is an incisive condensation of and reflection on the nature of their passion. Implicitly equating prenatal existence and death, Yseut manages to signal at once the thoroughly imaginary and narcissistic nature of their love, but also its deeper allegiance to the death drive. Placing them in the same 'womb' amounts to casting the two lovers as twins, the very incarnation of the double.[8] Yseut's image is also an allusion to Plato's myth of the origins of sexual difference: in death Tristan and Yseut are finally permanently reunited with their lost selves. In her study of androgyny, Carolyn Heilbrun stresses the symbolic resonance of the theme of opposite-sex twins:

---

[8] Twins have been considered magical since the earliest ages. Tribes in widely different parts of the world, J. G. Frazer informs us, regularly attribute supernatural powers for good or evil to twins (86–7).

Complementary, different in heredity and sex but identical in birth experience, the two seem to encompass between them complete human possibility. Throughout opposite-sex twin lore, the two are always seen as an original unit which has split, a unit destined to be reunited by sexual love, the ultimate symbol of human conjoining (34).

According to Heilbrun, the ultimate symbolic unity of the two finds its purest expression in the image of opposite-sex twins making love in the mother's womb.[9] An impossible image of identity-in-difference, Yseut's vision is the exact representation of the impossibility of achieving imaginary satisfaction in the symbolic order. Only the womb/grave can truly satisfy her passion. Yseut dreams of a peaceful death in the belly of the whale followed by rebirth into a common grave on dry land. If this image is free of any uncanny overtones, it is because her fantasy represents Eros harmoniously collapsing itself into death, the pleasure principle merging into the death drive. The beauty of this passage is an effect of the representation of the blissful pleasure achieved by the organism which truly has found its own path to death. Yet the *poem* does not end on this note of imaginary perfection. The question that remains to be answered is *why* the narrative refuses to come to the end so movingly evoked by Yseut.

NARRATIVE, PASSION, AND DEATH

For a poem entirely devoted to passion, Thomas's *Tristan* provides surprisingly little information about what happens when the lovers actually meet. It is the motif of *exile* or *absence*, not passion, that keeps the narrative going by furnishing a pretext for travels and by enabling the poem to narrativize its epistemological concerns. Set in the context of exile the drive for knowledge necessarily turns into a physical quest. This is not to deny that the lovers brave their perilous journeys because they are driven by passion, but it is to say that, at least in so far as Thomas is concerned, passion alone cannot produce a narrative. In this

9 Examples can be found in texts ranging from Edmund Spenser's *The Faerie Queene* to Christiane Rochefort's *Archaos ou le jardin étincelant*.

sense it is not so much the lovers who suffer from 'obstacle love' as Tony Tanner argues, as the narrator.[10] When Tristan, after having disguised himself as a leper, finally gains access to Yseut's 'marble chamber', Thomas describes their encounter as a 'break' or 'pause':

> Tristran a Ysolt se deduit.
> Après grant pose de la nuit
> Prent le congé à l'enjurnee
> E si s'en vet ver sa cuntree.

> (vv. 1995–8; Douce 723–6)

Tristan takes his pleasure with Yseut. After this break of one night he takes his leave at daybreak and then departs for his country.

On Tristan's second journey to England, Tristan and Kaherdin disguised as penitent pilgrims succeed in reaching King Mark's court without being recognized:

[10] Tanner's account of 'obstacle love' takes its cue from Rougemont's *Love in the Western World* and Freud's 1912 essay 'On the Universal Tendency to Debasement in the Sphere of Love'. This is not the place to argue the case in detail, but I will nevertheless briefly indicate why I think Freud's theory of 'obstacle love' does not apply to Thomas's *Tristan*. Freud's essay sets out to explain why it is that some men are impotent with women they love, whereas they are fully potent with 'debased' sexual objects such as prostitutes. Freud's argument is that these men suffer from a split between the affective and the sensual currents of their psyche, so that 'where they love they do not desire, and where they desire they do not love' (*SE* 11: 251). Such men unconsciously equate a loved woman with the mother, the forbidden sexual object par excellence. The incest taboo and its concomitant fear of castration prevent them from directing their desire towards the mother or her metonymical substitutes. For these men, then, sexual desire can only be directed towards women they neither respect nor cherish. There is no reason, however, to believe that Tristan unconsciously despises Yseut because he has sex with her, nor that he really loves or respects Yseut of the White Hands because he does not. It is equally unlikely to assume that Yseut of the White Hands is more of a mother figure to Tristan than the other Yseut. Wholly centred on the male, the obstacle love reading implies that *Tristan* is nothing but an account of male passion. Such a reading falls on its own implausibility: Yseut desires Tristan as much as he desires her. Are we to assume that Tristan unconsciously desires obstacles whereas Yseut does not? Dominant in a text like Andreas Capellanus's *De amore*, Freud's Oedipalized view of women as the passive objects of active male desire has no place at all in Thomas's *Tristan*.

> E venent a la curt le rei
> E parolent priveement
> E funt i mult de lur talent.
>
> (vv. 2064–6; Douce 792–4)

They arrived at the King's court, and spoke secretly together and took their pleasure fully.

The larger part of this episode, however, is devoted to a lengthy description of a tournament held by the King where Tristan and Kaherdin distinguish themselves before having to flee the country again. It is as if the lovers' presence to each other exceeds or undoes the narrative: the 'pause' referred to by Thomas is the pause in his narration, corresponding to a moment of maximal intensity in Tristan and Yseut's passion for each other. Representable reality, Thomas implies, is elsewhere: imaginary ecstasies can never be contained within the metonymic economy of narrative.

In relation to narrative, then, passion and death occupy similar positions. For if the attempt to represent the full presence of passion threatens to close the narrative down, so does the representation of death. This is why both topoi recur at the end of so many narratives. If Peter Brooks is right in his essay 'Freud's Masterplot', narratives may be theorized in the same way as the death drive. Texts as well as organisms, Brooks claims, are driven forward by the desire to find their own path to death:

> We emerge from reading *Beyond the Pleasure Principle* with a dynamic model that structures ends (death, quiescence, nonnarratability) against beginnings (Eros, stimulation into tension, the desire of narrative) in a manner that necessitates the middle as detour, as struggle towards the end under the compulsion of imposed delay, as arabesque in the dilatory space of the text. . . . As a dynamic-energetic model of narrative plot, *Beyond the Pleasure Principle* gives an image of how the nonnarratable existence is stimulated into the condition of narratability, to enter a state of deviance and detour (ambition, quest, the pose of a mask) in which it is maintained for a certain time, through an at least minimally complex extravagance, before returning to the quiescence of the nonnarratable (107–8).

On this theory of narrative desire, the vital question for any reader of Thomas's Tristan is *why* the text ends as it does. What exactly counts as *this* narrative's 'own' death? The question is all the more pressing given the number of hypothetical or fictional ends contained in the poem. It is as if Thomas rehearses one possible end after another only to discard them one by one in favour of yet another abortive attempt to close his poem down. It is also crucial here to distinguish between the end of the protagonists and the end of the narrative itself: in this poem, at least, the two have little in common.

Since Thomas is not about to rewrite the *Tristan* legend as comedy, there can be no question of ending the poem with the passionate reunion of the lovers. Instead such meetings serve as the necessary *detour* to keep the plot moving towards its own form of closure. In this specific sense, the principal narrative function of the lovers' presence to each other is to dynamize the themes of exile and absence, to motivate the protagonists for action rather than resignation. Death, then, would seem to be the only other logical option. Acutely aware of the fact that death can be represented in widely different ways, and thus conjures up a whole range of different connotations, Thomas's poem is rich in explorations of possible modes of death. As we have seen, Tristan *almost* freezes to death under the staircase in the manor house. To freeze to death is imperceptibly to cross the threshold between life and death, slowly increasing the degree of immobility and stasis in the organism. The quiet peace of this kind of death makes it a highly suitable illustration of the pleasure involved in simply giving in to the death drive. On the other hand there is very little emphasis on Eros here: fictionally speaking this is the death of somebody who has long since left Eros behind. This, then, is a 'hagiographical' death, not a heroic one.[11] From a sociological and 'courtly' point of view it would be unthinkable for a brave knight like Tristan to freeze to death: to safeguard his honour he has to die in armed combat. The obvious narrative reason why he doesn't in fact die

---

[11] I am grateful to Stephen G. Nichols for drawing my attention to the hagiographical nature of this episode. Nichols points out the parallels between Tristan's hiding away under the staircase with the episode in the 11th-cent. *Vie de Saint Alexis* where Alexis returns unrecognized to live as a beggar under the stairs in his patrician father's house in Rome.

under the staircase, however, would seem to be the impossibility of engineering a *common* death for the two lovers from this situation. Somehow it is hard to imagine Yseut crawling under the staircase with him. To have Tristan die alone would tend to obliterate the poem's elaborate representation of his drive for unity and merger with Yseut: in principle the narrative logic of the poem excludes the possibility of a solitary death for either of them.

'Then the same fish might eat us', sighs Yseut. Harmoniously merging Eros and the death drives, her incestuous image is *too* suitable, too pat to satisfy Thomas, who never indulges in senti-mentality, strenuously refusing to end on a tone of harmonious reconciliation of any kind. While Jean Charles Payen in his edition claims that 'Yseut's complaint on the ship verges on the ridiculous' (xii), Peter Brooks sees brother–sister incest as the very incarnation of a sameness that threatens to put a premature or 'improper' end to narrative:

> Throughout the Romantic tradition, it is perhaps most notably the image of incest (of the fraternal-sororal variety) that hovers as the sign of a passion interdicted because its fulfillment would be too perfect, a discharge indistinguishable from death, the very cessa-tion of narrative movement. ... Incest is only the exemplary version of a temptation of short-circuit from which the protagonist and the text must be led away, into detour, into the cure that prolongs narrative ('Masterplot', 109).

How, then, are we to read the actual death of the protagonists? In Thomas's poem, both of them come to a highly ambiguous and complex end. Tristan's death, for instance, can be read as the direct consequence of Yseut of the White Hands' treachery. On this reading, Thomas's *Tristan* becomes centrally concerned with the consequences of female jealousy, adding a misogynist discourse of its own to the rich medieval tradition in the field. Thomas's comment on Yseult of the White Hands' final lie to Tristan would seem to bear this out:

> Ire de femme est a duter
> Mult s'en deit chaschuns hum garder
> Car la u plus amé avra
> Illuc plus tost se vengera.
>
> (vv. 2595–8; Douce 1323–5)

> A woman's fury must be feared, and everyone must take great care
> to avoid it, for where she has loved the most, she will be the most
> eager to take revenge.

Echoing Medea's fury and Gudrun's final words in the *Laxdoela
Saga*: 'to him I was worst whom I loved the most' (195), Yseut of
the White Hands becomes a terrifying illustration of the cata-
strophic consequences of frustrated sexual desire in women.
On this reading Thomas would seem to share Andreas
Capellanus's view in *De Amore* of women as rapacious, bloodsucking leeches, who do not rest until they have sucked a man
dry.[12] To grasp its full implications Thomas's account of Yseut of
the White Hands should be compared to his treatment of the
jealous King Mark. Unlike the anonymous author of *Flamenca*,
for instance, who delights in depicting the cuckolded
Archambaut as nothing but a dishonoured fool, Thomas never
alludes to King Mark in less than respectful terms.[13]
Emphasizing the King's institutional duty to revenge himself,
Thomas never implies that the King should have managed to
control his wife in the first place. While this may well be
because the King has to deal with the consequences of a magical love potion, not simply his wife's wayward desires, no such
narrative charity is shown in the case of Yseut of the White
Hands. Fuelled by slighted desire, female jealousy is tempestu-
ous, powerful, and highly dangerous. A husband's jealousy on
the other hand is a matter of principle, institutional duty, and
honour. In Thomas's *Tristan*, then, female jealousy is a matter
of passion, male jealousy a matter of position.

While illuminating, such a 'jealousy-centred' reading of
Tristan's death tends to turn Tristan's poem into a far more
misogynist text than it is, necessarily ignoring a host of other
crucial factors in Thomas's narrative. For Yseut of the White

---

[12] For an exploration of Andreas's account of bloodsucking women, see
'Desire in Language: Andreas Capellanus and the Controversy of Courtly Love'
(Ch. 9, above). *La châtelaine de Vergi* also presents us with a chilling account of
murderous female jealousy.

[13] See Micha for a survey of the theme of the cuckold and the jealous
husband in medieval literature, and Dronke, 'The Rise' for an account of the
theme in the *fabliau*.

Hands alone does not kill Tristan: he dies as a consequence of the wound in his thigh, inflicted by Estout l'Orgueilleux's poisoned spear. There is no need to dwell on the sexual symbolism of this wound. By not having Tristan killed in battle but slowly dying from his wounds, the poem rescues Tristan's reputation as a heroic warrior while allowing the narrative to continue in search of an even more suitable end for another forty days. Thomas's reluctance to end the poem with a final battle scene is entirely understandable in so far as a purely action-oriented warrior's end would be highly inappropriate for a poem obsessed from the outset with psychological analysis of passion.

Tristan's final words are rich in implications:

> E turne sei vers la parei,
> Dunc dit: 'Deus salt Ysolt e mei!
> Quant a moi ne volez venir,
> Pur vostre amur m'estuit murir.
> Jo ne puis plus tenir ma vie:
> Pur vus muer, Ysolt, bele amie.
> N'avez pité de ma langur,
> Mais de ma mort avrez dolur.
> Ço m'est, amie, grant confort
> Que pité avrez de ma mort.'

> (vv. 3031–40; Douce 1759–68)

He turns to the wall and says: 'God save Yseut and me! Since you will not come to me, I must die because of my love for you. I can no longer hold on to life, I die for you, my beloved Yseut. You have no pity for my sufferings, but you will suffer when I die. It is a great comfort to me, my love, that you will have pity for my death.'

While presenting Queen Yseut as responsible for his death this passage also implies that Tristan *chooses* to die at this moment, partly to punish Yseut for her ill will in not coming to see him. This sounds more like the last words of a vindictive suicide than those of a heroic lover dying from the treachery of his jealous wife. Apparently Tristan's purpose here is above all to make Yseut feel guilty. And on seeing Tristan's dead body, Yseut takes her cue:

> Mort estes pur l'amur de mei:
> Par raisun vivre puis ne dei.

> (vv. 3085–6; Douce 1813–14)[14]

You are dead because of your love for me: it is clear that I should
no longer live.

Immediately casting herself as the cause of Tristan's death, the
Queen in a final irony dies in expiation for the crime of her
double, the other Yseut.

According to Thomas, then, Tristan's death is almost excessively overdetermined: it is caused by Tristan the Dwarf, Tristan's
own pride and generosity in helping out the other Tristan, by
Estout l'Orgueilleux and the poisoned spear, by Yseut of the
White Hands, epistemological confusion, Tristan's own death
wish, and—in the final instance—by Queen Yseut herself. All
these different causes of death are, in one way or another, directly
produced by passion. Such an accumulation of deadly instances
can only reinforce Thomas's analysis of the complex relationship
between the lovers' imaginary passion and death. Tristan's end,
while still containing an aspect of the harmonious death wished
for by Yseut (Tristan's 'letting go' of life), also exhibits all the ferocious hatred and anger provoked by frustrated desire and disappointed love.

Yseut's own death is somewhat less complex. As we have seen,
she dies in order to expiate her part in Tristan's death:

> Pur mei avez perdu la vie,
> E jo frai cum veraie amie:
> Pur vus voil murir ensement.

> (vv. 3113–15; Sn2 806–8)

You have lost your life for my sake, and I will act like a true lover:
I will die for you in return.

But the real cause of her death, the text implies, is the fact that
she arrived *too late*. Yseut herself laments her belatedness no less

---

[14] Having inserted a two-line repetition left out by Wind, Payen's text here
differs slightly from Douce where his v. 3085 cannot be found. While appearing
in reverse order, Douce 1812–13 are nevertheless almost identical to Payen
3085–6: 'Par raisun vivre puis ne dei. | Mort estes pur la meie amur.'

than *three* times (see vv. 3089, 3097, 3109; Douce 1815 and Sn2 790 and 802), with Thomas's own final summing-up further emphasizing the point:

> Tristrant murut pur sun desir,
> Ysolt, qu'a tens n'i pout venir.
> Tristran murut pur su amur
> E la bele Ysolt par tendrur.
>
> (vv. 3123–6; Sn2 816–19)

Tristan died of his desire, Yseut because she could not arrive on time. Tristan died for his love, and fair Yseut because of tender pity.

But Tristan too dies because Yseut arrives too late. The lovers die because they can never catch up with each other: instead, difference will inevitably catch up with them. If this final account is taken to be the poem's last word on the matter, the text's own preferred mode of death for its protagonists, their 'own path to death', it is strikingly ironic, a stark comment on the lovers' search for perfect unity. Unlike other authors Thomas makes no mention at all of the various accounts of the lovers' common burial. One version has it that Yseut of the White Hands had them buried together, another that two trees were planted on their graves and grew entwined. By leaving the lovers to die one after the other without any posthumous consolations, Thomas marks his sceptical distance from romantic sentimentality. Thomas's narrative, however, does not end with the demise of the lovers. In a little postscript of his own he insists on the truth and beauty of his tale:

> E dit ai tute la verur
> Si cum je pramis al primur,
> E diz e vers i ai retrait:
> Pur essamplë issi ai fait
> Pur l'estorië embelir
> Quë as amanz deive plaisir
> E que par lieus possent troveir
> Chose u se possent recorder:
> Aveir em poissent grant confort
> Encuntre change, encontre tort,
> Encuntre painë e dolur,
> Encuntre tuiz engins d'amur!
>
> (vv. 3135–46; Sn2 828–39)

And I have told the whole truth as I promised at the beginning. I have gathered stories and poems in order to hold up an example and to embellish the legend so that it will give pleasure to lovers. I hope that they may, here and there, find something to recognize, retell, and remember.[15] I hope they will find great comfort in it and that it will fortify them against inconstance and injustice, against pain and suffering, and against all the snares of love!

Announcing itself as didactic and prophylactic Thomas's narrative holds out an epistemological hope to its lovers/listeners: if they keep it alive by recognizing themselves in his tale, retelling and remembering it, they will learn to distinguish true from false. Triumphantly refusing to lie down, this tale insists that it is told to be repeated, not to come to an end. Qua narrator Thomas, unlike his characters, will have no truck with the temptations of the death drive. The fact that this is a highly traditional end to narrative poems does not alter its meaning. On the contrary: if so many texts end on this note it may precisely be because this topos allows the narrative to claim victory where its characters meet defeat. Such a coda serves at once to distance the text from its characters and to insist on the power of narrative. Repeating a tale is necessarily to change it. The difference that annihilates the lovers is the enabling condition of narrativity: in this tale the true champion of Eros is not Tristan the Lover but Thomas the Narrator.

[15] The translation of v. 3142 (Sn2 835) is difficult. My interpretation of the end of the poem turns on the meaning of the construction *se recorder*. Payen translates this as 'afin qu'ils y trouvent le miroir exemplaire de ce qu'ils vivent', Hatto has 'they may find some things to take to heart'. Various dictionaries indicate that *recorder* and *se recorder* together accumulate a cluster of meanings ranging from remember, tell, retell, repeat to report, confirm, reconcile, and so on. My translation is an evasion insofar as it simply accumulates various likely options instead of choosing one of them. The idea of repetition is nevertheless central to almost every one of the possible meanings of the term.

Intentions and Effects:
Rhetoric and Identification in Simone de Beauvoir's 'The Woman Destroyed' (1988)

Simone de Beauvoir's short story 'The Woman Destroyed',[1] first published in January 1968, is one of her most popular texts.[2] Neither as intellectually complex as *L'invitée* (*She Came to Stay*; 1943), nor as politically challenging as *The Mandarins* (1954), it is not among her most important literary works. It does, however, have the distinction of being the most persistently misunderstood, at least according to Beauvoir herself. In *All Said and Done* (1972), the fourth volume of her autobiography, she writes that when it was first published, the great majority of her female readers persisted in identifying with the heroine, Monique, whereas she had intended to portray her as a woman victimized by her own delusions, perversely refusing freedom and responsibility in

I am grateful to Elizabeth Fallaize and Peter Brooks for their comments on an earlier version of this paper.

[1] The English title sounds too melodramatic. 'A Broken Woman' would be a more literal translation of 'La femme rompue'.

[2] Exceptionally among Beauvoir's fiction, the story appeared in instalments in the popular women's magazine *Elle* in the autumn of 1967, that is to say a few months before it was published as the title story in a volume of three short stories in Jan. 1968. The volume was a runaway best-seller on publication. But already in the autumn of 1967, Beauvoir published the title story in a special volume illustrated by sixteen engravings by her sister, Hélène de Beauvoir. Beauvoir accepted serialization in *Elle*, accompanied by her sister's engravings, in order to get more publicity for this special edition. This somewhat complex publication history seems to be the reason why some sources give 1967 and some 1968 for the volume of short stories as a whole. The two other stories, 'The Age of Discretion' and 'The Monologue', however, were not published until Jan. 1968.

the face of reason. My own experience of teaching the text tends to confirm Beauvoir's impression: most of my students flatly reject the 'authorial' reading, take the unfaithful husband, Maurice, to be the scoundrel, and identify with the protagonist. Consequently they refuse to read the end of the story simply as bleak and despondent, insisting instead that it somehow must represent a new departure for Monique. The question I would like to address here is why this text provokes such persistent 'misreadings'. What rhetorical strategies contribute to produce such a conflict of interpretations? And why does the conflict turn on the question of sympathy or identification?

These questions raise the difficult problem of intentionality in literary texts. Without wanting to rehearse here the various arguments advanced on this issue, I think it is necessary to distinguish between the author's declared intentions on the one hand, and what one might want to call the intentionality of the text on the other, which I see as the 'logic' of the text as produced by the reader, or in other words the feeling that *this* is what the various elements studied are structured to add up to, whether the author knows it or not. In this paper I also sometimes use the term 'authorial reading' by which I understand an effort to read the text according to the author's own explicit intentions or comments. Needless to say I am not assuming that the author's intentions always allow for such an 'authorial reading': it will always be necessary to *show*, not simply to assume, that a plausible reading can in fact be derived from such a statement of intent. The implication is that, in principle at least, an explicit authorial intention need not have any discernible textual effects at all. In this paper, then, I will first examine Beauvoir's stated intentions, and then try to produce an 'authorial reading' based on it. Given the determined disagreement between the author and many of her readers on this score, I will also try to show that this particular short story generates a series of other textual effects (to do with language, meaning, and epistemology) which necessarily undermine the authorial reading. Finally, I examine the way in which the formal strategies of the text produce an impossible position for the reader, one in which she can only choose one perspective at the cost of blinding herself to another.

Before turning to these issues, I should say that I use the word 'author' and the name Simone de Beauvoir as synonymous with the 'speaking (or writing) subject' or the 'subject of the enunciation', in Kristeva's and Benveniste's sense of these terms.[3] Thus the female protagonist, Monique, is simultaneously part of the text of Beauvoir's *énoncé*, and the subject of her own act of enunciation, which is the writing of her diary. As such Monique is at once a double of Beauvoir—another writing subject—and simply an effect of her discourse.

THE EXISTENTIALIST READING

Simone de Beauvoir's own reading is entirely plausible, thoroughly consistent as it is with her own existentialist positions and her analysis of the female condition in *The Second Sex* (1949). In *All Said and Done*, Beauvoir claims that she has never written a more depressing piece of fiction than 'The Woman Destroyed':

> I had never written anything more sombre than 'The Woman Destroyed': the whole of the second part is one long cry of agony, and the final crumbling of the heroine is sadder than death itself (*ASD* 142; *TCF* 178).[4]

The fact that the story appeared in instalments in *Elle* before publication brought Beauvoir hundreds of thousands of new

[3] I am referring to Kristeva's theory of the speaking subject, and Benveniste's exploration of the act of enunciation. The reason why I mention Kristeva at all in the context of a paper where I only explicitly draw on Benveniste is to draw attention to the difference between Benveniste's transcendental ego and Kristeva's psychoanalytical speaking subject.

[4] All page references to works by Beauvoir are given in the text. Although I have been working with the French texts, I give all quotations in English. However, in order to facilitate rapid consultation of the original, I also supply page references to the French editions used. Full references to the editions used are given in the Works Cited. In some cases I have not been able to consult a published translation. In such cases, or where no English translation exists, I give only one page reference, to the French text, and supply my own translation.

I have no such scruples about quotations from other sources. In general, I have tried to use published English translations, but this has not always been possible. I give my own translations wherever I rely on an original text. The one page reference supplied is always to the edition listed in the Works Cited.

readers. They reacted passionately to the text. Beauvoir comments:

> Immediately I was overwhelmed with letters from women, destroyed, half-destroyed or in the act of being destroyed. They identified themselves with the heroine; they attributed all possible virtues to her and they were astonished that she should remain attached to a man so unworthy of her. Their partiality made it evident that as far as their husbands, their rivals and they themselves were concerned, they shared Monique's blindness. Their reactions were based upon an immense incomprehension [*un énorme contresens*] (*ASD* 142; *TCF* 177–8).

It is interesting—and somewhat puzzling—to note that the reactions of the readers of *Elle* in 1967 closely correspond to those of my own (and many of my colleagues') students in the late 1980s. Thus the advent of the women's movement would seem to have made no difference at all to this specific reading position. In 1967 and 1968, the critics in general disliked the book. According to Beauvoir, one of them, Bernard Pivot, even claimed that 'since "The Woman Destroyed" was appearing in a women's magazine it was therefore a shop-girl's romance with pink bows on it' (*ASD* 142; *TCF* 178).[5] On the whole Beauvoir did not take such criticisms and 'misreadings' seriously. But when some feminists objected that these stories had nothing militant about them, she was more affected, although not to the point of actually agreeing with them:

---

[5] Writing in the conservative *Figaro littéraire*, Pivot rushed into print on 30 Oct. 1967—that is to say, *before* the last instalments had appeared in *Elle*. It is only fair to point out that Pivot's aggression stems as much from his arrogant and sexist devaluation of *la presse féminine* as from his dislike of Beauvoir and her well-known political positions. 'Truly, "The Woman Destroyed" is a whole women's magazine by itself', he writes. 'It is *Elle* in *Elle*. So far, only the horoscope is missing' (29). Pivot's reaction, as well as that of Jacqueline Piatier, the influential critic of *Le Monde* (who, unlike Pivot, managed to wait until she had read the whole volume before reviewing it), raises the question of Beauvoir's status as a writer of popular fiction for women. The issue is far too complex to be broached here, but there can be no doubt that her best-selling status in many countries enables us to study her fiction and autobiographies from this angle. In 1988 I wrote: 'To my knowledge such a study has still to be undertaken'. In 1990, Elizabeth Fallaize published an interesting paper on 'The Woman Destroyed', precisely from the perspective of popular romance writing (see 'Resisting Romance').

'She has betrayed us!' they cried; and they sent me reproachful letters. There is no reason at all why one should not draw a feminist conclusion from 'The Woman Destroyed': Monique's unhappiness arose from her having agreed to be dependent. But I really do not feel obliged to choose exemplary heroines. It does not seem to me that describing failure, error and bad faith means betraying anyone at all (*ASD* 143–4; *TCF* 179).

But how did Beauvoir come to write such a gloomy story? Her own explanation is that the material came from her female friends and acquaintances. Around 1966, she tells us, several women in their forties confided in her their disarray at losing their husbands to another woman. In spite of the considerable differences between these women, they had one thing in common:

> the women could not even remotely understand what was happening to them; they thought their husband's behaviour contradictory, abnormal and deviant, and the rival unworthy of his love: their world was falling to pieces and they ended up by no longer knowing who they were (*ASD* 140; *TCF* 175).

In a striking turn of phrase Beauvoir goes on to say: 'L'idée m'est venue de donner à voir leur nuit' (*TCF* 175), which literally means that she wanted to 'make their night visible', and which Patrick O'Brian translates as 'I had the idea of speaking about their darkness and making it evident' (*ASD* 140). Here the story is presented as at once true and distant: as a problem which affects *other* women, not Simone de Beauvoir. Attributing a position of discursive and epistemological superiority to herself, Beauvoir seems to be insisting that *she* can expose the plight of these women precisely because she is not in the grip of their illusions. But perhaps she protests too much here? Is there not a whiff of denegation about this attempt to ascribe the problem of jealousy and loss of love to other and younger women? (Her informants are 'in their forties', whereas Beauvoir herself was 58 in 1966.) This suspicion is reinforced if one stops to consider that 'The Woman Destroyed' is only the last in a series of texts in which Beauvoir chooses to focus on the plight of a jealous woman. Many critics have been quick to point out that while female jealousy is surprisingly absent from Beauvoir's autobiography, it features often and insistently in her fiction and essays. Thus both her first published novel, *She Came to Stay*, and her last work of fiction, 'The Woman Destroyed', feature a female protagonist suffering agonies of jealousy. Jealousy is also discussed in some detail in *The Second Sex* and passionately exposed in the tragic case of Paule in *The Mandarins*. And Murielle, the cruel, paranoid, and narcissistic protagonist of the short story 'Monologue' (in *The Woman Destroyed*) can be read as at once a more obsessive version of Paule and a sadistic illustration of the narcissistic woman in love as described in *The Second Sex*.

The fact that Beauvoir here comes across as somewhat disingenuous and certainly as condescending, does not give us carte blanche to ignore her ostensible intentions. If she expresses her desire to expose other women's ignorance, it is overwhelmingly probable that it is because she wants to change the situation that brings it about. The language she uses ('reveal', 'make visible') is very similar to that of Sartre in his 1948 essay *What Is Literature?* And as late as 1964, in the great debate between *nouveaux romanciers* and existentialists on commitment in literature, Beauvoir still defended engagement in much the same terms as those first used by Sartre in 1948.[6] For Sartre and Beauvoir, to disclose or reveal (*dévoiler*) the world is to act on it. Here is Sartre's version of this view:

> Thus, by speaking, I reveal the situation by my very intention of changing it; I reveal it to myself and to others in order to change it. I strike at its very heart, I transfix it, and I display it in full view; at present I dispose of it; with every word I utter I involve myself a little more in the world. (*What Is Literature?* 37).

But Sartre's language here is not only a plea for engagement in literature, it is also—or first and foremost—a display of discursive power. In the two sentences quoted here, he manages to squeeze in no less than eight 'I' and three 'my' or 'myself', which is no little feat in itself. On the other hand, the modest 'and to others' is not repeated once, and consequently reads like a hurried afterthought, not as the very *raison d'être* of the writer's commitment. On this evidence, the politically engaged

---

[6] See Buin, with contributions from Yves Berger, Jean-Pierre Faye, Jean Ricardou, Jorge Semprun, and Sartre as well as from Beauvoir.

writer is at least as involved with his own prowess, his own capacity to reveal the truth (I reveal, I strike, I transfix, I display . . .), as with his political message. In the same way Beauvoir's genuine commitment to change is structured through a discursive position which signals power, superior insight, and a hierarchical mode of thought.

Implicitly, Beauvoir's autobiography displays the same emphasis on the superiority of the writer. Here every single text ever published by Beauvoir receives its own authorial interpretation: the autobiography becomes a repertoire of authorized readings, a series of efforts to enforce the law, or in other words, to police the reading of her own texts. On the whole she has been remarkably successful in this operation: to my knowledge very few critics indeed have set out—deliberately or not—to subvert her views. But there is of course also a sense in which the very intensity of Beauvoir's efforts to enforce the true meaning of her texts may make the sceptical reader wonder why she protests so much. Perhaps there is something in these texts which threatens to escape even Simone de Beauvoir?

The politics of Beauvoir's discursive enterprise is ambiguous. As we have seen, she herself claims that the story is compatible with feminist politics, but that is on two conditions only: first, that we accept her own interpretation, i.e. that Monique is the author of her own downfall, and secondly that we agree that the best feminist reading available is to turn Monique's tale into a terrible warning to others. A feminist who balks at submitting to so much authorial authority, will surely be cast out among the 'partial', 'blind', and 'incomprehending' readers of *Elle*.

This impression of discursive superiority is reinforced by Beauvoir's account of the structure of her short story. She finds Monique guilty of an unexpiable crime: that of seeking to escape from the truth (see *ASD* 140; *TCF* 175). In order to emphasize this point, she claims, she deliberately structured the narrative like a detective story, packing the text with clues pointing to the real author of the crime. Whereas Monique wants to make us believe that the scoundrel is Maurice, or possibly the evil rival Noëllie, Beauvoir points the finger at Monique herself. Her language signals the intensity of her engagement when Beauvoir sets out

clinically and methodically to construct a veritable witch-hunt in
which to trap her protagonist:

> the whole of Monique's efforts tend to obscure [the light]; from
> one page to another her diary contradicts itself—but it does so
> through fresh omissions and new falsehoods. She herself weaves
> the darkness in which she sinks far down, so far that she loses her
> own image. I hoped that people would read the book as a detec-
> tive-story; here and there I scattered clues that would allow the
> reader to find the key to the mystery—but only if he tracked
> Monique as one tracks down the guilty character [*à condition qu'on
> dépiste Monique comme on dépiste un coupable*] (*ASD* 140; *TCF* 175–6).

The repository of truth in the story is not Monique, but
Maurice, Beauvoir claims: 'Intellectually the husband is her superior by far and he has long since stopped loving her' (*ASD* 140;
TCF 175). It may not be intentional, but she does make this sound
rather as if the latter was a necessary consequence of the former.
However that may be, the reader now has a clear recipe for how
to read the story: accept everything Maurice says, particularly
when he is angry, and the truth will be clear. Since such an
estimable man likes her—even loves her—the independent
career woman Noëllie must be an excellent character, the dependent housewife Monique simply possessive and ignorant. For
most readers, whether or not they otherwise agree with the
author, the fact that Maurice has managed to lie to Monique
about his affairs with other women for over eight years makes this
interpretation somewhat uncomfortable. Curiously enough his
commonplace and petty avoidance of the sexual truth is not
supposed to cast a shadow over his heroic status in his author's
eyes, nor is it supposed to prevent him from representing reason
and the intellect in the text. In this sense, at least, there is more
than one parallel between the representation of Maurice in this
short story and the representation of Sartre in Beauvoir's
memoirs and in the *Lettres au Castor*.

From an existentialist perspective, Monique has made a series
of crucial errors. She is guilty of *mauvaise foi* (bad faith) in that
she persists in denying her own freedom and therefore also her
own responsibility for her life, choosing instead to define herself
as a 'relative being'. Having defined herself entirely through her

husband, Monique loses her own image when she loses him. Her definition of love is also cruelly flawed: she fails to realize that love is an active project, not a static essence. For Sartre and Beauvoir, to take the world as given (*donné*) is to deny freedom. The world is always already in process: every one of our actions transforms it, as it transforms us. If Maurice and Monique's interpretations of their marriage are radically opposed (see, for instance, the great scene between them on *ASD* 160–4; *TCF* 184–9), it is because he has changed through his struggle to realize his projects in the world, whereas she has remained faithful to a static image of herself, one originally reflected back to her by Maurice, but long since taken over by her and placed in some timeless realm outside history. In this sense he represents dynamism, activity, and transcendence, whereas she represents immanence, passivity, and inaction.

For an existentialist there is no such thing as a given, essential meaning of a situation. By choosing a project we shape our own identity, and create a position from which to interpret the world. But there is nothing inherent or necessary about this position or this project: it must always be renewed if it is to continue to define us. According to this view, if Monique slides helplessly from one interpretation to another, unable to get a grip on herself and the world, it is because her refusal to define herself through the recognition of her own freedom prevents her from forging a coherent position from which to perceive reality.

The fact that Monique gives up her own medical studies, and later refuses to take paid work, is crucial for the Beauvoirean reading of the story. Already in *The Second Sex* Beauvoir argued that economic liberation is the sine qua non of every other form of liberation. Her uncompromising message is clear: motherhood and marriage alone can never make a woman happy; paid work alone secures her independence. Monique is intended as a faithful illustration of this maxim.

To say that Monique derives her identity from her relationship with Maurice, is to say that when he no longer loves her, she is nobody. That she progressively loses her identity and slowly sinks into depression is a logical consequence of this position. For Monique, love made Maurice and her into a unity. They were each other, always and for ever. What she liked, he liked, and vice versa. Her constant use of 'we' indicates her incapacity to differentiate between them. Their very being is fixed once and for all in Monique's static image of their love. Maurice has no right to change: change can only signify falseness, lack of authenticity, superficiality, or a lack of reality. In emphasizing the theme of unity between her and her husband (*on ne fait qu'un*), Monique repeats the mistake of Françoise in *She Came to Stay*. 'Harmony between two individuals is never a *donnée*, it must be worked for continually', Beauvoir writes in *The Prime of Life* (*PL* 260; *FA* 299).

Monique's story also neatly illustrates Beauvoir's account of the dilemmas of the woman in love (*l'amoureuse*) in *The Second Sex*:

> It is, again, one of the loving woman's misfortunes to find that her very love disfigures her, destroys her; she is nothing more than this slave, this servant, this too ready mirror, this too faithful echo. When she becomes aware of this, her distress reduces her worth still further; in tears, demands and scenes she succeeds in losing all her attractiveness. An existent is what he does; but simply to be, she has come to rely on a consciousness not her own, and she has given up doing anything (*SS* 665; *DSb* 576).

But are there no mitigating circumstances? Even in *The Second Sex* Beauvoir takes pains to stress that it would be unfair to blame women for the negative and pathetic role they often come to play in patriarchal society: 'It is useless to apportion blame and excuses: justice can never be done in the midst of injustice' (*SS* 723; *DSb* 652). So why is she so determined to track Monique down like a criminal in this case? Already in 1947, two years before publishing *The Second Sex*, in *Pour une morale de l'ambiguïté*, she argues vigorously against blaming the victims of tyrannical regimes, such as slaves or the inmates of a harem, for their ignorance or indolence. But at the same time she stresses the necessity of seizing the very first opportunity of liberation:

> Ignorance and error are facts as ineluctable as the walls of a prison. The black slave in the eighteenth century or the Muslim woman locked up in a harem do not have any tools which allow them to attack, be it only in thought or through astonishment or anger, the society which oppresses them. Their behaviour can only be defined and can only be judged from within this fact. It is possible that in

their situation, which is limited as all human situations, they are already achieving a perfect affirmation of their freedom. But as soon as liberation appears as possible, not to take advantage of this possibility is to surrender one's freedom. This implies bad faith and is truly to be blamed (*une faute positive*) (*Pour une morale* 56; my translation).

If Monique is to be found guilty, it can only be because Simone de Beauvoir considered that by 1968 women had already gained their freedom. This is more than likely, since she argued the same thing as early as 1949: 'By and large we have won the game', she wrote in the introduction to *The Second Sex* (*SS* xxxiii; *DSa* 29). On this view of post-war society, Monique has no excuses: neither a slave nor imprisoned in a harem, she is free to act. The implications are clear: to read the text in accordance with Beauvoir's intentions amounts to rejecting the need for any further social or institutional liberation of women. To argue with the readers of *Elle* that Monique is deserving of sympathy and support, and to make her an object of identification is at least implicitly to recognize that the victimization of women cannot simply be turned into a question of the individual woman's complicity or guilt. It also means emphasizing the responsibility of the husband where Beauvoir's own reading lets him off the hook rather too quickly, mostly on the grounds of his superior intelligence. It is no wonder that a reading which tends to exonerate philandering husbands and instead blame their unsuspecting wives for not being interesting enough failed to appeal to the readers of *Elle*. Finally, it is interesting to note that while Beauvoir soon came to recognize the error of her social and political analysis of women's position (she declared her support for the new feminist movement in a famous interview published in *Le nouvel observateur* in 1972[7]), she apparently never changed her own reading of 'The Woman Destroyed'.

JEALOUSY, KNOWLEDGE, AND LANGUAGE

Although the conflicting interpretations of the text now can be seen to have their roots in an implicit political disagreement over how to

[7] See Alice Schwartzer's interview with Beauvoir, reprinted in *Simone de Beauvoir Today*.

read women's position in society, there are other reasons why the Beauvoirean reading, for all its coherence, fails to satisfy most of her readers. There is, for instance, no analysis of formal effects. The fact that 'The Woman Destroyed' has the distinction of being the only fictional text by Beauvoir which foregrounds the writing process, and that the text itself is a first person singular narrative, consisting of Monique's diary entries over a period of six and a half months (from 13 September to 24 March), is ignored. I shall return to the question of rhetorical and formal effects in the next section. There are nevertheless also a series of thematic and/or theoretical reasons why contemporary readers may fail to grasp Beauvoir's intentions. I now intend to examine three key issues here: the representation of jealousy, the representation of knowledge, and the implicit theory of language in 'The Woman Destroyed'.[8]

We have already seen that Beauvoir often returns to the theme of jealousy. Even more persistently, the question of knowledge haunts her texts. 'What is the truth—the truth about myself? about others? about the world?' is always the most pressing problem for her, whatever the genre she works in. For Beauvoir, knowledge represents control, power, self-confidence, self-reliance, solidity, and energy. Lucidity, intelligence, rationality are key values in her textual universe. These are of course the very Cartesian values which exercise such powerful influence on French education and culture in general. If Monique at one point becomes obsessed with the question of whether she is intelligent, it is not only because she is a product of Simone de Beauvoir's imagination: it is also because she is French.[9] For Beauvoir, the

---

[8] There are not many full-length readings of this short story. The two most important ones are Anne Ophir's study of the whole collection of stories, and Elizabeth Fallaize's chapter on the volume in her excellent study of Beauvoir's fiction. Mary Evans (88–90), while unaware both of the fact that her own socialist-feminist reading conflicts with the author's own and of the unreliability of Monique as a narrator, nevertheless produces some brief, but interesting remarks towards a possibly socially informed and politically transformative reading of this particular story. After publishing this essay, I have enjoyed reading Fallaize, 'Resisting Romance'. Terry Keefe's *Beauvoir: 'Les Belles Images'/'La Femme Rompue'* was published in 1991, but he does not take much notice of feminist work on these texts.

[9] It is nevertheless true to say that Beauvoir in no way questions such national values in this text.

theme of jealousy always involves that of knowledge,[10] and 'The Woman Destroyed' is no exception to this rule. The plot of the story casts Monique's breakdown as an effect of an increasingly frenzied quest for reliable knowledge. But jealousy breeds doubt, epistemological insecurity, and an increasingly paranoid obsession with interpretation.[11]

From this perspective, the jealous subject is more like the detective than the criminal in a traditional thriller. This, surely, is another reason why the author's intentions go unnoticed: she has given Monique the role of quasi-paranoid reader of signs normally reserved for the detective. So how can the reader guess that she is in fact the culprit? Perceiving the world as a set of confusing clues to a hidden truth, Monique now desperately tries to endow every sign with a stable meaning. But unlike the detective story, jealousy offers no solutions: the very process of constant interpretation and reinterpretation ensures that the final closure of the thriller is not to be had. In the end, no evidence is final: everything could always be interpreted differently. Othello's anguished plea for the 'proof, the ocular proof' is a plea for epistemological stability. But, as Monique knows, to the jealous subject visual evidence is no evidence at all: 'In any case, I should not have believed my eyes if I had seen him in bed with a woman' (*WD* 163; *FR* 188; TA). And Monique's efforts to trust other forms of knowledge—rumours, hearsay, graphology, even astrology—are shown to be vain as well as pathetic.

The first few entries in Monique's diary present us with what would seem to be firm epistemological ground. But an attentive reader will perceive the hollow note sounded already in the initial description of Les Salines. Looking at these eighteenth-century buildings, Monique thinks of their history and particularly of the fact that they never served any purpose: 'They are solid; they are real: yet their abandoned state changes them into a fantastic pretence [*simulacre*]—of what, one wonders' (*WD* 105; *FR* 123). This evocation of a useless and somewhat empty semblance of a

---

[10] The opposite is not necessarily true.

[11] For a somewhat different study of rhetorical jealousy see my essay on Andreas Capellanus's *De Amore* (Chapter 9 above).

city hiding an unknown reality is not the product of an easy and relaxed mind, as Monique would like us—and herself—to think. Whether one sees this image as a deliberate and rather heavy-handed authorial metaphor of Monique's ignorance of her own situation or as a first hint of the bleak final image in the book—that of the empty flat with the black windows and frightening doors behind which lurks the terrifying future (*WD* 220; *FR* 253), the salt works designed by Ledoux remain above all a monumental utopian project which failed.[12]

Monique's real or apparent peace of mind is soon shattered by the news that her husband is having an affair with another woman, Noëllie Guérard. From this moment on the narrative becomes a chronicle of the slow and meticulous shattering of every illusion Monique ever had. Her illusions are relatively easy to catalogue, in spite of the fact that one set tends to spawn another with disconcerting speed. When jealousy hits her, Monique has cast herself once and for all as the devoted wife, housewife, and mother, and as *grande amoureuse* as well. Her immediate reaction is simply to construct her rival, Noëllie, as her own negative mirror image. To describe herself and 'the other woman', she resorts to a simple pattern of depth v. surface, essence v. contingence:

> One thing that helps me is that I am not physically jealous. . . . She [Noëllie] is the incarnation of everything we dislike—desire to succeed at any price, pretentiousness, love of money, a delight in display. She does not possess a single idea of her own; she is fundamentally devoid of sensitivity—she just goes along with the fashion. There is such barefacedness and exhibitionism in her capers with men that indeed I wonder whether she may not be frigid (*WD* 120; *FR* 140).

But I am convinced of something that I cannot find adequate words for. With me Maurice has a relationship in depth, one to

---

[12] The place visited by Monique is the famous 'Salines de Ledoux', the work of the architect Claude Nicolas Ledoux (1736–1806), constructed between 1775 and 1779, and situated in the little village of Arc-et-Senans, near Besançon. Ledoux's masterplan was to design the central salt works surrounded by concentric circles of other industrial buildings. His 'ideal city' was never used as intended, but remains one of the most monumental set of buildings of 18-cent. France.

which his essential being is committed and which is therefore indestructible. He is only attached to Noëllie by his most superficial feelings—each of them might just as well be in love with someone else. Maurice and I are wholly conjoined (*WD* 171; *FR* 198).

If Monique is authentic (one of her favourite terms for herself, see for instance *WD* 136; *FR* 158 and *WD* 146; *FR* 169), Noëllie must be false and superficial. If Monique is simple and natural, Noëllie must be a sophisticated snob. If Monique gave her daughters a good education, Noëllie must be destroying her own daughter, and so on. The equation works both ways: if Noëllie loves money, lacks originality, and is a slave of fashion, it is the better to emphasize Monique's own sterling qualities. Monique's image of Noëllie is never corroborated by any other instance in the text, but neither is it contradicted: Maurice does not want to discuss her, and Monique's friends supply highly unreliable and contradictory information. So although the textual Noëllie comes across as nothing but the projection of Monique's hostility, the text surprisingly enough refrains from undercutting her account, and so comes to leave the question of Noëllie's 'real' nature fairly open.

As we have seen, Monique's sense of identity is bound up with her unshakeable belief in a fundamental unity between Maurice and herself. This belief cannot cope with the idea of difference. Monique therefore has to explain away the apparent difference in their interests and value judgements as an effect of ignorance, or more correctly, of incorrect knowledge. True knowledge, then, should theoretically help him to mend his ways:

> He is altogether gone from me if he likes being with someone I dislike so very much—and whom he ought to dislike if he were faithful to our code. Certainly he has altered. He lets himself be taken in by false values that we used to despise. Or he is simply completely mistaken about Noëllie. I wish the scales would drop from his eyes soon (*WD* 136; *FR* 158).

It is when Monique realizes that the 'superficial' or 'contingent' *histoire de peau* (*WD* 118, *FR* 138; *WD* 122, *FR* 141) that Maurice has with Noëllie is not simply an effect of ignorance, but real, that her whole epistemological system starts to break down. If she can no longer simply oppose surface to depth, false values to real values, Noëllie to herself, if the one set of terms surreptitiously starts to infect the other, chaos threatens to engulf her. Her *saison en enfer*—the two weeks she spends locked into her flat, dirty, drunk and desperate—expresses precisely this blurring of all categories.

LANGUAGE AND WRITING

As Monique grows increasingly jealous and desperate, references to the difficulties of writing, and particularly to the impossibility of seizing the truth in words, multiply. There is something paradoxical about the fact that Françoise, aspiring author and jealous protagonist of *She Came to Stay*, never utters a single reflection on the problems of language, whereas the crushed housewife of 'The Woman Destroyed' produces a running meta-commentary on questions of interpretation, communication, and language, so that it is in 'The Woman Destroyed' and not *She Came to Stay* that we find the most interesting reflections on the relationship between truth, knowledge, and language.

Monique's writing is a doomed attempt to capture an essential identity through language. But writing, she soon realizes, is no ally in such a struggle. In fact, the very act of writing signals lack: lack of insight, lack of happiness, lack of stability:

> Yes, something has changed, since here I am writing about him, about myself, behind his back. If he had done so, I should have felt betrayed. Each of us used to be able to see entirely into the other (*WD* 111; *FR* 131).

Nor do words ever convey reality, partly because writing always comes too late, *after* the event:

> Rages, nightmares, horror—words cannot encompass them. I set things down on paper when I recover strength, either in despair or in hope. But the feeling of total bewilderment, of stunned stupidity, of falling to pieces—these pages do not contain them (*WD* 194; *FR* 223; TA).

Sometimes the writing subject lacks insight. Writing the truth as one sees it, is just another illusion: 'I was lying to myself. How I lied to myself!' (*WD* 194; *FR* 224). Words are always open to reinterpretation; they offer no stability, no security. Rereading their old letters, Monique realizes that they now take on a different meaning from the one she thought they had, and earlier passages in her diary now strike her as false, wrong, or deceitful. But the same process of rereading and reinterpretation may itself be repeated. Thus we are given five different versions of the moment when she waved goodbye to Maurice at the airport in Nice and four different views on the picnic in Les Salines or of the moment of Maurice's confession. So how can she trust her most recent 'insight'? What's true and what's false? And what can words do for us anyway?

It is on this point, I think, that Beauvoir's own and her present-day readers' interpretation differ most sharply. Beauvoir claims that one of the clues to Monique's guilt is the fact that she constantly contradicts herself, whereas 'postmodern' readers tend to see this confusion not as a sign of her stupidity or blindness but as an excellent illustration of the treacherous, deconstructive nature of *all* language. To the same readers, Monique's increasing epistemological helplessness does not necessarily signal her specific lack of insight, but rather a correct insight into the unstable nature of knowledge in general. In this way, 'The Woman Destroyed' may paradoxically—and quite unintentionally—come across as a far more 'modern' text than any of Beauvoir's other writings. There is also a sense in which 'The Woman Destroyed', precisely by emphasizing the slippage of language and the disintegration of knowledge as much as it does, reveals a fundamental tension in Beauvoir's work in general: the tension between her conviction that she has full epistemological control and her fear of slipping into the irrational chaos of the body and the emotions.

In this text a similar tension surfaces as the contradiction between Monique's experience of a full-blown epistemological crisis and her espousal of a crudely realist theory of knowledge. After an unusually friendly conversation with Maurice, she concludes that language cannot change anything after all. In fact, when they give things different, more comfortable names, she feels cheated:

> It was delightful talking with him, like two friends, as we used to do. Difficulties grew smaller; questions wafted away like smoke; events faded; true and false merged in an iridescence of converging shades. Fundamentally, nothing had happened. I ended up by

believing that Noëllie did not exist. . . . Illusions: sleight of hand. In fact this comfortable talk has not changed anything in the very least. Things have been given other names: they have not altered in any way. I have learnt nothing. The past remains as obscure as ever; the future as uncertain (*WD* 180–1; *PR* 209).

Caught in her own homespun version of philosophical realism, one which divorces language from reality, she concludes that language is useless, a mere surface game which never influences the underlying reality in any way. Truth and reality become one and the same thing, equally abstract and absolute: both are inde-structible, outside language, outside time, fixed for all eternity: 'This love between us was real: it was solid—as indestructible as truth' (*WD* 195; *FR* 225). While ostensibly intended to protect truth and reality from the corroding effects of doubt, Monique's episte-mology, which turns her own experience of flux and uncertainty into non-knowledge, can only reinforce her suffering. Language will, for instance, be incapable of catching the very essence of what she proudly calls her 'sincerity'. This is doubly tragic, because she derives a large part of her own identity precisely from her sincer-ity: 'I try to say exactly what I think, what I feel; so does he; and there is nothing that seems more precious to us than this sincerity' (*WD* 137; *FR* 160). But in the light of her increasing distrust of language, the 'sincerity' Monique thought she and Maurice set above all other values can be nothing but a sham: the most sincere confession of true feeling will never change 'reality'.

There should be no need to emphasize the distance between such fatalism and Beauvoir's own view of language and action. Beauvoir is, after all, the woman who in 1962 declared that: 'I am an intellectual. I take words and the truth to be of value' (*FC* 378; *FCb* 120). From the author's perspective, Monique's lack of confi-dence in language turns out to be yet another trace of her prin-cipal crime: that of *not* being the bearer of knowledge and truth; that of not being an intellectual.

THE RHETORICS OF IDENTIFICATION

The readings outlined above are almost exclusively thematic: very little attention is being paid to the rhetorical strategies of the text.

In the case of this particular short story, however, perhaps the single most important factor to influence the reader is a purely formal structure: the diary form, with its characteristic use of the first-person singular narrator.

As we have already seen, Beauvoir intends to turn the reader into a detective. In one way this places the reader in a position of subservience to the author of the plot: she is after all simply decoding the puzzles set by the author, following the beaten path to the inevitable end, as it were. However, this strategy also assumes that the reader in the end will have accumulated all the knowledge the author alone originally possessed. As such it seeks to turn the reader into the author's double. In this way Beauvoir's rhetorical strategy aims for a Romantic identification between reader and author: an identification where the reader knows her place. Apart from being highly flattering for the author, this kind of hierarchical symbiosis is uncannily like Monique's deluded view of her relationship with Maurice: they are one—but *he* is the one they are. Thus Beauvoir is caught in a glaring contradiction between her thematic condemnation of her protagonist and her persistent efforts to enact the very same delusions on the rhetorical level.

But if Monique's marriage fails, so does Beauvoir's rhetorical struggle. This is first and foremost an effect of Monique's first-person singular narration. Her suffering and despair come across with a quite unusual intensity which rarely fails to elicit the reader's sympathy. In the Beauvoirean scheme of things, the intensity is more likely to be caused by the author's loathing for the hapless Monique, than by any great sympathy with her plight. There is a considerable gap between Beauvoir's cold-blooded plotting of her 'detective story' and the passionate suffering which, quite against all the rules of the traditional detective thriller, she attributes to the woman she claims to have set up as the criminal. If her rhetorical strategies do not work it is because she has failed to study the formal rules of the detective story closely enough. To make the criminal hide behind the mask of a first-person singular narrator, is extremely unusual, to say the least. When Agatha Christie tried it, in *The Murder of Roger Ackroyd*, her readers felt cheated. It is like making the counsel for the defence the murderer: it is violating the rules of the game by setting an illicit trap for the reader, and provides a far too easy way out for the author, who no longer has to construct a really clever set of 'licit' clues.

Monique's lack of knowledge makes her incapable of constructing a coherent narrative: Beauvoir makes her 'contradictions' one of the most incriminating pieces of evidence against her, accusing her, as we have seen, of 'weave[ing] the darkness in which she sinks far down', since 'from one page to another her diary contradicts itself'. These contradictions, moreover, are themselves a quagmire of ignorance, a set of 'fresh omissions and new falsehoods' (*ASD* 140; *TCF* 175). If Peter Brooks is right in his interpretation of Freud's *Dora*, for Freud the very fact of producing an incoherent narrative is a sign of neurosis (Brooks, 'Psychoanalytic' 54). But in this sense, Brooks points out, the work of analysis and that of detection have more than one feature in common:

> [The detective story] equates the incomplete, incoherent, baffling story with crime, whereas detection is the making of an intelligible, consistent and unbroken narrative. . . .The narrative chain, with each event connected to the next by reasoned causal links, marks the victory of reason over chaos, of society over the aberrancy of crime, and restitutes a world in which aetiological histories offer the best solution to the apparently unexplainable ('Psychoanalytic' 54).

One might add that the reason why the neurotic fails to produce coherence is that she lacks the power to impose her own connections on her reader/listener. Freud is very explicit about the way in which the analytic situation is a scene of struggle, if not in *Dora*, then in his papers on technique from 1911–15. In 'Remembering, Repeating and Working Through' (1914), he sees analysis as armed combat: 'The patient brings out of the armoury of the past the weapons with which he defends himself against the progress of the treatment—weapons which we must wrest from him one by one' (*SE* 12: 151). In 'The Dynamics of Transference' (1912) he summarizes his findings on transference by stressing the need for victory for the analyst: 'This struggle between the doctor and the patient, between intellect and instinctual life, between understanding and seeking to act, is played out almost exclusively in the phenomena of transference. It is on that field that the victory must be won— the victory whose expression is the permanent cure of the neurosis' (*SE* 12: 108). There is in 'The Woman Destroyed' more than a superficial similarity between Beauvoir's position in relation to her character, and that of Freud vis-à-vis Dora. In both cases, what is at stake in the narrative struggle is the right to claim one's own knowledge as truth, and as a corollary, the right to proclaim the guilt of one's defeated opponent.

But what exactly are the effects of the first-person singular narrative? For Émile Benveniste, before it is anything else, all actual use of language is an utterance, an act of enunciation. The act of enunciation produces (*instaure*) the discourse as discourse. This has a series of implications. First of all, the speaker cannot fail to signal her position as speaker (*locuteur*). Secondly, the very act of signalling one's place as a speaker establishes an 'other', a 'you' to whom the utterance is addressed. Finally, the act of enunciation is already, in its very formal effects, the 'expression of a certain relationship to the world' ('L'appareil' 82). This means that the enunciation always in some way or other reveals the 'attitudes of the enunciator towards that which he or she enounces' (85). And one of the main aims of the enunciation is to *influence* the listener, or in other words: every act of enunciation necessarily embodies a rhetorical strategy directed towards the 'you' implied by the speaking 'I'. As Gérard Genette has shown, this is no less true for texts which ostensibly signal their impersonality by extensive use of third-person narrative, the *passé simple*, and so on.[13] A monologue

---

[13] Benveniste changed his position on this point. My account is based on his 1970 paper 'L'appareil formel de l'énonciation'. But eleven years earlier, in a famous essay from 1959, 'Les relations de temps dans le verbe français', he sought to distinguish between two forms of enunciation, 'historical narrative' (*récit historique*) and discourse. The former he then defined as a mode of enunciation which excludes any 'autobiographical' trace in the language used. Prime examples were historical accounts, impersonal descriptions, and so on. 'Discourse' was defined in almost exactly the same terms as those used to characterize 'enunciation' in general in 1970, that is to say as language which presupposes a 'speaker and a listener and in the former the intention to influence the latter in any way' ('Relations' 242). But critics such as Gérard Genette and later Jonathan Culler were quick to point out that this distinction, although certainly

is no exception to this rule: it is simply a variation on the basic structure which is the dialogue. Fictional acts of enunciation are nevertheless more complex than ordinary utterances, in that they take place on at least two levels, that of the writer and that of her characters (see 'L'appareil' 88).

In 'The Woman Destroyed', there are two subjects of enunciation: the implicit I of the literary act of enunciation, which produces its own dialogic I/you relation, and that of the fictional character, the I of the *énoncé*, that is, the statement produced by the enunciation. The primary rhetorical relation which is to be established here is that between the author and the reader, where the reader is to be made to respond correctly to the clues laid down by the enunciator. Beauvoir's failure is the failure properly to establish this I/you relation. Instead, the competing I of the *énoncé* takes over as the predominant speaking subject, producing the reader in *her* image. The reader then becomes involved in doubling *her* perspective, endlessly inventing excuses for her, even ending up feeling cross with Beauvoir for placing Monique in such dire straits.

What happens here might best be described as a case of double transference: positive transference on to the character, negative on to the author. Transference may among other things be characterized as a relation of identification and as a demand for love. In his 'Observations on Transference-Love' (1915), Freud argues that: 'There can be no doubt that the outbreak of a passionate demand for love [in the analytic situation] is largely the work of resistance' (*SE* 12: 162). When this happens the patient becomes 'quite without insight' (*SE* 12: 162), and mobilizes the strongest drive-based opposition to the intellectual work of analysis. Much the same seems to be the case when an author writes for love. In 'The Woman Destroyed', the writing subjects both write to be loved. In

descriptive of different styles of language, in fact is untenable. Any utterance, however impersonally styled, necessarily intends to influence its readers/listeners. Or as Genette convincingly puts it: 'narrative exists nowhere, so to speak, in its strict form. The slightest adjective that is little more than descriptive, the most discreet comparison, the most modest "perhaps", the most inoffensive of logical articulations introduces into its web a type of speech that is alien to it, refractory as it were' (141–2). For Culler's critique of the same problem, see pp. 197–9.

Monique's case this is obvious; Beauvoir's is more complex. But in the *Memoirs of a Dutiful Daughter* (1958) she explicitly presents her vocation as a writer as one inspired by the desire for love and recognition. Crying over the destiny of George Eliot's Maggie Tulliver, she stresses her identification with Maggie, and then goes on to predict her future career as a writer: 'Through the heroine, I identified myself with the author: one day other adolescents would bathe with their tears a novel in which I would tell my own story' (*MDD* 140; *MJF* 195; TA). The trouble in 'The Woman Destroyed' is that if the reader recognizes the demands of the author, she will have to deny her sympathy to the character: it is difficult, to say the least, at one and the same time to identify with the mature lucidity of the author, and cherish the victim of that superior intellect.

As the subject of the enunciation, Beauvoir displays a markedly negative transference on to the subject of the *énoncé*, deliberately setting out to break or destroy her. The vehemence of her rhetorical sadism, however, ends up mobilizing the reader's support for the victimized Monique. There is nevertheless nothing automatic about this process, since similar support is not forthcoming in the case of the monologue of Murielle in the short story entitled 'The Monologue' (published in the same volume as 'The Woman Destroyed'). In the case of Murielle, it is clear that she is a wholly despicable character and, from the bourgeois point of view, also an obvious failure: she is a many-times divorced wife, and mother of a daughter who committed suicide to escape her control. In the case of Monique, however, the reader is presented with the epitome of a thoroughly nice and decent upper middle-class housewife. Beauvoir's story is a full-scale attempt to deprive the apparently successful bourgeois wife and mother of the last shreds of her claims to happiness: Monique loses her husband, her two daughters, and her own identity, and is left with absolutely nothing. The total absence of self-reflexive irony, or indeed of any kind of humour, points to the same transferential lack of distance to her subject matter.[14]

---

[14] Jacqueline Piatier, writing in *Le Monde*, deplores the lack of irony in relation to its subject matter. This point is intimately bound up with Piatier's distaste for women's magazines: 'It would have been intriguing if a story published in *Elle* actually was a parody of *Elle*', she notes.

There is a striking parallel between Monique's experience, where what she takes to be her own identity dissolves along with every other certainty, and Marx and Engels's graphic description of the constant revision and dissolution required by the bourgeois mode of production:

> Everlasting uncertainty and agitation distinguish the bourgeois epoch from all earlier ones. All fixed, fast-frozen relations, with their train of ancient and venerable prejudices and opinions are swept away, all new-formed ones become antiquated before they can ossify. All that is solid melts into air, all that is holy is profaned, and man is at last compelled to face with sober senses, his real conditions of life, and his relations with his kind (*Communist Manifesto* 83).

For Marx and Engels this process of disintegration is part of a larger dialectical structure, in which old illusions must be shed in order to open the way for new insights. Monique's breakdown, however, is decidedly undialectical: in this text the particular hallmark of Beauvoir's vision is the lack of *any* positive moment of reconstruction, however implicit. It is as if the text takes a perverse pleasure in slowly and deliberately blocking every issue for its protagonist, leaving her to face nothing but unlit windows and closed doors. It is in this sense that the feminists in 1968 were right to criticize the story: in the end it does not allow for change, let alone revolutionary transformation.

In 'Remembering, Repeating and Working Through', Freud writes that during the analysis, the patient 'does not listen to the precise wording of his obsessional ideas' (*SE* 12: 152). In other words: to be in the grip of transference is to neglect one's rhetoric. If Beauvoir's act of enunciation fails to persuade her readers to take up the position prepared for them, it is precisely because of the way in which the identificatory logic of transference prevents her from paying sufficient attention to the metonymical strategies of rhetorical displacement.[15] In this case,

---

[15] The relations between transference and rhetoric have been excellently analysed by Cynthia Chase. Other aspects of literary transference are discussed by Peter Brooks in 'Narrative Transaction'. Freud made some important further comments on transference in his two 1937 papers, 'Constructions in Analysis' and 'Analysis Terminable and Interminable'.

what is required in order to perceive the rhetorical logic of the text is neither a reader-detective, sharing the author's transferential investment in epistemological superiority, nor a reader-victim, identifying with the plight of the protagonist, but rather a reader-analyst who, in the words of Freud, will maintain 'the same "evenly-suspended attention" . . . in the face of all that one hears' ('Recommendations', *SE* 12: 111–12). That would seem to be the only way in which we might come to perceive the transferential play of rhetoric and identification or, as Peter Brooks puts it, 'understand narrative as both a story and the discourse that conveys it, seeking both to work on the text and to have the text work on us' ('Psychoanalytic' 74).

Works Cited

For individual essays published in anthologies or collections, cross-references have been used except for cases where it seemed unnecessarily fussy. For examples of the usual cross-reference, see the entries under Altieri and Cavell. For examples of cases where cross-references have not been used, see the entries under Baym and Howells.

Adams, Parveen, 'Of Female Bondage', in Brennan 247–65.
Alcoff, Linda, 'The Problem of Speaking for Others', *Cultural Critique* 20 (Winter 1991–2), 5–32.
Altieri, Charles, 'What Is at Stake in Confessional Criticism', in Veeser 55–67.
Andreas Capellanus, *The Art of Courtly Love*. See under Parry; Walsh.
L'Arc 61: *Simone de Beauvoir et la lutte des femmes* (1971).
Armengaud, Françoise, 'Pierre Bourdieu "grand témoin"?', *Nouvelles questions féministes* 14/3 (1993), 83–8.
Aronson, Ronald, and van den Hoven, Adrian (eds.), *Sartre Alive* (Detroit: Wayne State University Press, 1991).
Askew, Melvin W., 'Courtly Love: Neurosis as Institution', *Psychoanalytic Review* 52/1 (Spring 1965), 19–29.
Atack, Margaret, and Powrie, Phil (eds.), *Contemporary French Fiction by Women: Feminist Perspectives*. (Manchester: Manchester University Press, 1990).
Audry, Colette, *La statue* (Paris: Gallimard, 1983).
Austin, J. L., 'A Plea for Excuses' in *Philosophical Papers* (3rd edn. Oxford: Oxford University Press, 1979), 175–204.
Bandera, Cesar, *Mímesis conflictiva: ficción literaria y violencia en Cervantes y Calderón* (Madrid: Editorial Gredos, 1975).
Barteau, Françoise, *Les romans de Tristan et Iseut: Introduction à une lecture plurielle* (Paris: Larousse, 1972).
Barthes, Roland, *Mythologies*, trans. Annette Lavers (New York: The Noonday Press, 1972).
—— 'The Writer on Holiday', in *Mythologies* 29–31.
Bauer, Nancy, 'Recounting Woman: Simone de Beauvoir and Feminist Philosophy', unpublished diss. (Cambridge, Mass.: Harvard University, 1997).
Baym, Nina, 'The Madwoman and her Languages: Why I Don't Do Feminist Theory', in Shari Benstock (ed.), *Feminist Issues in Literary*

Scholarship. (Bloomington, Ind.: Indiana University Press, 1987), 45–61.

Beauvoir, Simone de, *All Men Are Mortal*, trans. Leonard M. Friedman, (Cleveland, Ohio: World Publishing, 1955); trans. of *Tous les hommes sont mortels* (Paris: Gallimard (Coll. Folio), 1946).

—— *All Said and Done*, trans. Patrick O'Brian (Harmondsworth: Penguin, 1987); trans. of *Tout compte fait* (Paris: Gallimard (Coll. Folio), 1972).

—— *America Day by Day*, trans. Carol Cosman (Berkeley and Los Angeles: University of California Press, 1999); trans. of *L'Amérique au jour le jour* (Paris: Gallimard, 1948).

—— *The Ethics of Ambiguity*, trans. Bernard Frechtman (New York: Philosophical Library, 1948); trans. of *Pour une morale de l'ambiguïté* (Paris: Gallimard (Coll. Idées), 1947).

—— *L'existentialisme et la sagesse des nations* (Paris: Nagel, 1948).

—— *Force of Circumstance*, trans. Richard Howard (Harmondsworth: Penguin, 1987); trans. of *La force des choses*, 2 vols. (Paris: Gallimard (Coll. Folio), 1963).

—— 'I am a feminist' in Beauvoir, *Simone de Beauvoir Today*, 29–48.

—— *The Mandarins*, trans. Leonard M. Friedman (London: Fontana, 1986); trans. of *Les mandarins*, 2 vols. (Paris: Gallimard (Coll. Folio), 1954).

—— *Memoirs of a Dutiful Daughter*, trans. James Kirkup (Harmondsworth: Penguin, 1987); trans. of *Mémoires d'une jeune fille rangée*, (Paris: Gallimard (Coll. Folio), 1958).

—— '*La phénoménologie de la perception* de Maurice Merleau-Ponty', *Les temps modernes*, 1/2 (Nov. 1945), 363–7.

—— *The Prime of Life*, trans. Peter Green (Harmondsworth: Penguin, 1988); trans. of *La force de l'âge*, 2 vols. (Paris: Gallimard (Coll. Folio), 1960).

—— *Pyrrhus et Cinéas* (Paris: Gallimard, 1944).

—— *The Second Sex*, trans. H. M. Parshley (New York: Vintage Books, 1989); trans. of *Le deuxième sexe*, 2 vols. (Paris: Gallimard (Coll. Folio), 1949).

—— *She Came to Stay*, trans. Yvonne Moyse and Roger Senhouse (London: Fontana, 1984); trans. of *L'invitée* (Paris: Gallimard (Coll. Folio), 1943).

—— 'Simone de Beauvoir' in Buin 73–92.

—— *Simone de Beauvoir Today: Conversations 1972–1982*, with Alice Schwartzer; trans. Marianne Howarth (London: Chatto, 1984).

—— *The Woman Destroyed*, trans. Patrick O'Brian (London: Fontana, 1987); trans. of *La femme rompue* (Paris: Gallimard (Coll. Folio), 1968).

Behar, Ruth. *Translated Woman: Crossing the Border With Esperanza's Story* (Boston: Beacon Press, 1993).

—— *The Vulnerable Observer: Anthropology That Breaks Your Heart* (Boston: Beacon Press, 1996).

Belsey, Catherine, and Moore, Jane (eds.), *The Feminist Reader: Essays in Gender and the Politics of Literary Criticism* (London: Macmillan, 1989).

Benhabib, Seyla, and Cornell, Drucilla (eds.), *Feminism as Critique: On the Politics of Gender* (Minneapolis: University of Minnesota Press, 1987).

Benton, John F., 'Clio and Venus: An Historical View of Medieval Love', In Newman 19–42.

—— 'The Court of Champagne as a Literary Center' *Speculum* 36/4 (Oct. 1961), 551–91.

Benveniste, Émile, 'L'appareil formel de l'énonciation', in *Problèmes de linguistique générale*, vol. ii (Paris: Gallimard (Coll. 'Tel'), 1974), 79–88.

—— 'Les relations de temps dans le verbe français', in *Problèmes de linguistique générale*, vol. i (Paris: Gallimard (Coll. 'Tel'.), 1966), 237–50.

Bergoffen, Debra B., *The Philosophy of Simone de Beauvoir: Gendered Phenomenologies, Erotic Generosities* (Albany, NY: State University of New York Press, 1997).

Bernheimer, Charles and Kahane, Claire (eds.), *In Dora's Case* (New York: Columbia University Press, 1985); 2nd expanded edn. published in 1990.

Bersani, Leo, *Marcel Proust: The Fiction of Life and Art* (New York: Oxford University Press, 1965).

Bettelheim, Bruno, *Freud and Man's Soul* (New York: Knopf, 1983).

Blakeslee, Merritt R., 'The Authorship of Thomas's *Tristan*', *Philological Quarterly* 64/4 (Fall 1985), 555–72.

Bleier, Ruth, *Science and Gender: A Critique of Biology and Its Theories on Women* (New York: Pergamon Press, 1984).

Bloch, Marc, *La société féodale*, ii. *Les classes et le gouvernement des hommes* (Paris: Albin Michel, 1940).

Bloom, Harold, *The Anxiety of Influence: A Theory of Poetry* (New York: Oxford University Press, 1973).

Blumstein, Andrée Kahn, *Misogyny and Idealization in the Courtly Romance* (Bonn: Bouvier Verlag Herbert Grundmann, 1977).

Bordo, Susan, 'The Cartesian Masculinization of Thought', in Harding and O'Barr 247–64.

Bornstein, Kate, *Gender Outlaw: On Men, Women and the Rest of Us* (New York: Routledge, 1994).

Boschetti, Anna, *Sartre et 'Les temps modernes'* (Paris: Minuit, 1985).

Bouchard, Constance B., 'The Possible Nonexistence of Thomas, Author of *Tristan and Isolde*', *Modern Philology* 79 (1981–2), 66–72.

Bourdieu, Pierre, *Ce que parler veut dire: L'économie des échanges linguistiques* (Paris: Fayard, 1982).

—— 'Champ du pouvoir, champ intellectuel et habitus de classe', *Scolies: Cahiers de recherches de l'École normale supérieure* 1 (1971), 7–26.

—— 'Champ intellectuel et projet créateur', *Les temps modernes* 246 (Nov. 1966), 865–905.

—— *Choses dites* (Paris: Minuit, 1987)

—— 'La construction sociale du sexe', unpublished ms., 1989.

—— *Distinction: A Social Critique of the Judgment of Taste*, trans. Richard Nice, (London: RKP, 1984); trans. of *La distinction: Critique sociale du jugement* (Paris: Minuit, 1979).

—— 'La domination masculine', *Actes de la recherches en sciences sociales* 84 (Sept. 1990), 2–31.

—— *La domination masculine* (Paris: Seuil, 1998).

—— 'Epreuve scolaire et consécration sociale: Les Classes préparatoires aux grandes écoles', *Actes de la recherche en sciences sociales* 39 (1981), 3–70.

—— 'Flaubert's Point of View', trans. Priscilla Parkhurst Ferguson, *Critical Inquiry* 14/3 (Spring 1988), 539–62.

—— 'He Whose Word Is Law', trans. Robin Buss, *Liber* 1: 12–13; suppl. to *Times Literary Supplement* (6–12 Oct. 1989).

—— *Homo Academicus*, trans. Peter Collier (Stanford, Calif.: Stanford University Press), trans. of *Homo Academicus* (Paris: Minuit, 1984).

—— *In Other Words: Essays Towards a Reflexive Sociology*, trans. Matthew Adamson (Stanford, Calif.: Stanford University Press, 1990).

—— *An Invitation to Reflexive Sociology*, ed. Loïc J. D. Wacquant (Chicago: University of Chicago Press, 1992).

—— 'A Lecture on the Lecture', trans. Matthew Adamson, in *In Other Words* 177–98; trans. of *Leçon sur la leçon* (Paris: Minuit, 1982).

—— *The Logic of Practice*, trans. Richard Nice (Stanford, Calif.: Stanford University Press, 1990), trans. of *Le sens pratique* (Paris: Minuit, 1980).

—— 'Le marché des biens symboliques', *L'année sociologique* 22 (1971), 49–126.

—— *Outline of a Theory of Practice*, trans. Richard Nice (Cambridge: Cambridge University Press, 1977).

—— *The Political Ontology of Martin Heidegger*, trans. Peter Collier (Stanford, Calif.: Stanford University Press, 1991).

—— 'The Production of Belief', *Media, Culture and Society* 2 (1980), 261–93.

—— *The Rules of Art: Genesis and Structure of the Literary Field*, trans. Susan Emanuel (Stanford, Calif.: Stanford University Press, 1995); trans. of *Les règles de l'art* (Paris: Seuil, 1992).

—— 'Sartre', *London Review of Books*, 2/22 (20 Nov. 1980), 11–12; rev. version repr. as 'The Total Intellectual and the Illusion of the Omnipotence of Thought', in *The Rules of Art* 209–13.

—— 'The Social Space and the Genesis of Groups', *Theory & Society* 14 (1985), 723–44.

—— *Sociology in Question*, trans. Richard Nice (London: Sage, 1993); trans. of *Questions de sociologie* (Paris: Minuit, 1984).

—— *The State Nobility: Elite Schools in the Field of Power*, trans. Lauretta C. Clough (Stanford, Calif.: Stanford University Press, 1996); trans. of *La noblesse d'état: Grandes écoles et esprit de corps* (Paris: Minuit, 1989).

—— and Passeron, Jean-Claude, *La reproduction: éléments pour une théorie du système d'enseignement* (Paris: Minuit, 1970).

—— —— *The Inheritors: French Students and Their Relation to Culture*, trans. Richard Nice (Chicago: University of Chicago Press, 1979); trans. of *Les héritiers: les étudiants et la culture* (Paris: Minuit, 1964).

—— and Saint-Martin, Monique de 'Les catégories de l'entendement professoral', *Actes de la recherche en sciences sociales* 3 (1975), 68–93.

Bowie, Malcolm, *Mallarmé and the Art of Being Difficult* (Cambridge: Cambridge University Press, 1978).

Bredsdorff, Thomas, *Tristans børn* (Copenhagen: Gyldendal, 1982).

Brennan, Teresa (ed.), *Between Feminism and Psychoanalysis* (London: Routledge, 1989).

Brooks, Peter, 'Freud's Masterplot: A Model for Narrative', in *Reading for the Plot*, 90–112.

—— 'Narrative Transaction and Transference', in *Reading for the Plot*, 216–37.

—— 'Psychoanalytic Constructions and Narrative Meanings', *Paragraph* 7 (Mar. 1986), 53–76.

—— *Reading for the Plot: Design and Intention in Narrative* (Oxford: Clarendon Press, 1984).

Brooks, W. K., *The Law of Heredity: A Study of the Cause of Variation, and the Origin of Living Organisms* (Baltimore: John Murphy, 1883).

Brown, Marshall (ed.), *Pierre Bourdieu and Literary History*, special issue of *Modern Language Quarterly* 58/4 (Dec. 1997), 367–508.

Brubaker, Rogers, 'Rethinking Classical Theory: The Sociological Vision of Pierre Bourdieu', *Theory & Society* 14 (1985), 745–75.

Buin, Yves (ed.), *Que peut la littérature* (Paris: UGE (Coll. 10/18), 1965).

Burton, Christine, 'Golden Threads', *Off Our Backs* 24/9 (Oct. 1994), 14–15.

Butler, Judith, *Bodies That Matter: On the Discursive Limits of 'Sex'* (New York: Routledge, 1993).

—— 'Critically Queer', *GLQ* 1/1 (1993), 17–32.

Butler, Judith, 'Gender as Performance', in Peter Osborne (ed.), *A Critical Sense: Interviews with Intellectuals* (London: Routledge, 1996), 109–25.

—— 'Gender Is Burning: Questions of Appropriation and Subversion', in *Bodies That Matter* 121–40.

—— *Gender Trouble: Feminism and the Subversion of Identity* (New York: Routledge, 1990).

—— 'Sex and Gender in Simone de Beauvoir's *Second Sex*', *Yale French Studies* 72 (1986), 35–49.

Bynum, Caroline, 'Why All the Fuss about the Body? A Medievalist's Perspective', *Critical Inquiry* 22/1 (Autumn 1995), 1–33.

Calhoun, Craig, 'Habitus, Field of Power and Capital: The Question of Historical Specificity', in Calhoun, LiPuma, and Postone 61–88.

—— LiPuma, Edward, and Postone, Moishe (eds.), *Bourdieu: Critical Perspectives* (Chicago: University of Chicago Press, 1993).

Calhoun, Randall, *Dorothy Parker: A Bio-Bibliography* (Westport, Conn.: Greenwood Press, 1993).

Carter, Angela, *The Passion of New Eve.* (1st pub. 1977; London: Virago, 1997).

Case, Mary Anne C., 'Disaggregating Gender from Sex and Sexual Orientation: The Effeminate Man in the Law and Feminist Jurisprudence', *Yale Law Journal* 105/1 (1995), 1–105.

Caughie, Pamela L., 'Let It Pass: Changing the Subject, Once Again', *PMLA* 112/1 (Jan. 1997), 26–39.

Cavell, Stanley, 'Aesthetic Problems of Modern Philosophy', in *Must We* 73–96.

—— 'Austin at Criticism' in *Must We* 97–114.

—— 'The Avoidance of Love: A Reading of *King Lear*', in *Must We* 267–353.

—— *The Claim of Reason: Wittgenstein, Skepticism, Morality, and Tragedy* (Oxford: Oxford University Press, 1979).

—— *Contesting Tears: The Hollywood Melodrama of the Unknown Woman* (Chicago: University of Chicago Press, 1996).

—— 'Knowing and Acknowledging', in *Must We* 238–66.

—— *Must We Mean What We Say? A Book of Essays* (Cambridge: Cambridge University Press, 1969).

—— 'Must We Mean What We Say?', in *Must We* 1–43.

—— *A Pitch of Philosophy: Autobiographical Exercises* (Cambridge, Mass.: Harvard University Press, 1994).

—— 'The Politics of Interpretation (Politics as Opposed to What?)', in *Themes Out of School: Effects and Causes* (Chicago: University of Chicago Press, 1984), 27–59.

Chanter, Tina, *Ethics of Eros: Irigaray's Rewriting of the Philosophers* (New York: Routledge, 1995).

Charle, Christophe, *Naissance des 'intellectuels' 1880–1900* (Paris: Minuit, 1990).

Chase, Cynthia, ' "Transference" as Trope and Persuasion', in Rimmon-Kenan 211–32.

Chodorow, Nancy, *The Reproduction of Mothering* (Berkeley and Los Angeles: University of California Press, 1978).

Christian, Barbara, 'The Race for Theory', in Kauffman 225–37, 1st pub. in *Cultural Critique* (Spring 1987), 51–63.

Cixous, Hélène, 'Sorties', in Cixous and Clément 63–132.

—— 'The Laugh of the Medusa', trans. Keith Cohen and Paula Cohen, in Marks and Courtivron 245–64; trans. of 'Le Rire de la Méduse', *L'Arc* 61 (1975), 39–54.

—— *Portrait de Dora* (Paris: des femmes, 1976); trans. as *Portrait of Dora* by Sarah Burd, *Diacritics* 12/1 (Spring 1983), 2–32; also trans. by Anita Barrows, in Simone Benmussa, *Benmussa Directs* (London: Calder, 1979), 9–67.

—— and Clément, Catherine, *The Newly Born Woman*, trans. Betsy Wing (Manchester: Manchester University Press, 1986); trans. of *La jeune née* (Paris: 10/18, 1975).

Copjec, Joan, 'Sex and the Euthanasia of Reason', in *Read My Desire: Lacan Against the Historicists* (Cambridge, Mass.: MIT Press, 1994), 201–36.

Culler, Jonathan, *Structuralist Poetics: Structuralism, Linguistics and the Study of Literature* (London: Routledge, 1975).

Curtis, Renée L., *Tristan Studies* (Munich: Fink, 1969).

d'Arcy, Martin C., *The Mind and Heart of Love. Lion and Unicorn: A Study in Eros and Agape* (London: Faber & Faber, 1945).

Danius, Sara, 'Själen är kroppens fängelse: om den vanskliga distinktionen mellan kön och genus', in Lindén and Milles 143–66.

Darwin, Charles, *The Descent of Man and Selection in Relation to Sex* (rev. edn., New York: Merrill and Baker, 1874).

Delphy, Christine, 'Rapports de sexe, genre et universalisme', interview with Myriam Lévy and Patrick Silberstein, *Utopie critique: Revue internationale pour l'autogestion* 2 (1995), 9–23.

Delsaut, Yvette, *Bibliographie des travaux de Pierre Bourdieu* (Paris: Centre de sociologie européenne, 1986); trans. Matthew Adamson as 'Bibliography of the works of Pierre Bourdieu, 1958–1988', in Bourdieu, *In Other Words* 199–218.

Denomy, Alexander J., *The Heresy of Courtly Love* (Gloucester, Mass.: Peter Smith, 1947).

Derrida, Jacques, *Limited Inc.* (Evanston, Ill.: Northwestern University Press, 1988).

—— *Marges de la philosophie* (Paris: Minuit, 1972).

Derrida, Jacques, *Of Spirit: Heidegger and the Question*, trans. Geoffrey Bennington and Rachel Bowlby (Chicago: Chicago University Press, 1989).

Deutsch, Felix, 'A Footnote to Freud's "Fragment of an Analysis of a Case of Hysteria" ', in Bernheimer and Kahane 35–43.

Diamond, Cora, 'Knowing Tornadoes and Other Things', *New Literary History* 22 (1991), 1001–15.

Donaldson, E. Talbot, *Speaking of Chaucer* (New York: Norton, 1970).

Dronke, Peter, 'André le Chapelain: Traité de l'amour courtois', *Medium Aevum* 45/3 (1976), 317–21.

—— 'The Rise of the Medieval Fabliau: Latin and Vernacular Evidence', *Romanische Forschungen* 85/3 (1973), 275–97.

Eagleton, Terry, *Criticism and Ideology* (London: New Left Books, 1976).

—— *Ideology: An Introduction* (London: Verso, 1991).

—— *The Illusions of Postmodernism* (Oxford: Blackwell, 1996).

Ebert, Teresa L., *Ludic Feminism and After: Postmodernism, Desire, and Labor in Late Capitalism* (Ann Arbor: University of Michigan Press, 1996).

Ellmann, Mary, *Thinking About Women* (New York: Harcourt, 1968).

Epstein, Julia, and Straub, Kristina (eds.), *Body Guards: The Cultural Politics of Gender Ambiguity* (New York: Routledge, 1991).

Evans, Mary, *Simone de Beauvoir: A Feminist Mandarin* (London: Tavistock, 1985).

Fabiani, Jean-Louis, *Les philosophes de la république* (Paris: Minuit, 1988).

Fallaize, Elizabeth, *The Novels of Simone de Beauvoir* (London: Croom Helm, 1988).

—— 'Resisting Romance: Simone de Beauvoir, "The Woman Destroyed" and the Romance Script', Atack and Powrie 15–23.

—— (ed.), *Simone de Beauvoir: A Critical Reader* (London: Routledge, 1998).

Fanon, Frantz, *Black Skin, White Masks*, trans. Charles Lam Markmann (New York: Grove Weidenfeld, 1967); trans. of *Peau noire, masques blancs* (Paris: Seuil, 1952).

Farnham, Marynia F., 'The Pen and the Distaff', *Saturday Review of Literature* (22 Feb. 1947), 7+.

Fausto-Sterling, Anne, 'The Five Sexes', *Sciences* (Mar./Apr. 1993), 20–4.

Feinberg, Leslie, *Stone Butch Blues* (Ithaca, NY: Firebrand Books, 1993).

—— *Transgender Warrior: Making History from Joan of Arc to Dennis Rodman* (Boston: Beacon Press, 1996).

Felman, Shoshana, *Jacques Lacan and the Adventure of Insight: Psychoanalysis in Contemporary Culture* (Cambridge, Mass.: Harvard University Press, 1987).

Felski, Rita, 'The Doxa of Difference', *Signs* 23/1 (1997), 1–21.

Fernald, Anne, 'A Room of One's Own: Personal Criticism and the Essay', *Twentieth Century Literature* 40/2 (Summer 1994): 165–89.

Fineman, Joel, 'The History of the Anecdote', *The Subjectivity Effect in Western Literary Tradition: Essays Toward the Release of Shakespeare's Will* (Cambridge, Mass.: October Books, 1991), 59–87.

Fish, Stanley, 'How Ordinary is Ordinary Language?', in *Is There* 97–111.

—— 'How To Do Things with Austin and Searle: Speech-Act Theory and Literary Criticism', in *Is There* 197–245.

—— *Is There A Text In This Class? The Authority of Interpretive Communities* (Cambridge, Mass.: Harvard University Press, 1980).

Fisher, John H., 'Tristan and Courtly Adultery', *Comparative Literature* 9 (1957), 150–64.

Flaubert, Gustave, *Madame Bovary* (1857; Paris: Le Livre de Poche, 1972).

'Forum', *PMLA* 111/5 (Oct. 1996), 1146–69.

Foucault, Michel, *The History of Sexuality: An Introduction*, Vol. i, trans. Robert Hurley (New York: Vintage Books, 1990).

Fox-Genovese, Elisabeth, *Feminism Without Illusions: A Critique of Individualism* (Chapel Hill, NC: UNC Press, 1991).

Frank, Francine Wattman, and Treichler, Paula A., *Language, Gender, and Professional Writing: Theoretical Approaches and Guidelines for Nonsexist Usage* (New York: MLA, 1989).

Franke, Katherine M., 'The Central Mistake of Sex Discrimination Law: The Disaggregation of Sex from Gender', *University of Pennsylvania Law Review* 144/1 (Nov. 1995), 1–99.

Frazer, J. G., *The Golden Bough: A Study in Magic and Religion* (1922; Abridged edn., London: Macmillan, 1974).

Freud, Sigmund, *The Standard Edition of the Complete Psychological Works*, ed. and trans. James Strachey (London: The Hogarth Press, 1953–74), 24 vols. (abbreviated to *SE*).

—— *Studienausgabe*, ed. Alexander Mitscherlich, Angela Richards, and James Strachey (Frankfurt am Main: Fischer Taschenbuch Verlag, 1982), 10 vols. plus an unnumbered supplementary vol.

—— 'The Aetiology of Hysteria' (1896), in *SE* 3: 189–221.

—— 'Analysis of a Phobia in a Five-Year Old Boy', [*Little Hans*] (1909), in *SE* 10: 1–150.

—— 'Analysis Terminable and Interminable' (1937), in *SE* 23: 209–54.

—— *Beyond the Pleasure Principle* (1920), in *SE* 18: 1–64.

—— ' "Civilized" Sexual Morality and Modern Nervous Illness' (1908), in *SE* 9: 177–204.

—— 'Constructions in Analysis' (1937), in *SE* 23: 255–70.

—— 'The Disposition to Obsessional Neurosis' (1913), in *SE* 12: 311–26.

—— 'The Dissolution of the Oedipus Complex' (1924), in *SE* 19: 173–82;

trans. of 'Der Untergang des Odipuskomplexes', in *Studienausgabe* 5: 243–51.

—— 'Dostoevsky and Parricide' (1928), in *SE* 21: 177–94.

—— 'The Dynamics of Transference' (1912), in *SE* 12: 97–108.

—— 'Fragment of an Analysis of a Case of Hysteria' [*Dora*] (1905), in *SE* 7: 1–122; trans. of 'Bruchstück einer Hysterie-Analyse', in *Studienausgabe* 6: 83–186.

—— *The Future of an Illusion* (1927), in *SE* 21: 1–56.

—— 'Instincts and Their Vicissitudes' (1915), in *SE* 14: 109–40; trans. of 'Triebe und Triebschicksale', in *Studienausgabe* 3: 75–102.

—— *The Interpretation of Dreams* (1900), in *SE* 4–5.

—— 'Leonardo da Vinci and a Memory of his Childhood' (1910), in *SE* 11: 59–138.

—— 'Notes Upon a Case of Obsessional Neurosis' [*The Rat Man*] (1909), in *SE* 10: 153–249.

—— 'Observations on Transference-Love' (1915), in *SE* 12: 157–71.

—— 'On the Universal Tendency to Debasement in the Sphere of Love' (1912), in *SE* 11: 177–90; trans. of 'Über die allgemeinste Erniedrigung des Liebeslebens', in *Studienausgabe* 5: 197–209.

—— 'Project for a Scientific Psychology' (1895), in *SE* 1: 283–387.

—— 'The Psychogenesis of a Case of Homosexuality in a Woman' (1920), *SE* 18: 147–72.

—— *The Psychopathology of Everyday Life* (1905), in *SE* 6.

—— 'Recommendations to Physicians Practicing Psycho-Analysis' (1912), in *SE* 12: 109–120.

—— 'Remembering, Repeating and Working Through' (1914), in *SE* 12: 145–56.

—— 'Some Psychical Consequences of the Anatomical Distinction between the Sexes' (1925), in *SE* 19: 241–260.

—— 'The Theme of the Three Caskets' (1913), in *SE* 12: 289–303.

—— *Three Essays on the Theory of Sexuality* (1905), in *SE* 7: 125–243.

—— *Totem and Taboo* (1913), in *SE* 13: 1–162.

—— 'The Uncanny' (1919), in *SE* 17: 217–56.

—— and Breuer, Joseph, *Studies on Hysteria* (1893–5), *SE* 2.

Fuss, Diana, *Essentially Speaking: Feminism, Nature and Difference* (New York: Routledge, 1989).

Gallop, Jane, *Feminist Accused of Sexual Harassment* (Durham, NC: Duke University Press, 1997).

—— *Thinking Through the Body* (New York: Columbia University Press, 1988).

—— Hirsch, Marianne and Miller, Nancy K., 'Criticizing Feminist Criticism', in Hirsch and Keller 349–69.

Garber, Marjorie, *Vested Interests: Cross-Dressing & Cultural Anxiety* (New York: Harper Perennial, 1993).

Gardner, Martin, 'The New New Math', *New York Review of Books* (24 Sept. 1998), 9–12.

Garnham, Nicholas, and Williams, Raymond, 'Pierre Bourdieu and the Sociology of Culture: An Introduction', *Media, Culture and Society* 2 (1980), 209–23.

Gatens, Moira, 'A Critique of the Sex/Gender Distinction' (1983), in Gunew 139–57; repr. in Moira Gatens, *Imaginary Bodies: Ethics, Power and Corporeality* (London: Routledge, 1996).

Gearhart, Suzanne, 'The Scene of Psychoanalysis: The Unanswered Questions of Dora', in Bernheimer and Kahane 105–27.

Geddes, Patrick, and Thomson, J. Arthur, *The Evolution of Sex* (London: Walter Scott, 1889).

Genette, Gérard, 'Frontiers of Narrative', in *Figures of Literary Discourse* (Oxford: Blackwell, 1982), 127–44.

Gilligan, Carol, *In a Different Voice* (Cambridge, Mass.: Harvard University Press, 1982).

Girard, René, *Deceit, Desire, and the Novel: Self and Other in Literary Structure*, trans. Yvonne Freccero (Baltimore: Johns Hopkins Press, 1965); trans. of *Mensonge romantique et vérité romanesque* (Paris: Grasset, 1961).

—— *Things Hidden Since the Foundation of the World*, trans. Stephen Bann and Michael Metteer (Stanford, Calif.: Stanford University Press, 1987); trans. of *Des choses cachées depuis la fondations du monde: Recherches avec Jean-Michel Oughourlian et Guy Lefort* (Paris: Grasset, 1978).

—— *To Double Business Bound: Essays on Literature, Mimesis and Anthropology* (Baltimore: Johns Hopkins Press, 1979).

—— *Violence and the Sacred*, trans. Patrick Gregory (Baltimore: Johns Hopkins Press, 1977); trans. of *La violence et le sacré* (Paris: Grasset, 1972).

Goethe, Johann Wolfgang von, 'Autobiographische Einzelheiten', *Autobiographische Schriften* (Hamburg: Christian Wegner Verlag, 1959), in *Goethes Werke*, 10: 529–47.

Gould, Timothy, 'The Unhappy Performative', in Parker and Sedgwick 19–44.

Greenberg, Karen, 'Reading Reading: Echo's Abduction of Language', in McConnell-Ginet, Borker, and Furman 300–9.

Greenblatt, Stephen, and Gunn, Giles (eds.), *Redrawing the Boundaries: The Transformation of English and American Literary Studies* (New York: MLA, 1992).

Grosz, Elizabeth, 'The Labors of Love', *Differences* 6/2–3 (Summer–Fall 1994), 274–94.

—— *Sexual Subversions: Three French Feminists* (Sydney: Allen & Unwin, 1989).

—— *Volatile Bodies: Toward a Corporeal Feminism* (Bloomington, Ind.: Indiana University Press, 1994).

Gubar, Susan, 'What Ails Feminist Criticism?', *Critical Inquiry* 24/4 (Summer 1998), 878–902.

Guillory, John, 'Bourdieu's Refusal', in Brown 367–98.

Gunew, Sneja (ed.), *A Reader in Feminist Knowledge.* (London: Routledge, 1991).

Gunnlaugsdottir, Alfrun (ed.), *Tristán en el norte*, trans. of *Saga af Tristram ok Isönd* (Reykjavik: Stofnun Arna Magnússonar, 1978).

Haraway, Donna J., ' "Gender" for a Marxist Dictionary', in *Simians, Cyborgs, and Women: The Reinvention of Nature* (New York: Routledge, 1991), 127–48.

Harding, Sandra, *The Science Question in Feminism* (Ithaca, NY: Cornell University Press, 1986).

—— and Hintikka, Merrill B. (eds.), *Discovering Reality: Feminist Perspectives on Epistemology, Metaphysics, Methodology and Philosophy of Science* (Dordrecht, Boston, and London: D. Reidel, 1983).

—— and O'Barr, Jean F. (eds.), *Sex and Scientific Inquiry* (Chicago: University of Chicago Press, 1987).

Harries, Elizabeth W., ' "Out in Left Field": Charlotte Smith's Prefaces, Bourdieu's Categories and the Public Sphere', in Brown 457–73.

Haslanger, Sally, 'Disembodying Race and Gender', unpublished lecture (Mar. 1996).

—— 'Natural Kinds and Social Construction: Butler on Subjects of Sex/Gender/Desire', unpublished manuscript (Dec.1995).

Hatto, Arthur Thomas, 'A Note on Thomas's *Tristran*', in Hatto 355–63.

—— (trans.), 'The "Tristran" of Thomas', in Gottfried von Strassburg, *Tristan*, with the 'Tristran' of Thomas (Harmondsworth: Penguin, 1967).

Haug, Frigga, *Female Sexualization* (London: Verso, 1987).

Hausman, Bernice L., *Changing Sex: Transsexualism, Technology, and the Idea of Gender* (Durham, NC: Duke University Press, 1995.)

Hegel, G. W. F., *The Philosophy of Right*, trans. T. M. Knox (Oxford: Oxford University Press, 1967).

Heilbrun, Carolyn G., *Toward a Recognition of Androgyny* (New York: Knopf, 1973).

Heinämaa, Sara, 'What Is a Woman? Butler and Beauvoir on the Foundations of the Sexual Difference', *Hypatia* 12/1 (1997), 20–39.

—— 'Woman—nature, Product, Style? Rethinking the Foundations of Feminist Philosophy of Science', in Lynn Hankinson Nelson and Jack Nelson (eds.), *Feminism, Science and the Philosophy of Science* (The Hague: Kluwer, 1996), 289–308.

Hirsch, Marianne, and Keller, Evelyn Fox, (eds.), *Conflicts in Feminism* (New York: Routledge, 1990).

Howard, Donald R., *The Three Temptations: Medieval Man in Search of the World* (Princeton: Princeton University Press, 1966).

Howells, Christina, 'Conclusion: Sartre and the Deconstruction of the Subject', in Christina Howells (ed.), *The Cambridge Companion to Sartre*, (Cambridge: Cambridge University Press, 1993), 318–52.

Huizinga, J., *The Waning of the Middle Ages* (1924; Harmondsworth: Penguin, 1965).

Hull, Carrie L., 'The Need in Thinking: Materiality in Theodor W. Adorno and Judith Butler', *Radical Philosophy* 84 (July/Aug. 1997), 22–35.

Ibsen, Henrik, *Et dukkehjem* (1879), in *Samlede Verker,* ii (Oslo: Gyldendal, 1993).

Irigaray, Luce, *Je, tu, nous: Toward a Culture of Difference*, trans. Alison Martin (New York: Routledge, 1993).

—— *Speculum of the Other Woman*, trans. Gillian Gill (Ithaca, NY: Cornell University Press, 1985); trans. of *Spéculum de l'autre femme* (Paris: Minuit, 1974).

—— *This Sex Which Is Not One*, trans. Catherine Porter with Carolyn Burke (Ithaca, NY: Cornell, 1985); trans. of *Ce sexe qui n'en est pas un* (Paris: Minuit, 1977).

Jameson, Fredric, 'Imaginary and Symbolic in Lacan: Marxism, Psychoanalytic Criticism, and the Problem of the Subject', *Yale French Studies* 55–56 (1977), 338–95.

—— *The Political Unconscious: Narrative as a Socially Symbolic Act* (London: Methuen, 1981).

Jeanson, Francis, *Simone de Beauvoir ou l'entreprise de vivre* (Paris: Seuil, 1966).

Kamuf, Peggy, 'To Give Place: Semi-Approaches to Hélène Cixous', *Yale French Studies* 87 (1995), 68–89.

Kaplan, Alice, *French Lessons: A Memoir* (Chicago: University of Chicago Press, 1993).

Kauffman, Linda (ed.), *Gender and Theory: Dialogues on Feminist Criticism* (Oxford: Basil Blackwell, 1989).

Keefe, Terry, *Beauvoir· 'Les Belles Images'/'La Femme Rompue'* (Glasgow: University of Glasgow French and German Publications, 1991).

Keller, Evelyn Fox, 'Feminism and Science', in Harding and O'Barr 233–46.

—— 'Gender and Science', in Harding and Hintikka 87–205.

—— *Reflections on Gender and Science* (New Haven: Yale University Press, 1985).

Kelly, Henry Ansgar, *Love and Marriage in the Age of Chaucer* (Ithaca, NY: Cornell University Press, 1975).

Keohane, Nannerl O., Rosaldo, Michelle Z., and Gelpi, Barbara C. (eds.), *Feminist Theory: A Critique of Ideology* (Chicago: Chicago University Press, 1982).

Kessler, Suzanne J., 'The Medical Construction of Gender: Case Management of Intersexed Infants', *Signs* 16/1 (Autumn 1990), 3–26.

Koenigsberg, Richard A., 'Culture and Unconscious Fantasy. Observations on Courtly Love', *Psychoanalytic Review* 54 (1967), 36–50.

Kofman, Sarah, 'Narcissistic Woman', in *The Enigma of Woman: Woman in Freud's Writings*, trans. Catherine Porter. Ithaca: Cornell, 1985; trans. of *L'Enigme de la femme: la femme dans les textes de Freud* (Paris: Galilée, 1980).

Köhler, Erich, 'Les troubadours et la jalousie', in *Mélanges Jean Frappier*. vol. i (Geneva: Droz, 1970), 543–59.

Krais, Beate, 'Gender and Symbolic Violence: Female Suppression in the Light of Pierre Bourdieu's Theory of Social Practice', in Calhoun, LiPouma, and Postone 156–77.

Kristeva, Julia, *Revolution in Poetic Language*, trans. Margaret Waller (New York: Columbia, 1984).

Kruks, Sonia, 'Simone de Beauvoir: Between Sartre and Merleau-Ponty', *Simone de Beauvoir Studies* 5 (1988), 74–80.

—— 'Simone de Beauvoir: Teaching Sartre about Freedom', in Aronson and van den Hoven 285–300.

—— *Situation and Human Existence: Freedom, Subjectivity and Society* (London: Unwin Hyman, 1990).

Lacan, Jacques, *Écrits* (Paris: Seuil, 1966).

—— 'Intervention on Transference', in Bernheimer and Kahane 92–104.

Lambert, Helen H., 'Biology and Equality: A Perspective on Sex Differences' (1978), in Harding and O'Barr 125–45.

Lamont, Michèle, 'How to Become a Dominant French Philosopher: The Case of Jacques Derrida', *American Journal of Sociology* 93/3 (Nov. 1987), 584–622.

Lang, Candace, 'Autocritique', in Veeser 40–54.

Laplanche, Jean, *Life and Death in Psychoanalysis*, trans. Jeffrey Mehlman (Baltimore: Johns Hopkins Press, 1976).

—— and Pontalis, J.-B., *The Language of Psycho-Analysis* (London: Hogarth Press, 1980).

Laqueur, Thomas, *Making Sex: Body and Gender from the Greeks to Freud* (Cambridge, Mass.: Harvard University Press, 1990).

Laxdœla Saga, trans. and intro. A. Margaret Arent (Seattle: University of Washington Press, 1964).

Le Dœuff, Michèle, *Hipparchia's Choice: An Essay Concerning Women, Philosophy, etc.*, trans. Trista Selous (Oxford: Blackwell, 1991); trans. of *L'Étude et le rouet: des femmes, de la philosophie etc.*, (Paris: Seuil, 1989).

—— 'Women and Philosophy', in Moi, *French* 181–209.

—— *The Philosophical Imaginary*, trans. Colin Gordon (London: Athlone, 1989); trans. of *L'imaginaire philosophique* (Paris: Payot, 1980).

—— *Le sexe du savoir* (Paris: Aubier, 1998).

Leclercq, Jean, *Monks and Love in Twelfth-Century France* (Oxford: Oxford University Press, 1979).

Lewis, C. S., *The Allegory of Love* (1936, Oxford: Oxford University Press, 1959).

Lindén, Claudia, and Milles, Ulrika (eds.), *Feministisk bruksanvisning* (Stockholm: Norstedts, 1995), 143–66.

Loesberg, Jonathan, 'Bourdieu's Derrida's Kant: The Aesthetics of Refusing Aesthetics' in Brown 417–36.

Lorde, Audre, 'The Master's Tools Will Never Dismantle the Master's House', in *Sister Outsider: Essays and Speeches* (Trumansburg, NY: The Crossing Press, 1984), 110–13.

Lundberg, Ferdinand, and Farnham, Marynia L. Foot, *Modern Woman: The Lost Sex* (New York: Harper and Brothers, 1947).

Lundgren-Gothlin, Eva, *Sex and Existence*, trans. Linda Schenck (Hanover: Wesleyan, 1996); trans. of *Kön och existens: studier i Simone de Beauvoirs Le Deuxième Sexe* (Gothenburg: Daidalos, 1991).

—— 'Simone de Beauvoir, Jean-Paul Sartre, Ethics, Desire and Ambiguity', *Hypatia* (forthcoming).

Macherey, Pierre, *A Theory of Literary Production*, trans. Geoffrey Wall (London: Routledge & Kegan Paul, 1978); trans. of *Pour une théorie de la production littéraire* (Paris: Maspéro, 1966).

Mackenzie, Catriona, 'Simone de Beauvoir: philosophy and/or the female body', in Carol Pateman and Elizabeth Gross (eds.), *Feminist Challenges: Social and Political Theory* (Boston: Northeastern University Press, 1987), 144–56.

MacKinnon, Catharine A., 'Feminism, Marxism, Method, and the State: an Agenda for Theory', in Keohane, Rosaldo, and Gelpi, 1–30.

Marks, Elaine, and Courtivron, Isabelle de (eds.), *New French Feminisms* (Brighton: Harvester, 1980).

Marx, Karl, and Engels, Friedrich, *The Communist Manifesto* (1848; Harmondsworth: Penguin, 1984).

Masson, Jeffrey, *The Assault on Truth: Freud's Suppression of the Seduction Theory* (Harmondsworth: Penguin, 1985).

McCarthy, Mary, 'Tyranny of the Orgasm', Review of *Modern Woman: The Lost Sex* by Ferdinand Lundberg and Marynia Farnham, *New Leader* (5 Apr. 1947), 10; repr. in *On the Contrary* (New York: Farrar, Straus and Cudahy, 1961), 167–73.

McConnell-Ginet, Sally, Borker, Ruth, and Furman, Nellie (eds.), *Women and Language in Literature and Society* (New York: Praeger, 1980).

McDougall, Joyce, *The Many Faces of Eros* (New York: Norton, 1995).

McDowell, Deborah, *'The Changing Same': Black Women's Literature, Criticism, and Theory* (Bloomington, Ind.: Indiana University Press, 1995).

—— *Leaving Pipe Shop* (New York: Norton, 1996).

—— 'Transferences. Black Feminist Thinking: The 'Practice' of 'Theory', in *Changing Same* 156–75.

McDowell, John, *Mind and World* (Cambridge, Mass.: Harvard University Press, 1994).

McIntosh, Mary, 'Review of *Gender Trouble*', *Feminist Review* 38 (Summer 1991) 113–14.

Mead, Margaret, 'Dilemmas the Modern Woman Faces', Review of *Modern Woman: The Lost Sex* by Ferdinand Lundberg and Marynia Farnham, *New York Times* (26 Jan. 1947), 18.

Merleau-Ponty, Maurice, *Phenomenology of Perception*, trans. Colin Smith (London: Routledge, 1962); trans. of *Phénoménologie de la perception* (Paris: Gallimard (Coll. 'Tel'), 1945).

Micha, Alexandre, 'Le mari jaloux dans la littérature romanesque des XIIᵉ et XIIIᵉ siècles', *Studi Medievali* (1951), 303–20.

Miller, Nancy, *Getting Personal: Feminist Occasions and Other Autobiographical Acts* (New York: Routledge, 1991).

Millot, Catherine, *Horsexe: Essay on Transsexuality*, trans. Kenneth Hylton (Brooklyn, NY: Autonomedia, 1990).

Milton, John, 'The Doctrine and Discipline of Divorce Restored to the Good of Both Sexes' (1643), in *John Milton*, eds. Stephen Orgel and Jonathan Goldberg (Oxford: Oxford University Press, 1991), 182–226.

Moi, Toril, 'Feminist, Female, Feminine', in Belsey and Moore 117–32.

—— *Feminist Theory and Simone de Beauvoir*, The Bucknell Lectures in Literary Theory (Oxford: Blackwell, 1990).

—— *Sexual/Textual Politics: Feminist Literary Theory* (London: Methuen, 1985).

—— *Simone de Beauvoir: The Making of an Intellectual Woman* (Oxford: Blackwell, 1994).

—— (ed.) *French Feminist Thought* (Oxford: Blackwell, 1987), 181–209.

Moller, Herbert, 'The Meaning of Courtly Love', *Journal of American Folklore* 73 (1960), 39–52.

Money, John, 'The Conceptual Neutering of Gender and the Criminalization of Sex', *Archives of Sexual Behavior* 14/3 (1985), 279–90.

——Hampson, Joan G., and Hampson, John L., 'An Examination of Some Basic Sexual Concepts: The Evidence of Human Hermaphroditism', *Bulletin of the Johns Hopkins Hospital* 97/1 (1955), 301–19.

Morón-Arroyo, Ciriaco, Review of Cesar Bandera, *Mímesis conflictiva, Diacritics* 8/1 (Mar. 1978), 75–86.

Mudimbe, V. Y., 'Reading and Teaching Pierre Bourdieu', *Transition* 61: 144–60.

Nelson, Lynn Hankins, and Nelson, Jack (eds.), *Feminism, Science and the Philosophy of Science* (The Hague: Kluwer, 1996), 289–308.

Newman, F. X. (ed.), *The Meaning of Courtly Love* (Albany, NY: State University of New York Press, 1968).

Nicholson, Linda. 'Interpreting Gender', *Signs* 20/1 (Autumn 1994), 79–105.

Ophir, Anne, *Regards féminins: Beauvoir/Etcherelli/Rochefort: Condition féminine et création littéraire* (Paris: Denoël/Gonthier, 1976).

Osborne, Peter (ed.), *A Critical Sense: Interviews with Intellectuals* (London: Routledge, 1996).

Painter, Nell Irvin, *Sojourner Truth: A Life, A Symbol* (New York: Norton, 1996).

Paris, Gaston, 'Lancelot du Lac 2: Le conte de la charrette', *Romania* 12 (1883).

Parker, Andrew, and Sedgwick, Eve Kosofsky (eds.), *Performativity and Performance: Essays from the English Institute* (New York: Routledge, 1995).

—— —— 'Introduction: Performativity and Performance', in Parker and Sedgwick 1–18.

Parry, John Jay (trans.), *The Art of Courtly Love*, by Andreas Capellanus (1941; New York: Columbia University Press, 1969).

Paulson, William, 'The Market of Printed Goods: On Bourdieu's Rules', in Brown 399–415.

Payen, Jean Charles, 'Lancelot contre Tristan: La conjuration d'un mythe subversif (réflexions sur l'idéologie romanesque au Moyen Age)', in *Mélanges Pierre Le Gentil* (Paris: SEDES, 1973), 617–32.

—— 'Ordre moral et subversion politique dans le *Tristan* de Béroul', in *Mélanges Jeanne Lods* (Paris: ENSJF, 1978)

—— (ed. and trans.), *Les Tristan en vers* (Paris: Garnier, 1974).

Pensom, Roger, 'Rhetoric and Psychology in Thomas's "Tristan"', *Modern Language Review* 78/2 (Apr. 1983), 285–297.

Piatier, Jacqueline, ' "La femme rompue" de Simone de Beauvoir', *Le Monde* (24 Jan. 1968).

Pivot, Bernard, 'Simone de Beauvoir: une vraie femme de lettres (pour le courrier du cœur)', *Le Figaro littéraire* (30 Oct. 1967), 29.

Prosser, Jay, 'No Place Like Home: The Transgendered Narrative of Leslie Feinberg's *Stone Butch Blues*', *Modern Fiction Studies* 41/3–4 (Fall–Winter 1995), 483–514.

Ramas, Maria, 'Freud's Dora, Dora's Hysteria: The Negation of a Woman's Rebellion', in Bernheimer and Kahane 149–80; a longer version 1st pub. in *Feminist Studies* 6 (Fall 1980), 472–510.

Rank, Otto, *The Double*, trans. and ed. with introd. by Harry Tucker Jr. (Chapel Hill, NC: University of North Carolina Press, 1971).

Raymond, Janice G., *The Transsexual Empire: The Making of the She-Male*, (New York: Teachers College Press, 1994).

Reiter, Rayna R. (ed.), *Toward an Anthropology of Women* (New York: Monthly Review Press, 1975).

Remnick, David, 'Inside-Out Olympics', *New Yorker* (5 Aug. 1996), 26–8.

Rimmon-Kenan, Shlomith, *Discourse in Psychoanalysis and Literature* (London: Methuen, 1987), 211–32.

Robertson, D. W., 'The Concept of Courtly Love as an Impediment to the Understanding of Medieval Texts', in Newman 1–18.

—— *A Preface to Chaucer* (1962; Princeton: Princeton University Press, 1969).

Rogers, Arthur, 'Legal Implications of Transsexualism', *The Lancet*, 341 (1993), 1085–6.

Rose, Jacqueline, 'Dora: Fragment of an Analysis', in Bernheimer and Kahane 128–48.

Rougemont, Denis de, *Love in the Western World*, trans. Montgomery Belgion (New York: Harcourt, Brace, 1956); trans. of *L'amour et l'occident* (Paris: Gallimard, 1939).

Rubin, Gayle, 'Thinking Sex: Notes for a Radical Theory of the Politics of Sexuality', in Vance 267–319.

—— 'The Traffic in Women: Notes on the "Political Economy" of Sex.' in Reiter, 157–210.

Russett, Cynthia Eagle, *Sexual Science: The Victorian Construction of Womanhood* (Cambridge, Mass.: Harvard University Press, 1989).

Sartre, Jean-Paul, *Anti-Semite and Jew*, trans. George Becker (New York: Schocken Books, 1948), trans. of *Réflexions sur la question juive* (Paris: Gallimard (Coll. 'Folio'), 1946).

—— *Being and Nothingness*, trans. Hazel E. Barnes (New York: Washington Square Press, 1992); trans. of *L'Être et le néant* (Paris: Gallimard (Coll. 'Tel'), 1943).

—— *The Family Idiot. Gustave Flaubert 1821–1857*, trans. Carol Cosman (Chicago: Chicago University Press, 1981); trans. of *L'idiot de la famille: Gustave Flaubert de 1821 à 1857* (Paris: Gallimard, 1971).

—— 'Introducing *Les temps modernes*', in *What Is* 249–67; trans. of 'Présentation des *temps modernes*', *Les temps modernes* 1/1 (Oct, 1945), 1–21.

—— *Lettres au Castor et à quelques autres*, ed. Simone de Beauvoir, 2 vols. (Paris: Gallimard, 1983).

—— —— *'What Is Literature?' And Other Essays*, introd. and ed. Steven Ungar (Cambridge, Mass.: Harvard University Press, 1988).

—— 'What Is Literature?', in *What Is* 21–238; trans. Bernard Frechtman; trans. of *Qu'est-ce que la littérature?* (Paris: Gallimard (Coll. idées), 1948).

Sayers, Janet, *Biological Politics: Feminist and Anti-Feminist Perspectives* (London: Tavistock, 1982).

Schor, Naomi, *Bad Objects: Essays Popular and Unpopular* (Durham, NC: Duke University Press, 1995).

—— 'French Feminism is a Universalism' in *Bad Objects* 3–27.

—— 'This Essentialism Which Is Not One: Coming to Grips with Irigaray', in *Bad Objects* 44–60.

Scott, Joan Wallach, 'Gender: A Useful Category of Historical Analysis', in *Gender and the Politics of History* (New York: Columbia, 1988), 28–50.

Sedgwick, Eve Kosofsky, *Epistemology of the Closet* (Berkeley and Los Angeles: University of California Press, 1990).

—— 'Gender Criticism', in Greenblatt and Gunn 271–302.

—— 'Queer Performativity: Henry James's *The Art of the Novel*', *GLQ* 1/1 (1993), 1–16.

Shakespeare, William, *The Merchant of Venice*, in *The Complete Works*, ed. Stanley Wells and Gary Taylor (Oxford: Clarendon Press, 1994).

Shepherd, Michael, 'Morbid Jealousy: Some Clinical and Social Aspects of a Psychiatric Symptom', *Journal of Mental Science* 107 (1961), 687–704.

Showalter, Elaine, 'Who's Afraid of Elaine Showalter? The MLA President Incites Mass Hysteria', with Emily Eakin, *Lingua Franca* 8/6 (Sept. 1998), 28–36.

Shumway, David R., 'The Star System in Literary Studies', *PMLA* 112/1 (Jan. 1997), 85–100.

Simons, Margaret (ed.), *Feminist Interpretations of Simone de Beauvoir* (University Park: Pennsylvania State University Press, 1995).

—— 'The Silencing of Simone de Beauvoir: Guess What's Missing from *The Second Sex*', *Women's Studies International Forum* 6/5 (1983), 559–64.

Simpson, David, *The Academic Postmodern and the Rule of Literature: A Report on Half-Knowledge* (Chicago: University of Chicago Press, 1995).

Soper, Kate, 'Feminism as Critique', *New Left Review* 176 (July/Aug. 1989), 91–112.

—— *Troubled Pleasures: Writings on Politics, Gender and Hedonism* (London: Verso, 1990).

—— *What Is Nature? Culture, Politics and the Non-Human* (Oxford: Blackwell, 1995).

Spelman, Elizabeth V., *Inessential Woman: Problems of Exclusion in Feminist Thought* (Boston: Beacon Press, 1988.)

Spivak, Gayatri Chakravorty, *Outside in the Teaching Machine* (New York: Routledge, 1993).

Stanley, Liz, and Wise, Sue, *Breaking Out: Feminist Consciousness and Feminist Research* (London: Routledge & Kegan Paul, 1983).

Steedman, Carolyn, *Landscape for a Good Woman: A Story of Two Lives* (London: Virago, 1986).

Stoller, Robert J., 'A Contribution to the Study of Gender Identity', *International Journal of Psychoanalysis* 45 (1964), 220–6.

—— *Sex and Gender: On the Development of Masculinity and Femininity* (New York: Science House, 1968).

Stone, Martin, 'Focusing the Law: What Legal Interpretation is Not', in Andrei Marmor (ed.), *Law and Interpretation: Essays in Legal Philosophy* (Oxford: Clarendon Press, 1995), 31–96.

Stone, Sandy, 'The Empire Strikes Back: A Posttranssexual Manifesto', in Epstein and Straub, 280–304.

Strindberg, August, *The Father*, in *Strindberg: Five Plays*, trans. Harry Carlson (New York: Signet, 1984); trans. of *Fadren* (1887), ed. Gunnar Ollén, in *August Strindbergs Samlade Verk* 27 (Stockholm: Almqvist & Wiksell, 1984).

Tang, Jesper, *Den oprørske elsker* (Copenhagen: Borgen, 1977).

Tanner, Tony, *Adultery in the Novel: Contract and Transgression* (Baltimore and London: Johns Hopkins Press, 1979).

Taylor, Charles, 'To Follow a Rule . . .', in Calhoun, LiPuma, and Postone 45–60.

Thernstrom, Melanie, 'Sexuality 101', *Details* (Feb. 1998), 96–100.

Thomas, *Tristan.* See Gunnlaugsdottir; Hatto, 'The "Tristran" of Thomas'; Payen; Wind.

Thompson, John B., *Studies in the Theory of Ideology* (Cambridge: Polity Press, 1984).

Tomasson, Sverrir, 'Hvenær var Tristrams sögu snúid?', with an English summary, in *Gripla* 2 (Reykjavik: Stofnum Arna Magnússonar, 1977), 47–78.

Tompkins, Jane,. *A Life in School: What the Teacher Learned* (Reading, Mass.: Addison-Wesley, 1996).

—— 'Me and My Shadow', in Kauffman 121–39.

Trebilcot, Joyce, 'Dyke Methods: or Principles for the Discovery/Creation of Withstanding', *Hypatia* 3/2 (Summer 1988), 1–13.

Vance, Carole S. (ed.), *Pleasure and Danger: Exploring Female Sexuality* (Boston: Routledge & Kegan Paul, 1984).

Van Doren, Dorothy, 'To Save Us from Women', Review of *Modern Woman: The Lost Sex* by Ferdinand Lundberg and Marynia Farnham, *New York Herald Tribune Weekly Book Review* (9 Feb. 1947: 16).

Veeser, H. Aram (ed.), *Confessions of the Critics* (New York: Routledge, 1996).

Vintges, Karen, *Philosophy as Passion: The Thinking of Simone de Beauvoir,* trans. Anne Lavelle (Bloomington, Ind.: Indiana University Press, 1996).

Walsh, P. G. (ed. and trans.), *Andreas Capellanus on Love* (London: Duckworth, 1982).

Ward, Julie K, 'Beauvoir's Two Senses of "Body" in *The Second Sex*', in Simons, *Feminist* 223–42.

Wertham, Frederic, 'Ladies in the Dark', Review of *Modern Woman: The Lost Sex* by Ferdinand Lundberg and Marynia Farnham, *New Republic* (10 Feb. 1947), 38.

West, Candace, and Zimmerman, Don H., 'Doing Gender', *Gender & Society* 1/2 (June 1987), 125–51.

White, Hayden, 'Ethnological "Lie" and Mythical "Truth" ', *Diacritics* 8/1 (Mar. 1978), 2–9.

Widerberg, Karin, *Kunnskapens kjønn: minner, refleksjoner, teori* (Oslo: Pax, 1994).

Wierzbicka, Anna, *Semantics, Culture, and Cognition: Universal Human Concepts in Culture-Specific Configurations* (New York: Oxford University Press, 1992).

Wind, Bartina H. (ed.), *Les fragments du Tristan de Thomas* (Leiden: Brill, 1950).

Wittgenstein, Ludwig, *Philosophical Investigations,* trans. G. E. M. Anscombe (3rd edn.; New York: Macmillan, 1968).

—— *Tractatus Logico-Philosophicus,* trans. D. F. Pears and B. F. McGuinness (London: Routledge, 1974).

Wittig, Monique, *The Straight Mind and Other Essays* (Boston: Beacon Press, 1992).

Wolff, Janet, *Feminine Sentences: Essays on Women and Culture* (Cambridge: Polity Press, 1990).

—— 'Textes et institutions: problèmes de la critique féministe', *Recherches sociologiques* 20/2–3 (1988), 175–93.

Woolf, Virginia, *A Room of One's Own* (1929; London: Granada, 1977).

Young, Iris Marion, *Throwing Like a Girl and Other Essays in Feminist Philosophy and Social Theory* (Bloomington, Ind.: Indiana University Press, 1990).

Index

Note: In order to avoid long strings of entries under frequently cited authors' names, entries have as far as possible been alphabetized under the relevant subject heading. Thus a concept such as 'symbolic capital' is not indexed under Bourdieu, but separately, as a subject heading in its own right. With the exception of the principal entry for each term, 'Simone de Beauvoir' has been abbreviated to 'SdB', and *The Second Sex* to *SS*. References of the type '348–55 *passim*' indicate that the subject matter of the heading is to be found in scattered passages throughout those pages of the text.